Magazine
Markets
for
Children's
Writers™
2006

Acknowledgments

The editors of this directory appreciate the generous contributions of our instructors and students and the cooperation of the magazine editors who made clear their policies and practices.

MARNI McNIFF, Editor

SUSAN TIERNEY, Articles Editor

CLAIRE BROWN, Assistant Editor

HEATHER BURNS-DeMELO, Assistant Editor

SHERRI KEEFE, Assistant Editor

Contributing Writers: EILEEN BYRNE, HEATHER BURNS-DeMELO, BARBARA COLE, CAROLINE LaFLEUR, PAMELA PURRONE

Cover Art: JOANNA HORVATH

International Standard Book Number 1-889715-29-8

1-800-443-6078. www.writersbookstore.com
email: services@writersbookstore.com

Contents

Submissions Guide   5

This section offers tips and step-by-step instructions for researching the market; writing query letters; preparing manuscript packages and bibliographies; initiating follow-up; and understanding copyrights, permissions, and other common publishing terms.

Gateway to the Markets   29

Contents (cont.)

Submissions Guide

Preparing to Sell

An idea has captivated you. You're sure it will be a fun and informative children's nonfiction article or an engaging story. Perhaps you've even written your piece and are ready for young readers to read it. Great! Your next step is to find those magazines whose editors and audiences will be most receptive to your writing.

You'll want to offer an editor the perfect match of quality, topic, and reader interest, making your work irresistible. Your goal is to identify the subjects those readers enjoy and then create material that engages them.

You might begin with a magazine you like and generate ideas for submissions specific to it, or begin with a good idea and no specific market in mind. Later you can research the topics of interest to various publications to find the best opportunities for placing your work. Here are some tips to launch your research.

What Captivates Young Readers?

You'll increase your publication odds if you know what topics interest children. Trust your own instincts, and hone these instincts throughout the market research process.

Researching potential subjects can begin by surveying the categories of magazines in *Magazine Markets for Children's Writers*. Start with the Category Index on pages 339-363, an excellent guide to finding magazines that publish the types of articles or stories you write on the subjects that interest you.

You'll find general interest publications, like *Highlights for Children* or *Spider*, and also special interest periodicals on topics such as health, sports, science, fiction, college, religion, history, and so on. Continue your research online or at libraries. Do Internet searches, and check the library or bookstores. What magazines are out there, for what ages, and what subjects do they cover? Along with magazines targeted specifically to children, be sure to check parenting, educational, and regional magazines.

You'll find that each magazine covers numerous subjects from month to month or year to year, even special interest publications that cover a niche more deeply than widely. Read several issues of each magazine to research which subjects a potential target magazine has covered recently and how it has approached particular subjects in the past. Begin to make a list of the magazines that cover subjects of interest to you. Use the Magazine Match List on page 7.

Roll Call: Who Are Your Readers?

Researching readers is intricately tied to subjects, but a magazine's target age and how the publication speaks to that age—voice and purpose—are important factors in the market research you perform. Select subjects and slants based on age-appropriateness. If you'd like to take on the subject of animals' sleep habits, for example, you'd write an article or story for early readers with less specific information than you would for a middle-grader, and with a different tone.

Once again, go to the Internet and other media, as well as to schools and children's activities, to get a feel for the interests and developmental levels of the readership that is drawing you. For example, go to www.google.com and select the directory. Click Kids and Teens. Look at the websites under preschool, school time, teen life, and other categories. The arts section has many interesting sites that can give you additional insights into every age group.

Look Deeper: Magazine Specifications

Create a magazine market file that seems to be a match with your interests. Use index cards, a notebook, or your computer to develop a file for each magazine for your initial list of publications. Request sample issues for the magazines and read them. Listings in *Magazine Markets for Children's Writers* will tell you if writers' guidelines, an editorial calendar, or a theme list are available, as well as the cost of a sample copy and the size of the envelope to send with your request. (See page 47 for a sample magazine listing.)

You may find the magazines you're targeting at your local library or newsstand, which will save you time and postage. Go to their websites—addresses are included in the listings.

Review each of the magazines in more detail for subjects related, or comparable, to yours. You should also check the *Reader's Guide to Periodical Literature* in your library to see if a target magazine has printed a piece similar to yours within the past two years. You may want to find another magazine or, depending on the publication, develop a new slant if you find that your topic is already well covered.

Study the Magazine and Its Guidelines

Sample issues. Use the Magazine Description Form (see example on page 8) to continue your detailed analysis of the publications, especially those you're beginning to hone in on as good matches. Record what you learn about each magazine. Evaluate how you could shape or present your manuscript to improve your chances of getting it published. If a particular idea or target magazine doesn't work out now, it may in the future—or it may lead to other ideas, angles, or possible markets. Review your market files periodically to generate ideas.

Writers' Guidelines. If the listing notes that a magazine offers writers' guidelines, you should send a letter requesting them with an SASE (see sample on page 9). Some magazines also list their writers' guidelines on their websites. This is specified in the listing. Read writers' guidelines, editorial calendars, and theme lists carefully. They may give you specific topics to write about,

but even if you're creating your own, take the guidelines seriously. They are key to the needs of publications and often new writers give them too little weight.

Some guidelines are more detailed and helpful than others, but virtually all will tell you something about the readership, philosophy, voice, and about such basics as word length requirements, submissions format, and payment. More than that, some guidelines can give writers specific insights into the immediate needs of a magazine. For example, *Odyssey* guidelines say, "The inclusion of primary research (interviews with scientists focusing on current research) are of primary interest to the magazine," while *Connecticut's County Kids* guidelines are directive in another way: "Use bullets and subheads to separate thoughts, especially in feature articles."

The guidelines will also indicate the rights a publication purchases, payment policies, and many more specifics—factors you'll consider as you get closer to submission. Many experienced writers do not sell all rights, unless the fee is high enough to be worth it; reselling articles or stories for reprint rights can be an additional source of income. (See the discussion of rights on page 23.)

Read with a Writer's Eye

Your review of sample magazines and guidelines should include:

Magazine Match List: Subjects

Idea Topic: _____

	Magazine	Audience Age	Similar/Related Subject	Slant	Date Published
1.	_____				
2.	_____				

• **Editorial objective.** Turn to the issue masthead, where the names of the editors are listed. Sometimes the magazine's editorial objective is also stated here. Does your story or article fit its purpose?

• **Audience.** What is the age range of the readers and the characters or children portrayed? For fiction, is your main character at the upper end of that range? Kids want to read about characters their own age or older.

• **Table of contents.** Study the table of contents. Usually, the stories and articles with bylines were written by freelancers like you. Compare the author names there with the editors and staff listed in the masthead to make sure that the publication is not primarily staff-written.

• **Article and story types.** Examine the types of articles and stories in the issue. Does one theme tie the articles and stories together? For example, does every article in a science magazine focus on plants, or do the articles cover a broader range of subjects? If the magazine issues a theme list, review it to see the range of topics. Think about the presentation as well: Is the magazine highly visual or does it rely primarily on text? Will photographs or illustrations be a consideration for you? Are there sidebars, and are you willing to provide those?

• **Style.** How is the writing impacted by the age of the audience? Read each story and article to get an idea of the style and tone the magazine prefers. Are there numerous three-syllable words, or mostly simple words? Are most sentences simple or complex, or a mixture of both? Is the tone upbeat and casual, or informative and educational? Do the writers speak directly to readers in a conversational way, or is the voice appropriately authoritative?

• **Editor's comments.** Note in the writers' guidelines particularly what *feel* for the magazine the editors provide. *Ladybug*'s guidelines include this important request: "[We] look for beauty of lan-

---

Magazine Description Form

Name of Magazine: U*S*Kids   **Editor:** Daniel Lee
Address: Children's Better Health Institute, 1100 Waterway Boulevard, P.O. Box 567, Indianapolis, IN 42606-0567

Freelance Percentage: 50%   **Percentage of Authors Who Are New to the Magazine:** 70%

Description
What subjects does this magazine cover? U*S*Kids features articles, stories, and activities related to health and fitness, science and nature, and multicultural and ethnic issues.

Readership
Who are the magazine's typical readers? Children ages 6 to 8

Articles and Stories
What particular slants or distinctive characteristics do its articles or stories emphasize? Articles and stories that spark a child's imagination and creativity while they learn something new.

Potential Market
Is this magazine a potential market? Yes. I have an article and activity to submit.

Ideas for Articles or Stories
What article, story, or department idea could be submitted? Submit an article on different types of physical fitness activities for young children.

guage and a sense of joy or wonder." *Magazine Markets for Children's Writers* includes a section called Editor's Comments in each listing. Study this section carefully as well. The editors give you tips on what they most want to see, or don't need.

Refine Your Magazine List

After you analyze your selected magazines, rank them by how well they match your idea, article or story's subject, style, and target age. Then return to the listings to examine other factors, such as the magazine's freelance potential, its receptivity to new or unpublished writers, rights purchased, and payment.

These facts reveal significant details about the magazine that you can use to your advantage as a freelance writer. For example, many published writers prefer magazines that:

- Publish a high percentage of authors who are new to the magazine;

- Respond in one month as opposed to three;

- Pay on acceptance rather than on publication.

If you're not yet published, however, writing for a nonpaying market may be worth the effort to earn the clips to build published credits. Once you've acquired credentials in these markets, you can list these published pieces in your queries to paying markets.

What to do if a magazine requests clips, but you've never been published before?

Many editors are open to new writers, so don't be discouraged if you haven't yet seen your name in a byline and think it's a vicious circle editors spin: To get published you need clips, but you can't have clips until you're published.

First, consider whether in fact you have been "published." Have you written anything substantial for a school or church newsletter (not a 100-word piece on the school lunch choices for the week), or a volunteer organization? If it's good, it might reveal your style well. If not, gather together unpublished samples. Try to select those that will be closest to the piece you're proposing, or include a portion of the piece itself. Be sure your samples are well written and have no errors.

Be honest with the editor in your query and call them *writing samples*, not *clips*; clips are published items.

Sample Guidelines Request

Name
Address
City, State, ZIP

Date

Dear (Name of Current Editor):

I would like to request a copy of your writers' guidelines and editorial calendar. I have provided a self-addressed, stamped envelope for your convenience.

Sincerely,

Your name

Submitting Your Work to an Editor

Your market study will prepare you to draft a query or cover letter that convinces the right editor of why your idea is suitable for the magazine and why *you* are the person to write it. When do you send a query, and when should you send a cover letter and manuscript? Should a query be accompanied by an outline or synopsis or other materials? Is a query ever appropriate for fiction?

In your research, you should already have begun to see the variety of submissions possibilities. Let's sort them out.

Know What Editors Want

Some editors want the query alone; it's efficient and provides them with enough information to make a decision about the article's appeal to their readers.

Others want queries accompanied by a synopsis, outline, or other information for an article. Yet other editors prefer to have a complete article or story before them to get a full sense of the work you do and whether the subject is a match for them. Expect that the editor who accepts a complete, unsolicited manuscript may require even more revisions or rewrites than if you had queried first.

In reality, queries for magazine fiction are rare, although they've become somewhat more common for book-length fiction. Magazine stories are short enough without being too much for an editor to review.

If the editor asks for a:	*Send:*
Query (nonfiction)	• One-page letter indicating article topic, slant, target readership, word count • Bibliography of research sources • One-page résumé (if requested) • SASE
Query (fiction)	• One-page letter containing a brief synopsis of the plot, indicating target readership and word count • SASE
Complete manuscript (nonfiction)	• Brief cover letter • Manuscript • Bibliography of research sources • List of people interviewed • SASE
Complete manuscript (fiction)	• Brief cover letter • Manuscript • SASE

Keys to Writing a Query Letter

Aquery tells the editor why your idea is appropriate for the magazine and why *you* are the person to write it. There are several advantages to using a query letter:

- Editors generally respond faster to queries than manuscripts.
- Your chances for a sale are increased because the piece is still in the "planning stage" and the editor can give you suggestions that help you tailor the article to the magazine.
- You save research and writing time by knowing exactly what the editor wants.

Do Your Homework

Before you write your query letter, refine your idea based on the sample issues you've read and the requirements described in the guidelines. Know the word limit the magazine prefers and whether or not it requires a bibliography of your sources. Most editors like articles with quotes from experts in the field you're writing about. Be prepared to tell the editor who you'll interview for the piece. For example, if you plan to write a science article and the magazine wants resourced and quoted articles, gather pertinent facts and include names of authorities you plan to interview. Know whether you can obtain photos—this can often swing a sale.

What Makes a Good Query Letter

A good query letter is short and to the point. If you can't get your idea across in one page or less, you're not yet ready to write the article.

Below are the basic steps in writing a query (see the examples on pages 12, 13, and 14):

- Direct your query to a specific editor.
- Begin with a lead paragraph that captures the editor's interest, conveys your slant, and reflects your knowledge of the editorial focus and writing style of the magazine.
- Include a one- or two-line description of your article that conveys your central idea. This should be very narrow in focus.

- Show how your idea meets the editorial goals of the targeted magazine.
- Indicate word length.
- Provide details as to what will be in the article—anecdotes, case histories, statistics, etc.
- Cite sources, research resources, and interviews to be done.
- Indicate number and type of photographs or illustrations available. If you can't provide any, don't mention them at all.
- List your publishing credentials briefly and, if enclosed, refer to your résumé, clips or writing samples. No need to tell the editor if you are unpublished.
- Close by asking if the magazine is interested; mention whether your query represents a simultaneous submission.
- Include other information if requested, such as an outline or bibliography.

Tips for Making a Good First Impression

Your query is the first impression the editor will have of you and your work, so take a few extra minutes to make sure it's ready to send.

- Use good quality bond paper (not erasable paper).
- Your font should be close to Courier or Times Roman 12. Type that's too small is hard on the eyes; large type is distracting. Only amateurs use script or other fancy type styles.
- Use a letter-quality printout, not dot matrix, and be sure your type is crisp and dark.
- Margins frame your words, so leave 1 to 1¼-inch margins on all four sides. Single spacing is preferred for query letters.
- Proofread for grammar, spelling, punctuation, and typos. If you're careless with this simple step, the editor will wonder if you're careless with your research, too.
- Make sure your name, address, phone number, and email address are on the query in case the editor wants to contact you. Always include a self-addressed, stamped envelope or postcard for the editor's reply.

Query Letter—Checklist

Your query letter will make the difference between a sale and a rejection in today's magazine market. The following checklist and sample query letter offer tips on how to avoid simple mistakes that can cost you a sale.

❶ Verify that you are writing to the current editor and correct address; double-check the spelling of the name and address. This is extremely important.

❷ Phrase the letter as if the article is in the planning stage. Editors prefer pieces written specifically for their publication, not generic articles.

❸ Give enough examples of what you will cover to allow the editor to get a feel for the article. Include any unique material, interviews, or primary sources that you will use.

❹ Note any background or experience you have that gives you credibility in writing this piece for this particular audience. **Include publishing credits if available.**

❺ No need to tell the editor if you are unpublished; let your work speak for you. If you have been published, give the editor your publishing history—but keep it brief.

Street Address
City, State ZIP
Phone Number
Email Address
Date

❶ (Name of Current Editor)
Guideposts for Kids
Suite 6, 1050 Broadway
Chesterton, IN 46304

Dear (Name of Current Editor):

Your teacher says that everyone in your class must do a project for the school science fair in a few weeks. You:
A. Groan
B. Wonder, "What in the world am I going to do for my project?"
C. Start to feel nervous and excited just thinking about the fair
D. All of the above

❷ ❸ With three to five million students participating in regional science fairs each year, chances are many of your readers can relate to this question. I feel my proposed article, "Help! I Hafta Do a Science Project" (700 words) would make an excellent featured article for your "School Scoop" section. With humor, insider's tips, and helpful advice, it covers everything readers need to know to do a great science fair project.

A sidebar contains links to helpful websites, including the Intel International Science Fair and Discovery Young Scientist Challenge, two competitions that reward the best budding scientists with cash for college.

❹ ❺ I am a former international science fair winner and judge, and the co-author of *You Have to Do a Science Fair Project* (John Wiley & Sons, 2002).

❻ "How to Do a Winning Science Fair Project" is available immediately upon request. I've enclosed an SASE and look forward to hearing from you.

Sincerely,

Heather Tomasello

❻ Keep the closing brief and professional; remember to include an SASE.

12

Sample Query & Article Outline

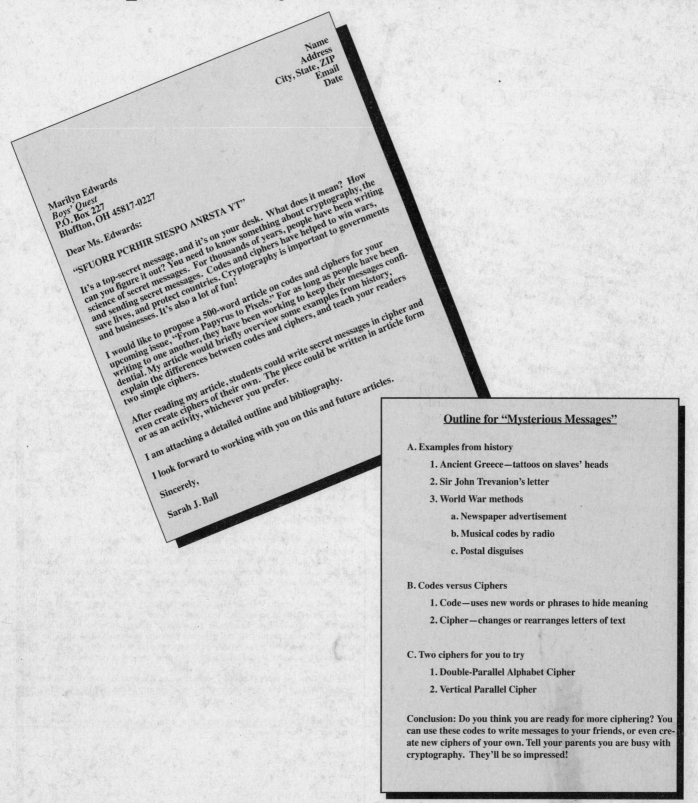

Name
Address
City, State, ZIP
Email
Date

Marilyn Edwards
Boys' Quest
P.O. Box 227
Bluffton, OH 45817-0227

Dear Ms. Edwards:

"SFUORR PCRHIR SIESPO ANRSTA YT"

It's a top-secret message, and it's on your desk. What does it mean? How can you figure it out? You need to know something about cryptography, the science of secret messages. For thousands of years, people have been writing and sending secret messages. Codes and ciphers have helped to win wars, save lives, and protect countries. Cryptography is important to governments and businesses. It's also a lot of fun!

I would like to propose a 500-word article on codes and ciphers for your upcoming issue, "From Papyrus to Pixels." For as long as people have been writing to one another, they have been working to keep their messages confidential. My article would briefly overview some examples from history, explain the differences between codes and ciphers, and teach your readers two simple ciphers.

After reading my article, students could write secret messages in cipher and even create ciphers of their own. The piece could be written in article form or as an activity, whichever you prefer.

I am attaching a detailed outline and bibliography.

I look forward to working with you on this and future articles.

Sincerely,

Sarah J. Ball

Outline for "Mysterious Messages"

A. Examples from history

    1. Ancient Greece—tattoos on slaves' heads

    2. Sir John Trevanion's letter

    3. World War methods

        a. Newspaper advertisement

        b. Musical codes by radio

        c. Postal disguises

B. Codes versus Ciphers

    1. Code—uses new words or phrases to hide meaning

    2. Cipher—changes or rearranges letters of text

C. Two ciphers for you to try

    1. Double-Parallel Alphabet Cipher

    2. Vertical Parallel Cipher

Conclusion: Do you think you are ready for more ciphering? You can use these codes to write messages to your friends, or even create new ciphers of your own. Tell your parents you are busy with cryptography. They'll be so impressed!

Sample Query Letters

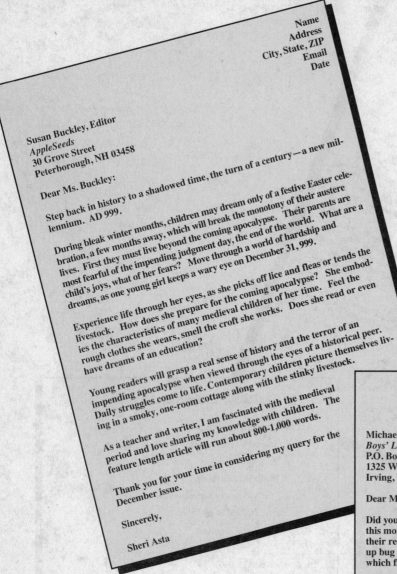

Name
Address
City, State, ZIP
Email
Date

Susan Buckley, Editor
AppleSeeds
30 Grove Street
Peterborough, NH 03458

Dear Ms. Buckley:

Step back in history to a shadowed time, the turn of a century—a new millennium. AD 999.

During bleak winter months, children may dream only of a festive Easter celebration, a few months away, which will break the monotony of their austere lives. First they must live beyond the coming apocalypse. Their parents are most fearful of the impending judgment day, the end of the world. What are a child's joys, what of her fears? Move through a world of hardship and dreams, as one young girl keeps a wary eye on December 31, 999.

Experience life through her eyes, as she picks off lice and fleas or tends the livestock. How does she prepare for the coming apocalypse? She embodies the characteristics of many medieval children of her time. Feel the rough clothes she wears, smell the croft she works. Does she read or even have dreams of an education?

Young readers will grasp a real sense of history and the terror of an impending apocalypse when viewed through the eyes of a historical peer. Daily struggles come to life. Contemporary children picture themselves living in a smoky, one-room cottage along with the stinky livestock.

As a teacher and writer, I am fascinated with the medieval period and love sharing my knowledge with children. The feature length article will run about 800-1,000 words.

Thank you for your time in considering my query for the December issue.

Sincerely,

Sheri Asta

Street Address
City, State ZIP
Phone Number
Email
Date

Michael Goldman, Senior Editor
Boys' Life
P.O. Box 152079
1325 West Walnut Hill Lane
Irving, TX 75015-2079

Dear Mr. Goldman:

Did you know you may have eaten a beetle when you licked that red lollipop this morning? Some red-colored food, like lollipops and red applesauce, get their red coloring from finely ground up, dried female beetles. This crunched up bug dust is known as cochineal. Every year, 500 tons of cochineal is made, which finds its way into shampoo, jellies, and juices.

I suspect your readers would love to know they may have eaten a bug. Would you be interested in an article about cochineal for your magazine? The article, tentatively entitled, "Beetles for Breakfast?" describes the cochineal beetles, how they are made into red dye, and their use now and in history. The article concludes with a practical application section which will excite the boys into looking at ingredients labels both at home and at the store.

The length of the piece is about 750 words, and it is geared towards 8- to 13-year-old boys. I have experience with this age group in the classroom as an English teacher in both junior high and high school.

If you would be interested in seeing this article, I would be happy to submit it for your consideration.

Sincerely,

Michelle Tripp

Enc. SASE

Sample Query Letters

Kim Griswell
Highlights for Children
803 Church Street
Honesdale, PA 18431

Street Address
City, State, Zip
Phone Number
Email Address
Date

Dear Ms. Griswell:

Working with clay is fun! You can smush it, squeeze it and shape it. It feels cool in your hands. Have you ever made a mobile? Did you know that you can make a clay mobile?

I am proposing a how-to article for 3–12-year-old children. This article would be tentatively called "Let's Make a Clay Mobile." The length of the article would be about 200 words. The article would provide step-by-step instructions that children must follow to make a clay mobile.

I have a BS in education with a minor in art. I have created craft ideas and used them in my work with children.

I am recently published in *Kids Holiday Craft Magazine* and will have an article in an upcoming issue of *Wee Ones*. I am also a member of the Society of Children's Book Writers and Illustrators.

If you are interested in seeing the article, I would be happy to submit it for your consideration. I can furnish photographs of work in progress and the finished product.

Sincerely,

Suzanne Miles

Street Address
City, State, Zip
Phone Number
Email Address

Date

Heather A. Delabre, Associate Editor
Spider
Cricket Magazine Group
P.O. Box 300
315 Fifth Street
Peru, IL 61354-0300

Dear Ms. Delabre:

Did you know some spiders' silk is so strong it can stop a bird in flight? That a thread of spider silk as big as a pencil could stop an airplane?

My proposed article titled "Web Masters" is a craft and science article of about 400 words. It shows children how to build a web like a spider, and shares some amazing spider facts.

I believe "Web Masters" would be a perfect fit for *Spider* (no pun intended).

My story "Just Luka and Me," is in *Simple Pleasures of Friendship*, published by Conari/Red Wheel/Weiser (January 2004). My activity article, "Snowflake Shake" is forthcoming in *Spider*.

If you are interested in seeing this article, I would be happy to submit it for consideration. I have enclosed an SASE for your convenience.

Yours Truly,

Keely Parrack

Enc.: SASE

Preparing a Manuscript Package

The following guide shows how to prepare and mail a professional-looking manuscript package. However, you should always adhere to an individual magazine's submission requirements as detailed in its writers' guidelines and its listing in this directory.

Cover Letter Tips

Always keep your cover letter concise and to the point. Provide essential information only.

If the letter accompanies an unsolicited manuscript submission (see below), indicate that your manuscript is enclosed and mention its title and word length. If you're sending the manuscript after the editor responded favorably to your query letter, indicate that the editor requested to see the enclosed manuscript.

Provide a *brief* description of the piece and a short explanation of how it fits the editor's needs. List any publishing credits or other pertinent qualifications. If requested in the guidelines or listing, note any material or sources you can provide. Indicate if the manuscript is being sent to other magazines as well (a simultaneous submission). Mention that you have enclosed a self-addressed, stamped envelope for return of the manuscript.

Sample Cover Letter

Street Address
City, State Zip
Phone Number
Email Address
Date

Manuscript Submissions
Highlights for Children
803 Church Street
Honesdale, PA 18431

Dear (Name of Current Editor):

If most chocolate chip cookie recipes include pretty much the same ingredients, why are some cookies crispy and thin with little hard nuggets of chocolate while others are chewy and moist, bursting with gooey melted chocolate?

The answer is a matter of science.

I have enclosed a 570-word nonfiction article entitled "Cookie Science." Almost everyone loves chocolate chip cookies, and I believe your older readers would enjoy learning about the chemical reactions involved in baking a great cookie.

Subject/ Specifications: A brief description of the topic and its potential interest to the magazine's readers. Word lengths, age range, availability of photos, and other submission details.

I am a member of SCBWI and an enthusiastic, experienced baker. I have taught writing at the high school and community college levels.

Publishing Credits or relevant experience

I have enclosed an SASE for the return of the manuscript if it does not meet your needs at this time.

Closing: Be formal and direct.

Thank you for your consideration.

Sincerely,

Ann Marie Pace

Put Your Best Foot Forward

Magazine editors prefer to receive a typewritten manuscript or a clear, letter-quality computer printout. Be sure your type is clear and not faded.

Use high-quality $8\frac{1}{2}$ x 11 white bond paper. If acceptable, you may send clear photocopies or submissions on a computer disk. For disk submissions, make sure your disk size and software system are compatible with the publication's—and always include a hard (paper) copy of the manuscript.

Some editors accept electronic (email) submissions. When this is the case, the publication's email address is given in its listing.

If requested in the guidelines or listing, include artwork according to specifications, a list of sources, a bibliography, or a biography.

Standard Manuscript Format

The format for preparing manuscripts is fairly standard—an example is shown below. Double-space manuscript text, leaving 1- to 1½-inch margins on the top, bottom, and sides. Indent 5 spaces for paragraphs.

In the upper left corner of the first page (also known as the title page), single space your name, address, phone number, and email address. In the upper right corner of that page, place your word count.

Center the title with your byline below it halfway down the page, approximately 5 inches. Then begin the manuscript text 4 lines below your byline.

In the upper left corner of the following pages, type your last name, the page number, and a word or two of your title. Then, space down 4 lines and continue the text of the manuscript.

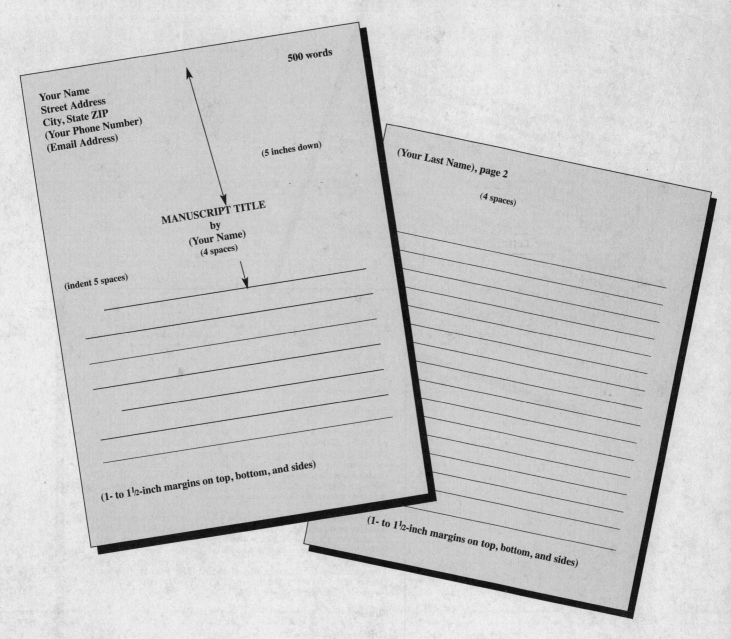

500 words

Your Name
Street Address
City, State ZIP
(Your Phone Number)
(Email Address)

(5 inches down)

MANUSCRIPT TITLE
by
(Your Name)
(4 spaces)

(indent 5 spaces)

(1- to 1½-inch margins on top, bottom, and sides)

(Your Last Name), page 2

(4 spaces)

(1- to 1½-inch margins on top, bottom, and sides)

Sample Cover Letters

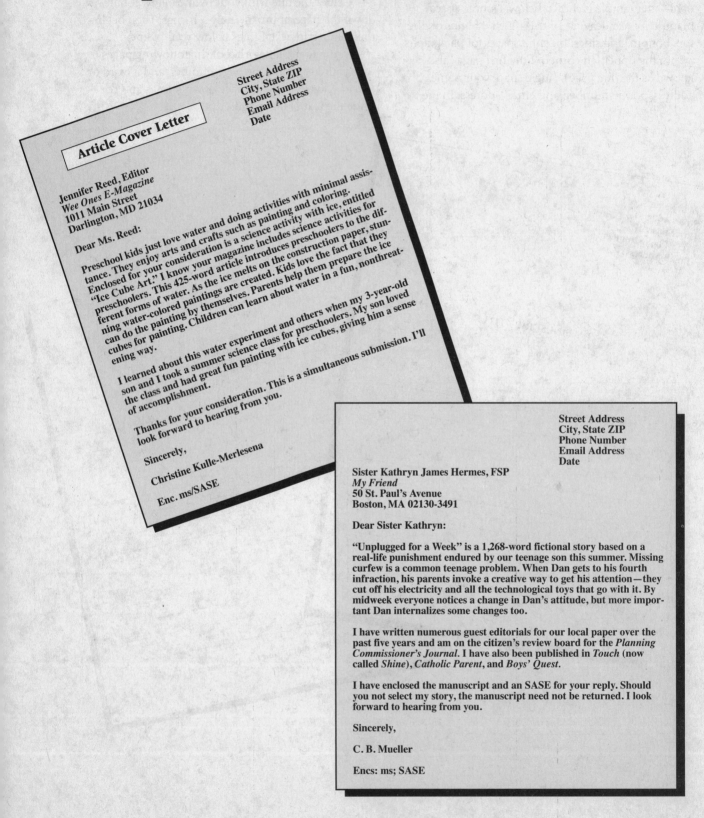

Article Cover Letter

Street Address
City, State ZIP
Phone Number
Email Address
Date

Jennifer Reed, Editor
Wee Ones E-Magazine
1011 Main Street
Darlington, MD 21034

Dear Ms. Reed:

Preschool kids just love water and doing activities with minimal assistance. They enjoy arts and crafts such as painting and coloring. Enclosed for your consideration is a science activity with ice, entitled "Ice Cube Art." I know your magazine includes science activities for preschoolers. This 425-word article introduces preschoolers to the different forms of water. As the ice melts on the construction paper, stunning water-colored paintings are created. Kids love the fact that they can do the painting by themselves. Parents help them prepare the ice cubes for painting. Children can learn about water in a fun, nonthreatening way.

I learned about this water experiment and others when my 3-year-old son and I took a summer science class for preschoolers. My son loved the class and had great fun painting with ice cubes, giving him a sense of accomplishment.

Thanks for your consideration. This is a simultaneous submission. I'll look forward to hearing from you.

Sincerely,

Christine Kulle-Merlesena

Enc. ms/SASE

Street Address
City, State ZIP
Phone Number
Email Address
Date

Sister Kathryn James Hermes, FSP
My Friend
50 St. Paul's Avenue
Boston, MA 02130-3491

Dear Sister Kathryn:

"Unplugged for a Week" is a 1,268-word fictional story based on a real-life punishment endured by our teenage son this summer. Missing curfew is a common teenage problem. When Dan gets to his fourth infraction, his parents invoke a creative way to get his attention—they cut off his electricity and all the technological toys that go with it. By midweek everyone notices a change in Dan's attitude, but more important Dan internalizes some changes too.

I have written numerous guest editorials for our local paper over the past five years and am on the citizen's review board for the *Planning Commissioner's Journal*. I have also been published in *Touch* (now called *Shine*), *Catholic Parent*, and *Boys' Quest*.

I have enclosed the manuscript and an SASE for your reply. Should you not select my story, the manuscript need not be returned. I look forward to hearing from you.

Sincerely,

C. B. Mueller

Encs: ms; SASE

Sample Cover Letters

Arun Toke
Skipping Stones Magazine
P.O. Box 3939
Eugene, OR 97403-0939

Street Address
City, State ZIP
Phone Number
Email Address
Date

Dear Mr. Toke:

What do you do when you wake up craving peanut butter in West Africa? In the U.S. most of us head to the cupboard and pull out a jar to satisfy our craving. But, in the village of Kerewan, The Gambia, getting peanut butter means doing a bit more.

With teaching credentials in hand, I headed to The Gambia as a Peace Corps Volunteer. I had many interesting experiences there that changed the way I viewed daily activities. Returning to the States to teach in California and then Alaska, I have never forgotten those experiences and draw on them frequently. I find that many of the cultural lessons I learned in West Africa can be applied to the village schools I travel to now.

The enclosed 500-word story entitled "Peanut Butter for Dinner," describes one of my favorite activities: making peanut butter from scratch with the women and children in my compound. I believe this article highlights the friendship and goodwill that people around the world have to offer. I hope you will consider it for an upcoming issue of *Skipping Stones Magazine.*

I have enclosed the manuscript and an SASE for your reply.

Sincerely

Tamra Wear

Date

Marvin Wengerd, Editor
Nature Friend Magazine
2673 TR421
Sugar Creek, OH 44681

Dear Mr. Wengerd:

On a recent trip to Washington I visited Mount St. Helens. I have been fascinated with the history of this great giant since its eruption in 1980. With the recent activity of this volcano, I suspect *Nature Friend* readers would be interested to know some of the details leading up to, and during her eruption as well as insight into the warning signs that we are experiencing today.

I have written an article titled "Sleeping Giant" which highlights the few weeks prior to, and the day of Mount St. Helens' eruption on May 18, 1980. My article highlights interesting facts about some of the people who were there, and vivid description of the pre-eruption.

The length of the article is about 700 words, and it includes some of my own observations regarding the choices people make, and how drawn we are to nature's beauty, yet hypnotized by its fury.

I have enclosed the complete ms for your review and consideration along with some photos and an SASE for your convenience.

Sincerely,

Shiela D. Hayes

Enc. ms/SASE

Sample Cover Letter & Bibliography

Street Address
City, State ZIP
Phone Number
Email Address

Date

Jonathan Shaw, Editor
The School Magazine
NSW Department of Education and Training
P.O. Box 1928
Macquarie Centre, NSW 2113 Australia

Dear Mr. Shaw:

I'm sure you've heard of Winnie-the-Pooh! Who hasn't? Do you know that Winnie was a real, live bear? *She* was born in 1914 near the town of White Water in the Canadian province of Manitoba. A trapper shot her mother while Winnie was still a cub. Normally, cubs don't survive in the wilderness when they lose their mother, but Winnie's case was different. The trapper caught Winnie and brought her to the train station in White River on a leash. A Canadian Army veterinary officer saw Winnie there and purchased her from the trapper. That began her rise from orphaned cub to international fame.

Children of all ages know and love Winnie-the-Pooh, but how many of them know her origin? The enclosed article, "Winnie-the-Who?" tells the story of Winnie's beginnings as an orphaned bear cub and of her benefactor, Lieutenant Harry Colebourn. I hope "Winnie" can find a place in the pages of *The School Magazine* where she will once again entertain and delight young readers who may have thought themselves too old for teddy bear stories.

I've enclosed a bibliography, a disposable manuscript, and an SAE/IRC for your reply. I look forward to hearing from you.

Sincerely,

Jim Slater

Enc: bibliography/ms/SAE/IRC

Bibliography

Colebourn, Fred, "Lt. Harry Colebourn and Winnie-the-Bear," original biographical sketch written by Harry Colebourn's son, Fred Colebourn, May 1988. Corrected and edited by CWO Gordon Crossley, Fort Garry Horse Museum and Archives, May 1999 to August 2000. www.fortgarryhorse.ca/HTML/winnie-the-bear.html

"Pooh Corner Biographies: A. A. Milne." www.pooh-corner.com/biomilne.html

Shushkewich, Val. The Real Winnie, A One-of-A-Kind Bear, Toronto, Ontario: Natural Heritage/Natural History Inc. 2003.

Snell, Gordon. Oh, no! More Canadians!: Hysterically Historical Rhymes, Toronto, McArthur & Company, 1998.

"Winne-the-Pooh-Disney and Pooh" www.just-pooh.com/disney.html

"Winnie-the-Pooh FAQ" www.lavasurfer.com/pooh-faq3.html#18

"Winnie the Pooh—History of Pooh" www.just-pooh.com/history

"Winnie the Pooh—Real Toys" www.just-pooh.com/toys.html

Bibliography

A solid indication of the sources you have identified is more and more a requirement of submissions to children's magazines. Much less common for fiction (with the possible exception of historical fiction) than for nonfiction, bibliographies show an editor that you have already thought through the viability of the project, that the finished piece is likely to be supported by strong evidence and research, and give the editor the tools to fact-check your work and feel confident it is of high quality.

Primary sources, interviews with experts or other relevant individuals (a profile subject and those who know him or her, for example), and a strong synthesis of research that is presented with a clarity and language your target age will appreciate—those are the strict demands of writing well for magazines for children. Articles on science or history or any other nonfiction subject, and stories with factual bases as well, can't rest on secondhand or encyclopedia-level information.

A well-constructed and balanced bibliography is an important tool in selling your writing to an editor. Several references are available and generally accepted for bibliographic format. Investing in one of these is highly recommended for writers: *The Chicago Manual of Style; Modern Language Association (MLA) Handbook;* or handbooks by such news organizations as the *New York Times* or Associated Press.

Sample Bibliography

Bibliography for "How the Birds Changed Their Colors"

Arnott, Kathleen. <u>Animal Folk Tales Around the World.</u> Henry Z. Walck, 1970. pp. 100–103.

Hilty, Steven L. <u>Birds of Venezuela.</u> Princeton University Press, 2002.

Ingersoll, Ernest. <u>Birds in Legend, Fable and Folklore.</u> Longmans Green & Co., 1923. p. 229.

Minnesota University. "Arawak."
http://emuseum.mnsu.edu/cultural/southamerica/arawak.html

Troughton, Joanna, ret. <u>How the Birds Changed Their Feathers: A South American Indian Folk Tale.</u> Peter Bedrick, 1976.

Preparing a Résumé

Several publications in this directory request that prospective writers send a list of publishing credits or enclose a résumé with their submission. As you read through the listings, you will notice that some editors want to see a résumé only, while others may request a résumé with a query letter, writing samples, or a complete manuscript.

By reviewing a résumé, an editor can determine if a prospective writer has the necessary experience to research and write material for that publication.

A résumé that you submit to a magazine is different from one you would submit when applying for a job, because it emphasizes writing experience, memberships in writing associations, and education. This type of résumé does not list all of your work experience or every association to which you belong, but should include only those credentials that demonstrate experience related to the magazine's editorial requirements. In the case of educational or special interest publications, be sure to include pertinent work experience.

No one style is preferred, but make sure your name and email address (if you have one) appear at the top of the page. Keep your résumé short and concise—it should not be more than one page long.

Sample Résumés

```
                    Joanna Coates
                      Address
                   City, State ZIP
                      Phone
                   Email Address

EDUCATION:
              University of Missouri, Columbia, MO
   1980          M.Ed. Reading
   1975          B.A. English Education

Missouri Certified Teacher of English and Reading
Specialist

TEACHING EXPERIENCE:
   1997—present  Instructor
                 Adult Continuing Education ESL Classes
                 Springfield College, Springfield, MO

   1981-1995     Classroom Teacher
                 Middle School English and Reading
                 John Jay Middle School, Thornfield, MO

EDUCATIONAL MATERIAL PUBLISHED:
                 Educational Insights
   1995            FUN WITH READING II
                     Story/activity kit
   1993            FUN WITH READING I
                     Story/activity kit
MEMBERSHIP:
Society of Children's Book Writers and Illustrators
```

```
                    Maria Lital
                      Address
                   City, State ZIP
                      Phone
                   Email Address

EDUCATION:
   1989          Bachelor of Arts
                 History/Journalism
                 University of North Carolina,
                 Chapel Hill, North Carolina

WORK EXPERIENCE:
   1998—present  Media Sales Representative,
                 Clarkson Ledger, Ripley, Tennessee

   1996-1998     Researcher/Librarian, Station
                 WBXI, Danville, Kentucky

   1993—1996     Researcher, Family News, Raleigh,
                 North Carolina

   1990—1993     Assistant Librarian, Public
                 Library; Edenton, North Carolina

RELATED ACTIVITIES:
   1998—present  Newsletter Editor, St. James
                 Church, Ripley, Tennessee

   1998—present  Historical Tour Guide, Ripley,
                 Tennessee, Historical Association

   1996—present  Active in Civil War Reenactments

MEMBERSHIP:
   1996—present  American Library Association
```

Copyright and Permissions

In the literary field, a copyright is legal ownership of an original written work. The owner or writer has the legal right to decide how a work is reproduced, and, for certain works, how it is performed or displayed. According to the Copyright Act of 1976 (effective January 1, 1978), this protection exists from the moment the work is recorded in a tangible medium, such as a computer file or on paper, without any need for legal action or counsel.

As a result of the Copyright Term Extension Act of 1998, you now own all rights to work you created during or after 1978 for your lifetime plus 70 years, until you choose to sell all or part of the copyright for this work. But remember that it is only your unique combination of words—how you wrote something— that the law protects and considers copyrighted. Ideas or facts that are expressed in your work cannot be copyrighted.

Do You Need to Register Your Work?

Once your manuscript is completed, your work is protected by the current copyright laws. You don't need to register your work with the United States Copyright Office. Editors want to buy your work; they have no need to steal it. A copy of the manuscript and a dated record of your submission will provide proof of creation.

Most editors view an author's copyright notice on manuscripts as a sign of amateurism, or a signal that the author doesn't trust the publication. However, if you decide to register your work, obtain an application form and directions on the correct way to file your copyright application. Write to the Library of Congress, Copyright Office, 101 Independence Ave. S. E., Washington, DC 20559-6000. These forms and directions are also available online in Adobe Acrobat format at: www.copyright.gov/forms. Copyright registration fees are currently $30.

If you have registered your unpublished manuscript with the Library of Congress, notify your editor of that fact once it is accepted for publication.

Rights Purchased by Magazines

Magazines request and purchase certain rights to publish manuscripts. A publisher is restricted by an agreement with you on when, how, and where he or she may publish your manuscript. Below is a list of common rights that are purchased by magazines:

All World Rights: The publisher purchases all rights to publish your work anywhere in the world any number of times. This includes all forms of media (both current and those which may be developed later). The publisher also has the right to all future use of the work, including reprints, syndication, creation of derivative works, and use in databases. You no longer have the right to sell or reproduce the work, unless you can negotiate for the return of certain rights (for example, book rights).

All World Serial Rights: The publisher purchases all rights to publish your work in newspapers, magazines, and other serial publications throughout the world any number of times. You retain all other rights, such as the right to use it as a chapter in a book.

First Rights: A publisher acquires the right to publish your work for the first time in any specified media. Electronic and nontraditional markets often seek these rights. All other rights, including reprint rights, belong to you.

Electronic Rights: Publishers use this as a catch-all for inclusion in any type of electronic publication, such as CD-ROM, websites, ezines or in an electronic database.

First North American Serial Rights: The publisher can publish your work for the first time in a U.S. or Canadian periodical. You retain the book and North American reprint rights, as well as first rights to a foreign market.

Second or Reprint Rights: This allows a publication non-exclusive rights to print the material for the second time. You may not authorize second publication to occur until after the work has appeared in print by the publisher who bought First Rights.

One-time Rights: Often bought by regional publications, this means the publication has bought the right to use the material once. You may continue to sell the material elsewhere; however, you should inform the publisher if this work is being simultaneously considered for publication in a competing magazine.

You should be aware that an agreement may limit a publisher to the right to publish your work in certain media (e.g., magazines and other periodicals only) or the agreement may include wider-ranging rights (e.g., the right to publish the manuscript in a book or an audio-cassette). The right may be limited to publishing within a specific geographic region or in a specific language. Any rights you retain allow you to resell the manuscript within the parameters of your agreement.

It is becoming increasingly common for magazines to purchase all rights, especially those who host Internet sites and make archives of previously published articles available to readers. Unless you have extensive publishing credentials, you may not want to jeopardize the opportunity to be published by insisting on selling limited rights.

Contracts and Agreements

Typically, when a publisher indicates an interest in your manuscript, he or she specifies what rights the publication will acquire. Then usually, but not always, a publisher will send you a letter of agreement or a standard written contract spelling out the terms of the agreement.

If a publisher does not send you a written contract or agreement and appears to be relying on oral consent, you need to consider your options. While an oral agreement may be legally binding, it is not as easy to enforce as a written one. To protect your interests, draft a letter outlining the terms as you understand them (e.g., a 500-word article without photos, first North American serial rights, paying on acceptance at $.05 a word). Send two copies of the letter to the editor (with a self-addressed, stamped envelope), asking him or her to sign one and return it to you if the terms are correct.

Work Made for Hire

Another term that is appearing more frequently in contracts is work made for hire. As a freelance writer, most editors treat you as an independent contractor (not an employee) who writes articles for their publication. Magazine editors can assign or commission articles to freelancers as works-made-for-hire, making the finished article property of the publisher.

Under current copyright laws, only certain types of commissioned works are considered works-made-for-hire, and only when both the publisher and the commissioned writer agree in writing. These works typically include items such as contributions to "col-

lective works" such as magazines. A contract or agreement clearly stating that the material is a work-made-for-hire must be signed by both parties and be in place before the material is written. Once a writer agrees to these terms, he or she no longer has any rights to the work.

Note that a pre-existing piece, such as an unsolicited manuscript that is accepted for publication, is not considered a commissioned work.

Guidelines for Permission to Quote

When you want to quote another writer's words in a manuscript you're preparing, you must get that writer's permission. If you don't, you could be sued for copyright infringement. Here are some guidelines:

- Any writing published in the U.S. prior to 1923 is in the public domain, as are works created by the U.S. government. Such material may be quoted without permission, but the source should be cited.

- No specific limits are set as to the length of permitted quotations in your articles: different publishers have various requirements. Generally, if you quote more than a handful of words, you should seek permission. Always remember to credit your sources.

- The doctrine of "fair use" allows quoting portions of a copyrighted work for certain purposes, as in a review, news reporting, nonprofit educational uses, or research. Contrary to popular belief, there is no absolute word limit on fair use. But as a general rule, never quote more than a few successive paragraphs from a book or article and credit the source.

- If you're submitting a manuscript that contains quoted material, you'll need to obtain permission from the source to quote the material before it is published. If you're uncertain about what to do, your editor should be able to advise you.

Resources

Interested in finding out more about writers and their rights under the law? Check these sources for further information:

The Publishing Law Center
www.publaw.com/legal.html
The Copyright Handbook: How to Protect and Use Written Works, 6th Edition by Attorney Stephen Fishman. Nolo, 2002.
The Writer's Legal Guide, 2nd Edition by Tad Crawford. Allworth Press, 1998

Last Steps and Follow Up

Before mailing your manuscript, check the pages for neatness, readability, and proper page order. Proofread for typographical errors. Redo pages if necessary. Keep a copy of the manuscript for your records.

Mailing Requirements

Assemble the pages (unstapled) and place your cover letter on top of the first page.

Send manuscripts over 5 pages in length in a 9x12 or 10x13 manila envelope. Include a same-size SASE marked "First Class." If submitting to a foreign magazine, enclose the proper amount of International Reply Coupons (IRC) for return postage. Mail manuscripts under 5 pages in a large business-size envelope with a same-size SASE folded inside.

Package your material carefully and address the outer envelope to the magazine editor. Send your submission via first-class or priority mail. Don't use certified or registered mail. (See Postage Information, page 28.)

Follow Up with the Editor

Some writers contend that waiting for an editor to respond is the hardest part of writing. But wait you must. Editors usually respond within the time period specified in the listings.

If you don't receive a response by the stated response time, allow at least three weeks to pass before you contact the editor. At that time, send a letter with a self-addressed, stamped envelope requesting to know the status of your submission.

The exception to this general rule is when you send a return postcard with a manuscript. In that case, look for your postcard about three weeks after mailing the manuscript. If you don't receive it by then, write to the editor requesting confirmation that it was received.

If more than two months pass after the stated response time and you don't receive any response, send a letter withdrawing your work from consideration. At that point, you can send your query or manuscript to the next publication on your list.

What You Can Expect

The most common responses to a submission are an impersonal rejection letter, a personalized rejection letter, an offer to look at your material "on speculation," or an assignment.

If you receive an impersonal rejection note, revise your manuscript if necessary, and send your work to the next editor on your list. If you receive a personal note, send a thank-you note. If you receive either of the last two responses, you know what to do!

Set Up a Tracking System

To help you keep track of the status of your submissions, you may want to establish a system in a notebook, in a computer file, or on file cards (see below).

This will keep you organized and up-to-date on the status of your queries and manuscripts and on the need to follow up with certain editors.

SENT QUERIES TO THE FOLLOWING PUBLICATIONS

Editor	Publication	Topic	Date Sent	Postage	Accepted/ Rejected	Rights Offered

SENT MANUSCRIPTS TO THE FOLLOWING PUBLICATIONS

Editor	Publication	Title	Date Sent	Postage	Accepted/ Rejected	Rights Offered

Frequently Asked Questions

How do I request a sample copy and writers' guidelines?

Write a brief note to the magazine: *"Please send me a recent sample copy and writers' guidelines. If there is any charge, please enclose an invoice and I will pay upon receipt."* The magazine's website, if it has one, offers a faster and less expensive alternative. Many companies put a part of the magazine, writers' guidelines, and sometimes a theme list or editorial calendar on the Internet.

How do I calculate the amount of postage for a sample copy?

Check the listing in this directory. In some cases the amount of postage will be listed. If the number of pages is given, use that to estimate the amount of postage by using the postage chart at the end of this section. For more information on postage and how to obtain stamps, see page 28.

I need to include a bibliography with my article proposal. How do I set one up?

The reference section of your local library can provide several sources that will help you set up a bibliography. A style manual such as *The Chicago Manual of Style* will show you the proper format for citing all your sources, including unpublished material, interviews, and Internet material. For information on bibliographies, see page 21.

What do I put in a cover letter if I have no publishing credits or relevant personal experience?

In this case, you may want to forego a formal cover letter and send your manuscript with a brief letter stating: *"Enclosed is my manuscript, [Insert Title], for your review."* For more information on cover letters, see pages 16.

How long should I wait before contacting an editor after I have submitted my manuscript?

The response time given in the listings can vary, and it's a good idea to wait three to four weeks after the stated response time before sending a brief note to the editor asking about the status of your manuscript. You might use this opportunity to add a new sales pitch or include additional material to show that the topic is continuing to generate interest. If you do not get a satisfactory response or you want to send your manuscript elsewhere, send a certified letter to the editor withdrawing the work from consideration and requesting its return. You are then free to submit the work to another magazine.

I don't need my manuscript returned. How do I indicate that to an editor?

With the capability to store manuscripts electronically and print out additional copies easily, some writers keep postage costs down by enclosing a self-addressed, stamped postcard (SASP) saying, *"No need to return my manuscript. Please use this postcard to advise me of the status of my manuscript. Thank you."*

Common Publishing Terms

All rights: Contractual agreement by which a publisher acquires the copyright and all use of author's material (see page 23).

Anthology: A collection of selected literary pieces.

Anthropomorphization: Attributing human form or personality to things not human (i.e., animals).

Assignment: Manuscript commissioned by an editor for a stated fee.

Bimonthly: A publication that appears every two months.

Biweekly: A publication issued every two weeks.

Byline: Author's name credited at the heading of an article.

Caption: Description or text accompanying an illustration or photograph.

CD-ROM (compact disc read-only-memory): Non-erasable compact disc containing data that can be read by a computer.

Clip: Sample of a published work.

Contributor's copies: Copies of the publication issue in which the writer's work appears.

Copyedit: To edit with close attention to style and mechanics.

Copyright: Legal rights that protect an author's work (see page 23).

Cover letter: Brief letter sent with a manuscript introducing the writer and presenting the materials enclosed (see page 16).

Disk submission: Manuscript that is submitted on a computer disk.

Early readers: Children 4 to 7 years.

Editorial calendar: List of topics, themes, or special sections that are planned for upcoming issues for a specific time period.

Electronic submission: Manuscript transmitted to an editor from one computer to another through a modem.

Email (electronic mail): Messages sent from one computer to another via computer network or modem.

English-language rights: The right to publish a manuscript in any English-speaking country.

Filler: Short item that fills out a page (e.g., joke, light verse, or fun fact).

First serial rights: The right to publish a work for the first time in a periodical; often limited to a specific geographical region (e.g., North America or Canada) [see page 23].

Genre: Category of fiction characterized by a particular style, form, or content, such as mystery or fantasy.

Glossy: Photo printed on shiny rather than matte-finish paper.

Guidelines: See **Writers' guidelines.**

In-house: See **Staff written.**

International Reply Coupon (IRC): Coupon exchangeable in any foreign country for postage on a single-rate, surface-mailed letter.

Kill fee: Percentage of the agreed-upon fee paid to a writer if an editor decides not to use a purchased manuscript.

Layout: Plan for the arrangement of text and artwork on a printed page.

Lead: Beginning of an article.

Lead time: Length of time between assembling and printing an issue.

Libel: Any false published statement intended to expose another to public ridicule or personal loss.

Manuscript: A typewritten or computer-printed version of a document (as opposed to a published version).

Masthead: The printed matter in a newspaper or periodical that gives the title and pertinent details of ownership, advertising rates, and subscription rates.

Middle-grade readers: Children 8 to 12 years.

Modem: An internal device or a small electrical box that plugs into a computer; used to transmit data between computers, often via telephone lines.

Ms/mss: Manuscript/manuscripts.

One-time rights: The right to publish a piece once, often not the first time (see page 23).

On spec: Refers to writing "on speculation," without an editor's commitment to purchase the manuscript.

Outline: Summary of a manuscript's contents, usually nonfiction, organized under subheadings with descriptive sentences under each.

Payment on acceptance: Author is paid following an editor's decision to accept a manuscript.

Payment on publication: Author is paid following the publication of the manuscript.

Pen name/pseudonym: Fictitious name used by an author.

Pre-K: Children under 5 years of age; also known as *preschool*.

Proofread: To read and mark errors, usually in printed text.

Query: Letter to an editor to promote interest in a manuscript or an idea.

Rebus story: A "see and say" story form, using pictures followed by the written words; often written for pre-readers.

Refereed journal: Publication that requires all manuscripts be reviewed by an editorial or advisory board.

Reprint: Another printing of an article or story; can be in a different magazine format, such as an anthology.

Reprint rights: See **Second serial rights.**

Response time: Average length of time for an editor to accept or reject a submission and contact the writer with his or her decision.

Résumé: Account of one's qualifications, including educational and professional background, as well as publishing credits.

SAE: Self-addressed envelope (no postage).

SASE: Self-addressed, stamped envelope.

SASP: Self-addressed stamped postcard.

Second serial rights: The right to publish a manuscript that has appeared in another publication; also known as *Reprint rights* (see page 23).

Semiannual: Occurring every six months or twice a year.

Semimonthly: Occurring twice a month.

Semiweekly: Occurring twice a week.

Serial: A publication issued as one of a consecutively numbered and indefinitely continued series.

Serial rights: See **First serial rights.**

Sidebar: A short article that accompanies a feature article and highlights one aspect of the feature's subject.

Simultaneous submission: Manuscript submitted to more than one publisher at the same time; also known as multiple submission.

Slant: Specific approach to a subject to appeal to a certain readership.

Slush pile: Term used within the publishing industry to describe unsolicited manuscripts.

Solicited manuscript: Manuscript that an editor has requested or agreed to consider.

Staff written: Prepared by members of the magazine's staff; also known as *in-house*.

Syndication rights: The right to distribute serial rights to a given work through a syndicate of periodicals.

Synopsis: Condensed description or summary of a manuscript.

Tabloid: Publication printed on an ordi-nary newspaper page, turned sideways and folded in half.

Tearsheet: A page from a newspaper or magazine (periodical) containing a printed story or article.

Theme list: See **Editorial calendar.**

Transparencies: Color slides, not color prints.

Unsolicited manuscript: Any manuscript not specifically requested by an editor.

Work-made-for-hire: Work specifically ordered, commissioned, and owned by a publisher for its exclusive use (see page 24).

World rights: Contractual agreement whereby the publisher acquires the right to reproduce the work throughout the world (see page 23); also known as *all rights*.

Writers' guidelines: Publisher's editorial objectives or specifications, which usually include word lengths, readership level, and subject matter.

Writing sample: Example of your writing style, tone, and skills; may be a published or unpublished piece.

Young adult: Readers 12 to 18 years.

Postage Information

How Much Postage?

When you're sending a manuscript to a magazine, enclose a self-addressed, stamped envelope with sufficient postage; this way, if the editor does not want to use your manuscript, it can be returned to you. To help you calculate the proper amount of postage for your SASE, here are the U.S. postal rates for first-class mailings in the U.S. and from the U.S. to Canada based on the latest increase (2002). Rates are expected to increase again, so please check with your local Post Office, or check the U.S. Postal Service website at usps.com.

Ounces	9x12 Envelope (Approx. no. of pages)	U.S. First-Class Postage Rate	Rate from U.S. to Canada
1	1–5	$ 0.37	$ 0.60
2	6–10	0.60	0.85
3	11–15	0.83	1.10
4	16–20	1.06	1.35
5	21–25	1.29	1.60
6	26–30	1.52	1.85
7	31–35	1.75	2.10
8	36–40	1.98	2.35

The amount of postage and size of envelope necessary to receive a sample copy and writers' guidelines are usually stated in the magazine listing. If this information is not provided, use the chart above to help gauge the proper amount of postage.

How to Obtain Stamps

People living in the U.S., Canada, or overseas can acquire U.S. stamps through the mail from the Philately Fulfillment Service Center. Call 800-STAMP-24 (800-782-6724) to request a catalogue or place an order. For overseas, the telephone number is 816-545-1100. You pay the cost of the stamps plus a postage and handling fee based on the value of the stamps ordered, and the stamps are shipped to you. Credit card information (MasterCard, Visa, and Discover cards only) is required for fax orders. The fax number is 816-545-1212. If you order through the catalogue, you can pay with a U.S. check or an American Money Order. Allow 3–4 weeks for delivery.

Gateway to the Markets

Read Me a Story Out Loud

The love of reading is often fostered in childhood at the knee of an adult armed with a good readaloud story. The pleasure in listening extends as far as adolescence, and even beyond: Around a campfire, under the covers, beneath a shady tree, or in front of a roaring fire, there is an enchantment about hearing a good story read out loud. To capture a listener as well as a reader, a story must have distinct qualities of content and style that give it appeal. Magazine editors are looking for creative, energetic readaloud stories for children of many ages.

Highlights for Children publishes six fictional stories each month, several of them considered readalouds, for ages 2 to 12. "We look for stories that older children will enjoy reading aloud and younger children will enjoy listening to," says Marileta Robinson, Senior Editor. "To appeal to a broad age range, they need to have a lively pace, tight writing, humor or suspense (or both), good rhythm, and a vocabulary that interests older children and appeals to young listeners."

"At *Ladybug*, our definition of a readaloud story hasn't changed in the 14 years I've been here: We simply look for engaging, age-appropriate stories told in beautiful language to please the ears and minds and hearts of young children. Stories must respect the child who listens and also the adult who reads," says Paula Morrow, Executive Editor of *Ladybug* and *Babybug*.

The Matter of Age

Though all ages love to hear good stories, the market for readalouds is still focused largely on babies to early reader, and the adults who read to them.

For *Ladybug*, which reaches a broader range of preschool and primary children, age appropriateness is more a matter of content and voice than of reading level. "Sadly, that's the one thing that's missing from the majority of manuscripts we receive. Too many writers give us the parent's or grandparent's viewpoint instead of the child's." *Babybug* doesn't use the typical readaloud story, Morrow explains. With a "readership" of infants and toddlers, *Babybug* stories consist of four to eight short sentences, totaling 20 to 30 words. "The shorter, the better!"

Age-appropriateness can be difficult to judge in a readaloud story due to the broad range of young listeners and school-aged readers. "Remember that a preschooler's listening comprehension is much higher than a primary child's reading ability," cautions Morrow. "Writers who want to see their work in *Ladybug* should study back issues to get a sense of our world and also spend time with young children to understand what they like and think and feel. Read a lot of other children's literature and avoid rehashing plots and characters you see everywhere else. And this goes without saying, but I'll say it anyway: Follow our guidelines."

Robinson counsels writers to become familiar with *Highlights* before submitting stories for consideration. "We publish stories for three- to eight-year-olds that are up to 500 words in length, and stories for more advanced readers that are up to 800 words in length. In both cases, the old adage *show, don't tell* applies. Readaloud stories need action and energy. Consider alliteration, assonance, playfulness, short sentence length, variety, and repetition."

Content & Character

Roger Hammer is Editor and Publisher of Read! America, a publishing concern aimed at encouraging children in grades three through six to read stories and poems. He agrees that writers must keep the reader's comprehension in the forefront of their minds when writing readaloud stories.

"Sentences need to be shorter for children, and vocabulary should be consistent with the reader's," says Hammer. "I often get manuscripts that use words that are too big or complex for young readers. Of course, stories that use bigger words that can be explained by a parent or teacher are useful to grow a child's vocabulary, but very young children need simplicity."

Read! America publishes material that is intended for reading program leaders to read aloud to their students. "We look for stories that can be read and reread. The characters should be fun, and the readers can relate to the dilemmas that they face. We like to see suspense, or a twist that keeps the reader actively listening and trying to figure out what will happen next. There is nothing better than a child who gets excited as they see a story form in their imagination," says Hammer.

The balance between style and content is an important one. "We want stories that challenge a child's mind and if they teach a lesson, it is done through example, rather than lecturing. Right now we're focusing on main characters who have disabilities. They are the heroes and heroines who overcome dilemmas. Most kids are in a limited developmental stage and know the frustration of not being able to do physically what they want. In this way, non-disabled children can relate to the physical limitations of those with disabilities."

Wee Ones Editor Jennifer Reed agrees. "For us, character-driven stories are important, even for the youngest readers. The language has to be age-appropriate and the problem something that children can relate to. I look for good, solid fiction, but when I read it out loud again, the words have to roll off my tongue. How it sounds when read out loud is important. How do the words flow? What is the pace like? Is it enjoyable to read? If I stumble over words, have to reread sections, then I probably won't accept the piece. I also have a child read it out loud and see how well they do with it."

Wee Ones is one of a growing number of magazines for children that publishes on the Internet (www.weeonesmag.com). "We are somewhat new to the marketplace," Reed explains. "Because we are on the Internet, our readaloud stories are relatively short, a maximum of 300 to 400 words. They are geared to children ages five to seven who are just learning to read, whether they are being read to or reading our stories on their own."

Story Mates, a Sunday school take-home paper for ages four to eight, uses readaloud stories to teach its young audience biblical lessons. "We are a conservative Mennonite publisher. As such, we look for material that is biblically sound and consistent with our applications of biblical principles," explains Crystal Shank, *Story Mates* Editor. "We seek stories that are true-to-life, rather than fantasy, with true-to-life characters, rather than talking animals. Most importantly, they need to have a spiritual lesson that helps children in their innocent years learn how to live in ways that please God."

> *Around a campfire, under the covers, beneath a shady tree, or in front of a roaring fire, there is enchantment in hearing a good story read out loud.*

Published monthly, *Story Mates* uses a format of four-page tear-out sections for each week. "Most weekly parts have one readaloud story of 800 or 900 words, or two shorter stories," says Shank. "With this age range, some children will be able to read the stories themselves, and some will need to have the stories read aloud to them. Most important, the stories must be interesting and suitable for the age group."

The Current Market

"It's not easy to write readalouds, and authors must realize that selling fiction is particularly tough," says Reed when asked about the current market for readaloud stories. "I buy them as I find good ones. I won't ask for rewrites or to resubmit a piece. If it doesn't work the first time I see it, that's it."

What works is best explained by reading and listening to stories publishers themselves hold up as good examples of the readaloud genre.

"'Mixing It Up,' by Linda Haas Manley (January 2004), is a good one," says Reed. "It was character-driven, relatively short, the conflict was age-appropriate, and it is easy to read. Another is 'Willy the Dirty Pirate,' by Anne Acosta (January 2005). It's a bit longer but there is a lot of action and dialogue and this makes it fun and easy to read."

According to Morrow, *Ladybug* has an almost three-year backlog of readaloud stories, so manuscripts accepted in 2006 will probably be published in 2009, perhaps even later. "We're still accepting good stories, and everything we accept will eventually be published. Nothing dies in the files here!"

Morrow is quick to highlight what distinguishes a good readaloud by identifying published stories she sees as aptly targeted to her readership. She cites "Cookie Moon," by Lori Menning (February 2005). "Normally we avoid bedtime stories because they're so overdone, but this one is quite uncommon. It has humor, carefully controlled repetition, and believable interactions between the two characters. A story that ends with the main character asleep is usually boring, but note that in 'Cookie Moon,' Jack is wide awake and active at the conclusion. As a bonus, this story offers interesting scientific information—the phases of the moon—without being at all teachy."

Another *Ladybug* example is "Weather Happens," by Audrey B. Baird (April 2005). Morrow says, "Now here's proof that a successful story can be very short. This is just over 200 words yet the lyrical language lets the reader share in the main character's emotions, from her initial disappointment through surprise to delight. Although neither character can be fully developed in such a short piece, the loving relationship between them is deftly, even poetically drawn."

At HighlightsKids.com, children and authors alike can hear recently published readaloud stories, including "Dexter Robin Learns to Fly," by Jennifer Gomoll (March 2005), "Belly Flops and Gutter Balls," by JoLynne Ricker Whalen (April 2005), and "What Dad Wanted," by Ann Devendorf (December 2004).

"One thing writers should keep in mind is that communication is a two-way street," says Hammer. "A story should be told well, but also must be understood by the person at the other end in order to be successful. We receive many manuscripts from writers who are so focused on what they want to say, that they forget about the reader. Above all, writers should remember to market the child you're targeting, not the editor."

Lights, Camera, Action— Adventure

Adventure can be the perfect read. It is a story a reader simply can't put down. It has a plot with enough cliff-hangers or twists and turns to keep a reader wanting to look around the next bend. In the end, it leaves readers of all ages and types satisfied—like a good meal. In a great adventure story, the action grows naturally out of narrative, setting, and character, and is accomplished without the need for a single exclamation point!!!

"For us, a good adventure story should be exciting and unpredictable," says Judy Burke, Associate Editor of *Highlights for Children.* "The child who is the main character should solve (or play a big part in helping to solve) the main problem in the story by using quick thinking." Burke says *Highlights* is always looking for good adventure stories. "Strong writing and a clever solution to the problem usually make a story stand out above the rest."

"A good adventure has a strong conflict and well thought-out plot," says Jennifer Reed, Editor of *Wee Ones*, an e-magazine for ages 5 to 10. "I also like to see a lot of action. Twists throughout the story add to the adventurous aspect of the story, too, and keep the reader guessing." She adds that if a story "is filled with action and has some twists and turns, I'll give it a second reading." Reed loves adventure stories but receives very few that excite her—a tale often told by children's editors.

Building on the Basics

Adventure, like any genre, depends on certain foundation elements: characters that readers can identify with, a story that rings true, realistic action, and an ending that is believable. Christina Malone, Managing Editor of *Shine,* a magazine for 9- to 14-year-old girls, looks for "engaging characters and characters that kids can relate to." In an adventure story, a character can and should face challenges, but they must be surmountable situations.

"Characters may be scared during their adventure, but they are brave enough to complete it," says Sandra Blanchard of *High Adventure*, a quarterly for boys 7 to 15 published by the General Council of the Assemblies of God. Blanchard is Administrative Coordinator to the denomination's National Commander of the National Royal Rangers.

Action may still be an outgrowth of character, however. "*Wee Ones* much prefers a character-driven story over any others," says Reed, but "if the story is set in an unusual setting, that will catch my attention."

What makes a good adventure plot? The story line needs to keep moving, literally. It needs to engage and progress through action rather than through internal conflict, although that also comes into play.

For Blanchard, "realistic situations and action sequences make a good adventure." *High Adventure* always wants adventures that fit the bill. Since it targets boys and is a Christian publication, she says, they look for the adventure, but built around "events that could happen and events that do not involve careless life-and-death risks."

Distinct Needs

Adventures can change with the times, despite their universal appeal. At *Highlights*, Burke says, "We like adventure stories that feel contemporary. As with any good story, the setting should be specific, not generic." In particular, she says, "We could always use more adventure stories set in foreign countries and more humorous adventure stories. If authors would like to improve their chances of success, I'd encourage them to study our editorial guidelines and to read several recent issues of *Highlights* at their local library. This will help authors to get a feel for the tone of our magazine and the types of stories that we like to publish."

Burke cites "Into the Cave," by Harriett Diller and Betty Hodges (July 2005). "I like this one a lot because the problem is universal (facing your fear) but the setting is unique (a cave in Guilin, China). The story is contemporary, which is a plus because so much of the world-cultures fiction that we receive has an old-timey folktale feel to it, which is okay for some folktales, but not for all stories!"

Another quality Burke says works in the story is that the protaganist struggles but grows.

> "We like adventure stories that feel contemporary. We could always use more adventures set in foreign countries and more humorous adventure stories."

"I like that the boy, Lin, finds the courage to do the right thing even though it's particularly tough for him, and I like that Lin appreciates his grandfather's point of view by the end."

At *Fun for Kidz*, timelessness is important, even in adventures. "We are different than a typical magazine. We don't change with the times. We don't get into current events. The issues are themed and timeless and children hang onto them because of it," says Editor in Chief Marilyn Edwards. "Every story has to have a moral, like helping someone out."

Edwards says that the best adventure she has read was a true story about a climb of Mount Everest. She would like to see more such nonfiction adventures, with pictures—"a true event told as an adventure story with photos that make it a true thing." She also "likes stories with a lot of dialogue, but it doesn't have to be that way."

Another adventure piece Edwards liked had an unusual format. The adventure story itself was in italics, but it alternated with paragraphs in regular type teaching readers how to write an adventure story of their own.

Ending on a Real Note

Adventure stories of course never end with the fairy tale happily-ever-after ending. But the end of the adventure is just as important as the beginning. The outcome needs to make sense. The ending should never disappoint the reader. The ending should not be too simple or unrealistic. "A lot of times, I'll receive an adventure story that is obvious," says Reed. "The plot or outcome of the story has a slow pace and I already know what is going to happen by the middle of the story."

Malone agrees and says the best advice she can give to writers interested in this kind of fiction is to keep it real. "A problem we see is that too many stories have what we call a pollyanna ending in which everything turns out perfectly. That's not real life. We want a realistic ending with believable twists and consequences to the actions of characters. In fact, we're seeking adventure stories that do not have a perfect ending."

Editors agree that one of the biggest challenges in writing successful adventure fiction for magazines is length. The maximum length is usually around 1,000 words, with many publications targeting younger readers looking for stories half that length.

"We welcome 800-word stories for 8- to 12-year-olds, and 500-word stories for 4- to 8-year-olds," says Burke at *Highlights*.

Fun for Kidz submissions should try to focus on the 8- to 10-year-old market, Edwards advises, although the subscribers range from 5 to 14. Stories are about 750 words.

"I think it's hard to write short adventure stories and our maximum word count is 500 words," says Reed. Malone says much the same. "We publish shorter stories—under 1,000 words. Often, it's difficult for writers to capture the elements we're looking for in so few words."

The answer is to keep it simple. Keep the number of characters to a minimum. Tell a story that takes place over a reasonable amount of time, one that lends itself to a shorter length. Finally, find a story that has something about it that will engage the reader from beginning to end.

"I get a lot of fiction but it's just boring stuff," says Reed. "It doesn't make me laugh or smile or move me in some way. I'm looking for stories that make me say, 'Wow! I never thought of that.'"

Crossing the Ocean of History

Ask anyone what they remember of history in grade school and they inevitably recite a ditty like, "In 1492 Columbus sailed the ocean blue." What we remember are the fun bits and stories that rang true or piqued our curiosity.

History is forever being rewritten as we find new ways to tell old stories and deliver new insights through primary sources. The demand for history writers is strong and editors look for those writers who can find a new way into a tried-and-true topic. "As for the current market need, I would say it is great," states Meg Chorlian, Editor of *Cobblestone*. "*Cobblestone* is closely tied to the school market, and we keep hearing that history and social studies departments are always looking for ways to make their subject engaging."

Schooled in History

Magazines driven by school curriculum needs are committed to bringing readers history that enriches required topics. These publications are all in the market for personal and untold stories, and stories with a fresh perspective.

Magazines like *Appleseeds* and *Cobblestone*, both from Carus Publishing, follow history as dictated by curriculum guidelines. "There are many discussions currently about how to get young people excited about history. Teachers are looking for options," says Chorlian. A successful writer can "breathe new life into an old or much covered topic. The job is made more difficult by the fact that while weaving a story, you need to remember to keep to the facts, especially in our case where we are trying to inform young people."

Chorlian cites a 2005 *Cobblestone* issue on 1776 and the Declaration of Independence as an example. "There have been many books written about the American Revolutionary War and there are lots of ways to approach the story of this important document. But how do you get kids to think in 1776 time, not 2006 time? We know that we won the Revolutionary War, but the people who lived in 1776 had no idea how it would turn out, and yet they were still willing to sacrifice their lives and livelihood to try. If kids can get that feeling of suspense and drama, history can be very exciting."

"Our aim is to make the past come alive so that readers take an interest in history and don't dismiss it as boring," says Susan Buckley, Editor of *Appleseeds*. "Because our readers range from 7 to 10, their historical background knowledge is limited. Our articles must engage their interest while providing sufficient historical context and background."

Appleseeds devotes one issue a year to some period of American history. The issue is called, "Growing Up in . . ." and focuses on a specific time period, as in "Growing Up in America Before 1492." A second issue each year is reserved for world history. In the past, this issue has been called "Children of . . ." but Buckley says that will change and the world history issue will soon take a new direction.

History will always be about facts, but as Buckley notes, a good writer knows how "to make the people, events, and situations of the past accessible and engaging for young readers."

Magazines also look for unique ways to present history, so the flexible writer is often one an editor will return to time and again. "Flexibility in our authors is important. An author might query on one subject, but if we have a specific need for something slightly different, the author who can shift gears and adjust to what we need is very valuable," says Buckley.

Chorlian cites as an example a writer who sent in a query that was of interest, but Chorlian asked that the writer take a different approach. "I asked her to treat the subject as a play, to make it more interactive for the readers. She had never done a play before, but she was willing to give it a try. When it came in, it needed virtually no editing!"

Buckley and Chorlian stress the need for fresh approaches to presenting history. "I like to include creative theme-related activities in each issue, but I don't get many queries for them."

"Good and bad writing for children have existed forever and in every field. But there have always been good writers who could tell the stories of history well," says Buckley. The ability to tell a good story is key to history writing. History is at its fundament, stories about real people. "We strive to include real stories of real people. They don't have to be famous. Daily life articles are great to provide some basic context to the subject and to help the readers imagine how life then was different from their own experiences today. Pull-out quotes provide *voices* to the history and also can be presented in a way that visually adds to the article," says Chorlian. In the fall of 2005, *Cobblestone* moved to a new format that lends itself to sidebars.

Inspiring, Don't You Know

Whatever the time period, a good story needs a good hook. "We have an increasing need for history articles, especially if they are accurate, succinct, and hook the reader with a question, anecdote, or something *present-day,*" something the reader can immediately relate to, says Kalen Marquis, Editor of *Mr. Marquis' Museletter,* a Canadian quarterly for ages 2 to 12. Marquis is interested in stories about inspirational historical figures. For history, she says, "We aim at informing our elementary school-aged readers with the thought that it will serve as trivia, a bit of *did-you-know?* In our winter 2005 issue, we published 'The Spirit of Christmas Long Ago.' It was an informative and timely article about a well-known Christmas tradition—the selection, cutting down, and lighting of Christmas trees that began so long ago."

Mr. Marquis' Museletter uses one history article for each of its quarterly issues. Marquis's best advice to writers looking for good historical material, "If it interests you, it will likely interest us. Ironically, in this time of great access to increasingly specialized information, a lot of common knowledge does not seem all that common anymore."

Chorlian agrees. "I can often tell that an author is excited by a topic because it comes through in the article. That's so important, to have a natural fascination and interest in the subject about which you are writing."

Writers who convey their own excitement about a given subject can also sometimes see pieces of history that are hidden to the casual observer. Things that Editor Rosanne Tolin of the e-zine *Guideposts for Kids,* or *GP4Kids,* calls the *cool factor.* "We do trivia-type pieces that are historical, such as accidental inventions. (Did you know an 11-year-old created the popsicle?)" Pieces like this work best for her e-zine, with cool links to other sites. Remember, stresses Tolin, to "make history come alive for the reader by asking yourself whether you would be interested in this fact or that fact. You don't want your reader asking 'so what?' or worse, falling asleep, before finishing your story."

Much of what Tolin uses for history fits under the category Famous Folks. These are profiles of historically important people. Tolin likes to see these written in a journalistic style, but says, "The writing should be short and snappy to appeal to our kid readers. But be historically accurate!" *GP4Kids* targets ages 6 to 12. Tolin purchases about a dozen pieces a year for the Famous Folks department. One example of a feature article that worked is "Rooting for Rootbeer." It is a longer piece, says Tolin, that the writer handled well by using a lot of subheads, sidebars, and links to other sites.

Like *Mr. Marquis' Museletter* and *GP4Kids,* *New Moon* is not based on the curriculum. It is interested in stories about real people who may be new to students or that are based on events not directly covered in school. Lacey A. Louwagie, Assistant Managing Editor, sees the need for such stories growing. "I think there has been more interest in topics that aren't necessarily covered in school, and I think that's great. Magazine articles about history should serve to fill in the gaps of what is left out at school—articles about women of color, for example, or other minorities who don't get a lot of formal recognition in school curriculum." *New Moon* appears six times a year and targets girls 8 to 14.

Tolin agrees that the role of children's magazines using history may be to fill in the blanks that curriculums do not cover in depth. "I think there's more being written about surprising aspects of historical figures and events—little known details that are difficult to decipher in textbooks. Because there is so much history at our fingertips through resources like the Internet, I think the best way to get kids interested is by including the wow factor in a manuscript. Give them something they didn't already know."

New Moon publishes one history article in each issue under the heading of "Herstory." Louwagie is interested in profiles of historical girls or women. "We like our historical profiles of women to be vivid and alive. We want girls to be able to relate to the women and girls they read about from history. While we give due appreciation to the girls and women who have had historical significance, we don't put them up on a pedestal. Articles should include specific anecdotes about who the historical figure was as a person—funny stories from her childhood or quirks she might have had."

Louwagie cites "The Tupperware Lady" (March/April 2005) about Brownie Wise, the woman behind the invention of Tupperware and her unique idea of marketing the product through Tupperware parties. "What made this article unique was that Brownie Wise grew up with minimal education but used her experience as a charming, talkative woman to help her get a job and support her family after she left her alcoholic husband. What she did was incredible, but underneath it all, she was a regular woman. We all know women like her."

New Moon is particularly interested in stories about minority women and women from cultures other than European and American.

Date, Time, Place

The journalistic golden rule of the five W's (*who, what, where, when, why*) are a necessary part of relating a historical story, but the trick is to avoid getting mired in the details. Young readers are overwhelmed by too much information and find it a turnoff. So do editors. "We don't want historical articles that are just a list of accomplishments," says Louwagie.

Another pitfall is the urgency to tell the whole story, when in fact a successful article is often one that encourages the young reader to be hungry for more. For us, says Marquis, "Your article is not meant to be exhaustive but, rather, serve as a springboard for further inquiry. Brevity and accuracy are important."

Most children's magazines have small word count specifications, and too many facts will make an 800-word article quickly lose its audience. What often works well is the use of sidebars to cover an important date or event that, should it appear in the running text, might take away from the narrative. "Details and facts," says Marquis, "must be balanced with a style or slant that holds the reader's interest."

> *History will always be about facts, but a good writer knows how "to make the people, events, and situations of the past accessible and engaging."*

The other key is to remember the age of your reader. For the younger reader, a history article in a magazine may be an introduction to the topic. A good writer needs to find a way to give context while telling a good story.

Because *Cobblestone* is aimed at ages 9 to 14, says Chorlian, an author "needs to assume that this may be the first time the reader is seeing information. Technical words should be explained or defined. Terminology should be chosen carefully. We like to introduce and define new words, but we also try to be careful about including too many defined words. Better to replace some of them with a more age-appropriate word than to have too many definitions distracting from the article's flow."

The biggest turnoff in a history article, says Chorlian, "is including too many dates. Dates are important for a reference, but we would rather get readers interested in the article before we hit them with that."

So if you choose to write about Columbus, talk about 1492 along with a description of the ocean blue—but with originality and flair—and your words will be remembered.

A Prime Market: Parenting Magazines

How many ways are there to raise a child? Let's count the ways: There's your way and then there's everyone else's. Parenting publications recognize that raising children is not a simple matter, but complex in needs and parameters. They are good resources for either getting advice for your parenting challenges or, as a writer, offering your experiences to them. Writing for this niche could seem deceptively simple, but as with any other specialty niche, there are guidelines and distinct requirements. As always, it's important to know the publication you're targeting.

Regional Markets

Many parenting magazines are regional in content. Editors look for articles with a local angle that is relevant to their readers.

Donna Willis, Editor of *Columbus Parent*, emphasizes, "We're specific to Central Ohio. All of my writers live, work, and raise their children here." Her goal of increasing usefulness to her audience requires that submissions have information pertinent to the region. Susan Holson, Managing Editor and Co-Publisher of *Kids VT*, agrees. "We favor anything with a local angle" including the author, subject matter, and quoted experts.

One of the reasons behind keeping things "native" is explained by Lynda Exley, Editor of *Arizona Parenting*. She says that as cities such as Phoenix grow larger and larger, parents crave more of a community feeling. One of the ways this is accomplished is by interviewing local experts and addressing local issues. "Yes, national experts are fine to quote, too, but the local flavor needs to be there," Exley says.

Getting the "newsy angle" is the target for Helen Freedman, Editor in Chief of *Big Apple Parent, Brooklyn Parent, Queens Parent,* and *Westchester Parent.* "It's the local news angle or the national news angle with local implica-

tions that gets our interest," she says. Our readers "look to us for cutting-edge info and sophisticated takes on parenting subjects, with the emphasis on local."

Authoritative, Substantial, Simple

Although editors and publishers believe that this niche market is holding its own and even growing, competition for readers remains high. The trend is toward serious information such as emotional and medical issues, underlining the need for reliable, solid information in articles that are fresh, thoroughly researched, nonbiased, and pertinent.

Exley wants at least three experts quoted for each article, with all sides of an issue represented. "We want content that will educate parents and improve the quality of life for their families," she explains. Brenda Hyde, Publisher of Families Magazines, sees health and medical issues becoming a larger part of the market's editorial content.

While local educational issues are common themes for parenting publications, many editors such as Exley say they're not afraid "to discuss controversial issues like spanking and masturbation." A two-part series on child abduction written by Jill McCullough was described by Willis as "the best feature we've put out this year" (March/April 2005). Freedman cites an article that dealt with teaching children how to bounce back from stressful situations as one of their best in 2005.

For many editors, first-person angles are acceptable only if the author is an expert on the subject. Both Exley and Freedman stated that they receive too many first-person accounts that read like essays. If an article is an essay or humorous, "I need to be blown away, or moved to tears by the writing," says Freedman. "We get too many general parenting pieces that we've read many times before, or blah essays. We need material that's new."

Shorter articles for readers who need good information quickly is a must for Hyde. "Parents don't want complex, intricate articles. They want an easy read," she says. Most moms don't have the time to research information or find resources on their own. "Our readers love bullets and pull-out points or quotes, so they can scan an article and see if there is anything of value in it before they invest time in reading it." Freedman concurs, and would like to see pieces no longer than 800 words and "short takes" with accompanying visuals.

Topics & Styles
Although overall content in parenting magazines is geared toward raising children, the scope of acceptable topics is growing, depending upon the publication.

Submission needs for Olya Fessard, Publisher of *Georgia Family*, cover a wide range to accommodate that publication's focus on parenting for ages birth through teen years, rather than just birth through ten. Its editorial content also includes articles on health, medical research affecting families, arts, sports, and a monthly feature about women themselves. "We try to address the total needs of children, not just the emotional and entertainment needs," says Fessard. "That means we have trouble finding articles on subjects not generally addressed in parenting magazines, such as sports, arts, and women's features."

Hyde would like to see more articles on women's health issues and personal stories of overcoming difficulties related to motherhood and parenting. She cites good articles that have appeared recently in her magazine: "Helping Your Child Cope with Bullies," "15 No-nonsense Strategies for Entrepreneurial Women," and "Getting Ready for Overnight Camp." Hyde explains, "We try to give something each month for parents of all ages of children."

Also of general interest to most parenting publications are guides for local or regional events, health and fitness resources, camps, cultural events, vacation ideas, and educational opportunities that provide parents with quick references and information.

Slightly different writing perspectives are also sought by specific magazines. Believing that there are too many frightful and scary things in the world today, Holson's editorial mission is to keep things upbeat, reminding readers "that parenting and family life can still be fun."

William Summey, Editor in Chief of *Parent-Life*, would like to see more articles about parenting children with special needs and about special situations such as single parenting. He states, "We're seeking honest, real personal experience parenting stories" written with a Christian point of view.

> *Parenting magazines tend to have a local feel because parents crave a community feeling, even on news with a national angle.*

A Bright Future
This market is viewed as stable with growth very likely in the future. Generally, parents have little free time and need publications that address their specific needs. Subtle changes may occur to keep abreast of changing demographics, however. Willis contends that as the baby boomers age, there might be a need to merge parenting publications with senior publications. These would support the up-and-coming "sandwich generation" that is called on to fulfill the needs of both their aging parents and their children.

Writers interested in this niche market will always find a need for solid, well-written information on child-rearing and family matters. Nearly every region has a parenting publication: Find yours, become familiar with its editorial focus, and contribute.

Intrigue with Science & Technology

Fascinating science, intriguing technology: They make for great reading by showing how the world works, opening children's minds to the wonders of the smallest bugs and the largest galaxies, and making every discovery an exciting event. With ongoing technological advances, new studies, and expanding data, writers can always find new opportunities to contribute to the knowledge base.

Science Activities Managing Editor Christine Polcino makes it crystal clear: "As long as there are children in school taking science courses, there will be a need for science and technology articles.

> *"As long as children in school take science courses, there will be a need for science and technology articles. It is important to educate children on science & technology for later in life."*

With the growing fields of technology and computers today, it is important to educate children in these subjects so they may be better prepared later in life. Although there is certainly not a shortage of article submissions to *Science Activities*, we are always looking for new ideas and activities to introduce to our readers."

From general interest to educational, publications cover the spectrum. Many science publications offer guides for teachers, special subscription deals for parents, and always consider what makes young readers read across the fields of science.

Capturing Imaginations

While science and technology are serious and often straightforward topics, various methods may be used to present technical information to children.

Hugh Westrup, Managing Editor of *Current*

Science, is aware that science isn't always the most popular subject for today's teens, so he looks for articles that help teachers in the classroom. One of his criteria is that articles "not only educate, but entertain." That doesn't mean, however, that he's looking for "fun science." Content needs to be "research-based, cutting-edge science." The entertaining aspect comes from the writing style and the way the information is presented.

One of the goals of *The Old Schoolhouse Magazine,* a publication that focuses on equipping and encouraging home school families, is to foster and encourage children's natural curiosity. "The level of knowledge that our children are attaining at a younger age is growing greater and greater and articles need to be tailored to speak to that interest," says Jessica Harvey, Secretary to the Publishers.

A different tack is taken by editors of *Science Weekly,* a classroom periodical exploring science and mathematics for students in kindergarten through sixth grades. Each issue has graded reading levels to accommodate the diverse abilities of its readers. "Writers for *Science Weekly* are expected to be able to research a topic and then develop the topic and related activities at six reading levels of difficulty," says Claude Mayberry, Publisher. Unsolicited manuscripts are not accepted by the publication; materials are assigned.

ChemMatters targets high school chemistry students. Editor Kevin McCue explains that ideas should be pitched in January when he has "a fresh budget to buy articles." McCue has noticed a growing tendency in this genre to include more access points to engage readers. By that he means sidebars, pull quotes, timelines, factoids, and activities. He admits that these attention-getters are attempts to capture and keep the readers' interest.

An educational approach to science is the

first threshold at *Science Activities.* Polcino says, "The current emphasis in teaching is inquiry-based learning, which stimulates children's abilities to ask pertinent questions that guide their understanding of a subject, rather than students learning simply by rote or being told the answers to unformed questions. Activities that employ inquiry-based teaching practices are especially welcome. Technology and computers are areas of interest not only to teachers, but to students, so activities involving these subjects are important. I also think that chemistry-related articles are of importance and of interest right now because of the growing need for medical researchers and doctors. Just think, a child doing a science lab one day could be the one to find the cure for cancer in 20 years. We need to cultivate young minds and get them interested and involved in science."

Content & Target Audiences

As one would imagine, the range of topics explored in science and technology publications covers a wide gamut. For instance, *Current Science* includes an excerpt from its Planning Guide for 2005–2006 on its website: Under the four major categories of earth science, physical science, health, and life science are such subjects as lightning, erosion, magnetism, minerals, genetic disorders, hygiene, ecology, classification, medical technology, and many others. Topics chosen by the publication support the National Science Education Standards.

"A superb article is written with the students' learning in mind. Whereas it may be easy to write an article for a teacher, it is more of a challenge to write and conduct an activity that children can participate in and relate to. Once we see these two components become one in an article, we know we've found something good," says Porcino.

She believes publishing in this field has made great strides. "Writing has definitely advanced in recent years, leaning more to the side of technology and inquiry. Students want to learn more about computers and technology. Their minds are growing, and they are

starting to ask, 'Why?' *Science Activities* strives to answer childrens' questions, giving them fun and useful activities that they can carry with them throughout their science education experiences."

Westrup reminds writers that articles must be of interest to young people, in addition to maintaining standards of science. "We look for matter with appeal to teens featuring today's latest technology and findings," he says, then adds that "too often we receive submissions that are not age-appropriate for teens." He advises writers to be aware of today's teen culture and what appeals to the kids themselves.

ChemMatters is also geared to teens, primarily tenth- and eleventh-grade students. "It's important to remember that these are older students," says McCue, and that they "are generally more knowledgeable about chemistry than the general public because they are currently studying it." According to McCue, the main thrust of *ChemMatters* is to explain "everyday chemistry with established science" rather than reporting cutting-edge science. Secondary sources are used for the articles, but primary sources are preferred for sidebars or those portions of the main article that feature contemporary data, to "expose students to the work of current researchers."

Geared to all ages from preschool to college students, *The Old Schoolhouse Magazine* takes another angle. Harvey says that each quarterly issue contains two or three science or technology features. "Articles are meant to be read by parents and put into practice or taught to younger children," but they are also meant to be read independently by older children and teenagers. Writing "must be congruent with the age scale," says Harvey. "Approach the article as a means to share your knowledge and excitement for a subject with children." It is also important to understand that *The Old Schoolhouse Magazine* focuses particularly on creation-based research that shows God is in all things.

Science Activities, says Porcino, publishes "articles for students of all ages, from elementary to middle school to high school. The scope of these articles is obviously very different. Articles tend to be 10 to 20 pages typed, and usually include photos, tables, charts, and graphs." The quarterly publishes about 20 articles a year, but freelancers should know that departments are also open. Porcino explains, "At the end of each journal, we also have special departments which include Computer News, Classroom Aides, News Notes, and Book Reviews. These shorter sections introduce students and teachers to the latest happenings in the science world today. Including these, we publish close to 36 articles a year." If writers want to count their articles among those, she recommends first conducting an "activity in an actual classroom setting. That way, they can see the do's and don'ts of the experiment. They will also be able to gauge if it is aimed at the correct age group. Of course, follow our guidelines for submission."

Individual Imprint

Just as each individual has a certain style and DNA imprint, so do publications. Westrup stresses that interviews and thorough research are important aspects for articles submitted to *Current Science,* while Harvey at *The Old Schoolhouse Magazine* welcomes bibliographies, photographs, and interviews. She also looks for articles "that share a love of learning with children because they have an amazing capacity to learn."

Articles cited by McCue in *ChemMatters* as excellent examples of what he looks for include "When Good Science Goes Bad!" by Tim Graham (October 2004), and "The Great Hartford Circus Fire," by Brendan Rimetz (February 2005). The Graham piece features real biochemistry/chemistry detective work that ultimately cleared a mother accused of poisoning her child. McCue describes the article on the Hartford circus fire as having "drama, a firsthand account, original pictures, and two scientifically relevant sidebars." Each article is enhanced with information separated into the following categories: Websites, Books, and Videos for additional information; Anticipating Student Questions; Suggestions for Student Projects; Connections to the

Chemistry Curriculum; Demonstrations and Lessons; Possible Student Misconceptions; and Connections to Chemistry Concepts.

Science Weekly's multiple educational levels are each divided into six learning departments that include new vocabulary words, a hands-on activity, a mathematical application, and a challenge to develop critical thinking skills. Harvey explains that hands-on activities are also important learning tools in *The Old Schoolhouse Magazine* because of the basic belief that involving the senses in education increases the retention of knowledge.

Delving into the wondrous world of science and technology brings out children's inherent inquisitiveness about the environment surrounding them. Presented in a lively fashion, these subjects have an ability to ignite a spark that can last a lifetime—the daily dream of editors and publishers.

A Recipe for Health & Fitness

Interest in improving fitness and health exploded across American culture in the last generation, and yet today the media reports repeatedly on the epidemic of childhood obesity. From both sides of this paradox, magazines for all kinds of readers look for articles on wellness. Some are general interest publications, some are family-oriented, and some are athletic magazines that incorporate health into their specific focus on the playing of a sport.

"There seems to be much more emphasis placed on providing information about good eating habits over the past few years, and about exercise routines you can do on your own or take to the gym," says *Sports Illustrated For Kids* Editor Nicholas Friedman.

American Cheerleader Editorial Director Sheila Noone says, "Health and fitness has become more of an issue for us over the last few years. We continue to see growth in this area."

USA Gymnastics has a section entitled Body Balance where, says Publications Director Luan Peszek, "We publish on nutrition, sport psychology, and other health-related issues." Peszek looks for articles that "touch our members and would have a wide audience."

Eye on the Ball

Concentrating on the ball—or the beam or the blade, on the sport itself—remains of utmost importance when approaching sports magazines. Find the right slant for that sport and a health article can be a winner.

"One particular interest involves informing teens about preparing themselves for more competitive sports teams, such as school or travel teams," says Friedman at *Sports Illustrated For Kids*. "Teen athletes want to know how they can get stronger, the ways they can gain a mental edge, and how they compare physically with other teen athletes their own age. In terms of slants or styles, Q&As with high level athletes about these subjects is attractive, as well as how-to articles."

"U.S. Figure Skating and *Skating* are committed to providing accurate training tips for our athletes, whether the focus is on stretching, mental health, warm-up, or nutrition. We have a health/fitness section in every issue," says Laura J. Fawcett, Interim Editor and Director of Online Services for U.S. Figure Skating.

Fawcett wants "to see more articles focusing on the variety of off-ice training skaters can do to enhance their physical well-being. For instance, weight training is an issue we haven't covered much with figure skaters, and it would be interesting to see a well-researched article on the kinds of weight training that would best benefit figure skaters. Other subject matters we haven't covered include yoga and pilates. In general, we would like to present a wide variety of off-the-ice training ideas to our readers."

For *USA Gymnastics*, Peszek says, "We're always interested in health topics of interest to gymnasts, such as how to care for your hands (rips from bars are common in gymnasts), what to eat prior to competitions, what type of supplements are good, what healthy snacks should you pack in your gym bag."

The need at *American Cheerleader* is for articles on "flexibility, conditioning, routine, something kids can do on their own," says Noone. Publications want to see ideas for "staying fit on the road because they are traveling a lot and usually just do their routine for exercise."

Points of Entry

Points awarded for good form are very high at sports publications.

"A few things make an article stand out

43

for us. One is an article with multiple *entry points,* such as sidebars, comparison charts, interesting stats, etc.," says Friedman. "Another standout feature is good writing and plenty of details—just as if the article were written for an adult publication."

Peszek also likes "tables, charts, bullet points, and illustrations that are kid-oriented," in articles of 1,000 words or less.

Clarity and directness are also well-exercised in queries, ideas, and in articles. Friedman likes "unique, concise ideas. We can't stress enough that writers interested in working with us read our magazine and get to know it well. Though our publication has the word *kids* in its title, we still like sophisticated stories. We also shy away from stories that have life lessons in them as they tend to turn off our readers." Writers for *Sports Illustrated For Kids* "should know that we have access to almost any big-name athlete in America. So, if the writer pitches us a story solely because he or she has a relationship with an athlete, we'll most likely not consider it. There needs to be much more substance to the idea." Interview fresh sources and provide the interview transcripts, plus all background research.

Noone also wants to see clarity and research sources indicated. "Articles should be 800 to 1,000 words and nothing too complicated. Remember the target audience is teen girls for *American Cheerleader* and younger for *American Cheerleader Jr.*" She needs 12 to 15 articles a year. "Practical and easy articles don't come our way often enough. I look for a very targeted query. Know what kids need. Put some thought into it and remember we *do not* cover professional cheerleading at all." Noone adds that an "original angle and seasonal tie-in are great."

At *Skating,* says Fawcett, "The majority of our readers are young girls. A fitness article

> *"We are committed to providing accurate training tips for our athletes, whether the focus is on stretching, mental health, warm-up, or nutrition."*

should not sound like a doctorate or be filled with complicated language. As an editor, if I can't understand and visualize the article while I am reading it, I know it's too technical for our readers."

She explains their process and preferences: "We publish 10 health and fitness articles every year, nearly all of them submitted by our Sports Medicine Committee. However, we are open to articles from freelance writers. All articles, regardless of their source, go through an approval process with our Sports Medicine Committee, so accurate facts are essential. All research/quotes/facts must be clearly documented."

Articles for *Skating* should be about 1,000 words. "For fitness articles, we only consider full manuscripts, not queries. Pay will be negotiable based on our rates for other articles in the magazine. Since most of our articles are organization-driven, we don't usually pay for fitness articles. But, as I said, that is negotiable for well-written, accurate, and unique training articles," says Fawcett. Quality artwork or photos that illustrate the article are required. Photos are also important at *American Cheerleader.*

Begin exercising those writing muscles, remain flexible in finding target audiences, and follow the rules of the game. Then take the field for health and nutrition article sales.

Listings

How to Use the Listings

The pages that follow feature profiles of 622 magazines that publish articles and stories for, about, or of interest to children and young adults. Throughout the year, we stay on top of the latest happenings in children's magazines to bring you new and different publishing outlets. This year, our research yielded over 90 additional markets for your writing. They are easy to find; look for the listings with a star in the upper right corner.

A Variety of Freelance Opportunities

This year's new listings reflect the interests of today's magazine audience. You'll find magazines targeted to readers interested in nature, the environment, computers, mysteries, child care, careers, different cultures, family activities, and many other topics.

Along with many entertaining and educational magazines aimed at young readers, we list related publications such as national and regional magazines for parents and teachers. Hobby and special interest magazines generally thought of as adult fare but read by many teenagers are listed too.

In the market listings, the Freelance Potential section helps you judge each magazine's receptivity to freelance writers. This section offers information about the number of freelance submissions published each year.

Further opportunities for selling your writing appear in the Additional Listings section on page 283. This section profiles a range of magazines that publish a limited amount of material targeted to children, young adults, parents, or teachers. Other outlets for your writing can be found in the Selected Contests and Awards section, beginning on page 321.

Using Other Sections of the Directory

If you are planning to write for a specific publication, turn to the Magazine and Contest Index beginning on page 364 to locate the listing page. The Category Index, beginning on page 339, will guide you to magazines that publish in your areas of interest. This year, the Category Index also gives the age range of each publication's readership. To find the magazines most open to freelance submissions, turn to the Fifty+ Free-lance index on page 338, which lists magazines that rely on freelance writers for over 50% of the material they publish.

Check the Market News, beginning on page 336, to find out what's newly listed, what's not listed and why, and to identify changes in the market that have occurred during the past year.

About the Listings

We revisited last year's listings and, through a series of mailed surveys and phone interviews, verified editors' names, mailing addresses, submissions and payment policies, and current editorial needs. All entries are accurate and up-to-date when we send this market directory to press. Magazine publishing is a fast-moving industry, though, and it is not unusual for facts to change before or shortly after this guide reaches your hands. Magazines close, are sold to new owners, or move; they hire new editors or change their editorial focus. Keep up to date by requesting sample copies and writers' guidelines.

Note that we do *not* list:

- Magazines that did not respond to our questionnaires or phone queries. Know that we make every effort to contact each editor before press date.

- Magazines that *never* accept freelance submissions or work with freelance writers.

To get a real sense of a magazine and its editorial slant, we recommend that you read several recent sample issues cover to cover. This is the best way to be certain a magazine is right for you.

Moo-Cow Fan Club

 — New listing

P.O. Box 165
Peterborough, NH 03458

Who to contact — Editor: Becky Ances

Profiles the publication, its interests, and readers

Description and Readership
Targeting children ages 8–12 who love learning, this magazine publishes mostly nonfiction that relates to a theme, folktales, interviews, quizzes, and crafts. It includes articles that explore the more unique aspects of topics that are not taught in school.
- **Audience:** 6–12 years
- **Frequency:** 4 times each year
- **Distribution:** 80% newsstand; 10% subscription; 10% schools
- **Circulation:** 3,000
- **Website:** www.moocowfanclub.com

Freelance Potential
10% written by nonstaff writers. Publishes 5 freelance submissions yearly; 100% by authors who are new to the magazine. Receives 8 queries monthly.

Designates the amount and type of freelance submissions published each year; highlights the publication's receptivity to unpublished writers

Provides guidelines for submitting material; lists word lengths and types of material accepted from free-lance writers

Submissions
Query with sample article. Accepts email queries to becky@moocowfanclub.com (no attachments), and computer printouts. SASE. Responds to queries in 3 weeks.
Articles: 300–550 words. Informational and how-to articles; profiles and interviews. Topics include nature, animals, science, sports, and travel.
Fiction: 300–550 words. Genres include folktales and folklore.
Depts/columns: Staff written.

Sample Issue
48 pages (no advertising): 5 articles; 6 stories; 6 depts/columns. Sample copy, $6 with 9x12 SASE ($1.46 postage). Guidelines and theme list available.
- "The Stonecutter's Wishes." Story tells of a stone-cutter who learns an important lesson after his wishes are granted by a mountain spirit.
- "The Spirit in All Things." Article takes a look at the different belief systems in Japan.
- "Stone and Water." Article discusses different types of Japanese Gardens.

Analyzes a recent sample copy of the publication; briefly describes selected articles, stories, departments, etc.

Lists types of rights acquired, payment rate, and number of copies provided to freelance writers

Rights and Payment
All rights. Written material, $50. Pays on acceptance. Provides 3 contributor's copies.

Editor's Comments
We are interested in articles that are both funny and smart. New writers have the best chance at publication with a general education article. Please note that all of our games and crafts are staff written.

Offers advice from the editor about the publication's writing style, freelance needs, audience, etc.

Icon Key

☆ New Listing   🔖 Epublisher   ⊗ Not currently accepting submissions

---

Abilities

Suite 401
340 College Street
Toronto, Ontario M5T 3A9
Canada

Managing Editor: Lisa Bendall

Description and Readership
This Canadian lifestyle magazine is read by people with disabilities, their families, and professionals involved in disability issues.
- **Audience:** Families with disabled members
- **Frequency:** Quarterly
- **Distribution:** 80% controlled; 10% newsstand; 10% other
- **Circulation:** 45,000
- **Website:** www.abilities.ca

Freelance Potential
50% written by nonstaff writers. Publishes 30–40 freelance submissions yearly; 5–10% by unpublished writers, 75% by authors who are new to the magazine. Receives 10 queries, 42 unsolicited mss monthly.

Submissions
Query with writing samples; or send complete ms. Accepts photocopies, computer printouts, and email submissions to lisa@abilities.ca. SAE/IRC. Responds in 2–3 months.
Articles: 1,500–2,000 words. Informational, self-help, and how-to articles; personal experience and opinion pieces; profiles; interviews; and humor. Topics include travel, health, sports, recreation, employment, education, transportation, housing, social policy, sexuality, reviews, and special events.
Depts/columns: 500–1,200 words. Crafts, cooking, and accessibility issues.

Sample Issue
56 pages (50% advertising): 7 articles; 6 depts/columns. Guidelines available.
- "Home Sweet Home." Feature article discusses successful elements of accessible housing.
- "Sayonara, Moto Ken!" Article talks about the adjustments that had to be made for a Canadian guide dog while visiting Japan.
- Sample dept/column: "The Lighter Side" offers a humorous story about uses for duct tape.

Rights and Payment
First and electronic rights. Written material, $25–$350. Kill fee, 50%. Pays 30 days after publication. Provides 2 contributor's copies.

Editor's Comments
Our goal is to expose readers to the multitude of Canadian resources that facilitate the self-empowerment of people with disabilities.

Above & Beyond

P.O. Box 408
Fort Madison, IA 52627

Editor: Donna Borst

Description and Readership
Above & Beyond is comprised of creative enrichment ideas for gifted learners and children in need of a challenge. It includes creative thinking ideas, thematic units, science experiments, problem-solving scenarios and brainteasers to expand students' thinking ability.
- **Audience:** Grades 5–8
- **Frequency:** 5 times each year
- **Distribution:** Subscription; other
- **Circulation:** 1,200
- **Website:** www.menageriepublishing.com

Freelance Potential
99% written by nonstaff writers. Publishes 60–100 freelance submissions yearly.

Submissions
Prefers complete ms; accepts queries. Prefers email submissions to donna@menageriepublishing.com. Will accept photocopies and computer printouts. SASE. Responds in 2–3 months.
Other: Science activites, writing exercises, problem-solving scenarios, brainteasers, and logic problems.

Sample Issue
64 pages: 26 activities. Sample copy, $5.25 with SASE. Guidelines available.
- "Enigmas from Ancient Times." Activity explains strange enigmas and mysteries from the past.
- "The Four Chaplains." Activity focuses on a journey of the USS *Dorchester.*
- "Reasonable or Ridiculous." Activity asks students to come up with both reasonable and ridiculous solutions to the problems listed.
- "Using Associative Thinking to Create a 'Glad About Me' Bag." Activity allows students to share personal feeling about themselves and combine them with abstract thinking.

Rights and Payment
First rights. Pays on publication. Written material, payment rates vary. Provides 1 contributor's copy.

Editor's Comments
Writers should request several sample copies for review prior to submitting material to us. We are a new publication that is striving break from the typical classroom-magazine mold. Send us story starters, logic puzzles, school projects, and enrichment activities. All submissions must include activities for students. We do not accept informational articles.

ADDitude Magazine

15th Floor
39 West 37th Street
New York, NY 10018

Editor & Publisher: Susan Caughman

Description and Readership
This lifestyle and self-help publication is written primarily for adults whose children have Attention Deficit Disorder, or who have AD/HD themselves. Health care professionals will also find the latest information on AD/HD.
• **Audience:** Adults
• **Frequency:** 6 times each year
• **Distribution:** Subscription; other
• **Circulation:** 40,000
• **Website:** www.additudemagazine.com

Freelance Potential
80% written by nonstaff writers. Publishes 25 freelance submissions yearly; 30% by unpublished writers, 30% by authors who are new to the magazine. Receives 4 queries each month.

Submissions
Query. No unsolicited mss. Accepts email submissions to susan@additudemag.com. Response time varies.
Articles: To 2,000 words. Informational articles and personal experience pieces. Topics include Attention Deficit Disorder, education, recreation, and child development.
Depts/columns: Word lengths vary. Profiles of schools and teachers; first-person experiences from parents; and AD/HD news and notes.

Sample Issue
62 pages (33% advertising): 4 articles; 13 depts/columns. Sample copy, $6.95. Guidelines available.
• "Applications 101." Article offers advice on how to help your teen with AD/HD keep up with the competitive nature of college admissions.
• "The Truth about TV and ADD." Article examines the latest research findings linking AD/HD in children to watching television.
• Sample dept/column: "Success at School" suggests ways to help your child get the most out of homework time.

Rights and Payment
First rights. All material, payment rates vary. Pays on publication. Kill fee, $75.

Editor's Comments
We are currently looking for articles that deal with adult ADD and offer advice on coping skills for the workplace and relationships.

Adoptalk

North American Council on Adoptable Children
Suite 106
970 Raymond Street
St. Paul, MN 55114-1149

Editor: Diane Riggs

Description and Readership
This newsletter focuses on topics related to adoption and foster care, special need education, and parent and professional resources.
• **Audience:** Adults
• **Frequency:** Quarterly
• **Distribution:** 100% controlled
• **Circulation:** 3,700
• **Website:** www.nacac.org

Freelance Potential
60% written by nonstaff writers. Publishes 4–6 freelance submissions yearly; 10% by unpublished writers, 50% by authors who are new to the magazine. Receives 1 query or unsolicited ms monthly.

Submissions
Query or send complete ms with biblipgraphy. Accepts photocopies, computer printouts, and email submissions to dianeriggs@nacac.org. Responds in 2–3 weeks.
Articles: To 2,000 words. Informational articles; personal experience pieces; and profiles. Topics include adoptive and foster care, parenting, recruitment, adoption news, conference updates, and NACAC membership news.
Depts/columns: Word length varies. Book reviews and first-person essays.

Sample Issue
20 pages (no advertising): 5 articles; 5 depts/columns. Sample copy, free with 9x12 SASE ($.83 postage). Guidelines available.
• "How to Mean Business without Being Mean." Article discusses how to maintain control when dealing with children and disciplinary consequences.
• "AFC Mentoring." Article explains about a program that builds personal relationships between adult volunteers and children.
• Sample dept/column: "Speak Out" offers first-person essays about adoption-related topics.

Rights and Payment
Rights policy varies. No payment. Provides 5 contributor's copies.

Editor's Comments
As always, we will consider submissions that focus on adoption and foster care. We are in special need of material that deals with children who have been diagnoses with RAD, ODD, FASD, and ADHD.

Adoptive Families

Suite 901
47 West 38th Street
New York, NY 10018

Submissions: Susan Coughman

Description and Readership
Adoptive Families offers parents, children, and other family members advice and support before, during, and after adoption. Each issue covers current topics of interest to adoptive families.
- **Audience:** Adoptive families
- **Frequency:** 6 times each year
- **Distribution:** 90% subscription; 10% other
- **Circulation:** 40,000
- **Website:** www.adoptivefamilies.com

Freelance Potential
75% written by nonstaff writers. Publishes 100 freelance submissions yearly; 20% by unpublished writers, 50% by authors who are new to the magazine. Receives 42–50 unsolicited mss monthly.

Submissions
Query or send complete ms. Accepts photocopies, computer printouts, Macintosh disk submissions (Microsoft Word), and email to letters@ adoptivefamilies.com. SASE. Responds in 4–6 weeks.
Articles: 500–1,800 words. Self-help, personal experience, and how-to articles; humor; and interviews. Topics include family issues, child development, health, teen topics, education, learning disabilities, careers, and multicultural issues.
Depts/columns: To 1,200 words. Opinion and personal experience pieces focusing on adoptions, singles parenting, and birth-parent issues; book and media reviews.
Other: Material on ethnic holidays, National Adoption Month, and Martin Luther King, Jr. Day.

Sample Issue
70 pages (40% advertising): 4 articles; 18 depts/ columns. Sample copy, $6.95. Guidelines available.
- "Unexpected Family." Article profiles three families who make contact with birth families overseas.
- "All through the Night." Article discusses ways to help a child fall asleep and stay asleep.
- "Single Parent" tells how one mother helped her daughter deal with grief.

Rights and Payment
All rights. All material, payment rates vary. Provides 2 contributor's copies.

Editor's Comments
We want to hear your insights and personal experiences about adoption.

Alateen Talk

Al-Anon Family Group
1600 Corporate Landing Parkway
Virginia Beach, VA 23454-5617

Associate Director, Member Services/Alateen:
Barbara Older

Description and Readership
Through the words of *Alateen Talk*, members share their experiences, strength, and hope. Their sharings relate to their personal lives, how their group is functioning, and ways in which to carry the Alateen message to young people still suffering from someone else's drinking.
- **Audience:** 6–18 years
- **Frequency:** Quarterly
- **Distribution:** 100% subscription
- **Circulation:** 4,000
- **Website:** www.al-anon.alateen.org.com

Freelance Potential
90% written by nonstaff writers. Publishes 100 freelance submissions yearly; 80–100% by unpublished writers, 80% by authors who are new to the magazine. Receives 16 unsolicited mss monthly.

Submissions
Accepts material from Alateen members only. Send complete ms. SASE. Responds in 2 weeks.
Articles: Word length varies. Self-help articles and personal experience pieces. Topics include alcoholism and its effects on friends and family members.
Depts/columns: Staff written.
Artwork: B/W line art.
Other: Poetry.

Sample Issue
8 pages (no advertising): 25 articles; 2 poems. Sample copy, free with 9x12 SASE ($.87 postage). Guidelines available to Alateen members.
- "I Can't Control Alcoholism." A girl relates how she works Step One and says the Serenity Prayer each day in order to face the world.
- "Today I Have Hope." A teen appreciates how going to Alateen changed her life and gave her hope.
- Other: Gratitude poem on how Alateen confers priceless gifts on those who seek its help.

Rights and Payment
All rights. No payment.

Editor's Comments
We only publish pieces by members of Alateen from all over the world. Frank, heartfelt testimonials about dealing with a family member's alcoholism and how teens cope with living with an alcoholic are always welcome. Other topics we want to see include lessons learned in Alateen and taking good care of ourselves.

Amazing Journeys Magazine ☆

3205 Highway 431
Spring Hill, TN 37174

Editor: Edward Knight

Description and Readership
A great mix of science fiction, fantasy, and poetry in the "golden age" style can be found between the covers of this magazine. Its readers include young adults and adults who enjoy a good speculative story.
- **Audience:** YA–Adult
- **Frequency:** Quarterly
- **Distribution:** 50% subscription; 50% other
- **Circulation:** Unknown
- **Website:** www.journeybookspublishing.com

Freelance Potential
90% written by nonstaff writers. Publishes 35 freelance submissions yearly; 40% by unpublished writers, 60% by authors who are new to the magazine. Receives 60 unsolicited mss monthly.

Submissions
Send complete ms. Accepts computer printouts and email (MS Word or RTF attachment). No simultaneous submissions. SASE. Responds in 2 months.
Fiction: 3,000–10,000 words. Genres include fantasy and science fiction.
Other: Poetry, 20–40 lines.

Sample Issue
44 pages (3% advertising): 8 stories; 2 poems; 1 editorial. Sample copy, $5.99 with 9x12 SASE ($1.52 postage). Guidelines available at website.
- "The Mercenary." Story tells of a woman who enlists the help of a man who carries the curse of death to rescue her daughter from a witch.
- "Sophie's Child." Story features a woman trying to do her part to help the planet by bringing a male child into the world to help fight aliens.

Rights and Payment
First North American serial rights. Written material, $.0025 per word. Poetry, $5 per poem. Provides 1 contributor's copy.

Editor's Comments
We are seeking short fiction, and prefer works within the 3,000–6,000 range. Material must have a G or PG rating. Absolutely no sexual content will be accepted. We accept works in most science fiction and fantasy genres, but we shy away from the really dark stuff, and do not publish gay or lesbian work. Those authors whose work generates the most interest from readers may be given an opportunity to participate in one of our upcoming anthologies.

American Baby

16th Floor
125 Park Avenue
New York, NY 10012

Editorial Assistant: Sarah Jones

Description and Readership
This magazine enjoys popularity with expectant and new parents, especially those having their first child. It covers issues related to pregnancy, infant care, and caring for children under the age of two.
- **Audience:** Parents
- **Frequency:** Monthly
- **Distribution:** 50% subscription; 50% controlled
- **Circulation:** 2.1 million
- **Website:** www.americanbaby.com

Freelance Potential
55% written by nonstaff writers. Publishes 24 freelance submissions yearly; 20% by unpublished writers. Receives 83 unsolicited mss monthly.

Submissions
Query with clips or writing samples; or send complete ms. Accepts photocopies, computer printouts, and simultaneous submissions if identified. SASE. Responds in 2 months.
Articles: 1,000–2,000 words. Informational and how-to articles; profiles; interviews; humor; and personal experience pieces. Topics include pregnancy, preconception, infants, child care, child development, and adoption.
Depts/columns: 1,000 words. Medical updates, relationships, new product information, and fashion.
Other: Submit seasonal material 3 months in advance.

Sample Issue
110 pages (50% advertising): 5 articles; 11 depts/columns. Sample copy, free with 9x12 SASE ($2 postage). Guidelines available.
- "Your Baby's Teething Timeline: What to Expect." Article provides an overview of teething signs and symptoms.
- "Help! I'm Raising a Brat!" Article suggests that a spoiled child is usually a product of his environment and offers tips for changing behavior.

Rights and Payment
First serial rights. Articles, to $2,000. Depts/columns, to $1,000. Pays on acceptance. Provides 5 contributor's copies.

Editor's Comments
Our magazine strives to provide an understanding shoulder to lean on, an experienced friend to lend a helping hand.

American Careers

6701 West 64th Street
Overland Park, KS 66202

Editor: Mary Pitchford

Description and Readership
This publication provides information, advice, and self-awareness tools for middle-grade and high school students who will soon enter the world of careers.
- **Audience:** 12–18 years
- **Frequency:** 1 time each year
- **Distribution:** 99% schools; 1% other
- **Circulation:** 400,000
- **Website:** www.carcom.com

Freelance Potential
90% written by nonstaff writers. Publishes 15 freelance submissions yearly; 20% by unpublished writers, 40% by authors who are new to the magazine. Receives 20+ queries monthly.

Submissions
Query with résumé and clips. Accepts photocopies and computer printouts. SASE. Responds in 2 months.
Articles: 300–750 words. Informational and how-to articles; and profiles. Topics include career planning, interview techniques, applications, education, business, technology, public administration, human services, and communications.
Artwork: Color prints, transparencies, or digital photos.
Other: Quizzes and self-assessments.

Sample Issue
64 pages (no advertising): 24 articles. Sample copy, $4 with 9x12 SASE (5 first-class stamps). Writers' guidelines available.
- "It's Your Future." Short article stresses early planning for a successful career.
- "You'll Find Good Jobs in Business." Informative article discusses the different positions available in business operations.
- "What Kind of Impression Will You Make?" Quiz on proper interview techniques.

Rights and Payment
All rights. All material, payment rates vary. Pays on publication. Provides 2 contributor's copies.

Editor's Comments
We continue to need age-appropriate articles and stories that will help students discover and explore career- and industry-related jobs, and the education needed to succeed. We offer three editions of our magazine—one for general employment, one for the health-care field, and one for business.

American Cheerleader

23rd Floor
110 William Street
New York, NY 10038

Editorial Director: Sheila Noone

Description and Readership
Young people who are on school or all-star cheerleading squads read this magazine for its complete coverage of competitions, as well as general interest articles and profiles.
- **Audience:** 13–18 years
- **Frequency:** 6 times each year
- **Distribution:** Subscription; newsstand
- **Circulation:** 200,000
- **Website:** www.americancheerleader.com

Freelance Potential
50% written by nonstaff writers. Publishes 10 freelance submissions yearly; 20% by unpublished writers, 20% by authors who are new to the magazine. Receives 1–2 queries and unsolicited mss monthly.

Submissions
Query with clips or send complete ms. Accepts computer printouts, Macintosh disk submissions, and email submissions to snoone@lifestyleventures.com. SASE. Responds in 3 months.
Articles: To 1,000 words. Informational and how-to articles; profiles; personal experience pieces; and photo essays. Topics include cheerleading, workouts, competitions, scholarships, fitness, college, careers, and popular culture.
Depts/columns: Word lengths vary. Product news, safety issues, health, nutrition, fundraising, beauty, and fashion.
Artwork: High resolution digital images; 35mm color slides.

Sample Issue
144 pages (40% advertising): 12 articles; 19 depts/columns. Sample copy, $3.99 with 9x12 SASE ($1.70 postage). Editorial calendar available.
- "Hey Now, You're An Allstar." Article offers advice on how to perfect solo skills and achieve camp-stand-out status.
- "Fab Fundraising." Article offers suggestions for creating a successful fundraiser.
- Sample dept/column: "Eating Smart" offers ways to help curb junk food cravings over the summer.

Rights and Payment
All rights. All material, payment rates vary. Pays 2 months after acceptance. Provides 1 author's copy.

Editor's Comments
We continue to seek cheerleading tips and skills.

American Cheerleader Junior

23rd Floor
110 William Street
New York, NY 10038

Editorial Director: Sheila Noone

Description and Readership

Articles and photos that capture the sport of cheerleading are featured in this publication. Each issue includes competition coverage, tips and techniques, and profiles of cheerleaders.
- **Audience:** 7–12 years
- **Frequency:** Quarterly
- **Distribution:** Subscription; newsstand
- **Circulation:** 65,000
- **Website:** www.americancheerleaderjunior.com

Freelance Potential

35% written by nonstaff writers. Publishes 10 freelance submissions yearly; 20% by unpublished writers, 30% by authors who are new to the magazine. Receives 6 queries and 2 unsolicited mss monthly.

Submissions

Query with clips; or send complete ms. Accepts computer printouts, Macintosh disk submissions, and email submissions to snoone@lifestyleventures.com. SASE. Responds in 3 months.
Articles: To 1,000 words. Informational and how-to articles; profiles; photo essays; and personal experience pieces. Topics include cheerleading, fitness, health, and popular culture.
Depts/columns: Word length varies. Cooking, information for parents, and fund-raising.
Artwork: High-resolution digital images; 35mm color slides.
Other: Activities, games, crafts and poetry.

Sample Issue

72 pages (40% advertising): 6 articles; 13 depts/columns. Sample copy, $4.99 with 9x12 SASE ($.77 postage). Guidelines available.
- "Behind the Scenes." Article takes a look at one squad's busy day at a national competition.
- "Fun-raising." Article offers details for holding a spirit garden fundraiser.
- Sample dept/column: "Practice Session" offers a session from Hawaii's Kekaha Panthers.

Rights and Payment

All rights. All material, payment rate varies. Pays 2 months after acceptance. Provides 1 author's copy.

Editor's Comments

We look for articles and cheers that introduce girls to the exciting world of cheerleading. Writing must be tailored to our audience of girls ages 7 to 14.

American Girl

Pleasant Company Publications
8400 Fairway Place
Middleton, WI 53562

Editorial Assistant

Description and Readership

American Girl offers articles that reinforce readers' self-confidence, curiosity, and self-esteem in order to successfully navigate adolescence.
- **Audience:** 8–12 years
- **Frequency:** 7 times each year
- **Distribution:** Subscription; newsstand; schools
- **Circulation:** 700,000
- **Website:** www.americangirl.com

Freelance Potential

10% written by nonstaff writers. Publishes 5 freelance submissions yearly; 5% by unpublished writers, 5% by authors who are new to the magazine. Receives 54 unsolicited mss monthly.

Submissions

Query for nonfiction. Send complete ms for fiction. Accepts photocopies, computer printouts, and simultaneous submissions if identified. SASE. Responds in 4 months.
Articles: 500–1,000 words. Informational articles; profiles; and interviews. Topics include crafts, hobbies, food, the arts, nature, sports, and culture.
Fiction: To 2,300 words. Contemporary historical, and multicultural fiction; and mystery.
Depts/columns: 175 words. Profiles, how-to pieces, and craft ideas.
Other: Word games and puzzles.

Sample Issue

48 pages (no advertising): 4 articles; 1 craft page. Sample copy, $3.95 with 9x12 SASE ($1.93 postage). Guidelines available.
- "Wish You Were Here!" Article offers ideas for making an at-home spring break seem more like a gone-away vacation.
- "Easter Egg-stravaganza." Crafty article suggests cool methods for dyeing decorative Easter eggs.
- Sample dept/column: "Friendship Matters" discusses the best ways to listen and talk to friends.

Rights and Payment

First North American serial rights. Written material, payment rate varies. Pays on acceptance. Provides 1 contributor's copy.

Editor's Comments

Our "Girls Express" section offers the most opportunities for freelance writers. We need true stories about girls who have had unusual experiences.

American Libraries

American Library Association
50 East Huron Street
Chicago, IL 60611

Acquisitions Editor: Beverly Goldberg

Description and Readership
Articles and reports covering issues affecting library professionals fill the pages of this publication. Read by members of the American Library Association, it also includes member updates and news.
- **Audience:** Librarians and library media specialists
- **Frequency:** 11 times each year
- **Distribution:** 100% membership
- **Circulation:** 56,000
- **Website:** www.ala.org/alonline

Freelance Potential
60% written by nonstaff writers. Publishes 50 freelance submissions yearly; 50% by authors who are new to the magazine. Receives 41 unsolicited mss each month.

Submissions
Send complete ms. Accepts electronic submissions to americanlibraries@ala.org, computer printouts, and IBM disk submissions (Microsoft Word). No simultaneous submissions. SASE. Responds in 8–10 weeks.
Articles: 600–2,500 words. Informational articles; profiles; and interviews. Topics include modern libraries, new technologies, and intellectual freedom.
Depts/columns: Word length varies. The Internet, books about library management, new technology, and opinion pieces.

Sample Issue
96 pages (27% advertising): 10 articles; 12 depts/columns. Sample copy, $6. Guidelines available.
- "Are You the Librarian?" Article discusses the professional development of library workers, the future of the profession, and recruitment challenges.
- "Google at the Gate." Article reports on expert assessments of the giant company Google, and what it may mean for libraries.
- Sample dept/column: "Internet Librarian" discusses library circulation models for music and videos.

Rights and Payment
First North American serial rights. Written material, $50–$400. Pays on acceptance. Provides 1+ contributor's copies.

Editor's Comments
We look for informative articles on hot topics affecting library professionals including technology and library funding issues. Our writing style is informal, however all factual material must be supported.

American School & University

9800 Metcalf Avenue
Overland Park, KS 66212

Executive Editor: Susan Lustig

Description and Readership
For 75 years this publication has been a resource for school administrators and other professional educators responsible for the planning, design, construction, maintenance, operations, and management of schools and universities.
- **Audience:** School administrators
- **Frequency:** Monthly
- **Distribution:** 100% controlled
- **Circulation:** 63,000
- **Website:** www.asumag.com

Freelance Potential
35% written by nonstaff writers. Publishes 40 freelance submissions yearly; 30% by authors who are new to the magazine. Receives 15 queries monthly.

Submissions
Query with outline. Prefers email submissions to slustig@primediabusiness.com. Will accept photocopies, computer printouts, and disk submissions (Microsoft Word or ASCII). Responds in 2 weeks.
Articles: 1,200 words. Informational and how-to articles. Topics include facilities management, maintenance, technology, energy, furnishings, and security.
Depts/columns: 250–350 words. New technologies, case histories, and new product information.

Sample Issue
46 pages (55% advertising): 6 articles; 6 depts/columns. Sample copy, $10. Guidelines and editorial calendar available.
- "Shared Vision." Article describes a new approach to having a new school accepted by the community by making it useful to the local residents.
- "Seeing the Big Picture." Article outlines the steps needed to reach an overall goal of saving energy costs while improving a school's environment.
- Sample dept/column: "Solutions Center" solves problems or questions put forth by readers concerning schools.

Rights and Payment
All rights. Payment rates and policy vary. Provides 2 contributor's copies.

Editor's Comments
We try to stay current with facility situations that face our educators. Although most of our material is developed in-house, freelance submissions will be considered if they provide solutions to our readers.

American Secondary Education

Ashland University, Weltmer Center
401 College Avenue
Ashland, OH 44805

Editor: James A. Rycik

Description and Readership
Serving those involved in public and private secondary education, this publication offers articles and reviews on current theories, issues, and practices that focus on middle and high school education.
- **Audience:** Secondary school educators
- **Frequency:** 3 times each year
- **Distribution:** 70% colleges and universities; 30% subscription
- **Circulation:** 450
- **Website:** www.ashland.edu/ase.html

Freelance Potential
100% written by nonstaff writers. Publishes 15 freelance submissions yearly. Receives 1 unsolicited ms monthly.

Submissions
Send 3 copies of complete ms with disk and 100-word abstract. No simultaneous submissions. SASE. Response times vary.
Articles: 10–30 double-spaced manuscript pages. Informational articles. Topics include secondary education research and practice.
Depts/columns: Book reviews, word lengths vary. "In the Schools" provides a personal look at innovative programs unique to a particular school district.

Sample Issue
92 pages (no advertising): 6 articles; 1 book review. Sample copy, free. Guidelines available.
- "Using Children's Stories in Secondary Mathematics." Article describes activities based upon children's literature used by teachers in making connections with fundamentals of mathematics in classrooms.
- "By Teens, For Teachers: A Descriptive Study of Adolescence." Article reports on a project based on essays by teens about issues specific to them.
- "Book Review." Review looks at a book that reports on misconceptions about public education.

Rights and Payment
All rights. No payment. Provides 1 contributor's copy.

Editor's Comments
We welcome articles about innovative schools and district programs; effective classroom practices; and issues relating to the achievement, lifestyles, attitudes, and culture of adolescents. Please include your educational affiliation, academic title, and other qualifications and experiences when submitting.

American String Teacher

4153 Chain Bridge Road
Fairfax, VA 22030

Editor: Tami O'Brien

Description and Readership
Members of the American String Teachers Association receive this magazine. Devoted to excellence in string teaching, it strives to enhance the professional development of teachers of all string instruments, including those who offer private lessons, direct ensembles, or teach in schools, colleges, and universities.
- **Audience:** String teachers and performers
- **Frequency:** Quarterly
- **Distribution:** 100% subscription
- **Circulation:** 11,500
- **Website:** www.astaweb.com

Freelance Potential
75% written by nonstaff writers. Publishes 30 freelance submissions yearly; 5% by unpublished writers, 50% by authors who are new to the magazine. Receives 2–3 queries and unsolicited mss monthly.

Submissions
Prefers query; accepts 5 copies of complete ms. Prefers email submissions to dlitmus@ksu.edu. Accepts photocopies and computer printouts. No simultaneous submissions. SASE. Responds in 3 months.
Articles: 1,000–3,000 words. Informational and factual articles; profiles; and association news. Topics include teaching methodology, techniques, competitions, and auditions.
Depts/columns: Word lengths vary. Teaching tips, opinion pieces, and industry news.

Sample Issue
104 pages (45% advertising): 5 articles; 8 depts/columns; 2 special sections. Sample copy, free with 9x12 SASE ($3.25 postage). Guidelines available.
- "Three Steps to Sight Reading Success." Article explains the importance of teaching sight reading to young students and that a lack of proficiency reveals much about overall skill, especially at auditions.
- Sample dept/column: "My Turn" features an essay by a string teacher who discusses how students can learn to take ownership of their musicianship.

Rights and Payment
All rights. No payment. Provides 5 contributor's copies.

Editor's Comments
Articles with a national perspective are welcome—an article that discusses how different teachers in different situations teach a similar technique, for instance.

Analog Science Fiction and Fact

Dell Magazine Fiction Group
475 Park Avenue South
New York, NY 10016

Editor: Stanley Schmidt

Description and Readership
Science fiction stories involving future technology is the specialty of this magazine. It offers short stories, novellas, and novelettes, as well as articles on current and future scientific interest.
- **Audience:** YA–Adult
- **Frequency:** 10 times each year
- **Distribution:** 80% subscription; 20% newsstand
- **Circulation:** 40,000
- **Website:** www.analgsf.com

Freelance Potential
100% written by nonstaff writers. Publishes 80–90 freelance submissions yearly; 10% by unpublished writers, 10% by authors who are new to the magazine. Receives 500 unsolicited mss monthly.

Submissions
Query for serials. Send complete ms for shorter works. Accepts photocopies and computer printouts. SASE. Responds in 6 weeks.
Articles: To 6,000 words. Informational articles. Topics include science and technology.
Fiction: Serials, 40,000–80,000 words; novella and novelette, 10,000–20,000 words; short stories, 2,000–7,000 words. Physical, sociological, and psychological science fiction; technological and biogenetic fiction.
Depts/columns: Staff written.

Sample Issue
144 pages (7% advertising): 3 novelettes; 5 stories; 1 article; 6 depts/columns. Sample copy, $5 with 6x9 SASE. Guidelines available.
- "Big Brother Inc.: Surveillance, Security, and the U.S. Citizen." Article stresses that powerful new information technologies must be handled with care.
- "Tomorrow's Strawberries." Short story about alien bubbles that invade a person's thoughts.
- "Smiling Vermin." Short story about a futuristic dolphin menace.

Rights and Payment
First North American serial and nonexclusive rights. Serials, $.04 per word; other written material, $.05–$.08 per word. Pays on acceptance. Provides 2 contributor's copies.

Editor's Comments
Stories must be strong and realistic, with believable people doing believable things.

Anime

15850 Parkway
Dallas, TX 75248

Editorial Director: Doug Kale

Description and Readership
Targeting collectors, this official guide to all Anime, pop culture, cards, games and products includes articles and reviews covering Inuysha, Yu-Gi-Oh!, Pokémon, and Full Metal Alchemist.
- **Audience:** YA–Adult
- **Frequency:** Monthly
- **Distribution:** 80% newsstand; 20% subscription
- **Circulation:** 250,000
- **Website:** www.beckettanime.com

Freelance Potential
50% written by nonstaff writers. Publishes 20 freelance submissions yearly; 10% by unpublished writers, 1% by authors who are new to the magazine.

Submissions
Prefers query with outline and clips. Accepts complete ms. Accepts photocopies, computer printouts, and email submissions to anime@beckett.com. SASE. Responds in 1–2 months.
Articles: 500–2,000 words. Informational articles; profiles; and reviews. Topics relating to Inuyasha, Yu-Gi-Oh, Pokémon, Dragon Ball, Duel Masters, Fullmetal Alchemist card and memorabilia collecting.
Fiction: Word lengths vary. Adventure stories.
Depts/columns: 500–750 words. Crafts and cooking.

Sample Issue
88 pages: 14 articles; 4 reviews; 3 contests; 3 price guides; 1 cartoon; 6 depts/columns. Sample copy, $6.99. Writers' guidelines available.
- "Anime Amour: Sango and Miroku." Article takes a look at the relationship between Sango and Miroku from the InuYasha series.
- "Tournament Terrific!." Article offers a review of the new Yu-Gi-Oh adventure game 7 Trials to Glory for the Game Boy Advance system.
- Sample dept/column: "Anime Stuff" offers information on new card games, a movie, a courier bag, and DVDs.

Rights and Payment
First North American serial rights. Articles and fiction, $150–$250. Depts/columns, $50–$200. Pays on acceptance. Provides 2 contributor's copies.

Editor's Comments
We are looking for up-to-date information on collecting and trading cards, the newest releases of videos and games, and hot reviews.

AppleSeeds

Cobblestone Publishing Company
30 Grove Street
Peterborough, NH 03458

Editor: Susan Buckley

Description and Readership
This multidisciplinary social studies magazine for children features scientifically and historically accurate articles, activities, and stories.
• **Audience:** 7–10 years
• **Frequency:** 9 times each year
• **Distribution:** 100% subscription
• **Circulation:** 5,000
• **Website:** www.cobblestonepub.com

Freelance Potential
90% written by nonstaff writers. Publishes 90–100 freelance submissions yearly; 20% by unpublished writers; 35% by authors who are new to the magazine. Receives 42 queries monthly.

Submissions
Prefers email queries to swbuc@aol.com. Accepts complete ms. Accepts photocopies and computer printouts. SASE. Responds to queries in 2–3 months; to mss only if interested.
Articles: 300-700 words. Informational articles; personal experience pieces; profiles; and interviews. Topics include nature, animals, the environment, the arts, biography, hobbies, health, fitness, history, mathematics, multicultural and ethnic issues, popular culture, science social issues, sports, and travel.
Fiction: Word length varies. Genres include folklore and contemporary fiction.
Depts/columns: 150–300 words. Theme-related activities and profiles.
Other: Poetry.

Sample Issue
34 pages (no advertising): 10 articles; 2 depts/columns. Writers' guidelines and theme list available at website.
• "Acting Through the Ages." Informative article discusses the history of the theater.
• "Behind the Scenes." Article explains the tasks of some nonacting show business jobs.
• Sample dept/column: "Puzzle Power" features a word game based on the dramatic arts.

Rights and Payment
All rights. Written material, $50 per page. Pays on publication. Provides 2 contributor's copies.

Editor's Comments
We want lively materials that exhibit an original approach to the theme and to stimulate young readers.

Aquila

Freepost BR 1158
Eastbourne BN21 2BR
United Kingdom

Editor: Jackie Berry

Description and Readership
Self-described as a "fun magazine for children who enjoy challenges," *Aquila* features math and word puzzles, science facts, art ideas, stories, jokes, and contests for middle-grade readers.
• **Audience:** 8–13 years
• **Frequency:** Monthly
• **Distribution:** 100% subscription
• **Circulation:** 8,000
• **Website:** www.aquila.co.uk

Freelance Potential
40% written by nonstaff writers. Publishes 4 freelance submissions yearly; 25% by unpublished writers, 25% by authors who are new to the magazine. Receives 16–20 queries monthly.

Submissions
Query with résumé. Accepts computer printouts and email queries to info@aquila.co.uk (Microsoft Word). SAE/IRC. Responds in 2–4 months.
Articles: 750–800 words. Informational and how-to articles; profiles; and interviews. Topics include pets, animals, the arts, crafts, hobbies, history, mathematics, nature, the environment, science, and technology.
Fiction: To 1,000 words. Genres include historical and contemporary fiction, science fiction, folklore, folktales, mystery, adventure, and horror. Also publishes stories about animals.
Artwork: Color prints and transparencies.
Other: Arts and crafts activities. Submit seasonal material 3 months in advance.

Sample Issue
24 pages (no advertising): 5 articles; 1 story; 8 activities. Sample copy, £2.60 with 9x12 SAE/IRC. Guidelines and editorial calendar available.
• "Save Energy." Article explains the need to conserve fossil fuels.
• "Wordworm." Article looks at writing in picture form and how our alphabet developed from the picture writing used by ancient Egyptians.

Rights and Payment
First rights. Articles and fiction, £60–£80. Artwork, payment rate varies. Pays on publication. Provides up to 6 contributor's copies.

Editor's Comments
Each month, we try to provide readers with an exciting journey of discovery.

Arizona Parenting

Suite 1185
2432 West Peoria Avenue
Phoenix, AZ 85029

Editor: Linda Exley

Description and Readership
Distributed free to parents living in Arizona, this magazine offers articles and tips, as well as information on regional events. Its editorial focus is on parenting and family issues.
- **Audience:** Parents
- **Frequency:** Monthly
- **Distribution:** 100% other
- **Circulation:** 80,000
- **Website:** www.azparenting.com

Freelance Potential
50% written by nonstaff writers. Publishes 20 freelance submissions yearly; 5% by unpublished writers, 25% by authors who are new to the magazine. Receives 35 queries, 25 unsolicited mss monthly.

Submissions
Query or send complete ms. Prefers email to linda.exley@azparenting.com. Accepts photocopies and disk submissions printouts. SASE. Responds to queries in 2–3 weeks.
Articles: 850–2,400 words. Informational articles; profiles; interviews; and humor. Topics include parenting, family issues, education, finances, health, travel, sports, computers, recreation, and fitness.
Depts/columns: 400–850 words. Child development, short news items, and family forums.
Artwork: B/W prints and transparencies. Line art.

Sample Issue
58 pages (50% advertising): 7 articles; 1 dept/column. Sample copy, free with 9x12 SASE ($2 postage). Editorial calendar available.
- "Children Secretly Like Chores." Article offers ideas on how to inspire children to do chores.
- "Prevent Summer Brain Drain." Article suggest learning activities for children to do over summer break.
- Sample dept/column: "Family F.Y.I." offers information on mosquitoes, a dance group, and way to encourage children to open a savings account.

Rights and Payment
First North American serial and electronic rights. Written material, $100+. Artwork, payment rates vary. Pays on publication. Provides 2–3 author's copies.

Editor's Comments
We strive to provide parents living in Arizona with up-to-date information and resources to aid them in doing their most important job, raising their children.

Art Education

College Of Education
Texas A&M University
4232-TAMU
College Station, TX 77843

Editor: B. Stephen Carpenter II

Description and Readership
Art Education publishes a variety of research articles of professional interest to a diverse audience of art educators who teach grades K through twelve.
- **Audience:** Art educators
- **Frequency:** 6 times each year
- **Distribution:** 70% subscription; 30% newsstand
- **Circulation:** 20,000
- **Website:** www.naea-reston.org/publications

Freelance Potential
100% written by nonstaff writers. Publishes 36 freelance submissions yearly; 25% by unpublished writers, 5% by authors who are new to the magazine. Receives 10 unsolicited mss monthly.

Submissions
Send 3 copies of complete ms. Accepts photocopies, computer printouts, disk submissions, and simultaneous submissions if identified. SASE. Responds in 8–10 weeks.
Articles: To 3,000 words. Informational articles; personal experience pieces; interviews; and profiles. Topics include the visual arts, curriculum planning, art history, and art criticism.
Depts/columns: To 2,750 words. "Instructional Resources" features lesson plan ideas.
Artwork: 8x10 or 5x7 B/W prints, slides, or digital images.

Sample Issue
52 pages (3% advertising): 7 articles; 1 dept/column. Sample copy, $1.25 with 9x12 SASE ($.87 postage). Guidelines available.
- "Teaching Real Art Making." Article discusses the importance of making art with meaning.
- "Object Design." Article explains 12 art concepts for students to know, understand, and apply.
- Sample dept/column: "Instructional Resources" suggests methods for interpreting visual stories.

Rights and Payment
All rights. No payment. Provides 2 contributor's copies.

Editor's Comments
We always need fresh material for our "Instructional Resources" department. Instructional resources should state an objective and have immediate and practical classroom applications for teachers. Content must be derived from artwork and must relate the works to each other and to the objective.

Arts & Activities

12345 World Trade Drive
San Diego, CA 92128

Editor-in-Chief: Maryellen Bridge

Description and Readership
Informative, inspirational material for art teachers are the focus of this publication. It offers articles that stress creative visual expression, techniques for engaging students, and programs that expand students' appreciation of art.
- **Audience:** Art educators, grades K–12
- **Frequency:** 10 times each year
- **Distribution:** 100% subscription
- **Circulation:** 20,000
- **Website:** www.artsandactivities.com

Freelance Potential
95% written by nonstaff writers. Publishes 100–125 freelance submissions yearly; 70% by unpublished writers, 50% by authors who are new to the magazine. Receives 25 unsolicited mss monthly.

Submissions
Send complete ms. Accepts photocopies, computer printouts, and disk submissions with hard copy. No simultaneous submissions. SASE. Responds in 2–6 months.
Articles: Word length varies. Informational, how-to, and practical application articles; and personal experience pieces. Topics include art education, program development, collage, printmaking, art appreciation, and composition.
Depts/columns: Word length varies. New product information, short news items, and book reviews.
Other: Lesson plans for classroom projects.

Sample Issue
54 pages (29% advertising): 15 articles; 5 depts/columns. Sample copy, $3 with 9x12 SASE ($2 postage). Guidelines and theme list available.
- "Fun with Yarnikin Dancers." How-to article explains how to use yarn figures to introduce the concept of drawing bodies.
- Sample dept/column: "Arts Update" highlights news items in the field of art education.

Rights and Payment
All First North American serial rights. All material, payment rates vary. Pays on publication. Provides 3 contributor's copies.

Editor's Comments
We are seeking articles and lesson plans for ceramic and clay projects, as well as ideas for fiber art and three-dimensional artwork.

Asimov's Science Fiction

Dell Magazine Group
475 Park Avenue, 11th Floor
New York, NY 10016

Editor: Sheila Williams

Description and Readership
This well-known magazine of science fiction and fantasy publishes original stories, novellas, and novelettes. It considers its material to be "serious, accessible fiction" that holds a reader's interest.
- **Audience:** YA–Adult
- **Frequency:** 10 times each year
- **Distribution:** 87% subscription; 13% newsstand
- **Circulation:** 60,000
- **Website:** www.asimovs.com

Freelance Potential
97% written by nonstaff writers. Publishes 85 freelance submissions yearly; 10% by unpublished writers, 30% by authors who are new to the magazine. Receives 800 unsolicited mss monthly.

Submissions
Send complete ms. No queries. Accepts photocopies and computer printouts. SASE. Responds in 6–8 weeks.
Fiction: To 20,000 words. Genres include science fiction and fantasy.
Depts/columns: Word length varies. Book and website reviews.
Other: Poetry, to 40 lines.

Sample Issue
144 pages (10% advertising): 3 short stories, 2 novelettes, 1 novella, 5 poems; 4 depts/columns. Sample copy, $5. Writers' guidelines available.
- "The Edge of Nowhere." Novelette about a woman who owns two rather unusual dogs.
- "The Ice-Cream Man." Short story set in the future, where normal items are in short supply.

Rights and Payment
First worldwide English language serial rights. Fiction, $.06–$.08 per word. Poetry, $1 per line. Depts/columns, payment rate varies. Pays on acceptance. Provides 2 contributor's copies.

Editor's Comments
Although most of our published material is science fiction, we will consider borderline fantasy, but no sword and sorcery, please. Neither are we interested in explicit sex or violence. Write your story in a way that examines or illustrates some aspect of human existence, but with a backdrop of science fiction. New writers are welcome.

ASK

Carus Publishing
Suite 1450
140 S. Dearborn Street
Chicago, IL 60603

Editor

Description and Readership
This arts and sciences magazine features articles on topics that fascinate young readers and help them understand how the world works and how discoveries are made.
- **Audience:** 7–10 years
- **Frequency:** 9 times each year
- **Distribution:** Subscription; newsstand
- **Circulation:** 32,000
- **Website:** www.cricketmag.com

Freelance Potential
80% written by nonstaff writers. Of the freelance submissions published each year, 10% are by authors who are new to the magazine. Receives 4–5 queries each month.

Submissions
All material is commissioned from experienced authors. Send résumé and clips. Response time varies.
Articles: To 1,500 words. Informational articles; interviews; and photo essays. Topics include animals, pets, science, the environment, nature, computers, technology, history, math, and the arts. Also publishes special issues devoted to biographies.
Depts/columns: Word length varies. News items.

Sample Issue
32 pages (no advertising): 4 articles; 7 depts/columns; 1 pull-out section. Sample copy available at website. Guidelines available.
- "Is This a Giant Squid?" Article takes a look at the elusive giant squid.
- "Shark!" Article discusses the habitat and habits of the great white shark.
- "Sea Monsters in Kansas." Article tells about the fossils of sea creatures found in the middle of the United States.

Rights and Payment
Rights policy varies. Written material, payment rates and policy varies.

Editor's Comments
Our magazine is about the real world. We like to see proposals for articles that cover anything from dinosaurs to cathedrals—from distant stars to microbes. Material should draw the reader in, and make learning fun. All material is assigned to experienced writers.

Atlanta Baby

Suite 101
2346 Perimeter Park
Atlanta, GA 30341

Editor: Alison Amoroso

Description and Readership
Parents of newborns and children under the age of two turn to this tabloid for information on regional programs and resources, as well as articles on parenting issues and concerns.
- **Audience:** Parents
- **Frequency:** Twice each year
- **Distribution:** 100% controlled
- **Circulation:** 30,000
- **Website:** www.atlantaparent.com

Freelance Potential
25% written by nonstaff writers. Publishes 50 freelance submissions yearly; 5% by unpublished writers, 30% by authors who are new to the magazine. Receives 260 unsolicited mss monthly.

Submissions
Send complete ms. Accepts photocopies, computer printouts, disk submissions (WordPerfect or ASCII), email submissions to aamoroso@atlantaparent.com. SASE. Responds in 6 months.
Articles: 600–1,200 words. Informational and how-to articles; and humor. Topics include pregnancy, childbirth, child development, early education, health and fitness, and parenting.
Depts/columns: Word length varies. Short essays and resource guides.
Other: Submit seasonal material 6 months in advance.

Sample Issue
34 pages (50% advertising): 4 articles; 4 depts/columns. Sample copy, $2 with 9x12 SASE. Guidelines available.
- "Moms Have a Choice." Article discusses alternative birthing methods, including waterbirth, natal hypnotherapy, and acupuncture.
- "Dads & Their Babies." Article on how some fathers have adjusted their business schedules to allow more time with their children.
- Sample dept/column: "Nursery Giggles" takes a look a the Mild-Wild Child syndrome.

Rights and Payment
One-time rights. Written material, $35–$50. Pays on publication. Provides 1 tearsheet.

Editor's Comments
All articles should focus on the needs of children from birth to age two.

Atlanta Parent

Suite 101
2346 Perimeter Park Drive
Atlanta, GA 30341

Managing Editor: Alison Amoroso

Description and Readership
Aimed at parents with children from birth to 16 years old, this tabloid offers articles, notices of regional events, and family resources related to the Atlanta metropolitan area.
• **Audience:** Parents
• **Frequency:** Monthly
• **Distribution:** 100% controlled
• **Circulation:** 100,000
• **Website:** www.atlantaparent.com

Freelance Potential
25% written by nonstaff writers. Publishes 50 freelance submissions yearly; 5% by unpublished writers, 30% by authors who are new to the magazine. Receives 22 unsolicited mss monthly.

Submissions
Send complete ms. Accepts photocopies, disk submissions (WordPerfect or ASCII), and email submissions to aamoroso@atlantaparent.com. SASE. Responds in 6 months.
Articles: 600–1,200 words. Informational and how-to articles; and humor. Topics include education, child care, child development, health, fitness, and parenting issues.
Depts/columns: Word length varies. Short essays and resource guides.
Other: Submit secular holiday material 6 months in advance.

Sample Issue
88 pages (50% advertising): 6 articles; 6 depts/columns. Sample copy, $2 with 9x12 SASE. Writers' guidelines available.
• "'Lessons from a Lemonade Stand." Article recounts what can be learned from opening a neighborhood drink stand, from a mom's point of view.
• "Childcare Concerns: Are They Valid?" Article discusses some of the problems involved in finding a good day care program.
• Sample dept/column: "Humor in the House" is a short essay about a not-so-handy husband.

Rights and Payment
One-time rights. Written material, $35–$50. Pays on publication. Provides 1 tearsheet.

Editor's Comments
Down-to-earth, activity-based articles appeal to our readers. Include quotes from local experts.

Atlanta Sporting Family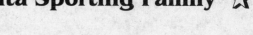

Suite 300
3650 Brookside Parkway
Alpharetta, GA 30022

Editor: Michael J. Pallerino

Description and Readership
Families residing in the Atlanta, Georgia, area read this magazine for its articles, resources, and up-to-date information relating to sports and recreation, and staying healthy. It also includes a calendar of events in the region.
• **Audience:** Parents
• **Frequency:** 6 times each year
• **Distribution:** Schools; subscription
• **Circulation:** Unavailable
• **Website:** www.sportingfamily.com

Freelance Potential
30% written by nonstaff writers. Publishes 10 freelance submissions yearly; 10% by authors who are new to the magazine. Receives 50 queries, 10 unsolicited mss monthly.

Submissions
Query or send complete ms. Accepts email submissions to editor@sportingfamily.com. Queries must be pasted in email. Send complete ms as a Microsoft Word attachment only. Responds in 1 month.
Articles: Word length varies. Informational and how-to articles; profiles; and personal experience pieces. Topics include health, fitness, recreation, social issues, and sports.
Depts/columns: Word length varies. News, health and wellness, and recreation ideas.

Sample Issue
48 pages: 7 articles; 7 depts/columns. Writers' guidelines available.
• "In the Driver's Seat." Article describes a driving program that provides teens with hands-on improvement skills.
• "Bike Like Lance." Article explores bikes and gear for children, and offers cycling tips.
• Sample dept/column: "Health & Wellness" offers nutrition tips for teens.

Rights and Payment
First and electronic rights. Written material, payment rate varies. Pays on publication.

Editor's Comments
We look for material that meets the needs of our readers, active families living in Georgia. Articles and news covering sports, health and wellness, and social issues, as well as destination pieces on family-friendly places in the region are of interest to us.

Austin Family

P.O. Box 7559
Round Rock, TX 78683-7559

Editor: Monica Davis

Description and Readership
Austin's parenting community looks forward to each new issue of this guide to local events and destinations for family fun. *Austin Family* also serves as a source of child-raising advice and up-to-date information on creating a healthy home.
- **Audience:** Parents
- **Frequency:** Monthly
- **Distribution:** 80% controlled; 10% schools
  5% subscription; 5% other
- **Circulation:** 35,000
- **Website:** www.austinfamily.com

Freelance Potential
70% written by nonstaff writers. Publishes 15 freelance submissions yearly; 10% by unpublished writers, 50% by authors who are new to the magazine. Receives 67 queries and unsolicited mss monthly.

Submissions
Query or send complete ms. Accepts photocopies, computer printouts, simultaneous submissions if identified, and email submissions to editor@austinfamily.com. Availability of artwork improves chance of acceptance. SASE. Responds in 3 months.
Articles: 800 words. Informational, practical application, and how-to articles. Topics include parenting, the family, the environment, recreation, ethnic and multicultural issues, hobbies, crafts, computers, careers, college, pets, current events, and health.
Depts/columns: 800 words. Local news and events, humor, and parenting tips.
Artwork: B/W prints.
Other: Submit seasonal material 6 months in advance.

Sample Issue
40 pages (50% advertising): 4 articles; 10 depts/columns. Sample copy, free.
- "Sink Some Line with the Kids on the Texas Coast." Article spotlights family fishing destinations.
- Sample dept/column: "Health Notes" discusses health issues related to summer camp and overseas travel.

Rights and Payment
First and second serial rights. Payment rates and payment policy vary.

Editor's Comments
We'd like to review more submissions that relate to parenting teens. More student- and teacher-oriented material is needed as well.

BabagaNewz

90 Oak Street
Newton, MA 02464

Production Editor: Aviva Werner

Description and Readership
BabagaNewz is a classroom magazine that accurately and thoughtfully analyzes major news stories, religious holidays, cultural events, and youth trends that play an important part in the lives of Jewish children.
- **Audience:** 9–13 years
- **Frequency:** 8 times each year
- **Distribution:** Schools; subscription
- **Circulation:** 41,029
- **Website:** www.babaganewz.com

Freelance Potential
All material is written on assignment.

Submissions
Query or send complete ms. Accepts photocopies and computer printouts. SASE. Response time varies.
Articles: Word length varies. Informational and how-to articles; profiles; and interviews. Topics include renewal, friendship, personal satisfaction, peace, caring for the environment, truth, responsibility, heroism, health, seder, the Torah, Jewish holidays, history, political science, social studies, geography, language, and sports.
Depts/columns: Word length varies. Science news, short profiles, and world news.

Sample Issue
20 pages (no advertising): 3 articles; 8 depts/columns. Sample copy and guidelines available by email request to aviva@babaganewz.com.
- "Lisa Fuld and Dawn Henning." Article recounts how two young girls found peace and family in a Jewish foster home.
- "Daniela Aharoni: Celebrity Host." Interview with Israel's Los-Angeles-based consul for tourism.
- Sample dept/column: "Recreate" provides instruction for making a sweet, crunchy Pesach side dish.

Rights and Payment
All rights. Written material, payment rate varies. Pays on acceptance. Provides contributor's copies upon request.

Editor's Comments
Each of our monthly issues focuses on a specific Jewish value and includes a teacher's guide. Although all of our material is written on assignment, we will consider queries for themed articles that speak to our Jewish readers and provide information that will become part of their background.

Babybug

Cricket Magazine Group
P.O. Box 300
315 5th Street
Peru, IL 61354

Submissions Editor

Description and Readership
Babybug is a looking and listening magazine for infants and toddlers and for the adults who read to them. Published by the well-known Cricket Magazine Group, it offers full-color illustrated stories and poems that express simple words and concepts.
• **Audience:** 6 months–2 years
• **Frequency:** 10 times each year
• **Distribution:** 90% subscription; 10% newsstand
• **Circulation:** 50,000
• **Website:** www.cricketmag.com

Freelance Potential
100% written by nonstaff writers. Publishes 30–40 freelance submissions yearly; 50% by authors who are new to the magazine. Receives 200 unsolicited mss each month.

Submissions
Send complete ms. Accepts photocopies, computer printouts, and simultaneous submissions if identified. SASE. Responds in 3–4 months.
Articles: 10 words. Simple ideas and concepts.
Fiction: 3–6 short sentences. Concrete stories and age-appropriate humor.
Other: Rhyming and rhythmic poetry, to 8 lines. Parent/child activities, to 8 lines.

Sample Issue
22 pages (no advertising): 4 stories; 2 poems. Sample copy, $5. Guidelines available.
• "Kim and Carrots." Illustrated story continues the saga of a little girl and her stuffed rabbit.
• "Which Water?" Picture story shows the different ways we use water.
• "Buddy Bear." Poem about a muddy, then cuddly, bear friend.

Rights and Payment
Rights vary. Written material, $25 minimum. Pays on publication. Provides 6 contributor's copies.

Editor's Comments
Our magazine brings parents and young children together to share words and pictures about the world around them. We always need stories, articles, and poems with unique treatments of everyday things in a toddler's world. We are seeing far too much material dealing with body parts, bathtime, and bedtime. Our standards are very high, and we will accept only top-quality material.

Baby Dallas

Lauren Publications
Suite 146
4275 Kellway Circle
Addison, TX 75001

Editor: Shelly Pate

Description and Readership
Striving to meet the needs of families residing in the Dallas area, this parenting magazine offers informative and entertaining articles with a focus on children from prenatal through adolescence.
• **Audience:** Parents
• **Frequency:** Twice each year
• **Distribution:** 90% controlled; 10% subscription
• **Circulation:** 120,000
• **Website:** www.babydallas.com

Freelance Potential
25% written by nonstaff writers. Publishes 12–15 freelance submissions yearly; 20% by authors who are new to the magazine. Receives 20 queries monthly.

Submissions
Query with résumé. Accepts photocopies, computer printouts, simultaneous submissions if identified, and email queries to editorial@dallaschild.com. SASE. Responds in 2–3 months.
Articles: 1,000–2,500 words. Informational, self-help, and how-to articles; profiles; interviews; humor; and personal experience pieces. Topics include parenting, education, current events, social issues, multicultural and ethnic issues, health, fitness, crafts, and computers.
Depts/columns: 800 words. Health updates, safety issues, baby care, and parent resources.

Sample Issue
30 pages (14% advertising): 1 article; 7 depts/columns. Sample copy, free with 9x12 SASE. Guidelines available.
• "The Many Emotions of Motherhood." Article discusses the overwhelming range of intense emotions motherhood can bring, and offers tips to help manage them.
• Sample dept/column: "Birthing Options" takes a look at the four stages of labor.
• Sample dept/column: "Early Childhood" offers information on baby talk, infant toys, and a test to find out if a baby has a metabolic disorder.

Rights and Payment
First rights. Written material, payment rate varies. Pays on publication. Provides author's copies upon request.

Editor's Comments
We look for resourceful parenting information that will offer guidelines, advice, comfort and a sense of humor. Keep in mind that we target first-time parents.

Baby Talk

The Parenting Group
3rd Floor
135 West 50th Street
New York, NY 10020

Senior Editor: Patty Onderko

Description and Readership
Expectant mothers and parents of toddlers up to eighteen months of age turn to this resourceful magazine for its articles and tips on pregnancy, caring for babies, child development, nutrition, and health.
- **Audience:** Parents
- **Frequency:** 10 times each year
- **Distribution:** 100% controlled
- **Circulation:** 2 million
- **Website:** www.babytalk.com

Freelance Potential
70% written by nonstaff writers. Publishes 40 freelance submissions yearly; 20% by authors who are new to the magazine. Receives 42 queries monthly.

Submissions
Query with clips or writing samples. No simultaneous submissions. SASE. Responds in 2 months.
Articles: 1,500–2,000 words. Informational and how-to articles; and personal experience pieces. Topics include pregnancy, baby care, infant health, juvenile equipment and toys, day care, marriage, and relationships.
Depts/columns: 500–1,200 words. News, advice, women's and infant health, and personal experiences from new parents.

Sample Issue
92 pages (50% advertising): 6 articles; 10 depts/columns. Sample copy, free with 9x12 SASE ($1.60 postage). Guidelines and theme list available.
- "Everything You Need to Know about Fever." Article offers information on what to do when a child spikes a high temperature.
- "Stressed about SIDS?" Article discusses Sudden Infant Death Syndrome and information on ways to help protect babies from it.
- Sample dept/column: "Your Body" offers energy booster ideas for new moms.

Rights and Payment
First rights. Articles, $1,000–$2,000. Depts/columns, $300–$1,200. Pays on acceptance. Provides 2–4 contributor's copies.

Editor's Comments
We look for articles that will provide our readers with the hands-on information they need on topics related to caring for infants and toddlers. It is important to include expert advice to back up your material.

Baltimore's Child

11 Dutton Court
Baltimore, MD 21228

Editor: Dianne R. McCann

Description and Readership
Packed with resourceful information, this magazine for families in the Baltimore metro area includes articles on topics such as parenting, education, healthcare, and social issues. It also offers news, tips, and information on regional events and services.
- **Audience:** Parents
- **Frequency:** Monthly
- **Distribution:** Unavailable
- **Circulation:** 55,000
- **Website:** www.baltimoreschild.com

Freelance Potential
95% written by nonstaff writers. Publishes 250 freelance submissions yearly.

Submissions
Prefers query; accepts ms. Accepts photocopies, computer printouts, and email submissions to baltochild@aol.com. SASE. Response time varies.
Articles: 1,000–1,500 words. Informational articles. Topics include parenting issues, education, health, fitness, child care, social issues, and regional news.
Depts/columns: Word lengths vary. Family issues, travel, opinion, baby care, book and music reviews, new product reviews, parenting teens, and parenting children with special needs.

Sample Issue
80 pages: 6 articles; 13 depts/columns. Guidelines and calendar available at website.
- "Baby Basics: The Bare Necessities of Life." Article rates different baby care items and lists supplies to keep on hand.
- "Bored with Summer? Give Board Games a Spin." Article explores and reviews different board games that the whole family can enjoy.
- Sample dept/column: "A Woman's Place" offers suggestions to help stop excessive worrying.

Rights and Payment
One-time rights. Written material, payment rates and policies vary.

Editor's Comments
We are looking for articles that emphasize positive, constructive and practical advice that will help parents make informed choices. All material must be specific to the Baltimore metropolitan area. Please note that while each issue includes information on a theme topic, it also offers other material as well.

Bay Area Baby

Suite 120
2280 Vehicle Drive
Rancho Cordova, CA 95670

Special Sections Editor: Corrie Pelc

Description and Readership
Distributed to new and expectant parents in the Greater San Francisco Bay area, this magazine offers well-researched articles about parenting concerns.
- **Audience:** Parents
- **Frequency:** 3 times each year
- **Distribution:** 100% controlled
- **Circulation:** 80,000
- **Website:** www.bayareaparent.com

Freelance Potential
50% written by nonstaff writers. Publishes 21 freelance submissions yearly; 50% by authors who are new to the magazine. Receives 8 queries and unsolicited mss monthly.

Submissions
Query or send complete ms. Accepts photocopies, computer printouts, and simultaneous submissions if identified. SASE. Responds in 1–2 months.
Articles: 1,200–1,400 words. Informational, self-help, and how-to articles; personal experience pieces; profiles; interviews; and humor. Topics include pregnancy, prenatal care, childbirth, and infant care.
Depts/columns: 800 words. Parenting updates.
Artwork: 8x10 B/W or color prints. No slides.
Other: Submit seasonal material 6 months in advance.

Sample Issue
36 pages: 5 articles; 2 depts/columns. Sample copy, free with 9x12 SASE (5 first-class stamps). Guidelines and theme list available.
- "Helping Older Children Cope with a Newly Mobile Sibling." Article looks at preparing preschoolers with strategies for protecting space and possessions.
- "What to Look for in a Preschool or Childcare Program." Article helps parents choose the best childcare options for their loved ones.
- "How Children Learn to Speak." Informative article explains the speech process, and what to do if parents suspect a problem.

Rights and Payment
Regional rights. Written material, payment rate varies. Pays on publication. Provides 1 contributor's copy.

Editor's Comments
Although most of our articles are written on assignment, we will consider local material geared to parents of children of all ages.

Bay State Parent

800 Main Street
P.O. Box 617
Holden, MA 05120

Editor: Susan Scully Petroni

Description and Readership
Formerly listed as *Today's Parent,* this publication focuses on the needs of families and parents in the Massachusetts Bay area.
- **Audience:** Parents
- **Frequency:** Monthly
- **Distribution:** Newstand; subscription; libriaries
- **Circulation:** 71,000
- **Website:** www.baystateparent.com

Freelance Potential
80% written by nonstaff writers. Publishes 10 freelance submissions yearly; 10% by unpublished writers, 20% by authors who are new to the magazine. Receives 25+ queries monthly.

Submissions
Query. Accepts email queries (Microsoft Word) to spetroni@rcn.com. Artwork improves chance of acceptance. Responds in 30 days.
Articles: To 2,000 words. Informational and how-to articles; and humor. Topics include regional and local events, travel, books, arts and crafts, family finance, and computers.
Fiction: To 1,000 words. Contemporary, mainstream, and literary fiction.
Depts/columns: To 1,500 words. Accepts seasonal material 4 months in advance.
Artwork: B/W and color prints. JPEGS/200dpi

Sample Issue
68 pages: 10 articles; 1 story; 4 depts/columns. Sample copy, free. Guidelines available.
- "Planning: The Great Family Weekend." Article describes one family's camping excursion.
- "Children of the World." Article reports on a mulitcultural city in Westborough.
- Sample dept/column: "Parent Prose" features essays on family life from parents.

Rights and Payment
Massachusetts exclusive rights. Pays on publication. Payment rate varies.

Editor's Comments
All of our material has a regional focus. We are not interested in general parenting articles at this time. We look for multi-source articles and articles that present more than one viewpoint. At this time we are seeking articles on education, health, and parenting trends.

Becoming Family

718 S. Loomis
Chicago, IL 60607

Editor: Peg Short

Description and Readership
Becoming Family is dedicated to celebrating and strengthening family life in America. It offers ideas, advice, and encouragement, as well as inspiring stories of families striving to grow stronger.
- **Audience:** Families
- **Frequency:** Quarterly
- **Distribution:** Subscription; newsstand; other
- **Circulation:** 90,000
- **Website:** www.becomingfamily.com

Freelance Potential
70% written by nonstaff writers. Publishes 10 freelance submissions yearly.

Submissions
Query. Accepts photocopies, computer printouts, and email queries to pshort@becomingfamily.com. SASE. Responds to queries in 1 month.
Articles: Word lengths vary. Informational articles; profiles; and personal experience pieces. Topics include family and social issues, recreation, education, health, and careers.
Fiction: Word lengths vary. Mainstream fiction depicting strong family life.
Depts/columns: Word lengths vary. Entertainment, health and safety, and community building.

Sample Issue
80 pages: 87 articles; 9 stories; 10 depts/columns. Sample copy, $3.95 with 9x12 SASE. Writers' guidelines available.
- "United They Stand." Profile of a military family who share their secrets of happiness despite long separations and the stresses of war.
- "A Stroke of Genius." Article profiles a young girl whose artwork has appeared in the best galleries in the world.
- Sample dept/column: "Management Matters" features tips on taking your family out of the fast lane.

Rights and Payment
All rights. Pays on acceptance. Written material, payment rates vary. Provides 1 contributor's copy.

Editor's Comments
We are looking for stories about "real" families that can serve as models for family values. Articles of interest to us have an upbeat and encouraging tone and show our readers that good families just don't happen; they require work and nurturing.

Better Homes and Gardens

Meredith Corporation
1716 Locust Street
Des Moines, IA 50309-3023

Department Editor

Description and Readership
Focusing on the home, community, and family, this magazine features articles and photos on topics such as entertaining, travel, health, the environment, home design, garden and outdoor living, and food and nutrition. It also includes features on education and parenting, and a section just for kids.
- **Audience:** Adults
- **Frequency:** Monthly
- **Distribution:** Subscription; newsstand
- **Circulation:** 7.6 million
- **Website:** www.bhg.com

Freelance Potential
10% written by nonstaff writers. Publishes 25–30 freelance submissions yearly; 25% by authors who are new to the magazine. Receives 20 queries monthly.

Submissions
Query with résumé and clips or writing samples. No unsolicited mss. Accepts photocopies and computer printouts. SASE. Responds in 1 month.
Articles: Word length varies. Informational and how-to articles; personal experience pieces; and profiles. Topics include food and nutrition, home design, gardening and outdoor living, travel, the environment, health, fitness, holidays, education, parenting, and child development.

Sample Issue
284 pages: 34 articles. Sample copy, $2.99 at newsstands. Guidelines available.
- "Small Spaces." Article describes how antiques dealers transformed their home into a cottage that reflected the history of their community.
- "Color Comes of Age." Article tells how one couple updated the palette of their whole house.
- "Plantings." Article takes a look at how to add carefree color to gardens.

Rights and Payment
All rights. Written material, payment rate varies. Pays on acceptance. Provides 1 contributor's copy.

Editor's Comments
Only a small percentage of our editorial comes from freelance writers. Therefore, make sure you only send your best work. We suggest new writers try submitting a piece in the areas of health, travel, parenting, or education. Please note that we rarely publish fiction, poetry, or beauty articles.

Big Apple Parent

4th Floor
9 East 38th Street
New York, NY 10016

Editor: Judy Antell

Description and Readership
News, feature stories about education and current events, and commentaries of interest to New York City parents fill each issue of this publication, along with articles on family finance, health, and child-related household concerns.
- **Audience:** Parents
- **Frequency:** Monthly
- **Distribution:** 100% controlled
- **Circulation:** 70,000
- **Website:** www.parentsknow.com

Freelance Potential
50% written by nonstaff writers. Publishes 30 freelance submissions yearly; 10% by unpublished writers, 20% by authors who are new to the magazine. Receives 100 queries and unsolicited mss monthly.

Submissions
Query or send complete ms. Accepts photocopies, computer printouts, and email submissions to judy@parentsknow.com. SASE. Responds in 1 month.
Articles: 800–1,000 words. Informational and how-to articles; profiles; interviews; and personal experience pieces. Topics include family issues, health, nutrition, fitness, crafts, current events, gifted and special education, nature, and regional news.
Depts/columns: 750 words. News and reviews.
Other: Submit seasonal material 4 months in advance.

Sample Issue
88 pages: 9 articles; 15 depts/columns; 1 calendar of events. Sample copy, free with 10x13 SASE. Guidelines available.
- "Children Living with Asthma." Article presents the latest findings on the causes and treatment of asthma in children under the age of 18.
- "A Watery Road to Success." Article reports on an afterschool program where high school kids build a boat, then launch it on the Bronx River.
- Sample dept/column: "Reflections" features an essay about becoming a mom at the age of 44.

Rights and Payment
First New York area rights. Articles, $50. Pays 2 months after publication. Provides 1 contributor's copy.

Editor's Comments
News pieces are what we'd most like to see. We're always looking for good journalistic stories for New York City's parents on new trends or education topics.

Birmingham Christian Family

P.O. Box 382724
Birmingham, AL 35238

President: Laurie Stroud

Description and Readership
Targeting families in the Birmingham area, this Christian publication provides articles and tips on positive living, including entertainment, healthy living, parenting, local personalities, and inspirational literature.
- **Audience:** Families
- **Frequency:** Monthly
- **Distribution:** 95% newsstand; 5% subscription
- **Circulation:** 35,000
- **Website:** www.birminghamchristian.com

Freelance Potential
50% written by nonstaff writers. Publishes 60 freelance submissions yearly; 5% by unpublished writers, 2–3% by authors who are new to the magazine. Receives 8–9 queries monthly.

Submissions
Query with photos if applicable. Accepts email submissions to laurie@birminghamchristian.com. Availability of artwork improves chance of acceptance. SASE. Responds in 1 month.
Articles: To 500 words. Informational, self-help, and how-to articles; profiles; interviews; and personal experience pieces. Topics include animals, pets, the arts, crafts, hobbies, current events, fitness, music, recreation, religion, travel, and sports.
Fiction: To 500 words. Features inspirational fiction and humorous stories.
Depts/columns: To 500 words. Book and music reviews, regional news, humor, money matters, and recipes.

Sample Issue
30 pages (25% advertising): 3 articles; 16 depts/columns. Sample copy, free with 9x12 SASE ($3 postage). Editorial calendar available.
- "A New Pet: Are You Ready?" Article takes a look at things to consider before adopting a pet, including doing research and the commitment.
- Sample dept/column: "Senior Scene" offers tips for maintaining a healthy senior diet.

Rights and Payment
Rights vary. No payment.

Editor's Comments
Articles that inspire readers to grow and develop their Christian faith are of interest to us. New writers have the best chance at publication with a cover story.

The Black Collegian

140 Carondelet Street
New Orleans, LA 70130

Editorial Assistant: Caroline Wilson

Description and Readership
This award-winning publication for African American college students offers articles that cover topics relating to career and self-development, including trends in the industry, career reports, and job opportunities.
- **Audience:** African Americans, 18–22 years
- **Frequency:** 2 times each year
- **Distribution:** Internet; college campuses
- **Circulation:** 125,000
- **Website:** www.black-collegian.com

Freelance Potential
95% written by nonstaff writers. Publishes 20 freelance submissions yearly; 33% by authors who are new to the magazine. Receives 2 queries monthly.

Submissions
Prefers email queries to jim@imdiversity.com. Accepts photocopies, computer printouts, and IBM disk submissions (Microsoft Word). SASE. Responds in 3 months.
Articles: 1,500–2,000 words. Informational, self-help, and how-to articles; profiles; and personal experience pieces. Topics include careers, personal development, job hunting, colleges, financial aid, history, technology, and multicultural and ethnic issues.
Depts/columns: Word lengths vary. Health issues and African American book and art reviews.
Artwork: 5x7 and 11x14 B/W and color transparencies. B/W and color line art.

Sample Issue
96 pages: 21 articles; 3 depts/columns. Writers' guidelines available.
- "Got an Internship?" Article discusses how internships and co-op positions are becoming a more frequent part of the academic experience.
- "Engineering: Trends and Opportunities within the Industry." Article takes a look at important trends that will impact the engineering workforce.
- Sample dept/column: "Campus Advisor" offers advice on adjusting to college life.

Rights and Payment
One-time rights. Written material, payment rate varies. Pays after publication. Provides 1 author's copy.

Editor's Comments
We seek information that will help our reader prepare for the job market, including writing résumés, dressing for success, interviewing, and coping with stress.

Book Links

American Library Association
50 East Huron Street
Chicago, IL 60611

Editor: Laura Tillotson

Description and Readership
Published by the American Library Association, this magazine publishes bibliographies, essays, and retrospective reviews to provide educators with classroom ideas to connect children with books.
- **Audience:** Librarians, teachers, and parents
- **Frequency:** 6 times each year
- **Distribution:** 98% subscription; 2% controlled
- **Circulation:** 20,577
- **Website:** www.ala.org/booklinks

Freelance Potential
90% written by nonstaff writers. Publishes 60 freelance submissions yearly; 20% by unpublished writers, 30% by authors who are new to the magazine. Receives 8 queries monthly.

Submissions
Query. No unsolicited mss. SASE. Response time varies.
Articles: Word length varies. Informational articles; personal experience pieces; interviews; and profiles. Topics include children's books, current and historical events, nature, the environment, and ethnic and multicultural subjects.
Depts/columns: Classroom ideas for curriculum enrichment, 800–1,200 words. Book lists for specific countries, locales, or themes, 250–300 words. Interviews with authors and illustrators, word length varies.

Sample Issue
64 pages (28% advertising): 12 articles; 3 depts/columns. Sample copy, $6. Writers' guidelines and theme list available.
- "Working Short Stories into the Curriculum." Article suggests ways to use short stories to add depth, richness, and historical context to classroom lessons.
- "Gung Hay Fat Choy!" Article lists book titles about celebrating the Chinese New Year
- "Talking with Leo & Diane Dillon." Interview with an interracial couple who gave up their personal styles to make art together.

Rights and Payment
All rights. Articles, $100. Pays on publication. Provides 2 contributor's copies.

Editor's Comments
We want material that supports the classroom use of children's trade books. Gear your articles to the curriculum needs of teachers, librarians, and library media specialists.

Bop

Suite 700
6430 Sunset Boulevard
Hollywood, CA 90028

Editor-in-Chief: Leesa Coble

Description and Readership
Fun articles, hot photos, and the latest news and gossip on today's favorite teen celebrities can be found in this magazine. In addition, it offers cool fashion ideas, posters, crafts, and contest information.
• **Audience:** 10–16 years
• **Frequency:** Monthly
• **Distribution:** 90% newsstand; 10% newsstand
• **Circulation:** 200,000
• **Website:** www.bopmag.com

Freelance Potential
5% written by nonstaff writers. Publishes 2 freelance submissions yearly; 50% by authors who are new to the magazine. Receives 2 queries monthly.

Submissions
Query with résumé and clips for celebrity angle only. Accepts photocopies, computer printouts, and simultaneous submissions if identified. SASE. Responds in 2 months.
Articles: To 700 words. Celebrity interviews; profiles of film and television personalities and recording stars; and behind-the-scenes reports on the entertainment industry.
Depts/columns: Staff written.
Other: Quizzes and puzzles. Submit seasonal material 3–5 months in advance.

Sample Issue
82 pages (15% advertising): 19 articles; 18 depts/columns; 16 posters. Sample copy, $3.99 at newsstands.
• "The Best and Worst of Ashlee Simpson." Article discusses good and bad personality traits of actress/singer Ashlee Simpson.
• "Just a Girl." Article takes a look at the lifestyle of star Jamie Lynn Spears.
• "Between You and Jesse." Article tells what celebrity Jesse McCartney thinks of crushes and flirting.

Rights and Payment
All rights. Written material, payment rates vary. Pays on publication. Provides 2 contributor's copies.

Editor's Comments
We are looking for more celebrity interviews, items, and angles. Our tween audience turns to us for up-front and personal information that makes them feel closer to their favorite celebrities. We look for the latest news and juiciest rumors.

The Boston Parents' Paper

670 Centre Street
Jamaica Plain, MA 02130

Senior Editor: Allison Murray

Description and Readership
Parents living in the Boston area find practical, useful information that can help them improve their parenting skills in this free magazine, which also publicizes local family events and service providers.
• **Audience:** Parents
• **Frequency:** Monthly
• **Distribution:** 98% controlled; 2% subscription
• **Circulation:** 70,000
• **Website:** www.bostonparentspaper.com

Freelance Potential
75% written by nonstaff writers. Publishes 3 freelance submissions yearly; 10% by unpublished writers, 20% by authors who are new to the magazine. Receives 21 queries monthly.

Submissions
Query with clips or writing samples. Accepts photocopies and computer printouts. Availability of artwork improves chance of acceptance. SASE. Response time varies.
Articles: Word length varies. Informational articles; profiles; and interviews. Topics include child development, education, parenting, family issues, fitness, and health.
Depts/columns: To 1,800 words. Short news items, parenting tips, and profiles.
Artwork: B/W prints. Line art.
Other: Submit seasonal material 6 months in advance.

Sample Issue
68 pages (45% advertising): 3 articles; 9 depts/columns; 1 calendar of events. Guidelines and theme list available.
• "Small but Sure." Article reports on Boston's creation of smaller, more effective high schools.
• Sample dept/column: "Family Travel" highlights the attractions in Quebec City.

Rights and Payment
First North American serial and electronic rights. All material, payment rates vary. Pays within 30 days of publication. Provides 5 contributor's copies.

Editor's Comments
With your article, enclose a list of Boston-area resources that parents can contact if they want to pursue your subject further. Remember, our audience of busy parents wants a quick read, so distill your major points into bulleted lists for easy reading.

Boutique Magazine

P.O. Box 1162
Newtown, PA 18940

Editor: Angela Hughes

Description and Readership
Specializing in products for infants and young children, this resource for upscale shoppers offers informational articles on unusual products and accessories including fashions, home decor, literature, and stationery. It also includes reviews, and interviews.
• **Audience:** Families
• **Frequency:** 6 times each year
• **Distribution:** 70% subscription; 30% newsstand
• **Circulation:** Unavailable
• **Website:** www.boutiquemagazineonline.com

Freelance Potential
20% written by nonstaff writers. Publishes 12 freelance submissions yearly.

Submissions
Query or send complete ms. Accepts photocopies and computer printouts. SASE. Response time varies.
Articles: Word length varies. Informational articles; profiles; interviews; and reviews. Topics include clothes, shoes, toys, gifts, books, home decor, and accessories; all for children up to the age of 10.
Depts/columns: Word lengths vary. Decorating, Internet sites, gift ideas, book reviews.

Sample Issue
44 pages: 5 articles; 8 depts/columns.
• "Flea Market Babies." Article describes a book that offers suggestions and tips for decorating children's rooms with a vintage look.
• "Dressing for Fall." Article takes a look at the combination of styles mixing the fashions of the past and present in the upcoming fall fashions for children.
• Sample dept/column: "Online" offers information on on Internet sites for children's books, clothing, shoes, and stationery.

Rights and Payment
One-time rights. Written material, payment rates vary. Pays on publication.

Editor's Comments
We are always looking for unique articles as they pertain to the children's fashion industry from writers who know the market. We look for material that provides shoppers with an opportunity to see how far children's products have come, and strive to provide them with suggestions for finding the perfect gift. Keep in mind that our readers are from affluent families with children up to the age of 10.

Boys' Life

Boy Scouts of America
P.O. Box 152079
1325 West Walnut Hill Lane
Irving, TX 75015-2079

Senior Editor: Michael Goldman

Description and Readership
The Boy Scouts of America has been publishing this magazine since 1911. It offers nonfiction on any subject of interest to boys, as well as fiction.
• **Audience:** 6–18 years
• **Frequency:** Monthly
• **Distribution:** 95% subscription; 5% other
• **Circulation:** 1.3 million
• **Website:** www.boyslife.org

Freelance Potential
80% written by nonstaff writers. Publishes 50 freelance submissions yearly; 1% by unpublished writers, 25% by authors who are new to the magazine. Receives 8+ queries monthly.

Submissions
Query for articles and depts/columns. Query or send complete ms for fiction. Accepts computer printouts. SASE. Responds to queries in 4–6 weeks, to mss in 6–8 weeks.
Articles: 500–1,500 words. Informational and how-to articles; profiles; and humor. Topics include sports, science, American history, geography, animals, nature, and the environment.
Fiction: 1,000–1,500 words. Genres include mystery, adventure, humor, and science fiction.
Depts/columns: 300–750 words. Cars, music, collecting, space and aviation, computers, and pets.
Other: Puzzles and cartoons.

Sample Issue
54 pages (18% advertising): 4 articles; 1 story; 4 depts/columns; 4 comics. Sample copy, $3.60 with 9x12 SASE. Guidelines available.
• "This Was the Worst." Article reports on Scout cleanup efforts in Florida after the 2004 hurricanes.
• "10,000 Cookies." Story tells of a boy who organizes a Christmas cookie drive for the troops in Iraq.
• Sample dept/column: "Heads Up!" describes an ancient Hawaiian sport that is making a comeback.

Rights and Payment
First rights. Articles, $400–$1,500. Fiction, $750+. Depts/columns, $150–$400. Pays on acceptance. Provides 2 contributor's copies.

Editor's Comments
You'll stand a better chance of acceptance if you submit a piece for one of our columns or a short story. All of our articles are commissioned.

Boys' Quest

P.O. Box 227
Bluffton, OH 45817-0227

Associate Editor: Virginia Edwards

Description and Readership
Timeless topics of interest to boys are the mainstay of this children's magazine. It features theme-related articles, stories, and activities.
- **Audience:** 6–13 years
- **Frequency:** 6 times each year
- **Distribution:** 60% school libraries; 40% newsstand
- **Circulation:** 10,000
- **Website:** www.boysquest.com

Freelance Potential
100% written by nonstaff writers. Publishes 100 freelance submissions yearly; 20% by unpublished writers, 50% by authors who are new to the magazine. Receives 208 queries and unsolicited mss monthly.

Submissions
Prefers complete ms. Accepts queries. Accepts photocopies, computer printouts, and simultaneous submissions if identified. SASE. Responds to queries in 1–2 weeks, to mss in 2–3 months.
Articles: 500 words. Informational and how-to articles; personal experience pieces; profiles; and humor. Topics include family, culture and customs, sports, building, and cars.
Fiction: 500 words. Multicultural fiction, adventure, mystery, rebus stories, and stories about animals, sports, and nature.
Depts/columns: 300–500 words. Science projects.
Artwork: Prefers B/W prints; accepts color prints.
Other: Puzzles, activities, riddles, and cartoons.

Sample Issue
48 pages (no advertising): 2 articles; 6 stories; 7 depts/columns; 5 puzzles. Sample copy, $4 with 9x12 SASE. Guidelines and theme list available with #10 SASE.
- "Sammy in the Suitcase." Story about a homeless man's dog who finds a new place to live.
- "Treetop Orphans." Informative article tells about the residents of a wildlife rescue center.

Rights and Payment
First and second rights. Articles and fiction, $.05 per word. Depts/columns, $35. Poems and activities. $10+. Artwork, $5–$10. Pays on publication. Provides 1 contributor's copy.

Editor's Comments
We are looking for lively, wholesome material written from a boy's point of view.

Bread for God's Children

P.O. Box 1017
Arcadia, FL 34265-1017

Editorial Secretary: Donna Wade

Description and Readership
Bread for God's Children is dedicated to spreading the Gospel of Jesus Christ with special emphasis on the Word of God for children and parents. It features stories written from a child's viewpoint.
- **Audience:** Families
- **Frequency:** 6–8 times each year
- **Distribution:** 100% subscription
- **Circulation:** 10,000
- **Website:** www.breadministries.com

Freelance Potential
25% written by nonstaff writers. Publishes 15–20 freelance submissions yearly; 20% by unpublished writers, 20% by authors who are new to the magazine. Receives 25 unsolicited mss monthly.

Submissions
Send complete ms. Accepts photocopies, computer printouts, and simultaneous submissions if identified. No email submissions. SASE. Responds to mss in 2–3 months.
Articles: 600–800 words. Informational and personal experiences that inspire readers to grow in their spiritual lives.
Fiction: Christian theme-based stories for younger children, 500–800 words. Stories for middle-grade and young adult readers, 800–1,000 words.
Depts/columns: To 800 words. Parenting issues, family activities, and issues of interest to teens.
Other: Filler and crafts.

Sample Issue
28 pages (no advertising): 3 stories; 8 depts/columns; 1 Bible story. Sample copy, free with 9x12 SASE (5 first-class stamps). Guidelines available at website.
- "Tiffy Disappears." A young boy trusts that God will lead him to where his lost dog can be found.
- "The Ride of His Life." Boy relates needing help to escape an elevator to accepting God as his Savior.
- Sample dept/column: "Heroes of the Faith" recalls an author and Bible teacher who passed away.

Rights and Payment
First rights. Pays on publication. Articles, $30; fiction, $40–$50. Short filler, $10. Provides 3 copies.

Editor's Comments
We want to see stories for younger children on their learning godly principles of life such as commitment and following through.

Breakaway

Focus on the Family
8605 Explorer Drive
Colorado Springs, CO 80920

Editor: Mike Ross

Description and Readership
Striving to inspire and challenge teenage boys to live for God, this colorful magazine brings readers adventure and excitement with its articles and short stories.
- **Audience:** 12–18 years
- **Frequency:** Monthly
- **Distribution:** 97% subscription; 3% other
- **Circulation:** 95,000
- **Website:** www.breakawaymag.com

Freelance Potential
20% written by nonstaff writers. Publishes 5 freelance submissions yearly; 1% by unpublished writers, 1% by new authors. Receives 50 unsolicited mss monthly.

Submissions
Send complete ms. Accepts electronic submissions through website at www.breakawayfamily.org, and computer printouts. SASE. Responds in 8–10 weeks.
Articles: 600–1,200 words. How-to and self-help articles; personal experience pieces; profiles; interviews; and humor. Topics include religion, sports, and multicultural issues.
Fiction: 1,500–2,200 words. Contemporary, religious, and inspirational fiction; suspense; adventure; humor; and stories about sports.
Depts/columns: Word lengths vary. Advice, Scripture readings, and Bible facts.
Other: Filler. Submit seasonal material about religious holidays 6–8 months in advance.

Sample Issue
32 pages (9% advertising): 4 articles; 1 story; 5 depts/columns. Sample copy, $1.75 with 9x12 SASE (2 first-class stamps). Guidelines available.
- "Wiping Out at the Wedge." Essay shares a teen's experience of riding the waves at the end of the Balboa Peninsula in California.
- "Bethany Hamilton Rides the Wave." Article tells the story of a young surfer who lost her arm to a shark, and her mission to spread the Word of Christ.
- Sample dept/column: "Epic Truth" shares the story of a disabled man who was once a pole-vaulter.

Rights and Payment
First or one-time rights. Written material, $.15 per word. Pays on acceptance. Provides 5 author's copies.

Editor's Comments
We are looking for more personal profiles of Christians, such as pro athletes, missionaries, and actors.

Brilliant Star

1233 Central Street
Evanston, IL 60201

Associate Editor: Susan Engle

Description and Readership
Following the beliefs of the Bahá'í faith, this magazine exposes young readers to diverse articles, stories, and activities that help them in their everyday lives.
- **Audience:** 8–12 years
- **Frequency:** 6 times each year
- **Distribution:** 75% subscription; 25% other
- **Circulation:** 7,000
- **Website:** www.brilliantstarmagazine.org

Freelance Potential
5% written by nonstaff writers. Publishes 5 freelance submissions yearly; 30% by unpublished writers, 80% by authors who are new to the magazine. Receives 120 unsolicited submissions yearly.

Submissions
Query with clips for nonfiction. Send complete ms for fiction. Accepts photocopies, computer printouts, and simultaneous submissions if identified. SASE. Responds in 6–8 weeks.
Articles: To 700 words. Informational and how-to articles; personal experience pieces; profiles; and biographies. Topics include the Bahá'í faith, historical Bahá'í figures, religion, history, ethnic and social issues, travel, music, nature, and the environment.
Fiction: To 700 words. Early reader fiction. Genres include ethnic, multicultural, historical, contemporary, and problem-solving fiction.
Depts/columns: To 600 words. Religion and ethics.
Other: Puzzles, activities, games, recipes, and poetry.

Sample Issue
30 pages (no advertising): 1 article; 1 story; 1 comic; 9 activities; 10 depts/columns. Sample copy, $3 with 9x12 SASE (5 first-class stamps). Guidelines, theme list, and editorial calendar available.
- "A New Culture." Story features a girl who learns about different cultures around the world.
- "Take the Plunge!" Article offers offers ways to speak up and make new friends.
- Sample dept/column: "Music Cafe" offers music and lyrics from songs from around the world.

Rights and Payment
All or one-time rights. No payment. Provides 2 contributor's copies.

Editor's Comments
We're looking for problem-solving fiction with sincere characters who have a sense of humor.

Brio

Focus on the Family
8605 Explorer Drive
Colorado Springs, CO 80920

Associate Editor: Krishana Kraft

Description and Readership
The goal of this magazine is to teach creatively, to entertain, to challenge readers toward a healthy self-concept, and draw them closer in their relationship with Jesus Christ.
• **Audience:** 12–15 years
• **Frequency:** Monthly
• **Distribution:** Subscription; newsstand
• **Circulation:** 200,000
• **Website:** www.briomag.com

Freelance Potential
10% written by nonstaff writers. Publishes 20–30 freelance submissions yearly; 1% by unpublished writers, 5% by authors who are new to the magazine. Receives 25 queries, 25 unsolicited mss monthly.

Submissions
Query or send complete ms. Accepts photocopies, computer printouts, and email submissions to krishana.kraft@fotf.org. SASE. Responds in 4–6 weeks.
Articles: To 2,000 words. Informational and how-to articles; personal experience pieces; profiles and interviews. Topics include Christian living, peer relationships, family life, and contemporary issues.
Fiction: To 2,000 words. Genres include contemporary fiction, romance, and humor with Christian themes.
Depts/columns: Staff written.
Other: Cartoons, anecdotes, and quizzes.

Sample Issue
48 pages (6% advertising): 6 articles; 1 story; 7 depts/columns. Sample copy, $1.50 with 9x12 SASE ($.52 postage). Guidelines available.
• "When You're Not the One." Article tells how to handle unwelcome feelings of rejection.
• "Fren-emies." Article helps readers deal with the odd-one-out problem when they are involved in a three-way friendship.

Rights and Payment
First rights. Written material, $.08–$.15 per word. Pays on acceptance. Provides 3 contributor's copies.

Editor's Comments
Send us fun, action-oriented articles on subjects teen girls are into, such as wearing the "right" clothes, organizing school items, and spending money. Tell us about ordinary teens you know who are doing extraordinary things to help others.

Brio and Beyond

Focus on the Family
8605 Explorer Drive
Colorado Springs, CO 80920

Associate Editor: Krishana Kraft

Description and Readership
Inspiring stories and advice for older teen girls can be found in this magazine. It strives to provide information to foster a deeper relationship with God.
• **Audience:** 16–20 years
• **Frequency:** Monthly
• **Distribution:** 100% subscription
• **Circulation:** 50,000
• **Website:** www.briomag.com

Freelance Potential
10% written by nonstaff writers. Publishes 20–30 freelance submissions yearly; 70% by unpublished writers, 50% by authors who are new to the magazine.

Submissions
Send complete ms. Accepts computer printouts, disk submissions, and email submissions to krishana.kraft@fotf.org. Availability of artwork improves chance of acceptance. SASE. Responds in 1 month.
Articles: Word lengths vary. Informational and how-to articles; profiles; interviews; reviews; and personal experience pieces. Topics include the arts, college, careers, crafts, hobbies, health, fitness, music, popular culture, religion, multicultural and social issues, sports, and travel. Also publishes humorous pieces.
Fiction: Word lengths vary.
Depts/columns: Staff written.
Artwork: Color prints or transparencies. Line art.
Other: Submit seasonal material 6 months in advance.

Sample Issue
46 pages (no advertising): 13 articles; 1 story; 3 depts/columns; 1 quiz; 1 comic. Sample copy, free. Guidelines available.
• "Facing Change with Confidence." Article offers suggestions for handling change.
• "Going Deeper: Would Jesus Church-Hop?" Article tells the importance of belonging to one church.
• "The Sanctity of Marriage." Article explores marriage as a religious institution ordained by God.

Rights and Payment
First or second rights. All material, payment rates vary. Pays on acceptance. Provides 2 copies.

Editor's Comments
We look for articles that provide our readers with faith building tools they can use in their daily lives.

Brooklyn Parent

Busy Family Network

25 8th Avenue
Brooklyn, NY 11217

Editor: Judy Antell

Publisher: Gina Ritter

Description and Readership

Chock full of parenting information, this regional tabloid includes informational articles, news, and tips on pregnancy, child development, and other issues relating to parenting.
- **Audience:** Parents
- **Frequency:** Monthly
- **Distribution:** 100% controlled
- **Circulation:** 50,000
- **Website:** www.parentsknow.com

Description and Readership

A number of family-oriented e-zines can be found at this website, including *Natural Family Online*, which offers a "bridge between mainstream and granola parenting"; *Busy Family Network*, which offers expert advice; and *Busy Homeschool*.
- **Audience:** Parents
- **Frequency:** Monthly
- **Distribution:** 100% Internet
- **Circulation:** 10,000
- **Website:** www.busyfamilynetwork.com

Freelance Potential

95% written by nonstaff writers. Publishes 450 freelance submissions yearly; 25% by authors who are new to the magazine. Receives 75 queries, 75 unsolicited mss monthly.

Freelance Potential

95% written by nonstaff writers. Publishes 140 freelance submissions yearly; 5% by unpublished writers, 50% by new authors. Receives 20 mss monthly.

Submissions

Query or send complete ms. Accepts photocopies, computer printouts, and email submissions to hellonwheels@parentsknow.com and judy@ parentsknow.com. SASE. Responds in 1 week.
Articles: 800–1,000 words. Informational articles; profiles; interviews; and personal experience pieces. Topics include family issues, health, nutrition, fitness, crafts, current events, gifted education, humor, nature, and regional news.
Depts/columns: 750 words. News and reviews.
Other: Submit seasonal material 4 months in advance.

Submissions

Send complete ms with brief author bio via email only to publisher@busyfamilynetwork.com. No attachments. Responds in 1–3 months.
Articles: 700–1,000 words. Informational and how-to articles; profiles; photo-essays; and personal experience pieces. Topics include nature, animals, crafts, hobbies, gifted and special education, health, fitness, popular culture, multicultural and ethnic issues, social issues, sports, and travel.
Fiction: 500–3,000 words. Genres include contemporary, historical, and multicultural fiction; adventure; folktales; and stories about sports. Also features read-aloud stories.
Depts/columns: 500–1,000 words.
Other: Filler, activities, and games. Interviews and profiles, 500–1,000 words.

Sample Issue

54 pages: 5 articles; 12 depts/columns. Sample copy, free with 10x13 SASE. Guidelines available.
- "Has Motherhood Fried Your Brain?" Article discusses the effects of brain power during motherhood.
- "Stop Your Crying." Article describes a class on how to calm a fussy baby.
- Sample dept/column: "Health Bites" offers tips on sun care for kids and snacks on the go.

Sample Issue

Sample copies of each publication, along with guidelines and editorial calendars, available at website.
- "Barb Silvestro, Dyer of Silks." Article interviews a mom about her wearable art business.
- "Top 10 Ways to Raise More Responsible Children." Tells how to develop good habits at a young age.

Rights and Payment

First New York area rights. Articles, $50. Depts/ columns, payment rate varies. Pays 2 months after publication. Provides 1 contributor's copy.

Rights and Payment

First North American serial or reprint rights and 1-year archival rights. Payment policy and payment rates vary.

Editor's Comments

We look for articles covering hot topics related to parenting and child development, and up-to-date information on available resources and regional events.

Editor's Comments

We look for good resource material that serves parents on their terms.

ByLine

P.O. Box 5240
Edmond, OK 73083-5240

Articles Editor: Marcia Preston
Fiction Editor: Carolyn Wall
Poetry Editor: Sandra Soli

Description and Readership

Since its founding in 1981, this writers' newsletter has featured articles on the craft and business of writing, as well as the first work of fiction and nonfiction writers, and poets.
- **Audience:** Writers
- **Frequency:** 11 times each year
- **Distribution:** 100% subscription
- **Circulation:** 3,500
- **Website:** www.bylinemag.com

Freelance Potential

80% written by nonstaff writers. Publishes 198 freelance submissions yearly. Receives 300 queries and unsolicited mss monthly.

Submissions

Query or send complete ms. Accepts photocopies, computer printouts, and simultaneous submissions if identified. SASE. Responds in 1–2 months.
Articles: 1,500–1,800 words. Informational and how-to articles. Topics include writing and marketing fiction, nonfiction, and poetry; finding an agent; grammar; and writing humor.
Fiction: 2,000–4,000 words. Contemporary, mainstream, and literary fiction.
Depts/columns: 200–400 words. Humor, marketing tips, and contest information.
Other: Poetry, to 30 lines.

Sample Issue

34 pages (8% advertising): 3 articles; 1 story; 13 depts/columns. Sample copy, $5 with 9x12 SASE. Writers' guidelines available.
- "Who's Afraid of Semicolons?" Article concisely explains the correct use of this grammatical device.
- "Writing a Killer Mystery Series." Article offers ten tips to keep the momentum going throughout a series.
- Sample dept/column: "EndPiece" is a column written by various professional authors.

Rights and Payment

First rights. Articles, $75. Fiction, $100. Depts/columns, $15–$35. Pays on acceptance. Provides 1–3 copies.

Editor's Comments

We like to encourage and advise novice and published writers, and we publish the work of beginners and veterans alike. *ByLine* sponsors contests to motivate writers by providing deadlines and competition.

Byronchild

P.O. Box 971
Mullumbimby, New South Wales 2482
Australia

Editor: Kali Wendorf
U.S. Editorial Contact: Lisa Reagan

Description and Readership

A parenting journal, *Byronchild* addresses family life from a social change perspective. Topics covered include political, spiritual, social, global, and environmental issues.
- **Audience:** Parents
- **Frequency:** Quarterly
- **Distribution:** Subscription; newsstand
- **Circulation:** 8,000
- **Website:** www.byronchild.com

Freelance Potential

90% written by nonstaff writers. Publishes 90 freelance submissions yearly; 50% by unpublished writers, 50% by authors who are new to the magazine.

Submissions

Query or send complete ms with list of references and sources. Accepts email submissions to Kali@byronchild.com (Microsoft Word attachments). Response time varies.
Articles: 2,000 words. Factual, informational, and how-to articles; personal experience pieces; and interviews. Topics include child care, health, relationships, pregnancy, and social issues.
Depts/columns: Word lengths vary. Humor, household tips, and media reviews.

Sample Issue

60 pages (30% advertising): 9 articles; 5 depts/columns. Sample copy, $8.95 with 9x12 SASE. Writers' guidelines available.
- "Making the Switch: The Thinking Family's Guide to Sustainable Living." Article offers environment-friendly alternative to household items.
- "Yelling Is Worse than Spanking." Article describes how a parents' yell can do more damage to a child than a spank.
- "22 Alternatives to Losing It." Article provides parents with ways to calm down before disciplining a child."

Rights and Payment

First rights. No payment. Provides 1–3 copies.

Editor's Comments

Our content is based on the belief that each parent innately knows what is right for his or her own child. We are interested in current parenting trends and ways to help parents raise socially-aware children. Review several sample issues prior to submitting.

BYU Magazine

218 UPB
Provo, UT 84602

Editor: Jeff McClellan

Description and Readership
Read by alumni, students, and staff of Brigham Young University, *BYU Magazine* includes thought-provoking commentary, college updates, personal essays, and informational articles.
- **Audience:** YA–Adult
- **Frequency:** Quarterly
- **Distribution:** 98% controlled; 2% schools
- **Circulation:** 180,000
- **Website:** www.magazine.byu.edu

Freelance Potential
45% written by nonstaff writers. Publishes 10 freelance submissions yearly; 5% by authors who are new to the magazine. Receives 10 queries monthly.

Submissions
Query with writing samples. Accepts photocopies and computer printouts. SASE. Responds in 6–12 months.
Articles: 2,000–4,000 words. Informational, factual, and how-to articles; self-help and personal experience pieces; and humor. Topics include college life, careers, computers, current events, health, fitness, religion, science, technology, sports, and family issues.
Depts/columns: To 1,500 words. Campus news, book reviews, commentary, and alumni updates.
Artwork: 35mm color prints or transparencies.
Other: Word length varies. BYU trivia.

Sample Issue
80 pages (15% advertising): 3 articles; 12 depts/columns. Sample copy, free. Guidelines available.
- "Where Will It Lead?" Personal experience essay about where the different paths of life may lead.
- "On the Shoulders of Giants." Article examines how students at BYU study their heritage.
- Sample dept/column: "Family Focus" poses questions to ask when considering adoption.

Rights and Payment
First North American serial rights. Articles, $.35 per word. Pays on publication. Provides 10 contributor's copies.

Editor's Comments
We are devoted to keeping graduates and friends informed and connected to the University, and are looking for material that sparks interest and motivates involvement in our establishment.

Cadet Quest

Calvinist Cadet Corps
P.O. Box 7259
Grand Rapids, MI 49510

Editor: G. Richard Broene

Description and Readership
Published for members of the Christian youth organization Calvinist Cadet Corps, this magazine teaches Christian principles through articles and stories with a Christian perspective.
- **Audience:** 9–14 years
- **Frequency:** 7 times each year
- **Distribution:** 100% subscription
- **Circulation:** 8,000
- **Website:** www.calvinistcadets.org

Freelance Potential
78% written by nonstaff writers. Publishes 25 freelance submissions yearly; 5% by unpublished writers, 10% by authors who are new to the magazine. Receives 33 unsolicited mss monthly.

Submissions
Send complete ms. Accepts photocopies, computer printouts, and simultaneous submissions if identified. SASE. Responds in 1 month.
Articles: 400–1,000 words. Informational and factual articles; profiles; and interviews. Topics include religion, spirituality, camping skills, crafts and hobbies, sports, nature study, the environment, stewardship, and serving God.
Fiction: 900–1,600 words. Adventure and sports stories with a Christian perspective.
Depts/columns: Word length varies. Cadet Corps news and Bible stories.
Other: Puzzles and cartoons.

Sample Issue
20 pages (5% advertising): 4 articles; 6 Bible lessons; 1 profile. Sample copy, free with 9x12 SASE ($1.01 postage). Guidelines and theme list available.
- "Planning Pays." Story about teamwork, hard work, and success.
- "Parts Are Parts." Article compares the church to the human body—all the parts must work as a whole.

Rights and Payment
First and second rights. Written material, $.04–$.05 per word. Other material, payment rates vary. Pays on acceptance. Provides 1 contributor's copy.

Editor's Comments
Our readers are active, inquisitive, imaginative boys from different Protestant denominations. Each issue of *Cadet Quest* deals with a specific theme or topic that will help boys make the right choices in life.

Calliope

Exploring World History

Cobblestone Publishing
Suite C, 30 Grove Street
Peterborough, NH 03458

Co-Editor: Rosalie F. Baker

Description and Readership
Each issue is devoted to a single historical theme and material is presented in a lively, attention-keeping style geared to middle-grade students.
- **Audience:** 8–14 years
- **Frequency:** 9 times each year
- **Distribution:** 100% subscription
- **Circulation:** 12,000
- **Website:** www.cobblestonepub.com

Freelance Potential
95% written by nonstaff writers. Publishes 75 freelance submissions yearly; 25% by unpublished writers, 30–40% by authors who are new to the magazine. Receives 25 queries monthly.

Submissions
Query with outline, bibliography, and clips or writing samples. All material submitted must relate to upcoming themes. SASE. Responds in 4 months.
Articles: Features, 700–800 words; sidebars, 300–600 words. Informational articles and profiles. Topics include Western and Eastern history.
Fiction: To 800 words. Historical and biographical fiction, adventure, retold legends, and plays.
Depts/columns: 300–600 words. Current events, archaeology, languages, and book reviews.
Artwork: B/W or color prints and slides. B/W or color line art.
Other: Activities, games, crafts, puzzles, and recipes, to 700 words.

Sample Issue
44 pages (no advertising): 12 articles; 8 depts/columns; 3 activities. Sample copy, $4.95 with 9x12 SASE ($2 postage). Writers' guidelines and theme list available.
- "Who Was Cleopatra?" Article details the culture and lifestyle in existence during Cleopatra's era.
- Sample dept/column: "From Past to Present" depicts how Cleopatra has been perceived over the years.

Rights and Payment
All rights. Articles and fiction, $.20–$.25 per word. Other material, payment rate varies. Pays on publication. Provides 2 contributor's copies.

Editor's Comments
We strive for material related to world history that is educational and entertaining. Each issue presents several aspects of a single theme.

Camping Magazine

American Camping Association
5000 State Road 67 North
Martinsville, IN 46151-7902

Editor-in-Chief: Harriet Gamble

Description and Readership
This magazine is written specifically for professionals who work for recreational children's camps. It mixes articles on camp industry news and trends with innovative programming ideas and the latest research on youth development.
- **Audience:** Camp managers and educators
- **Frequency:** 6 times each year
- **Distribution:** 100% subscription
- **Circulation:** 7,000
- **Website:** www.ACAcamps.org

Freelance Potential
98% written by nonstaff writers. Publishes 30 freelance submissions yearly; 50% by unpublished writers, 50% by authors who are new to the magazine. Receives 8 queries monthly.

Submissions
Query with outline. Prefers email submissions to magazine@acacamps.org. Accepts IBM disk submissions and simultaneous submissions. SASE. Response time varies.
Articles: 1,500–4,000 words. Informational and how-to articles. Topics include camp management, special education, social issues, careers, health, recreation, crafts, and hobbies.
Deptsp/columns: 800–1,000 words. Opinion pieces, health issues related to camping, marketing ideas, and building and construction information.
Artwork: B/W and color prints and slides.

Sample Issue
56 pages (20% advertising): 6 articles; 13 depts/columns. Sample copy, $4.50 with 9x12 SASE. Guidelines and editorial calendar available.
- "Year-Round Schools? No Worries, Mate." Article examines the types of children's camps available in Australia.
- "'This Old Camp' Goes Green." Article talks about things to consider when choosing camp lighting, flooring, and bathroom facilities.

Rights and Payment
All rights. No payment. Provides 2 copies.

Editor's Comments
We are primarily interested in articles written by people who have had first-hand experience with organized children's camps. Our emphasis is on practical, useful ideas.

Campus Life

Christianity Today
465 Gunderson Drive
Carol Stream, IL 60188

Editor: Chris Lutes

Description and Readership

First-person articles that capture teen life experiences and show the strength in having Christian values and beliefs are featured in this magazine for teens that are in high school or early college.
- **Audience:** 13–19 years
- **Frequency:** 9 times each year
- **Distribution:** 100% subscription
- **Circulation:** 100,000
- **Website:** www.campuslife.com

Freelance Potential

60% written by nonstaff writers. Publishes 20–30 freelance submissions yearly; 10% by unpublished writers, 10% by authors who are new to the magazine. Receives 25 queries monthly.

Submissions

Query with one-page synopsis. No unsolicited mss. Accepts photocopies, computer printouts, and simultaneous submissions if identified. SASE. Responds in 3–6 weeks.
Articles: 750–1,500 words. Personal experience pieces and humor. Topics include Christian values, beliefs, and Christian education.
Fiction: 1,000–1,500 words. Genres include contemporary fiction with religious themes.
Depts/columns: Staff written.

Sample Issue

64 pages (30% advertising): 4 articles; 27 depts/columns. Sample copy, $3 with 9x12 SASE (3 first-class stamps). Writers' guidelines available.
- "Page Turners" Article takes a look at some awesome books to read over the summer.
- "My Grandpa...the Stranger." Essay tells how a boy grows closer to his grandfather after spending time with him over the summer.
- "Rock On!" Article follows a youth group as it attends a music festival in Illinois over the summer.

Rights and Payment

First rights. Written material, $.20–$.25 per word. Pays on acceptance. Provides 2 contributor's copies.

Editor's Comments

We are looking for first-person stories that share a lesson that is well learned. Stories should be sense and dialogue driven, and demonstrate Christian values and beliefs. Articles that are moralistic, preachy, or lack respect and empathy for teens will be rejected.

Canadian Children's Literature

4th Floor, MacKinnon Building, University of Guelph
Guelph, Ontario, N1G 2W1
Canada

Administrator: Benjamin Lefebvre

Description and Readership

Focusing on children's literature, this academic journal includes critical essays and reviews of recent Canadian books, films, videos, drama, and television shows. It also features profiles of authors.
- **Audience:** Educators, scholars, and librarians
- **Frequency:** Quarterly
- **Distribution:** 70% subscription; 3% newsstand; 27% other
- **Circulation:** 900
- **Website:** www.uoguelph.ca/ccl

Freelance Potential

99% written by nonstaff writers. Publishes 100 freelance submissions yearly; 10% by unpublished writers, 40% by authors who are new to the magazine. Receives 10 unsolicited mss monthly.

Submissions

Query with summary; or send 3 copies of complete ms. Accepts photocopies, computer printouts, and email submissions to ccl@uoguelph.ca. SAE/IRC. Responds to queries in 6 weeks, to mss in 6 months.
Articles: 2,000–6,000 words. Informational articles; reviews; profiles; and interviews. Topics include children's literature; film, videos, and drama for children; and children's authors.

Sample Issue

96 pages (2% advertising): 5 articles; 17 reviews; 6 mini reviews. Sample copy, $10. Guidelines and theme list/editorial calendar available.
- "A Defense of Potter, or When Religion is Not Religion." Article offers an analysis of the controversy surrounding objections to the J.K. Rowling's Harry Potter series.
- "The Race for the Pole: Peary, Cook, and *Winnie-the-Pooh*." Article takes a look at the link between the controversy over who was the first person to reach the North Pole and the book of *Winnie-the-Pooh*.

Rights and Payment

First serial rights. No payment. Provides 1 contributor's copy.

Editor's Comments

Submissions on children's and young adult literature, video, film, and drama from various perspectives are welcome. Keep in mind that we are an academic journal, and provide in-depth coverage. In addition to theme issues, we also publish general issues.

Canadian Guider

50 Merton Street
Toronto, Ontario M4S 1A3
Canada

Publications Manager: Catherine Bryant

Description and Readership
For over 70 years, this magazine has been providing leaders of the Girl Guide organization with resourceful information on camping, life skills, and the great outdoors. It also includes articles on leadership, education, and hands-on activities.
- **Audience:** Girl Guide leaders
- **Frequency:** 3 times each year
- **Distribution:** 100% controlled
- **Circulation:** 40,000
- **Website:** www.girlguides.ca

Freelance Potential
20% written by nonstaff writers. Publishes 3–5 freelance submissions yearly. Receives 2 queries monthly.

Submissions
Query with résumé. SAE/IRC. Responds in 1 month.
Articles: To 200 words. Informational and how-to articles. Topics include fitness, health, camping, nature, the environment, the arts, social issues, and leadership and life skills.
Depts/columns: Word lengths vary. Activity ideas and leadership tips.
Artwork: B/W and color photos; digital images. Submission information at our website.

Sample Issue
44 pages (12% advertising): 13 articles; 10 depts/columns. Sample copy, $3 with 9x12 SAE/IRC. Editorial calendar and theme list available.
- "Sea Kayaking in the Gulf Islands." Article describes a sea kayaking adventure that thirteen girls and guiders went on.
- "A Rookie Guider Goes to Camp." Article shares a leader's first experience camping.
- Sample dept/column: "Outdoor Guider" takes a look at exploring non-camping outdoor activities and tips for organizing them.

Rights and Payment
All rights. No payment. Provides 2 author's copies.

Editor's Comments
We're always looking for articles that highlight exploring adventures and camping trips. Use an active voice with a friendly tone. Also, if you have an idea for a program related craft or activity, we'd love to see it. Samples, photographs, and diagrams are welcome. New writers have the best chance at publication with an article covering the environment or camping.

Capper's

1503 SW 42nd Street
Topeka, KS 66609

Editor-in-Chief: Andrea Skalland

Description and Readership
Capper's is a national distributed tabloid for families who live in the rural Midwest. It uses family-oriented articles, fiction, and poetry.
- **Audience:** Families
- **Frequency:** 26 times each year
- **Distribution:** 100% subscription
- **Circulation:** 120,000
- **Website:** www.cappers.com

Freelance Potential
90% written by nonstaff writers. Publishes 40–50 freelance submissions yearly; 50% by unpublished writers, 70% by authors who are new to the magazine. Receives 40 unsolicited mss monthly.

Submissions
Send complete ms with photos for articles; query for fiction. Accepts photocopies and computer printouts. SASE. Responds to queries in 1 month; to mss in 3–4 months.
Articles: 700 words. General interest, historical, inspirational, and nostalgic articles. Topics include family life, travel, hobbies, and occupations.
Fiction: To 25,000 words. Serialized novels.
Depts/columns: 300 words. Personal experience pieces humor, and essays.
Artwork: 35mm color slides, transparencies, or prints.
Other: Jokes, 5–6 per submission.

Sample Issue
36 pages (3% advertising): 15 articles; 6 depts/columns; 1 recipe page. Sample copy, $1.95. Writers' guidelines available.
- "More Males Take up Knitting Needles." Article covers the trend for men and boys to learn to knit.
- "First Ferris Wheel Designed for 1893 World's Fair." Article discusses the history of the Ferris wheel.
- "A Moving Experience." Short story about two young friends who pretend to date each other so their parents will become more than friends.

Rights and Payment
Shared rights. Articles, $2.50 per column inch; serialized novels, $75–$300. Pays on publication for nonfiction; on acceptance for fiction. Provides up to 5 contributor's copies.

Editor's Comments
We will consider freelance material for items that reflect local pride and volunteerism, and jokes.

Careers and Colleges

Suite 100
2 LAN Drive
Westford, MA 01886

Managing Director: Jane Ponnington

Description and Readership
The goal of this publication is to help students achieve their academic, career, and financial goals. Each issue focuses on a single theme and is intended to serve as a complete reference guide for future use.
- **Audience:** 15–18 years
- **Frequency:** 4 times each year
- **Distribution:** 99% schools; 1% subscription
- **Circulation:** 752,000
- **Website:** www.careersandcolleges.com

Freelance Potential
80% written by nonstaff writers. Publishes 4 freelance submissions yearly; 10% by by authors who are new to the magazine. Receives 8 queries monthly.

Submissions
Query with clips or writing samples. No unsolicited mss. Accepts photocopies and computer printouts. SASE. Responds in 2 months.
Articles: 800–2,400 words. Informational and how-to articles; personal experience pieces; profiles; and interviews. Topics include career choices, post-secondary education, independent living, social issues, and personal growth.
Depts/columns: Staff written.

Sample Issue
48 pages (29% advertising): 9 articles; 2 depts/columns. Sample copy, $6.95 with 10x13 SASE ($1.75 postage). Guidelines available.
- "10 Tips for Taking the New SAT." Informative article provides information on successfully completing the new version of the SAT.
- "Making the Grade." Article offers advice on choosing college courses, selecting a major, dealing with professors, and financial aid.
- "Bring It On?" Article reveals the diverse world of life after high school.

Rights and Payment
First North American serial and electronic rights. Articles, $300–$800. Pays 2 months after acceptance. Provides 2 contributor's copies.

Editor's Comments
Most articles include a list of relevant websites and other resources, plus interactive tools to help students manage their lives. Because much of our editorial is updates of prior material, freelance opportunities are somewhat limited.

Carolina Parent

Suite 201
5716 Fayetteville Road
Durham, NC 27713

Editor: Cathy Ashby

Description and Readership
Published as a resource for parents, this publication provides a wealth of information for area families with children from the ages of newborn through teens. Its readers include parents, educators, and daycare and health care providers throughout the community.
- **Audience:** Parents
- **Frequency:** Monthly
- **Distribution:** 100% distribution
- **Circulation:** 55,000
- **Website:** www.carolinaparent.com

Freelance Potential
50% written by nonstaff writers. Publishes 40 freelance submissions yearly; 20% by unpublished writers, 30% by authors who are new to the magazine.

Submissions
Accepts queries from established writers. New writers, send complete ms. Accepts photocopies, computer printouts. and email submissions to editorial@carolinaparent.com (Microsoft Word attachments). SASE. Response time varies.
Articles: Word length varies. Informational and how-to articles; profiles; and personal experience pieces. Topics include college, careers, computer, crafts, hobbies, gifted education, health, fitness, humor, music, nature, environment, recreation, regional news, science, technology, self-help, social issues, sports, and travel.
Depts/columns: Word length varies. Family finances, family issues, news, events, and health.

Sample Issue
68 pages: 7 articles; 10 depts/columns; 1 special section. Guidelines and editorial calendar available.
- "Summer Storm Safety for All Ages." Article takes a look at how to stay safe during thunderstorms.
- "Island Hopping, Family Style." Article explores a few family-friendly island resorts in Georgia, South Carolina, and North Carolina.
- Sample dept/column: "Changing Families" offers an essay by a single father on parenting.

Rights and Payment
First and electronic rights. Written material, $50–$75. Pays on publication.

Editor's Comments
Submissions from freelance writers are welcome and should be exclusive within our region.

Catholic Digest

P.O. Box 180
Mystic, CT 06355

Articles Editor: Julie Rattey

Description and Readership
Articles that apply the riches of Catholic faith and tradition to the challenges of everyday life can be found in this digest-sized publication.
- **Audience:** Adults
- **Frequency:** Monthly
- **Distribution:** 92% subscription; 8% other
- **Circulation:** 350,000
- **Website:** www.catholicdigest.com

Freelance Potential
50% written by nonstaff writers. Publishes 100–200 freelance submissions yearly; 10% by unpublished writers. Receives 400 unsolicited mss monthly.

Submissions
Send complete ms. Accepts photocopies, computer printouts, disk submissions, and email submissions to cdsubmissions@bayardpubs.com. No simultaneous submissions. SASE. Responds in 6–8 weeks.
Articles: 1,000–3,500 words. Informational articles; profiles; and personal experience pieces. Topics include religion, prayer, spirituality, relationships, family issues, history, science, and nostalgia.
Depts/columns: 50–500 words. True stories about faith, spotlights of community organizations, and profiles of volunteers.
Other: Filler, to 500 words.

Sample Issue
128 pages (13% advertising): 8 articles; 18 depts/columns. Sample copy, free with 6x9 SASE ($1 postage). Guidelines available.
- "The Hidden Strength of The Magnificat." Article explores what Mary's prayer says about the person she really was.
- "Miracle in a Bottle." Article discusses the Lourdes Marian Center, one of the sources for the ailing and the devout to obtain Lourdes healing water.
- Sample dept/column: "Be Well" reports on strokes and how to reduce the risk of having one.

Rights and Payment
One-time rights. Articles, $100–$400. Depts/columns, $2 per published page. Pays on publication. Provides 2 contributor's copies.

Editor's Comments
We are looking for topics that inspire, entertain, and inform our readers while reinforcing Catholic values. Study previous issues to see what we are all about.

Catholic Forester

P.O. Box 3012
335 Shuman Boulevard
Naperville, IL 60566-7012

Associate Editor: Patricia Baron

Description and Readership
This Catholic magazine offers articles on a wide array of topics of interest to members of the Catholic Order of Foresters. It also keeps members aprised of organizational news and developments.
- **Audience:** Catholic Forester members
- **Frequency:** Quarterly
- **Distribution:** 100% controlled
- **Circulation:** 100,000
- **Website:** www.catholicforester.com

Freelance Potential
20% written by nonstaff writers. Publishes 4–8 freelance submissions yearly; 5% by unpublished writers, 20% by authors who are new to the magazine. Receives 20 unsolicited mss monthly.

Submissions
Send complete ms. Accepts computer printouts. SASE. Responds in 3–4 months.
Articles: 1,000 words. Informational and inspirational articles. Topics include money management, fitness, health, family life, investing, senior issues, careers, parenting, and nostalgia.
Fiction: 1,000 words. Topics include inspriational, humorous, and light fiction.
Other: Cartoons.

Sample Issue
40 pages (no advertising): 7 articles; 2 activities; 6 depts/columns. Sample copy, free with 9x12 SASE (3 first-class stamps). Guidelines available.
- "Try a Little Kindness." Article looks at a national kindness movement that emerged from the Columbine tragedy.
- "Unique Heartsaving Device." Article examines a cutting-edge development in life-saving technology.
- Sample dept/column: "Spiritual" reminds readers of the meaning of the Eucharist.

Rights and Payment
First North American serial rights. Written material, $.30 per word. Cartoons, one-time rights, $30. Pays on acceptance. Provides 3 contributor's copies.

Editor's Comments
We are looking for material that projects personal experience into informational topics. Complete articles that have a good lead, style, and rhythm that hold the reader's interest have the best chance of acceptance.

Catholic Library World

Suite 224
100 North Street
Pittsfield, MA 01201-5109

Editor: Mary S. Gallagher, SSJ

Description and Readership
As the official publication of the Catholic Library Association, this tool for librarians includes articles and reviews of books. Its readers include professionals, volunteers, and others interested in librarianship.
- **Audience:** Adults
- **Frequency:** Quarterly
- **Distribution:** 99% subscription; 1% other
- **Circulation:** 1,100
- **Website:** www.cathla.org

Freelance Potential
25% written by nonstaff writers. Publishes 12 freelance submissions yearly. Receives 1 unsolicited ms each month.

Submissions
Query or send complete ms. Accepts photocopies, computer printouts, and email submissions (Microsoft Word attachments) to cla@cathla.org. SASE.
Articles: Word length varies. Informational articles and reviews. Topics include books, reading, library science, and Catholic Library Association news.
Reviews: 150–300 words. Topics include theology, spirituality, pastoral issues, church history, education, history, literature, library science, philosophy, and reference; children's and young adult topics include biography, fiction, multicultural issues, picture books, reference, science, social studies, and values.
Artwork: B/W and color prints and transparencies. Line art.

Sample Issue
78 pages (2% advertising): 4 articles; 114 book reviews; 1 media review. Sample copy, $15. Reviewers' guidelines available.
- "Library Connections: Where Ideas Begin." Article describes a program that creates inner-city school library media centers.
- "Living with Dignity: Character with Developmental Disabilities in Children's Literature." Article takes a look at books that have characters with developmental disabilities who break down stereotypes and whose lives have value and dignity.

Rights and Payment
No payment. Provides 1 contributor's copy.

Editor's Comments
We are looking for articles on topics such as academic libraries and high school and children's libraries.

Catholic Parent

Our Sunday Visitor
200 Noll Plaza
Huntington, IN 46750-4304

Associate Editor: York Young

Description and Readership
In print since 1993, this magazine offers articles and essays for Catholic parents on issues relating to raising their children in today's changing world.
- **Audience:** Parents
- **Frequency:** 6 times each year
- **Distribution:** 95% subscription; 5% religious instruction
- **Circulation:** 24,000
- **Website:** www.osv.com

Freelance Potential
95% written by nonstaff writers. Publishes 4–6 freelance submissions yearly; 10% by authors who are new to the magazine. Receives 200 queries and unsolicited mss monthly.

Submissions
Query or send complete ms. Accepts email submissions to cparent@osv.com, photocopies, and computer printouts. SASE. Responds to queries in 3 months, to mss in 3–6 months.
Articles: To 1,200 words. Informational and how-to articles. Topics include religion, relationships, marriage, family life, teen issues, and child development.
Depts/columns: Word lengths vary. Short news items, media reviews, and parenting tips.
Other: Submit seasonal material 8 months in advance.

Sample Issue
50 pages (27% advertising): 10 articles; 7 depts/columns. Sample copy, $5. Guidelines available.
- "Beating Boredom." Article discusses boredom, ways to identify what it is, and how-to overcome it.
- "Do You Have a Vocation?" Article explores the three distinct senses of personal vocation, and how to discern what God wants us to do to serve Him.
- Sample dept/column: "Heart Land" offers an essay on how to explain tragedy to children.

Rights and Payment
First rights. Written material, payment rates vary. Pays on acceptance.

Editor's Comments
We seek well-written, first-person accounts on topics of concern to Catholic parents. Share your experiences as a parent, but do not preach. Keep writing short and concise. We are mostly an assignment-only publication, but queries are welcome.

Celebrate

6401 The Paseo
Kansas City, MO 64131

Submissions: Denise Willemin

Description and Readership
Young children attending Sunday school enjoy this take-home paper for its bright, colorful appearance and its fun activities, Bible stories, and poems. It strives to provide material that will connect Sunday school learning with daily life.
• **Audience:** 3–6 years
• **Frequency:** Weekly
• **Distribution:** 100% subscription
• **Circulation:** 40,000
• **Website:** www.wordaction.com

Freelance Potential
40% written by nonstaff writers. Publishes 50 freelance submissions yearly; 30% by unpublished writers, 35% by authors who are new to the magazine. Receives 10 queries monthly.

Submissions
Query. Accepts photocopies, computer printouts, and email queries to dwillemin@nazrene.org (Microsoft Word attachment). SASE. Responds in 2–4 weeks.
Other: Poetry, 4–8 lines. Songs, finger plays, action rhymes, crafts, activities, and recipes.

Sample Issue
4 pages (no advertising): 1 Bible story; 1 poem; 1 recipe; 2 activities. Sample copy, free with #10 SASE (1 first-class stamp). Writers' guidelines and theme list available.
• "The Basket Lunch." Bible story tells of the time when a large crowd gathered to hear Jesus speak and He turned five loaves of bread and two fish into enough food for everyone.
• "Squishy Sculptures." Activity offers instructions for making fish sculptures.
• "Fish and Bread Maze." Activity lets preschooler follow the fish or loaves to find Jesus and the people.
• "Jesus Meets My Needs." Poem reflects on the miracle of Jesus feeding a large hungry crowd with fish and bread.

Rights and Payment
Rights and payment policy vary.

Editor's Comments
We look for activities, crafts, and songs that celebrate the love of Jesus. Each week our publication ties together a Bible story, craft, recipe, and activity. Please make sure your writing style matches the level of understanding of our young audience.

Central Penn Parent

2nd Floor
101 North Second Street
Harrisburg, PA 17101

Editor: Karren Johnson

Description and Readership
This award-winning publication includes informational articles on parenting topics and family activities, as well as regional news and resources. It is distributed free to families living in the central Pennsylvania area.
• **Audience:** Parents
• **Frequency:** Monthly
• **Distribution:** 100% controlled
• **Circulation:** 35,000
• **Website:** www.centralpennparent.com

Freelance Potential
50% written by nonstaff writers. Publishes 10 freelance submissions yearly; 20% by unpublished writers, 10% by authors who are new to the magazine. Receives 8 queries monthly.

Submissions
Request guidelines first. Query. Accepts email submissions to karrenm@journalpub.com. Availability of artwork improves chance of acceptance. SASE. Responds in 2 weeks.
Articles: 1,200–1,500 words. Informational articles and reviews. Topics include local family events and activities, health, nutrition, discipline, education, home life, technology, literature, parenting issues, and travel.
Depts/columns: 700 words. Parenting and health news, infants, family finances, and perspectives from fathers.
Artwork: Color prints and transparencies. Line art.
Other: Submit seasonal material at least 2 months in advance.

Sample Issue
56 pages (50% advertising): 3 articles; 19 depts/columns. Sample copy, free. Guidelines available.
• "What Does a Didgeri-Doo?" Article offers multicultural musical craft projects for summertime fun.
• "Party Planning Guide." Article offers advice on planning successful birthday parties.
• Sample dept/column: "Family Site-Seeing" offers kid-friendly websites for children of all ages.

Rights and Payment
All rights. Articles, $35–$125. Dept/columns, $30. Pays on publication. Provides contributor's copies upon request.

Editor's Comments
We are looking for family-friendly activities, as well as informational articles on parenting issues.

Characters

P.O. Box 708
Newport, NH 03773

Editor: Cindy Davis

Description and Readership
Original fiction by children and teens is spotlighted in this magazine. Four issues each year offer a range of writing styles on a variety of themes.
- **Audience:** 7–18 years
- **Frequency:** Quarterly
- **Distribution:** 100% subscription
- **Circulation:** Unavailable
- **Website:** www.cdavisnh.com

Freelance Potential
100% written by nonstaff writers. Publishes 40 freelance submissions yearly; 75% by unpublished writers, 50% by authors who are new to the magazine. Receives 35 unsolicited mss monthly.

Submissions
Send complete ms with short biography. Accepts email submissions (no attachments) to hotdog@nhvt.net, and simultaneous submissions if identified. SASE. Responds in 2–4 weeks.
Fiction: 1,500 words. Contemporary and historical fiction, mystery, humor, adventure, Westerns, romance, fantasy, nature and animal stories, and science fiction.
Other: Poetry, to 18 lines; to 3 poems per submission.

Sample Issue
36 pages (no advertising): 8 stories; 1 poem. Sample copy, $5.75. Guidelines available.
- "Grandma Gets a Gameboy." Short story about a grouchy, stubborn old woman who discovers a challenging new interest.
- "An Oldfangled Tale." Story offers a new twist on the timeless enchanted frog tale.
- "Troublesome Words at Findley's." Humorous tale about a talking parrot with a less-than-appropriate and sometimes embarrassing vocabulary.

Rights and Payment
One-time and electronic rights. Written material, $5. Payment policy varies. Provides 1 copy.

Editor's Comments
We publish the work of young authors, and occasionally, adults. The important thing to keep in mind when writing for our publication is to match the vocabulary to the audience. We see too many stories with an adult voice or an adult main character. Your characters should be children, act like children, and speak like them.

Charlotte Parent

Suite 253
2125 South End Drive
Charlotte, NC 28230

Editor: Kathleen Conroy

Description and Readership
This thematic journal is full of information for parents in the Charlotte metro area. Each issue includes articles and tips, as well as news and regional events.
- **Audience:** Parents
- **Frequency:** Monthly
- **Distribution:** 54% controlled; 35% schools 10% libraries; 1% subscription
- **Circulation:** 55,000
- **Website:** www.charlotteparent.com

Freelance Potential
40% written by nonstaff writers. Publishes 60 freelance submissions yearly; 15% by unpublished writers, 25% by authors who are new to the magazine. Receives 25 queries, 50 unsolicited mss monthly.

Submissions
Query or send complete ms with resume and bibliography. Prefers email to editor@charlotteparent.com. Accepts photocopies, Macintosh disk submissions, and simultaneous submissions. SASE. Responds if interested.
Articles: 500–1,000 words. Informational and how-to articles. Topics include parenting, family life, finances, education, health, fitness, vacations, entertainment, regional activities, and the environment.
Depts/columns: Word length varies. Restaurant and media reviews; children's health, ages and stages.
Artwork: High-density Macintosh format artwork.
Other: Activities. Submit seasonal material 2–3 months in advance.

Sample Issue
84 pages (35% advertising): 9 articles; 2 reviews; 15 depts/columns. Sample copy, free with 9x12 SASE (5 first-class stamps). Guidelines and editorial calendar available at website.
- "Trading Places: Home Exchange for Families." Article discusses home exchange vacation options for families and offers tips to help make it work.
- Sample dept/column: "Kids Health" reports on using hypnosis to cope with pain.

Rights and Payment
First and web rights. Written material, payment rates vary. Pays on publication. Provides 1 copy.

Editor's Comments
Interesting and informative articles on topics other than each issue's theme list will also be considered.

ChemMatters

American Chemical Society
1155 16th Street NW
Washington, DC 20036

Editor: Kevin McCue

Description and Readership
Striving to make chemistry exciting and interesting for high school students, this magazine offers articles that incorporate real-world applications to help students understand how a theory works.
- **Audience:** 4–18 years
- **Frequency:** 5 times each year
- **Distribution:** 80% schools; 20% subscription
- **Circulation:** 40,000
- **Website:** www.chemistry.org/education/chemmaters.html

Freelance Potential
90% written by nonstaff writers. Publishes 2 freelance submissions yearly; 10% by unpublished writers, 90% by new authors. Receives 2–3 queries monthly.

Submissions
Query with abstract, outline, related material that conveys the scientific content, and a writing sample. Prefers email queries to chemmatters@acs.org. Accepts photocopies. SASE. Responds in 5 days.
Articles: 1,400–2,100 words. Informational articles. Topics include the human body, food, history, current events, and chemical matters.
Depts/columns: 1,400–2,100 words. "ChemSumer" reports on new products for teens and explains their chemistry. "Mystery Matters" explains how forensic chemistry solves crimes.
Artwork: JPEG or GIF line art.
Other: Chemistry-oriented puzzles and activities.

Sample Issue
20 pages (no advertising): 3 articles; 4 depts/columns. Sample copy, available free at website. Guidelines and theme list available.
- "Antimatter." Article discusses how antimatter is created, where it can be found, and its practical uses.
- "Mustard Gas." Article takes a look at the effects and uses of mustard gas and ways to help ban it.
- Sample dept/column: "GreenChemistry" discusses the use of biodiesel as a form of fuel.

Rights and Payment
All rights. Articles, $500–$1,000. Pays on acceptance. Provides 5 contributor's copies.

Editor's Comments
We look for stimulating and motivating articles on topics of interest to young people that reveal an underlying chemical story. The concepts should be easy enough for the average reader, and challenging.

Chesapeake Family

Suite 307
929 West Street
Annapolis, MD 21401

Editor

Description and Readership
This free publication is found in libraries, doctors' offices, grocery stores, and other outlets in the counties surrounding Annapolis. Its articles are written for parents of school-aged children seeking information on local family events and health and education news.
- **Audience:** Parents
- **Frequency:** Monthly
- **Distribution:** 55% schools; 15% newsstand; 5% subscription; 25% other
- **Circulation:** 40,000
- **Website:** www.chesapeakefamily.com

Freelance Potential
80% written by nonstaff writers. Publishes 4–6 freelance submissions yearly; 5% by unpublished writers, 10% by new authors. Receives 20 mss monthly.

Submissions
Send complete ms. Accepts photocopies and computer printouts. SASE. Response time varies.
Articles: 1,000–1,200 words. Informational and how-to articles and profiles. Topics include parenting, the environment, music, regional news, current events, education, entertainment, health, and family travel destinations.
Fiction: "Just for Kids" features stories and poems by local 4- to 17-year-old children.
Depts/columns: 700–900 words. Education, child development, and health.
Other: Submit seasonal material 3–6 months in advance.

Sample Issue
64 pages (45% advertising): 2 articles; 9 depts/columns; 4 events calendars. Guidelines and editorial calendar available.
- "Independence: How Much Should You Give Your Tween?" Article offers advice to parents wondering how much independence their pre-teens can handle.
- Sample dept/column: "Family Fun" reviews biking trails on the Delmarva Peninsula.

Rights and Payment
Geographic print rights; electronic rights negotiable. Features, $75–$110. Depts/columns, $50. Reprints, $35. Payment policy varies.

Editor's Comments
We'd like to see more submissions on fun family activities in the area, as well as community news.

Chess Life

U.S. Chess Federation
Suite 100
3068 US Route 9W
New Windsor, NY 12553

Editor: Glenn Petersen

Description and Readership
Chess Life is the official publication of the United States Chess Federation. Each issue covers news of major chess events, instruction, and historical articles. It emphasizes the triumphs and exploits of American chess players.
- **Audience:** YA–Adult
- **Frequency:** Monthly
- **Distribution:** 90% subscription; 10% newsstand
- **Circulation:** 60,000–80,000
- **Website:** www.uschess.org

Freelance Potential
45% written by nonstaff writers. Publishes 30 freelance submissions yearly; 30% by unpublished writers. Receives 30–50 queries monthly.

Submissions
Query with clips or writing samples. Accepts photocopies, computer printouts, and IBM disk submissions (ASCII). SASE. Responds in 1–3 months.
Articles: 800–3,000 words. Informational, how-to, and historical articles; personal experience and opinion pieces; profiles; and humor. Topics include chess games and strategies, tournaments, and events.
Depts/columns: To 1,000 words. Book reviews, product information, short how-to's, and player profiles.
Other: Cartoons, contests, and games.

Sample Issue
78 pages (16% advertising): 14 articles; 21 depts/columns. Sample copy, free with 9x12 SASE. Guidelines available.
- "Arthur Bisguier, Dean of American Chess." Article profiles a chess champion and Grandmaster.
- "Chess Trip to Mexico." Article reports on a chess group from Barrington, Illinois, that traveled to Mexico to participate in a tournament.
- Sample dept/column: "The Chess Detective" offers ways to pick up clues that help win games.

Rights and Payment
All rights. Written material, $100 per page. Kill fee, 50%. Pays on publication. Provides 2 copies.

Editor's Comments
Our feature section is open to freelance writers. We are interested in articles on relatively unknown chess personalities and "chess in everyday life." Our only rule is that the game of chess must be central to every item.

Chicago Parent

141 South Oak Park Avenue
Chicago, IL 60302

Associate Publisher/Editor: Susy Schultz

Description and Readership
A lively editorial mix with a distinctly local focus is offered by this regional tabloid. Feature articles tackle a range of timely topics for families and parents.
- **Audience:** Parents
- **Frequency:** Monthly
- **Distribution:** 90% controlled; 10% subscription
- **Circulation:** 138,000
- **Website:** www.chicagoparent.com

Freelance Potential
85% written by nonstaff writers. Publishes 100-200 freelance submissions yearly; 10% by unpublished writers, 40% by authors who are new to the magazine. Receives 40–50 queries monthly.

Submissions
Query with résumé and clips. Accepts photocopies, computer printouts, and email queries to spedersen@chicagoparent.com. SASE. Responds in 6 weeks.
Articles: 1,500–2,500 words. Informational articles and profiles. Topics include local resources, regional events, parenting, grandparenting, maternity, foster care, child development, adoption, day care, careers, education, and family issues.
Depts/columns: 850 words. Opinion pieces, children's health, media reviews, travel, and fathering.
Other: Submit seasonal material 2 months in advance.

Sample Issue
192 pages (60% advertising): 14 articles; 18 depts/columns. Sample copy, $3.95. Guidelines and editorial calendar available.
- "Flying High." Article looks at local places that provide a birds-eye perspective on different things.
- "Finding Nature." Informative article suggests places to visit with nature themes, including farms, nature centers, and conservatories.
- "Get Out of Town." Article covers state parks and campgrounds in the six-county area.

Rights and Payment
One-time and Illinois exclusive rights. Articles, $125–$350. Depts/columns, $75–$100. Kill fee, 10%. Pays on publication. Provides contributor's copies upon request.

Editor's Comments
We prefer to use local writers who know what's what in Chicago.

Child

Meredith Corporation
9th Floor
375 Lexington Avenue
New York, NY 10017-4024

Submissions Editor

Description and Readership
This widely-distributed magazine seeks to provide its readers with the tools they need to raise children in a changing, time-pressed world. It focuses on health, development, behavior, and parenting and marital relationships.
- **Audience:** Parents
- **Frequency:** 10 times each year
- **Distribution:** 92% subscription; 8% newsstand
- **Circulation:** 1,020,000
- **Website:** www.child.com

Freelance Potential
70% written by nonstaff writers. Publishes 50 freelance submissions yearly; 10% by unpublished writers, 30% by authors who are new to the magazine. Receives 150 queries monthly.

Submissions
Query with published clips. Accepts computer printouts. SASE. Responds in 2 months.
Articles: Word lengths vary. Informational and how-to articles; profiles; interviews; and personal experience pieces. Topics include pets, computers, crafts, hobbies, current events, gifted and special education, health, fitness, popular culture, science, sports, travel, fashion, and lifestyles.
Depts/columns: Word lengths vary. Food, nutrition, media reviews, safety, beauty, and dining out.
Other: Submit seasonal material 6–8 months in advance.

Sample Issue
152 pages (47% advertising): 6 articles; 24 depts/columns. Sample copy, $3.50 at newsstands. Guidelines and editorial calendar available.
- "Raising an Introvert in an Extrovert World." Article offers advice for parents who have quiet, reserved children.
- Sample dept/column: "Family Traveler" looks at fun family activities in the Atlanta area.

Rights and Payment
First rights. Written material, payment rate varies. Pays on acceptance. Provides contributor's copies.

Editor's Comments
Keep in mind that our focus is on raising children under the age of 12. You must be an established writer whose work has appeared in national publications to work for us.

Child Care Information Exchange

P.O. Box 3249
Redmond, WA 98073-3249

Editor: Bonnie Neugebauer

Description and Readership
Targeting early childhood care professionals, this magazine focuses on effectively managing child-care centers, current trends in the field of child care, and practical solutions to problems.
- **Audience:** Child-care professionals
- **Frequency:** 6 times each year
- **Distribution:** 100% subscription
- **Circulation:** 26,000
- **Website:** www.childcareexchange.com

Freelance Potential
65–75% written by nonstaff writers. Publishes 75 freelance submissions yearly; 50% by unpublished writers, 60% by authors who are new to the magazine. Receives 12 queries monthly.

Submissions
Query with outline and writing samples. Accepts photocopies, computer printouts, and Macintosh disk submissions. SASE. Responds in 1 week.
Articles: 1,500 words. Informational, practical application, and how-to articles; and self-help pieces. Topics include education, current events, multicultural and ethnic subjects, and social issues.
Depts/columns: Word length varies. Infant and toddler care, staff training and development, and parent perspectives.

Sample Issue
88 pages: 15 articles; 8 depts/columns. Sample copy, $8. Guidelines and theme list available.
- "Culture and Leadership." Article examines ways to stimulate thinking and share cross-cultural perspectives among early care leaders.
- "Teaching Health Habits." Article discusses different methods for teaching proper hand-washing technique to young children.
- Sample dept/column: "From a Parent's Perspective" suggests weekly family meetings to keep everyone organized and cooperative.

Rights and Payment
All rights. Articles, $300. Other material, payment rate varies. Pays on publication. Provides 2 copies.

Editor's Comments
We seek articles that educate childcare professionals in better management techniques, inform them of current social issues and solutions, and help them develop a rewarding care environment.

Childhood Education

Association for Childhood Education International
Suite 215
17904 Georgia Avenue
Olney, MA 20832

Editor: Anne W. Bauer

Description and Readership
Topics, such as pets, hobbies, and sports, are in this magazine for girls. Its philosophy is that every girl deserves the right to be young before becoming an adult.
- **Audience:** Educators and child-care professionals
- **Frequency:** 6 times each year
- **Distribution:** 100% controlled
- **Circulation:** 10,000
- **Website:** www.acei.org

Freelance Potential
98% written by nonstaff writers. Publishes 40 freelance submissions yearly; 75% by authors who are new to the magazine. Receives 10 unsolicited mss monthly.

Submissions
Send 4 copies of complete ms. Accepts photocopies, computer printouts, and Macintosh or IBM disk submissions. SASE. Responds in 3 months.
Articles: 1,400–3,500 words. Informational articles. Topics include innovative learning strategies, the teaching profession, research findings, parenting and family issues, communities, drug education, and safe environments for children.
Depts/columns: 1,000 words. Classroom technology, reviews of professional books and books for children, and current educational issues.

Sample Issue
252 pages (15% advertising): 6 articles; 10 depts/columns. Sample copy, free with 9x12 SASE (3 first-class stamps). Writers' guidelines and editorial calendar available.
- "Merging Literacies." Articles describes how a pair of teachers immersed their classrooms in the arts.
- "A Glimpse into Kibbutz Education." Article demonstrates how teachers in similar settings address parallel issues.
- "Teaching Religious Diversity through Children's Literature." Article focuses on the need for teachers to learn about religious differences in our diverse nation.

Rights and Payment
All rights. No payment. Provides 5 contributor's copies.

Editor's Comments
We look for articles on innovative classroom topics and interviews with leaders in the field of education.

Children and Families

1651 Prince Street
Alexandra, VA 22310

Associate Editor: Julie Konieczny

Description and Readership
This award-winning publication for early childhood professionals presents articles and information on administrative topics, parenting and teaching skills, child development, initiating and developing programs, as well as solutions to problems in the field.
- **Audience:** Early child care professionals and educators
- **Frequency:** Quarterly
- **Distribution:** 90% subscription; 10% other
- **Circulation:** 15,000
- **Website:** www.nhsa.org

Freelance Potential
90% written by nonstaff writers. Publishes 25 freelance submissions yearly; 70% by unpublished writers, 70% by authors who are new to the magazine. Receives 2 mss monthly.

Submissions
Send complete ms. Accepts email submissions to julie@nhsa.org. Responds in 1–12 weeks.
Articles: 1,600–4,000 words. Informational and how-to articles. Topics include computers, gifted education, health, fitness, mathematics, multicultural issues, music, science and technology, and special education.
Depts/columns: 500–1,400 words. Learning activities, curriculum fun, and early literacy.
Artwork: Color prints and transparencies.
Other: Submit seasonal material 4 months in advance.

Sample Issue
76 pages (25% advertising): 6 articles; 11 depts/columns. Guidelines and theme list available.
- "The Head Start National Reporting System." Article offers a critique of an achievement test for 4- and 5-year-olds in Head Start.
- "Literacy for All Children." Article discusses the importance of having all children, including those with special needs, participate in literacy activities.
- Sample dept/column: "Curriculum Fun" offers activities for teaching children about different sizes.

Rights and Payment
First rights. No payment. Provides 2+ author's copies.

Editor's Comments
We look for detailed articles that provide new insights on topics of interest to our readers. Material should be well-crafted, descriptive, and offer practical advice.

Children's Advocate Newsmagazine

Action Alliance for Children, The Hunt House
1201 Martin Luther King, Jr., Way
Oakland, CA 94612-1217

Editor: Jean Tepperman

Description and Readership
Published in both English and Spanish, this newsmagazine offers articles, news, and reports that covers public policy issues and current trends that affect young children in California.
- **Audience:** Children's advocates
- **Frequency:** 6 times each year
- **Distribution:** 50% newsstand; 30% subscription; 20% controlled
- **Circulation:** 15,000
- **Website:** www.4children.org

Freelance Potential
40% written by nonstaff writers. Publishes 18 freelance submissions yearly. Receives few queries monthly.

Submissions
All articles assigned. Send résumé with clips or writing samples. Accepts photocopies and computer printouts. SASE. Responds in 1 month.
Articles: 500–1,500 words. Informational articles; program descriptions; policy analysis pieces; and how-to articles. Topics include families, foster care, child care, education, child welfare, violence prevention, health, nutrition, poverty, and mental health.
Depts/columns: Short news items, 300–500 words. Public policy analysis, 500–1,100 words. Book reviews, word length varies.

Sample Issue
16 pages (4% advertising): 14 articles; 3 depts/columns. Sample copy, $3. Guidelines available.
- "Selling Obesity." Article discusses junk food marketing and how activists take a stand against it.
- "Going Out to the Community." Article describes how mobile clinics are a key strategy for improving access to health care in rural areas.
- Sample dept/column: "Hands On" offers tips to get young children moving to music.

Rights and Payment
First North American serial rights. Written material, to $.25 per word. Pays on acceptance. Provides 3 contributor's copies.

Editor's Comments
We look for features on current policy issues, and descriptions of model programs or community action projects. Writers must have experience writing about children's issues. Avoid technical language.

Children's Digest

Children's Better Health Institute
1100 Waterway Boulevard
Indianapolis, IN 46202

Editor: Penny Rasdall

Description and Readership
This magazine of short stories, articles, activities, and poetry stresses a healthy lifestyle. Information about good health habits, sports, or fitness is a key component of everything it publishes.
- **Audience:** Pre-teens
- **Frequency:** 6 times each year
- **Distribution:** 100% subscription
- **Circulation:** 60,000
- **Website:** www.childrensdigest.com

Freelance Potential
50% written by nonstaff writers. Publishes 30 freelance submissions yearly; 70% by unpublished writers. Receives 100 unsolicited mss monthly.

Submissions
Query only. No unsolicited mss. Accepts email queries to p.rasdall@cdhl.org, photocopies and computer printouts. SASE. Responds in 3 months.
Articles: To 1,200 words. Informational and how-to articles; profiles; interviews; and personal experience pieces. Topics include health, exercise, safety, hygiene, drug education, and nutrition.
Fiction: To 1,500 words. Genres include multicultural and ethnic fiction, science fiction, fantasy, adventure, mystery, humor, and stories about animals and sports.
Depts/columns: To 1,200 words. Book reviews, recipes, and information about personal health.
Other: Puzzles, activities, and games. Poetry, to 25 lines. Submit seasonal material 8 months in advance.

Sample Issue
34 pages (6% advertising): 2 articles; 1 story; 3 depts/columns; 4 poems; 6 activities. Sample copy, $1.25 with 9x12 SASE. Guidelines available.
- "Vegetable Trivia." Article helps kids understand how various vegetables grow.
- "Planting Potatoes." Article provides instructions for cultivating potatoes in your garden.
- Sample dept/column: "Science Award Winner" reviews a book about chemists, physicists, biologists, and other scientists.

Rights and Payment
All rights. Written material, $.12 per word. Pays prior to publication. Provides 10 contributor's copies.

Editor's Comments
We'd like to see submissions about new or unusual sports, especially those in which kids can participate.

Children's Ministry

1515 Cascade Avenue
Loveland, CO 80538

Associate Editor: Jennifer Hooks

Description and Readership
This Christian publication offers practical articles for adult youth leaders and educators to help children grow spiritually.
- **Audience:** Church youth leaders
- **Frequency:** 6 times each year
- **Distribution:** Subscription; other
- **Circulation:** 90,000
- **Website:** www.cmmag.com

Freelance Potential
60–65% written by nonstaff writers. Publishes 150 freelance submissions yearly; 30% by unpublished writers, 30% by authors who are new to the magazine. Receives 200 queries and unsolicited mss each month.

Submissions
Query or send complete ms. Prefers email submissions to jhooks@cmmag.com; accepts computer printouts. Responds in 2–3 months.
Articles: 500–1,700 words. Informational and how-to articles; and personal experience pieces. Topics include Christian education, family issues, child development, and faith.
Depts/columns: 50–300 words. Educational issues, activities, devotionals, family ministry, parenting, crafts, and resources.
Other: Activities, games, and tips. Submit seasonal mateial 6–8 months in advance.

Sample Issue
144 pages (50% advertising): 9 articles; 18 depts/columns. Sample copy, $5.95 with 9x12 SASE. Wirters' guidelines available.
- "The Secret to an Irresistible Church." Informative article explains how relationships can attract people to a church, or send them packing.
- "Saying the Hard Things." Article discusses how to "speak truthfully in a loving manner."
- Sample dept/column: "Leading Volunteers" suggests ways to boost volunteer turnout.

Rights and Payment
All rights. Articles, to $350. Depts/columns, $40–$75. Pays on acceptance. Provides 1 contributor's copy.

Editor's Comments
We're seeking inspirational articles that deal with children's faith, morals, and church community. All material should strongly stress a Christian lifestyle.

Children's Playmate

Children's Better Health Institute
1100 Waterway Boulevard
P.O. Box 567
Indianapolis, IN 46206-0567

Editor: Terry Harshman

Description and Readership
This magazine teaches good health and safety habits through its stories, articles, and activities written to appeal to beginning readers.
- **Audience:** 6–8 years
- **Frequency:** 6 times each year
- **Distribution:** 100% subscription
- **Circulation:** 80,000
- **Website:** www.childrensplaymatemag.org

Freelance Potential
25% written by nonstaff writers. Publishes 30 freelance submissions yearly; 10% by unpublished writers, 50% by authors who are new to the magazine. Receives 75 unsolicited mss monthly.

Submissions
Send complete ms. Accepts photocopies and computer printouts. SASE. Responds in 2–3 months.
Articles: To 500 words. Humorous and how-to articles. Topics include health, nature, fitness, the environment, science, hobbies, crafts, multicultural and ethnic issues, and sports.
Fiction: To 100 words. Rebus stories.
Depts/columns: Staff written.
Other: Puzzles, activities, games, and recipes. Poetry, to 20 lines. Submit seasonal material about unusual holidays 8 months in advance.

Sample Issue
36 pages (no advertising): 2 articles; 2 stories; 16 poems; 10 activities; 1 recipe; 2 depts/columns. Sample copy, $1.75 with 9x12 SASE. Writers' guidelines available.
- "Skin-Sational Skin Facts." Article illustrates basic facts about skin.
- "A Salute to Animal Fathers." Article looks at four male creatures that assume responsibility for the birth of their young.
- "Helmet Head." Rebus tells of a young bike rider who avoided several different head injuries during one short ride by keeping her helmet on.

Rights and Payment
All rights; returns book rights upon request. Written material, $.17 per word. Pays on publication. Provides up to 10 contributor's copies.

Editor's Comments
We're looking for more health or safety related activities, and we always need articles on these topics as well.

Children's Voice

3rd Floor
440 First Street NE
Washington, DC 20001-2085

Editor-in-Chief: Steven Boehm

Description and Readership
Published by the Child Welfare League of America, this magazine offers in-depth articles and news on issues and events that affect the well being of children, youth, and families.
• **Audience:** Child welfare professionals
• **Frequency:** 6 times each year
• **Distribution:** Subscription; membership
• **Circulation:** 25,000
• **Website:** www.cwla.org/pubs

Freelance Potential
10% written by nonstaff writers. Publishes 2–3 freelance submissions yearly; 25% by authors who are new to the magazine. Receives 6+ queries monthly.

Submissions
Query. Accepts email queries (text only) to voice@cwla.org. Availability of artwork improves chance of acceptance. SASE. Responds in 1 week.
Articles: 1,500–3,000 words. Informational and how-to articles; profiles; interviews; and personal experience pieces. Topics include social issues, current events, and regional news as they relate to children and child-welfare issues.
Depts/columns: 100–200 words. Legislative updates; agency and organizational news.

Sample Issue
38 pages (20% advertising): 3 articles; 7 depts/columns. Sample copy, $10. Guidelines available.
• "Unlocking Mental Health Services for Youth in Care." Article discusses strategies to meet the mental needs of youth in foster care.
• "Ten Things Your Student with Autism Wishes You Knew." Article takes a look at ways to understand the world as special-needs children experience it.
• Sample dept/column: "Health Beat" stresses the importance of seat belts and having children ride in the back seat of cars.

Rights and Payment
All rights. No payment. Provides contributor's copies, and a free, one-year subscription.

Editor's Comments
We look for in-depth articles on topics of interest to professionals in the fields related to child welfare. Two times each year we publish special issues highlighting single subjects in child welfare and related fields. Style should be feature-oriented rather than scholarly.

Children's Writer

Institute of Children's Literature
95 Long Ridge Road
West Redding, CT 06896-1124

Editor: Susan Tierney

Description and Readership
This newsletter for writers features information on publishers, markets, genres, and trends in book and magazine publishing. It offers timely, helpful advice together with solid sources.
• **Audience:** Children's writers
• **Frequency:** Monthly
• **Distribution:** 100% subscription
• **Circulation:** 14,000
• **Website:** www.childrenswriter.com

Freelance Potential
100% written by nonstaff writers. Publishes 75 freelance submissions yearly; 10% by unpublished writers, 15% by authors who are new to the magazine. Receives 5+ queries monthly.

Submissions
Query with outline, synopsis, and résumé. Prefers email submissions through website. Accepts disk submissions with hard copy. SASE. Responds to queries in 2 months.
Articles: 1,500–2,000 words. Reports on children's book and magazine publishing markets that include interviews with editors and writers. Topics include industry trends, new markets, and publishers. Also publishes features on writing technique, research, motivation, and business issues.
Depts/columns: To 750 words, plus 125-word sidebar. Practical pieces about writing technique and careers, inside tips, and children's publishing.

Sample Issue
12 pages (no advertising): 2 articles; 4 depts/columns. Sample copy, free with #10 SASE (1 first-class stamp). Writers' guidelines available with SASE or at website.
• "Tales of the Dark Side." Article highlights why gothic and supernatural literature still hold such a draw for children and teens.
• Sample dept/column: "Commentary" offers an editor's viewpoint against picture book dummies.

Rights and Payment
First North American serial rights. Articles, $135–$350. Pays on publication.

Editor's Comments
Our newsletter is a writer's handy tool, so we look for articles that provide up-to-date information, beneficial tips, and interviews with editors and authors.

Child Welfare Report

E3430 Mountainview Lane
P.O. Box 322
Waupaca, IL 54981

Editor: Mike Jacquart

Description and Readership
This newsletter offers professionals working in the field of child welfare up-to-date and useful information on issues affecting the well-being of children and teens. Its three inserts provide additional information.
• **Audience:** Child welfare professionals
• **Frequency:** Monthly
• **Distribution:** 100% subscription
• **Circulation:** 500
• **Website:** www.impact-publications.com

Freelance Potential
40% written by nonstaff writers. Publishes several freelance submissions yearly; 90% by authors who are new to the magazine. Receives 10+ queries monthly.

Submissions
Query with outline. Accepts photocopies, computer printouts, and IBM disk submissions (Microsoft Word). Availability of artwork improves chance of acceptance. SASE. Responds in 1 month.
Articles: Word length varies. Informational and how-to articles; personal experience and opinion pieces; interviews, and new product information. Topics include gifted and special education, disabilities, government programs, foster care, career choices, family life, parenting, psychology, mentoring, and multicultural and ethnic issues.

Sample Issue
8 pages (no advertising): 4 articles; 3 inserts; 1 resource page. Sample copy, $6.95 with #10 SASE (1 first-class stamp). Guidelines available.
• "Child Neglect: Where Do We Go from Here?" Article addresses inconsistencies in the definition and handling of child neglect.
• "Understanding Rett Syndrome." Article examines the characteristics of this autism-related disease.
• Sample dept/column: "Teen Connections" relays the latest findings on teenage alcohol consumption.

Rights and Payment
First rights. Written material, payment rates vary. Pays on publication. Provides 5 contributor's copies.

Editor's Comments
We are seeking articles on child and youth homelessness, juvenile and mental health courts, and balancing an organization's budget with reality. We are also looking for material for our new insert, "Mental Health Matters," which deals with children and teen mental health.

Christian Camp & Conference Journal

P.O. Box 62189
Colorado Springs, CO 80962-2189

Editor: Alison Hayhoe

Description and Readership
This magazine is published for adults who serve at Christian camps, conference centers, and retreat centers. Its articles address those who fill a variety of roles in the areas of food service, management, health, maintenance, and guest services.
• **Audience:** Adults
• **Frequency:** 6 times each year
• **Distribution:** 95% subscription; 5% other
• **Circulation:** 9,000
• **Website:** www.ccca-us.org

Freelance Potential
90% written by nonstaff writers. Publishes 2 freelance submissions yearly. Receives 1–2 queries monthly.

Submissions
Query with résumé and writing samples. Accepts email submissions to editor@ccca-us.org. Availability of artwork may improve chance of acceptance. SASE. Responds in 1 month.
Articles: 800–1,500 words. Informational and how-to articles; profiles; and interviews. Topics include biography, crafts, hobbies, health and fitness, multicultural and ethnic issues, nature, the environment, popular culture, recreation, religion, social issues, and sports.
Depts/columns: Staff written.
Artwork: B/W and color prints and transparencies.
Other: Submit seasonal material 6 months in advance.

Sample Issue
38 pages (25% advertising): 7 articles; 8 depts/columns. Sample copy, $4.95 with 9x12 SASE ($1.40 postage). Guidelines and theme list available.
• "Twenty-First Century Staff." Article advises camp managers to minister to their incoming staff as they provide training for them.
• "Older and Wiser." Article explains why it's a good idea to invite retirees to work at youth camps.

Rights and Payment
First rights. Written material, $.16 per word. Artwork, $25–$250. Pays on publication. Provides 1 contributor's copy.

Editor's Comments
New writers stand a better chance of publication with the submission of a profile, an interview, or a how-to piece. Articles should contain a practical or inspirational element that applies to leaders in organized Christian camping.

Christian Home & School

3350 East Paris Avenue SE
Grand Rapids, MI 49512-3054

Senior Editor: Roger Schmurr

Description and Readership
This magazine promotes Christian education and addresses a variety of topics of interest to parents who send their children to Christian schools.
- **Audience:** Parents
- **Frequency:** 6 times each year
- **Distribution:** 95% schools; 5% subscription
- **Circulation:** 66,000
- **Website:** www.csionline.org/chs

Freelance Potential
75% written by nonstaff writers. Publishes 40–45 freelance submissions yearly; 10% by unpublished writers, 30% by authors who are new to the magazine. Receives 5 queries, 25 unsolicited mss monthly.

Submissions
Query or send complete ms. Accepts photocopies, computer printouts, email submissions to rogers@ csionline.org, and simultaneous submissions if identified. SASE. Responds in 7–10 days.
Articles: 1,000–2,000 words. Informational, how-to, and self-help articles; and personal experience pieces. Topics include education, parenting, life skills, decision making, self-control, discipline, family travel, faith, and social issues.
Fiction: Word length varies. Christian stories and first-person narratives about Christian life.
Depts/columns: "Parentstuff," 100–250 words. Reviews and profiles, word length varies.

Sample Issue
34 pages (15% advertising): 4 articles; 11 depts/ columns; 8 book reviews. Sample copy, free with 9x12 SASE ($1.06 postage). Guidelines available.
- "When Parents Fail." Article explains that it's OK to make mistakes with children.
- "Christian Schools in the City." Article examines the challenges faced by urban Christian schools.
- Sample dept/column: "Profiles" takes a look at a Christian school in Minneapolis, Minnesota.

Rights and Payment
First rights. Written material, $175–$250. "Parentstuff," $25–$40. Pays on publication. Provides 5 contributor's copies.

Editor's Comments
We would like more material that highlights the advantages of a Christian education. Articles should reflect a mature, biblical perspective.

Christian Parenting Today

Christian Today International
465 Gundersen Drive
Carol Stream, IL 60188

Managing Editor: Caryn Rivadeneira

Description and Readership
Building strong families based on solid Christian values is the goal of this publication. Positive articles focus on parenting skills, contemporary family concerns, and parent/child relationships.
- **Audience:** Parents
- **Frequency:** Quarterly
- **Distribution:** 85% subscription; 15% newsstand
- **Circulation:** 90,000
- **Website:** www.christianparenting.net

Freelance Potential
90% written by nonstaff writers. Publishes 24–30 freelance submissions yearly; 20% by unpublished writers, 20% by authors who are new to the magazine. Receives 100–125 queries monthly.

Submissions
Query with résumé, outline, and clips or writing samples. Accepts photocopies and computer printouts. SASE. Responds in 6–8 weeks.
Articles: 1,000–2,000 words. Informational articles; and humor. Topics include parenting, family life, spiritual development, personal values, prayer, faith, and discipline.
Depts/columns: Word length varies. Single parenting, child development, and faith.
Other: Submit seasonal material 6 months in advance.

Sample Issue
48 pages (40% advertising): 5 articles; 12 depts/ columns. Sample copy, $4.95 at newsstands. Guidelines available at website.
- "Boys Will Be Boys!" Humorous article about being a parent of boys.
- "What Jordan Taught." First-person account of a boy with a phenomenal sense of faith.
- Sample dept/column: "Discipline Matters" discusses the positive power of praise.

Rights and Payment
First North American serial rights. Articles, $.12–$.25 per word. Other material, $25–$250. Pays on acceptance for articles; on publication for depts/columns. Provides 1 contributor's copy.

Editor's Comments
Our readers are looking for Christian approaches to raising their families. Material should emphasize ways to solve parenting issues using traditional Christian principles.

The Christian Science Monitor

1 Norway Street
Boston, MA 02115

Kid Space and Home Forum Editor: Owen Thomas

Description and Readership
Analytical pieces covering national and international events, unique stories, and poetry can be found in this daily newspaper. It also has a kids page that appears once a week.
- **Audience:** Adults, children
- **Frequency:** Daily
- **Distribution:** 95% subscription; 5% newsstand
- **Circulation:** 80,000
- **Website:** www.csmonitor.com

Freelance Potential
30% written by nonstaff writers. Publishes 750 freelance submissions yearly; 15% by unpublished writers. Receives 500 queries monthly.

Submissions
Query with résumé and clips for articles. Send complete ms for depts/columns. Accepts computer printouts and email submissions to homeforum@csmonitor.com. SASE. Responds in 1 month.
Articles: To 1,000 words. Creative nonfiction and personal experience pieces; humor; and essays for the "Home Forum" page. Topics include nature, the environment, the arts, pets, wildlife, and nostalgia.
Depts/columns: 400–800 words. News and reviews.
Artwork: Color negatives, slides, JPEG or PDF files.
Other: Puzzles, activities, and poetry.

Sample Issue
20 pages (15% advertising): 13 articles; 14 depts/columns. Sample copy and guidelines, $1.
- "Court Hits Jury Race Bias." Article discusses the rulings by the Supreme Court to challenge racial bias in the jury selection process.
- "Rich-Poor Gap Gaining Attention." Article discusses the increase in the income gap between the rich and the rest of the U.S. population.
- Sample dept/column: "Learning" discusses merit pay for teachers.

Rights and Payment
Exclusive rights. All material, payment rate varies. Pays on publication. Provides 1 contributor's copy.

Editor's Comments
The asset we value most in freelance writers is quality of thought. Nearly all of our prose pieces are provided by first-time and established freelance writers. Our "Kidspace" department requires more expertise. Send us something thought-provoking and intriguing.

Christian Work at Home Moms Ezine

Editor: Jill Hart

Description and Readership
For over five years, this online publication has been offering Christian mothers resources to help them find work at home, as well as career information on balancing a work-at-home position and a family. It includes articles and essays on running a home-based business, profiles, reviews, job listings, business listings, and spiritual encouragement.
- **Audience:** Women ages 20–65
- **Frequency:** Weekly
- **Distribution:** 100% Internet
- **Circulation:** 2,300
- **Website:** www.cwahm.com

Freelance Potential
50% written by nonstaff writers. Publishes 500 freelance submissions yearly; 75% by unpublished writers, 80% by authors who are new to the magazine.

Submissions
Send ms through website. Response time varies.
Articles: Word lengths vary. Informational and how-to articles; profiles; reviews; and personal experience pieces. Topics include college and career.
Depts/columns: Word lengths vary. Employment information, information on careers.

Sample Issue
Guidelines available at website.
- "Honesty." Article discusses how to be honest as well as business savvy.
- "Partnership Parenting—Parenting with the Mind of Christ." Article discusses how to trust in the Lord and give him the control.
- "Can't Find a Boss, So Become One." Article takes a look at home-based businesses, how to select one, start one, and help it grow.

Rights and Payment
Electronic rights. No payment.

Editor's Comments
Our goal is to provide our readers with the information they need to make contact with and have ready access to organizations and resources that will help them be more informed and more effective. We seek inspirational and informational articles on topics related to work at home jobs, home businesses, and other information of special interest to Christian parents who desire to work from home. Submissions must be family-friendly and have a Christian slant.

Church Educator

165 Plaza Drive
Prescott, AZ 86303

Editor: Linda Davidson

Description and Readership
This resourceful publication offers a wealth of practical information for Christian educators. It includes how-to articles on ministries for children and youth, as well as adults, and covers topics such as workshops, curriculums, Bible lessons and review, worshiping, and activities.
- **Audience:** Christian educators
- **Frequency:** Monthly
- **Distribution:** 100% subscription
- **Circulation:** 3,000
- **Website:** www.educationalministries.com

Freelance Potential
90% written by nonstaff writers. Publishes 100 freelance submissions yearly; 10% by unpublished writers, 5% by authors who are new to the magazine. Receives 25 unsolicited mss monthly.

Submissions
Send complete ms. Accepts computer printouts. SASE. Responds in 1 month.
Articles: 500–1,500 words. How-to articles. Topics include faith education, spirituality, and religion.

Sample Issue
38 pages: 20 articles. Sample copy, free with 9x12 SASE ($.83 postage). Writers' guidelines and theme list available.
- "How Much Is Enough?" Article discusses evaluating our attitude towards our possessions.
- "It's a Snap." Article offers ways to utilize photographs as a tool for Christian education and other church programs.
- "Small Groups That Succeed." Article explores small groups in churches and offers guidelines for building strong foundations within them.

Rights and Payment
One-time rights. Written material, $.03 per word. Pays on publication. Provides 2 contributor's copies.

Editor's Comments
For this upcoming year we are looking for articles on changing school curriculums that focus on new programs that are working. Material for youth programs should include an outline for discussion format, and guidelines for activities and encounters. Keep in mind that we publish creative practical material that will help educators in spreading the Word of God, including lessons, activities, stories, prayers and liturgies.

Cicada

Cricket Magazine Group
P.O. Box 300
315 5th Street
Peru, IL 61354

Submissions Editor

Description and Readership
Entertaining, high-quality fiction for young adults can be found in this literary journal. Part of the Cricket Magazine Group, its pages include essays, novellas, personal experience pieces, short stories, and poems.
- **Audience:** 14–21 years
- **Frequency:** 6 times each year
- **Distribution:** 95% subscription; 5% newsstand
- **Circulation:** 18,500
- **Website:** www.cricketmag.com

Freelance Potential
98% written by nonstaff writers.

Submissions
Send complete ms. Accepts photocopies, computer printouts, and simultaneous submissions if identified. SASE. Responds in 2–3 months.
Articles: To 5,000 words. Essay and personal experience pieces.
Fiction: To 5,000 words. Genres include adventure, fantasy, humor, and historical, contemporary, and science fiction. Plays and stories presented in a sophisticated cartoon format. Novellas, to 15,000 words.
Depts/columns: 300–500 words. Book reviews. "Expressions" features readers' opinions and observations on everything from school life to concerns about social and cultural issues, 350–1,000 words.
Other: Cartoons. Poetry, to 25 lines.

Sample Issue
128 pages (no advertising): 8 stories; 6 poems; 1 book review; 1 dept/column. Sample copy, $8.50. Guidelines available.
- "Nightingales." Story explores the challenges an African American girl faces as a scholarship student at a private elite school for girls.
- "The Voice Lesson." Story tells of a college student who takes voice lessons to fill her music requirement and ends up really enjoying herself.
- Sample dept/column: "Expressions" offers an essay of the author's trip to Spain and her encounter with a mandolinist and a young boy.

Rights and Payment
All rights. Payment rates vary. Pays on publication.

Editor's Comments
We welcome fresh, well-written YA fiction of any genre—especially coming of age themes with humor. We prefer original stories over reprint material.

Circle K

Circle K International
3636 Woodview Trace
Indianapolis, IN 46268-3196

Executive Editor: Christopher Martz

Description and Readership
Members of Circle K International, a collegiate community service organization, are the audience for this magazine. Articles cover a variety of areas—from career choices to social and community issues.
- **Audience:** YA–Adult
- **Frequency:** 6 times each year
- **Distribution:** Subscription; schools; controlled
- **Circulation:** 10,000
- **Website:** www.circlek.org

Freelance Potential
50% written by nonstaff writers. Publishes 12 freelance submissions yearly; 50% by unpublished writers, 50% by authors who are new to the magazine. Receives 4+ unsolicited mss monthly.

Submissions
Prefers query with clips or writing samples. Accepts complete ms. Accepts photocopies and computer printouts. SASE. Responds in 2 weeks.
Articles: 1,000–1,800 words. Informational and self-help articles. Topics include social issues, collegiate trends, community involvement, leadership, and career development.
Depts/columns: Word length varies. News and information about Circle K activities.
Artwork: 5x7 or 8x10 glossy prints; emailed TIFF or JPEG files of 300 dpi or better.

Sample Issue
16 pages (no advertising): 3 articles; 4 depts/columns. Sample copy, $.75 with 9x12 SASE ($.75 postage). Guidelines available.
- "Global 'Classroom'." Article highlights three international study programs that help students absorb and share a wealth of experience beyond their home campus environment.
- Sample dept/column: "Spotlight" examines various Circle K activities and programs across the U.S.

Rights and Payment
First North American serial rights. Written material, $150–$400. Artwork, payment rate varies. Pays on acceptance. Provides 3 contributor's copies.

Editor's Comments
Articles that help service-minded student leaders become better individuals, personally and professionally, are needed by our editors. Send us material about successful Circle K programs.

The Claremont Review

4980 Wesley Road
Victoria, British Columbia V8Y 1Y9
Canada

Business Editor: Sue Field

Description and Readership
Featuring the works of young Canadian authors, this literary journal publishes short stories, poetry, short plays, and author interviews. *The Claremont Review* also sponsors annual fiction and poetry contests for students in grades six through twelve.
- **Audience:** 13–19 years
- **Frequency:** Twice each year
- **Distribution:** 20% newsstand; 20% schools; 15% subscription; 45% other
- **Circulation:** 600
- **Website:** www.theclaremontreview.ca

Freelance Potential
99% written by nonstaff writers. Publishes 150 freelance submissions yearly; 90% by unpublished writers, 90% by authors who are new to the magazine. Receives 12 unsolicited mss monthly.

Submissions
Send complete ms with biography. Accepts photocopies and computer printouts. SAE/IRC. Responds in 1 month.
Articles: Word length varies. Interviews with contemporary authors and editors.
Fiction: To 5,000 words. Traditional, literary, experimental, and contemporary fiction. Also publishes adventure and sports stories.
Artwork: B/W and color prints and transparencies.
Other: Poetry, no line limit.

Sample Issue
128 pages (2% advertising): 11 stories; 35 poems. Sample copy, $10 with 9x12 SASE. Guidelines available at website.
- "Jim's Biological Clock Short-Circuits." Grim tale of a confused young man.
- "Abduction." Story about two children who are waiting for the appearance of UFOs.
- "The Guy in the Black Fedora." Short story gives a glimpse of the imagination of a teenager.

Rights and Payment
Rights vary. Payment policies vary. Payment rates varies. Provides 1 contributor's copy.

Editor's Comments
We are looking for original work that reveals something novel about the human condition. Such material can be traditional or experimental. We do not publish science fiction, fantasy, or anything that mimics prime-time television.

The Clearing House

Heldref Publications
1319 18th Street
Washington, DC 20036

Managing Editor: Sarah Erdreich

Description and Readership
Teaching strategies, educational innovations, and testing and standards are the focus of this journal for middle school and high school educators. *The Clearing House* features reports on new methods and practices, as well as research findings and opinion pieces.
- **Audience:** Educators
- **Frequency:** 6 times each year
- **Distribution:** Subscription; other
- **Circulation:** 1,500
- **Website:** www.heldref.org/tch.php

Freelance Potential
100% written by nonstaff writers. Publishes 65 freelance submissions yearly; 5% by unpublished writers, 50% by authors who are new to the magazine. Receives 10 unsolicited mss monthly.

Submissions
Send 2 copies of complete ms. Accepts photocopies and computer printouts. Does not return mss. Responds in 3–4 months.
Articles: To 2,500 words. Informational and how-to articles. Topics include teaching methods, special education, learning styles, and educational testing and measurement.
Depts/columns: Word length varies. Educational news and opinion pieces.

Sample Issue
42 pages (no advertising): 7 articles. Sample copy, $14.50. Guidelines available in each issue.
- "Assessing Teacher Candidate Growth Over Time: Embedded Signature Assessments." Article reports on a pilot program in California that offers an alternative to the Performance Assessment for California Teachers (PACT).
- "Helping New Teachers Enter and Stay in the Profession." Examines the importance of individualized teacher support and professional development.

Rights and Payment
All rights. No payment. Provides 2 author's copies.

Editor's Comments
Ours is a peer-reviewed journal. We look for articles that report on useful practices, research findings, and experiments. We also publish a limited number of first-person accounts and opinion pieces on controversial issues. Articles on educational trends, effective schools, curriculum, and learning styles are welcome.

Cleveland/Akron Family

Suite 224
35475 Vine Street
Eastlake, OH 44095-3147

Editor: Frances Richards

Description and Readership
This magazine serves as a resource guide for parents and expectant parents residing in northeastern Ohio. Family calendars and directories of preschools, childcare centers, and maternity services are examples of the kind of information it provides, along with parenting advice.
- **Audience:** Parents
- **Frequency:** Monthly
- **Distribution:** 100% controlled
- **Circulation:** 65,000
- **Website:** www.clevelandakronfamily.com

Freelance Potential
50% written by nonstaff writers. Publishes 40 freelance submissions yearly; 33% by authors who are new to the magazine. Receives 400 queries monthly.

Submissions
Query. Accepts email to editor@tntpublications.com. Responds only if interested.
Articles: 500+ words. Informational, self-help, and how-to articles; profiles; and reviews. Topics include animals, the arts, computers, crafts, health, fitness, gifted education, popular culture, sports, the environment, religion, and regional issues.
Depts/columns: Word length varies. Media reviews, health, and education.
Artwork: High resolution JPEG and TIFF files.

Sample Issue
40 pages (50% advertising): 5 articles; 9 depts/columns; 1 family calendar. Editorial calendar available.
- "Dealing with Disabilities." Article discusses how families are affected when there is a child with a hidden disability in the home.
- "Sex(tuplets) and the City." Article reports on the birth of the Hanselman sextuplets of Cuyahoga Falls and on the progress they made during their first few weeks.
- Sample dept/column: "Monthly Matters" features feedback from readers on the topic of chores.

Rights and Payment
Exclusive rights. Written material, payment rate varies. Pays on publication. Provides 1 contributor's copy.

Editor's Comments
We're looking for more articles that present solid information for our readers and fewer first-person, slice-of-life, reflection pieces.

Click

Carus Publishing
Suite 1450
140 S. Dearborn Street
Chicago, IL 60603

Editor

Description and Readership
Click is a magazine of investigation and discovery for young readers. Its articles introduce children to the world of ideas and knowledge in a challenging, age-appropriate way.
• **Audience:** 3–7 years
• **Frequency:** 9 times each year
• **Distribution:** Subscription; newsstand
• **Circulation:** 54,000
• **Website:** www.cricketmag.com

Freelance Potential
90% written by nonstaff writers. Of the freelance submissions published each year, 10% are by authors who are new to the magazine. Receives 4–5 queries each month.

Submissions
All material is commissioned from experienced authors. Send résumé and clips. Response time varies.
Articles: To 1,000 words. Informational articles; interviews; and photo essays. Topics include the natural, physical, and social sciences; the arts; technology; math; and history. Also publishes special issues devoted to biographies.
Depts/columns: Word length varies. News items.

Sample Issue
32 pages (no advertising): 4 articles; 3 stories; 3 depts/columns; 1 pull-out section. Sample copy, $5. Guidelines available.
• "Click & the Kids." Illustrated serial story about a mouse and his human friends.
• "Sea Otters at Home." Informative article about the natural habitat of sea otters.
• "Nick's Sharks." Story about a little boy who is afraid of sharks, but finally learns that they are not really scary after all.

Rights and Payment
Rights policy varies. Written material, payment rates and policy varies.

Editor's Comments
We need material that introduces children to the process of investigation and observation, and encourages them to be active participants in the search for knowledge and understanding of their world. We will consider stories, articles, poems, photo essays, and activities. All of our freelance work is commissioned.

Club Connection

Assemblies of God
1445 North Boonville Avenue
Springfield, MO 65802-1894

Associate Editor: Sherrie Batty

Description and Readership
Offering fun, upbeat articles and activities with inspirational themes, *Club Connection* is published for elementary school girls who are members of Missionettes, a Christian club for girls. Published by the Assemblies of God, it also offers resource materials for Missionettes' leaders.
• **Audience:** 6–12 years
• **Frequency:** Quarterly
• **Distribution:** 100% subscription
• **Circulation:** 9,000
• **Website:** www.clubconnection.ag.com

Freelance Potential
60% written by nonstaff writers. Publishes 30 freelance submissions yearly; 45% by unpublished writers, 80% by authors who are new to the magazine. Receives 15–17 unsolicited mss monthly.

Submissions
Send complete ms. Accepts photocopies, computer printouts, and simultaneous submissions if identified. SASE. Responds in 1–2 months.
Articles: 300–700 words. Profiles; interviews; and biographical pieces. Topics include religion, missions, hobbies, health, fitness, music, nature, the environment, multicultural and ethnic subjects, camping, pets, sports, recreation, science, and technology.
Depts/columns: Word length varies. Book and music reviews, club news, science, and advice.
Other: Puzzles, games, trivia, and recipes.

Sample Issue
32 pages (5% advertising): 6 articles; 10 depts/columns; 3 devotionals; 3 games; 2 crafts. Sample copy, $2 with 9x12 SASE ($.77 postage). Guidelines and editorial calendar available.
• "His Creation." Article explains why you don't have to be perfect or flawless for God to love you, and presents five things you can do to help you understand how much you mean to God.
• "Emailing God." Features one girl's email conversation with God.

Rights and Payment
First or one-time rights. Articles, $25–$50. Pays on publication. Provides 2 contributor's copies.

Editor's Comments
Material you submit should address girls' common interests while also offering a salvation message.

Cobblestone

Discover American History

Cobblestone Publishing
Suite C, 30 Grove Street
Peterborough, NH 03458

Editor: Meg Chorlian

Description and Readership

This award-winning magazine offers middle school students an exciting look at history. Each issue includes articles, stories, and activities that spotlight both well-known and not-so-famous people.
- **Audience:** 8–14 years
- **Frequency:** 9 times each year
- **Distribution:** 100% subscription
- **Circulation:** 29,000
- **Website:** www.cobblestonepub.com

Freelance Potential

85% written by nonstaff writers. Publishes 80 freelance submissions yearly; 15% by unpublished writers, 25% by new authors. Receives 50 queries monthly.

Submissions

Query with outline, bibliography, and clips or writing samples. All queries must relate to a specific theme. Accepts photocopies and computer printouts. SASE. Responds in 5 months.
Articles: Features, 700–800 words. Sidebars, 300–400 words. Informational articles; interviews; and profiles of historical figures—all as they relate to American history.
Fiction: To 800 words. Historical, multicultural, and biographical fiction; retold legends; and adventure.
Artwork: Color prints and slides. Line art.
Other: Puzzles, activities, and games. Poetry relating to the issue's theme.

Sample Issue

48 pages (no advertising): 9 articles; 12 depts/columns; 2 activities; 1 cartoon. Sample copy, $4.95 with 9x12 SASE ($1.24 postage). Guidelines available.
- "Creating the Tree Army." Article discusses a plan by Franklin Delano Roosevelt to create a civilian conservation corps that later became a law.
- "Closing the Camps." Article shares the results the Civilian Conservation Corps had on America.
- Sample dept/column: "Flashback" takes a look at the life of Franklin D. Roosevelt.

Rights and Payment

All rights. Written material, $.20–$.25 per word. Artwork, payment rates vary. Pays on publication. Provides 2 contributor's copies.

Editor's Comments

We are looking for more activities and good historical nonfiction. We want more than a broad overview.

College Bound Teen Magazine

Suite 202
1200 South Avenue
Staten Island, NY 10314

Editor-in-Chief: Gina LaGuardia

Description and Readership

Young adults who are considering college find useful information about college life in this magazine. It offers real-life accounts and expert advice on all aspects of campus life.
- **Audience:** 14–18 years
- **Frequency:** Monthly for regional editions; 2 times each year for national edition
- **Distribution:** 85% schools; 15% subscription
- **Circulation:** 775,000 national; 100,000 regional
- **Website:** www.collegeboundteen.com

Freelance Potential

60% written by nonstaff writers. Publishes 175 freelance submissions yearly; 60% by unpublished writers, 60% by authors who are new to the magazine. Receives 50 queries monthly.

Submissions

Query with clips or writing samples. Accepts photocopies and email queries to editorial@collegebound.net. SASE. Responds in 6–8 weeks.
Articles: 600–1,000 words. Informational and how-to articles; profiles; interviews; and personal experience pieces. Topics include choosing a college, college survival, dorm life, and joining a fraternity or sorority.
Depts/columns: Word length varies. Reviews of college guides and resources, financial aid, lifestyle issues, and athletics.
Other: Submit seasonal material 4 months in advance.

Sample Issue

130 pages (48% advertising): 13 articles; 13 depts/columns. Sample copy, free with 9x12 SASE. Guidelines available.
- "The Hidden Enemy." Article addresses the often hidden signs of mental health issues.
- "Matt Long Keeps It Real." Article profiles this TV star.
- Sample dept/column: "Cash Crunch" looks at three college students who are getting financial help from comedian Bill Cosby.

Rights and Payment

First and second rights. Articles, $50–$100. Depts/columns, $15–$70. Pays on publication. Provides 3–5 contributor's copies.

Editor's Comments

We are seeing too many submissions about "Freshman 15," roommate issues, long distance relationships, and how to pay for college.

College Outlook

20 East Gregory Boulevard
Kansas City, MO 64114-1145

Editor: Ryan Deo

Description and Readership
This resourceful publication offers a wealth of information for prospective college students. Each issue includes up-to-date material on admission processes, financial aid, money management, and current trends in career choices. It is published once in the spring for high school juniors, and once in the fall for high school seniors.
- **Audience:** College-bound students
- **Frequency:** Twice each year
- **Distribution:** 100% controlled
- **Circulation:** Spring, 440,000; fall, 710,000
- **Website:** www.townsend-outlook.com

Freelance Potential
60% written by nonstaff writers. Publishes 5–10 freelance submissions yearly; 95% by unpublished writers, 95% by authors who are new to the magazine. Receives 8 queries and unsolicited mss monthly.

Submissions
Query with clips or writing samples; or send complete ms. Accepts photocopies and computer printouts. SASE. Responds in 1 month.
Articles: To 1,500 words. How-to articles; personal experience pieces; and humor. Topics include school selection, financial aid, scholarships, student life, extracurricular activities, money management, and college admissions procedures.
Artwork: 5x7 B/W and color transparencies.
Other: Gazette items on campus subjects, including fads, politics, classroom news, current events, leisure activities, and careers.

Sample Issue
48 pages (15% advertising): 4 articles; 1 academic chart. Sample copy, free. Guidelines available.
- "Unleashed." Article discusses how to use the Internet when researching and applying for scholarships.
- "Where Does the Money Come From?" Article takes a look at different types of financial aid available to help pay for college.

Rights and Payment
All rights. No payment. Provides 2 author's copies.

Editor's Comments
We look for articles that will help guide our readers as they begin to think about life after high school. Topics relating to smart money management, career planning, and choosing the right college are of interest to us.

Columbus Parent

Suite F
670 Lakeview Plaza Boulevard
Worthington, OH 43085

Editor: Donna Willis

Description and Readership
Fresh, innovative articles on parenting and family issues can be found in this tabloid. Distributed free to parents in the Columbus region, it also includes information on local events and resources.
- **Audience:** Parents
- **Frequency:** Monthly
- **Distribution:** 90% newsstand; 10% subscription
- **Circulation:** 125,000
- **Website:** www.columbusparent.com

Freelance Potential
40% written by nonstaff writers. Publishes 120 freelance submissions yearly; 40% by authors who are new to the magazine. Receives 83 queries monthly.

Submissions
Query. Accepts email queries to dwillis@thisweeknews.com.
Articles: 700 words. Informational and how-to articles; profiles; interviews; and reviews. Topics include the arts, current events, health and fitness, humor, music, recreation, self-help, and travel.
Fiction: 300 words. Humor.
Depts/columns: 300 words. Local events, food, health, book reviews, travel, and local personalities.
Artwork: Color prints and transparencies.
Other: Submit seasonal material 2 months in advance.

Sample Issue
64 pages (50% advertising): 3 articles; 14 depts/columns; 1 guide. Sample copy, free at newsstands. Guidelines and theme list available.
- "Calming the Family Storm." Article offers tips to build family relationships out of mutual respect.
- "Father Power." Article discusses the importance of having positive male involvement during the teenage years.
- Sample dept/column: "Family Media" reviews books that focus on dads.

Rights and Payment
No rights. Written material, $.10 per word. Pays on publication.

Editor's Comments
We are looking for well-researched features. Writers should use an active voice, with simple sentences. All material must have a local slant. We are currently not accepting submissions for our personal column or essays, as we have enough of these.

Complete Woman

Suite 3434
875 North Michigan Avenue
Chicago, IL 60611-1901

Executive Editor: Lora Wintz

Description and Readership
This magazine offers articles that help readers understand what it means to be a complete woman in today's society, including family commitments, social issues, and personal concerns.
- **Audience:** Adults
- **Frequency:** 6 times each year
- **Distribution:** Subscription; newsstand
- **Circulation:** 350,000

Freelance Potential
90% written by nonstaff writers. Publishes 75 freelance submissions yearly; 20% by unpublished writers, 30% by authors who are new to the magazine. Receives 60 queries monthly.

Submissions
Query or send complete ms with clips and résumé. Accepts photocopies, computer printouts, and simultaneous submissions if identified. SASE. Responds in 3 months.

Articles: 800–1,200 words. Informational articles; and personal experience pieces. Topics include health, exercise, beauty, skin care, fashion, relationships, romance, self-help, business, sex, and self-improvement.

Depts/columns: Word length varies. Careers, new products, beauty, and news.

Sample Issue
96 pages: 32 articles; 8 depts/columns. Sample copy, $3.99 at newsstands.
- "Crossing Over." Interview with psychic medium John Edward tells readers how to tap into their psychic abilities.
- "Bottoms Up!" Article profiles the lives of female bartenders in South Beach, Florida.
- Sample dept/column: "Living Right" highlights new products for women.

Rights and Payment
Rights policy and payment policy vary. Pays on publication. Provides 1 contributor's copy.

Editor's Comments
We welcome all nonfiction manuscripts that address the concerns of today's woman. Our readers want to learn more about contemporary trends and issues that affect women of all ages. For a better understanding of what our magazine is all about, be sure to review a recent issue.

Connect

P.O. Box 60
Brattleboro, VT 5302-0060

Associate Editor: Heather Taylor

Description and Readership
This education publication is used as a resource for developing problem-solving skills, hands-on learning, and interdisciplinary approaches in the classroom.
- **Audience:** Teachers, grades K–8
- **Frequency:** 5 times each year
- **Distribution:** 100% subscription
- **Circulation:** 2,000
- **Website:** www.synergylearning.org

Freelance Potential
75% written by nonstaff writers. Publishes 25 freelance submissions yearly; 66% by unpublished writers, 75% by authors who are new to the magazine. Receives 2 queries and unsolicited mss monthly.

Submissions
Query or send complete ms. Prefers email submissions to connect@synergylearning.org. Accepts photocopies, computer printouts, and disk submissions. SASE. Responds in 1 month.

Articles: To 1,400 words. Informational and how-to articles; personal experience pieces; and interviews. Topics include communication, animals, algebra, diversity, health, technology, and the environment.

Depts/columns: Book reviews and news, word length varies. Resource reviews, 50–300 words.

Other: Classroom activities, 250–300 words.

Sample Issue
24 pages (no advertising): 5 articles; 1 story; 2 depts/columns; 16 reviews; 1 project. Sample copy, free with 9x12 SASE. Guidelines available.
- "Silkworm Time." Article explains how to use silkworms to demonstrate the cycle of life.
- "Howard, Minuta, and Turtle." Story uses a Native American myth to explain the concept of time.
- Sample dept/column: "Technology for Learning" discusses websites for weather and climate studies.

Rights and Payment
First rights. Honorarium for full-length articles. Provides 5 contributor's copies and a 1-year subscription.

Editor's Comments
Each of our issues supports a particular educational theme. We are looking for specific examples of children's learning, either through anecdotes or children's work. Material should be easy to understand and stress interdisciplinary instruction and cross-curriculum study.

Connect for Kids

1625 K Street NW
Washington, DC 20006

Editor: Susan Phillips

Description and Readership
Focusing on children and families, this online publication offers articles on issues that affect children including early childhood development, education, health, crime, politics, and volunteering and mentoring. It also includes tips and tools for advocating.
- **Audience:** Children and families
- **Frequency:** Weekly
- **Distribution:** Online
- **Circulation:** Unavailable
- **Website:** www.connectforkids.org

Freelance Potential
25% written by nonstaff writers. Publishes 20–24 freelance submissions yearly; 25% by authors who are new to the magazine.

Submissions
Query. Accepts photocopies, computer printouts, and email to susan@connectforkids.org. SASE. Response times vary.
Articles: 900–1,500 words. Informational articles; profiles; reviews; and photo-essays. Topics include adoption, foster care, the arts, child abuse and neglect, health, child care and early development, kids and politics, community building, learning disabilities, crime and violence prevention, parent involvement in education, development, diversity and awareness, parenting, education, family income and poverty, and volunteering and mentoring.

Sample Issue
Guidelines available at website.
- "Lowering the Voting Age: A Tough Sell." Article reports on a group of teens who worked hard to convince their city council to support a referendum that would lower the voting age to 16.
- Sample dept/column: "Speak Out!" reports on a summer essay contest for teens.

Rights and Payment
All rights. Payment rates and policies vary.

Editor's Comments
We are currently looking for stories dealing with early childhood development and care, environmental issues that affect kids, and juvenile justice. Please note that we are not looking for over-broad "issue" stories with no compelling central person/program, or parenting topics, as we are seeing too many of these.

Connecticut Parent

Suite 18
420 East Main Street
Branford, CT 06405

Editor & Publisher: Joel MacClaren

Description and Readership
Parents living in Connecticut receive this resourceful magazine free of charge. Each issue is packed with articles on all aspects of parenting, as well as information on regional events, programs, and schools.
- **Audience:** Parents
- **Frequency:** Monthly
- **Distribution:** 95% controlled; 5% subscription
- **Circulation:** 50,000
- **Website:** www.ctparent.com

Freelance Potential
20% written by nonstaff writers. Publishes 36 freelance submissions yearly; 25% by unpublished writers. Receives 50 unsolicited mss monthly.

Submissions
Send complete ms. Accepts photocopies, and computer printouts. SASE. Response time varies.
Articles: 500–1,000 words. Self-help articles; profiles; and interviews. Topics include parenting, regional news, family relationships, social issues, education, special education, health, fitness, entertainment, and travel.
Depts/columns: 600 words. Family news, new product information, and media reviews.

Sample Issue
92 pages (60% advertising): 4 articles; 5 depts/columns. Sample copy, $5 with 9x12 SASE. Writers' guidelines available.
- "Camp Decisions." Article discusses at what age you should send young children to sleep away camp.
- "Family Travel." Article takes a look at different family-friendly vacation destinations in the Bahamas.
- Sample dept/column: "Small Talk" tells of a St. Patrick's Day classic race in Fairfield, Connecticut.

Rights and Payment
One-time rights. All material, payment rates vary. Pays on publication. Provides 1 contributor's tearsheet.

Editor's Comments
We welcome ideas for articles related to parenting topics such as education, health, and marriage. Material should be fresh and relevant to our target audience, parents of children prenatal to age twelve. We are also looking for family-friendly travel pieces, as well as crafts, recipes, and activities for children. When possible, photos should accompany articles. Your cover letter should include your degree and area of expertise.

Connecticut's County Kids

877 Post Road East
Westport, CT 06880

Editor: Linda Greco

Description and Readership
This local resource for parents of children in Fairfield and New Haven counties in Connecticut provides useful information on growth and development, education, parenting, and local activities.
- **Audience:** Parents
- **Frequency:** Monthly
- **Distribution:** 99% controlled; 1% subscription
- **Circulation:** 32,000
- **Website:** www.countykids.com

Freelance Potential
85% written by nonstaff writers. Publishes 70 freelance submissions yearly; 2% by unpublished writers, 20% by authors who are new to the magazine. Receives 150 queries and unsolicited mss monthly.

Submissions
Query or send complete ms. Prefers email submissions to countykids@ctcentral.com. Accepts photocopies. Responds only if interested.
Articles: 600–1,200 words. Informational articles; profiles; and personal experience pieces. Topics include nature, animals, arts and crafts, ethnic subjects, and sports.
Depts/columns: 500–800 words. Parenting, pediatric health issues, child growth and development, and family issues.

Sample Issue
48 pages (50% advertising): 11 articles; 10 depts/columns, 1 special section. Sample copy, free with 10x13 SASE. Writers' guidelines and editorial calendar available.
- "Money Saving Tips for Your Child's Wardrobe." Article offers frugal tips concerning children's clothing.
- "Inside the Heart and Head of Single Dads." Article looks at the unique challenges and rewards of being a single father.
- Sample dept/column: "Active Family" offers ideas on how to spark a child's interest in gardening.

Rights and Payment
First rights. Written material, $.05 per word. Artwork, payment rate varies. Pays on publication. Provides 2 contributor's copies.

Editor's Comments
Currently we are looking for articles that deal with issues surrounding homeschooling, kids' fashion, and sibling rivalry.

The Conqueror

United Pentecostal Church International
8855 Dunn Road
Hazelwood, MO 63042-2299

Editor: Shay Mann

Description and Readership
Inspirational articles and stories that focus on spiritual growth and development can be found in this publication for young adults. It also includes missionary-related stories and current events.
- **Audience:** 12–18 years
- **Frequency:** 6 times each year
- **Distribution:** 80% churches; 20% subscription
- **Circulation:** 5,200
- **Website:** http://pentecostalyouth.org

Freelance Potential
95% written by nonstaff writers. Publishes 55 freelance submissions yearly; 5% by unpublished writers, 5% by authors who are new to the magazine. Receives 10 unsolicited mss monthly.

Submissions
Send complete ms. Accepts photocopies, computer printouts, and simultaneous submissions if identified. SASE. Responds in 3 months.
Articles: Features. 1,200–1,800 words. Shorter articles, 600–800 words. Personal experience pieces and profiles. Topics include religion, missionary-related subjects, spiritual growth, social issues, and current events.
Fiction: 600–900 words. Real-life fiction with Christian themes. Genres include humor and romance.
Depts/columns: Word lengths vary. Book and music reviews; opinion and first-person pieces by teens; and reports on church events.

Sample Issue
16 pages (11% advertising): 4 articles; 1 story; 5 depts/columns; 1 quiz. Sample copy, free with 9x12 SASE (2 first-class stamps). Guidelines available.
- "His Glory His Way." Article discusses putting our way aside and letting God show His glory His way.
- "The Dragon Fly." Story features a water beetle that changes into a beautiful blue-tailed butterfly.
- Sample dept/column: "God Speaks" offers a poem reflecting on God's never ending love.

Rights and Payment
All rights. All material, $15–$50. Pays on publication. Provides 1 contributor's copy.

Editor's Comments
We favor descriptive writing that uses active verbs and modern language. Use anecdotes and illustrations. Show what you mean rather than just telling it.

Countdown for Kids

Juvenile Diabetes Research Foundation
19th Floor
120 Wall Street
New York, NY 10005

Editor: Rachel Lewinson

Description and Readership
Published by the Juvenile Diabetes Research Foundation, *Countdown for Kids* appears in conjunction with *Countdown for a Cure* and provides inspirational and informative articles for tweens and teens dignosed with Type 1 diabetes.
• **Audience:** 12+ years
• **Frequency:** Quarterly
• **Distribution:** Subscription; other
• **Circulation:** Unavailable
• **Website:** www.jdrf.org

Freelance Potential
25% written by nonstaff writers. Publishes 25 freelance submissions yearly.

Submissions
Query or send complete ms. Accepts photocopies and computer printouts. SASE. Response time varies.
Articles: Word length varies. Informational, factual, and self-help articles; profiles; interviews; and personal experience pieces. Topics include coping with Type 1 diabetes, health, fitness, careers, college, popular culture, social issues, and diabetes research.
Depts/columns: Word length varies. Diabetes news; career profiles; advice.

Sample Issue
16 pages (1% advertising): 4 articles; 2 depts/columns. Sample copy available.
• "Don't Pick on Me!" Article explains that having diabetes can make kids vulnerable to teasing and explains ways they can protect themselves.
• "Why Your Body Thrives on Exercise." Article points out the many benefits of exercising.
• Sample dept/column: "Fun Stuff" features recipes and profiles of interesting people.

Rights and Payment
First North American serial rights. All material, payment rates vary. Pays on publication. Provides 1 contributor's copy.

Editor's Comments
We need uplifting articles that deal with the social and practical issues of living with diabetes. We like to see material that kids can relate to, with a specific relevance to what they deal with on a day-to-day basis living with Type 1 diabetes. Articles that inspire community involvement and provide hope are what we are looking for.

Cousteau Kids

The Cousteau Society
710 Settlers Landing Road
Hampton, VA 23669-4035

Editor: Melissa Norkin

Description and Readership
To meet its goal of educating children about the world's oceans and the forms of life found there, this magazine features information on all areas of science that relate to the global water system.
• **Audience:** 8–12 years
• **Frequency:** 6 times each year
• **Distribution:** 100% membership
• **Circulation:** 80,000
• **Website:** www.cousteaukids.org

Freelance Potential
10% written by nonstaff writers. Publishes 4 freelance submissions yearly; 50% by authors who are new to the magazine. Receives 4 queries monthly.

Submissions
Query. Accepts photocopies, computer printouts, and simultaneous submissions if identified. SASE. Responds only if interested.
Articles: 400–600 words. Shorter pieces, to 250 words. Informational articles. Topics include unique aquatic organisms, underwater habitats, ocean phenomena, the environment, and the physical properties of water.
Depts/columns: Staff written.
Artwork: Color slides.
Other: Games based on scientific fact, original science experiments, and art projects related to an ocean theme.

Sample Issue
22 pages (no advertising): 5 articles; 1 comic strip; 2 quizzes; 2 depts/columns. Sample copy, $2 with 9x12 SASE (3 first-class stamps). Guidelines available.
• "On the Road to Antarctica." Article follows the first leg of Jacques Cousteau's historic trip to explore Antarctica.
• "Cuttlefishes." Article looks at an unusual invertebrate of the ocean.

Rights and Payment
One-time and reprint rights; worldwide translation rights for use in other Cousteau Society publications. Articles, $100–$300. Shorter pieces, $15–$100. Pays on publication. Provides 3 contributor's copies.

Editor's Comments
We want to instill a sense of environmental awareness in our readers so that they will become advocates of the oceans and their ecosystems.

Creative Kids

Prufrock Press
P.O. Box 8813
Waco, TX 76714

Editor: Jenny Robins

Description and Readership
Written by and for children, this publication includes stories, poetry, artwork, activities, and articles. All work is submitted by students or their teachers.
- **Audience:** 6–14 years
- **Frequency:** Quarterly
- **Distribution:** Subscription; schools
- **Circulation:** 3,600
- **Website:** www.prufrock.com

Freelance Potential
97% written by nonstaff writers. Publishes 150 freelance submissions yearly; 95% by unpublished writers, 80% by authors who are new to the magazine. Receives 500 unsolicited mss monthly.

Submissions
Send complete ms. Accepts photocopies, and computer printouts. Availability of artwork improves chance of acceptance. SASE. Responds in 4–6 weeks.
Articles: 800–900 words. Informational, self-help, and how-to articles; humor; photo-essays; and personal experience pieces. Topics include animals, pets, social issues, sports, travel, and gifted education.
Fiction: 800–900 words. Genres include real-life and problem-solving stories; inspirational, historical, and multicultural fiction; mystery; suspense; folktales; humor; and stories about sports and animals.
Artwork: B/W and color prints and transparencies. Line art on 8½x11 white paper.
Other: Poetry, songs, word puzzles, games, and cartoons. Submit seasonal material 1 year in advance.

Sample Issue
34 pages (no advertising): 5 articles; 6 depts/columns; 12 poems; 8 games. Guidelines available.
- "Wild Winter Weekend." Essay shares the author's memory of a weekend of weird winter weather.
- "Mister Socks." Essay recalls a boy's love for his wonderful cat.
- "Tom's Great Escape." Story tells how a turkey escapes from a farm where he was to be the Thanksgiving turkey.

Rights and Payment
Rights vary. No payment. Provides 3–4 copies.

Editor's Comments
We continue to seek high-quality work from students ages 8 to 14 including poetry, games, activities, artwork, photographs, and original stories.

Cricket

Cricket Magazine Group
P.O. Box 300
315 5th Street
Peru, IL 61354

Submissions Editor

Description and Readership
The pages of this fun magazine for children and young teens offer a collection of folktales, adventures, fantasy, nonfiction, poems, and crafts.
- **Audience:** 9–14 years
- **Frequency:** Monthly
- **Distribution:** 92% subscription; 8% newsstand
- **Circulation:** 70,000
- **Website:** www.cricketmag.com

Freelance Potential
100% written by nonstaff writers. Publishes 150 freelance submissions yearly; 30% by unpublished writers, 50% by new authors. Receives 1,000 mss monthly.

Submissions
Send ms; include bibliography for nonfiction. Accepts photocopies, computer printouts, and simultaneous submissions. SASE. Responds in 2–3 months.
Articles: 200–1,500 words. Informational and how-to articles; biographies; and profiles. Topics include science, technology, history, social science, archaeology, architecture, geography, foreign culture, travel, adventure, and sports.
Fiction: 200–2,000 words. Genres include humor, mystery, fantasy, science fiction, folktales, fairy tales, mythology, and historical and contemporary fiction.
Depts/columns: Staff written.
Other: Poetry, to 25 lines. Puzzles, games, crafts, recipes, and science experiments; word length varies.

Sample Issue
64 pages (no advertising): 8 stories; 1 serial; 4 poems; 1 puzzle. Sample copy, $5 with 9x12 SASE. Writers' guidelines available.
- "Dust from a Cat's Tail." Story tells of how a poor boy tricks a jeweler and ends up wealthy from the gold dust he collects from a cat's tail.
- "Old Sultan." Story tells of an old cat who plans a scheme with a wolf to get on his owner's good side.
- "Elijah the Cat." Story details how a cat brings together two old friends during Passover.

Rights and Payment
Rights vary. Articles and fiction, to $.25 per word. Poetry, to $3 per line. Pays on publication. Provides 6 contributor's copies.

Editor's Comments
We would like to see more humorous contemporary fiction and contemporary multicultural fiction.

Crinkles

3401 Stockwell Street
Lincoln, NE 68506

Managing Editor: Deborah Levitov

Description and Readership
Crinkles is designed to stimulate a child's curiosity about people, places, things, and events. Each issue includes articles with accompanying activities such as paper figures, word puzzles, and models.
- **Audience:** 7–11 years
- **Frequency:** 6 times each year
- **Distribution:** 100% subscription
- **Circulation:** 6,000
- **Website:** www.crinkles.com

Freelance Potential
70% written by nonstaff writers. Publishes 2–3 freelance submissions yearly; 30% by authors who are new to the magazine. Receives 3 queries monthly.

Submissions
Query with résumé. Accepts computer printouts and email queries to deborah.levitov@lu.com. SASE. Responds in 1 month.
Articles: Word lengths vary. Informational, factual, and how-to articles. Topics include history, culture, multicultural and ethnic subjects, social issues, science, animals, nature, the environment, the arts, and sports.
Other: Puzzles, games, and crafts.

Sample Issue
48 pages (no advertising): 13 articles; 13 activities. Guidelines available.
- "Zebras." Informative article tells about the different types of zebras and their habitat; includes a maze.
- "Beautiful Daughters, Snakes, and Spirits Galore." Article retells a Zimbabwe folktale about a girl and a a special snake; includes paper dolls and a list of websites to learn more about Zimbabwe.
- "Black & White Photography." Article explains how photography works; includes a picture to color in shades of gray.

Rights and Payment
All rights. Written material, $150. Payment policy varies. Provides contributor's copies upon request.

Editor's Comments
We want material that makes more "crinkles" in a child's brain. Most of our authors are leaders in the field of education. If you fit the bill, send us your idea for a well-researched article and hands-on activities that will develop the reader's skills in critical thinking, independent research, and study skills.

Current Health 1

Weekly Reader Publishing
P.O. Box 120023
200 First Stamford Place
Stamford, CT 06912-0023

Editor: Jessica Cohn

Description and Readership
In print since 1977, this magazine is used as part of the health curriculum for students in grades five through seven. It covers topics such as nutrition, safety, and drug awareness.
- **Audience:** Grades 5–7
- **Frequency:** 8 times each year
- **Distribution:** 100% schools
- **Circulation:** 163,793
- **Website:** www.weeklyreader.com\ch1

Freelance Potential
90% written by nonstaff writers. Publishes 50 freelance submissions yearly; 30% by authors who are new to the magazine.

Submissions
All articles are assigned. Query with letter of introduction; list of areas of expertise, publishing credits, and clips. Accepts email queries to currenthealth@ weeklyreader.com. No unsolicited mss. Responds in 1–4 months.
Articles: 850–2,000 words. Informational articles about subjects related to middle-grade health curriculum. Topics include health, fitness, safety, first aid, nutrition, disease, drug education, psychology, and relationships.
Depts/columns: Activities, Q&A, and health updates.

Sample Issue
32 pages (no advertising): 7 articles; 4 depts/columns. Sample copy available. Guidelines provided upon agreement.
- "Beat the Cold." Article discusses why it is important to dress wisely during the winter and offers tips for recognizing frostbite and hypothermia.
- "Mean Screens." Article takes a look at the problem of developing eye problems from playing video and computer games.
- Sample dept/column: "Pulse" tells of a virus that attacks koalas in Austrialia and nearsightedness in guide dogs.

Rights and Payment
All rights. Articles, $150+. Provides 2 author's copies.

Editor's Comments
We look for material that uses current news to make topics relevant to students, and helps them make the right health choices and resist peer pressure. Please note that our articles are written on assignment only.

Current Health 2

Weekly Reader Publishing
P.O. Box 120023
200 First Stamford Place
Stamford, CT 06912-0023

Editor: Anne Flounders

Description and Readership

Offered as a supplement to the health education curriculum of junior and high school students, this magazine covers topics such as nutrition, psychology, human sexuality, and substance abuse.
- **Audience:** Grades 7–12 years
- **Frequency:** 8 times each year
- **Distribution:** 100% schools
- **Circulation:** 195,000
- **Website:** www.weeklyreader.com\ch2.

Freelance Potential

90% written by nonstaff writers. Publishes 50 freelance submissions yearly; 30% by authors who are new to the magazine. Receives 5 queries monthly.

Submissions

Query with letter of introduction listing areas of expertise, publishing credits, and clips. Accepts email queries to currenthealth@weeklyreader.com. No unsolicited mss. Responds in 1–4 months.
Articles: 900–2,500 words. Informational articles on subjects related to the middle school and high school curricula. Topics include fitness, exercise, nutrition, disease, psychology, first-aid, safety, human sexuality, and drug education.
Depts/columns: Word lengths vary. Health updates and Q&A on health-related issues.

Sample Issue

30 pages (1% advertising): 9 articles; 4 depts/columns. Sample copy available. Guidelines provided upon assignment.
- "Hurts So Bad." Article discusses the problems and reasons behind self-injury.
- "The Facts of Lunch." Article takes a look at the importance of reading the nutrition facts label on packages.
- Sample dept/column: "Speak Up" offers pros and cons of gastric bypass surgery.

Rights and Payment

All rights. Articles, $150+. Pays on publication. Provides 2 contributor's copies.

Editor's Comments

We look for articles and news on health related issues that will provide our readers with the information they need to make wise choices when it comes to their health. Make sure your writing style matches our target audience of preteens and teens.

Current Science

Weekly Reader Corporation
200 First Stamford Place
P.O. Box 120023
Stamford, CT 06912-0023

Managing Editor: Hugh Westrup

Description and Readership

This magazine uses current news to make science more relevant to students in grades six through ten. Each issue covers an aspect of the science curriculum, from life, earth, and physical science to health and technology.
- **Audience:** 11–17 years
- **Frequency:** 16 times each year
- **Distribution:** 100% schools
- **Circulation:** 1 million
- **Website:** www.weeklyreader.com/features.cs.html

Freelance Potential

40% written by nonstaff writers. Publishes 30 freelance submissions yearly; 10% by authors who are new to the magazine. Receives 2 queries monthly.

Submissions

Query with résumé. No unsolicited mss. Availability of artwork improves chance of acceptance. SASE. Response time varies.
Articles: Word length varies. Informational articles. Topics include nature, science, the environment, technology, animals, physics, and earth science.
Depts/columns: Word length varies. Science-related news and Q&A.
Artwork: Color prints.
Other: Science-related photos, trivia, and puzzles.

Sample Issue

16 pages (no advertising): 3 articles; 3 depts/columns. Sample copy, free with 9x12 SASE.
- "Wave Action." Article explains the theory of energy behind bodysurfing.
- "Cell Division." Article describes the moral implications of stem cell research, and its alternatives.
- Sample dept/column: "Discoveries" covers a rare liver condition, musical "bloom boxes," and paper made from roo poo.

Rights and Payment

All rights. Written material, payment rates vary. Pays on acceptance. Provides contributor's copies.

Editor's Comments

We want dynamic nonfiction material that engages students, reinforces the science curriculum, increases student performance, and helps teachers meet state and national standards. Freelance writers are encouraged to send us queries for inquiry-based learning activities that make science come alive.

Curriculum Review

The Dabbling Mum

Paperclip Communications
125 Patterson Avenue
Little Falls, NJ 07424

Editor: Frank Sennett

9919 Marilyn Collins Way
Knoxville, TN 37931

Editor: Alyice Edrich

Description and Readership
Up-to-date news, trends in education, textbook reviews, and other teaching resources and strategies can be found in this professional educators' newsletter. It covers elementary through high school education and provides information from around the U.S.
• **Audience:** Teachers and school administrators
• **Frequency:** 9 times each year
• **Distribution:** 100% subscription
• **Circulation:** 5,000
• **Website:** www.curriculumreview.com or www.paper-clip.com

Description and Readership
This Christian online magazine is a positive publication geared toward helping busy parents balance their lives by offering inspiring, encouraging, true-to-life articles and stories.
• **Audience:** Parents
• **Frequency:** Monthly
• **Circulation:** 23,000 hits per month
• **Website:** www.thedabblingmum.com

Freelance Potential
2% written by nonstaff writers. Publishes 10 freelance submissions yearly. Receives 2 mss monthly.

Freelance Potential
90% written by nonstaff writers. Publishes 48–120 freelance submissions yearly; 40% by unpublished writers, 60% by authors who are new to the magazine. Receives 100 queries monthly.

Submissions
Send complete ms. Responds in 1 month.
Articles: To 4,000 words. Informational articles; resource reviews; and conference reports. Teaching techniques and classroom ideas, to 500 words.
Depts/columns: Word length varies. Short news items about educational programs and practices; interviews with educators and administrators.

Submissions
Query with samples. Accepts online submissions only. Responds in 4–8 weeks.
Articles: 500–1,500 words. Informational and how-to articles; and personal experience pieces. Topics include family life, parenting, women's issues, home businesses, Christian living, marriage, entertainment, education, child development, teen issues, and contemporary social concerns.

Sample Issue
16 pages (no advertising): 7 articles; 8 depts/columns. Sample copy, free with 9x12 SASE (2 first-class stamps).
• "What's Working in Education?" Article offers activities to help jumpstart learning excitement in the classroom and break out of the usual routines.
• "Delivering Breakfast on the Go." Article reports on a school in Pennsylvania that offers kids a breakfast cart before school starts.
• Sample dept/column: "Socialstudious" tells of a teacher who follows a dog-sled race in Alaska and posts race-related lesson plans on the Web.

Sample Issue
7 articles; 1 story. Sample copy, free at website. Writers' guidelines available.
• "Chit Chat." Article tells about a mom who is facing the fact her children are growing up.
• "For the Love of Bobby." First-person story describes the joy and fulfillment of volunteering.
• "Something to Teach, Something to Learn." Feature article tells of a parent who learned to trust God's teachings more often.

Rights and Payment
One-time rights. Written material, payment rates vary. Provides contributor's copies.

Rights and Payment
Three-month online rights; indefinite archival rights. Written material, $20–$30. Pays on publication.

Editor's Comments
Articles should be written in a journalistic style. Please avoid overly academic language. Fresh material that provides hands-on activities that can be easily applied to the classroom are welcome. Most of our freelance contributions come from writers with educational backgrounds.

Editor's Comments
We want to help our readers be better parents, build successful businesses, and form closer relationships with our Lord. We need articles that provide honest, helpful answers that our readers can put to use immediately. Try to write your material in a conversational tone with a journalistic twist, and make instructions easy to follow. New writers will have the best luck with a submission of a recipe or story.

Dallas Child

Lauren Publications
Suite 146
4275 Kellway Circle
Addison, TX 75001

Editor: Shelley Hawes Pate

Description and Readership
Emphasizing stories pertinent to the Dallas metropolitan area, this magazine includes articles on local issues and resources, as well as profiles and interviews with regional personalities.
- **Audience:** Parents
- **Frequency:** Monthly
- **Distribution:** 90% controlled; 10% subscription
- **Circulation:** 80,000
- **Website:** www.dallaschild.com

Freelance Potential
50% written by nonstaff writers. Publishes 10–20 freelance submissions yearly; 20% by authors who are new to the magazine. Receives 33 queries monthly.

Submissions
Query with résumé. Accepts photocopies, computer printouts, and simultaneous submissions if identified. SASE. Responds in 2–3 months.
Articles: 1,000–2,000 words. Informational and how-to articles; personal experience and self-help pieces; profiles; interviews; and humor. Topics include parenting, education, child development, family travel, regional news, recreation, entertainment, current events, social issues, multicultural and ethnic subjects, health, fitness, and crafts.
Depts/columns: 800 words. Local events, travel, and health news.

Sample Issue
92 pages (14% advertising): 7 articles; 2 depts/columns. Sample copy, free with 9x12 SASE. Guidelines available.
- "Have to Give You Credit." Article explains Texas Child and Dependent Care Credits, and how they affect working families.
- "Cut Through the Red Tape." Informative article supplies website addresses for state and local government offices.

Rights and Payment
First rights. Written material, payment rates vary. Pays on publication. Provides contributor's copies upon request.

Editor's Comments
We prefer to work with writers from the Metroplex area. Parenting is important to our readers, so give them what they want—information and ideas about raising a family, what to do, and where to go.

Dallas Teen

Lauren Publication
Suite 146
4275 Kellway Circle
Addison, TX 75001

Submissions Editor: Shelly Hawes Pate

Description and Readership
Distributed free to families with teenagers in the Dallas, Texas area, this magazine offers articles on issues related to parenting teens, as well as activities that strengthen relationships and communication between teens and parents.
- **Audience:** Parents and teens
- **Frequency:** Quarterly
- **Distribution:** Controlled; subscription
- **Circulation:** Unavailable
- **Website:** www.dallaschild.com

Freelance Potential
60% written by nonstaff writers. Publishes 12–15 freelance submissions yearly; 20% by authors who are new to the magazine. Receives 20 queries monthly.

Submissions
Query with résumé. Accepts photocopies and computer printouts. SASE. Responds in 2–3 months. Writers' guidelines available.
Articles: 1,000–2,500 words. Informational articles; profiles; and personal experience pieces. Topics include gifted education, health and fitness, recreation, regional news, social issues, and sports.
Depts/columns: 800 words. Health news and media reviews.

Sample Issue
46 pages (15% advertising): 7 articles; 6 depts/columns. Sample copy, free. Guidelines available.
- "Frank Talk about Teens and Sex." Article discusses keeping communication open when discussing boys and sex to teenage girls.
- "Who's Watching Your Teen Online?" Article takes a look at the dangers of online chat lines and installing monitoring software.
- Sample dept/column: "College Planner" discusses grade-level planning for college.

Rights and Payment
First rights. Written material, payment rates vary. Pays on publication.

Editor's Comments
Our readers include parents of teens as well as teenagers. We continue to seek media reviews and articles on topics related to health, education, and parenting issues. Also, activities that promote strengthening family relationships and keeping the lines of communication flowing are on our want list.

Dance Magazine

11th Floor
333 7th Avenue
New York, NY 10001

Editor-in-Chief: Wendy Perron

Description and Readership
Published for dancers of all ages, this magazine features articles on dance, interviews of dancers and dance companies, and news of dance-related events.
- **Audience:** YA-Adult
- **Frequency:** Monthly
- **Distribution:** Subscription; newsstand
- **Circulation:** 75,000
- **Website:** www.dancemagazine.com

Freelance Potential
75% written by nonstaff writers. Publishes 25 freelance submissions yearly; 20% by unpublished writers, 50% by authors who are new to the magazine. Receives 83 queries and unsolicited mss monthly.

Submissions
Query or send complete ms. Accepts photocopies and computer printouts. SASE. Response time varies.
Articles: Word lengths vary. Informational articles; profiles; and interviews. Topics include dance, dance instruction, choreography, the arts, family, and health concerns.
Fiction: To 4,000 words. Ethnic and multicultural fiction related to dance.
Depts/columns: Word lengths vary. New product information, reviews, dance news, and instruction.

Sample Issue
104 pages (33% advertising): 6 articles; 13 depts/columns. Sample copy, $4.95 with 9x12 SASE. Guidelines available.
- "The Heat Is On." Article profiles the dance work of Hubbard Street Dance Chicago.
- "Meet Your Maker." Article discusses the symbiotic relationship between ballerinas and the makers of dance shoes.
- Sample dept/column: "Transitions" covers recent news in the world of dance, including retirements, deaths, and births.

Rights and Payment
Rights negotiable. Written material, $.30 per word. Payment policy varies.

Editor's Comments
We need material that appeals to all types of dancers, and to those who have a passion for dance. New writers are encouraged to contribute a piece on young dancers who are proving to be extraordinary contributors to the dance world.

Dance Teacher

Lifestyle Media, Inc.
Floor 23
110 William Street
New York, NY 10038

Senior Editor: Katia Bachko

Description and Readership
This resource for dance educators, students, and studio owners offers teaching techniques, management tips, health and exercise advice, business ideas, and information on costume and shoe design.
- **Audience:** Dance teachers and students
- **Frequency:** Monthly
- **Distribution:** 100% subscription
- **Circulation:** 20,000
- **Website:** www.dance-teacher.com

Freelance Potential
50% written by nonstaff writers. Publishes 75 freelance submissions yearly; 10% by unpublished writers, 15% by authors who are new to the magazine. Receives 12 queries monthly.

Submissions
Query. Accepts computer printouts, email submissions to kbachko@lifestylemedia.com. Availability of artwork improves chance of acceptance. SASE. Responds in 2 months.
Articles: 1,000–2,000 words. How-to articles; profiles; and personal experience pieces. Topics include dance education, nutrition, health, publicity, and management as it relates to dance businesses.
Depts/columns: 700–1,200 words. Media reviews and news from the dance world.
Artwork: Slides, transparencies, and prints; prefers color, accepts B/W.

Sample Issue
120 pages (50% advertising): 8 articles; 16 depts/columns. Sample copy, free with 9x12 SASE ($1.37 postage). Guidelines and theme list available.
- "To See or Not to See." Article takes a look at the choices available for allowing parents to observe their children in dance class.
- "Trick or Treat." Article discusses how and when to incorporate acrobatics into dance routines.
- Sample dept/column: "Problem Solved!" offers ideas for thanking devoted students and their parents.

Rights and Payment
All rights. Articles, $200–$300. Depts/columns, $100–$150. Pays on acceptance. Provides 1 contributor's copy.

Editor's Comments
We seek practical ideas for business management, as well as articles on anatomy and health issues.

Dane County Kids

P.O. Box 8457
2001 Fish Hatchery Road
Madison, WI 53708-8457

Editor: Teresa Peneguy Paprock

Description and Readership
This resourceful tabloid offers parents and grandparents living in Madison, Wisconsin, articles and tips on issues relating to parenting. It also includes events and services available in the region.
- **Audience:** Parents
- **Frequency:** Monthly
- **Distribution:** 100% controlled
- **Circulation:** 28,000
- **Website:** www.ericksonpublishing.com

Freelance Potential
80% written by nonstaff writers. Publishes 40 freelance submissions yearly; 70% by authors who are new to the magazine. Receives 20 queries and unsolicited mss monthly.

Submissions
Query or send complete ms. Accepts photocopies, computer printouts, and disk submissions (RTF format). SASE. Response time varies.
Articles: To 1,000 words. Informational articles; personal experience pieces; profiles; and interviews. Topics include parenting, family issues, gifted and special education, multicultural issues, hobbies and crafts, animals, computers, and careers.
Depts/columns: To 750 words. Personal experiences, local school news, health and safety issues, and book reviews.

Sample Issue
26 pages (50% advertising): 17 articles; 6 depts/columns. Sample copy, $2. Guidelines and theme list/editorial calendar available.
- "Options Old and New Abound for Expectant Parents Here." Article discusses the many options for childbirth and support that are available to parents.
- "Family Garden Provides Learning Opportunity." Article discusses the benefits of family gardening.
- Sample dept/column: "Health and Wellness" reports on the dangers of childhood obesity.

Rights and Payment
Rights negotiable. All material, payment rates vary. Pays on publication.

Editor's Comments
Our readers turn to us to keep them up to date on services available in the region. We look for practical articles that focus on issues such as children's health and educational related issues.

Daughters

Suite 200
34 East Superior Street
Duluth, MN 55802

Editor: Helen Cordes

Description and Readership
Published by the national educational and advocacy organization Dads and Daughters, this newsletter provides parents with the tools they need to strengthen relationships with daughters ages nine to sixteen.
- **Audience:** Parents
- **Frequency:** 6 times each year
- **Distribution:** 100% subscription
- **Circulation:** 25,000
- **Website:** www.daughters.com

Freelance Potential
65% written by nonstaff writers. Publishes 10 freelance submissions yearly; 90% by unpublished writers, 10% by authors who are new to the magazine. Receives 2–3 queries and unsolicited mss monthly.

Submissions
Send complete ms for "Mothering Journey" and "Fathering Journey." Query for all other material. Accepts computer printouts and email submissions to editor@daughters.com (Microsoft Word attachments). SASE. Responds in 1–2 months.
Articles: 600 words. Informational and self-help articles; personal experience pieces; profiles; and interviews. Topics include adolescent girls, health, fitness, social issues, body image, sexuality, education, communication, and parenting.
Depts/columns: 375 words. First-person pieces about parenting adolescent girls.

Sample Issue
16 pages (no advertising): 8 articles; 1 interview; 4 depts/columns. Guidelines available.
- "Margo Maine on Mom's Body Influence." Article discusses how mothers can instill a sense of personal body satisfaction in their daughters.
- "When Her Friends Make Bad Choices." Article tells how to help young girls negotiate friendship issues.

Rights and Payment
All rights. Written material, $.30–$.50 per word. Pays on publication. Provides 3 contributor's copies.

Editor's Comments
We want to send our readers the message that we should value our daughters for who they are rather than how they look. We need effective parenting and communication techniques tailored specifically for parents of girls in all stages of adolescence.

Davey and Goliath

Devotions for Families on the Go

Augsburg Fortress Publishers
P.O. Box 1209
Minneapolis, MN 55440-1209

Development Editor: Arlene Flancher

Description and Readership
Targeting Christian families with children ages five through eleven, this publication offers retellings of Bible stories, family prayers, discussion questions, fun Bible activities, prayers, and real-life ideas for sharing faith with others.
- **Audience:** Families
- **Frequency:** Quarterly
- **Distribution:** Subscription
- **Circulation:** 50,000
- **Website:** www.augsburgfortress.org/ag

Freelance Potential
100% written by nonstaff writers. Publishes 30 freelance submissions yearly; 25% by unpublished writers, 75% by authors who are new to the magazine. Receives less than 1 query monthly.

Submissions
Query with 6x9 SASE (2 first-class stamps). All work assigned on a contract basis. Accepts email to dg@augsburgfortress.org. Responds in 1 month.
Articles: 100–125 words. Bible stories; how-to articles on sharing and celebrating the word of God.
Fiction: 100–125 words. Bible stories.
Depts/columns: 500 words. Bible facts, prayers, and activities.
Other: Puzzles, games, and mazes.

Sample Issue
64 pages (15% advertising): 13 Bible stories; 27 activities. Sample copy and guidelines provided free to prospective writers.
- "Baby Moses." Story tells of the birth of Moses, who went on to lead the Hebrew people out of slavery.
- "The Storm at Sea." Story tells of how Jesus stopped a storm that came across the sea.
- Sample dept/column: "Bible Activity" discusses hosting a family game night for friends.

Rights and Payment
All rights. Written material, payment rates vary. Pays on acceptance. Provides 2 contributor's copies.

Editor's Comments
We look for devotions and activities that will allow families to spend time together everyday and share in the word of God in an easy, fun way. If you have an idea for something that fits our needs, send us a query. Please keep in mind that all of our freelance work is done on a contract basis only.

Devo'Zine

1908 Grand Avenue
P.O. Box 340004
Nashville, TN 37203-0004

Editor: Sandy Miller

Description and Readership
Two months worth of devotionals, stories, and prayers are included in each issue of this Christian publication. It helps readers develop a better relationship with God and with each other.
- **Audience:** YA
- **Frequency:** 6 times each year
- **Distribution:** 100% subscription
- **Circulation:** 105,000
- **Website:** www.devozine.org

Freelance Potential
100% written by nonstaff writers. Publishes 378 freelance submissions yearly; 50% by authors who are new to the magazine.

Submissions
Query. Accepts photocopies, computer printouts, disk submissions, email queries to devozine@upperroom.org. SASE. Responds in 4 months.
Articles: 150–500 words. Daily meditations, 150–250 words. Informational articles; personal experience pieces; and profiles. Topics include Christian faith, mentoring, independence, courage, teen parenting, creativity, social issues, and relationships.
Fiction: 150–250 words. Genres include contemporary and inspirational fiction.
Other: Prayers and poetry, 10–20 lines. Submit seasonal material 6–8 months in advance.

Sample Issue
64 pages (no advertising): 62 devotionals. Sample copy, $3.90. Guidelines and theme list available.
- "A New Perspective." Devotional teaches how a relationship with God can offer a new outlook on life.
- "Agents on Assignment." Devotional helps readers reflect on how their work helps the Lord.
- "Prayer Changes." Devotional discusses how prayer changes the one who prays.

Rights and Payment
First and second rights. Features, $100. Meditations, $25. Pays on acceptance.

Editor's Comments
Our magazine consists mostly of daily devotionals for our readers to help them strengthen their faith and belief in God. Freelance writers should also have strong faith in Christ, and be able to write for a young-adult audience. Personal experience pieces about personal growth are needed.

Dig

Suite C
Cobblestone Publishing
30 Grove Street
Peterborough, NH 03458

Editor: Rosalie F. Baker

Description and Readership
This magazine geared to archaeology for middle-grade students makes digging for facts and history fascinating and fun. Each issue relates to a specific theme and explores many aspects relating to it.
- **Audience:** 9–14 years
- **Frequency:** 9 times each year
- **Distribution:** Subscription; newsstand
- **Circulation:** 19,000
- **Website:** www.cobblestonepub.com

Freelance Potential
80% written by nonstaff writers. Publishes 40 freelance submissions yearly; 40% by unpublished writers, 60% by authors who are new to the magazine. Receives 8 queries monthly.

Submissions
All submissions must relate to an upcoming theme. Query with outline, bibliography, and clips or writing samples. SASE. Responds in 4 months.
Articles: Word length varies. Informational articles and photo essays. Topics include nature, animals, science, and technology.
Fiction: Word length varies. Stories related to the theme of each issue.
Depts/columns: Word length varies. Art, archaeology facts, quizzes, and projects.

Sample Issue
34 pages (no advertising): 8 articles; 6 depts/columns; 4 activities. Sample copy, $4.95 at newsstands. Guidelines and theme list available.
- "Long March to Taipei." Article reenacts the transference of China's imperial art collection from the Forbidden City in Beijing to the Taipei Palace Museum in Taiwan that took 32 years to complete.
- "War in the First Cities." Article traces the origins of war to the first civilized cities and shows how war strategies developed through the years.
- Sample dept/column: "Stones & Bones" explores ancient artifacts and what they meant.

Rights and Payment
First rights. Pays on publication. Written material, $.20–$.25 per word. Provides 2 contributor's copies.

Editor's Comments
Become familiar with our publication's style and how each issue's material is interrelated. If you're interested in writing for us, please send for a theme list.

Dimensions

1908 Association Drive
Reston, VA 20191

Editor: Traci Molnar

Description and Readership
High school students interested in marketing, management, and entrepreneurship read this magazine for its coverage of the business world, as well as articles on leadership development, communication skills, community service, and preparing for college.
- **Audience:** 14–18 years
- **Frequency:** Quarterly
- **Distribution:** Subscription; membership
- **Circulation:** 180,000
- **Website:** www.deca.org

Freelance Potential
60% written by nonstaff writers. Publishes 9 freelance submissions yearly; 50% by unpublished writers, 50% by authors who are new to the magazine.

Submissions
Query or send complete ms with short author bio. Accepts photocopies, computer printouts, Macintosh disk submissions (RFT files), simultaneous submissions if identified, and email submissions to traci–molnar @deca.org. SASE. Response time varies.
Articles: 800–1,200 words. Informational and how-to articles; profiles; interviews; and personal experience pieces. Topics include general business, management, marketing trends (domestic and international), sales, ethics, leadership development, entrepreneurship, franchising, personal finance, advertising, e-commerce, technology, careers, college admissions, and school-to-work incentives.
Depts/columns: 400–600 words. DECA chapter news and short business news items.

Sample Issue
24 pages (45% advertising): 7 articles; 5 depts/columns. Sample copy, free with 9x12 SASE. Writers' guidelines available.
- "Get Ready for Your New Life Now." Article discusses important things to consider during the months before starting college.
- Sample dept/column: "Short Stuff" offers information on a tattoo pen and a three-wheeled vehicle.

Rights and Payment
First North American serial rights. Written material, payment rates vary. Pays on publication.

Editor's Comments
Practical articles on dressing professionally are of interest to us. Please write in a conversational tone.

Dimensions of Early Childhood

Southern Early Childhood Association
P.O. Box 55930
Little Rock, AR 72215-5930

Dimensions Manager: Jennifer Bean

Description and Readership
Designed to foster the professional growth of individuals working with young children and their families, this journal seeks to enhance the quality of children's lives through early care and education.
- **Audience:** Early childhood professionals
- **Frequency:** Quarterly
- **Distribution:** 100% subscription
- **Circulation:** 19,000
- **Website:** www.southernearlychildhood.org

Freelance Potential
99% written by nonstaff writers. Publishes 40 freelance submissions yearly; 90% by unpublished writers, 80% by authors who are new to the magazine. Receives 7 unsolicited mss monthly.

Submissions
Send 4 copies of complete ms with bibliography. Prefers email submissions to melissa@southernearlychildhood.org. Accepts photocopies and disk submissions. SASE. Responds in 3–4 months.
Articles: Word length varies. Informational articles. Topics include emergent curriculum for children, effective classroom practices, theory and research, program administration, family relationships, and resource systems.
Depts/columns: Word length varies. Book reviews, support strategies, and SECA updates.

Sample Issue
40 pages (20% advertising): 5 articles; 4 depts/columns. Sample copy, $5. Guidelines available.
- "Build Trust with Diverse Families and Communities." Article discusses how to build greater trust among teachers, families, and communities.
- "Scaffolding Play for English Language Learners." Article uses examples to demonstrate using pretend play to encourage players to communicate.
- Sample dept/column: "Strategies to Support Children" takes a look at play re-enactments.

Rights and Payment
All rights. No payment. Provides 1 contributor's copy.

Editor's Comments
We seek material that addresses both the continuing interests of early childhood professionals and emerging ideas and issues in the field. We occasionally publish theme issues that address timely, critical topics related to early childhood education.

Dogs for Kids

P.O. Box 6050
Mission Viejo, CA 92690-6050

Managing Editor: Roger Sipe

Description and Readership
This magazine for young dog owners and enthusiasts offers information on all aspects of dog care, from health and nutrition to training and traveling with a pet in tow. Young readers can learn about proper pet care and how to be a responsible owner, while enjoying colorful photos and interesting articles.
- **Audience:** 10–15 years
- **Frequency:** Quarterly
- **Distribution:** Subscription; newsstand
- **Circulation:** Unavailable
- **Website:** www.dogsforkids.com

Freelance Potential
50% written by nonstaff writers. Publishes 15–25 freelance submissions yearly; 20% by authors who are new to the magazine. Receives 100 queries monthly.

Submissions
Query with writing samples. Accepts photocopies and computer printouts. SASE. Responds in 8–10 weeks.
Articles: 1,200–1,800 words. Informational and how-to articles; profiles; photo essays; and personal experience pieces. Topics include animals and pets.
Depts/columns: To 650 words. Tips on dog behavior, health, breeds, nutrition, and new products.
Other: Puzzles, activities, and games.

Sample Issue
48 pages (10% advertising): 6 articles; 11 depts/columns; 7 breed reviews. Sample copy, $2.99 with 9x12 SASE. Guidelines available.
- "Walk This Way." Article reminds readers to keep safety in mind while walking their dogs.
- "The Agility Biz." Article profiles a Texan dog trainer who got the idea for her business from house sitting.
- Sample dept/column: "K9 Kitchen" offers ideas for making tasty canine treats.

Rights and Payment
First rights. All material, payment rates vary. Pays on publication. Provides 2 contributor's copies.

Editor's Comments
We are interested in material that offers training tips, information on volunteering, nutrition and recipes for dogs, and profiles of working dogs. All articles must be written in an upbeat tone that appeals to our 10- to 15-year-old readers, but keep in mind that they are knowledgeable about dogs.

Dovetail

A Journal By and For Jewish/Christian Families

775 Simon Greenwell Lane
Boston, KY 40107

Editor: Debi Tenner

Description and Readership
This publication explores the spiritual and religious dimensions of an interfaith household, and provides readers with educational and networking venues and opportunities.
- **Audience:** Interfaith families
- **Frequency:** 6 times each year
- **Distribution:** Subscription; other
- **Circulation:** 500
- **Website:** www.dovetailinstitute.org

Freelance Potential
80% written by nonstaff writers. Publishes 18 freelance submissions yearly; 90% by unpublished writers, 80% by authors who are new to the magazine. Receives 4 queries and unsolicited mss monthly.

Submissions
Query or send complete ms. Accepts photocopies, computer printouts, Macintosh and text file submissions, email submissions to debiT4RLS@aol.com, and simultaneous submissions if identified. SASE. Responds in 1–2 months.
Articles: 800–1,000 words. Informational articles; personal experience pieces; profiles; interviews; and reviews. Topics include the interfaith community, parenting, anti-semitism, gender roles, religious holidays, family issues, social concerns, and education.
Other: Poetry, line length varies.

Sample Issue
16 pages (no advertising): 9 articles. Sample copy, $5.50 with 9x12 SASE ($.78 postage). Guidelines and theme list available.
- "Jewish Homes Anchored by Non-Jewish Women." Article discusses the special responsibility non-Jewish women have in maintaining Jewish households.
- "Who Do You Think You Are?" Article examines the different household roles assigned to Jewish and Gentile spouses.

Rights and Payment
One-time rights. Articles, $25. reviews, $15. Pays on publication. Provides 2 contributor's copies.

Editor's Comments
We have no denominational affiliation or agenda. Articles may reflect a variety of approaches and strategies, but should not have a proselytizing or negative tone. Personal experiences are welcome, as are articles based on research.

Dragon

Suite 201
2700 Richards Road
Bellevue, WA 98005

Editor-in-Chief: Erik Mona

Description and Readership
Targeting Dungeons and Dragons players, masters, and fans of the game, this magazine offers articles that provide new feats, races, spells, magic items, equipment, and rule systems.
- **Audience:** YA–Adult
- **Frequency:** Monthly
- **Distribution:** Subscription; newsstand
- **Circulation:** 63,000
- **Website:** www.paizo.com/dragon

Freelance Potential
80% written by nonstaff writers. Publishes 350 freelance submissions yearly; 20% by unpublished writers, 20% by authors who are new to the magazine.

Submissions
Query with clips. Prefers email submissions to dragon@ paizo.com. Accepts photocopies, and computer printouts. No simultaneous submissions. SASE. Responds in 3 months.
Articles: Word lengths vary. Informational articles that provide new feats, weapons, spells, magic items, equipment, or prestige classes.
Depts/columns: Word lengths vary. Game strategies, advice.
Other: Comics.

Sample Issue
98 pages: 5 articles; 5 depts/columns; 3 comics. Sample copy, $6.99 at newsstands. Guidelines available at website.
- "Dreams of Arabia." Article takes a look at six new creatures derived from and inspired by Akkadia, Arabian, Egyptian, and Persian myths.
- "Fires of Alchemy." Article reviews the real-world history of Greek fire, and offers suggestions on how to incorporate it into games.
- Sample dept/column: "Bazaar of the Bizarre" takes a look at an arsenal of magic war items.

Rights and Payment
All rights. Written material, $.05 per word. Pays on publication.

Editor's Comments
We usually don't assign specific ideas to freelancers. It is better to write about subjects that interest you. Our favorites include information for players on both sides of the DM screen, with compelling writing and inspiration to satisfy those who aren't experts.

Dramatics

Educational Theatre Association
2343 Auburn Avenue
Cincinnati, OH 45219

Editor: Donald Corathers

Description and Readership
Articles and stories related to theatre can be found in this magazine. Topics such as acting, production, directing, and industry news are covered. It targets high school drama teachers and their students.
- **Audience:** High school students and teachers
- **Frequency:** 9 times each year
- **Distribution:** 100% subscription
- **Circulation:** 37,000
- **Website:** www.edta.org

Freelance Potential
90% written by nonstaff writers. Publishes 41 freelance submissions yearly; 5% by unpublished writers, 50% by authors who are new to the magazine. Receives 15 unsolicited mss monthly.

Submissions
Send complete ms. Accepts photocopies and email submissions to dcorathers@edta.org. SASE. Responds in 2–4 months.
Articles: 750–4,000 words. Informational articles; profiles; interviews; and book reviews. Topics include playwriting, musical theatre, acting, auditions, stage makeup, set design, and production.
Fiction: 500–3,500 words. Full-length and one-act plays suitable for high school audiences.
Artwork: 5x7 or larger B/W prints or 35mm or larger color transparencies. B/W line art. High-resolution JPGs or TIFFs.

Sample Issue
44 pages (40% advertising): 5 articles; 1 dept/column; 1 play. Sample copy, $3 with 9x12 SASE. Writers' guidelines available.
- "The Playwright's Mirror." Article provides an interview with playwright Nilo Cruz.
- "The Breath Experiments." Article offers breathing experiments to aid in vocal training.
- Sample dept/column: "Strut and Fret" spotlights the 2005 ARTS Gold Award winner and information on an award that aims to encourage songwriters.

Rights and Payment
First rights. Written material, $50–$400. Pays on acceptance. Provides 5 contributor's copies.

Editor's Comments
We are looking for material that informs and educates students about pursuing careers in theatre from authors with experience in live theatre.

Drink Smart

Suite 200
110 Eglinton Avenue W
Toronto, Ontario M4R 1A3
Canada

Managing Editor: Julie Crljen

Description and Readership
One of several online publications produced by Young People's Press, *Drink Smart* looks at the issue of alcohol consumption from the point of view of young people ages 14 to 24. In addition to factual articles, it includes opinion pieces from young adults seeking to express their ideas about this emotionally charged subject. Personal experience pieces from alcohol abusers as well as from those who have been victims of alcohol abuse are other major features.
- **Audience:** YA–Adult
- **Frequency:** Unavailable
- **Distribution:** 100% Internet
- **Hits per month:** Unavailable
- **Website:** www.drinksmart.org

Freelance Potential
95% written by nonstaff writers. Publishes 150–200 freelance submissions yearly; 70% by unpublished writers, 75% by authors who are new to the magazine.

Submissions
Send complete ms. Accepts email submissions to media@ypp.net. Responds immediately.
Articles: 400–1,000 words. Informational articles and opinion and personal experience pieces. Topics include the alcohol culture, responsible drinking, the effects of alcohol consumption, drinking and driving, domestic abuse, and the effects of alcohol abuse on careers, health, and relationships.
Depts/columns: 80–120 words. CD, movie, and website reviews.

Sample Issue
Sample copy and guidelines available at website.
- "Drunk Driver Destroys a Dream." Personal experience piece recounts how two lives changed the night a young woman's car was hit by a drunk driver.
- "You Can Rock, But Don't Roll." Article reports on an American/Canadian coalition of rock stars, actors, and athletes who have launched a poster campaign to promote their anti-drunk-driving message.

Rights and Payment
Rights, payment rates, and payment policy vary.

Editor's Comments
We need good writers, and we provide emerging young writers with the opportunity to have their work showcased at our website. Share with us your thoughts about the use of alcohol and alcohol abuse.

Earlychildhood News

Suite 125
2 Lower Ragsdale
Monterey, CA 93940

Director of Publishing: Megan Shaw

Description and Readership

This publication is read by parents, teachers, and professionals working with children up to the age of eight. Each issue includes articles, activities, and professional development material.
- **Audience:** Early childhood professionals and parents
- **Frequency:** 6 times each year
- **Distribution:** Subscription; controlled
- **Circulation:** 50,000
- **Website:** www.earlychildhoodnews.com

Freelance Potential

90% written by nonstaff writers. Publishes 10 freelance submissions yearly; 5% by unpublished writers, 15% by authors who are new to the magazine. Receives 8 queries and unsolicited mss monthly.

Submissions

Query with clips and writing samples; or send complete ms. Accepts email submissions to mshaw@ excelligencemail.com. SASE. Responds in 2 months.
Articles: 600–1,200 words. Informational and self-help articles; success stories; and interviews. Topics include early childhood education; health and safety; advocacy; testing; multicultural subjects; family, social, and emotional issues; and professional development.
Depts/columns: 500 words. Topics vary.

Sample Issue

50 pages (50% advertising): 4 articles; 5 depts/columns. Sample copy available. Guidelines and editorial calendar available.
- "10 Ideas for Including Music in the Classroom." Article describes ways to integrate the universal language of music into the classroom.
- "Fostering Goodness & Caring." Article discusses the importance of teaching moral development.
- Sample dept/column: "Tips & Tidbits" suggests ways to help an only child adjust to the arrival of a new sibling.

Rights and Payment

First rights. Written material, $75–$200. Depts/columns, payment rates vary. Pays on acceptance. Provides 1 contributor's copy.

Editor's Comments

We would like to see articles focusing on school readiness, literacy, math, special needs, and infant/toddler topics.

Early Childhood Today

Scholastic Inc.
5th Floor
557 Broadway
New York, NY 10012-3999

Editor-in-Chief: Diane Ohanesian

Description and Readership

Professional educators working with children in preschool through first grade turn to this journal for ideas about program and curriculum development. It also offers informative articles on child development issues, family concerns, and health and safety.
- **Audience:** Early childhood professionals
- **Frequency:** 8 times each year
- **Distribution:** Subscription; schools
- **Circulation:** 55,000
- **Website:** www.scholastic.com

Freelance Potential

20% written by nonstaff writers. Publishes 5 freelance submissions yearly; 10% by unpublished writers, 50% by authors who are new to the magazine. Receives 8–9 queries monthly.

Submissions

Query. Accepts computer printouts. SASE. Responds in 1 month.
Articles: Word length varies. Informational, educational, and how-to articles. Topics include child advocacy, child development, special needs, communication, physical development, family issues, health, technology, and multicultural issues.
Depts/columns: Word length varies. News about early childhood issues, teaching tips, and teaching with technology.

Sample Issue

56 pages (8% advertising): 2 articles; 10 depts/columns; 1 interview; 1 activity page. Sample copy and guidelines, $3 with SASE.
- "The Surprising Truth about Why Children Lie." Article explains that lying follows a developmental progression.
- "Lauren Lawson on Art, Writing, and Young Children." Interview with a successful early childhood teacher and mentor.
- Sample dept/column: "Physical Development" suggests creative ways to improve indoor playtime.

Rights and Payment

All rights. Written material, payment rates vary. Pays on acceptance. Provides 3 contributor's copies.

Editor's Comments

We welcome queries from all educators. At this time, we are interested in helpful and inspiring classroom ideas that show respect for all learners.

East of the Web

361 Manhattan Building
Fairfield Road
London E32UL
England

Editor: Alex Patterson

Description and Readership
Showcasing top-notch short stories, this website is read by fiction lovers, agents, the press, film makers, schools, colleges, and other publishers. Each issue includes a mix of genres including romance, horror, humor, science fiction, and hyperfiction.
- **Audience:** All ages
- **Frequency:** Unavailable
- **Distribution:** 100% Internet
- **Circulation:** 40,000+
- **Website:** www.eastoftheweb.com

Freelance Potential
96% written by nonstaff writers. Publishes 150 freelance submissions yearly; 50% by unpublished writers, 85% by authors who are new to the magazine. Receives 500+ unsolicited mss monthly.

Submissions
Send complete ms. Accepts email submissions to submissions@eastoftheweb.com (TEXT, RTF files, or Microsoft Word attachments). SASE. Responds in 3–4 months.
Fiction: Word lengths vary. Genres include contemporary fiction; mystery; folktales; fairy tales; humor; science fiction; and stories about animals.

Sample Issue
Guidelines available at website.
- "Mr. Sticky." Story tells of a girl who finds a small water snail in her fish tank and then thinks her mother killed it while she was cleaning the tank.
- "The Dragon Rock." Story tells what happens when a town goes dry from no rain and a rock shaped like a dragon awakens and makes a lake by sneezing.
- "The Tale of Princess Laughing Dove." Story tells a tale of an ugly man who follows a dove and meets the woman he ends up marrying.

Rights and Payment
Non-exclusive rights. No payment.

Editor's Comments
We are an open submissions site and are always on the lookout for 'fresh new voices.' We receive a large amount of submissions and failure to adhere to our submissions guidelines will severely decrease the chance of your submission. All submissions are judged on the quality of writing, regardless of the author's experience. If you think you have what it takes, we'd love to hear from you.

The Edge

2 Overlea Boulevard
Toronto, Ontario M4H 1P4
Canada

Editor: John McAlister

Description and Readership
As the editors declare in their mission statement, the purpose of *The Edge* is to celebrate youth and to assist and encourage them in their spiritual growth. Each issue presents articles that focus on the spiritual side of young people, some whom are media stars. *The Edge* is the official Christian youth magazine of The Salvation Army in Canada.
- **Audience:** 14–18 years
- **Frequency:** 10 times each year
- **Distribution:** 90% controlled; 10% subscription
- **Circulation:** 5,000

Freelance Potential
80% written by nonstaff writers. Publishes 20 freelance submissions yearly; 50% by unpublished writers, 50% by authors who are new to the magazine. Receives 4 queries and unsolicited mss monthly.

Submissions
Query or send complete ms. Accepts disk submissions and email submissions to edge@can.salvationarmy.org (Microsoft Word attachments). Availability of artwork improves chance of acceptance. SAE/IRC. Responds in 2 weeks.
Articles: 400–500 words. How-to articles; profiles; and personal experience pieces. Topics include biography, humor, health, music, the environment, religion, social issues, sports, popular culture, computers, and college.
Fiction: 300 words. Problem-solving stories, humor, inspirational fiction, and stories about sports.
Depts/columns: 200 words. Advice and reviews.
Artwork: Color prints and transparencies.

Sample Issue
24 pages (no advertising): 10 articles; 1 dept/column. Guidelines available.
- "Crack Cocaine." Article outlines the risks of cocaine use and its effects on the body and the brain.
- "Avoid the Family Feud." Article explains the three R's for improving family relationships: respect, responsibility, and resolution of conflicts.

Rights and Payment
First rights. All material, payment rates vary. Pays on publication. Provides 3 contributor's copies.

Editor's Comments
If you're thinking of submitting, remember that everything we publish offers a Christian perspective.

Educational Horizons

Pi Lambda Theta
P.O. Box 6626
4101 East Third Street
Bloomington, IN 47407-6626

Managing Editor

Description and Readership
Offering an international perspective on educational issues, this journal includes articles, research reports, and scholarly essays.
- **Audience:** Pi Lambda Theta members
- **Frequency:** Quarterly
- **Distribution:** 90% controlled; 10% subscription
- **Circulation:** 17,000
- **Website:** www.pilambda.org

Freelance Potential
95% written by nonstaff writers. Publishes 10–15 freelance submissions yearly; 75% by authors who are new to the magazine. Receives 5 queries, 10 unsolicited mss monthly.

Submissions
Query with outline/synopsis; or send complete ms with biography. Accepts photocopies, computer printouts, and simultaneous submissions if identified. Availability of artwork improves chance of acceptance. SASE. Responds to queries in 1 month, to mss in 3–4 months.
Articles: 3,500–5,000 words. Informational articles; research reports; and scholarly essays on national and international trends.
Depts/columns: 500–750 words. Multicultural education, educational topics in the news, international perspectives on education, legal issues, and book reviews.
Artwork: B/W prints and camera-ready illustrations.

Sample Issue
82 pages (4% advertising): 6 articles; 6 depts/columns. Sample copy, $5 with 9x12 SASE ($.87 postage). Writers' guidelines and theme list available at website.
- "NCLB and High-Stakes Accountability." Article reports on problems with the No Child Left Behind Act and accountability for its flaws.
- "Seize the Day." Article discusses a presentation on positive alternatives that can come out of the No Child Left Behind Act.
- Sample dept/column: "Legal Update" discusses the impact of the Children's Internet Protection Act.

Rights and Payment
First rights. No payment. Provides 5 author's copies.

Editor's Comments
We look for up-to-date material that reports on political, cultural, and international educational issues.

Educational Leadership

1703 North Beauregard Street
Alexandria, VA 22311-1714

Editor: Margaret Scherer

Description and Readership
Addressing all aspects of effective teaching and learning, this magazine features articles by leading educators, interpretations of research, reports of effective programs and practices, and book reviews. It is published by the Association for Supervision and Curriculum Development.
- **Audience:** Educators
- **Frequency:** 8 times each year
- **Distribution:** 90% subscription; 10% schools
- **Circulation:** 170,000
- **Website:** www.ascd.org

Freelance Potential
90% written by nonstaff writers. Publishes 200 freelance submissions yearly; 50% by unpublished writers. Receives 125 unsolicited mss monthly.

Submissions
Send complete ms. Accepts computer printouts. Does not return mss. Responds in 1–2 months.
Articles: 1,500–2,500 words. How-to articles and personal experience pieces. Topics include health, fitness, computers, special and gifted education, social issues, religion, nature, science, technology, and multicultural and ethnic subjects.
Depts/columns: Word length varies. Association and education news, and opinion pieces. Also includes policy, book, and website reviews.

Sample Issue
96 pages (25% advertising): 14 articles; 10 depts/columns. Sample copy, $6. Guidelines and theme list available at website.
- "Bridging the Generation Gap." Article discusses ways school leaders can act to build integrated professional cultures in which new and experienced teachers collaborate regularly.
- "Let Kids Come First." Article explores the importance of letting new teachers connect meaningfully with their students.
- Sample dept/column: "The Principal Connection" reports on meeting the range of needs of teachers.

Rights and Payment
First rights. No payment. Provides 5 author's copies.

Editor's Comments
We look for material with practical examples that illustrate key points. Writing must be conversational in style. Keep in mind we are a thematic publication.

Education Forum

60 Mobile Drive
Toronto, Ontario M4A 2P3
Canada

Managing Editor: Marianne Clayton

Description and Readership
Articles that focus on educational issues affecting educators in Ontario can be found in this magazine. It also includes teaching strategies and techniques, activities, reviews, and teacher profiles.
- **Audience:** Teachers
- **Frequency:** 3 times each year
- **Distribution:** 90% membership; 10% subscription
- **Circulation:** 48,000
- **Website:** www.osstf.on.ca

Freelance Potential
90% written by nonstaff writers. Publishes 35 freelance submissions yearly; 20% by unpublished writers, 80% by authors who are new to the magazine. Receives 4 queries and unsolicited mss monthly.

Submissions
Query with clips or writing samples; or send complete ms. Accepts photocopies. No simultaneous submissions. SAE/IRC. Responds to queries in 1–2 months.
Articles: To 2,500 words. How-to and practical application articles on education trends; discussions of controversial issues; and teaching techniques for use in secondary school classrooms.
Depts/columns: "Openers" features news and opinion pieces, to 300 words. "Forum Picks" uses media and software reviews.
Artwork: B/W prints and line art for nonfiction pieces. Color prints and transparencies.
Other: Classroom activities, puzzles, and games. Submit seasonal material 8 months in advance.

Sample Issue
40 pages (18% advertising): 4 articles; 6 depts/ columns. Sample copy, free with 9x12 SAE/IRC (Canadian postage). Guidelines available.
- "Devastating Conflicts." Article takes a look at the ongoing humanitarian crisis in the world.
- "Commercialization." Article explores alternative funding sources for schools in Ontario.
- Sample dept/column: "Openers" discusses using films in classes to explore basic human values.

Rights and Payment
First North American serial rights. No payment. Provides 5 contributor's copies.

Editor's Comments
We seek information on regional and global educational issues and welcome works from new writers.

Education Week

Suite 100
6935 Arlington Road
Bethesda, MD 20814-5233

Managing Editor: Greg Chronister

Description and Readership
This tabloid offers articles and news that explore the latest in educational issues. It targets elementary and secondary teachers, school administrators, and other professionals in the education field.
- **Audience:** Educators
- **Frequency:** 44 times each year
- **Distribution:** Subscription; schools; newsstand
- **Circulation:** 50,000
- **Website:** www.edweek.org

Freelance Potential
8% written by nonstaff writers. Publishes 125 freelance submissions yearly; 80% by unpublished writers, 75% by authors who are new to the magazine. Receives 50 unsolicited mss monthly.

Submissions
Send complete ms. Accepts IBM disk submissions (WordPerfect or Microsoft Word) and MacIntosh disk submissions (plain text). SASE. Responds in 6–8 weeks.
Articles: 1,200–1,500 words. Essays on child development and education related to grades K–12, for use in "Commentary" section.
Depts/columns: Staff written.

Sample Issue
48 pages (25% advertising): 26 articles; 18 depts/ columns. Sample copy, $3 with 9x12 SASE ($1 postage). Guidelines available.
- "Teachers Resign After Peer Is Fired in Mo. District." Article tells of a teacher who is fired after advocating on behalf of the safety of a student.
- "States Report Reading First Yielding Gains." Article reports on states benefiting as a result of the federal government's Reading First initiative.
- "Record Numbers of Students Enrolled in the Public Schools." Article reports on the federal government's latest education statistics on school enrollment.

Rights and Payment
First rights. "Commentary," $200. Pays on publication. Provides 2 contributor's copies.

Editor's Comments
We focus on pre-college education and are seeking freelance submissions for our Commentary section. Material should take the form of an opinion essay rather than a scholarly paper. Writing should be detailed and presented in an analytical way.

EduGuide

321 North Pine
Lansing, MI 48933

Office Manager: Jan Mason

Description and Readership
Previously listed as *Learning Guide*, this resourceful
magazine offers three editions for parents covering the
elementary, middle school, and high school years. It
includes articles and tips on educational issues.
- **Audience:** Parents
- **Frequency:** 3 times each year
- **Distribution:** 50% subscription; 50% schools
- **Circulation:** 300,000
- **Website:** www.partnershipforlearning.org

Freelance Potential
85% written by nonstaff writers. Publishes 25–30 freelance submissions yearly; 10% by unpublished writers,
60% by new authors. Receives 4 mss monthly.

Submissions
Send complete ms. Accepts computer printouts and
email submissions to jan@partnershipforlearning.org.
SASE. Responds in 4–6 weeks.
Articles: 500–1,000 words. Informational and how-to
articles; profiles; interviews; and personal experience
pieces. Topics include the arts, college, careers, computers, gifted education, health, fitness, history,
humor, mathematics, music, science, technology, special education, and issues related to elementary and
secondary education.
Depts/columns: Word lengths vary. Advice and opinion pieces.
Artwork: Color prints and transparencies. Line art.
Other: Reviews, 200 words. Submit seasonal material
3 months in advance.

Sample Issue
32 pages (no advertising): 3 articles; 2 depts/
columns; 1 quiz. Sample copy, $3 with 9x12 SASE
($1 postage). Writers' guidelines and theme list/editor-
ial calendar available.
- "Warning Signs on Your Career Path." Article takes a
  look at opportunities for students to explore and
  prepare for careers.
- Sample dept/column: "Parent Primer" offers steps to
  take in high school to help prepare for college.

Rights and Payment
First or second rights. All material, payment rates vary.
Pays on acceptance. Provides 5 copies.

Editor's Comments
We are looking for coverage of topics and trends in
education that will guide parents in making choices.

Edutopia

P.O. Box 3494
San Rafael, CA 94912

Managing Editor: Sarah Fallon

Description and Readership
This magazine, from the George Lucus Educational
Foundation, is for educators, policy makers, and
active parents of public school children. It addresses
the educational issues of today and seeks to reach
teachers as people, as well as professionals.
- **Audience:** Educators; parents
- **Frequency:** 7 times each year
- **Distribution:** 90% subscription; 10% newsstand
- **Circulation:** 85,000
- **Website:** www.edutopia.org

Freelance Potential
80% written by nonstaff writers. Publishes 50–60 freelance submissions yearly; 5% by authors who are new
to the magazine. Receives 10–20 queries monthly.

Submissions
Query with résumé. Prefers email queries to edit@
edutopia.org. Response time varies.
Articles: 300–2,500 words. Informational and how-to
articles; and personal experience pieces. Topics
include computers education, current events, gifted,
health and fitness, nature, the environment, popular
culture, recreation, science, technology, social issues,
and travel.
Depts/columns: 700 words. Health, education, and
ethnic and multicultural issues.

Sample Issue
58 pages (30% advertising): 3 articles; 10 depts/
columns. Sample copy, $4.95. Guidelines available.
- "School's Out." Article looks at the reasons half of
  new teachers leave the job within five years.
- "Brave New School." Article profiles a mother with an
  autistic son who started her own charter school that
  integrates disabled and nondisabled students.
- Sample dept/column: "Border Crossing" looks at a
  school that adds depth and meaning to education by
  taking its students abroad.

Rights and Payment
First North American rights. Written material, payment
rates vary. Pays on acceptance. Provides 2 contributor's copies.

Editor's Comments
We're looking for a witty and sharp writing syle that
deals with today's ever-changing world of education.
Our features, front of book, and lifestyle sections are
most open to freelance writers.

Elementary School Writer

Writer Publications
P.O. Box 718
Grand Rapids, MN 55744-0718

Editor: Emily Benes

Description and Readership
The pages of this newspaper are devoted to featuring the works of elementary school students. Each issue includes poetry, essays, and stories about life, social issues, and school experiences. It is used as a teaching tool in elementary school classrooms.
• **Audience:** Elementary school students
• **Frequency:** 6 times each year
• **Distribution:** 100% schools
• **Circulation:** Unavailable

Freelance Potential
100% written by nonstaff writers. Publishes 300 freelance submissions yearly; 95% by unpublished writers, 75% by authors who are new to the magazine. Receives 3,000 unsolicited mss monthly.

Submissions
Accepts submissions from elementary students of subschools only. Send complete ms. Accepts photocopies, computer printouts, email submissions to writer@mx3.com (ASCII text only), and simultaneous submissions if identified. SASE. Response time varies.
Articles: To 1,000 words. Informational and how-to articles; profiles; and personal experience pieces. Topics include current events, humor, multicultural and ethnic issues, nature, the environment, popular culture, recreation, sports, and travel.
Fiction: To 1,000 words. Genres include humor and science fiction, stories about nature, the environment, and sports.
Other: Poetry, no line limit. Seasonal material.

Sample Issue
8 pages (no advertising): 19 articles; 11 stories; 25 poems. Sample copy, free. Guidelines available in each issue.
• "A Flag of Remembrance and Beauty." Essay expresses the symbolic meaning the author sees when looking at the American flag.
• "Saving the World from a Tasty Treat." Story features a boy who becomes a hero when he saves the neighborhood from marshmallow goo.

Rights and Payment
One-time rights. No payment.

Editor's Comments
We only publish original submissions written by elementary school students of subscribing schools.

Ellery Queen's Mystery Magazine

11th Floor
475 Park Avenue South
New York, NY 10016

Editor: Janet Hutchings

Description and Readership
For more than 60 years, this magazine has published original mysteries ranging from realistic stories of police procedure to imaginative, "impossible" crimes.
• **Audience:** YA–Adult
• **Frequency:** 10 times each year
• **Distribution:** 90% subscription; 10% newsstand
• **Circulation:** 180,780
• **Website:** www.themysteryplace.com

Freelance Potential
100% written by nonstaff writers. Publishes 125 freelance submissions yearly; 7% by unpublished writers, 25% by authors who are new to the magazine. Receives 200 unsolicited mss monthly.

Submissions
Send complete ms. Accepts computer printouts and simultaneous submissions if identified. SASE. Responds in 3 months.
Fiction: Feature length, 2,000–12,000 words. Minute Mysteries, 250 words. Novellas by established authors, to 20,000 words. Contemporary and historical crime fiction, psychological thrillers, mystery, suspense, and detective and private-eye stories.
Other: Poetry, line length varies.

Sample Issue
144 pages (6% advertising): 1 article; 8 stories; 6 book reviews; 1 translation. Sample copy, $5. Writers' guidelines available.
• "The Drum." A first-published crime story about a young Indian woman, a jealous cousin, and a special drum.
• "I Know Where You Live." Short story about a killer for hire.
• "The Occupational Rehabilitation of Cousin Henry." Story about a man who chooses to be an "insurance" salesman, much to the chagrin of his family.

Rights and Payment
First and anthology rights. All material, $.05–$.08 per word. Pays on acceptance. Provides 3 contributor's copies.

Editor's Comments
Classic whodunits are on our wish list for this year. We are especially interested in reviewing first stories by authors who have never before published fiction professionally. First-story submissions should be addressed to our Department of First Stories.

ePregnancy

Suite 113
5742 W. Harold Gatty Drive
Salt Lake City, UT 84116

Editor: Misty Bott

Description and Readership
Published in print and online, *ePregnancy* focuses on pregnancy, labor, and delivery as well as on post-partum issues such as breastfeeding, depression, exercise, and infant care.
- **Audience:** Expectant parents
- **Frequency:** 10 times each year
- **Distribution:** Internet; subscription; newsstand
- **Circulation:** 345,000
- **Website:** www.epregnancy.com

Freelance Potential
95% written by nonstaff writers. Publishes 300 freelance submissions yearly. Receives 80 queries and unsolicited mss monthly.

Submissions
Prefers query. Accepts complete ms. Accepts photocopies, computer printouts, and email submissions to editorial@mjstc.net. SASE. Response time varies.
Articles: 500–2,500 words. Informational, self-help, and how-to articles; profiles; interviews; humor; and reviews. Topics include preconception, pregnancy, and postpartum issues; health; fitness; social issues; education; and travel.
Depts/columns: Word length varies. Expert advice, fitness, and personal essays.

Sample Issue
128 pages: 16 articles; 22 depts/columns. Sample copy, $4.99 at newsstands. Guidelines available at website.
- "Infertility and PCOS." Article reports on a syndrome that is known to be one of the leading causes of infertility in women.
- "Pregnancy over 40." Article details the physical, mental, and spiritual differences of women in their 20s, 30s, and 40s.
- Sample dept/column: "Birth Stories" features readers' accounts of their babies' births.

Rights and Payment
First print rights. Written material, $25–$50; $10 for reprints and first-person essays. Pays on publication.

Editor's Comments
Journalists and others with appropriate writing skills are invited to query or send a submission. We look for research-based articles that feature a friendly tone, and we like articles that include quotes from people who are considered experts in their fields.

eSchoolNews

Suite 900
7920 Norfolk Avenue
Bethesda, MD 20814

Editor: Greg Downey

Description and Readership
Educational professionals read this tabloid for its articles on all aspects of school technology news, issues, products, services, and strategies, as well as the business and political issues impacting school technology.
- **Audience:** K-12 educators
- **Frequency:** Monthly
- **Distribution:** 100% subscription
- **Circulation:** Unavailable
- **Website:** www.eschoolnews.com

Freelance Potential
20% written by nonstaff writers. Publishes 6–8 freelance submissions yearly. Receives 1 unsolicited ms each month.

Submissions
Prefers query. Accepts ms. Accepts photocopies, computer printouts, and email to GDowney@eschoolnews.com. SASE. Response time varies.
Articles: Word lengths vary. Informational and how-to articles; profiles; and reviews. Topics include gifted children, science, technology, social issues, and special education.
Depts/columns: Word lengths vary. News, reviews, grants and funding, community relations, technology.

Sample Issue
30 pages (45% advertising): 2 articles; 19 depts/columns.
- "eSN Special Feature." Article reports on new effective network administration software that saves school IT managers time and money.
- "Readers' Choice Awards." Article takes a look at multimedia creation tools that came out on top according to an online survey.
- Sample dept/column: "Best Practices" offers information on a visual presenter that allows students to show and share assignments with the rest of the class, and a wireless laptop initiative.

Rights and Payment
Rights vary. Written material, payment rates vary. Pays on acceptance.

Editor's Comments
We provide school decision-makers with the information they need to make the best choices possible when it comes to achieving their educational goals through the use of technology and the Internet. Send us something on technology that will excite readers.

Exceptional Parent

551 Main Street
Johnstown, PA 15901

Editor-in-Chief: Dr. Rick Rader

Description and Readership
This publication seeks to improve communication between persons with disabilities and their caregivers. Its articles focus on working together, respect, and consideration.
- **Audience:** Parents, teachers, and professionals
- **Frequency:** Monthly
- **Distribution:** Subscription; controlled
- **Circulation:** 70,000
- **Website:** www.eparent.com

Freelance Potential
95% written by nonstaff writers. Publishes 50–60 freelance submissions yearly; 50% by unpublished writers, 50% by authors who are new to the magazine. Receives 8+ queries monthly.

Submissions
Prefers query by email to epedit@aol.com. Accepts photocopies, computer printouts, and Macintosh disk submissions. SASE. Responds to queries in 3 weeks.
Articles: To 2,000 words. Informational articles; personal experience pieces; profiles; and interviews. Topics include the social, psychological, legal, political, technological, financial, and educational concerns faced by individuals with disabilities.
Depts/columns: Word length varies. Opinion and personal experience pieces, news items, new product information, and media reviews.

Sample Issue
76 pages (50% advertising): 8 articles; 9 depts/columns. Sample copy, $4.99 with 9x12 SASE ($2 postage). Guidelines and editorial calendar available.
- "A Team Approach." Article follows an *Extreme Makeover Home Edition* program as it renovates a home to help people with special needs.
- "At Walter Reed There are People Who Scare Dogs." Article takes a looks at this military hospital, its patients, and the people who help them.
- Sample dept/column: "Living with Disability" offers an essay on coping with being disabled.

Rights and Payment
First North American serial rights. Written material, to $60. Pays on acceptance. Provides 2 copies.

Editor's Comments
Your article should summarize the topic in the first two paragraphs; this enables readers to decide if the information is pertinent to their interests.

Faces

Cobblestone Publishing Company,
Division of Carus Publishing
Suite C
30 Grove Street
Peterborough, NH 03458

Assistant Editor: Peg Lopata

Description and Readership
This thematic magazine explores the people, cultures, and places around the world. Through its articles and essays, it allows middle-grade readers to learn about geography, history, customs, language, and religion.
- **Audience:** 9–14 years
- **Frequency:** 9 times each year
- **Distribution:** 100% subscription
- **Circulation:** 15,000
- **Website:** www.cobblestonepub.com

Freelance Potential
80% written by nonstaff writers. Publishes 80 freelance submissions yearly; 10% by unpublished writers, 35% by new authors. Receives 30 queries monthly.

Submissions
Query with outline, bibliography and clips or writing samples. Accepts email queries to facesmag@ yahoo.com. SASE. Responds in 5 months.
Articles: 800 words. Informational articles and personal experience pieces related to the theme of each issue. Supplemental articles, 300–600 words.
Fiction: To 800 words. Stories, legends, and folktales from countries around the world, related to each issue.
Depts/columns: 500 words. Crafts and cooking.
Artwork: Color prints and transparencies.
Other: Games, crafts, puzzles, and activities, to 700 words. Poetry, to 100 lines.

Sample Issue
48 pages (no advertising): 9 articles; 1 story; 11 depts/columns; 2 activities. Sample copy, $4.95 with 9x12 SASE ($2 postage). Writers' guidelines and theme list available at website.
- "Making a Difference." Article takes a look at a student from Australia who started an organization of young people that helps other young people.
- "Do You Speak Strine?" Article explores the history of Australia's lingo and rhyming slang.
- "School of the Air?" Article describes the use of a two-way satellite system for interactive distance learning.

Rights and Payment
All rights. Articles and fiction, $.20–$.25 per word. Pays on publication. Provides 2 contributor's copies.

Editor's Comments
We like articles that are lively and offer in-depth coverage of a culture. Artwork is always welcome.

Face Up

75 Orwell Road
Rathgar, Dublin 6
Ireland

Editor: Gerard Moloney

Description and Readership
Published by the Irish Redemptorists, this magazine is read by young men with a mission to spread the word of God through the media.
- **Audience:** 14–18 years
- **Frequency:** 10 times each year
- **Distribution:** 80% schools; 15% subscription; 5% newsstand
- **Circulation:** 12,000
- **Website:** www.faceup.ie

Freelance Potential
100% written by nonstaff writers. Publishes 60 freelance submissions yearly; 30% by unpublished writers, 70% by authors who are new to the magazine. Receives 42 unsolicited mss monthly.

Submissions
Send complete ms. Accepts email submissions to info@faceup.ie. Availability of artwork improves chance of acceptance. SAE/IRC. Responds in 1 month.
Articles: 900 words. Informational and how-to articles; personal experience pieces; profiles; and interviews. Topics include college, careers, current events, health, fitness, music, popular culture, and sports.
Depts/columns: 500 words. Opinion pieces, advice, health issues, the Internet, and reviews.
Artwork: Color prints and transparencies.
Other: Submit seasonal material on Christmas, Easter, and on final exams 3 months in advance.

Sample Issue
38 pages (5% advertising): 5 articles; 1 profile; 12 depts/columns. Sample copy, guidelines, theme list, and editorial calendar available.
- "Relationships." Article discusses the benefits and frustrations of having friends and family.
- "Stress Head." Article offers three steps for coping with school, exams, parents, and money.
- "Body, Mind & Spirit." Article looks at how procrastination affects everything you do.

Rights and Payment
Rights vary. Payment rate varies. Pays on publication. Provides 2 contributor's copies.

Editor's Comments
We need articles that relate to contemporary teenage issues and concerns. Material should emphasize positive values and help readers make positive choices in their lives.

Faith & Family

432 Washington Avenue
North Haven, CT 06473

Editorial Assistant: Robyn Lee

Description and Readership
A Catholic viewpoint of family life and general daily issues is expressed throughout this publication. Readers also find inspirational ideas on education, spiritual pursuits, child rearing, and entertainment.
- **Audience:** Catholic families
- **Frequency:** Quarterly
- **Distribution:** 90% subscription; 10% other
- **Circulation:** 32,000
- **Website:** www.faithandfamilymag.com

Freelance Potential
90% written by nonstaff writers. Publishes 35 freelance submissions yearly; 15% by unpublished writers, 10% by authors who are new to the magazine. Receives 25 unsolicited mss monthly.

Submissions
Prefers queries via email to editor@ faithandfamilymag.com. Responds in 2–3 months.
Articles: 600–2,000 words. Informational, how-to, and self-help articles; personal experience pieces; profiles; interviews; and media reviews. Topics include Catholic family life, and social and political issues.
Depts/columns: Word length varies. Marriage; entertainment reviews; and family meals.
Artwork: Prefers color photos and slides.

Sample Issue
96 pages (30% advertising): 7 articles; 14 depts/columns. Sample copy, $4.50. Guidelines available.
- "Nasty Girls." Article details how effective girls can be at bullying, formerly a problem thought to be only associated with boys.
- "Second-Chance Christmas." Article profiles people who were given a second chance at living, and because of these gifts, changed their perspective on the way they conduct their lives.
- Sample dept/column: "Family Matters" looks at how a couple pulled through some tough times after enrolling in a church study group.

Rights and Payment
First North American serial rights. Written material, $.33 per word. Pays on publication.

Editor's Comments
We prefer proposals by email and rarely accept unsolicited material. Proposals should target a specific section of the magazine and show that the writer has studied our publication.

Family Circle

Gruner + Jahr Publishing
375 Lexington Avenue
New York, NY 10017

Senior Editor: Angela Ebron

Description and Readership
This popular magazine is chock full of information on issues of interest to women and families. It covers topics such as family relationships, finance, social issues, child care, and personal development.
- **Audience:** Families
- **Frequency:** 15 times each year
- **Distribution:** 50% subscription; 50% newsstand
- **Circulation:** 5 million
- **Website:** www.familycircle.com

Freelance Potential
80% written by nonstaff writers. Publishes 50 freelance submissions yearly; 50% by unpublished writers, 20% by authors who are new to the magazine. Receives 25 queries monthly.

Submissions
Query with outline and 2 clips or writing samples. No simultaneous submissions. SASE. Responds in 6–8 weeks.
Articles: 2,000–2,500 words. Profiles of women who make a difference; reports on contemporary family issues; and real-life inspirational issues.
Depts/columns: 750–1,500 words. Beauty, fashion, health, legal issues, parenting, relationships, home decorating, food, and fitness.

Sample Issue
202 pages (48% advertising): 30 articles; 6 depts/columns. Sample copy, $2.50 at newsstands. Guidelines available.
- "Marriage: It's the Little Things That Count." Article offers some insights from experts that strive to bring married couples closer.
- "Everyday Blessings." Article shares the experiences and challenges of a family with seven siblings who are all battling cancer.
- Sample dept/column: "Circle This" includes information on teen spas, a parenting book, a round crib company, and a hotel where the Beatles stayed.

Rights and Payment
Rights negotiable. Written material, $1 per word. Kill fee, 10%. Pays on acceptance. Provides 1 copy.

Editor's Comments
We are looking for articles on family issues; health; decorating; family-friendly crafts and recipe ideas; and dramatic, inspirational personal experience pieces. Send us a query for something we haven't seen.

Family Digest

P.O. Box 40137
Fort Wayne, IN 46804

Manuscript Editor: Corine B. Erlandson

Description and Readership
The Family Digest publishes material devoted to the joy and fulfillment of Catholic family life, and how families relate to the Catholic parish.
- **Audience:** Catholic families
- **Frequency:** 6 times each year
- **Distribution:** 100% controlled
- **Circulation:** 150,000

Freelance Potential
95% written by nonstaff writers. Publishes 60 freelance submissions yearly; 40% by authors who are new to the magazine. Receives 100 unsolicited mss each month.

Submissions
Send complete ms. Accepts photocopies and computer printouts. No simultaneous submissions; previously published material will be considered. SASE. Responds in 1–2 months.
Articles: 750–1,300 words. Informational, how-to, and inspirational articles; and self-help and personal experience pieces. Topics include family and parish life, spiritual living, church traditions, prayer, religious saints' lives, and seasonal material.
Depts/Columns: Staff written.
Other: Humorous anecdotes, 25–100 words. Cartoons. Submit seasonal material 7 months in advance.

Sample Issue
48 pages (no advertising): 10 articles; 5 depts/columns. Sample copy, free with 6x9 SASE (2 first-class stamps). Guidelines available.
- "A Day's Dawning." First-person article about finding gentle reminders of God's grace.
- "These Forty Days." Short story about finding riches amidst Lenten sacrifices.
- "We Reenacted a Last Supper." Story about the lasting results of a First Communion project.

Rights and Payment
First North American serial rights. Articles, $40–$60. Anecdotes, $25. Pays 1–2 months after acceptance. Provides 2 contributor's copies.

Editor's Comments
We are looking for upbeat articles that affirm the simple ways the Catholic faith can be expressed in daily life. We are also in need of articles and stories about youth and church holidays.

Family Doctor

P.O. Box 38790
Colorado Springs, CO 80937-8790

Managing Editor: Leigh Ann Hubbard

Description and Readership
Written almost exclusively by health-care professionals, this family medical magazine focuses on mainstream medicine and looks at alternative treatments from a scientific, studied point of view.
- **Audience:** Adults and parents
- **Frequency:** 4 times each year
- **Distribution:** Unavailable
- **Circulation:** 100,000
- **Website:** www.familydoctormag.com

Freelance Potential
100% written by nonstaff writers. Publishes 100 freelance submissions yearly; 1% by unpublished writers, 1% by authors who are new to the magazine. Receives 12 queries and unsolicited mss monthly.

Submissions
Query with writing samples. Prefers email submissions to managingeditor@familydoctormag.com. Accepts photocopies and computer printouts. SASE. Responds in 1 month.
Articles: 1,500 words. Informational articles; and personal experience pieces. Topics include health, fitness, nutrition, and preventive medicine.
Depts/columns: 200–400 words. Medical studies and breakthroughs.
Other: Filler, 200–400 words.

Sample Issue
64 pages (2% advertising): 8 articles; 28 depts/columns. Sample copy available at newsstands. Guidelines available.
- "Meredith's Club." Article describes one journalist's quest to help overweight children.
- "Beat the Heat." Article offers ways to play it cool and safe in the summer.
- Sample dept/column: "Housecalls" looks at how to recognize a depressed teenager.

Rights and Payment
First North American serial, exclusive syndication for one-year, and nonexclusive rights. Pays on publication. Written material, $.30 per word.

Editor's Comments
We are a source for upbeat, reliable, up-to-date medical information and advice. We seek summaries and analyses of recent medical studies, and in-depth articles on disease treatment and prevention. Most of our authors have medical degrees.

FamilyFun

Disney Publishing
244 Main Street
Northampton, OH 01060

Features Editor

Description and Readership
Since 1996, *FamilyFun* has been catering to families with children ages 3 to 12. It features articles on cooking, vacations, parties, and holidays, as well as ideas on building strong, healthy families.
- **Audience:** Parents
- **Frequency:** 10 times each year
- **Distribution:** Subscription; newsstand
- **Circulation:** 1.85 million
- **Website:** www.familyfun.com

Freelance Potential
50% written by nonstaff writers. Publishes 100+ freelance submissions yearly; 1% by unpublished writers, 5% by authors who are new to the magazine.

Submissions
Query with clips or writing samples. No unsolicited mss. Accepts photocopies and letter-quality computer printouts. SASE. Responds in 2–3 months.
Articles: 750–3,000 words. Informational and how-to articles. Topics include cooking, games, crafts, activities, educational projects, sports, holiday parties, travel, and creative solutions to household problems.
Depts/columns: 100–1,500 words. News items about family travel, media reviews, and inspirational or humorous pieces focusing on family life.
Other: Submit seasonal material 6 months in advance.

Sample Issue
112 pages (47% advertising): 6 articles; 9 depts/columns. Sample copy, $3.50 at newsstands. Guidelines available at website.
- "Family Reunions." Article gives tips on organizing everything from small get-togethers to large family gatherings.
- "Tin Can Train." Everything you need to know to make a shiny toy train from recyclable materials.
- Sample dept/column: "Learning" offers ways to make writing fun for children.

Rights and Payment
All rights. Articles, $1.25 per word. Other material, payment rate varies. Pays on acceptance.

Editor's Comments
Craft ideas that busy families can make and enjoy are a top priority with us. We also welcome articles on family activities that are fun, affordable, and easy to do. We are launching a new magazine this year so check our website for updates.

Family Safety & Health

1121 Spring Lake Drive
Itasca, IL 60143

Editor: Tim Hodson

Description and Readership
Promoting home, recreational, and traffic safety, this magazine features articles and tips for the entire family. Published by the National Safety Council, it covers topics such as nutrition, health, sports, equipment, and the Internet.
• **Audience:** 6–12 years
• **Frequency:** Quarterly
• **Distribution:** 70% subscription; 30% newsstand
• **Circulation:** 225,000
• **Website:** www.nsc.org

Freelance Potential
5% written by nonstaff writers. Publishes 5 freelance submissions yearly; 20% by authors who are new to the magazine.

Submissions
Send résumé only via email to hodsont@nsc.org. No unsolicited submissions. All work is done on a work-for-hire basis. Response time varies.
Articles: 1,200 words. Informational and how-to articles. Topics include home and traffic safety, nutrition, fitness, and technology.
Depts/columns: Staff written.

Sample Issue
26 pages (15% advertising): 6 articles; 3 depts/columns. Sample copy, $4 with 9x12 SASE ($.77 postage). Guidelines available.
• "Cyberbully: The Schoolyard Bully's Turf Moves Online." Article discusses the problem of cyberbullies and how they work.
• "In Season." Article takes a look at children and sports and things parents can do to help prevent injuries.
• "Teen Driving Safety." Article presents evidence defining the risks teen drivers face, ways to reduce those risks, and ways for parents to get involved.

Rights and Payment
All rights. Written material, payment rates vary. Pays on acceptance. Provides 2 contributor's copies.

Editor's Comments
If you would like to be considered for a writing assignment, send us your résumé. We are currently not accepting unsolicited submissions. We look for writers who can present a topic using facts and statistics. Check our editorial calendar and past issues to see what we are all about and whether you are a good fit.

FamilyWorks Magazine

4 Joseph Court
San Rafael, CA 94903

Editor: Lew Tremaine

Description and Readership
A regional publication available free of charge in Marin and Sonoma counties, *FamilyWorks* presents articles aimed at strengthening the family unit. It was launched in 1978.
• **Audience:** Parents, caregivers, and professionals
• **Frequency:** Monthly
• **Distribution:** 50% newsstand; 40% schools; 10% subscription
• **Circulation:** 30,000
• **Website:** www.familyworks.org

Freelance Potential
90% written by nonstaff writers. Publishes 18 freelance submissions yearly; 25% by unpublished writers, 25% by authors who are new to the magazine. Receives 8 unsolicited mss monthly.

Submissions
Send complete ms. Accepts computer printouts, Macintosh disk submissions, and email submissions to familynews@familyworks.org. Availability of artwork improves chance of acceptance. SASE. Responds in 1 month.
Articles: 1,000 words. Informational articles; profiles; and interviews. Topics include parenting, family issues, recreation, education, finance, crafts, hobbies, sports, health, fitness, nature, and the environment.
Depts/columns: Word length varies. Reviews, recipes, and organizational news.
Artwork: B/W and color prints.

Sample Issue
32 pages (46% advertising): 8 articles; 3 depts/columns. Sample copy, free. Guidelines available.
• "Think Your Teen Needs Counseling?" Article offers guidelines for exasperated parents seeking help for their troubled teens.
• "Kids' Allowances: Save or Spend?" Article looks at the benefits of giving an allowance and letting kids be responsible for their own spending decisions.
• "Keep Your Cool with Icy Cold Goodies." Article offers refreshing recipes for hot-weather days.

Rights and Payment
One-time rights. No payment. Provides 3 copies.

Editor's Comments
Community leaders and others who care about parents, kids, and the family are invited to submit. First-person stories as well as feature articles are welcome.

Faze Teen

Suite 2400
4936 Yonge Street
Toronto, Ontario M2N 6S3
Canada

Editor: Lorraine Zander

Description and Readership
Available both online and in print, this magazine for Canadian teenagers offers articles and information on the latest news, celebrities, technology, entertainment, health and beauty, careers, and social issues.
- **Audience:** 13–18 years
- **Frequency:** 6 times each year
- **Distribution:** Subscription; newsstand; school libraries; Internet
- **Circulation:** 250,000
- **Website:** www.fazeteen.com

Freelance Potential
80% written by nonstaff writers. Publishes 100+ freelance submissions yearly; 90% by authors who are new to the magazine. Receives 8 queries, 2 unsolicited mss monthly.

Submissions
Query. Accepts email queries to editor@fazeteen.com. Response time varies.
Articles: Word length varies. Informational and factual articles; personal experience pieces; profiles; and interviews. Topics include current affairs, real-life issues, famous people, entertainment, science, travel, business, technology, and health.
Depts/columns: Word length varies. Media reviews.

Sample Issue
66 pages (3% advertising): 13 articles; 11 depts/columns. Sample copy, $3.50 Canadian. Guidelines available at website.
- "Anatomically Incorrect!" Article discusses how the media presents supermodels and actresses who are unnaturally thin.
- "When Friends Want to Die: How to Help." Article reports on teen suicide and how to intervene.
- Sample dept/column: "Careers" takes a look at some non-traditional careers such as ironworkers, roofers, funeral directors, and firefighters.

Rights and Payment
All rights. Written material, $50–$300. Payment policy varies. Provides 1 contributor's copy.

Editor's Comments
The majority of our material is written by teens and other young adults. We are currently looking for more articles by college-age/journalism majors. Topics of interest include unique travel pieces, information on the latest social issues, and technology.

FitPregrancy

21100 Erwin Street
Woodland Hills, CA 91367

Executive Editor: Sharon Cohen

Description and Readership
This magazine strives to encourage women to stay healthy and fit and have fun during pregnancy. It offers articles on health, nutrition, and psychology, as well as fashion and beauty issues.
- **Audience:** Adults
- **Frequency:** 6 times each year
- **Distribution:** 60% subscription; 40% newsstand
- **Circulation:** 500,000
- **Website:** www.fitpregnancy.com

Freelance Potential
75% written by nonstaff writers. Publishes 50 freelance submissions yearly; 3% by unpublished writers, 5% by authors who are new to the magazine. Receives 30 queries monthly.

Submissions
Query with clips. Accepts photocopies and computer printouts. SASE. Responds in 1 month.
Articles: 1,200–2,400 words. Informational articles and personal experience pieces. Topics include health, fitness, family issues, psychology, postpartum issues, and breastfeeding.
Fiction: Word lengths vary. Publishes humorous fiction.
Depts/columns: 600 words. Nutrition, baby care, food, fashion, beauty, news items, and new product information.

Sample Issue
132 pages (42% advertising): 9 articles; 17 depts/columns. Sample copy, $4.95 at newsstands. Writers' guidelines available.
- "Winds of Change." Article showcases the latest in maternity wear.
- "The First Time." Article offers information for first-time moms on caring for a newborn.
- Sample dept/column: "Time Out" discusses how swimming offers a mom a way to reflect on the past and present.

Rights and Payment
Rights vary. Written material, payment rates vary. Pays on publication. Provides 2 contributor's copies.

Editor's Comments
Our features cover broad, timely topics. Features for which we accept freelance writing include: prenatal fitness, nutrition and food, and psychology. Send us a query and tell us why your idea is unique.

Florida Leader

Oxendine Publishing
P.O. Box 14081
Gainesville, FL 32604-2081

Associate Editor: Stephanie Reck

Description and Readership

Focusing on student leadership, this magazine offers articles on topics related to college life, careers, and student government. It is read by students interested in attending college and universities in Florida.
- **Audience:** 15–22 years
- **Frequency:** 3 times each year
- **Distribution:** 95% schools; 5% subscription
- **Circulation:** 45,000
- **Website:** www.floridaleader.com

Freelance Potential

10% written by nonstaff writers. Publishes 5 freelance submissions yearly; 50% by unpublished writers, 80% by authors who are new to the magazine. Receives 12 queries monthly.

Submissions

Query. No unsolicited mss. Accepts photocopies, computer printouts, and simultaneous submissions if identified. SASE. Responds in 3 weeks.
Articles: 1,000 words. Informational, self-help, and how-to articles. Topics include colleges, universities, undergraduate life, financial aid, admissions requirements, majors, and student leadership.
Depts/columns: Word lengths vary. Information on careers and education.
Artwork: B/W and color prints and slides.

Sample Issue

46 pages (50% advertising): 10 articles. Sample copy, guidelines, and editorial calendar available.
- "Best Homecoming." Article describes the University of Central Florida's homecoming week.
- "Best Halloween." Article takes a look at the Art Institute of Ft. Lauderdale's annual Halloween parade.
- "Best Fundraiser." Article reports on a fundraiser by the Mud Pi ceramics club of Florida Keys Community College, where members sold ceramic plates.

Rights and Payment

All rights. All material, payment rates vary. Provides 2 contributor's copies.

Editor's Comments

We look for articles and tips that will help empower students to make a difference in their college community and take on leadership roles. While our publication is theme oriented, submissions for general content will be considered for the September issue.

Focus on the Family Clubhouse

8605 Explorer Drive
Colorado Springs, CO 80902

Associate Editor: Suzanne Hadley

Description and Readership

Articles, stories, and activities for children can be found in this Christian publication. It teaches children about God and the Bible and includes adventure, action, excitement, humor, and mystery stories.
- **Audience:** 8–12 years
- **Frequency:** Monthly
- **Distribution:** 100% subscription
- **Circulation:** 115,000
- **Website:** www.clubhousemagazine.com

Freelance Potential

20% written by nonstaff writers. Publishes 12–15 freelance submissions yearly; 5% by unpublished writers, 5% by authors who are new to the magazine. Receives 95 unsolicited mss monthly.

Submissions

Send complete ms. Accepts photocopies and computer printouts. SASE. Responds in 4–6 weeks.
Articles: 800–1,000 words. Informational, how-to, and factual articles; interviews; personal experience pieces; and humor. Topics include sports, nature, history, fantasy, religion, current events, and multicultural issues.
Fiction: 500–1,500 words. Genres include historical, contemporary, and religious fiction; parables; humor; and mystery.
Other: Activities and Bible-related comics. Submit Christian holiday material 7 months in advance.

Sample Issue

24 pages (5% advertising): 1 article; 4 stories; 5 depts/columns; 3 activities; 1 comic. Sample copy, $1.50 with 9x12 SASE (2 first-class stamps). Guidelines available.
- "A Very Merry Unbirthday." Personal experience piece describes a surprise birthday party that was held 7 months early.
- "April Showers." Story features a teen who is blamed for an April Fools prank she didn't do.
- Sample dept/column: "MailBag" offers a poem, puzzle, and pizza bagel recipe.

Rights and Payment

First rights. Written material, to $200. Pays on acceptance. Provides 5 contributor's copies.

Editor's Comments

We look for wholesome, educational material with moral insight that pleases both the parent and child.

Focus on the Family Clubhouse Jr.

8605 Explorer Drive
Colorado Springs, CO 80920

Associate Editor: Suzanne Hadley

Description and Readership
This magazine offers inspirational and entertaining material that teaches young children Christian values. It includes articles, stories, poetry, and activities.
- **Audience:** 4–8 years
- **Frequency:** Monthly
- **Distribution:** 98% subscription; 2% newsstand
- **Circulation:** 105,000
- **Website:** www.clubhousemagazine.org

Freelance Potential
20% written by nonstaff writers. Publishes 6–12 freelance submissions yearly; 1% by unpublished writers, 5% by authors who are new to the magazine. Receives 60 unsolicited mss monthly.

Submissions
Send complete ms. Accepts photocopies and computer printouts. No simultaneous submissions. SASE. Responds in 4–6 weeks.
Articles: To 600 words. Informational articles. Topics include the environment, nature, hobbies, health, and fitness.
Fiction: 250–1,000 words. Genres include Bible stories; humor; folktales; and religious, contemporary, and historical fiction.
Other: Puzzles, activities, games, cartoons, and poetry with biblical themes. Submit seasonal material 6 months in advance.

Sample Issue
24 pages (no advertising): 1 article; 3 stories; 4 activities; 1 comic; 1 poem. Sample copy, $1.50 with 9x12 SASE (2 first-class stamps). Guidelines available.
- "Growing with Goats." Article shares a young girl's experience of growing up with goats.
- "Corrie's New Heart." Story about a young girl who learns about prayer and Jesus filling her heart.
- Sample dept/column: "Stuff Kids Love" offers information on an audio series, books, and a CD set.

Rights and Payment
First North American one-time rights. Written material, to $200. Pays on acceptance. Provides 2 author's copies.

Editor's Comments
We look for fresh, creative fiction that is built upon a solid foundation of Christian beliefs and wholesome family values. We also seek articles about real children or adults with interesting spiritual experiences.

Footsteps

Cobblestone Publishing
Suite C
3 Grove Street
Peterborough, NH 03458

Associate Editor: Rosalie F. Baker

Description and Readership
This children's magazine of African American history, culture, and heritage features theme-based issues focusing on the contributions of African Americans.
- **Audience:** 9–14 years
- **Frequency:** 5 times each year
- **Distribution:** 100% subscription
- **Circulation:** 6,000
- **Website:** www.footstepsmagazine.com

Freelance Potential
80% written by nonstaff writers. Publishes 100 freelance submissions yearly; 40% by unpublished writers, 60% by authors who are new to the magazine. Receives 25 queries monthly.

Submissions
Query with résumé. Accepts photocopies, computer printouts, and Macintosh disk submissions. SASE. Responds in 2–4 months.
Articles: 200–1,000 words. Informational articles; profiles; and interviews. Topics include history and multicultural issues. Also publishes biographies.
Depts/columns: 200–1,000 words. Reviews, poems, and artwork.
Artwork: B/W and color prints or transparencies. Line art.
Other: Theme-related activities.

Sample Issue
50 pages (no advertising): 15 articles; 4 depts/columns; 4 activities. Sample copy, $4.50 with 9x12 SASE ($1.24 postage). Writers' guidelines and theme list available.
- "Four Food 'Greats'." Article discusses the role four African Americans played in making some familiar foods cheap, safe, and widely available.
- "Never Stop." Article tells how a young girl made a childhood idea an award-winning reality.
- Sample dept/column: "Let's Find Out" features moments in history that involved African Americans.

Rights and Payment
All rights. Written material, $.20 per word. Artwork, payment rate varies. Pays on publication. Provides 2 contributor's copies.

Editor's Comments
Each of our issues focuses on a specific theme relating to African American history. All submissions should correspond to our editorial topics.

Fort Myers Magazine

Suite 189
15880 Summerlin Road
Ft. Myers, FL 33908

Creative Director: Andrew Elias

Description and Readership
This regional magazine celebrates living in southwest Florida. It offers articles and information and family entertainment for residents and visitors.
- **Audience:** Parents
- **Frequency:** 6 times each year
- **Distribution:** 5% controlled; 2% subscription; 97% other
- **Circulation:** 20,000
- **Website:** www.ftmyersmagazine.com

Freelance Potential
85% written by nonstaff writers. Publishes 20–35 freelance submissions yearly; 50% by unpublished writers, 50% by authors who are new to the magazine. Receives 250 unsolicited queries monthly.

Submissions
Query or send complete ms. Accepts photocopies, computer printouts, Macintosh disk submissions, and email submissions to ftmyers@optonline.net. SASE. Responds in 1–6 weeks.
Articles: 500–2,000 words. Informational articles; profiles; interviews; reviews; and local news. Topics include the arts, media, entertainment, travel, computers, crafts, current events, health and fitness, history, popular culture, recreation, social and environmental issues, and parenting.
Depts/columns: Word length varies. Sports, recreation, and book reviews.
Artwork: JPG, Tiff, or PDF.

Sample Issue
26 pages (40% advertising): 1 article; 8 depts/columns; 1 calendar of events. Sample copy, $3 with 9x12 SASE. Guidelines and editorial calendar available.
- "Kasey: An Outback Angel Grows Up." Feature article highlights the life of Australian singer-songwriter Kasey Chambers.
- Sample dept/column: "Sports & Recreation" profiles the coach of the Florida Flame basketball team.

Rights and Payment
One-time rights. Pays 30 days from publication. Written material, $.10 per word. Provides 1 contributor's copy.

Editor's Comments
We want succinct, fun, reader-friendly, informative, and entertaining articles that deal with events and personalities in Lee County.

Fort Worth Child

Lauren Publications
Suite 146
4275 Kellway Circle
Addison, TX 75001

Editor: Shelly Pate

Description and Readership
Informative and entertaining articles on parenting and family issues are featured in this magazine. Read by families living in Fort Worth, Texas, it also includes information on local resources, services, and events.
- **Audience:** Parents
- **Frequency:** Monthly
- **Distribution:** 90% controlled; 10% subscription
- **Circulation:** 120,000
- **Website:** www.fortworthchild.com

Freelance Potential
25% written by nonstaff writers. Publishes 12–15 freelance submissions yearly; 20% by authors who are new to the magazine. Receives 20 queries monthly.

Submissions
Query with résumé. Accepts photocopies, computer printouts, and simultaneous submissions if identified. SASE. Responds in 2–3 months.
Articles: 1,000–2,500 words. Informational, self-help, and how-to articles; humor; profiles; and personal experience pieces. Topics include family, parenting, education, health, nutrition, exercise, travel, crafts, hobbies, computers, regional news, and multicultural and ethnic issues.
Depts/columns: 800 words. Health news and reviews.

Sample Issue
46 pages (14% advertising): 2 articles; 8 depts/columns. Sample copy, free with 9x12 SASE. Writers' guidelines available.
- "Kids' Activities." Article discusses the importance of examining registration forms for kids' activities carefully before signing them.
- Sample dept/column: "Education" offers tips on ways to help prepare children at home for academic success.

Rights and Payment
First rights. Written material, payment rates vary. Pays on publication. Provides contributor's copies upon request.

Editor's Comments
We would like to see more articles on local child advocacy issues, as well as up-to-date, need-to-know parenting information on safety issues and finance. Keep in mind that all of the material we offer must have a connection to the Fort Worth area.

Fostering Families Today

3614 Cardinal Ridge Drive
Greensboro, NC 27410

Editor: Cynthia Peck

Description and Readership
Articles on issues relating to adoption and foster care are featured in this magazine. Its readers include families and professionals interested in domestic, international, and national adoption and foster care.
- **Audience:** Parents
- **Frequency:** 4 times each year
- **Distribution:** Subscription
- **Circulation:** Unavailable
- **Website:** www.fosteringfamiliestoday.com

Freelance Potential
75% written by nonstaff writers. Publishes several freelance submissions yearly.

Submissions
Send complete ms. Accepts photocopies, computer printouts, IBM disk submissions (Microsoft Word or ASCIII), and email to ffteditor@bellsouth.net. SASE. Response time varies.
Articles: 500–1,200 words. Informational and how-to articles; profiles; and personal experience pieces. Topics include parenting, pertinent research, health and family, adoption, single parenting, adolescence, special-needs children, foster parenting, multicultural families, issues in education, and legal issues.
Depts/columns: Word length varies. Parenting topics, events, cultural information, identity formation, legal issues, and reviews.

Sample Issue
62 pages (no advertising): 17 articles; 12 depts/columns. Guidelines available.
- "Aiming for the Future." Article describes how Minnesota Vikings quarterback Daunte Culpepper, who was adopted as an infant, encourages foster kids to look to their future.
- "Life Skills 101." Article offers information on teaching teens life skills they need to know by setting examples and stressing the importance of family.
- Sample dept/column: "Everyday Heroes" profiles the founder and executive director of Rocky Mountain Children's Law Center, Shari Shink.

Rights and Payment
One-time rights. No payment. Provides 2 contributor's copies and a 1-year subscription.

Editor's Comments
We look for personal stories that share the excitement, frustration, hope, and joy of adoption.

The Friend

The Church of Jesus Christ of Latter-day Saints
24th Floor
50 East North Temple
Salt Lake City, UT 84150

Managing Editor: Vivian Paulsen

Description and Readership
Contents of this magazine support and strengthen the teachings and lessons of the Mormon church. Stories, based on biblical events, are used to build character and provide ideas for conflict resolution.
- **Audience:** 3–11 years
- **Frequency:** Monthly
- **Distribution:** 100% subscription
- **Circulation:** 252,000
- **Website:** www.www.lds.org

Freelance Potential
60% written by nonstaff writers.

Submissions
Send complete ms. Accepts photocopies and computer printouts. SASE. Responds in 2 months.
Articles: To 1,200 words. Informational and factual articles; profiles; personal experience pieces; and true stories. Topics include spirituality, the Mormon church, personal faith, and conflict resolution.
Depts/columns: Word length varies. Profiles of Mormon elders and children from different countries.
Other: Poetry, word length varies. Puzzles, activities, crafts, and cartoons. Submit seasonal material 8 months in advance.

Sample Issue
50 pages (no advertising): 13 articles; 3 stories; 4 depts/columns; 5 activities; 1 poem. Sample copy, $1.50 with 9x12 SASE (4 first-class stamps). Guidelines available.
- "Trust in Others and Yourself." Article recounts how the author learned from his father how to be trustworthy and trusting as a boy.
- "You Must Choose for Yourself." Article retells a historic incident about a family that chooses to join a new church and the ensuing consequences.
- "The Ugliest, Most Wonderful Car." Story depicts how even a mistake can turn out to be a positive experience if we're honest about our efforts.

Rights and Payment
All rights. Pays on acceptance. Articles 200–400 words, $100; 400+ words, $250. Poems, $50. Other material, $15+. Provides 2 contributor's copies.

Editor's Comments
We are always looking for pieces that are humorous and that have a universal appeal. Keep in mind that our age range is preschool to middle school.

Fun For Kidz

P.O. Box 227
Bluffton, OH 45817-0227

Associate Editor: Virginia Edwards

Description and Readership
Each theme-oriented issue of this magazine offers activity-based stories and articles that deal with timeless topics of interest to children.
- **Audience:** 6–13 years
- **Frequency:** 6 times each year
- **Distribution:** 80% subscription; 20% newsstand
- **Circulation:** 3,000
- **Website:** www.funforkidz.com

Freelance Potential
100% written by nonstaff writers. Publishes many freelance submissions yearly; 5% by unpublished writers, 15% by authors who are new to the magazine.

Submissions
Send complete ms. Accepts computer printouts and simultaneous submissions if identified. SASE. Availability of artwork improves chance of acceptance. Responds in 4–6 weeks.
Articles: 500 words. Informational and how-to articles. Topics include pets, nature, careers, cooking, and sports.
Fiction: 500 words. Humorous fiction, animal stories, and adventure.
Depts/columns: Word length varies. Puzzles, science, and collecting.
Artwork: B/W and color prints or transparencies. Line art.
Other: Activities, filler, games, jokes, and puzzles. Submit seasonal material 6–12 months in advance.

Sample Issue
48 pages (no advertising): 11 articles; 6 depts/columns; 9 puzzles. Sample copy, $4. Guidelines and theme list available.
- "The Castaways." Ongoing story follows the adventures of a family of hares that was shipwrecked on a deserted island.
- Sample dept/column: "Stunts & Puzzles" gives instructions for making a tall paper tree.

Rights and Payment
First or reprint rights. Written material, $.05 per word. Artwork, payment rate varies. Pays on publication. Provides 1 contributor's copy.

Editor's Comments
All submissions must center on an activity. Fiction is acceptable, but should be accompanied by a hands-on activity featured in the story.

Games

Suite 200
6198 Butler Pike
Blue Bell, PA 19422-2600

Editor-in-Chief: R. Wayne Schmittberger

Description and Readership
Games is a unique publication aimed at entertaining and intellectually challenging its readers. Although its readership spans a wide range of ages, all readers share the joy of exercising their minds in new and playful ways.
- **Audience:** YA–Adult
- **Frequency:** 10 times each year
- **Distribution:** 70% subscription; 30% newsstand
- **Circulation:** 75,000

Freelance Potential
86% written by nonstaff writers. Publishes 200+ freelance submissions yearly; 10% by unpublished writers, 20% by authors who are new to the magazine. Receives 80 queries and unsolicited mss monthly.

Submissions
Query with outline for articles. Send complete ms for longer pieces. Accepts photocopies and computer printouts. SASE. Responds to queries in 6–8 weeks.
Articles: 1,500–3,000 words. Informational articles; humor; and profiles. Topics include game-related events and people, wordplay, and human ingenuity. Game reviews by assignment only.
Depts/columns: Staff written except for "Gamebits."
Artwork: Visual and verbal puzzles, quizzes, contests, two-play games, and adventures.

Sample Issue
80 pages (8% advertising): 1 article; 4 depts/columns; 2 contests; 19 activities. Sample copy, $4.50 with 9x12 SASE ($1.24 postage). Guidelines available.
- "Game of the Decade?" Article profiles game designer Klaus Teuber, and describes his award-winning game, Settlers of Catan.

Rights and Payment
All North American serial rights. Articles, $500–$1,200. "Gamebits," $100–$250. Pays on publication. Provides 1 contributor's copy.

Editor's Comments
We offer our readers a vast variety of games, puzzles, and brain-teasers. While our game reviews and departments are written by staff writers, we are open to article submissions, profiles, interviews, historically important advancements, and humor. We look for imaginative proposals that appeal to a wide age range and to both male and female readers. Please review our magazine and guidelines for the type of material that interests us.

Genesee Valley Parent

Suite 204
1 Grove Street
Pittsford, NY 14534

Managing Editor: Margo Perine

Description and Readership
Articles and reviews covering parenting and child development are featured in this magazine. Targeting parents in the greater Rochester, New York, area, it also includes resources and events in the region.
• **Audience:** Parents
• **Frequency:** Monthly
• **Distribution:** 65% controlled; 30% schools; 5% other
• **Circulation:** 37,000
• **Website:** www.gvparent.com

Freelance Potential
75% written by nonstaff writers. Publishes 50 freelance submissions yearly; 5% by authors who are new to the magazine. Receives 20 queries monthly.

Submissions
Query with clips or writing samples. Accepts photocopies and simultaneous submissions if identified. SASE. Responds in 1–3 months.
Articles: 700–1,200 words. Informational and how-to articles; personal experience pieces; interviews; reviews; and humor. Topics include regional events and concerns, special and gifted education, social issues, family problems, health and fitness, and parenting.
Depts/columns: 500–600 words. Short news items, health, and family finances.
Other: Submit seasonal material 4 months in advance.

Sample Issue
50 pages (50% advertising): 4 articles; 8 depts/columns; 1 calendar of events. Guidelines and editorial calendar available.
• "Making the Most of a College Visit." Article discusses the importance of visiting college campuses before deciding on which college to attend.
• "Fairs, Festivals and Family Fun." Article explores fun summer activities for the whole family to enjoy.
• Sample dept/column: "Parents Exchange" takes a look at things most dads have in common.

Rights and Payment
Second rights. Articles, $30–$45. Depts/columns, $25–$30. Pays on publication. Provides 1 tear sheet.

Editor's Comments
Accurate and well-researched articles on topics related to raising children are of interest to us.

GeoParent

719 Octavia Street
New Orleans, LA 70115

Editor: Jennifer Newton Reents

Description and Readership
The *GeoParent* website features informational articles, interactive tools, and a support community for parents of children from birth through the teen years. It includes material on family health, lifestyles, and relationships, along with parenting tips.
• **Audience:** Parents
• **Frequency:** Weekly
• **Distribution:** 100% Internet
• **Website:** www.geoparent.com

Freelance Potential
90% written by nonstaff writers. Publishes 50 freelance submissions yearly. Receives 50 queries and unsolicited mss monthly.

Submissions
Prefers query. Accepts complete ms. Accepts photocopies, computer printouts, email submissions to feedback@coincide.com, and submissions through their website. SASE. Response time varies.
Articles: 500–2,500 words. Informational articles and advice. Topics include parenting, child development, family issues, child care, gifted education, and special education.
Depts/columns: Word lengths vary. Parenting advice.

Sample Issue
Sample copy and guidelines available at website.
• "Jaundice in Breastfed Babies." Article explains the causes of jaundice and tells why it is common in newborns.
• "Bringing Your New Baby into a Blended Family." Article discusses the special needs of older siblings when a new baby joins a blended family.
• "Babies and Sleep." Article offers tips about the erratic sleep patterns of babies.

Rights and Payment
Rights vary. Written material, $25–$50; $10 for reprints. Pays on publication.

Editor's Comments
We try to offer a unique, interactive edge for parents of children of all ages. We seek information from experts in a variety of fields, as well as features written by journalists and others with appropriate writing skills and style. The best guide for writers is the site itself. We are not seeking personal essays or opinion pieces at this time.

Gifted Education Press Quarterly

P.O. Box 1586
10201 Yuma Court
Manassas, VA 20109

Editor & Publisher: Maurice D. Fisher

Description and Readership
This education newsletter is written for adults who work with gifted children. Each issue offers practical articles on various issues in gifted education.
- **Audience:** Educators, administrators, and parents
- **Frequency:** Quarterly
- **Distribution:** 100% subscription
- **Circulation:** 4,500
- **Website:** www.giftedpress.com

Freelance Potential
90% written by nonstaff writers. Publishes 15 free-lance submissions yearly; 50% by unpublished writers, 90% by authors who are new to the magazine. Receives 2 queries monthly.

Submissions
Query. SASE. Responds in 2 weeks.
Articles: 3,000–5,000 words. Informational and how-to articles; personal experience pieces; interviews; and profiles. Topics include gifted education, home-schooling, multiple intelligence, parent advocates, social issues, science, history, the environment, and popular culture.

Sample Issue
14 pages (no advertising): 4 articles. Sample copy, $4 with 9x12 SASE.
- "Experience and Processing: The Funnel and Cylinder Analogy of Giftedness." Article uses an easily under-stood analogy to help readers understand how children process information.
- "Teaching Physics to Gifted Students." Article explains how to transform a physics problem into basic mathematical symbols and diagrams and then use the laws of physics to transform those symbols into equations of motion.
- "The Buck Stops Here." Literary tribute to Harry S. Truman, one of the most gifted presidents of the United States.

Rights and Payment
All rights. No payment. Provides 5 copies.

Editor's Comments
We would like to see more material on science programs for gifted children. We also like articles on national legislation that has an impact on gifted education. Prospective writers should have a solid base in the field, and be able to document the material used in their submission.

Girls' Life

4517 Harford Road
Baltimore, MD 21214

Executive Editor: Kelly White

Description and Readership
In addition to features on fashion and beauty, pre-teen and young teenage girls can find articles on friendship and family issues; reviews of music, books, and movies; profiles of girls who are making contributions to their communities; and the views and opinions of other teen girls in each issue of *Girls' Life*.
- **Audience:** 10–14 years
- **Frequency:** 6 times each year
- **Distribution:** Subscription; newsstand
- **Circulation:** 400,000
- **Website:** www.girlslife.com

Freelance Potential
40–50% written by nonstaff writers. Publishes 100+ freelance submissions yearly; 10% by unpublished writers, 10% by authors who are new to the magazine. Receives 83 unsolicited mss monthly.

Submissions
Query or send complete ms with résumé and 2 clips. SASE. Responds in 3 months.
Articles: 1,200–2,500 words. Informational, service-oriented articles. Topics include self-esteem, body image, friendship, relationships, sibling rivalry, school success, facing challenges, and setting goals.
Depts/columns: 300–800 words. Celebrity spotlights; newsworthy stories about real girls; service pieces about friends, guys, and life; decorating tips; easy-to-do crafts and activities; and media reviews.

Sample Issue
96 pages (30% advertising): 9 articles; 1 story; 20 depts/columns. Sample copy, $5. Guidelines and editorial calendar available at website or with SASE.
- "Make This School Year Your Best One Yet." Article presents back-to-school tips.
- "The Silent Scream." Article discusses the emotional issue of cutting.
- Sample dept/column: "GL Friends" has advice for girls who feel neglected when their best friends find boyfriends.

Rights and Payment
All or first rights. All material, payment rates vary. Pays on publication. Provides 1 contributor's copy.

Editor's Comments
All the information we offer must be entirely trustwor-thy. If your topic involves research, please use primary sources and provide us with a complete list of names.

Go-Girl

Rumholtz Publishing
Suite 202
1200 South Avenue
Staten Island, NY 10314

Editor-in--Chief: Gina LaGuardia

Description and Readership
This online publication is packed with information and tips for college-bound teenage girls. It includes light-hearted and informative articles on topics such as finances, beauty, social issues, health, careers, fashion, and coping with college life.
• **Audience:** 14–18 years
• **Frequency:** 6 times each year
• **Distribution:** Internet
• **Hits per month:** 350,000
• **Website:** www.go-girl.com

Freelance Potential
50% written by nonstaff writers. Publishes 100 freelance submissions yearly; 50% by unpublished writers, 70% by authors who are new to the magazine. Receives 42 queries monthly.

Submissions
Query with clips. Accepts email queries to editorial@collegebound.net, and photocopies. SASE. Responds in 5 weeks.
Articles: 200–600 words. Informational, factual, and how-to articles; profiles; interviews; and personal experience pieces. Topics include health, fashion, beauty, fitness, relationships, family, friends, celebrities, hobbies, college, careers, sports, music, popular culture, and education.
Depts/columns: 100–300 words. Fashion, beauty, health, fitness, entertainment, and academic advice.

Sample Issue
Guidelines available at website.
• "Trippin'." Article offers information on learning about other cultures and how to help make a difference in the world.
• "Ashley Gets a Little Help from Friends." Article describes one girl's remarkable experiences of living on her own and meeting her television idol.
• Sample dept/column: "Go Beauty" offers 25 beauty secrets on looking good.

Rights and Payment
All or first rights. Written material, $50–$75. Depts/columns, $25–$40. Pays on publication.

Editor's Comments
We are looking for fresh stories on topics that haven't been covered before. We are receiving too many submissions on "freshman 15," roommate issues, long distance relationships, and how to pay for college.

Great Lakes Family Magazine

P.O. Box 714
Kalamazoo, MI 49004

Editor & Publisher: Cynthia L. Schrauben

Description and Readership
Great Lakes Family Magazine is a local magazine dedicated to providing southwest Michigan parents with information vital to raising healthy, well-adjusted children. Its goal is to help parents solve problems with information from local and national experts.
• **Audience:** Parents
• **Frequency:** 6 times each year
• **Distribution:** Subscription; newsstand
• **Circulation:** 47,000
• **Website:** www.glfamily.com

Freelance Potential
90% written by nonstaff writers. Publishes 18–20 freelance submissions yearly. Receives 100+ unsolicited mss monthly.

Submissions
Query or send complete ms. Accepts photocopies, computer printouts, and email submissions to editor@glfamily.com. SASE. Response time varies.
Articles: Word lengths vary. Informational articles. Topics include infant and child care, health, fitness, family safety, and family travel destinations.
Fiction: Word lengths vary. Genres include contemporary fiction.
Depts/columns: Word lengths vary. Local events, book reviews, and family recipes.

Sample Issue
32 pages: 4 articles; 8 depts/columns. Sample copy and guidelines available.
• "Beyond Band-Aids." Article explains how parents can evaluate emergencies and determine if medical intervention is necessary.
• "Parenting with Success." Article discusses how to help young children learn to be patient.
• "Kids Dig Dirt." Article shows that gardening with children can be a satisfying activity for all involved.

Rights and Payment
Rights vary. Written material, payment rates vary. Pays on publication.

Editor's Comments
Our audience consists of all types of parents, from those just expecting, to parents of infants and toddlers, to parents of older children. Our region covers the areas of Barry, Kent, Calhoun, Allegan, and Kalamazoo; material from writers from those areas will receive a second look.

Green Teacher

95 Robert Street
Toronto, Ontario M5S 2K5
Canada

Co-Editors: Tim Grant & Gail Littlejohn

Description and Readership
Care for planet Earth is the focus of this educational magazine for teachers and students. It contains a mix of information and classroom activities.
• **Audience:** Teachers, grades K–12
• **Frequency:** Quarterly
• **Distribution:** 50% newsstand; 40% subscription; 10% other
• **Circulation:** 7,500
• **Website:** www.greenteacher.com

Freelance Potential
90% written by nonstaff writers. Publishes 40 freelance submissions yearly; 90% by unpublished writers, 90% by authors who are new to the magazine. Receives 5 unsolicited mss monthly.

Submissions
Prefers summary or outline before sending complete ms. Accepts photocopies, computer printouts, disk submissions (ASCII) with hard copy, fax submissions to 416-925-3474, and email submissions to tim@ greenteacher.com. Availability of artwork improves chance of acceptance. SAE/IRC. Responds in 2 months.
Articles: 1,500–3,000 words. Informational and how-to articles. Topics include the environment, science, education, and mathematics.
Depts/columns: Word length varies. Resources, reviews, and announcements.
Artwork: B/W and color prints and transparencies. Line art.
Other: Submit material for Earth Day 6 months in advance.

Sample Issue
48 pages (12% advertising): 8 articles; 3 depts/columns. Sample copy, $7. Guidelines available.
• "Paradise Lost? How Do We Define Progress?" Article explains how a sixth-grade class compared the present day local environment to its condition during their grandparents' era.
• Sample dept/column: "Inside the Internet" shows how to integrate projects and Internet resources.

Rights and Payment
Rights negotiable. No payment. Provides 5 copies.

Editor's Comments
Our articles focus on how to teach environmental and conservation values and ideas, rather than on scientific facts.

Grit

1503 SW 42nd Street
Topeka, KS 66609-1265

Editor-in-Chief: Andrea Skalland

Description and Readership
Striving to be America's favorite publication and to brighten its readers' lives, this upbeat magazine includes inspirational articles and stories.
• **Audience:** Families
• **Frequency:** 12 times each year
• **Distribution:** 100% subscription
• **Circulation:** 100,000
• **Website:** www.gritmagazine.com

Freelance Potential
90% written by nonstaff writers. Publishes 150–200 freelance submissions yearly; 50% by unpublished writers, 50% by authors who are new to the magazine. Receives 200 unsolicited mss monthly.

Submissions
Send complete ms with photos, résumé, and clips or writing samples. Accepts Macintosh CD submissions with hard copy. SASE. Response time varies.
Articles: 800–1,500 words. Factual and how-to articles; profiles; and personal experience pieces. Topics include American history, family lifestyles, parenting, pets, crafts, community involvement, and antiques.
Fiction: 1,000+ words. Serials, romance, mysteries, Westerns, and stories with strong moral principles.
Depts/columns: 500–1,500 words. Topics include pets, animals, nostalgia, true stories, family issues, health, cooking, and gardening.
Artwork: Color slides. B/W prints for nostalgia pieces.
Other: Poetry. Submit seasonal material 6 months in advance.

Sample Issue
48 pages (40% advertising): 9 articles; 1 story; 10 depts/columns. Sample copy, $4. Guidelines available.
• "Making WAVES." Article profiles a woman from Ohio who hand sews military uniforms for dolls.
• "A Place of Hope." Article shares the history of St. Jude's Chapel of Hope in North Carolina.
• Sample dept/column: "Under Our Roof" discusses using edible flowers to enhance the flavor of meals.

Rights and Payment
Shared rights. Articles, to $.15 per word. Depts/columns, payment rates vary. Artwork, $15–$25. Pays on publication. Provides 1 contributor's copy.

Editor's Comments
We look for true uplifting stories that reflect true American values that readers can relate to.

Group

Group Publishing, Inc.
P.O. Box 481
Loveland, CO 80539-0481

Associate Editor: Kathy Dieterich

Description and Readership
This magazine claims to be the world's most widely-read youth ministry resource publication. It caters to Christian youth ministers by providing information on running successful programs, providing effective outreach, and working with kids and parents.
- **Audience:** Adults
- **Frequency:** 6 times each year
- **Distribution:** 100% subscription
- **Circulation:** 55,000
- **Website:** www.grouppublishing.com

Freelance Potential
60% written by nonstaff writers. Publishes 200 freelance submissions yearly; 50% by unpublished writers, 80% by authors who are new to the magazine. Receives 25 queries monthly.

Submissions
Query with outline/synopsis and clips or writing samples. Accepts photocopies and computer printouts. State if artwork is available. SASE. Responds in 8–10 weeks.
Articles: 500–1,700 words. Informational and how-to articles. Topics include youth ministry strategies, recruiting and training adult leaders, understanding youth culture, professionalism, time management, leadership skills, and the professional and spiritual growth of youth ministers.
Depts/columns: "Try This One," to 300 words. "Hands-on Help," to 175 words.
Artwork: B/W or color illustration samples. Send artwork to art department. No photographs.

Sample Issue
114 pages (30% advertising): 5 articles; 24 depts/columns. Sample copy, $2 with 9x12 SASE. Guidelines available.
- "Stopping the Middle School Drop Off." Article explores ways to keep kids involved in church activities once they reach middle school.
- Sample dept/column: "Youth-Led Worship Service" offers ideas for Mother's Day and Father's Day.

Rights and Payment
All rights. Articles, $125–$225. Depts/columns, $40. Pays on acceptance.

Editor's Comments
Remember, we believe that young people learn best by doing. Send practical youth ministry ideas.

Guide

Review and Herald Publishing Association
55 West Oak Ridge Drive
Hagerstown, MD 21740

Assistant Editor: Rachel Whitaker

Description and Readership
A mix of true stories, games, puzzles, and Bible lessons appear in this Christian magazine for pre-teens and teens.
- **Audience:** 10–14 years
- **Frequency:** Weekly
- **Distribution:** 100% subscription
- **Circulation:** 29,000
- **Website:** www.guidemagazine.org

Freelance Potential
100% written by nonstaff writers. Publishes 50 freelance submissions yearly; 15% by unpublished writers, 20% by authors who are new to the magazine. Receives 30–40 unsolicited mss monthly.

Submissions
Send complete ms. Prefers email submissions to guide@rhpa.org. Accepts photocopies, computer printouts, and simultaneous submissions if identified. SASE. Responds in 4–6 months.
Articles: To 1,200 words. True stories with inspirational and personal growth themes; true adventure pieces; and humor. Nature articles with a religious emphasis, 750 words.
Other: Puzzles, activities, and games. Submit seasonal material about Thanksgiving, Christmas, Mother's Day, and Father's Day 8 months in advance.

Sample Issue
32 pages (no advertising): 5 articles; 2 Bible lessons; 5 activities. Sample copy, free with 9x12 SASE (2 first-class stamps). Guidelines available.
- "The Foolish Bandit." Story tells of a greedy robber who ends up losing more money than he stole.
- "Stopped at the Edge." Story describes how a boy riding a bike avoids a dangerous fall and believes his guardian angel saved him.
- "Media and Entertainment." Lesson discusses why children watch so much television.

Rights and Payment
First and second rights. Written material, $.06–$.12 per word. Pays on acceptance. Provides 3 contributor's copies.

Editor's Comments
We are looking for fresh stories on God at work in young peoples' lives at home and school. Make sure your writing style matches our target audience. Also, use plenty of dialogue and word pictures.

Guideposts for Kids Online

Suite 6
1050 Broadway
Chesterton, IN 46304

Managing Editor: Rosanne Tolin

Description and Readership
Guideposts for Kids Online seeks to provide an "interactive, entertaining, and empowering place for kids to play and learn."
- **Audience:** 6–12 years
- **Frequency:** Unavailable
- **Distribution:** 100% Internet
- **Hits per month:** 3.5 million
- **Website:** www.gp4k.com

Freelance Potential
90% written by nonstaff writers. Publishes 120 freelance submissions yearly; 1% by unpublished writers, 15% by authors who are new to the magazine. Receives 100 queries and unsolicited mss monthly.

Submissions
Query for nonfiction. Send complete ms for fiction. Accepts photocopies, computer printouts, and email submissions to rtolin@guideposts.org. SASE. Responds in 2–3 months.
Articles: To 700 words. Thought-provoking, issue-oriented articles. Topics include current events, science, animals, school, sports, and general subjects of interest to kids.
Fiction: To 900 words. Includes historical and contemporary fiction and mysteries.
Depts/columns: 50–150 words. Profiles of 6- to 12-year-old kids who volunteer.
Artwork: 8x10 B/W and color prints. Line art.
Other: Puzzles, jokes, trivia, quizzes, crafts, poetry, and recipes. Submit seasonal material 6 months in advance.

Sample Issue
48 pages (15% advertising): 7 articles; 1 story; 8 depts/columns. Sample copy, $4 with 9x12 SASE ($.77 postage). Guidelines available.
- "Herman." Story about two brothers who set out at the crack of dawn in hopes of catching a legendary fish, Herman.
- "How to Catch a Dog Food Snatcher." Story about a boy who is determined to catch the thief who's stealing his dog's food.

Rights and Payment
Electronic and non-exclusive rights. All material, payment rates vary. Pays on acceptance.

Editor's Comments
We're interested in fashion/beauty articles for tweens and nonfiction on school and sports.

Guideposts Sweet 16

Suite 6
1050 Broadway
Chesterton, IN 46304

Associate Editor: Allison Ruffing

Description and Readership
This magazine focuses on wholesome, inspiring relationships and real-life teen issues, and offers true stories about real teens.
- **Audience:** 12–18 years
- **Frequency:** 6 times each year
- **Distribution:** 100% subscription
- **Circulation:** 200,000
- **Website:** www.guidepostssweet16mag.com

Freelance Potential
60% written by nonstaff writers. Publishes 100 freelance submissions yearly; 17% by unpublished writers, 55% by authors who are new to the magazine. Receives 50 queries monthly.

Submissions
Query or send complete ms. Accepts photocopies, computer printouts, and and email submissions to writers@guidepostssweet16mag.com SASE. Responds in 1 month.
Articles: 750–1,500 words. Real-life and first-person stories; profiles; and interviews. Topics include adventure, relationships, dating, friendship, peer pressure, and celebrities.
Depts/columns: 300–500 words. Fashion, beauty, "miracle" stories, teen profiles, and quizzes.

Sample Issue
44 pages (no advertising): 3 articles; 9 stories; 5 depts/columns. Sample copy, $4.50. Writers' guidelines available.
- "Learning to Love Again." True story about a girl who turns to a horse to help her through the loss of her brother.
- "Perfect Boyfriend Alert." Profile of successful teen actor, Jared Padalecki.
- Sample dept/column: "Ask Ginger" answers readers' questions about friends, school, and siblings.

Rights and Payment
All rights. Articles, $150–$500. Depts/columns, $175–$400. Pays on acceptance. Provides 2–5 contributor's copies.

Editor's Comments
We need light stories about finding a date and learning to drive, as well as catch-in-your-throat stories about contemporary teen issues. Language and subject matter must be current, uplifting, and teen-friendly. Our readers do not like being lectured to.

Gumbo Magazine

1818 North Dr. Martin Luther King Drive
Milwaukee, WI 53212

Managing Editor: Tiffany Klynn
Submissions: Ty Finke

Description and Readership
Written for and by teens, this magazine strives to keep readers informed about contemporary teen issues, educational, social and political issues, and the latest fashions, sports, and entertainment news.
- **Audience:** 13–19 years
- **Frequency:** 6 times each year
- **Distribution:** 50% schools; 40% libraries; 10% subscription
- **Circulation:** 25,000
- **Website:** www.mygumbo.com

Freelance Potential
25% written by nonstaff writers. Publishes 75 freelance submissions yearly; 85% by unpublished writers, 20% by authors who are new to the magazine. Receives 8 queries monthly.

Submissions
Query. Accepts email queries to ty@mygumbo.com. SASE. Responds in 2 weeks.
Articles: 700–1,000 words. Personal experience pieces, profiles, interviews, and reviews. Topics include college; career; computers; current events; health; fitness; music; popular culture; recreation; science; technology; sports; and self-help, multicultural, and social issues.
Depts/columns: Word length varies. Current events, technology, fashion, and book and music reviews.
Other: Poetry, less than 500 words. Submit seasonal material 6 months in advance.

Sample Issue
60 pages (30% advertising): 15 articles; 10 depts/columns; 1 poem. Sample copy, $3 with 8x10 SASE ($1.23 postage). Guidelines and theme list available.
- "The Drive." Article reports on a program that allows teens to learn about driving safety.
- "It's about That Time!" Article discusses why teens smoke and how to become smoke-free.
- Sample dept/column: "Holiday" takes a look at Valentine's Day and the history of St. Patrick's Day.

Rights and Payment
One-time rights. Written material, $25. Pays on publication. Provides 10 contributor's copies.

Editor's Comments
We would like to see human-interest stories, and articles on money management, technology, and health. We have enough on entertainment, music, and sports.

Gwinnett Parents Magazine

Suite 325
3651 Peachtree Parkway
Suwanee, GA 30024

Editor: Terry Porter

Description and Readership
Created exclusively for and by parents of Gwinnett County Georgia, this magazine offers articles that educate and entertain parents on everyday parenting issues and decisions such as child care, after-school activities, education, safety, healthcare, and finances.
- **Audience:** Parents
- **Frequency:** Monthly
- **Distribution:** Subscription; newsstand
- **Circulation:** Unavailable
- **Website:** www.gwinnettparents.com

Freelance Potential
40% written by nonstaff writers. Publishes several freelance submissions yearly.

Submissions
Query or send complete ms. Accepts email submissions only to editor@gwinnettparents.com. Include "Editorial Submission" in the subject line or they will not be read. Responds in 3–4 weeks.
Articles: 500–1,500 words. Informational articles; profiles; and personal experience pieces. Topics include finances, homeschooling, recreation, health, after-school activities, and other parenting issues.
Depts/columns: Word lengths vary. Health, parenting, ages and stages, family fun time.

Sample Issue
38 pages: 5 articles; 15 depts/columns. Sample copy, $4 with 9x12 SASE ($.77 postage). Guidelines available at website.
- "Before the Prom." Article offers tips for teaching teenagers financial responsibility when developing a prom budget.
- "Are You Qualified to Home School?" Article offers steps to become a successful and qualified home schooling parent.
- Sample dept/column: "Healthy Child" discusses how to buy braces for your child.

Rights and Payment
First and non-exclusive online archival rights. Articles, $75. Depts/columns, $50. Pays on publication.

Editor's Comments
Articles that are concise, timely, professionally presented, and well-written have the best chance of being published. Topics with a "local flair" are preferable to those citing sources and incidents or quoting individuals from other areas outside of the region.

Happiness

P.O. Box 388
Portland, TN 37148

Editor: Sue Fuller

Description and Readership
In addition to being a television guide, this publication offers positive articles, puzzles, poems, and children's stories. It has been in print for over 37 years.
- **Audience:** Families
- **Frequency:** Weekly
- **Distribution:** Subscription
- **Circulation:** Unavailable
- **Website:** www.happiness.com

Freelance Potential
50% written by nonstaff writers.

Submissions
Send complete ms. Accepts computer printouts. Availability of artwork improves chance of acceptance. SASE. Responds in 3 months.
Articles: 500 words. Informational, how-to, self-help, and inspirational articles and personal experience pieces. Topics include education, health, fitness, crafts, hobbies, animals, pets, nature, the environment, recreation, and travel. Also publishes humor and biographical articles.
Fiction: 500 words. Inspirational fiction, real-life stories, and stories about animals.
Depts/columns: 25–75 words. Crafts, cooking, and tips from readers.
Artwork: Color prints.
Other: Puzzles, activities, and poetry. Submit seasonal material 4 months in advance.

Sample Issue
40 pages (no advertising): 2 articles; 1 story; 6 depts/columns; 7 activities. Guidelines available.
- "Step Out of the Crowd." Article discusses how to be an extraordinary person.
- "Read the Instructions Carefully." Personal experience piece describes how a failed pancake recipe ends up turning into a delightful breakfast.
- Sample dept/column: "Happiness Within" discusses appreciating the simple things in life.

Rights and Payment
First rights. All material, payment rates vary. Pays on publication.

Editor's Comments
We are looking for heartwarming, true-life stories that focus on self-improvement and are upbeat. Please note that we do not need any more children's stories as we have enough of these.

Healthy Beginnings

1450 Pilgrim Road
Birmingham, MI 48009

Executive Editor: Alice R. McCarthy, Ph.D.

Description and Readership
The goal of this award-winning newsletter is to help parents and caregivers teach children to make health decisions and to support the teaching of health in schools. Targeting families of children in kindergarten through third grade, it offers articles and tips on child development topics, nutrition, and education. It also includes book reviews.
- **Audience:** Parents
- **Frequency:** Twice each year
- **Distribution:** 75% schools; 25% hospitals
- **Circulation:** 70,000
- **Website:** www.bridge-comm.com

Freelance Potential
10% written by nonstaff writers. Publishes 4 freelance submissions yearly; 5% by authors who are new to the magazine.

Submissions
Query with writing sample. Accepts email queries to bridgecomm@aol.com. Response time varies.
Articles: 300–400 words. Informational and how-to articles; and personal experience pieces. Topics on parenting issues, nutrition, and child development.
Depts/columns: Short fillers, 200–300 words. Health, nutrition, and parenting topics.

Sample Issue
4 pages: 5 articles; 4 depts/columns. Sample copy, $.85.
- "The Confident Child." Article discusses things parents can do to develop resiliency in children, such as identifying their strengths and encouraging them.
- "Child Rearing by the Book." Article takes a look at how parents can decide if a book is reliable.
- Sample dept/column: "Resources for Parents" offers five book reviews.

Rights and Payment
All rights. Written material, $.12 per word. Pays on publication.

Editor's Comments
We look for educational articles for parents on topics related to keeping young children healthy. Our readers look for practical tips they can use. Resources for parents including book reviews on topics such as manners, safety issues, nutrition, social issues, and reading, are of interest to us. New writers have the best opportunity with a short filler.

Healthy Choices

1450 Pilgrim Road
Birmingham, MI 48009

Executive Editor: Alice R. McCarthy, Ph.D.

Description and Readership
Articles, news, tips, and book reviews for families of pre-adolescents in grades six through eight can be found in this newsletter. Striving to offer information to help make positive health choices, it includes articles on topics such as nutrition, drugs, bullying, teen sex, and other educational issues.
• **Audience:** Parents
• **Frequency:** Twice each year
• **Distribution:** 75% schools; 25% hospitals
• **Circulation:** 70,000
• **Website:** www.bridge-comm.com

Freelance Potential
10% written by nonstaff writers. Publishes 4 freelance submissions yearly; 5% by authors who are new to the magazine.

Submissions
Query with writing sample. Accepts email queries to bridgecomm@aol.com. Response time varies.
Articles: 300–400 words. Informational and how-to articles. Topics include parenting and child care issues.
Depts/columns: Short fillers, 200–300 words. Parenting topics.

Sample Issue
4 pages: 5 articles; 2 depts/columns. Sample copy, $.85.
• "Bullies and Preteens." Article discusses the problem of bullying at school and offers advice on how to help if your child is being bullied.
• "Another Ploy: Flavored Cigarettes." Article discusses cigarette marketing campaigns and products that are specifically marketed to youth and non-smokers.
• Sample dept/column: "Books for Parents" offers six book reviews for parents.

Rights and Payment
All rights. Written material, $.12 per word. Pays on publication. Provides 12 contributor's copies.

Editor's Comments
We provide readers with practical and useful material, and look for articles with supporting research on topics that are of interest to families of pre-adolescents. Sidebars with additional information are a plus. Please make sure all information is accurate. If you have an idea for a topic, send us a query. Short fillers provide the best opportunity for new writers.

Healthy Growing

1450 Pilgrim Road
Birmingham, MI 48009

Executive Editor: Alice R. McCarthy, Ph.D.

Description and Readership
Targeting families of children in grades four and five, this newsletter features articles, tips, and resourceful information on parenting issues, finance, healthy eating, child development, and educational issues. It strives to offer material that will promote a healthy family lifestyle.
• **Audience:** Parents
• **Frequency:** Twice each year
• **Distribution:** 75% schools; 25% hospitals
• **Circulation:** 70,000
• **Website:** www.bridge-comm.com

Freelance Potential
10% written by nonstaff writers. Publishes 4 freelance submissions yearly; 5% by authors who are new to the magazine.

Submissions
Query with writing sample. Accepts email queries to bridgecomm@aol.com. Responds in 1 month.
Articles: 300–400 words. Informational and how-to articles. Topics include parenting and child care issues.
Depts/columns: Short fillers, 200–300 words. Money, health, parenting topics.

Sample Issue
4 pages: 7 articles; 2 depts/columns. Sample copy, $.85.
• "Ways to Show Love for Your Early Teen." Article offers ideas on ways to express love to early teens, including setting good examples, encouragement, and guidance.
• "Tips to Help Kids Learn to Manage Money." Article offers tips for parents to help kids learn about managing money effectively.
• Sample dept/column: "Resources for Parents" offers six book reviews for parents.

Rights and Payment
All rights. Written material, $.12 per word. Pays on publication. Provides 12 contributor's copies.

Editor's Comments
We need material that is informative and practical. Our readers look for tips on topics related to parenting children ages 8–12. Keep in mind that we focus on positive parenting, and look for materials that will boost self-esteem, and allow parents to teach children how to be healthy and enjoy life.

High Adventure

The General Council of the Assemblies of God
1445 North Boonville Avenue
Springfield, MO 65802-1894

Editor: Jerry Parks

Description and Readership
This periodical for boys from kindergarten through high school is designed to provide readers with captivating reading, while challenging them to greater sprirual ideals.
- **Audience:** Boys grades K–12
- **Frequency:** Quarterly
- **Distribution:** 95% charter; 5% subscription
- **Circulation:** 87,000
- **Website:** www.royalrangers.ag.org

Freelance Potential
70% written by nonstaff writers. Publishes 125 freelance submissions yearly; 5% by unpublished writers, 30% by authors who are new to the magazine. Receives 30–40 unsolicited mss monthly.

Submissions
Send complete ms. Accepts photocopies, computer printouts, IBM disk submissions, email submissions to jparks@ag.org, and simultaneous submissions. SASE. Responds in 1–2 months.
Articles: To 1,000 words. Informational, how-to, and self-help articles; profiles; humor; and personal experience pieces. Topics include religion, geography, nature, travel, sports, college, and multicultural issues.
Fiction: 1,000 words. Includes inspirational, historical, religious, adventure, and multicultural fiction; problem-solving stories; and humor.
Nonfiction: Historical, inspirational, and religious topics.
Depts/columns: 500 words. Crafts and cooking.
Artwork: Color prints.
Other: Puzzles, activities, and jokes.

Sample Issue
16 pages (no advertising): 3 articles; 2 stories; 1 dept/column. Sample copy, free with 9x12 SASE. Guidelines available.
- "A Gadget-Crazy World." Article compares a high-tech GPS system with the sextant.
- Sample dept/column: "Devotionals for Boys" offers hands-on activites to teach Christian principles.

Rights and Payment
First or all rights. All material, payment rates vary. Pays on publication. Provides 2 contributor's copies.

Editor's Comments
We are looking for articles that perpetuate the spirit of the Royal Rangers ministry through stories, crafts, ideas, and illustrations.

Higher Things
Dare To Be Lutheran

P.O. Box 580111
Pleasant Prairie, WI 53158-8011

Executive Editor: Rev. Todd A. Peperkorn, STM

Description and Readership
The goal of *Higher Things* is to enrich the spiritual lives of Lutheran teens. With a focus on God's work in Christ for salvation, it offers articles that demonstrate how the Gospel message can be applied to the everyday lives of Christian youth.
- **Audience:** 13–19 years
- **Frequency:** Quarterly
- **Distribution:** Subscription; other
- **Circulation:** Unavailable
- **Website:** www.higherthings.org

Freelance Potential
25% written by nonstaff writers. Publishes 20 freelance submissions yearly.

Submissions
Query or send complete ms. Accepts photocopies, computer printouts, and email to peperkorn@ higherthings.org. SASE. Response time varies.
Articles: 500–800 words. Informational and how-to articles; profiles; interviews; and personal experience pieces. Topics include religion, current events, recreation, social issues, and travel.
Depts/columns: Staff written.

Sample Issue
32 pages (10% advertising): 5 articles; 6 depts/columns. Sample copy, $3. Guidelines available.
- "The Myths of Evolution." Article outlines four concepts of the theory of evolution and questions whether they are fact or fiction.
- "Life in the Blood." Article discusses embryonic stem cell research and advocates finding a way to harvest stem cells without destroying life.
- "Love Songs for Jesus?" Article studies the portrayal of God in contemporary Christian music.

Rights and Payment
Rights vary. Articles, $50–$100. Pays on publication.

Editor's Comments
Your writing should be fresh, lively, and appealing to our readers, who include young teens still innocent in their interests to older teens who may be experimenting with sex or cigarettes. Consider our audience carefully in terms of vocabulary, readability, and subject matter as you prepare your submission. Remember that our primary purpose is to enrich the faith of our youth by focusing on Christ and His work for us and our salvation.

Highlights for Children

803 Church Street
Honesdale, PA 18431

Manuscript Submissions

Description and Readership
Striving to make reading educational and fun for children, this popular magazine offers articles, stories, poetry, art, and activities.
- **Audience:** 2–12 years
- **Frequency:** Monthly
- **Distribution:** 100% subscription
- **Circulation:** More than 2.5 million
- **Website:** www.highlights.com

Freelance Potential
98% written by nonstaff writers. Publishes 200 freelance submissions yearly; 30% by unpublished writers, 40% by new authors. Receives 665 mss monthly.

Submissions
Send complete ms for fiction; query for nonfiction. Accepts computer printouts. SASE. Responds to queries in 2–4 weeks, to mss in 4–6 weeks.
Articles: To 800 words. Informational articles; interviews; profiles; and personal experience pieces. Topics include nature, animals, science, crafts, hobbies, world culture, and sports.
Fiction: To 400 words for ages 3–7; to 800 words for ages 8–12. Rebuses, to 120 words. Genres include mystery, adventure, and multicultural fiction. Also features stories about sports and retellings of traditional stories.
Depts/columns: Word length varies. Science, crafts, and pets.
Other: Puzzles, activities, riddles, games, and jokes.

Sample Issue
44 pages (no advertising): 5 articles; 5 stories; 10 depts/columns; 12 activities; 1 rebus; 12 poems. Sample copy, free with 9x12 SASE (4 first-class stamps). Guidelines available.
- "Calvin's Cock-a-Doodle-Do." Story tells of a rooster that only crows in the evening.
- "Poles Apart." Article takes a look at the differences between the Arctic and the Antarctic.
- Sample dept/column: "Nature Watch" offers information on hummingbirds.

Rights and Payment
All rights. Written material, payment rates vary. Pays on acceptance. Provides 2 contributor's copies.

Editor's Comments
We continue to seek nonfiction articles and contemporary stories with strong characters.

The High School Journal

CB#3500 University of North Carolina
Editorial Office, School of Education
Chapel Hill, NC 27599

Submissions Editor

Description and Readership
Founded in 1918, *The High School Journal* focuses on secondary education by publishing research, informed opinion pieces, and articles about successful educational practices. Its audience includes both teachers and school administrators.
- **Audience:** Secondary school educators and administrators
- **Frequency:** Quarterly
- **Distribution:** 100% subscription
- **Circulation:** 1,500
- **Website:** http://muse.jhu.edu/

Freelance Potential
100% written by nonstaff writers. Publishes 20–30 freelance submissions yearly; 25% by unpublished writers, 85% by authors who are new to the magazine. Receives 27 unsolicited mss monthly.

Submissions
Send 3 copies of complete ms. Accepts photocopies and computer printouts. SASE. Responds in 3 months.
Articles: 1,500–2,500 words. Informational articles on adolescent issues as they affect school practices; reports on successful teaching practices; and research reports on teacher, administrator, and student interaction in school settings.
Depts/columns: 300–400 words. Book reviews.
Artwork: Line art.

Sample Issue
52 pages (no advertising): 6 articles. Sample copy, $7.50 with 9x12 SASE. Guidelines available.
- "Shooting for Stars: A Case Study of the Mathematics Achievement and Career Attainment of an African American Male High School Student." Article tells how one high school student petitioned to have a calculus course offered at his school.
- "Secondary Mathematics Teachers' Perceptions of the Achievement Gap." Study surveys teachers on ways to improve achievement among minority students.

Rights and Payment
All rights. No payment. Provides 3 copies.

Editor's Comments
This is a peer-reviewed journal. We look for serious, substantial articles and case studies about secondary education.

High School Writer

Junior High Edition

Writer Publications
P.O. Box 718
Grand Rapids, MN 55744-0718

Editor: Emily Benes

Description and Readership
Creating a forum of expression for junior high and middle school students, this publication offers articles, stories, and poetry. It only accepts submissions from students whose teachers subscribe to the paper.
- **Audience:** Junior high school students
- **Frequency:** 6 times each year
- **Distribution:** 100% schools
- **Circulation:** 44,000

Freelance Potential
100% written by nonstaff writers. Publishes 300 freelance submissions yearly; 95% by unpublished writers, 75% by authors who are new to the magazine. Receives 3,000 unsolicited mss monthly.

Submissions
Accepts submissions from students of subscribing teachers in junior high school only. Send complete ms. Accepts photocopies, computer printouts, and simultaneous submissions if identified. SASE. Response time varies.
Articles: To 2,000 words. Informational and how-to articles; profiles; and personal experience pieces. Topics include family, religion, health, social issues, careers, college, multicultural issues, travel, nature, the environment, science and computers.
Fiction: To 2,000 words. Genres include historical and contemporary fiction, science fiction, drama, adventure, suspense, mystery, humor, fantasy, and stories about sports and nature.
Artwork: B/W and line art.
Other: Poetry, no line limit.

Sample Issue
8 pages (15% advertising): 12 articles; 6 stories; 25 poems. Sample copy, free. Guidelines available in each issue.
- "Ridiculing Is Ridiculous." Article discusses how making fun of someone or judging them is wrong.
- "Owen." Personal experience piece shares the author's joy of meeting his young cousin.
- "Loosing My Mind." Story tells what it would be like looking for a lost mind.

Rights and Payment
One-time rights. No payment

Editor's Comments
We look for creative works from junior high and middle school students. Seasonal material is okay too.

High School Writer

Senior High Edition

Writer Publications
P.O. Box 718
Grand Rapids, MN 55477-0718

Editor: Emily Benes

Description and Readership
The pages of this newspaper are filled with the works of high school seniors. Each issue includes a mix of articles, stories, and poems. Submissions are only accepted from subscribing schools.
- **Audience:** Senior high school students
- **Frequency:** 6 times each year
- **Distribution:** 100% schools
- **Circulation:** 44,000

Freelance Potential
100% written by nonstaff writers. Publishes 300 freelance submissions yearly; 95% by unpublished writers, 75% by authors who are new to the magazine. Receives 3,000 unsolicited mss monthly.

Submissions
Accepts submissions from students of subscribing teachers in senior high school only. Send complete ms. Accepts photocopies, computer printouts, email submissions to writer@mx3.com (ASCII text), and simultaneous submissions if identified. SASE. Response time varies.
Articles: To 2,000 words. Informational and how-to articles; profiles; and personal experience pieces. Topics include current events, humor, multicultural and ethnic issues, nature, environment, popular culture, recreation, sports, and travel.
Fiction: To 2,000 words. Genres include humor, science fiction, adventure, and stories about sports.
Other: Poetry, no line limit. Seasonal material.

Sample Issue
8 pages (15% advertising): 12 articles; 6 story; 25 poems. Sample copy, free. Guidelines available in each issue.
- "Time with Daddy." Essay shares the author's experience of seeing a different side of her father.
- "Dance." Essay reflects on how being part of the dance team shaped the author's life.
- "Spider Bite." Story shares a spider's thoughts of man being a rude creature.

Rights and Payment
One-time rights. No payment.

Editor's Comments
We create a place for high school students to share their original stories and ideas with their peers. We will consider all submissions, but are most interested in topics that are morally uplifting.

Alfred Hitchcock's Mystery Magazine

475 Park Avenue South
New York, NY 10016

Editor: Linda Landrigan

Description and Readership
Original crime fiction is the mainstay of this mystery magazine. All stories are related to a crime, or involve the threat or fear of a crime.
- **Audience:** Adults
- **Frequency:** 10 times each year
- **Distribution:** Subscription; newsstand
- **Circulation:** 150,000
- **Website:** www.themysteryplace.com

Freelance Potential
99% written by nonstaff writers. Publishes 10 free-lance submissions yearly; 10% by unpublished writers, 10% by authors who are new to the magazine. Receives 100 unsolicited mss monthly.

Submissions
Send complete ms. Accepts photocopies and computer printouts. No simultaneous submissions. SASE. Responds in 3 months.
Fiction: To 12,000 words. Classic crime mysteries, detective stories, suspense, private-eye tales, court-room drama, and espionage.
Depts/columns: Word length varies. Reviews, puzzles, bookstore profiles.

Sample Issue
144 pages (2% advertising): 7 stories; 1 mystery, 9 depts/columns, 1 puzzle. Sample copy, $5. Guidelines available.
- "Shanks Goes Hollywood." Short story involves a mystery writer who helps the police solve a crime, and gets ideas for a new book in the process.
- "Small-Town God." Story about two best friends, when one turns to stealing.
- "The Stolen Story." Short story follows what happens after a man unknowingly publishes a story that was written by someone else.

Rights and Payment
First serial, anthology, and foreign rights. Written material, payment rates vary. Pays on acceptance. Provides 3 contributor's copies.

Editor's Comments
Finding new authors is a great pleasure for us, and we look forward to reading all submissions. We are interested in all types of crime-related mysteries, and we sometimes consider ghost stories or supernatural tales, but they must involve a crime. Please note that we do not accept true crime stories.

Hit Parader

Suite 211
210 Route 4 East
Paramus, NJ 07652

Managing Editor: Renée Daigle

Description and Readership
Articles and photos covering the hard rock and heavy metal scene are featured in this magazine. It includes profiles and interviews of bands, information on upcoming concerts and groups, and industry trends.
- **Audience:** YA
- **Frequency:** Monthly
- **Distribution:** Subscription; newsstand
- **Circulation:** 150,000
- **Website:** www.hitparader.com

Freelance Potential
10% written by nonstaff writers. Publishes 10 free-lance submissions yearly; 50% by new authors.

Submissions
Query. Accepts computer printouts. Availability of art-work improves chance of acceptance. SASE. Responds in 1–3 months.
Articles: 1,000 words. Lifestyle articles; profiles; and interviews. Topics include hard rock and heavy metal musicians and popular bands.
Depts/columns: Word lengths vary. Reports on instruments and sound equipment; profiles of new bands; and reviews of video games, music videos, and new music releases.
Artwork: 3x5 and 5x7 B/W prints and color transparencies.
Other: Submit seasonal material about anniversaries or notable events 4 months in advance.

Sample Issue
98 pages (50% advertising): 11 articles; 14 depts/columns. Sample copy, $4.99 at newsstands. Guidelines available.
- "Hoobastank: A Delicate Situation." Article takes a look at the hard rocking Los Angeles based band Hoobastank and how they take things to extremes.
- "All-time Top 100 Hard Rock Songs." Article lists the *Hit Parader's* version of the greatest hard rock/heavy metal songs of all time.
- Sample dept/column: "Over the Edge" takes a look at the music of Bleeding Through and My Ruin.

Rights and Payment
First rights. Articles, $75–$100. Other material, payment rates vary. Pays on publication. Provides 1 copy.

Editor's Comments
We are looking for interviews of hot new groups from freelance writers with ties to the industry.

Home Education Magazine

P.O. Box 1083
Tonasket, WA 98855

Managing Editor: Helen Hegener

Description and Readership
In print for over 20 years, this resourceful magazine offers informative, how-to, and personal experience pieces on topics related to homeschooling children. It is read by parents living across the country.
- **Audience:** Parents
- **Frequency:** 6 times each year
- **Distribution:** 50% subscription; 20% controlled; 30% other
- **Circulation:** 60,000
- **Website:** www.homeedmag.com

Freelance Potential
90% written by nonstaff writers. Publishes 50 freelance submissions yearly; 25% by unpublished writers, 50% by authors who are new to the magazine. Receives 42 queries and unsolicited mss monthly.

Submissions
Query or send complete ms with résumé. Prefers email submissions to articles@homeedmag.com. Accepts photocopies and computer printouts. SASE. Responds in 1–2 months.
Articles: 1,000–1,500 words. Informational, how-to, and personal experience articles. Topics include homeschooling, education, and parenting.
Depts/columns: Staff written.
Artwork: B/W prints and color slides.

Sample Issue
58 pages (13% advertising): 6 articles; 12 depts/columns. Sample copy, $6.50 with 9x12 SASE. Guidelines available.
- "Oh, Fer Pete's Sake." Essay takes a humorous look at getting creative when homeschooling.
- "An Attitude of Gratitude." Essay discusses having gratitude in your life, and offers the author's homeschooling gratitude list.
- "A Dozen Reasons for Not Mowing the Lawn." Article describes plants and animals that live in lawns.

Rights and Payment
First North American serial and electronic rights. Articles, $50–$100. Artwork, $10–$100. Pays on acceptance. Provides 1 contributor's copy.

Editor's Comments
We strictly publish real-life experiences from parents who are homeschooling their children. Humorous personal experience pieces on homeschooling and interviews with homeschooling personalities are welcome.

Homeschooling Today

P.O. Box 436
Barker, TX 77413

Editor-in-Chief: Stacy McDonald

Description and Readership
This publication offers parents encouragement and information on homeschooling. Each issue includes unit studies and lessons, book reviews, child training tips, and family ideas. The majority of its material is written with a Christian slant.
- **Audience:** Parents
- **Frequency:** 6 times each year
- **Distribution:** Subscription; newsstand
- **Circulation:** 30,000
- **Website:** www.homeschoolingtoday.com

Freelance Potential
90% written by nonstaff writers. Publishes 10–20 freelance submissions yearly; 10% by unpublished writers, 5% by new authors. Receives 5–10 mss monthly.

Submissions
Send complete ms. Accepts photocopies and email submissions to editor@homeschoolingtoday.com. (Microsoft Word or RTF attachments). SASE. Responds to queries in 3–6 months.
Articles: 1,000–2,500 words. Informational and how-to articles; profiles; interviews; and personal experience pieces. Topics include education, music, technology, special education, the arts, history, mathematics, and science. Also publishes self-help articles.
Depts/columns: Word lengths vary. Study units, media and book reviews, and new product information.

Sample Issue
76 pages: 3 articles; 14 depts/columns. Sample copy, $5.95. Guidelines available.
- "Get the Kids Out!" Article reports on a conference that focuses on getting children out of harmful schools and into honest education.
- "Celebrating the End of Homeschooling." Article offers ways to celebrate seniors graduating from homeschooling.
- Sample dept/column: "Lessons for Little Ones" offers a lesson for youngsters about trees.

Rights and Payment
First rights. Written material, $.08 per word. Pays on publication. Provides 1 contributor's copy.

Editor's Comments
We consider ourselves a homeschooling tool, and strive to provide practical information and resources to parents who homeschool their children. Articles with a Christian slant are preferred.

Hopscotch

P.O. Box 164
Bluffton, OH 45817-0164

Associate Editor: Virginia Edwards

Description and Readership
This popular magazine affirms that every girl has the right to be a young girl before she becomes a young adult. All articles and stories are wholesome and age-appropriate.
- **Audience:** 6–13 years
- **Frequency:** 6 times each year
- **Distribution:** 70% subscription; 30% newsstand
- **Circulation:** 15,000
- **Website:** www.hopscotchmagazine.com

Freelance Potential
100% written by nonstaff writers. Publishes 100–200 freelance submissions yearly; 20% by unpublished writers, 50% by authors who are new to the magazine. Receives more than 400 queries and unsolicited mss each month.

Submissions
Query or send complete ms. Include photographs with nonfiction. Accepts photocopies, computer printouts, disk, and simultaneous submissions. SASE. Responds to queries in 1–2 weeks, to mss in 2–3 months.
Articles: To 500 words. Informational articles; personal experience pieces; and profiles. Topics include emotions, communication, babies, courage, and animals.
Fiction: To 1,000 words. Historical and multicultural fiction, mystery, and adventure.
Depts/columns: 500 words. Crafts, cooking, and science activities.
Artwork: Prefers B/W prints. Accepts color prints.
Other: Puzzles, activities, and poetry.

Sample Issue
48 pages (no advertising): 1 article; 6 stories; 4 poems; 1 puzzle; 1 comic; 1 activity; 1 recipe page. Sample copy, $4 with 9x12 SASE. Guidelines and theme list available with #10 SASE.
- "Terror on the Trestle." Heart-pounding story involving two girls and a train.
- "Smell a Rain Forest." Article sends readers on a hunt for the smells and tastes of the rain forest.

Rights and Payment
First and second rights. Written material, $.05 per word. Artwork, payment rate varies. Pays on publication. Provides 1 contributor's copy.

Editor's Comments
Our magazine is read by young girls—leave the dating, sex, fashion, and romance for other publications.

The Horn Book Magazine

Suite 200
56 Roland Street
Boston, MA 02129

Editor-in-Chief: Roger Sutton

Description and Readership
In print since 1924, this resourceful publication offers readers who want to know about children's and young adult literature in-depth and timely reviews, as well as lively articles and essays.
- **Audience:** Parents, teachers, and librarians
- **Frequency:** 6 times each year
- **Distribution:** 70% subscription; 10% newsstand; 20% other
- **Circulation:** 16,000
- **Website:** www.hbook.com

Freelance Potential
70% written by nonstaff writers. Publishes 12–15 freelance submissions yearly; 10% by unpublished writers, 30% by authors who are new to the magazine. Receives 20 queries, 10 unsolicited mss monthly.

Submissions
Query or send complete ms. Accepts photocopies and computer printouts. SASE. Responds in 4 months.
Articles: To 2,800 words. Interviews with children's authors, illustrators, and editors; critical articles about children's and young adult literature; and book reviews.
Depts/columns: Word lengths vary. Perspectives from illustrators; children's publishing updates; and special columns.

Sample Issue
128 pages (20% advertising): 9 articles; 73 reviews; 6 depts/columns. Sample copy, free with 9x12 SASE. Guidelines and editorial calendar available.
- "The Bones of Story." Article discusses the basic elements of good storytelling.
- "On Spies and Purple Socks and Such." Article discusses books with characters that children can relate to in discovering their own identities.
- Sample dept/column: "The Beaten Path" takes a look at different series books for children.

Rights and Payment
All rights. Written material, payment rates vary. Pays on publication. Provides 1 contributor's copy.

Editor's Comments
We strive to provide our readers with up-to-date information on the latest and greatest in children's and young adult books, as well as exposing the worst, and what falls in between. Our readers include parents, librarians, teachers, writers, and publishers.

Horsemen's Yankee Pedlar

83 Leicester Street
North Oxford, MA 01537

Editor: Molly Johns

Description and Readership
For more than 45 years, this publication has been covering the equine industry in the Northeast. Each issue is chock full of news, events, and features on horse care, health, nutrition, training, and education.
- **Audience:** YA–Adult
- **Frequency:** Monthly
- **Distribution:** Newsstand; subscription; schools
- **Circulation:** 50,000
- **Website:** www.pedlar.com

Freelance Potential
50% written by nonstaff writers. Publishes 40 freelance submissions yearly; 5% by authors who are new to the magazine. Receives 30 queries, 20 unsolicited mss monthly.

Submissions
Query or send complete ms. Accepts photocopies, computer printouts, and simultaneous submissions if identified. SASE. Responds to queries in 1–2 weeks, to mss in 2–3 months.
Articles: 500–800 words. Informational and how-to articles; personal experience pieces; interviews; and reviews. Topics include horse breeds, disciplines, training, health care, and equestrian equipment.
Depts/columns: Word lengths vary. Regional news, book reviews, business issues, nutrition, and legal issues.
Artwork: B/W and color prints.

Sample Issue
243 pages (75% advertising): 63 articles; 15 depts/columns. Sample copy, $3.99 with 9x12 SASE (7 first-class stamps). Guidelines available.
- "Home Schooling." Article offers a how-to description for building cross-country fences for schooling.
- Sample dept/column: "Trail Talk" reports on a horse camping facility in Massachusetts.

Rights and Payment
First North American serial rights. Written material, $2 per published column inch. Show coverage, $75 per day. Pays 30 days after publication. Provides 1 tearsheet.

Editor's Comments
We look for well-written, how-to and informational articles from New England writers on topics related to the equestrian industry in that region, as well as interviews with riders, breeders, and trainers.

Horsepower

P.O. Box 670
Aurora, Ontario L4G 4J9
Canada

Managing Editor: Susan Stafford

Description and Readership
Young horse fans enjoy this magazine for its articles on the care, riding, and training of horses. Appearing as an insert of *Horse-Canada*, it also includes activities, puzzles, and horse stories.
- **Audience:** 8–16 years
- **Frequency:** 6 times each year
- **Distribution:** 80% subscription; 10% schools; 10% controlled
- **Circulation:** 10,000
- **Website:** www.horse-canada.com

Freelance Potential
80% written by nonstaff writers. Publishes 10–12 freelance submissions yearly; 10% by unpublished writers, 10% by new authors. Receives 2–3 mss monthly.

Submissions
Query with outline or synopsis; or send complete ms with résumé. Accepts photocopies, computer printouts, IBM disk submissions (ASCII or WordPerfect), and email submissions to info@horse-canada.com. SAE/IRC. Responds to queries in 1–2 weeks, to mss in 2–3 months.
Articles: 500–1,000 words. Informational and how-to articles; profiles; and humor. Topics include breeds, training, stable skills, equine health, and tack.
Fiction: 500 words. Adventure, humorous stories, and sports stories related to horses.
Depts/columns: Staff written.
Artwork: B/W and color prints.
Other: Horse-themed activities, games, and puzzles.

Sample Issue
16 pages (20% advertising): 3 articles; 4 depts/columns; 2 activities; 2 puzzles; 1 poster. Sample copy, $3.95. Guidelines and theme list available.
- "Cavalia." Article profiles Ricky Suarez, a rosin-back rider in the Canadian show Cavalia.
- "Drilling on Horseback." Article describes how drilling can help maintain and improve riding skills and a horse's performance.

Rights and Payment
First North American serial rights. Written material, $50–$90. Artwork, $10–$75. Pays on publication. Provides 1 contributor's copy.

Editor's Comments
Send us something that will inform and entertain our readers on their favorite topic, horses.

Hudson Valley Parent

174 South Street
Newburgh, NY 12550

Editor: Leah Black

Description and Readership
Published for parents in the mid-Hudson Valley of New York, this magazine covers parenting issues, local resources, and regional events.
- **Audience:** Parents
- **Frequency:** Monthly
- **Distribution:** 100% other
- **Circulation:** 70,000
- **Website:** www.excitingread.com

Freelance Potential
95% written by nonstaff writers. Publishes 100 freelance submissions yearly; 50% by unpublished writers, 50% by authors who are new to the magazine. Receives 8 queries, 20 unsolicited mss monthly.

Submissions
Query with writing samples or send complete ms. Prefers email queries to editor@excitingread.com. Accepts computer printouts. SASE. Responds in 3–6 weeks.
Articles: 700–1,200 words. Informational and how-to articles; and practical application pieces. Topics include parenting, grandparenting, recreation, computers, technology, health, fitness, sports, hobbies, and the home.
Depts/columns: 700 words. Health, education, and adolescent issues.
Other: Submit seasonal material 6 months in advance. "Vida y Familia Hispana," Spanish section.

Sample Issue
62 pages (50% advertising): 6 articles; 8 depts/columns. Sample copy, free with 9x12 SASE. Guidelines and editorial calendar available.
- "Five Tips to Stop the Summer 'Brain Drain.'" Article offers suggestions to keep kids involved in learning over the summer.
- "Better Shop Around." Article offers money-saving tips for stocking up on new baby supplies.
- "Water Safety Tips for Your Family." Article urges families to take basic precautions to stay safe around water.

Rights and Payment
One-time rights. Written material, $25–$70. Pays on publication. Provides contributor's copies.

Editor's Comments
Local authors are best—they know what our area has to offer families.

Humpty Dumpty's Magazine

Children's Better Health Institute
1100 Waterway Boulevard, P.O. Box 567
Indianapolis, IN 46206-0567

Editor: Phyllis Lybarger

Description and Readership
Committed to improving the health and well-being of children, this magazine offers read-aloud stories, articles, poems, and activities that make learning fun.
- **Audience:** 4–6 years
- **Frequency:** 6 times each year
- **Distribution:** 100% subscription
- **Circulation:** 236,000
- **Website:** www.humptydumptymag.org

Freelance Potential
10% written by nonstaff writers. Publishes 25 freelance submissions yearly; 10% by unpublished writers, 25% by authors who are new to the magazine.

Submissions
Send complete ms. Accepts photocopies and computer printouts. SASE. Responds in 10–12 weeks.
Articles: To 250 words. Factual, observational, and how-to articles. Topics include health, fitness, sports, science, nature, the environment, animals, crafts, hobbies, and multicultural and ethnic subjects.
Fiction: To 300 words. Genres include early reader contemporary and multicultural fiction; stories about sports; fantasy; folktales; mystery; drama; and humor.
Depts/columns: Word lengths vary. Recipes and health and fitness news.
Other: Puzzles, activities, and games. Submit seasonal material 8 months in advance.

Sample Issue
36 pages (2% advertising): 2 articles; 3 stories; 1 dept/column; 13 activities. Sample copy, $1.25. Writers' guidelines available.
- "I Learn to Swim." Story tells how a boy is taught to float and swim.
- "Plant a Garden." Article offers directions for planting a vegetable garden.
- "Will You Help Me?" Story teaches counting using number characters helping each other.

Rights and Payment
All rights. Written material, $.22 per word. Pays on publication. Provides 10 contributor's copies.

Editor's Comments
Characters in realistic stories should be up-to-date. Many of our readers are working mothers and/or come from single-parent homes. We need more stories that reflect these changing times, while also communicating good, wholesome values.

The Illuminata

Tyrannosaurus Press
P.O. Box 8337
New Orleans, LA 70181-8337

Submissions

Description and Readership
Readers and writers of speculative fiction enjoy this free online publication for its articles, reviews, and stories. It publishes the works of both new and established authors.
- **Audience:** YA–Adult
- **Frequency:** Monthly
- **Distribution:** 100% internet
- **Circulation:** 300
- **Website:** www.TyrannosaurusPress.com

Freelance Potential
20% written by nonstaff writers. Publishes 10–15 freelance submissions yearly; 5% by unpublished writers, 10% by authors who are new to the magazine. Receives several queries monthly.

Submissions
Query with form available on website. Accepts email queries to Submissions@TyrannosaurusPress.com (no attachments). SASE. Responds in 1–3 months.
Articles: 1–2 pages in length. Informational articles. Topics related to writing science fiction and fantasy.
Fiction: Word length varies. Genres include fantasy, horror, and science fiction.
Depts/columns: Book reviews, 500–1,000 words. Reviews of science fiction and fantasy.

Sample Issue
16 pages. Sample copy and writers guidelines available on website.
- "Ten Things Tolkien Got Away With (But You Won't)." Article discusses the writing style of well-known fantasy author J.R.R. Tolkien.
- "Character Profiling (Part V): Conclusions." Article discusses different grouping systems authors use.
- Sample dept/column: "Reviews" offers reviews of 6 science fiction/fantasy books.

Rights and Payment
Rights vary. No payment. Copies available online.

Editor's Comments
We are seeking both regular and occasional contributors. Our greatest needs are for reviews and original fiction, though we gladly accept submissions in other categories. Reviews may be negative, but they cannot be cruel; negative reviews must be grounded in fact or they will not be included. We are also open to suggestions, so if you have your own idea, please share it. See our website to fill out an online query form.

Imperial Valley Family

P.O. Box 1397
El Centro, CA 92243

Publisher: Cheryl Von Flue

Description and Readership
Parents living in Imperial County, California, including the communities of Calexico, Niland, Winterhaven, and Ocotillo, read this free tabloid for its articles on parenting issues, lists of resources, and regional family-friendly events.
- **Audience:** Parents
- **Frequency:** Monthly
- **Distribution:** 50% schools; 50% other
- **Circulation:** 30,000
- **Website:** www.imperialvalleyfamily.org

Freelance Potential
40% written by nonstaff writers. Publishes 10–20 freelance submissions yearly; 10% by unpublished writers, 10% by authors who are new to the magazine. Receives 5–10 unsolicited mss monthly.

Submissions
Send complete ms. Accepts photocopies, computer printouts, and email submissions to impvalleyfamily@aol.com. SASE. Responds in 2 weeks.
Articles: 500–600 words. Informational and how-to articles; profiles; personal experience pieces; humor; and photo-essays. Topics include parenting, family issues, recreation, popular culture, music, nature, the environment, social issues, college, and careers.
Depts/columns: 500–600 words. Book reviews.
Artwork: B/W prints or transparencies.
Other: Filler, activities, games.

Sample Issue
12 pages: 3 articles; 3 depts/columns; 1 community calendar. Sample copy, free with 9x12 SASE.
- "Ten Common Sense Rules for Fathers." Article takes a look at ideas to help fathers be effective.
- "Travel'n Tots, Teens, and Tweens." Article offers child friendly steps to take when vacation planning.
- Sample dept/column: "Readers' Circle" offers a review of five summer reading books for children.

Rights and Payment
All rights. Payment rates and policies vary. Provides 1 contributor's copy.

Editor's Comments
We look for practical articles and tips on parenting issues and local news, as well as up-to-date information on resources, and events and activities for families in the area. Topics related to education, community issues, and safety are of interest to us.

Indy's Child

1901 Broad Ripple Avenue
Indianapolis, IN 46220

Editorial Assistant: Lynette Rowland

Description and Readership
Serving readers in the Indianapolis metropolitan area, this tabloid paper provides parents with complete and reliable information on raising children.
• **Audience:** Parents
• **Frequency:** Monthly
• **Distribution:** 50% newsstand; 30% controlled; 10% religious instruction; 10% schools
• **Circulation:** 144,000
• **Website:** www.indyschild.com

Freelance Potential
98% written by nonstaff writers. Publishes 75 freelance submissions yearly; 20% by new authors. Receives 83 unsolicited mss each month.

Submissions
Send complete ms. Accepts Macintosh disk submissions and email submissions to editor@indyschild.com. SASE. Responds in 3–4 months.
Articles: 1,000–2,000 words. Informational and self-help articles; personal experience pieces; profiles; interviews; and humor. Topics include the arts, careers, hobbies, current events, education, health, multicultural and ethnic subjects, music, popular culture, recreation, social issues, sports, and travel.
Depts/columns: To 1,000 words. Women's and family health, single parenting, and museum reviews.
Artwork: Color prints, transparencies or digital images.
Other: Puzzles, activities, filler, games, and jokes.

Sample Issue
44 pages (50% advertising): 8 articles; 14 depts/columns. Sample copy, free. Guidelines and editorial calendar available.
• "From Bottles to Board Rooms." Article discusses how to prepare for the return from maternity leave.
• "Gaining a Window Into Your Baby's Mind." Article tells how simple sign language helps babies build self-confidence.
• Sample dept/column: "Healthy Kids" stresses family travel safety.

Rights and Payment
First or second rights. Written material, $100. Pays on publication. Provides contributor's copies.

Editor's Comments
We look for material with a distinct Indianapolis focus. Keep it clear and concise.

InQuest Gamer

151 Wells Avenue
Congers, NY 10920

Editor: Kyle Ackerman

Description and Readership
Game lovers of all skill levels enjoy this magazine for its pages filled with information on all types of games. It includes articles, new product reviews, previews, and news and information on computer games, video games, collectible card games, roleplaying games, and board games.
• **Frequency:** Monthly
• **Distribution:** Subscription
• **Circulation:** Unavailable
• **Website:** www.wizarduniverse.com

Freelance Potential
40% written by nonstaff writers. Publishes many freelance submissions yearly.

Submissions
Query or send complete ms. Accepts email submissions to kackerman@wizarduniverse.com. Response time varies.
Articles: Word length varies. Opinion pieces; new product information; and media reviews. Topics include audio, video, software, computers, entertainment, and games.
Depts/columns: Word length varies. Games, news, notes, previews, computer information.

Sample Issue
104 pages: 7 articles; 16 depts/columns. Sample copy, $4.99.
• "Kings of Oblivion." Article describes a challenging upcoming roleplaying game filled with character types and skills that improve through play.
• "Swords, Sandals and Starships." Article explores a multiplayer online game that thrusts the player into an ongoing conflict between Rome and its enemy.
• Sample dept/column: "Best Bytes" reviews the collectible card game, Phantom Dust.

Rights and Payment
Rights and payment policy vary.

Editor's Comments
Our readers love a challenge, and look forward to hearing about what is going on in the gaming world. We strive to provide gamers with the latest information on up-and-coming releases, and detailed overviews and strategies. This upcoming year we are looking for more coverage of computer games. We look for articles and previews that will pique our readers' interest and have them coming back for more.

Insight

55 West Oak Ridge Drive
Hagerstown, MD 21740-7390

Editor: Dwain Neilson Esmond

Description and Readership
Informational articles and inspirational stories can be found in this publication. Published by the Seventh-Day Adventist Church, it targets high school and college students. All material has a Christian slant.
- **Audience:** 14–21 years
- **Frequency:** Weekly
- **Distribution:** 10% subscription; 90% other
- **Circulation:** 20,000
- **Website:** www.insightmagazine.org

Freelance Potential
99% written by nonstaff writers. Publishes 150 freelance submissions yearly; 50% by unpublished writers, 70% by authors who are new to the magazine. Receives 83 unsolicited mss monthly.

Submissions
Send complete ms. Accepts photocopies, computer printouts, disk submissions (Microsoft Word), and email submissions to insight@rhpa.org. SASE. Responds in 1–3 months.
Articles: 500–1,500 words. Informational articles; profiles; biographies; reports on volunteer and mission trips; and humor. Topics include social issues, religion, music, and careers.
Depts/columns: Word lengths vary. True-to-life stories and personal experience pieces.
Other: Submit material about Christmas, Easter, Mother's Day, Father's Day, and Valentine's Day 6 months in advance.

Sample Issue
14 pages (2% advertising): 4 articles; 2 depts/columns. Sample copy, $2 with 9x12 SASE (2 first-class stamps). Guidelines available.
- "When to Betray a Friend." Article discusses when betraying a friend is the right thing to do.
- "God on the Job." Article takes a look at the connection between a job and a spiritual life.
- Sample dept/column: "On the Case" answers the questions of who started Seventh-Day Adventism.

Rights and Payment
First rights. Written material, $50–$125. Pays on acceptance. Provides 3 contributor's copies.

Editor's Comments
We look for true stories that provide factual details, build suspense, and provide character growth. Use sensory impressions—show, don't tell your readers.

Instructor

Scholastic Inc.
557 Broadway
New York, NY 10016

Editor: Francine Cabreja

Description and Readership
Kindergarten through eighth-grade teachers read *Instructor* and contribute much of its content. Each issue covers subjects such as classroom management, trends in education, and professional development. Activities and lesson plans are also included.
- **Audience:** Teachers
- **Frequency:** 8 times each year
- **Distribution:** 40% subscription; 30% newsstand; 30% schools
- **Circulation:** 250,000
- **Website:** www.scholastic.com/instructor

Freelance Potential
70% written by nonstaff writers. Publishes 50 freelance submissions yearly; 20% by unpublished writers, 25% by authors who are new to the magazine. Receives 40 unsolicited mss monthly.

Submissions
Send complete ms. Accepts photocopies. Availability of artwork improves chance of acceptance. SASE. Responds in 3–4 months.
Articles: 1,200 words. Informational and how-to articles and personal experience pieces. Topics include animals, pets, the arts, biographies, college, career, computers, current events, mathematics, science, music, nature, the environment, and special education.
Depts/columns: News items, Q&As, and computers, word length varies. Classroom activities, to 250 words. Humorous or poignant personal essays, to 400 words.
Artwork: Color prints or transparencies. Line art.
Other: Games, puzzles, and activities, 400–800 words. Submit seasonal material 6 weeks in advance.

Sample Issue
72 pages (40% advertising): 3 articles; 5 depts/columns; 8 activities. Sample copy, $3 with 9x12 SASE. Guidelines and theme list available.
- "Poems to Teach By." Article examines the use of poetry as a way to enrich communication.
- Sample dept/column: "End of the Day" is a personal experience piece from a kindergarten teacher.

Rights and Payment
All rights. Articles, $600. Depts/columns, $250–$300. Pays on publication. Provides 2 contributor's copies.

Editor's Comments
We welcome submissions that call attention to current practices and activities that enhance learning.

Inteen

P.O. Box 436987
Chicago, IL 60643

Editor: Aja Carr

Description and Readership
Sunday school lessons for African American teens living in urban areas are presented in this award-winning magazine. Each issue includes stories, Bible lessons, and activities.
- **Audience:** 15–17 years
- **Frequency:** Quarterly
- **Distribution:** 80% subscription; 20% newsstand
- **Circulation:** 75,000
- **Website:** www.inteen.com

Freelance Potential
95% written by nonstaff writers. Publishes 52 freelance submissions yearly; 60% by unpublished writers, 50% by new authors. Receives 30 queries monthly.

Submissions
All material is written on assignment. Send résumé with writing samples. SASE. Responds in 3–6 months.
Articles: Word lengths vary. Bible study guides and Bible lessons; how-to articles; profiles; interviews; and reviews. Topics include religion, biography, colleges, careers, black history, multicultural and ethnic subjects, social issues, and music.
Fiction: Word lengths vary. Stories are sometimes included as part of study plans. Includes inspirational, multicultural, and ethnic fiction, as well as real-life and problem-solving stories.
Other: Puzzles, activities, and poetry. Submit seasonal material 1 year in advance.

Sample Issue
32 pages (no advertising): 2 articles; 14 Bible study guides; 1 activity; 1 poem. Guidelines available.
- "Get a Job!" Article offers tips on how to prepare for an interview and get a job.
- "Make Your Choice." Bible study guide focuses on the importance of personal responsibility in spiritual growth.
- "Forever." Bible study guide includes scripture and discussion about the Book of Daniel.

Rights and Payment
All rights for work-for-hire material. One-time rights for features and poetry. Written material, payment rate varies. Artwork, payment rate varies. Pays 2 months after acceptance. Provides 2 contributor's copies.

Editor's Comments
We look for features that bring readers closer to Christ and help strengthen their commitment to him.

InTeen Teacher

P.O. Box 436987
Chicago, IL 60643

Editor: Aja Carr

Description and Readership
In print for over 35 years, this publication includes Sunday school lessons and features that explore Bible passages. It targets teachers in urban settings who work with African American students.
- **Audience:** Religious educators
- **Frequency:** Quarterly
- **Distribution:** 80% subscription; 20% newsstand
- **Circulation:** 75,000
- **Website:** www.urbanministries.com

Freelance Potential
95% written by nonstaff writers. Publishes 52 freelance submissions yearly; 60% by unpublished writers, 50% by authors who are new to the magazine. Receives 30 queries monthly.

Submissions
All material is written on assignment. Send résumé with writing samples. SASE. Responds in 3–6 months.
Articles: Word length varies. Offers Bible study plans and teaching guides for teaching Christian values to African American teens.
Fiction: Word length varies. Stories are sometimes included as part of study plans. Includes inspirational, multicultural, and ethnic fiction, as well as real-life and problem-solving stories.
Other: Puzzles, activities, and poetry. Submit seasonal material 1 year in advance.

Sample Issue
80 pages (no advertising): 14 teaching plans; 14 Bible study guides. Guidelines available.
- "Keep the Faith." Teaching plan focuses on realizing the importance of obeying God's laws, having faith in God, and that God punishes disobedience.
- "Select Good Leaders." Bible study guide teaches students the biblical qualifications for church leadership and why it is important to encourage and appreciate church leadership and its members.

Rights and Payment
All rights for work-for-hire material. One-time rights for features and poetry. Payment rate varies. Pays 2 months after acceptance. Provides 2 contributor's copies.

Editor's Comments
We strive to provide religious education teachers with the tools necessary to share God's Word with teens and to foster their relationship with Christ and others.

International Gymnast

P.O. Box 721020
Norman, OK 73070

Editor: Dwight Normile

Description and Readership
Articles and photos covering the gymnastics scene can be found in this magazine. Targeting young gymnasts and their coaches, it includes information on competitions, nutrition, fitness, training, and techniques. It also includes profiles of gymnasts.
• **Audience:** 10–16 years
• **Frequency:** 10 times each year
• **Distribution:** 95% subscription; 5% newsstand
• **Circulation:** 17,000
• **Website:** www.intlgymnast.com

Freelance Potential
10% written by nonstaff writers. Publishes 5 freelance submissions yearly; 50% by unpublished writers, 50% by authors who are new to the magazine. Receives fewer than 1 unsolicited ms monthly.

Submissions
Send complete ms. Accepts photocopies, computer printouts, and simultaneous submissions if identified. SASE. Responds in 1 months.
Articles: 1,000–2,250 words. Informational articles; profiles; and interviews. Topics include gymnastics competitions and coaching and personalities involved in the sport around the world.
Fiction: To 1,500 words. Stories about gymnastics.
Depts/columns: 700–1,000 words. News, training tips, and opinion pieces.
Artwork: B/W prints. 35mm color slides for cover.

Sample Issue
54 pages (14% advertising): 4 articles; 10 depts/columns. Sample copy, $5 with 9x12 SASE. Writers' guidelines available.
• "Super Sixth for Georgia." Article reports on Georgia capturing its sixth NCAA team title.
• "Code Comparison." Article takes a look at three subjectively judged sports other than gymnastics.
• Sample dept/column: "Catching Up With" offers an update on the lives of gymnasts Alexander Tkatchev and Linda Gorbik.

Rights and Payment
All rights. Written material, $15–$25. Artwork, $5–$50. Pays on publication. Provides 1 author's copy.

Editor's Comments
We are looking for in-depth interviews with top figures in artistic/rhythmic gymnastics, or sports acrobatics that uncover unknown facts about the person.

Iowa Parent

P.O. Box 957
Des Moines, IA 50304

Editor: Craig S. Black

Description and Readership
Thematic articles, camp and school directories, event schedules, and craft ideas are featured in each issue of this regional tabloid for families in central Iowa.
• **Audience:** Parents
• **Frequency:** Monthly
• **Distribution:** 100% controlled
• **Circulation:** 35,000
• **Website:** www.iowaparent.com

Freelance Potential
90% written by nonstaff writers. Publishes 15 freelance submissions yearly; 50% by authors who are new to the magazine. Receives 8 unsolicited mss each month.

Submissions
Send complete ms. Accepts disk submissions and email submissions to editor@iowaparent.com. SASE. Response time varies.
Articles: 700–800 words. Informational, self-help, and how-to articles; and profiles. Topics include parenting, the arts, summer camps, family travel, pediatric health, fathering, child care, homework, traditions, social issues, and education.
Depts/columns: 700–800 words. Essays on family life, medical advice, and party planning.

Sample Issue
24 pages (50% advertising): 10 articles; 1 events insert. Sample copy, $2 with 10x12 SASE. Writers' guidelines and theme list available.
• "The Big To-Do." Article offers 46 places to go and things to do to stay busy in the spring.
• "Dinner Table Game Helps Families Connect." Article highlights a new game developed by a family to help open lines of communication.
• "From Trash to Trendy." Article explains how to transform empty juice packs into jazzy purses.

Rights and Payment
One-time, non-exclusive rights. Articles, $25. Pays on publication. Provides 2 contributor's copies.

Editor's Comments
Check our editorial calendar before submitting your material. Articles that fit a designated theme or a specific holiday will have a better chance of being accepted. Keep it local—we like to see articles that discuss current national issues and trends with a regional twist, as well as profiles of area personalities.

Jack And Jill

Children's Better Health Institute
1100 Waterway Boulevard
P.O. Box 567
Indianapolis, IN 46206-0567

Editor: Daniel Lee

Description and Readership
Children in second and third grade enjoy this popular magazine for its articles, stories, and activities. It strives to offer material that promotes good health.
- **Audience:** 7–10 years
- **Frequency:** 6 times each year
- **Distribution:** 100% subscription
- **Circulation:** 200,000
- **Website:** www.jackandjillmag.org

Freelance Potential
10% written by nonstaff writers. Publishes 10 freelance submissions yearly; 70% by authors who are new to the magazine. Receives 100 unsolicited mss each month.

Submissions
Send complete ms. Accepts photocopies and computer printouts. SASE. Responds in 3 months.
Articles: 500–600 words. Informational and how-to articles; humor; profiles; and biographies. Topics include sports, health, exercise, safety, nutrition, and hygiene.
Fiction: 500–900 words. Genres include mystery, fantasy, folktales, humor, science fiction, as well as stories about sports and animals.
Artwork: Submit sketches to Andrea O'Shea, art director; photos to Daniel Lee, editor.
Other: Poetry, games, puzzles, activities, and cartoons. Submit seasonal material 8 months in advance.

Sample Issue
34 pages (4% advertising): 5 articles; 1 story; 3 depts/columns; 4 activities; 1 poem. Sample copy, $6.50 ($2 postage). Guidelines available.
- "The Right Track." Story tells how a girl uses her speed in running to help her with a math test.
- "It's Bubble Time!" Article offers ideas to get kids comfortable with the water when learning to swim.
- "Hats All, Folks!" Article takes a look at different reasons why people wear hats.

Rights and Payment
All rights. Articles and fiction, to $.17 per word. Other material, payment rates vary. Pays on publication. Provides 10 contributor's copies.

Editor's Comments
We seek to provide interesting and entertaining material that educates children on the importance of living a healthy lifestyle. Fun activities are welcome.

Journal of Adolescent & Adult Literacy

International Reading Association
800 Barksdale Road, P.O. Box 8139
Newark, DE 19714-8139

Editorial Assistant: Carol Nicholls

Description and Readership
In this membership journal, reading professionals find ideas for improving the quality of their reading instruction. Circulated around the globe, the magazine reaches an audience that includes classroom teachers, reading specialists, psychologists, librarians, media specialists, and parents.
- **Audience:** Reading education professionals
- **Frequency:** 8 times each year
- **Distribution:** 100% subscription
- **Circulation:** 16,000
- **Website:** www.reading.org

Freelance Potential
100% written by nonstaff writers. Publishes 50 freelance submissions yearly; 20% by unpublished writers, 10% by authors who are new to the magazine. Receives 21 unsolicited mss monthly.

Submissions
Send 2 copies of complete ms with disk and hard copy. SASE. Responds in 2–3 months.
Articles: 1,000–6,000 words. Informational and how-to articles and personal experience pieces. Topics include reading theory, research, and practice; and trends in teaching literacy.
Depts/columns: Word lengths vary. Opinion pieces, reviews, and technology information.

Sample Issue
92 pages (7% advertising): 5 articles; 3 depts/columns. Sample copy, $10. Guidelines available.
- "Poetry Connections Can Enhance Content Area Learning." Article reveals that poetry has been successfully used for many years to help students at all levels learn concepts, procedures, theories, and terms across the curriculum.
- "From Dialogue to Two-Sided Argument." Article reports on a writing workshop that used structured reading, oral debate, and reflection to strengthen students' written arguments.

Rights and Payment
All rights. No payment. Provides 5 contributor's copies for articles; 2 copies for depts/columns.

Editor's Comments
For us, an ideal article is one that has a clear purpose, discusses a topic in some depth, and is written in a straightforward style. Remember, your article must appeal to readers around the world.

Journal of Adventist Education

12501 Old Columbia Pike
Silver Spring, MD 20904-6600

Editor: Beverly J. Rumble

Description and Readership
Articles and news on a variety of topics pertinent to Adventist education can be found in this publication. Its readers include Seventh-day Adventist teachers and administrators.
- **Audience:** Educators, school board members
- **Frequency:** 5 times each year
- **Distribution:** Subscription; religious instruction; controlled
- **Circulation:** 15,000
- **Website:** http://education.gc.adventist.org/JAE

Freelance Potential
90% written by nonstaff writers. Publishes 30–40 freelance submissions yearly. Receives 2–4 queries each month.

Submissions
Query. Accepts photocopies, disk submissions (Microsoft Word or WordPerfect files) and computer printouts. Availability of artwork improves chance of acceptance. SASE. Responds in 3 weeks.
Articles: To 2,000 words. Informational and how-to articles. Topics include parochial, gifted, and special education; mathematics; religion; science; and technology.
Artwork: B/W and color prints and transparencies. Line art.

Sample Issue
48 pages (5% advertising): 8 articles; 1 dept/column. Sample copy, $3.50 with 9x12 SASE ($.68 postage). Guidelines available.
- "Ten Things Faculty Can Do to Nurture College Students Spiritually." Article offers opportunities teachers can use to integrate faith and learning.
- "Christian Radio for a Hurting World." Article discusses the benefits of having Christian radio stations on educational campuses.
- "The Scholar and the Administrator: Twin Pillars of Truth." Article takes a look at the roles of the administrator and the scholar in the life of the church.

Rights and Payment
First North American serial rights. Articles, to $100. Artwork, payment rates vary. Pays on publication. Provides 2 contributor's copies.

Editor's Comments
We are seeking fresh articles on new teaching methods and approaches, as well as religious activities.

Journal of School Health

American School Health Association
P.O. Box 708
7263 State Route 43
Kent, OH 44240-0708

Managing Editor: Tom Reed

Description and Readership
Through this publication, the American School Health Association seeks to promote the health of children and youth by providing research papers and educational articles on school health programs.
- **Audience:** School health professionals
- **Frequency:** 10 times each year
- **Distribution:** Subscription
- **Circulation:** 5,000
- **Website:** www.ashaweb.org

Freelance Potential
90% written by nonstaff writers. Publishes 60 freelance submissions yearly; 90% by authors who are new to the magazine. Receives 10 queries monthly.

Submissions
Query or send 4 copies of complete ms; include 150-word abstract for articles and research papers. SASE. Responds to queries in 2 weeks; to mss in 3–4 months.
Articles: 2,500 words. Informational articles; research papers; commentaries; and practical application pieces. Topics include teaching techniques, health services in the school system, nursing, medicine, substance abuse, nutrition, counseling, and ADD/ADHD.

Sample Issue
36 pages (no advertising): 4 articles; 2 research papers; 1 commentary. Sample copy, $8.50 with 9x12 SASE. Guidelines available.
- "School Nurse Perceptions of Barriers and Supports for Children with Diabetes." Article reports on how support for diabetic students can be facilitated through better education of staff and students.
- "A Role for School Health Personnel in Supporting Children and Families Following Childhood Injury." Commentary highlights the need for increased awareness in schools regarding the vulnerability of injured children and the role of school health professionals as resources.

Rights and Payment
All rights. No payment. Provides 2 copies.

Editor's Comments
We want health professionals that can provide original, data-based research papers, position papers, documented analyses of current or controversial issues, reflective treatments of health-related topics, and innovative ideas concerning health instruction.

Juco Review

Suite 103
1755 Telstar Drive
Colorado Springs, CO 80920

Submissions: Wayne Baker

Description and Readership
As the official publication of the National Junior College Athletic Association, this magazine features articles on association news, school athletes and coaches, and health and fitness.
- **Audience:** YA–Adult
- **Frequency:** 9 times each year
- **Distribution:** 90% controlled; 10% subscription
- **Circulation:** 2,700
- **Website:** www.njcaa.org

Freelance Potential
10% written by nonstaff writers. Publishes 5–7 freelance submissions yearly; 90% by unpublished writers, 80% by authors who are new to the magazine. Receives less than 1 unsolicited ms monthly.

Submissions
Send complete ms. Accepts photocopies and computer printouts. Availability of artwork improves chance of acceptance. SASE. Responds in 2 months.
Articles: 1,500–2,000 words. Informational articles. Topics include sports, college, careers, health, fitness, and NJCAA news.
Artwork: B/W prints and transparencies.

Sample Issue
24 pages (25% advertising): 19 articles. Sample copy, $4 for current issue; $3 for back issue with 9x12 SASE. Editorial calendar available.
- "NJCAA Elects Two Executive Committee Members and Three Board Members." Article profiles the newest members of the National Junior College Athletic Association.
- "Why Get Involved with the NJCAA?" Article explains how active participation helps the organization.
- "NJCAA President Karen Sykes." Profile of the organization's president.

Rights and Payment
All rights. No payment. Provides 3 copies.

Editor's Comments
We are looking for up-to-date information on our member schools. Tell us what's going on in their sports programs, who's up and coming, and when sports events are happening. We always need profiles and interviews with athletes and their coaches, and information on teams that are doing well. Our readers also like articles on health, fitness, and nutrition, and how to stay in shape off-season.

Juniorway

P.O. Box 436987
Chicago, IL 60643

Editor: Katherine Steward

Description and Readership
Articles, stories, and activities that spread the joy and love of Christ appear in this magazine. Targeting young Christian African Americans in urban areas, it is used as a tool in Sunday school.
- **Audience:** 9–11 years
- **Frequency:** Quarterly
- **Distribution:** 100% religious education
- **Circulation:** 75,000
- **Website:** www.urbanministries.com

Freelance Potential
95% written by nonstaff writers. Publishes 52 freelance submissions yearly. Receives 20 queries each month.

Submissions
Send résumé and writing samples. All material is written on assignment. Response time varies.
Articles: Word lengths vary. Personal experience pieces; photo-essays; and humor. Topics include religion, social issues, ethnic and multicultural subjects, hobbies, crafts, nature, the environment, pets, and African American studies.
Fiction: Word lengths vary. Inspirational stories with multicultural or ethnic themes; adventure stories; humor; and folktales.
Artwork: B/W and color prints and transparencies.
Other: Activities, games, puzzles, jokes, and filler. Accepts seasonal material for vacation Bible school.

Sample Issue
32 pages (no advertising): 13 Bible lessons; 1 article; 1 story; 6 activities; 1 prayer; 1 cartoon. Sample copy, $1.90. Writers' guidelines and theme list available.
- "You're Special!" Bible lesson tells how all human beings are created in God's image.
- "When I Grow Up." Story tells how a woman's dream as a child of being a nurse came true because she worked hard and had faith in God.

Rights and Payment
All rights. All material, payment rates vary. Pays on publication.

Editor's Comments
We are looking for fresh ideas. New writers have the best chance at publication with short stories, games, jokes, and activities. In order to write for us, you must be a practicing Christian who is familiar with Sunday school curriculum, and knows the Bible.

Juniorway Teacher

P.O. Box 436987
Chicago, IL 60643

Editor: Katherine Steward

Description and Readership
Striving to provide ease in understanding God's Word, this Bible study publication offers articles, lesson plans, study questions, and discussion ideas. It targets teachers working with urban black middle school children.
- **Audience:** Religious educators
- **Frequency:** Quarterly
- **Distribution:** 100% religious instruction
- **Circulation:** Unavailable
- **Website:** www.urbanministries.com

Freelance Potential
95% written by nonstaff writers. Publishes 52 freelance submissions yearly. Receives 20 queries each month.

Submissions
Query with résumé. All material is written on assignment. Response time varies.
Articles: Word lengths vary. Informational and how-to articles; personal experience pieces; and teaching guides. Topics include religion, science, technology, social issues, crafts, hobbies, animals, pets, and African-American history.
Artwork: B/W and color prints and transparencies.

Sample Issue
96 pages (no advertising): 3 articles; 13 teaching plans; 13 Bible study guides. Sample copy, $1.90. Guidelines and theme list available.
- "Jesus and Juniors: Rapping with My Hero." Article discusses introducing Jesus to Juniors as the ultimate hero.
- "Growing Stronger." Teaching plan discusses being faithful to God's teaching and offers suggested reading materials for background information.
- "Do Good Works." Bible study guide focuses on creative ways in which students' Christian beliefs can be translated into good works in the community.

Rights and Payment
All rights. All material, payment rates vary. Pays on publication.

Editor's Comments
We look for articles and teaching guides that will aid teachers in spreading God's Word in a manner that will reach children. We are also looking for puzzles and activities, as well as teaching tips that have proven to be effective in the classroom.

Justine Magazine

Suite 430
6263 Poplar Avenue
Memphis, TN 38119

Editorial Director/Publisher: Jana Pettey

Description and Readership
Targeting girls between the ages of 13 and 18, this magazine offers cool, crafty projects, decorating ideas, and beauty tips. In addition, it offers advice on family issues and diet and nutrition. Its editorial content is entertaining and wholesome.
- **Audience:** 13–18 years
- **Frequency:** 6 times each year
- **Distribution:** 70% subscription; 30% newsstand
- **Circulation:** Unavailable
- **Website:** www.justinemagazine.com

Freelance Potential
15–20% written by nonstaff writers. Publishes 20–30 freelance submissions yearly.

Submissions
Query with résumé and clips. Accepts photocopies and computer printouts. SASE. Response time varies.
Articles: Word length varies. Informational articles; profiles; and personal experience pieces. Topics include room decorating, beauty, health, nutrition, family issues, recreation, travel, and fashion.
Depts/columns: Word length varies. Health, fashion, exercise, entertainment, media and book reviews.

Sample Issue
98 pages: 4 articles; 33 depts/columns.
- "Fancy Footwork." Article takes a look at different flip-flops and pedicures for summer wear.
- "Sushi, Anyone?" Article offers ideas for planning and hosting a sushi-making party for friends, including preparing, recipes, and chef secrets.
- Sample dept/column: "Just' Beauty" takes a look at different types of makeup brushes.

Rights and Payment
Rights vary. Written material, payment rates vary. Pays 30 days after publication.

Editor's Comments
We look for material that fits in with our goal of relating to all of our readers on every level. Our magazine includes up-to-date information on the latest in fashion and makeup, as well as articles on eating healthy, exercise, decorating ideas, ways to deal with family issues, and self-confidence. Make sure your writing style matches our audience. Send us a query for something new, stylish, and entertaining. Please do not send us anything that would make our readers blush.

Kansas School Naturalist

Department of Biological Sciences
Emporia State University
1200 Commercial Street
Emporia, KS 66801-5087

Editor: John Richard Schrock

Description and Readership
Each issue of this publication contains one in-depth research article relating to natural history and nature education. Topics are both teacher- and student-oriented and relate to Kansas in some manner. *Kansas School Naturalist* is read by teachers, students, school administrators, librarians, conservationists, other educational personnel, and anyone else interested in natural history or nature education.
- **Audience:** Teachers, librarians, and conservationists
- **Frequency:** Irregular
- **Distribution:** 70% schools; 30% other
- **Circulation:** 9,700
- **Website:** www.emporia.edu/ksn

Freelance Potential
75% written by nonstaff writers. Publishes less than one freelance submission yearly; 50% by authors who are new to the magazine. Receives 2 unsolicited mss each month.

Submissions
Query or send complete ms. Accepts photocopies, computer printouts, and IBM disk submissions. SASE. Response time varies.
Articles: Word length varies. Informational and how-to articles. Topics include natural history, nature, science, technology, animals, health, and education—all with a Kansas focus.
Artwork: B/W and color prints and transparencies.
Other: Seasonal material.

Sample Issue
16 pages (no advertising): 1 article. Sample copy, free.
- "Biological Smoke Detectors." Article is a toxicology primer with useful suggestions and practical guidance to enhance the quality, meaningfulness, and safety of experiments that are pursued by careful and thoughtful students, their teachers, and other research mentors.

Rights and Payment
All rights. No payment. Provides contributor's copies.

Editor's Comments
We publish scientific articles that are useful to students and educators. While we encourage a conversational language style, we also maintain high standards of exacting, scientific research. All articles relate in some way to the natural history or nature of the state of Kansas.

Keynoter

Key Club International
3636 Woodview Trace
Indianapolis, IN 46268-3196

Executive Editor: Shanna Mooney

Description and Readership
Keynoter is published for members of Key Club, a service organization for students interested in helping others and improving their schools and communities.
- **Audience:** 14–18 years
- **Frequency:** 8 times each year
- **Distribution:** 100% membership
- **Circulation:** 200,000
- **Website:** www.keyclub.org/magazine

Freelance Potential
65% written by nonstaff writers. Publishes 16 freelance submissions yearly; 10% by unpublished writers, 40% by authors who are new to the magazine. Receives 10 queries monthly.

Submissions
Query with outline/synopsis and clips or writing samples. Accepts photocopies, computer printouts, and simultaneous submissions if identified. SASE. Responds in 1 month.
Articles: 1,200–1,500 words. Informational, self-help, and service-related articles. Topics include education, teen concerns, community service, leadership, school activities, social issues, and careers.
Depts/columns: Staff written.
Artwork: Color prints and illustrations.
Other: Submit seasonal material about back to school, college, and summer activities 3–7 months in advance.

Sample Issue
18 pages (5% advertising): 3 articles; 3 depts/columns. Sample copy, free with 9x12 SASE ($.65 postage). Guidelines available.
- "Car Safety." Informative article about how Key Club members can enlighten parents and children about life-saving car-safety measures.
- "Later . . ." Article offers simple suggestions for achieving instant motivation and determination to complete a task.

Rights and Payment
First North American serial rights. Pays on acceptance. All material, $150–$350. Provides 3 contributor's copies.

Editor's Comments
We are looking for general interest feature articles that help Key Club members become better students and better Club members.

Keys for Kids

P.O. Box 1001
Grand Rapids, MI 49510

Editor: Hazel Marett

Description and Readership
This publication offers devotionals for children and their families. Each booklet includes devotionals for two month's of study, as well as stories and Scripture readings to inspire and enhance personal faith.
- **Audience:** 9–12 years
- **Frequency:** 6 times each year
- **Distribution:** 100% controlled
- **Circulation:** 50,000
- **Website:** www.cbhministries.org

Freelance Potential
100% written by nonstaff writers. Publishes 60 free-lance submissions yearly; 50% by unpublished writers, 50% by authors who are new to the magazine. Receives 14 unsolicited mss monthly.

Submissions
Send complete ms. Accepts photocopies, computer printouts, and simultaneous submissions if identified. SASE. Responds in 2 months.
Articles: 400 words. Devotionals. Topics include contemporary social issues, family life, trust, friendship, salvation, witnessing, prayer, marriage, and faith.

Sample Issue
80 pages (no advertising): 61 devotionals. Sample copy, free with 6x9 SASE. Guidelines available.
- "Fleas and Friendship." Devotional explains why we should choose our friends carefully.
- "Something Beautiful." Devotional shows that God is at work in all things.
- "Just a Sub." Devotional discusses God's commandment to obey.

Rights and Payment
First, second, and reprint rights. Written material, $25. Pays on acceptance. Provides 1 contributor's copy.

Editor's Comments
Each devotional should focus on one lesson relevant to young readers. The four parts of our devotional are: a scriptural passage, generally three to ten verses; a story (not a Bible story) with a spiritual application; a practical application the readers can use to further understand the idea of the story; and a key verse that sums up the point of the devotional. Because our readers are young, humor is good way to explain spiritual principles—make sure you use language they can understand. Seasonal material should be submitted four months in advance.

Kickoff Magazine

23rd Floor
110 William Street
New York, NY 10038

Editor: Mitchell Lavnick

Description and Readership
Articles and photos covering the sport of football appear on the pages of this colorful magazine. Targeting football players and enthusiasts from ages seven to fourteen, it includes articles on techniques, coaching, and teamwork, along with profiles and interviews of players and teams.
- **Audience:** 7–14 years
- **Frequency:** Monthly
- **Distribution:** Subscription; newsstand
- **Circulation:** 80,000
- **Website:** www.kickoffmag.com

Freelance Potential
50% written by nonstaff writers. Publishes 5 freelance submissions yearly.

Submissions
Query with clips. Accepts photocopies, computer printouts, and Macintosh disk submissions. SASE. Responds in 3 months.
Articles: To 1,000 words. Informational and how-to articles; profiles; and interviews. Topics related to football including coaching, teamwork, techniques, drills and strategies, fundraising, and sportsmanship.
Depts/columns: Word lengths vary. Collectibles, news, and tips, techniques and strategies.
Other: Cartoons, quizzes, activities.

Sample Issue
72 pages: 4 articles; 19 depts/columns; 1 cartoon, 1 poster. Sample copy, $4 with 9x12 SASE ($.77 postage). Guidelines available.
- "The Rookie Phenom." Article takes a look at the successful record of Ben Roethlisberger as a rookie quarterback for Pittsburgh.
- "Football Camp." Article offers tips on getting the most out of a summer football session, and advice on choosing a good camp. ·
- Sample dept/column: "Parents' Page" offers advice on teaching kids good sportsmanship.

Rights and Payment
All rights. Written material, payment rates vary. Pays 2 months after acceptance.

Editor's Comments
Writers who have experience coaching or playing are invited to submit a query for a how-to article on effective drills and strategies, and techniques that work. Also, up-to-date information on players is welcome.

Kids Discover

12th Floor
149 5th Avenue
New York, NY 10010-6801

Editor: Stella Sands

Description and Readership

Kids Discover features themed issues that cover a wide range of subjects including nature, the environment, archaeology, geography, ecology, weather, travel, entertainment, the media, science, history, architecture, and animals.
- **Audience:** 6–12 years
- **Frequency:** Monthly
- **Distribution:** Subscription
- **Circulation:** 500,000
- **Website:** www.kidsdiscover.com

Freelance Potential

100% written by nonstaff writers. Receives 10 queries monthly.

Submissions

Send resumé. No unsolicited mss. SASE. Response time varies.
Articles: Word length varies. Informational and general interest articles; and profiles. Topics include geology, lakes, ecology, the Mississippi River, World War I, ancient Egypt and China, Thomas Jefferson, weather, the solar system, earthquakes, knights and castles, the Industrial Revolution, Ellis Island, and George Washington.

Sample Issue

16 pages (no advertising): 6 articles; 1 puzzle; 1 recipe; 1 activity. Sample copy available upon email request to editor@kidsdiscover.com.
- "Volcanoes Inside Out." Article explains how volcanoes occur.
- "Rifts, Rafts, & Hot Spots." Article discusses the various places magma can displace the earth's crust.
- "Living with Volcanoes." Article describes what life is like in areas prone to volcanic eruptions.

Rights and Payment

Rights and payment policy vary.

Editor's Comments

All of our articles are written by assignment only. Most of our writers have been working for us for a long time, so freelance work is scarce. If you are still interested in pursuing freelance work with us, we would like to see ideas for material that interests and inspires young readers to learn more about the topic. Review our past publications to see what we have already covered and send us ideas for something new.

The Kids Hall of Fame® News

3 Ibsen Court
Dix Hills, NY 11746

Publisher: Victoria Nesnick

Description and Readership

This magazine spotlights the extraordinary, positive achievements of kids under the age of 20. Its goal is to provide positive, peer role models for readers of all ages.
- **Audience:** 6 years–Adult
- **Frequency:** Quarterly
- **Hits per month:** 8,000
- **Website:** www.thekidshalloffame.com

Freelance Potential

40% written by nonstaff writers. Publishes 300 freelance submissions yearly; 10% by unpublished writers, 20% by authors who are new to the magazine. Receives 100 unsolicited mss monthly.

Submissions

Send complete ms. Accepts photocopies and computer printouts. SASE. Responds in 1–2 months.
Articles: 1,000–2,000 words. Informational and self-help articles; personal experience pieces; photo essays; profiles; and interviews. Topics include the arts, college, careers, hobbies, gifted and special education, music, sports, and multicultural issues.
Artwork: 8½x11 B/W or color prints. Line art.
Other: Poetry, no line limit. Filler.

Sample Issue

28 pages (no advertising): 28 articles. Sample copy available at website. Guidelines available.
- "7-Year-Old Nominee Musician Aaron Yi Huang." Profile of an accomplished young violinist.
- "9-Year-Old Nominee Humanitarian Jamie Ridgely." Profile of a girl who started a program to help the hungry in her community.
- "Parental Techniques for Developing a Child's Self-Confidence." Article suggests nineteen ways to boost a child's self-esteem.

Rights and Payment

Rights policy varies. Pays on acceptance. Payment rates vary.

Editor's Comments

We want to see articles that inspire readers to say "if that kid can do it, so can I," and "I can do it better." We are looking for information on kids under 20 who are champions, contest winners, equestrians, entertainers, entrepreneurs, environmentalists, founders, fund-raisers, humanitarians, life savers, musicians, spokespersons, volunteers, and web designers.

Kids Life Magazine

3014 11th Avenue East
Tuscaloosa, AL 33405

Publisher: Mary Jane Turner

Description and Readership

Full of information for raising children, this publication also features events and resources around the Tuscaloosa region. It is distributed free of charge to families in west Alabama.
- **Audience:** Parents
- **Frequency:** 6 times each year
- **Distribution:** Subscription; newsstand; schools
- **Circulation:** 30,000
- **Website:** www.kidslifemagazine.com

Freelance Potential

50% written by nonstaff writers. Publishes 10 freelance submissions yearly; 50% by unpublished writers, 10% by authors who are new to the magazine. Receives 9 queries and unsolicited mss monthly.

Submissions

Query or send complete ms. Accepts computer printouts and email submissions to kidslife@comcast.net. SASE. Responds to email in 2 weeks.
Articles: 1,000 words. Informational articles; reviews; and personal experience pieces. Topics include parenting, education, child care, religion, cooking crafts, health, and current events.
Artwork: Color prints or transparencies. Line art.
Other: Puzzles, activities, games, and filler.

Sample Issue

42 pages (60% advertising): 9 articles; 5 depts/columns. Sample copy, free.
- "Inspire Your Child." Article discusses ways to help a child make the world a better place for others by volunteering and helping in the community.
- "Help! There's a Teen in the House." Article articulates different ways to interact, teach, and accept teens in order to help them come to terms with their world.
- "Escape for a Date." Article reminds readers that maintaining a relationship between a husband and wife is important despite hectic lifestyles.

Rights and Payment

Rights policy varies. Written material, to $30. Pays on publication. Provides 1 contributor's copy.

Editor's Comments

Our magazine is dedicated to families living in Alabama. Submissions should focus on life in the area, with an emphasis on parenting or local personalities and other subjects of interest to Alabama readers.

Kids VT

10½ Alfred Street
Burlington, VT 05401

Editor: Susan Holson

Description and Readership

Although some of the information in this tabloid offers general parenting information and advice, most of its content is related to resources and activities in the greater Burlington area.
- **Audience:** Parents
- **Frequency:** 10 times each year
- **Distribution:** 100% other
- **Circulation:** 22,000
- **Website:** www.kidsvt.com

Freelance Potential

75% written by nonstaff writers. Publishes 50 freelance submissions yearly; 25–50% by authors who are new to the magazine. Receives 40–80 unsolicited mss each month.

Submissions

Send complete ms. Accepts faxes to 802-865-0595, email to editorial@kidsvt.com, and simultaneous submissions if identified. Response time varies.
Articles: 500–1,500 words. Informational articles; profiles; interviews; and humor. Topics include the arts, education, recreation, nature, the environment, music, camps, maternity issues, and infancy.
Depts/columns: Word length varies. News and book reviews.
Other: Activities and games. Submit seasonal material 2 months in advance.

Sample Issue

26 pages (50% advertising): 4 articles; 8 depts/columns; 1 activity; 1 poem. Theme list available.
- "Help Your Child Develop the 'Write' Stuff." Article lists ideas that will help children of all ages improve their writing skills.
- "Positive Adoption Language." Article explains which positive words and phrases to use when referring to an adopted child or the adoption process.
- Sample dept/column: "Science from the Montshire" gives a scientific cooking experiment about how emulsifiers work in recipes.

Rights and Payment

Exclusive Vermont rights. Written material, $15–$40. Pays on publication. Provides 1–2 author's copies.

Editor's Comments

Submitted material should be relevant to our local readers. We like to see submissions on parenting issues portray child rearing in a positive manner.

Know Your World Extra

200 First Stamford Place
Stamford, CT 06912

Senior Managing Editor: Deb Nevins

Description and Readership
This entertaining and educational magazine is aimed at below-level readers. It offers fiction and nonfiction that is designed to keep the interest of middle school and high school students.
- **Audience:** 10–18 years
- **Frequency:** Monthly
- **Distribution:** 50% controlled; 30% schools
- **Circulation:** 80,000
- **Website:** www.weeklyreader.com

Freelance Potential
30% written by nonstaff writers. Publishes 5 freelance submissions yearly; 10% by unpublished writers, 30% by authors who are new to the magazine. Receives 2 queries and unsolicited mss monthly.

Submissions
Query with writing samples. SASE. Response time varies.
Articles: 350–500 words. How-to articles, plays, profiles, and interviews. Topics include animals, current events, health and fitness, history, humor, music, popular culture, science, technology, and sports.
Fiction: 1,200 words. Topics include adventure, contemporary, fantasy, horror, humor, inspirational, multicultural, real life issues, science fiction, and sports.
Depts/columns: 150–200 words. Current events, health, animals, and sports.
Other: Crosswords, riddles, and puzzles.

Sample Issue
16 pages (no advertising): 1 article; 1 play; 6 depts/columns. Sample copy, free with 9x12 SASE. Writers' guidelines available.
- "Going to Extremes." Article profiles a boy who uses stilts that let him jump 6 feet and run 15 mph.
- "A Brush with Fame." Play is about two kids who try to get into the *Guinness World Records*.
- Sample dept/column: "Debate It" looks at whether or not wearing low-rider pants should be legal.

Rights and Payment
One-time rights. Written material, payment rates vary. Pays on approval. Provides 5 contributor's copies.

Editor's Comments
We need articles, stories, and plays that are teen-based and positive. Our magazine seeks to provide our teenage readers with upbeat information and advice on how to positively handle adolescence.

Ladies' Home Journal

Meredith Corporation
125 Park Avenue
New York, NY 10017

Deputy Editor: Margot Gilman

Description and Readership
Women enjoy this lifestyles magazine for its articles and news on topics such as careers, celebrities, fashion, health, parenting, finances, and family life.
- **Audience:** Women
- **Frequency:** Monthly
- **Distribution:** Newsstand; subscription
- **Circulation:** 4.1 million
- **Website:** www.lhj.com

Freelance Potential
85% written by nonstaff writers. Publishes 25 freelance submissions yearly; 1% by an unpublished writer, 5% by authors who are new to the magazine. Receives 200 queries monthly.

Submissions
Query with résumé, outline, and clips or writing samples for nonfiction. Accepts fiction through literary agents only. SASE. Responds in 1–3 months.
Articles: 1,500–2,000 words. Informational, how-to, and personal experience articles; profiles; and interviews. Topics include family issues, parenting, social concerns, fashion, beauty, and women's health.
Fiction: Word length varies. Accepts agented submissions only.
Depts/columns: Word length varies. Short news items, fashion and beauty advice, and marriage and family issues.

Sample Issue
214 pages (15% advertising): 22 articles; 16 depts/columns. Sample copy, $2.49 at newsstands.
- "Connections." Article describes how two families share their love of extended family by sharing dinner together every night.
- "This House Saved My Son's Life." Article tells how a Habitat home was built for a family tailored to their son's medical needs.
- Sample dept/column: "Health Journal" reports on the dangers of diet pills.

Rights and Payment
All rights. All material, payment rates vary. Pays on acceptance. Provides 2 contributor's copies.

Editor's Comments
We are currently looking for dramatic family stories and newsworthy health stories. Send us a query for something unique. Our column, "A Woman Today" provides the best chance for freelance writers.

Ladybug

The Magazine for Young Children

Cricket Magazine Group
P.O. Box 300,
315 5th Street
Peru, IL 61354
Submissions Editor

Description and Readership
This magazine of stories, poetry, and learning activities also includes nonfiction that presents concepts, vocabulary words, and simple explanations of the things a small child encounters in the world.
- **Audience:** 2–6 years
- **Frequency:** Monthly
- **Distribution:** 92% subscription; 8% other
- **Circulation:** 130,000
- **Website:** www.cricketmag.com

Freelance Potential
100% written by nonstaff writers. Publishes 100 freelance submissions yearly. Receives 200 unsolicited mss monthly.

Submissions
Send complete ms with exact word count. Accepts photocopies, computer printouts, and simultaneous submissions. SASE. Responds in 3–4 months.
Articles: To 300 words. Informational, humorous, and how-to articles. Topics include nature, animals, family, the environment, and other age-appropriate topics.
Fiction: 100–800 words. Read-aloud, early reader, picture, and rebus stories. Genres include adventure, humor, mild suspense, folktales, and contemporary fiction.
Other: Puzzles, activities, games, crafts, finger plays, and songs. Poetry, to 20 lines.

Sample Issue
36 pages (no advertising): 5 stories; 1 rebus; 4 poems; 1 song; 2 activities. Sample copy, $5. Writers' guidelines available.
- "Max and Kate." Story depicts Kate and Max making cardboard wings so they can pretend to fly like the wild geese.
- "Bad Day, Good Day." Story shows a day that starts off sadly for Little Turtle but turns happy when Little Rabbit asks if they can be friends again.

Rights and Payment
Rights vary. Articles and fiction, $.25 per word. Other material, payment rates vary; $25 minimum. Pays on publication. Provides 6 contributor's copies.

Editor's Comments
Please do not query first. We must see a complete manuscript to evaluate it for beauty of language and a sense of joy or wonder.

Language Arts

University of Arizona
515 College of Education
Tucson, AZ 85721

Editor: Kathy G. Short

Description and Readership
This magazine provides educators of children in preschool through middle school an opportunity to explore learning and teaching language arts in classrooms across the U.S. Published by the National Council of Teachers, it includes research articles and personal experience pieces.
- **Audience:** Teachers
- **Frequency:** 6 times each year
- **Distribution:** 100% subscription
- **Circulation:** 22,000
- **Website:** www.ncte.org

Freelance Potential
85% written by nonstaff writers. Publishes 35–40 freelance submissions yearly; 15% by unpublished writers, 25% by authors who are new to the magazine. Receives 20 unsolicited mss monthly.

Submissions
Send 4 copies of complete ms along with an electronic Word or PDF file. Accepts photocopies, computer printouts, and IBM or Macintosh disk submissions. 2 SASEs. Responds in 3–9 months.
Articles: 2,500–6,500 words. Research articles; position papers; personal experiences; and opinion pieces. Topics include language arts, linguistics, and literacy.
Depts/columns: Word length varies. Profiles of children's authors and illustrators; reviews of children's trade books and professional resources; and theme-related research papers.

Sample Issue
80 pages (8% advertising): 6 articles; 4 depts/columns. Sample copy, $5 with 9x12 SASE. Guidelines and theme list available.
- "The Donut House: Real World Literacy in an Urban Kindergarten Classroom." Article discusses characteristics and strategies of schooled literacy.
- Sample dept/column: "Profile" examines the works and contributions of a world-renowned scholar and her impact on understanding literacy learning.

Rights and Payment
All rights. No payment. Provides 2 author's copies.

Editor's Comments
We are seeking topics related to literacy and technology/popular culture, literacy in multilingual classrooms, and literacy from an inquiring perspective.

Launch Pad

Teen Missions International
885 East Hall Road
Merritt Island, FL 32953

Editor: Linda Maher

Description and Readership
Articles and photos portraying the activities and evangelical work by teen missions around the world can be found in this tabloid. Read by supporters and current and former members, it features articles, essays, current events, and profiles of members.
- **Audience:** YA–Adult
- **Frequency:** Twice each year
- **Distribution:** Unavailable
- **Circulation:** Unavailable
- **Website:** www.teenmissions.org

Freelance Potential
10% written by nonstaff writers. Publishes 10 freelance submissions yearly; 15% by unpublished writers, 15% by authors who are new to the magazine. Receives 8–10 queries monthly.

Submissions
Query. Accepts photocopies and computer printouts. SASE. Response time varies.
Articles: Word lengths vary. Informational and factual articles; personal experience pieces; profiles; interviews; and photo-essays. Topics include mission work and teen evangelism in different counties.
Fiction: Word lengths vary. Inspirational, multicultural, and ethnic fiction.
Depts/columns: Word lengths vary. Alumni news and teen mission opportunities.

Sample Issue
8 pages (5% advertising): 3 articles; 5 depts/columns. Sample copy available.
- "Work Groups–Zambia Sewing Team." Article reports on orphan rescue units, which help make clothing for children, to be placed in villages of Zambia.
- "Matrons' House Update." Article provides an update on a program that provides housing and support for girls living in Katembula, Zambia.
- Sample dept/column: "Global Ministry of Teen Missions International" highlights teen missions from around the world.

Rights and Payment
Rights policy varies. No payment.

Editor's Comments
We are looking for photo-essays and inspirational pieces that cover the activities and projects that our dedicated teen missions are involved in. All material is Christian based, and should be positive in tone.

Leadership for Student Activities

National Association of Secondary School Principals
1904 Association Drive
Reston, VA 20191-1537

Editor: Lyn Fiscus

Description and Readership
Advisors who work with student councils or Honor Society chapters in middle schools and high schools turn to this magazine for information on all aspects of student activity advising and student leadership development. Students in leadership positions also read this publication.
- **Audience:** Student leaders and advisors
- **Frequency:** 9 times each year
- **Distribution:** 95% subscription; 5% other
- **Circulation:** 51,000
- **Website:** www.nhs.us/leadershipmag

Freelance Potential
67% written by nonstaff writers. Publishes 18–25 freelance submissions yearly; 75% by unpublished writers, 50% by authors who are new to the magazine. Receives 1–2 queries, 4 unsolicited mss monthly.

Submissions
Query with clips; or send complete ms. Accepts photocopies, computer printouts, Macintosh disk submissions, and email to FiscusL@principal.org. SASE. Responds to queries in 2 weeks, to mss in 1 month.
Articles: 1,200–1,700 words. Informational and how-to articles; profiles; and interviews. Topics include student activities, leadership development, and careers.
Depts/columns: Reports on special events, 100–350 words; advice for and by activity advisors, 1,000–1,500 words; national and regional news, leadership plans, and opinion pieces, word lengths vary.
Artwork: B/W and color prints and transparencies.
Other: Submit seasonal material 4 months in advance.

Sample Issue
48 pages (21% advertising): 6 articles; 10 depts/columns. Sample copy, free with 9x12 SASE ($1.24 postage). Guidelines and theme list available.
- "Making the Most of Summer." Article profiles a Delaware student council whose members spend their summer planning events for the new school year.
- Sample dept/column: "Leadership Lessons" offers an activity that sharpens critical thinking skills.

Rights and Payment
All rights. Payment rates and policies vary. Provides 5 contributor's copies.

Editor's Comments
In your article, include a discussion of barriers overcome and provide details about planning and process.

Leading Edge

4198 JFSB
Provo, UT 84602

Fiction Director

Description and Readership
Leading Edge focuses on the science fiction and fantasy genres in its short stories, novelettes, novellas, and poetry, as well as in the nonfiction it presents. Its nonfiction offerings include book reviews, interviews with successful authors, and articles that discuss science, mythology, and related subjects.
- **Audience:** YA–Adult
- **Frequency:** Twice each year
- **Distribution:** 30% subscription; 70% other
- **Circulation:** 500
- **Website:** http://tle.byu.edu

Freelance Potential
90% written by nonstaff writers. Publishes 15 freelance submissions yearly; 90% by unpublished writers, 90% by authors who are new to the magazine. Receives 50 unsolicited mss monthly.

Submissions
Send complete ms. Accepts photocopies and computer printouts. No simultaneous submissions. SASE. Responds in 2–3 months.
Articles: 1,000–10,000 words. Informational articles; interviews; and book reviews. Topics include science fiction, science, fantasy, mythology, and speculative anthropology.
Fiction: To 17,000 words. Genres include science fiction and fantasy.
Depts/columns: Staff written.
Other: Poetry, no line limit.

Sample Issue
180 pages (no advertising): 3 articles; 6 stories; 4 poems; 6 depts/columns. Sample copy, $4.95. Guidelines available.
- "Summer of the Brides." Story revolves around a tailor and the dresses she works on for six brides from the fairy world.
- "Do Insomniacs Dream of Eclectic Sheep?" Essay turns the practice of counting sheep into an adventurous tale of unusual sheep encounters.

Rights and Payment
First North American serial rights. Written material, $.01 per word. Artwork, payment rate varies. Pays on publication. Provides 2 contributor's copies.

Editor's Comments
To help new authors, we critique story submissions. Let us know if you'd rather we didn't critique yours.

Leading Student Ministry

One Life Way Plaza
Nashville, TN 37234-0174

Editor-in-Chief: Paul Turner

Description and Readership
This denominational magazine is written for youth ministers affiliated with Southern Baptist churches. Its articles are intended to present youth leaders with the kind of information they need to successfully reach out to young adults ages 12 and up.
- **Audience:** Youth ministers and leaders
- **Frequency:** Quarterly
- **Distribution:** Unavailable
- **Circulation:** 10,000
- **Website:** www.lifeway.com

Freelance Potential
85% written by nonstaff writers.

Submissions
Query or send complete ms with résumé. Accepts email submissions to paul.turner@lifeway.com (Microsoft Word documents). Responds to queries in 2–3 days, to mss in 2–3 weeks.
Articles: 1,000–1,800 words. How-to articles; profiles; interviews; and personal experience pieces.
Topics include college, careers, current events, health, fitness, music, popular culture, religion, adolescent ministry, and parenting teens. Also publishes humorous articles.
Depts/columns: 500–1,000 words. Youth culture, adolescent development and counseling, college ministry, parent ministry, teaching tips, and resource reviews.
Artwork: B/W and color prints and transparencies. Line art.
Other: Jokes. Submit seasonal material 3 months in advance.

Sample Issue
62 pages (no advertising): 6 articles; 11 depts/columns. Sample copy, $3.95. Guidelines available.
- "Surviving in a Declining Area." Article addresses the unique needs of churches located in declining neighborhoods.
- Sample dept/column: "College Ministry" explains how to decide if your church needs a collegiate minister.

Rights and Payment
All rights. Written material, $.10 per word. Artwork, rate varies. Pays on acceptance. Provides 3 copies.

Editor's Comments
Many of our articles are written on assignment, but we are open to freelance work that follows our guidelines.

Learning and Leading with Technology

International Society for Technology in Education
480 Charnelton Street
Eugene, OR 97401-2626

Editor: Kate Conley

Description and Readership
Articles that cover the latest in classroom technology appear in this publication for teachers and administrators. In addition, it provides material on leadership and policy as related to education.
- **Audience:** Educators
- **Frequency:** 8 times each year
- **Distribution:** 90% subscription; 10% libraries
- **Circulation:** 12,000
- **Website:** www.iste.org/LL

Freelance Potential
90% written by nonstaff writers. Publishes 50 freelance submissions yearly; 50% by unpublished writers; 75% by authors who are new to the magazine.

Submissions
Check website for latest submissions information. Query. Accepts email queries to submission@iste.org and simultaneous submissions if identified. Response time varies.
Articles: 600–2,000 words. Informational and how-to articles; and personal experience pieces. Topics include computers, software, technology, media applications, teaching methods, and telecommunications.
Depts/columns: Word lengths vary. Research, software, reviews, and curriculum ideas.
Artwork: B/W prints. Line art.

Sample Issue
64 pages (20% advertising): 3 articles; 13 depts/columns. Sample copy, free with 9x12 SASE (3 first-class stamps). Guidelines and editorial calendar available at website.
- "Establishing a Framework for Digital Images in the School Curriculum." Article describes a framework for integrating digital imaging into the classroom.
- Sample dept/column: "Products and Services" offers a review of a collection of software.

Rights and Payment
All rights; returns limited rights to author upon request. No payment. Provides 3 contributor's copies.

Editor's Comments
Our readers turn to us to provide them with up-to-date information on improving teaching and learning through effective technology. Keep in mind that our teachers work with students with various learning styles and performance levels. We look for interesting, practical materials that will engage students.

The Learning Edge

Clonlara School
1289 Jewett
Ann Arbor, MI 48104

Editor: Susan Andrews

Description and Readership
Published by the Clonlara School Home Based Education Program, this newsletter keeps school members abreast of news, events, and educational resources related to its classes.
- **Audience:** Clonlara School members
- **Frequency:** 6 times each year
- **Distribution:** 100% subscription
- **Circulation:** 1,500
- **Website:** www.clonlara.org

Freelance Potential
25% written by nonstaff writers. Publishes 1 freelance submission yearly; 10% by unpublished writers, 1% by authors who are new to the magazine. Receives 1 query monthly.

Submissions
Query. Accepts photocopies and computer printouts. SASE. Responds in 2 months.
Articles: Word length varies. Informational and how-to articles; personal experience pieces; and profiles. Topics include homeschooling, education, technology, career choices, and college.
Depts/columns: Word length varies. School programs, membership news and information, and curriculum resources.
Other: Puzzles and activities.

Sample Issue
12 pages (no advertising): 2 articles; 5 depts/columns. Sample copy available upon request.
- "Etched in Stone." Article takes a look at some of the reasons why members purchased etched bricks for the school walkway.
- "Happenings at Clonlara." Article highlights new programs, classes, and workshops available for winter enrichment.
- Sample dept/column: "News of Our Families" provides news about Clonlara graduates.

Rights and Payment
All rights. No payment.

Editor's Comments
Clonlara School is committed to illuminating educational rights and freedoms. Our students are homeschooled by parents and other family members. We need material and resources that provide practical information that can be individualized for each child's educational program.

Lexington Family Magazine

3529 Cornwall Drive
Lexington, KY 40503

Publisher: Dana Tackett

Description and Readership
This regional tabloid focuses on the needs and interests of families in eastern Kentucky. It features articles focusing on parenting, as well as consumer-interest material for adults.
- **Audience:** Parents
- **Frequency:** Monthly
- **Distribution:** 50% schools; 50% other
- **Circulation:** 30,000
- **Website:** www.lexingtonfamily.com

Freelance Potential
50% written by nonstaff writers. Publishes 5 freelance submissions yearly; 20% by unpublished writers, 10% by authors who are new to the magazine. Receives 10 unsolicited mss monthly.

Submissions
Query or send complete ms. Accepts photocopies and computer printouts. SASE. Response time varies.
Articles: 500–1,500 words. Informational and how-to articles. Topics include the arts, hobbies, current events, education, health, fitness, regional history, multicultural issues, popular culture, recreation, science, technology, and family travel.
Depts/columns: 800 words. Media reviews and news; pediatric medicine.
Artwork: B/W and color prints. Line art.
Other: Puzzles, activities, and poetry.

Sample Issue
32 pages (50% advertising): 6 articles; 9 depts/columns; 1 calendar of events; 1 party guide. Sample copy, free with 9x12 SASE ($1.50 postage). Guidelines and theme list available.
- "Explorium: A Landmark by Any Other Name." Article looks at a local children's museum that has been updated to appeal to visitors of all ages.
- "When Children Get Short of Breath, It May Not Be Asthma." Informative article describes exercise-induced bronchospasm.
- Sample dept/column: "Passages" highlights some of the problem areas in child and youth development.

Rights and Payment
All rights. Payment rate varies. Pays on publication. Provides 25 contributor's copies.

Editor's Comments
We always need more material that relates to our female readers, such as articles on women's health.

Library Media Connection

Suite L
40 East Wilson Bridge Road
Worthington, OH 43085

Editor: Shelley Glantz

Description and Readership
Guidance, information, and motivation are the keys to this specialized publication. Each issue includes specific articles, advice, reviews, and resources.
- **Audience:** School librarians and media specialists
- **Frequency:** 7 times each year
- **Distribution:** 100% subscription
- **Circulation:** 15,000
- **Website:** www.linworth.com

Freelance Potential
100% written by nonstaff writers. Publishes 215 freelance submissions yearly; 75% by unpublished writers, 25% by authors who are new to the magazine. Receives 12 queries, 12 unsolicited mss monthly.

Submissions
Query or send complete ms with résumé. Accepts computer printouts, disk submissions (Microsoft Word or ASCII), and email submissions to linworth@linworthpublishing.com. SASE. Responds in 2 weeks.
Articles: Word length varies. Informational and how-to articles; personal experience pieces; and opinions. Topics include library science, research, technology, education, computers, and media services.
Depts/columns: Word lengths vary. Teaching tips, handouts, reviews, and opinions.
Other: Submit seasonal material 6 months in advance.

Sample Issue
96 pages (15% advertising): 10 articles; 9 depts/columns. Sample copy, $11 with 9x12 SASE. Guidelines and theme list available.
- "Book Folders for High School Readers." Article discusses the benefits of book folders as an effective way of assessing and encouraging high school students.
- "Ready, Set, Motivate!" Article offers food-related ideas to help children make connections to books.
- Sample dept/column: "Author Profile" highlights *ElfQuest* authors Wendy and Richard Pini.

Rights and Payment
All rights. Payment rates vary. Pays on publication. Provides 4 contributor's copies.

Editor's Comments
We are looking for practical, how-to articles based on real-life situations, as well as articles that correspond with upcoming themes. We also want material on the application of technology to the information process and daily life in the library media center.

Library Sparks

P.O. Box 800
W5527 State Road 106
Fort Atkinson, WI 53580

Managing Editor: Michelle McCardell

Description and Readership
In each issue of *Library Sparks*, elementary school teachers and children's librarians find practical information and ready-to-use ideas for their programs or reading and literature classes. The purpose of the magazine is to create enthusiasm for reading and to encourage lifelong reading habits.
- **Audience:** Librarians and teachers
- **Frequency:** 9 times each year
- **Distribution:** Subscription; other
- **Circulation:** Unavailable
- **Website:** www.librarysparks.com

Freelance Potential
90% written by nonstaff writers. Publishes 5 freelance submissions yearly; 40% by unpublished writers, 10% by authors who are new to the magazine. Receives 2 queries and unsolicited mss monthly.

Submissions
Query or send complete ms. Accepts photocopies, computer printouts, and email submissions to librarysparks@highsmith.com. SASE. Response time varies.
Articles: Word length varies. Informational articles and profiles. Topics include connecting literature to the curriculum, lesson plans for librarians, library skills, children's authors and illustrators, and ideas for motivating students to read.
Depts/columns: Word length varies. Reading skills and book review activities, ready-made lessons, fingerplays and storytelling activities, booktalks, and reader's theater scripts.
Other: Reproducible games and activities, crafts.

Sample Issue
50 pages (no advertising): 1 article; 11 depts/columns. Sample copy available at website. Guidelines and editorial calendar available.
- "Math Awareness Month." Article suggests ways to practice math skills across the curriculum.
- Sample dept/column: "Keep 'em Reading" discusses the popularity of parody and lists resources.

Rights and Payment
Rights vary. Written material, payment rates vary. Pays on publication. Provides 1 contributor's copy.

Editor's Comments
We welcome submissions from teachers and librarians with lessons, creative ideas, or activities to share.

The Lion

Lions Club International
300 22nd Street
Oak Brook, IL 60523-8842

Senior Editor: Robert Kleinfelder

Description and Readership
For over 85 years, this publication has been providing Lion's Club members with informational articles, news, and family-oriented photo essays, as well as member profiles and articles on service activism and worldwide achievements.
- **Audience:** Members of the Lions Club
- **Frequency:** 10 times each year
- **Distribution:** Unavailable
- **Circulation:** 600,000
- **Website:** www.lionsclub.org

Freelance Potential
40% written by nonstaff writers. Publishes 40 freelance submissions yearly; 5% by unpublished writers, 20% by authors who are new to the magazine. Receives 20 queries, 5 unsolicited mss monthly.

Submissions
Prefers query; accepts complete ms. Accepts photocopies and computer printouts. SASE. Responds to queries in 10 days, to mss in 2 months.
Articles: 300–2,000 words. Informational articles; humor; and family-oriented photo-essays. Topics include Lions Club service projects, disabilities, social issues, and special education.
Depts/columns: Staff written.
Artwork: 5x7 glossy prints and slides.

Sample Issue
56 pages (6% advertising): 12 articles; 9 depts/columns. Sample copy, free. Guidelines available.
- "Marvel at China's Wonders." Article explores and highlights the big cities and famous sites in China.
- "Provide a Lions Legacy for Your Community." Article discusses how a Lions Club offers opportunities to help meet the needs of a community.
- "Relief, Recovery and Rebuilding: Lions and the Tsunami Disaster." Article takes a look at the outpouring of support from Lions around the world for the Asia disaster.

Rights and Payment
All rights. Written material, $100–$700. Pays on acceptance. Provides 4–10 contributor's copies.

Editor's Comments
We welcome travel stories or articles on technology, finance, or consumer issues and are also interested in photo-essays that illustrate our members' commitment to helping people in need globally.

Listen Magazine

55 West Oak Ridge Drive
Hagerstown, MD 21740

Editor: Céleste Perrino-Walker

Description and Readership
This classroom tool features articles, stories, and poetry that focuses on total abstinence from tobacco, alcohol, and other drugs.
- **Audience:** 12–18 years
- **Frequency:** 9 times each year
- **Distribution:** 60% subscription; 40% newsstand
- **Circulation:** 40,000
- **Website:** www.listenmagazine.com

Freelance Potential
75% written by nonstaff writers. Publishes 50 freelance submissions yearly; 15% by unpublished writers, 30% by authors who are new to the magazine. Receives 500 unsolicited mss monthly.

Submissions
Query or send complete ms. Accepts photocopies, computer printouts, email submissions to editor@listenmag.org, and simultaneous submissions. SASE. Responds in 6 weeks.
Articles: 1,000–1,100 words. Informational articles; self-help pieces; and profiles. Topics include peer pressure, decision making, family conflict, self-discipline, self-esteem, suicide, and hobbies.
Fiction: 1,000–1,100 words. Contemporary fiction based on true events.
Depts/columns: Word length varies. Opinion pieces and short pieces on social issues.
Other: Poetry, word length varies.

Sample Issue
30 pages (no advertising): 12 articles; 6 depts/columns. Sample copy, $2 with 9x12 SASE (2 first-class stamps). Writer's guidelines and editorial calendar available.
- "Too Young to Die." Article discusses the problem of teenage suicide and offers telltale signs.
- "A Deeper Shade of Blue." Article discusses recognizing depression and how to get treatment for it.
- Sample dept/column: "Good for You!" looks at the healthy aspects of smoothies.

Rights and Payment
All rights. Written material, $.05–$.10 per word. Pays on acceptance. Provides 3 contributor's copies.

Editor's Comments
We are looking for more creative stories on how teens have made positive choices in resisting drugs and alcohol. Check our theme list for current topics.

Live

The General Council of the Assemblies of God
1445 North Boonville Avenue
Springfield, MO 65802-1894

Editor: Paul Smith

Description and Readership
This weekly journal of practical Christian living is used in adult Sunday school classes. Each issue includes true stories about God's will and love.
- **Audience:** 18+ years
- **Frequency:** Quarterly, in weekly sections
- **Distribution:** 100% religious instruction
- **Circulation:** 65,000
- **Website:** www.radiantlife.org

Freelance Potential
100% written by nonstaff writers. Publishes 110 freelance submissions yearly; 20% by unpublished writers, 50% by authors who are new to the magazine. Receives 180 queries and unsolicited mss monthly.

Submissions
Query or send complete ms. Accepts photocopies, computer printouts, email to rl-live@gph.org, and simultaneous submissions if identified. SASE. Responds in 6 weeks.
Articles: 800–1,200 words. Informational articles; personal experience pieces; and humor. Topics include family issues, parenting, and religious history.
Fiction: 800–1,200 words. Inspirational and historical fiction, adventure stories, and stories about family celebrations and traditions.
Other: Poetry, 12–25 lines. Filler, 200–700 words. Submit seasonal material 1 year in advance.

Sample Issue
8 pages (no advertising): 2 articles; 1 poem. Sample copy, free with #10 SASE ($.37 postage). Writers' guidelines available.
- "The Worst Day of My Life." Story about a father who comes to terms with his teenage daughter's pregnancy, with the help of prayer.
- "Like Little Children." Story reveals that with forgiveness, all things are possible.

Rights and Payment
First and second rights. Written material, $.10 per word for first rights; $.07 for second rights. Pays on acceptance. Provides 2 contributor's copies.

Editor's Comments
We continue to need more material about the sanctity of life. We also need short stories and articles about special days and holidays, including Valentine's Day, Easter, Mother's Day, Father's Day, Thanksgiving, Christmas, and patriotic days.

Living

1251 Virginia Avenue
Harrisburg, VA 22802

Editor: Melodie Davis

Description and Readership
Practical, positive articles on challenging issues families face in their daily lives can be found in this tabloid. It is written from a Christian perspective with a gentle approach.
- **Audience:** Families
- **Frequency:** Quarterly
- **Distribution:** 100% controlled
- **Circulation:** 150,000
- **Website:** www.churchoutreach.com

Freelance Potential
85% written by nonstaff writers. Publishes 55 freelance submissions yearly; 5% by unpublished writers, 30% by authors who are new to the magazine. Receives 50 unsolicited mss monthly.

Submissions
Send complete ms. Accepts email submissions to melodiemd@msn.com. Include name of magazine and title of article in the subject line; also include your email address in the body of the email. Accepts photocopies, computer printouts, and simultaneous submissions if identified. SASE. Responds in 3–4 months.
Articles: 500–1,000 words. Informational, factual, and how-to articles; opinion and personal experience pieces. Topics include health and fitness, recreation, religion, social issues, education, and multicultural and ethnic issues.
Depts/columns: Staff written.

Sample Issue
32 pages (20% advertising): 12 articles; 4 depts/columns. Sample copy, free with 9x12 SASE (4 first-class stamps). Guidelines available at website.
- "Resurrection Kittens and a Heavy Heart." Essay describes the healing a litter of kittens brings to a woman grieving the death of her son.
- "The Better Side of ADHD." Article discusses how parents of children with ADHD should look at the good qualities of the child.

Rights and Payment
One time and second rights. Articles, $30–$60. Pays on publication. Provides 2 contributor's copies.

Editor's Comments
We cover a wide variety of topics that people face in the home and workplace. We like shorter features as sidebars and fillers. Send us something inspirational that the whole family can enjoy.

Living Safety

Canada Safety Council
1020 Thomas Spratt Place
Ottawa, Ontario K1G 5L5
Canada

General Manager: Jack Smith

Description and Readership
The publication of an independent, not-for-profit safety organization, Living Safety is a family magazine that emphasizes safety awareness at home, in the car, and while enjoying recreational activities.
- **Audience:** All ages
- **Frequency:** Quarterly
- **Distribution:** 100% subscription
- **Circulation:** 80,000
- **Website:** www.safety-council.org

Freelance Potential
75% written by nonstaff writers. Publishes 25 freelance submissions yearly; 65% by unpublished writers, 10% by authors who are new to the magazine. Receives 2–3 queries monthly.

Submissions
Query with résumé and clips or writing samples. Accepts photocopies and computer printouts. SAE/IRC. Responds in 2 weeks.
Articles: 1,500–2,500 words. Informational articles. Topics include recreational, home, traffic, and school safety; and health issues.
Depts/columns: Word lengths vary. Safety news, research findings, opinions, and product recalls.
Other: Children's activities.

Sample Issue
32 pages (no advertising): 4 articles; 4 depts/columns; 1 kids' page. Sample copy, free with 9x12 SAE/IRC. Guidelines available.
- "Dial Privacy." Article discusses the efforts underway in Canada to create a national Do Not Call List to shield residents from telemarketers.
- "Survive the Summer Heat." Article outlines some of summer's hazards, including sun damage to eyes and skin, dehydration, and heat stress disorders.
- Sample dept/column: "Info Bits" reports on trans fats, fake charities, and pest prevention.

Rights and Payment
All rights. Articles, to $500. Depts/columns, payment rates vary. Pays on acceptance. Provides 1–5 contributor's copies.

Editor's Comments
Our goal is to create in our readers a 24-hour safety consciousness. Because our magazine is national in scope, we like to include articles that residents of all provinces and regions can relate to.

Living with Teenagers

One LifeWay Plaza
Nashville, TN 37234-0174

Editor: Ivey Beckman

Description and Readership
Christian parents seeking guidance on raising their teenagers according to biblical principles turn to this magazine for advice, inspiration, and encouragement.
- **Audience:** Parents
- **Frequency:** Monthly
- **Distribution:** Subscription; religious instruction
- **Circulation:** 42,000
- **Website:** www.lifeway.com

Freelance Potential
90% written by nonstaff writers.

Submissions
No queries or unsolicited mss. Work done by assignment only. Submit writing samples if you wish to be considered for an assignment. SASE.
Articles: 600–2,000 words. Informational, self-help, and how-to articles; profiles; interviews; and reviews. Topics include parenting; colleges; current events; health; fitness; recreation; religion; and social, spiritual, multicultural, and ethnic issues.
Depts/columns: Staff written.

Sample Issue
34 pages (no advertising): 6 articles; 10 depts/columns. Sample copy, free.
- "Holes in Their Hearts." Article suggests that teens are turning to sex because they have unfulfilled emotional needs.
- "Playing It Safe in an Unsafe World." Article explains how parents can teach personal safety habits to their teens.
- "Inside Out." Article advises parents to look beyond appearances and to get to know their teenagers' dates for what they are inside.

Rights and Payment
All rights with non-exclusive license to the writer. Articles, $100–$300. Pays on acceptance. Provides 3 contributor's copies.

Editor's Comments
We highly value qualified writers who deliver professional Christian journalism, but, to better meet the needs of our readers, we no longer accept unsolicited freelance submissions. We prefer to assign an article conceived by our staff to a trained journalist who can then develop the idea and craft the article. If you think you'd like to write for us, please visit our website and follow the prompts for writer interest.

Long Island Mothers Journal

P.O. Box 220
Lawrence, NY 11559

Creative Director: Andrew Elias

Description and Readership
Informative, entertaining, reader-friendly material about women's, children's, and family issues are the focus of this regional tabloid. It also offers insightful interviews with leaders in the field of education, healthcare, business, and the media.
- **Audience:** Parents, educators, and caregivers.
- **Frequency:** 6 times each year
- **Distribution:** 5% subscription; 95% other
- **Circulation:** 35,000

Freelance Potential
90% written by nonstaff writers. Publishes 25–50 freelance submissions yearly; 80% by unpublished writers, 90% by authors who are new to the magazine. Receives 300–500 unsolicited mss monthly.

Submissions
Send complete ms. Accepts email submissions (Microsoft Word) to limjedit@optonline.net. Responds in 1–6 weeks.
Articles: 500–2,000 words. Informational and how-to articles; personal experience pieces; profiles; and interviews. Topics include family issues, media, arts, entertainment, health, fitness, home and garden, food, travel, recreation, and sports.
Depts/columns: 500–2,000 words. Family vacations, reviews, reflections, and anecdotes.
Artwork: JPGS, Tiff, or PDF files.

Sample Issue
30 pages (3% advertising): 3 articles; 6 depts/columns; 1 calendar of events. Sample copy available. Guidelines and editorial calendar available.
- "Memories & Motherhood." Interview with Long Island native author Jodi Picoult.
- "The 7 Stages of Motherhood." Article looks at a new book about how to make the most of the "Mom Years."
- Sample dept/column: "Being Well" discusses how to stay healthy, happy, and strong.

Rights and Payment
One-time rights. Pays 30 days after publication. Written material, $.10 per word. Provides 1 copy.

Editor's Comments
Our editors are interested in informative articles about local, regional, and national news and issues of special interest to women concerned about their children, their families, and themselves.

Long Island Woman

P.O. Box 176
Malverne, NY 11565

Publisher: Arie Nadboy

Description and Readership
Distributed free to women residing on Long Island, this magazine features articles on health, recreation, lifestyles and family, news, travel, fashion, decorating, gardening, and other issues of interest to women. It also includes interviews with inspirational females.
- **Audience:** Women 35–65 years
- **Frequency:** Monthly
- **Distribution:** 100% controlled
- **Circulation:** 40,000
- **Website:** www.liwomanonline.com.

Freelance Potential
85% written by nonstaff writers. Publishes 30 free-lance submissions yearly. Receives 62 unsolicited mss monthly.

Submissions
Send ms. Accepts email submissions to editor@liwomanonline.com. Availability of artwork improves chance of acceptance. SASE. Response time varies.
Articles: 350–2,000 words. Informational and how-to articles; profiles; and interviews. Topics include health, recreation, regional news, family, fashion, decorating, entertainment, and gardening.
Depts/columns: 500–1,000 words. Health, money, website information, local attractions and events.
Artwork: Electronic B/W and color prints. Line art.
Other: Submit seasonal material 90 days in advance.

Sample Issue
38 pages (60% advertising): 5 articles; 4 depts/columns. Sample copy, $5. Guidelines available.
- "Managing Your Money." Article offers tips on finding a financial planner who will meet your needs.
- "B. Smith Living with Style." Article offers an interview with top-model turned self-professed minister of style, Barbara Smith.
- Sample dept/column: "Good Advice" takes a look at a non-surgical approach to facial rejuvenation.

Rights and Payment
One time and electronic rights. Written material, $35–$150. Kill fee, 33%. Pays on publication. Provides 1 tearsheet.

Editor's Comments
Our editorial content targets baby-boomer women and we are looking for articles that cover fashion. New writers have the best chance with a piece on fashion decorating. We do not publish poetry or fiction.

Look-Look Magazine

6685 Hollywood Boulevard
Los Angeles, CA 90028

Associate Editor: Lauren Edson

Description and Readership
The pages of this magazine showcase the works of amateur writers and artists ages 14–20. Each issue includes a mix of articles, stories, photo-essays, poems, art, and ruminations.
- **Audience:** 14 to Adult
- **Frequency:** 2 times each year
- **Distribution:** 95% newsstand; 5% subscription
- **Circulation:** 55,000
- **Website:** www.look-lookmagazine.com

Freelance Potential
99% written by nonstaff writers. Publishes 500 freelance submissions yearly; 100% by unpublished writers, 100% by authors who are new to the magazine.

Submissions
Query with submission. Accepts submissions through website.
Articles: To 2,000 words. How-to articles; profiles; interviews; and personal experience pieces. Topics include the arts and popular culture.
Fiction: To 2,000 words. Genres include contemporary, humorous, and multicultural fiction.
Artwork: B/W and color prints and transparencies. Line art.
Other: Poetry. Submit seasonal material 4 months in advance.

Sample Issue
104 pages (5% advertising): 1 article; 5 stories; 4 photo-essays; 1 interview. Sample copy, $5.95 with 9x12 SASE. Writers' guidelines and editorial calendar available at website.
- "The Fan." Story shares how a Washington State University fan deals with the emotions of the team losing a championship game.
- "A Rush of Blood to the Head." Story details the events of the day leading up to the death of the author from a car accident.
- "Mind's Eye." Photo-essay describes and captures the author's family at home in Columbus, Ohio.

Rights and Payment
All rights. No payment. Provides 2 author's copies.

Editor's Comments
Our magazine offers a way for young writers and artists to share their works with others. We are open to any style of writing, and would like to see more on environmental and political issues at this time.

Lowcountry Parent

1277 Stiles Bee Avenue
Charleston, SC 29412

Submissions Editor: Christina Bean

Description and Readership
Distributed free to parents living in the Charleston, South Carolina area, this resourceful magazine covers topics relating to parenting and family issues, child development, health, and education.
- **Audience:** Parents
- **Frequency:** 10 times each year
- **Distribution:** 80% subscription; 20% controlled
- **Circulation:** 38,000
- **Website:** www.lowcountryparent.com

Freelance Potential
90% written by nonstaff writers. Publishes many freelance submissions yearly; 40% by authors who are new to the magazine. Receives 100 mss monthly.

Submissions
Query with sample pages; or send complete ms with biography. Accepts email submissions to editor@lowcountryparent.com. Responds in 3 days.
Articles: Word lengths vary. Informational and factual articles; and personal experience pieces. Topics include parenting, child development, family issues, education, vacations, holidays, and pets.
Depts/columns: Word lengths vary. Infant, preteen, and teen development; health issues; and media reviews.
Artwork: B/W or color prints.
Other: Word lengths vary. Jokes, puzzles, and filler.

Sample Issue
38 pages (50% advertising): 3 articles; 7 depts/columns; 1 calendar of events; 1 directory. Sample copy, free. Guidelines available.
- "Preschool Philosophy 101." Article discusses the various styles and approaches to early childhood education.
- "Strengthen Your Relationship." Article offers tips for parents to help keep their relationship exciting and energized.
- Sample dept/column: "Teen Years" discusses the benefits of part-time jobs for teens.

Rights and Payment
One-time rights. Written material, $15–$100. Pays on publication. Provides 3 contributor's copies.

Editor's Comments
Topics for parenting middle-age children are of interest to us. Material should provide insight and solutions to help face the challenges of parenting.

The Magazine of Fantasy & Science Fiction

P.O. Box 3447
Hoboken, NJ 07030

Editor: Gordon Van Gelder

Description and Readership
Fun and fantasy burst to life within the pages of this pocket-sized digest, entertaining readers with improbable, but maybe possible, scenarios that border on dreams and nightmares. Reviews and odd bits of information are also included.
- **Audience:** YA–Adult
- **Frequency:** Monthly
- **Distribution:** Subscription; newsstand
- **Circulation:** 45,000
- **Website:** www.sfsite.com/fsf

Freelance Potential
90% written by nonstaff writers. Publishes 60–90 freelance submissions yearly; 10% by unpublished writers, 15% by authors who are new to the magazine. Receives 500–650 unsolicited mss monthly.

Submissions
Send complete ms. Accepts photocopies and computer printouts. No simultaneous or electronic submissions. SASE. Responds in 1 month.
Fiction: 1,000–25,000 words. Novellas, novelettes, and short stories. Includes fantasy, science fiction, and humor.
Depts/columns: Staff written.

Sample Issue
162 pages (1% advertising): 2 novelettes; 6 short stories; 5 departments. Sample copy, $5. Writers' guidelines available.
- "The Secret Sutras of Sally Strumpet." Novelette about an author who creates a novel and rides an emotional rollercoaster through the process of publication.
- "A Friendly Little Oasis." An amusing short story about a vampire's account of moving to a new neighborhood and being recognized by its citizens.
- "Black Deer." Short story depicts the slow awakening of a woman to the reality of her past and present.

Rights and Payment
First world rights with option of anthology rights. Pays on acceptance. Written material, $.06–$.09 word. Provides 2 contributor's copies.

Editor's Comments
Humor is always good—we don't get enough of it from authors. Our stories are character-driven science fiction, with elements of fantasy and range from possible reality to totally otherworldly.

Magic the Gathering

15850 Dallas Parkway
Dallas, TX 75248

Editorial Director: Doug Kale

Description and Readership
Players and collectors of Magic the Gathering read this magazine for its articles and information on trading and collecting of cards and memorabilia, as well as its extensive pricing guide.
- **Audience:** YA–Adults
- **Frequency:** Monthly
- **Distribution:** 80% newsstand; 20% subscription
- **Circulation:** 250,000
- **Website:** www.beckettmagic.com

Freelance Potential
50% written by nonstaff writers. Publishes 20 freelance submissions yearly; 10% by unpublished writers, 1% by authors who are new to the magazine.

Submissions
Prefers query with outline and clips. Accepts complete mss. Accepts photocopies and computer printouts. SASE. Responds in 1–2 months.
Articles: 500–2,000 words. Informational articles; profiles; and reviews. Topics include card and memorabilia collecting.
Fiction: Word lengths vary. Includes adventure stories.
Depts/columns: 500–750 words. News related to memorabilia collecting and events.

Sample Issue
88 pages: 7 articles; 10 depts/columns; 2 contests; 2 price guides. Sample copy, $5.99. Writers' guidelines available.
- "The Complete Magic Player." Article discusses the most fashionable accessories Magic players use.
- "Better Than You Think." Article takes a look at ten cards a lot of drafters undervalue that could prove to be useful.
- Sample dept/column: "Magic Hot List" offers information on the hottest cards available.

Rights and Payment
First North American serial rights. Articles and fiction, $150–$350. Depts/columns, $50–$200. Pays on acceptance. Provides 2 contributor's copies.

Editor's Comments
We look for writers that can give readers the hard facts on trading and collecting, including what cards are in demand and why players and collectors like them. We are a new publication and are looking for writers who know the ins and outs of the industry.

Mahoning Valley Parent

Suite 210
100 DeBartolo Place
Youngstown, OH 44512

Editor & Publisher: Amy Leigh Wilson

Description and Readership
Parents residing in northeast Ohio and western Pennsylvania are the target audience of this resourceful magazine. Its pages include articles on topics related to education, parenting, health, and family issues.
- **Audience:** Parents
- **Frequency:** Monthly
- **Distribution:** Subscription; newsstand; schools
- **Circulation:** 50,000
- **Website:** www.forparentsonline.com

Freelance Potential
85% written by nonstaff writers. Publishes 35 freelance submissions yearly; 5% by unpublished writers, 20% by authors who are new to the magazine. Receives 21 unsolicited mss monthly.

Submissions
Send complete ms. Accepts photocopies, computer printouts, and email submissions to editor@ mvparentmagazine.com. Retains all material on file for possible use; does not respond until publication. Include SASE if retaining ms is not acceptable.
Articles: 1,000–1,800 words. Informational and how-to articles; profiles; and reviews. Topics include regional news, current events, parenting, the environment, nature, crafts, travel, recreation, hobbies, and ethnic and multicultural subjects.
Depts/columns: Word length varies. Parenting issues, book reviews, events for kids.
Artwork: B/W and color prints.
Other: Seasonal material.

Sample Issue
42 pages (70% advertising): 6 articles; 6 depts/columns. Sample copy, free with 9x12 SASE. Writers' guidelines and editorial calendar available.
- "Kids Enjoy Benefits of Special Needs Camp." Article explores opportunities at special needs camps.
- "Easy-Does-It Discipline." Article tells of a system that gets kids to listen and behave positively.
- Sample dept/column: "Single Parenting" discusses myths about divorce.

Rights and Payment
One-time rights. Articles, $20–$50. Pays on publication. Provides tearsheets.

Editor's Comments
We are always on the lookout for unique personality profiles and regional newsworthy items.

The Majellan: Champion of the Family

P.O. Box 43
Brighton, Victoria 3186
Australia

Editor: Father Paul Bird, C.S.S.R.

Description and Readership

Based on Catholic viewpoints, this publication offers short items related to living in a manner that will leave the world a better place. Thoughtful ruminations are pertinent to Catholic families and individuals.
- **Audience:** Parents
- **Frequency:** Quarterly
- **Distribution:** 100% subscription
- **Circulation:** 25,000
- **Website:** www.majellan.org.au

Freelance Potential

60% written by nonstaff writers. Publishes 15 freelance submissions yearly; 10% by unpublished writers, 20% by authors who are new to the magazine. Receives 4 queries, 4 unsolicited mss monthly.

Submissions

Prefers complete ms; will accept query. Accepts photocopies, computer printouts, and email submissions to majellan@hotkey.net.au (attachments in Microsoft Word or Rich Text format). SASE. Response time varies.
Articles: 750–1,500 words. Informational articles and personal experience pieces about marriage and family life situations.

Sample Issue

48 pages (15% advertising): 9 articles; 1 photo-essay; 4 depts/columns.
- "The Mothers' Saint." Article relates the story of Saint Gerard Majella who helped many mothers, and after his death became the patron saint of mothers.
- "Tears and Healing." Article describes a woman's personal experience of losing her teenage son, then finding strength by helping others in need.
- "Boundaries." Article contemplates the usefulness of boundaries, both visible and invisible, in maintaining relationships and personal respect.
- Sample dept/column: "Youth Section" highlights the efforts of a youngster who goes beyond the normal kindnesses to make the world a better place.

Rights and Payment

Rights vary. Written material, $50–$80 Australian. Pays on acceptance.

Editor's Comments

Our material is geared to foster strong Christian values in families. We are always interested in articles featuring teens and healthy family relationships.

Maryland Family

10750 Little Patuxent Parkway
Columbia, MD 21044

Editor: Betsy Stein

Description and Readership

This award-winning publication provides parents in the greater Baltimore area with information on all aspects of family life, as well as regional events.
- **Audience:** Maryland families
- **Frequency:** Monthly
- **Distribution:** Subscription; newsstand; other
- **Circulation:** 50,000
- **Website:** www.marylandfamilymagazine.com

Freelance Potential

40% written by nonstaff writers. Publishes 10 freelance submissions yearly; 10% by unpublished writers, 10% by authors who are new to the magazine. Receives 30–50 queries monthly.

Submissions

Query with description of your experience in proposed subject. Accepts photocopies and computer printouts. SASE. Responds in 1 month.
Articles: 800–1,000 words. Practical application pieces, how-to articles, and profiles. Topics include family issues, parenting, college, careers, summer camp, and national trends looked at from a local angle.
Depts/columns: 500–750 words. Health, education, books, cooking, crafts, money, recreation, safety, teens, and travel.
Artwork: Color prints and transparencies.
Other: News briefs on timely, local subjects and "Family Matters," 100–400 words. Submit seasonal material about holidays and events 2–3 months in advance.

Sample Issue

50 pages (50% advertising): 2 articles; 7 depts/columns; 1 calendar; 1 activity. Sample copy, free with 9x12 SASE.
- "A Place to Play." Article discusses different types of playhouses for children.
- "Sharing Seder." Article describes how one family celebrates Passover.
- Sample dept/column: "Recreation" offers information on an award-winning precision jump rope team.

Rights and Payment

First and electronic rights. Written material, payment rate varies. Pays on publication. Provides 1 copy.

Editor's Comments

We provide resourceful information for busy parents and look for coverage of events and parenting articles.

Mentoring Bigtime

Young People's Press
374 Fraser Street
North Bay, Ontario P1B 3W7
Canada

Editor

Description and Readership
This e-zine showcases Big Brother Big Sister programs across Canada by publishing the personal stories of adults and children who have been involved in this mentoring program.
- **Audience:** Adults and children involved in mentoring programs
- **Frequency:** 5 times a year
- **Distribution:** 100% Internet
- **Circulation:** Unavailable
- **Website:** www.mentoringbigtime.org

Freelance Potential
95% written by nonstaff writers. Publishes 50 freelance submissions yearly; 70% by unpublished writers, 75% by authors who are new to the magazine.

Submissions
Send complete ms. Accepts email submissions to mentoringbigtime@onlink.net. Response time varies.
Articles: 500–1,500 words. Informational and how-to articles; profiles; interviews; and personal experience pieces. Features articles that describe successful mentoring relationships and news about the Big Brother Big Sister program in Canada.
Artwork: JPEG and GIF images.

Sample Issue
Sample copy available on website.
- "The Best Sister." Article profiles a 17-year-old girl from Edmonton who was named Little Sister of the Year and describes the rewarding experiences she has had as part of the program.
- "Joyful Hands." Article describes a new Big Brother/ Sister program in Halifax that matches hearing-impaired children with hearing-impaired adults.
- "A Road Map for Youth." Article details the Life Skills Mentoring program offered by Big Brothers and Sisters of Edmonton.

Rights and Payment
Rights vary. Payment rate and policy vary.

Editor's Comments
We look for submissions that highlight some of the magic performed in various Big Brother Big Sister programs in Canada. These can be individual stories or descriptions of successful programs, including in-school programs or couple-matching programs. Log on to our website and you'll see the types of success stories we use.

Metro Parent Magazine

Suite 150
24567 Northwestern Highway
Southfield, MI 48075

Managing Editor: Susan DeMaggio

Description and Readership
Focusing on the needs of families in southeast Michigan, this magazine offers insightful articles and information on parenting issues and trends.
- **Audience:** Parents
- **Frequency:** Monthly
- **Distribution:** 75% newsstand; 25% subscription
- **Circulation:** 80,000
- **Website:** www.metroparent.com

Freelance Potential
75% written by nonstaff writers. Publishes 250 freelance submissions yearly; 5% by unpublished writers, 35% by authors who are new to the magazine. Receives 80+ unsolicited mss monthly.

Submissions
Send complete ms. Accepts email submissions to sedemaggio@metroparent.com. SASE. Responds in 1–2 days.
Articles: 1,500–2,500 words. Informational, self-help, and how-to articles; personal experience pieces; and interviews. Topics include parenting, family life, childbirth, education, social issues, child development, crafts, vacation travel, personal finance, fitness, health, and nature.
Fiction: Word length varies. Inspirational and contemporary fiction, humor, problem-solving stories, and sports-related stories.
Depts/columns: 850–900 words. Family fun, media reviews, new product information, crafts, computers, and women's health.

Sample Issue
82 pages (60% advertising): 4 articles; 12 depts/ columns. Sample copy, free. Guidelines available.
- "Young and Mobile." Article discusses how to set rules and guidelines for children with cell phones.
- Sample dept/column: "Chalk Talk" answers readers' questions about topics such as special needs and school bullies.

Rights and Payment
First rights. Articles and fiction, $150–$300. Depts/columns, $50–$100. Pays on publication. Provides 1 contributor's copy.

Editor's Comments
Timeless topics with a regional twist are what we are seeking. Our audience consists of families with children from infants to twelve years old.

Midwifery Today

P.O. Box 2672
Eugene, OR 97402

Managing Editor: Amanda Bird

Description and Readership
Striving to promote responsible midwifery and child-birth education around the world, this resourceful magazine includes articles, essays, and reviews for birth practitioners and families.
- **Audience:** Childbirth practitioners
- **Frequency:** Quarterly
- **Distribution:** 80% subscription; 10% newsstand; 10% other
- **Circulation:** 4,000
- **Website:** www.midwiferytoday.com

Freelance Potential
90% written by nonstaff writers. Publishes 40+ freelance submissions yearly; 5% by unpublished writers, 5–10% by authors who are new to the magazine. Receives 12 queries monthly.

Submissions
Send complete ms or query with author background. Accepts email submissions to editorial@midwiferytoday.com (Microsoft Word or RTF files). No simultaneous submissions. SASE. Responds in 1 month.
Articles: 800–1,500 words. Informational and instructional articles; profiles; interviews; personal experience pieces; and media reviews. Topics include feminism, health and fitness, medical care and services, diet and nutrition, and multicultural and ethnic issues—all as they relate to childbirth.
Depts/columns: "Question of the Quarter," 100–800 words.
Artwork: B/W and color prints.

Sample Issue
72 pages (10% advertising): 23 articles; 9 depts/columns. Sample copy, $12.50. Writers' guidelines and editorial calendar available.
- "Protocols." Article discusses the slow change in guidelines and protocols for midwives.
- "Antiretroviral Basics." Article offers an overview of the current use of antiretrovirals in the U.S.
- Sample dept/column: "Question of the Quarter" examines the changes in protocols for midwives.

Rights and Payment
Joint rights. No payment. Provides 2 copies and a 1-year subscription for articles over 800 words.

Editor's Comments
We would like to see more articles on clinical and technical issues surrounding birth and pregnancy.

Mission

223 Main Street
Ottawa, Ontario K1S 1C4
Canada

Editor: Peter Pandimakil

Description and Readership
This Christian scholarly journal offers young adult and adult readers essays and reviews on interreligious and intercultural topics.
- **Audience:** 14 years–Adult
- **Frequency:** 2 times each year
- **Distribution:** 90% subscription; 10% other
- **Circulation:** 500
- **Website:** www.ustpaul.ca.com

Freelance Potential
95% written by nonstaff writers. Publishes 3–5 freelance submissions yearly; 60% by unpublished writers, 40% by authors who are new to the magazine. Receives 3 queries monthly.

Submissions
Send complete ms with résumé. Accepts disk submissions (RTF), email submissions to ppandimakil@ustpaul.ca and simultaneous submissions if identified. Availability of artwork improves chance of acceptance. SASE. Responds to mss in 1–2 months.
Articles: 8,000–10,000 words. Bilingual articles; reviews; and personal experience pieces. Topics include current events; history; religion; and multicultural, ethnic, and social issues. Also includes dialogue.
Fiction: Word length varies. Includes historical, multicultural, and ethnic fiction; and problem-solving.
Artwork: 8x10 B/W and color prints.

Sample Issue
404 pages (no advertising): 9 articles; 6 book reviews. Sample copy, $12 U.S. with 8x6 SAE/IRC. Writers' guidelines available.
- "Trinitarian Theology at al-Azhar." Essay examines the principles of Trinity within the context of other religions.
- "Confessing the Trinity in Interreligious Dialogue." Essay analyzes interfaith dialogue.
- Sample book review: "Recensions" reviews various books on the topic of religious theology.

Rights and Payment
Rights policy varies. No payment. Provides 3 contributor's copies.

Editor's Comments
We are seeking scholarly material on Christian topics of interest. Our Praxis section allows the presentation of personal experiences and reflections and is open to freelance writers.

Momentum

National Catholic Educational Association
Suite 100
1077 30th Street NW
Washington, DC 20007-3852

Editor: Brian Gray

Description and Readership
The official publication of the National Catholic Educational Association, *Momentum* covers education methods and trends, and financial development concerning catechetical schools.
- **Audience:** Teachers, school administrators, parents
- **Frequency:** Quarterly
- **Distribution:** 100% controlled
- **Circulation:** 23,000
- **Website:** www.ncea.org

Freelance Potential
95% written by nonstaff writers. Publishes 90 freelance submissions yearly; 25% by unpublished writers, 80% by authors who are new to the magazine. Receives 11 queries and unsolicited mss monthly.

Submissions
Send complete ms with résumé and bibliography. Accepts computer printouts, disk submissions (Microsoft Word), and email submissions to momentum@ncea.org. SASE. Responds in 1–3 months.
Articles: 1,000–1,500 words. Informational and scholarly articles on catechetical education. Topics include teacher and in-service education, educational trends, technology, research, management, and public relations—all as they relate to Catholic education.
Depts/columns: Book reviews, 300 words. "Trends in Technology," 900 words. "From the Field," 700 words.

Sample Issue
92 pages (20% advertising): 20 articles; 7 depts/columns. Sample copy, free with 9x12 SASE ($1.05 postage). Guidelines and editorial calendar available.
- "Teachers Experience Firsthand the Joys of Literacy." Article describes a group of teachers who taught Indian women to read and write in their native language.
- "Small School, Big City." Article looks at a small school in the heart of New York City.
- Sample dept/column: "Technology Trends" examines the culture of information overload.

Rights and Payment
First rights. Articles, $75. Depts/columns, $50. Pays on publication. Provides 2 contributor's copies.

Editor's Comments
Professional ideas for "From the Field" that can be replicated elsewhere are on this year's wish list. Please remember that we only want material that has relevance to Catholic education.

MOMSense

2370 South Trenton Way
Denver, CO 80231-3822

Editor: Mary Darr

Description and Readership
Striving to nurture and support mothers of preschoolers, this publication offers inspirational and informative articles on issues relating to motherhood and womanhood. All material has a Christian perspective.
- **Audience:** Mothers
- **Frequency:** 7 times each year
- **Distribution:** 95% subscription; 5% other
- **Circulation:** 100,000
- **Website:** www.mops.org

Freelance Potential
40% written by nonstaff writers. Publishes 20 freelance submissions yearly; 40% by unpublished writers, 40% by authors who are new to the magazine. Receives 8 queries, 33 unsolicited mss monthly.

Submissions
Query or send complete ms. Accepts computer printouts, and email submissions to MOMSense@mops.org (Microsoft Word attachments). Availability of artwork improves chance of acceptance. SASE. Response time varies.
Articles: 500–1,000 words. Informational articles; profiles; and personal experience pieces. Topics include parenting, religion, and humor.
Depts/columns: Word lengths vary. Parenting and family life articles.
Artwork: B/W and color prints and transparencies.
Other: Accepts seasonal material 6–12 months in advance.

Sample Issue
24 pages (no advertising): 7 articles; 9 depts/columns. Sample copy, free. Guidelines available.
- "Doing What Matters." Article offers advice on ways to prioritize and streamline family activities to gain a sense of balance.
- "Dads Are Cool." Article takes a look at why kids think dads are special.
- Sample dept/column: "Mothering Matters" offers tips for making preschoolers comfortable on vacation.

Rights and Payment
First rights. Payment rates and terms vary. Provides contributor's copies.

Editor's Comments
We look for material that celebrates motherhood, and seek ideas that will challenge and help women regardless of where they are in their spiritual life.

MomsVoice.com

27909 NE 26th Street
Redmond, WA 98053

President: Krista Sweeney

Description and Readership
This online publication offers a wide variety of articles and tips for mothers and mothers-to-be. Topics include party-planning, education, tips for babies and children of all ages, focus issues, book reviews, local communities, and health and wellness.
• **Audience:** Moms
• **Frequency:** Unavailable
• **Distribution:** 100% online
• **Circulation:** Unavailable
• **Website:** momsvoice.com

Freelance Potential
100% written by nonstaff writers. Publishes 100 freelance submissions yearly; 10% by unpublished writers, 20% by authors who are new to the magazine. Receives 20 queries monthly.

Submissions
Query with sample or actual material to be published. Accepts email queries to kristasweeney@momsvoice.com (Word attachment, or in body of email). SASE. Responds in 1 week. Guidelines and editorial calendar available
Articles: 2,500 words. Informational and how-to articles; profiles; personal experience pieces; and reviews. Topics include crafts, hobbies, current events, gifted education, health and fitness, regional news, social issues, special education, travel, and parenting topics.
Fiction: 2,500 words. Genres include humor, real life, and inspirational fiction.
Depts/columns: 2,500 words. Crafts, parenting tips, recipes, health, book reviews.
Other: Activities and fillers.

Sample Issue
Guidelines available at website.
• "Why Pregnancy Yoga." Article discusses how pregnancy yoga benefits a woman's labor.
• Sample dept/column: "Mother Nurture" offers tips on ways to help develop a greater self-awareness.

Rights and Payment
First rights for 2 months. No payment. Provides 2 author's copies.

Editor's Comments
We are looking for articles on dining, recipes, single moms, stay-at-home moms, pregnancy, working moms, step-moms, family travel, women in finance, party-planning, tips for babies, and crafts.

Montessori Life

281 Park Avenue South
New York, NY 10010

Submissions: Marcy Krever

Description and Readership
Thought provoking articles relating to the Montessori method of education are featured in this magazine for educators, school administrators, and parents.
• **Audience:** Educators; parents
• **Frequency:** Quarterly
• **Distribution:** 99% subscription; 1% other
• **Circulation:** 10,500
• **Website:** www.amshq.org

Freelance Potential
90% written by nonstaff writers. Publishes 40 freelance submissions yearly; 30% by unpublished writers, 30% by authors who are new to the magazine. Receives 10–20 unsolicited mss monthly.

Submissions
Send complete ms. Prefers email submissions to mary@amshq.org. Accepts photocopies and computer printouts. SASE. Responds in 3 months.
Articles: 1,000–4,000 words. Informational, academic, and how-to articles; profiles; interviews; and humor. Topics include educational trends, social issues, gifted and special education, and family life–all with some connection to Montessori education.
Fiction: 1,000–1,500 words. Publishes allegorical fiction.
Depts/columns: 500–1,000 words. Montessori community news, events, media reviews, and parenting.

Sample Issue
50 pages (25% advertising): 11 articles; 3 depts/columns. Sample copy, $5 with 9x12 SASE. Guidelines available.
• "The Common Vision: Parenting and Education for Wholeness." Article discusses the common vision of child raising and education of three early 20th century spiritual teachers.
• "Fine Designs from Italy." Article outlines and compares Montessori education and the Reggio approach.

Rights and Payment
All rights. Written material, $90 per published page. Pays on publication. Provides 1–5 author's copies.

Editor's Comments
We are looking for reviews of research and books for parents, as well as features pertinent to Montessori parents and educators. Illustrations are helpful.

Moo-Cow Fan Club Mothering

P.O. Box 165
Peterborough, NH 03458

Editor: Becky Ances

Description and Readership
Targeting children ages 6–12 who love learning, this magazine publishes mostly nonfiction that relates to a theme, folktales, interviews, quizzes, and crafts. It includes articles that explore the more unique aspects of topics that are not taught in school.
- **Audience:** 6–12 years
- **Frequency:** 4 times each year
- **Distribution:** 80% newsstand; 10% subscription; 10% schools
- **Circulation:** 3,000
- **Website:** www.moocowfanclub.com

Freelance Potential
10% written by nonstaff writers. Publishes 5 freelance submissions yearly; 100% by authors who are new to the magazine. Receives 8 queries monthly.

Submissions
Query with sample article. Accepts email queries to becky@moocowfanclub.com (no attachments), and computer printouts. SASE. Responds to queries in 3 weeks.
Articles: 300–550 words. Informational and how-to articles; profiles and interviews. Topics include nature, animals, science, sports, and travel.
Fiction: 300–550 words. Genres include folktales and folklore.
Depts/columns: Staff written.

Sample Issue
48 pages (no advertising): 5 articles; 6 stories; 6 depts/columns. Sample copy, $6 with 9x12 SASE ($1.46 postage). Guidelines and theme list available.
- "The Stonecutter's Wishes." Story tells of a stone-cutter who learns an important lesson after his wishes are granted by a mountain spirit.
- "The Spirit in All Things." Article takes a look at the different belief systems in Japan.
- "Stone and Water." Article discusses different types of Japanese Gardens.

Rights and Payment
All rights. Written material, $50. Pays on acceptance. Provides 3 contributor's copies.

Editor's Comments
We are interested in articles that are both funny and smart. New writers have the best chance at publication with a general education article. Please note that all of our games and crafts are staff written.

P.O. Box 1690
Santa Fe, NM 87504

Senior Editor: Ashisha

Description and Readership
The articles in this magazine stress the value of family life in the development of the full potential of parents and children. Articles on health, pregnancy, birth, and innovative approaches to education appear along with discussions of the spiritual side of nurturing children.
- **Audience:** Parents
- **Frequency:** 6 times each year
- **Distribution:** 70% subscription; 30% newsstand
- **Circulation:** 250,000
- **Website:** www.mothering.com

Freelance Potential
90% written by nonstaff writers. Publishes 100+ freelance submissions yearly; 20% by unpublished writers, 80% by authors who are new to the magazine. Receives 9 queries monthly.

Submissions
Query with outline/synopsis. Accepts photocopies and computer printouts. SASE. Responds in 2–4 weeks.
Articles: 2,000 words. Informational and factual articles; profiles; and personal experience pieces. Topics include pregnancy, childbirth, midwifery, health, homeopathy, teen issues, and organic foods.
Depts/columns: Word length varies. Inspirational pieces; parenting news; health updates; and book and product reviews.
Artwork: 5x7 B/W or color prints.
Other: Children's activities and arts and crafts. Poetry about motherhood and families. Submit seasonal material 6–8 months in advance.

Sample Issue
88 pages (35% advertising): 2 articles; 7 depts/columns. Sample copy, $5.95 with 9x12 SASE. Guidelines available.
- "The Flu Vaccine and You." Article provides important information for parents concerning the new recommendations.
- Sample dept/column: "Art of Mothering" discusses how our children reflect ourselves.

Rights and Payment
First rights. Written material, $200+. Artwork, payment rate varies. Pays on publication. Provides 2 contributor's copies and a 1-year subscription.

Editor's Comments
If you'd like to write for us, tackle a subject you know well or an area in which little information exists.

Mother Verse Magazine

2663 Highway 3
Two Harbors, MN 55616

Editor: Melanie Mayor Laakso

Description and Readership
This magazine is dedicated to the biological, cultural, psychological, and universal state of motherhood. It features intelligent, thoughtful pieces from mothers around the world. It appears both online and in print.
- **Audience:** Parents
- **Frequency:** Quarterly
- **Distribution:** 50% subscription; 50% Internet
- **Circulation:** 15,000
- **Website:** www.motherverse.com

Freelance Potential
90% written by nonstaff writers. Publishes 30 freelance submissions yearly; 50% by unpublished writers, 75% by authors who are new to the magazine.

Submissions
Query or send complete ms. Accepts email submissions only to submissions@motherverse.com (as RTF attachment or in the body of an email). Accepts simultaneous submissions if identified. SASE. Responds in 2–4 weeks.
Articles: To 5,000 words. Essays; personal experience pieces. Topics include issues that are affecting parents in the modern day.
Fiction: 400 words. Stories related to motherhood.
Depts/columns: Column "Muddy Path," up to 1,500 words. Includes personal accounts of life. Book reviews, up to a half a page in length. "Literary Shorts," up to 250 words.
Artwork: 8x10 B/W low resolution.
Other: Poetry, up to 4 poems per submission.

Sample Issue
50 pages: 2 articles; 1 story; 6 poems; 1 dept/column. Sample copy, $3.50. Guidelines available at website.
- "Think of a Time You Were Happy." Story features a woman dealing with her father's aneurysm and reflecting on other challenging issues in her life.
- Sample dept/column: "Muddy Path" discusses the stress that comes along with taking the Alpha Fetal Protein test during pregnancy.

Rights and Payment
One-time rights. No payment. Provides 2 contributor's copies or a 1-year subscription.

Editor's Comments
We are currently accepting submissions for poetry, creative nonfiction, short fiction, and essays, and are always looking for fresh, diverse voices.

Mr. Marquis' Museletter

Box 29556
Maple-Ridge, British Columbia V2X 2V0
Canada

Editor: Kalen Marquis

Description and Readership
The creative works of young writers and artists can be found in this newsletter. Its pages include short stories, book reviews, poems, and artwork.
- **Audience:** 2–21 years
- **Frequency:** Quarterly
- **Distribution:** 100% subscription
- **Circulation:** 150

Freelance Potential
90% written by nonstaff writers. Publishes 40 freelance submissions yearly; 90% by unpublished writers, 90% by authors who are new to the magazine. Receives 40 queries and unsolicited mss monthly.

Submissions
Query with writing samples; or send complete ms. Accepts photocopies, computer printouts, simultaneous submissions if identified, and email submissions to kmarquis@sd42.ca. SAE/IRC. Responds in 4 months.
Articles: 300 words. Personal experience pieces and book reviews. Topics include nature, animals, pets, the arts, current events, history, multicultural and ethnic issues, music, and popular culture. Also features biographies of painters, writers, and inventors.
Fiction: 300 words. Genres include adventure; problem-solving stories; and contemporary, inspirational, and multicultural fiction.
Artwork: Line art.
Other: Poetry, 4–16 lines. Accepts seasonal material 6 months in advance.

Sample Issue
10 pages (no advertising): 7 poems; 1 story; 2 depts/columns. Sample copy, $2 with #10 SASE. Writers' guidelines available.
- "The Spirit of Christmas Long Ago." Article tells how the custom of the first Christmas tree began.
- "Bookfest 2004." Article reports on a bookfest with the author of an adventure sports series.
- "Morning Watch." Poem describes a grandmother's morning ritual of rocking in her rocking chair.

Rights and Payment
One-time rights. No payment. Provides 1 copy.

Editor's Comments
We are looking for inspirational stories and poems (triumph over adversity), line art, and book reviews, and welcome submissions from young writers. We happily publish as many young writers as possible.

MultiCultural Review

194 Lenox Avenue
Albany, NY 12208

Editor: Lyn Miller-Lachmann

Description and Readership
Celebrating multicultural diversity, this glossy magazine offers articles and book and media reviews that explore and create an awareness of ethnic, racial, and religious diversity.
- **Audience:** Teachers and librarians
- **Frequency:** Quarterly
- **Distribution:** 80% subscription; 20% newsstand
- **Circulation:** 3,500+
- **Website:** www.mcreview.com

Freelance Potential
80% written by nonstaff writers. Publishes 30 freelance submissions yearly; 10% by unpublished writers, 20% by authors who are new to the magazine. Receives 10 unsolicited mss monthly.

Submissions
Send complete ms. Accepts photocopies, computer printouts, and disk submissions. SASE. Responds in 3–4 months.
Articles: 2,000–6,000 words. Informational and how-to articles; profiles; and opinion pieces. Topics include the arts; education; writing; and social, multicultural, and ethnic issues.
Depts/columns: 1,500–2,000 words. News.
Other: Book and media reviews, 200–300 words.

Sample Issue
122 pages (10% advertising): 4 articles; 5 depts/columns; 132 reviews. Sample copy, $15. Guidelines and theme list available.
- "Multicultural Children's Publishing: A Family Affair." Article shares the experiences of award-winning children's publishers and their families.
- Sample dept/column: "Bridges on the I-Way: Multicultural Resources Online" offers information on websites with multicultural art content.

Rights and Payment
First serial rights. Articles, $50–$200. Depts/columns, $50. Reviews, no payment. Pays on publication. Provides 2 contributor's copies.

Editor's Comments
We are looking for more articles that cover cultural diversity in film, music, and the Internet, as well as review essays. We are seeing too many theoretical articles. Book reviewers in all subject areas are always needed. Please include information concerning areas of interest, specific format, and expertise.

MultiMedia & Internet Schools

Suite 102
14508 NE 20th Avenue
Vancouver WA 98646

Editor: David Hoffman

Description and Readership
Articles that explore the use of new technologies in kindergarten through grade 12 classrooms can be found in this publication. It is read by teachers, media specialists, and technology coordinators.
- **Audience:** Librarians, teachers, and technology coordinators
- **Frequency:** 6 times each year
- **Distribution:** Unavailable
- **Circulation:** 12,000
- **Website:** www.mmischools.com

Freelance Potential
90% written by nonstaff writers. Publishes 20–24 freelance submissions yearly; 20% by unpublished writers, 20% by authors who are new to the magazine.

Submissions
Query or send complete ms. Accepts disk submissions and email submissions to hoffman@infotoday.com. Availability of artwork improves chance of acceptance. SASE. Responds in 6–8 weeks.
Articles: 1,500 words. Informational, factual, and how-to articles. Topics include K–12 education, the Internet, multimedia and electronic resources, technology-based tools, and curriculum integration.
Artwork: 300 dpi TIFF format.

Sample Issue
80 pages (15% advertising): 15 articles; 5 depts/columns. Sample copy and guidelines, $7.95 with 9x12 SASE.
- "The Net Works." Article explores the use of a plug-in external viewer application called RealAudio to deliver sound information to computers.
- "Teaching High School Mathematics with Technology." Article discusses using software tools for exploring and visualizing mathematics in the classroom.

Rights and Payment
First rights. Written material, $.05 per word. Artwork, payment rate varies. Pays on publication. Provides 2 contributor's copies.

Editor's Comments
We look for practical, how-to articles that explain the benefits of technology-based tools in the classroom environment. Material should stress the do's and don'ts and tips and techniques that can be applied to the readers' situations. Language should be straightforward. Please avoid technical jargon.

Muse

Carus Publishing
Suite 1450
140 S. Dearborn Street
Chicago, IL 60603

Editor

Description and Readership
Published in conjunction with *Smithsonian Magazine*, *Muse* is a nonfiction magazine that presents important ideas and concepts underlying the principal areas of human knowledge.
- **Audience:** 8–14 years
- **Frequency:** 10 times each year
- **Distribution:** 95% subscription; 5% newsstand
- **Circulation:** 51,000
- **Website:** www.cricketmag.com

Freelance Potential
95% written by nonstaff writers. Of the freelance submissions published yearly, 20% are by authors who are new to the magazine. Receives 2 unsolicited mss monthly.

Submissions
All material is commissioned from experienced authors. Send résumé and clips. Response time varies.
Articles: To 1,500 words. Informational articles; interviews; and photo-essays. Topics include animals, pets, science, the environment, nature, computers, technology, history, math, and the arts. Also publishes special issues devoted to biographies.
Depts/columns: Word length varies. News items.

Sample Issue
48 pages (16% advertising): 4 articles; 8 depts/columns. Sample copy, $5. Guidelines available.
- "The Neverending Project." Informative article describes the work involved in determining if a piece of art is genuine.
- "Random Knots." Article explains why rope always ends up in a knot.
- "Fairy Circles." Article offers a theory about the mysterious plantless circles peppering the Namib, the world's oldest desert.

Rights and Payment
Rights policy varies. Written material, payment rates and policy varies.

Editor's Comments
Material should take children seriously as developing intellects by assuming the ideas and concepts of the article will be of interest to them. Treat the topic with competence and humor. All articles are commissioned, and we will let you know if we are interested in your query.

Music Educators Journal

MENC
1806 Robert Fulton Drive
Reston, VA 20191

Editor: Frances S. Ponick

Description and Readership
Published by the National Association for Music Education, this journal covers topics of interest to members and teachers of music. Its articles address the latest developments in music education.
- **Audience:** Music teachers
- **Frequency:** 5 times each year
- **Distribution:** 100% membership
- **Circulation:** 80,000
- **Website:** www.menc.org

Freelance Potential
90% written by nonstaff writers. Publishes 40 freelance submissions yearly; 5% by unpublished writers. Receives 20 unsolicited mss monthly.

Submissions
Send 5 copies of complete ms. Accepts photocopies and computer printouts. SASE. Responds in 3 months.
Articles: 1,800–3,000 words. Instructional and informational articles; and historical studies of music education. Topics include teaching methods, professional philosophy, and current issues in music teaching and learning.
Depts/columns: Word length varies. Personal experience pieces, product reviews, commentary from music teachers, and MENC news.
Other: Submit seasonal material 8–12 months in advance.

Sample Issue
80 pages (40% advertising): 7 articles; 9 depts/columns. Sample copy, $6 with 9x12 SASE ($2 postage). Guidelines available.
- "Whose Music?" Article examines the politics that surround school music.
- "Colliding Perspectives?" Article suggests that teachers who teach culturally diverse music should be aware of its social and political roles.
- Sample dept/column: "MENC Today" covers the latest news and events of MENC.

Rights and Payment
All rights. No payment. Provides 2 contributor's copies.

Editor's Comments
We encourage submissions on all phases of music education in schools and communities about practical instruction, professional philosophy, and current issues in teaching and learning music.

My Friend

Pauline Books & Media/Daughters of St. Paul
50 Saint Pauls Avenue
Boston, MA 02130-3491

Editor: Sister Maria Grace Dateno, FSP

Description and Readership
This Catholic magazine for kids provides readers with a fun way to receive a solid grounding in the Christian faith and values that are most important for a healthy and happy life.
- **Audience:** 7–12 years
- **Frequency:** 10 times each year
- **Distribution:** 80% subscription; 20% newsstand
- **Circulation:** 8,000
- **Website:** www.myfriendmagazine.org

Freelance Potential
60% written by nonstaff writers. Publishes 30 freelance submissions yearly; 5% by unpublished writers, 65% by authors who are new to the magazine. Receives 100 unsolicited mss monthly.

Submissions
Send complete ms. Accepts photocopies and computer printouts. No email. SASE. Responds in 2 months.
Articles: 150–900 words. Informational, self-help, and how-to articles and biographies—all with some connection to the Catholic faith.
Fiction: 750–1,000 words. Genres include inspirational, contemporary, and multicultural fiction.
Depts/columns: Staff written.

Sample Issue
32 pages (no advertising): 3 articles; 1 story; 20 depts/columns. Sample copy, $3.95 with 9x12 SASE ($1.29 postage). Guidelines and theme list available.
- "Detective Writing Duo." Article profiles a nephew and uncle writing team.
- "The Day I Met Fred." Story about a boy who manages to stay happy, even though his family doesn't have a television.
- Sample dept/column: "Craft Page" offers easy-to-follow instructions on how to make a weaving out of words of peace.

Rights and Payment
First worldwide rights. Written material, $80–$150. Pays on acceptance. Provides contributor's copies.

Editor's Comments
We are currently looking for more articles about Lent and other holidays besides Christmas. The best material uses our theme list in a creative and innovative manner. Fiction should include realistic dialogue, including current lingo, and not be too "preachy."

Nashville Christian Family

P.O. Box 1425
Nashville, TN 37065

Editor: Paula Morrison

Description and Readership
Designed to provide Christians living in Nashville, Tennessee, with material to promote positive living, this magazine includes articles and news on entertaining, marriage and family issues, and parenting.
- **Audience:** Parents
- **Frequency:** Monthly
- **Distribution:** 95% newsstand; 5% subscription
- **Circulation:** 30,000

Freelance Potential
30% written by nonstaff writers. Publishes 60 freelance submissions yearly; 5% by unpublished writers, 2–3% by authors who are new to the magazine. Receives 8 queries monthly.

Submissions
Query with photos if applicable. Accepts photocopies and computer printouts. SASE. Responds in 1 month.
Articles: To 500 words. Informational and how-to articles; and personal experience pieces. Topics include regional news, travel, entertainment, recreation, animals, crafts, hobbies, health, fitness, and music.
Fiction: To 500 words. Genres humorous and inspirational fiction.
Depts/columns: To 500 words. Marriage, careers, student issues, family finances, and profiles of church leaders.
Other: Activities. Submit seasonal material 2 months in advance.

Sample Issue
20 pages: 2 articles; 7 depts/columns. Sample copy, free with 9x12 SASE ($3 postage). Editorial calendar available.
- "Christ Church Choir Premiers New CD." Article reports on the debut of the latest release from a Christian choir.
- "Keeping Marriages Afloat." Article discusses clothing yourself in Christ from within to keep a marriage from wearing out.
- Sample dept/column: "House & Home" offers creative decorating projects to do with children.

Rights and Payment
Rights vary. No payment. Provides 1 author's copy.

Editor's Comments
We seek positive articles that demonstrate living a Christian lifestyle in the Nashville region.

Nashville Parent Magazine

2228 Metro Center Boulevard
Nashville, TN 37228

Editor: Susan B. Day

Description and Readership
Residents of Davidson, Sumner, and Wilson counties in central Tennessee can pick up this publication free of charge at various outlets in the area. In addition to providing information about baby and child care, each issue offers significant coverage of upcoming regional events for families with young children.
- **Audience:** Parents
- **Frequency:** Monthly
- **Distribution:** 50% newsstand; 10% subscription; 10% schools; 30% other
- **Circulation:** 73,000
- **Website:** www.parentworld.com

Freelance Potential
60% written by nonstaff writers. Publishes 400 freelance submissions yearly; 40% by authors who are new to the magazine. Receives 40 mss monthly.

Submissions
Send complete ms. Accepts computer printouts, Macintosh disk submissions with hard copy, and email to npinfo@nashvilleparent.com. Artwork improves chance of acceptance. SASE. Responds in 2 weeks.
Articles: 800–1,000 words. Informational and how-to articles; profiles; interviews; photo-essays; and personal experience pieces. Topics include parenting, family issues, current events, social issues, health, music, travel, recreation, religion, the arts, crafts, computers, and multicultural and ethnic issues.
Depts/columns: Staff written.
Artwork: B/W prints.
Other: Submit seasonal material related to Christmas, Easter, and Halloween 2 months in advance.

Sample Issue
112 pages (50% advertising): 6 articles; 13 depts/columns; 1 family calendar. Sample copy, free with 9x12 SASE. Guidelines available.
- "Top 10 Questions to Ask Your OB." Article lists vital questions newly pregnant women should ask.
- "Coaching Kids in Sports." Article explores the traits that make a person a successful coach.

Rights and Payment
One-time rights. Written material, $35. Pays on publication. Provides 3 contributor's copies.

Editor's Comments
Remember that our readers are busy parents looking for information from clear, easy-to-read articles.

NASSP Bulletin

National Assoc. of Secondary School Principals
1904 Association Drive
Reston, VA 20191-1537

Editor

Description and Readership
For more than 80 years, this professional journal has provided middle school and high school principals and administrators with informative articles and resources.
- **Audience:** Secondary school educators and administrators
- **Frequency:** Quarterly
- **Distribution:** 100% subscription
- **Circulation:** 35,000
- **Website:** www.principals.org

Freelance Potential
98% written by nonstaff writers. Publishes 30 freelance submissions yearly; 2% by unpublished writers, 20% by authors who are new to the magazine. Receives 16 unsolicited mss monthly.

Submissions
Send complete ms with bibliography and abstract. Accepts computer printouts, IBM disk submissions, and email to bulletin@principals.org (Microsoft Word attachments). SASE. Responds in 4–6 weeks.
Articles: 4,000 words. Informational articles about education, school administration, and leadership.
Depts/columns: Word length varies. Book, media, and product reviews.

Sample Issue
84 pages (1% advertising): 5 articles; 4 depts/columns. Sample copy, free with 8x10 SASE. Guidelines available.
- "Implementing and Sustaining Standards-Based Curricular Reform." Article presents the latest research findings on standards-based curriculum.
- "Action Research as Instructional Supervision: Suggestions for Principals." Article examines student supervision and how it affects teaching and learning.
- Sample dept/column: "Grant Opportunities" suggests possibilities for program funding.

Rights and Payment
All North American serial rights. No payment. Provides 2 contributor's copies.

Editor's Comments
We look for data-based writing that advances the vision and performance of middle level and high school principals. We seek articles that are timely and thought-provoking. Each issue follows a variety of themes, a list of which can be found at our website. Even so, we publish material on a wide variety of topics.

National Geographic Kids

National Geographic Society
1145 17th Street NW
Washington, DC 20036-4688

Editor: Julie Agnone

Description and Readership
Fresh ways to entertain and educate children is the focus of this magazine. Each issue includes articles on science, entertainment, current events, and cultures from around the world.
- **Audience:** 6–14 years
- **Frequency:** 10 times each year
- **Distribution:** 100% subscription
- **Circulation:** 1.2 million
- **Website:** www.nationalgeographic.com.ngkids

Freelance Potential
85% written by nonstaff writers. Publishes 20 freelance submissions yearly; 1% by unpublished writers, 50% by authors who are new to the magazine. Receives 30 queries monthly.

Submissions
Query with relevant clips. No unsolicited mss. SASE. Response time varies.
Articles: Word lengths vary. Informational articles. Topics include geography, archaeology, paleontology, history, science, technology, culture, natural history, engineering, entertainment, the environment, community service, diversity, and business.
Depts/columns: Word lengths vary. Fun facts, jokes, games, and amazing animals.
Other: Original games.

Sample Issue
44 pages (20% advertising): 5 articles; 11 depts/columns. Sample copy, $3.95. Guidelines available.
- "10 Cool Things About Dolphins." Article reports on the surprising abilities of these clever sea creatures.
- "Amazing Animal Friends." Photo-essay of five true stories of an unusual friendship between animals.
- Sample dept/column: "Kids Did it!" offers a true story of how one family escaped the cruelties of the Taliban government in Afghanistan.

Rights and Payment
All rights. Written material, payment rate varies. Artwork, $100–$600. Pays on acceptance. Provides 3–5 contributor's copies.

Editor's Comments
Although our staff generates most of our story ideas, we would like to hear from you about stories with kid appeal. New writers are invited to submit to "Kids Did It!," a column that highlights youth who have accomplished a superior achievement.

Nature Friend Magazine

2673 TR421
Sugarcreek, OH 44681

Editor: Marvin Wengerd

Description and Readership
This magazine takes children on a journey exploring the wonders of God's creations. Each issue includes fun-to-read stories, interesting articles, nature puzzles, and art projects.
- **Audience:** 6–12 years
- **Frequency:** Monthly
- **Distribution:** 100% subscription
- **Circulation:** 12,000

Freelance Potential
80% written by nonstaff writers. Publishes 36 freelance submissions yearly; 5% by unpublished writers, 10% by authors who are new to the magazine. Receives 40–60 unsolicited mss monthly.

Submissions
Send complete ms. Accepts photocopies and computer printouts. SASE. Response time varies.
Articles: 300–900 words. Informational and how-to articles. Topics include nature and wildlife.
Fiction: 300–900 words. Outdoor adventures and wholesome stories about wildlife, the environment, and enjoying God's creations.
Artwork: 4x6 or larger prints.
Other: Puzzles and projects related to nature and science.

Sample Issue
24 pages (no advertising): 7 articles; 1 story; 8 activities. Sample copy, $2.50 with 9x12 SASE ($.87 postage). Guidelines available for $4 with 9x12 SASE.
- "In the Beginning God Created Snow Flakes." Article discusses how snow flakes are formed and how God sees the perfection in them.
- "Bats: Flying Mammals." Article takes a look at these interesting creatures including where they live, what they eat, and their size.
- "The Squirrels in Wintertime." Story tells of a family watching the behavior of squirrels in their yard, and how God wants us to help the animals.

Rights and Payment
One-time rights. Written material, $.05 per word. Pays on publication. Artwork, payment rates variy. Provides 1 tearsheet.

Editor's Comments
We are looking for how-to articles on nature and science experiments for children ages 6–12. Make sure material includes step-by-step procedures.

Neopets Magazine

Beckett Publishing
15850 Dallas Parkway
Dallas, TX 75248

Editorial Director: Doug Kale

Description and Readership
Fans of Neopets enjoy this magazine for its game hints, site news, previews, merchandise reviews, trading card game advice, and stories and art.
- **Audience:** YA–Adult
- **Frequency:** 6 times each year
- **Distribution:** 80% newsstand; 20% subscription
- **Circulation:** 250,000
- **Website:** www.neopetsmagazine.com

Freelance Potential
50% written by nonstaff writers. Publishes 20 freelance submissions yearly; 10% by unpublished writers, 1% by authors who are new to the magazine.

Submissions
Query with 4–5 article ideas. Accepts photocopies and computer printouts. SASE. Responds to queries in 1–2 months.
Articles: 800–2,000 words. Informational articles; profiles; opinion pieces; and reviews. Topics include game hints, site news, previews, merchandise reviews, and trading card game advice.
Fiction: Word lengths vary. Adventure stories.
Depts/columns: 500–700 words. New card reviews, collecting news and information.

Sample Issue
96 pages: 18 articles; 1 story; 5 depts/columns; 1 poster; 1 contest. Sample copy, $9.99. Writers' guidelines available.
- "Keys to Creating a Successful Guild." Article takes a look at how to create a place to gather with other people from the Neopets site who share a common interest.
- "NeoBoards." Article offers information on how to chat with other users about Neopets-related topics on the Neoboards.
- Sample dept/column: "Neopets TCG Secrets" offers information on a returning card and cards that are new releases.

Rights and Payment
First North American serial rights. Articles, $150–$350. Depts/columns, $50–$200. Pays on publication. Provides 2 contributor's copies.

Editor's Comments
We are interested in articles related to Neopets, news about collectibles, and gaming advice. If you are an expert player with an idea, send us a query.

New & Fox Valley Kids

P.O. Box 45050
Madison, WI 53744-5050

Editor: Karin Mahony

Description and Readership
Formerly *Fox Valley Kids*, this parenting publication is distributed free to parents residing in the Wisconsin towns of Appleton, Ashwaubenon, Green Bay, Kimberly, Kaukauna, Little Chute, Menasha, Oshkosh, Sheboygan, and Two Rivers.
- **Audience:** Parents
- **Frequency:** Monthly
- **Distribution:** Schools; libraries; other
- **Circulation:** 40,000
- **Website:** www.newandfoxvalleykids.com

Freelance Potential
90% written by nonstaff writers. Publishes 19 freelance submissions yearly; 5% by unpublished writers, 10% by authors who are new to the magazine. Receives 17 queries and unsolicited mss monthly.

Submissions
Query or send complete ms. Accepts photocopies, computer printouts, and disk submissions (RFT files). SASE. Response time varies.
Articles: To 750 words. Informational articles and humorous pieces. Topics include parenting, family issues, education, gifted and special education, regional and national news, crafts, hobbies, music, the arts, health, fitness, sports, animals, pets, travel, popular culture, and multicultural and ethnic issues.
Depts/columns: To 750 words. Women's and children's health, school news, and essays.
Artwork: B/W and color prints. Line art.
Other: Submit seasonal material 4 months in advance.

Sample Issue
20 pages (60% advertising): 3 articles; 12 depts/columns. Sample copy, free with 9x12 SASE. Guidelines and editorial calendar available.
- "Scatter Joy!" Article tells how two neighbors joined together to open a store.
- "Books Are Bringing People Together." Article reports on the increase of book discussions on the Internet.
- Sample dept/column: "Rookie Dad" discusses geting children to do chores.

Rights and Payment
Rights negotiable. All material, payment rates vary. Pays on publication. Provides 2 contributor's copies.

Editor's Comments
We seek parenting tips and regional news and events. Check our theme list for upcoming topics.

New Expression

Columbia College
Suite 207
600 South Michigan Avenue
Chicago, IL 60605

Editorial Advisor: Anita Bryant

Description and Readership
Teen staffers write the feature stories and news briefs that appear in this newspaper for young adult readers. Its content focuses exclusively on issues that pertain to teenagers and on individuals who are teenagers.
- **Audience:** YA–Adults
- **Frequency:** 9 times each year
- **Distribution:** 90% schools; 5% subscription; 5% other
- **Circulation:** 45,000
- **Website:** www.newexpression.org

Freelance Potential
20–25% written by nonstaff writers. Publishes 40–50 freelance submissions yearly; 50% by unpublished writers, 50% by authors who are new to the magazine. Receives 3–4 unsolicited mss monthly.

Submissions
Send complete ms. Accepts email submissions only to newexpress@aol.com. Availability of artwork improves chance of acceptance. Response times vary.
Articles: No word limit. Informational articles; reviews; and personal experience pieces. Topics include current events, music, popular culture, and social issues.
Depts/columns: Word lengths vary. News briefs.
Artwork: B/W JPEG files.
Other: Poetry.

Sample Issue
28 pages (10% advertising): 4 articles; 10 depts/columns. Sample copy, $1. Guidelines and editorial calendar available.
- "Teens Complain of Army Recruiting Tactics in High Schools." Article reports that many high school students have found that Army recruiters use aggressive, deceitful tactics to get them to enlist.
- Sample dept/column: "Teens Mean Business" profiles several teen entrepreneurs who have started their own successful businesses.

Rights and Payment
All rights. No payment.

Editor's Comments
Although our newspaper is staffed by local students who supply our editorial content, we will consider freelance submissions from teens. Please note that we accept manuscripts via email only.

New Moon
The Magazine for Girls and Their Dreams

Suite 200
34 East Superior Street
Duluth, MN 55802

Editorial Department

Description and Readership
This magazine features articles, fiction, and poetry written by girls between the ages of 8 and 14. It strives to present girl-centered pieces that portray girls as smart, powerful, and in control of their own lives.
- **Audience:** Girls, 8–14 years
- **Frequency:** 6 times each year
- **Distribution:** 90% subscription; 10% newsstand
- **Circulation:** 25,000
- **Website:** www.newmoon.org

Freelance Potential
85% written by nonstaff writers. Publishes 10–15 freelance submissions yearly; 70% by unpublished writers, 20% by authors who are new to the magazine. Receives 30 queries and unsolicited mss monthly.

Submissions
Query or send complete ms. Accepts photocopies, computer printouts, and email submissions to girl@newmoon.org. SASE postcard. Does not return mss. Responds in 4–6 months.
Articles: 300–900 words. Profiles and interviews. Topics include careers, health, fitness, recreation, science, technology, and social issues.
Fiction: 900–1,200 words. Genres include contemporary, inspirational, multicultural, and ethnic fiction.
Depts/columns: Word length varies. Material about women and girls.
Other: Poetry from girls ages 8–14 only.

Sample Issue
48 pages (no advertising): 4 articles; 2 poems; 23 depts/columns. Sample copy, $6.50. Guidelines available at website.
- "Fitting In." Article traces the evolution of women's clothing from the 1800s to the 1980s.
- Sample dept/column: "Sister to Sister" shares the experiences of a Yale student who has found a way to stop cancer cells from multiplying.

Rights and Payment
All rights. Written material, payment rates vary. Pays on publication. Provides 3 contributor's copies.

Editor's Comments
Our magazine is written by girls, for girls. Adult submissions are considered, but a piece that has been written by a girl will take precedence over one on a similar topic written by an adult. Remember that good writing does not resort to stereotyping or preachiness.

New York Family

Suite 302
141 Halstead Avenue
Mamaroneck, NY 10543

Senior Editor: Heather Hart

Description and Readership
Distributed free to parents living in New York City, this magazine includes articles on issues of interest to families, including education, social issues, and parenting topics. It also features information on local events and resources.
- **Audience:** Parents
- **Frequency:** 11 times each year
- **Distribution:** 96% controlled; 4% subscription
- **Circulation:** 50,000
- **Website:** www.parenthood.com

Freelance Potential
80% written by nonstaff writers. Publishes 40 freelance submissions yearly; 40% by authors who are new to the magazine. Receives 50 queries monthly.

Submissions
Query with clips. Accepts photocopies and computer printouts. SASE. Response time varies.
Articles: 800–1,200 words. Informational articles; profiles; interviews; photo-essays; and personal experience pieces. Topics include gifted education, music, recreation, regional news, social issues, special education, travel, and women's interests.
Depts/columns: 400–800 words. News and reviews.

Sample Issue
62 pages: 2 articles; 1 story; 10 depts/columns; 1 calendar of events. Sample copy, free with 9x12 SASE. Guidelines available.
- "Birth Order." Article takes a look at birth-order research and theory, and how much of our personalities are influenced by the order in which we are born.
- "Daddy Do-Right." Article offers responses by several men on how much fatherhood has changed since they were children.
- Sample dept/column: "Health Notes" takes a look at the link between global warming and asthma.

Rights and Payment
First rights. Written material, $25–$200. Pays on publication. Provides 1 contributor's copy.

Editor's Comments
We look for material that will help provide readers with the resources they need to meet their parenting needs. Thought-provoking and service-oriented editorials are of interest to us. If you know the city, and have an idea for something that will inform and empower our readers, send us a query.

New York Times Upfront

Scholastic Inc.
557 Broadway
New York, NY 10012-3999

Editor

Description and Readership
The New York Times collaborates with Scholastic Inc. to publish this magazine and website for high school students. The focus is on current events, with an emphasis on stories that relate to school social studies curricula.
- **Audience:** 14–18 years
- **Frequency:** 18 times each year
- **Distribution:** 95% schools; 5% subscription
- **Circulation:** 250,000
- **Website:** www.upfrontmagazine.com

Freelance Potential
10% written by nonstaff writers. Publishes 2 freelance submissions yearly; 10% by authors who are new to the magazine. Receives 12 queries monthly.

Submissions
Query with résumé and published clips. Accepts photocopies and computer printouts. Availability of artwork improves chance of acceptance. SASE. Responds in 2–4 weeks only if interested.
Articles: 500–1,200 words. Informational articles; profiles; and interviews. Topics include popular culture, current events, social issues, history, careers, college, the arts, the environment, technology, science, politics, government, business, and multicultural subjects.
Depts/columns: Word length varies. News and trends, first-person accounts from teens.
Artwork: High-resolution color prints or transparencies.

Sample Issue
14 pages (18% advertising): 6 articles; 2 depts/columns. Sample copy, $2.25. Writer's guidelines available.
- "Life in a Village." Article portrays the life of a teen living in Yaftal, a village in northeast Afghanistan.
- "I've Started to Care About My Future." First-person piece written by a "troubled" teen who attends an alternative high school near Washington, D.C.

Rights and Payment
All rights. All material, payment rates vary. Pays on publication.

Editor's Comments
Material should be written for teens who are smart and aware of the world. We look for timely, interesting stories that relate to high school coursework.

The Next Step Magazine

86 West Main Street
Victor, NY 14564

Editor-in-Chief: Laura Jeanne Hammond

Description and Readership
Targeting high school juniors and seniors, this magazine includes information about college planning, career exploration, and life skills, such as public speaking, credit-card management, and résumé writing.
• **Audience:** 14–21 years
• **Frequency:** 5 times each year
• **Distribution:** 100% controlled
• **Circulation:** 800,000
• **Website:** www.nextstepmag.com

Freelance Potential
35% written by nonstaff writers. Publishes 20 freelance submissions yearly.

Submissions
Query. Accepts email queries to laura@nextSTEPmagazine.com. Response time varies.
Articles: 700–1,000 words. Informational, self-help, and how-to articles; profiles; interviews; personal experience pieces; humor; and essays. Topics include college planning, financial aid, campus tours, choosing a career, useful life skills, résumé writing, public speaking, personal finances, computers, multicultural and ethnic issues, social issues, sports, and special education.

Sample Issue
62 pages: 16 articles. Sample copy available at website. Guidelines available.
• "Get Organized." Article discusses getting organized as a senior to be more successful in college.
• "Online Learning." Article takes a look at some of the pros and cons of Internet-based college courses.
• "You Are the Leaders of Tomorrow!" Article lists some of the basic traits a leader should possess.

Rights and Payment
All rights. Articles, payment rate varies. Pays on publication.

Editor's Comments
Our readers turn to us for up-to-date information and tips on preparing for college. We look for articles that cover some aspect of the college-planning process, such as financial aid, campus tours, and how to choose a major. Keep the language personal, refer to readers as "you." Interviews with college faculty and experts are highly regarded. If you have an idea for something resourceful, send us a query.

Nick Jr. Family Magazine

7th Floor
1633 Broadway
New York, NY 10019

Deputy Editor: Wendy Smolen

Description and Readership
The pages of this family magazine are filled with informational articles on parenting topics, vacations, and health. It also includes activities, recipes, and crafts.
• **Audience:** Families
• **Frequency:** 9 times each year
• **Distribution:** 46% subscription; 53% subscription; 1% other
• **Circulation:** 1 million+
• **Website:** www.nickjr.com

Freelance Potential
40% written by nonstaff writers. Publishes 10 freelance submissions yearly; 50% by authors who are new to the magazine. Receives 50 queries and unsolicited mss monthly.

Submissions
Query or send ms. Accepts photocopies, and computer printouts. SASE. Responds in 3 months.
Articles: To 300 words. Informational and how-to articles. Topics include nature, the environment, music, social issues, popular culture, special education, animals, crafts, hobbies, pets, mathematics, current events, and multicultural and ethnic subjects.
Fiction: Word length varies. Humor; adventure; stories about nature animals; and the environment.
Other: Activities and games.

Sample Issue
116 pages (45% advertising): 17 articles; 4 depts/columns; 4 activities. Sample copy, $2.95 at newsstands.
• "What's Your Family's Vacation Style?" Article offers a quiz on different types of family vacations and possible destinations.
• "Monkey Business." A read-together story tells of a brother/sister April Fool's prank.
• Sample dept/column: "Cooking with Kids" offers international variations derived from a basic chicken soup recipe.

Rights and Payment
All rights. Written material, payment rates vary. Pays on publication. Provides 10 contributor's copies.

Editor's Comments
We seek well-written articles on new topics related to parenting issues, family-friendly travel, and health. We are also looking for fun and creative activities and crafts that parents and children can do together.

No Crime

Suite 201
374 Fraser Street
North Bay, Ontario P1B 3W7
Canada

Managing Editor: Ken Sitter

Description and Readership
This electronic publication includes the writings of young adults along with articles from professional staffers that explore what individuals, groups, and communities are doing to help young people avoid involvement in criminal activity. *No Crime* is published by Young People's Press.
- **Audience:** YA–Adult
- **Frequency:** 6 times each year
- **Distribution:** 100% Internet
- **Hits per month:** 24,000
- **Website:** www.nocrimetime.net

Freelance Potential
100% written by nonstaff writers. Publishes 150–200 freelance submissions yearly; 70% by unpublished writers, 75% by authors who are new to the magazine.

Submissions
Send complete ms. Accepts email submissions to media@ypp.net. Responds immediately.
Articles: Word length varies. Informational articles and personal experience pieces. Topics include youth justice, youth crime, and community-based programs in crime prevention.

Sample Issue
8 articles. Sample copy and guidelines available at website.
- "A Lesson Learned." Article reports on a Lethbridge, Alberta, program called Youth in Action that helps prepare at-risk youth for employment.
- "A Cleaner Hip Hop Lifestyle." Article profiles a band that gives hip hop a cleaner image and encourages its fans to live cleaner, too.
- "Judo, the Gentle Way to Confidence." Article describes a program that uses judo to change thinking and behaviors, build confidence, and boost self-esteem.

Rights and Payment
Rights, payment rates, and payment policy vary.

Editor's Comments
Our stories are often printed in more than 220 daily and weekly newspapers across Canada, and some papers publish the stories from Young People's Press regularly. If you're between the ages of 14 and 24, we'd like your input on youth crime prevention in Canada. If you'd like to try writing for us, check out our detailed guidelines posted at our website.

Northern Michigan Family Magazine

P.O. Box 579
Indian River, MI 49749

Editor: L. Scott Swanson

Description and Readership
Distributed free to parents living in Northern Michigan, this magazine offers articles on topics such as child development, parenting, and family life. It also lists regional resources and information on events.
- **Audience:** Parents
- **Frequency:** 6 times each year
- **Distribution:** 100% controlled
- **Circulation:** 6,000

Freelance Potential
50% written by nonstaff writers. Publishes 20 freelance submissions yearly; 25% by unpublished writers, 50% by authors who are new to the magazine. Receives 100 queries and unsolicited mss monthly.

Submissions
Query or send complete ms. Accepts photocopies, computer printouts, email to submissionseditor@resorter.com, and simultaneous submissions if identified. Availability of artwork improves chance of acceptance. SASE. Response time varies.
Articles: 200–1,500 words. Informational, self-help, and how-to articles; profiles; interviews; and personal experience pieces. Topics include parenting, family life, gifted and special education, current events, music, nature, the environment, regional news, recreation, and social issues.
Depts/columns: Word lengths vary. Family news and resources, health information, area events, and perspectives from parents.

Sample Issue
24 pages: 6 articles; 5 depts/columns. Sample copy, free with 9x12 SASE. Guidelines available.
- "Becoming an Involved Parent." Article discusses the importance of parents spending time with their children, listening to them, and helping them learn.
- Sample dept/column: "Health Hints" offers steps to take to have a healthy heart.

Rights and Payment
All rights. Pays $10–$25 for unsolicited articles and reprints; pays $25–$100 for assigned articles. Payment policy varies.

Editor's Comments
We are looking for well-written articles on overcoming health issues, as well as tips and strategies on raising kids. Material should include quotes from experts. Kid-friendly crafts and recipes are always welcome.

The Northland

Northwest Baby & Child

P.O. Box 841
Schumacher, Ontario P0N 1G0
Canada

Submissions Editor

15417 204th Avenue SE
Renton, WA 98059

Editor: Betty Freeman

Description and Readership
Published by the Diocese of Moosonee of the Anglican Church of Canada, this publication is a source of information and enlightenment for church members.
- **Audience:** Adults
- **Frequency:** Quarterly
- **Distribution:** 100% subscription
- **Circulation:** 500

Freelance Potential
100% written by nonstaff writers. Publishes several freelance submissions yearly. Receives few unsolicited mss monthly.

Submissions
Send complete ms. Accepts photocopies and computer printouts. SASE. Response time varies.
Articles: Word length varies. Informational articles. Topics include the Anglican church, ministry, faith, prayer, church rites, baptism, confirmation, worship, and sermon ideas.
Depts/columns: Word length various. Local church news and events.

Sample Issue
24 pages (no advertising): 9 articles. Sample copy available.
- "Lent and Easter: Frequently Asked Questions." Informative article supplies the answers to common questions about the celebration of Easter and Lent, including the meaning of the liturgical color purple, and the reason for fasting during Lent.
- "Rector's Ramblings." Short essay on celebrating Rogation Sunday, and the parable of the sower and the seed.
- Sample dept/column: "Moose Notes" highlights news from various Canadian parishes.

Rights and Payment
Rights policy varies. No payment.

Editor's Comments
This small magazine is a resource for our church family. Each issue includes local and regional information on what is happening in our parishes, as well as in-depth information on the church as a whole. We like to include articles on current and upcoming religious celebrations and what they mean today to our members. We also include sermons, prayers, and photos of church events. Occasionally we publish first-person essays on spiritual events.

Description and Readership
Informative and entertaining articles on issues that are of interest to expectant parents and parents of young children can be found in this regional tabloid. It also includes local activities and events for families.
- **Audience:** Expectant and new parents
- **Frequency:** Monthly
- **Distribution:** 75% public distribution; 10% schools; 5% subscription; 10% other
- **Circulation:** 32,000
- **Website:** www.nwbaby.com

Freelance Potential
70% written by nonstaff writers. Publishes 75 freelance submissions yearly; 25% by unpublished writers, 25% by authors who are new to the magazine. Receives 66 queries monthly.

Submissions
Query. Accepts email queries to editor@nwbaby.com (no attachments). SASE. Responds in 2–3 months if interested.
Articles: 750 words. Informational and how-to articles; personal experience pieces; profiles; and interviews. Topics include early education, party ideas, home-based businesses, pregnancy and childbirth, family life, travel holidays, and traditions.
Depts/columns: Word length varies. Health, parenting tips, activities, and regional resources.

Sample Issue
12 pages (15% advertising): 5 articles; 2 depts/columns; 1 calendar of events. Sample copy, free with 9x12 SASE ($1.48 postage). Guidelines and editorial calendar available.
- "Attracting Your Child to Healthy Food." Article offers suggestions on how to get children to eat more nutritious foods and how to stay away from treats.
- "Baby Diaper Service is Environmentally Sound." Article reports on a baby diaper service that recycles diapers and sells them as rags.
- Sample dept/column: "Health and Safety" reports on what newborns can see.

Rights and Payment
First rights. Written material, $10–$40. Pays on publication. Provides 1–2 contributor's copies.

Editor's Comments
We need articles on life with newborns, infants, and toddlers; discipline; working at home; and nature activities.

OC Family

The News Magazine for Parents

Suite 201
1451 Quail Street
Newport Beach, CA 92660

Editor: Craig Reem

Description and Readership

In print since 1998, this parenting magazine offers families in Orange County, California articles, tips, and information on regional events. Topics include health, finance, education, child development, and other issues related to parenting.
- **Audience:** Families
- **Frequency:** Monthly
- **Distribution:** Newsstand; subscription; controlled
- **Circulation:** 80,000
- **Website:** www.ocfamily.com

Freelance Potential

82% written by nonstaff writers. Publishes 50 freelance submissions yearly; 1% by unpublished writers, 1% by new authors. Receives 12 queries monthly.

Submissions

Query. Accepts photocopies and email queries to OCFmag@aol.com. SASE. Responds in 1 month.
Articles: 800–2,500 words. Informational articles and profiles. Topics include education, the Internet, family activities, health, stay-at-home moms, fatherhood, sports, fine arts, regional food and dining, consumer interests, and grandparenting.
Depts/columns: Word length varies. Family life, personal finances, book and software reviews, and women's health.
Artwork: B/W and color prints.

Sample Issue

194 pages (60% advertising): 3 articles; 23 depts/columns; 2 guides; 1 directory. Sample copy, free. Editorial calendar available.
- "Breath of Life." Article reports on the rise of childhood asthma and possible causes.
- "All About: Breastfeeding." Article discusses the benefits of breastfeeding for mothers.
- Sample dept/column: "Family Finance" offers ideas for teaching children about the value of money.

Rights and Payment

One-time rights. Articles, $100–$500. Artwork, $90. Kill fee, $50. Pays 45 days after publication. Provides 3 contributor's copies.

Editor's Comments

We are seeking queries for articles on nutrition, fitness, and education. Remember that we are a regional publication. We are seeing too many essay-type submissions that are not specific to Orange County.

Odyssey

Carus Publishing
Suite C
30 Grove Street
Peterborough, NH 03458

Senior Editor: Elizabeth E. Lindstrom

Description and Readership

The pages of this thematic glossy are filled with interesting and amazing material that explores the world of science, math, and technology. Targeting middle school students, it includes articles, photos, and activities that make learning fun and exciting.
- **Audience:** 10–16 years
- **Frequency:** 9 times each year
- **Distribution:** 100% subscription
- **Circulation:** 21,000
- **Website:** www.odysseymagazine.com

Freelance Potential

90% written by nonstaff writers. Publishes 40 freelance submissions yearly; 5% by unpublished writers, 25% by authors who are new to the magazine. Receives 12 queries monthly.

Submissions

Query with outline, biography, and clips or writing samples. Availability of artwork improves chance of acceptance. SASE. Responds in 5 months.
Articles: 750–1,000 words. Informational articles; interviews; and biographies.
Depts/columns: Word lengths vary.
Other: Activities, to 500 words. Seasonal material about notable astronomy or space events placed in current context, experiments, and science projects.

Sample Issue

48 pages (no advertising): 8 articles; 6 depts/columns; 4 activities. Sample copy, $4.50 with 9x12 SASE (4 first-class stamps). Guidelines and theme list available.
- "Skin to Skin: The Science of Touch." Article discusses the research and details involved in the science of touch.
- "Skin That Can Make Your Skin Crawl." Article takes a look at how some animals use their skin to their advantage.
- Sample dept/column: "What's Up" offers a sky chart and information on sky and meteor showers.

Rights and Payment

All rights. Written material, $.20–$.25 per word. Other material, payment rates vary. Pays on publication. Provides 2 contributor's copies.

Editor's Comments

We are looking for articles with an interactive approach and science-related stories relating to a theme.

The Old Schoolhouse

The Magazine for Homeschool Families

P.O. Box 185
Cool, CA 95614

Publisher: Gena Suarez

Description and Readership
Parents who homeschool their children receive guidance and practical information from the articles presented in this magazine. Written from a Christian perspective, it addresses a variety of teaching styles and features authoritative material written by well-known members of the homeschooling community.
- **Audience:** Homeschooling families
- **Frequency:** Quarterly
- **Distribution:** Unavailable
- **Circulation:** 22,000
- **Website:** www.thehomeschoolmagazine.com

Freelance Potential
20% written by nonstaff writers. Publishes 30–50 freelance submissions yearly; 75% by unpublished writers, 75% by authors who are new to the magazine. Receives 16 queries monthly.

Submissions
Query with outline, sample paragraphs, and biography. Accepts email queries to publishers@tosmag.com. No simultaneous submissions. SASE. Response time varies.
Articles: 1,000–2,000 words. Informational and how-to articles and personal experience pieces. Topics include homeschooling, education, family life, art, music, spirituality, literature, child development, teen issues, science, history, and mathematics.
Depts/columns: Word lengths vary. Short news items, teaching styles, opinion pieces, children with special needs, humor.

Sample Issue
192 pages (40% advertising): 3 articles; 18 depts/columns. Sample copy available. Guidelines available at website.
- "Homeschooling Pioneers." Part one in a series profiles a couple who were among the first to take part in the homeschooling movement back in the 1970s.
- Sample dept/column: "Styles" discusses notebooking and the Charlotte Mason style of education.

Rights and Payment
First rights. Written material, $.05 per word. Artwork, payment rates vary. Pays on publication. Provides 2 contributor's copies.

Editor's Comments
We welcome queries from homeschoolers. Be sure to include the components listed above with your letter.

Once Upon a Time . . .

553 Winston Court
St. Paul, MN 55118

Editor/Publisher: Audrey B. Baird

Description and Readership
A support publication for children's writers and illustrators, *Once Upon a Time* serves as a forum for readers to communicate, commiserate, share successes, and gather information. Now in its 15th year of publication, the magazine does not publish fiction or poetry for children, but will accept short poems about writing or illustrating.
- **Audience:** Children's writers and illustrators
- **Frequency:** Quarterly
- **Distribution:** 100% subscription
- **Circulation:** 1,000
- **Website:** http://onceuponatime.com

Freelance Potential
50% written by nonstaff writers. Publishes 160 freelance submissions yearly; 20% by unpublished writers, 20% by authors who are new to the magazine. Receives 17 unsolicited mss monthly.

Submissions
Send complete ms. No queries. Accepts photocopies and computer printouts. SASE. Responds in 2 months.
Articles: To 900 words. Informational, self-help, how-to articles; and personal experience pieces. Topics include writing and illustrating for children.
Depts/columns: Staff written.
Artwork: B/W line art.
Other: Poetry, to 24 lines.

Sample Issue
32 pages (2% advertising): 17 articles; 22 poems; 15 depts/columns. Sample copy, $5. Writers' guidelines available.
- "The Revenge of the Rejection Letter." Article relates how one writer's rejection letter took first prize in a "Worst Rejection Letter" contest.
- "Using a Journal to Explore Character." Article suggests going on a journey with your character and writing down all that the character learns, sees, and experiences.

Rights and Payment
One-time rights. No payment. Provides 2 contributor's copies; 5 copies for cover art.

Editor's Comments
Too many submissions come in that reflect on the experience of rejection. What we really need instead are nuts-and-bolts types of how-to articles on the subjects of children's writing and illustration.

On Course

General Council on the Assemblies of God
1445 North Boonville Avenue
Springfield, MO 65802-1894

Associate Editor: Heather Van Allen

Description and Readership
The official publication of the General Council of the Assemblies of God, *On Course* offers its teenage readers upbeat and inspirational articles on contemporary issues. Articles, interviews, profiles, and personal experience pieces about living a Christian lifestyle are included in its editorial mix.
- **Audience:** 12–18 years
- **Frequency:** Quarterly
- **Distribution:** 100% controlled
- **Circulation:** 160,000
- **Website:** www.oncourse.ag.org

Freelance Potential
85% written by nonstaff writers. Publishes 32 freelance submissions yearly; 30% by unpublished writers, 40% by authors who are new to the magazine. Receives 16 queries and unsolicited mss monthly.

Submissions
Send résumé with clips and writing samples. All work is done on assignment only.
Articles: To 1,000 words. How-to articles, profiles, interviews, humor, and personal experience pieces. Topics include social issues, music, health, religion, sports, careers, college, and multicultural subjects.
Depts/columns: Word lengths vary.

Sample Issue
30 pages (33% advertising): 4 articles; 7 depts/columns. Sample copy, free. Guidelines available.
- "Boost Your Brain Power." Article offers students ways to manage homework and excel.
- "10 Things You Need to Know about Copyright." Article discusses ten ways to ensure that your downloaded music is legal.
- Sample dept/column: "Face" profiles the animator of *Veggie Tales*, Michael Nawrocki.

Rights and Payment
First and electronic rights. Articles, $.10 per word. Provides 5 contributor's copies.

Editor's Comments
This year we are seeking articles, supported by the true stories of real people, about hard-hitting topics like substance abuse, underage drinking, and peer pressure. In contrast, lighter subject matters that incorporate pop culture, the latest trends, and entertainment into a Christian-based message are also welcome.

On the Line

Mennonite Publishing House
616 Walnut Avenue
Scottsdale, PA 15683-1999

Editor: Mary Clemens Meyers

Description and Readership
Articles, stories, verse, and activities that demonstrate Christian values can be found in this magazine for children of the Mennonite faith.
- **Audience:** 9–12 years
- **Frequency:** Monthly
- **Distribution:** 90% subscription; 10% other
- **Circulation:** 5,000
- **Website:** www.mph.org/otl

Freelance Potential
90% written by nonstaff writers. Publishes 85 freelance submissions yearly; 10% by unpublished writers, 30% by new authors. Receives 100 mss monthly.

Submissions
Send ms. Prefers email to otl@mph.org. Accepts photocopies, computer printouts, and simultaneous submissions if identified. SASE. Responds in 1 month.
Articles: 350-500 words. Informational, how-to, and self-help articles; profiles; bibliographies; and photo-essays. Topics include animals, history, sports, hobbies, crafts, and social and ethnic issues, environmental concerns, and peacemaking.
Fiction: 1,000–1,800 words. Genres include adventure; humor; mystery; and contemporary, ethnic, and multicultural fiction.
Artwork: Full color.
Other: Interesting facts, recipes, quizzes, puzzles, jokes, and cartoons. Poetry, 3–24 lines. Submit seasonal material 4–6 months in advance.

Sample Issue
24 pages (no advertising): 1 articles; 3 stories; 6 activities; 2 puzzles. Sample copy, $2 with 8x10 SASE (2 first-class stamps). Guidelines available.
- "Thinking Straight." Story tells how a city boy discovers the wonders of nature while attending sleep away camp at a lake.
- "Lies in Disguise." Story features a young boy who learns that practical jokes aren't funny.

Rights and Payment
One-time rights. Articles and fiction, $.04–$.05 per word. Puzzles and quizzes, $10–$15. Poetry, $10–$25. Cartoons, $10. Pays on acceptance. Provides 2 contributor's copies.

Editor's Comments
We look for material that encourages and empowers children to grow toward a commitment to God.

Organic Family Magazine

P.O. Box 1614
Wallingford, CT 06492-1214

Editor: Catherine Wong

Description and Readership
The purpose of this magazine is to encourage the adoption of a more natural lifestyle. Articles focus on the growing, buying, and consuming of organic foods and the resulting environmental benefits. Intelligent political commentary, media reviews, stories, essays, and poems with environmental themes are some of its other features.
- **Audience:** Families
- **Frequency:** Quarterly
- **Distribution:** Unavailable
- **Circulation:** Unavailable
- **Website:** www.organicfamilymagazine.com

Freelance Potential
90% written by nonstaff writers. Publishes 40 freelance submissions yearly.

Submissions
Query or send complete ms. Prefers email submissions to sciencelibrarian@hotmail.com. Accepts photocopies and computer printouts. SASE. Response time varies.
Articles: Word length varies. Informational articles; interviews; and personal experience pieces. Topics include nature, organic agriculture, conservation, parenting, natural pet care, herbs, gardening, nutrition, progressive politics, health, wellness, and environmental issues.
Fiction: Word length varies. Stories about nature and the environment.
Depts/columns: Word length varies. New product reviews; recipes; profiles of conservation organizations; and book, movie, and website reviews.
Other: Poetry.

Sample Issue
36 pages: 18 articles; 7 depts/columns; 1 poem; 1 contest.
- "Windowsill Gardening." Article explains how to cultivate vegetables and herbs indoors.
- "Herbal Approaches to Hay Fever." Article examines various herbs that help alleviate allergy symptoms.

Rights and Payment
One-time rights. No payment. Provides 1 author's copy.

Editor's Comments
We have a high acceptance rate and love to publish first-time writers. Are you involved in a community project? Tell us how you're making a difference.

Our Children

National PTA
Suite 1300
541 North Fairbanks Court
Chicago, IL 60611-3396

Editor: Marilyn Anderson

Description and Readership
Established a century ago, this magazine provides informational and practical articles on educational issues and improving the welfare of children. It is the official publication of the National PTA.
- **Audience:** Parents, educators, school administrators
- **Frequency:** 6 times each year
- **Distribution:** 90% membership; 10% subscription
- **Circulation:** 31,000
- **Website:** www.pta.org

Freelance Potential
50% written by nonstaff writers. Publishes 20–25 freelance submissions yearly; 75% by authors who are new to the magazine. Receives 15–20 queries and unsolicited mss monthly.

Submissions
Query or send complete ms. Accepts email submissions to m_anderson@pta.org. No simultaneous submissions. Final submissions must be sent on disk. SASE. Responds in 2 months.
Articles: 600–1,100 words. Informational and how-to articles. Topics include education, child welfare, and family life.
Depts/columns: Word length varies. Short updates on parenting and education issues.
Artwork: 3x5 or larger color prints and slides.
Other: Submit seasonal material 3 months in advance.

Sample Issue
22 pages (no advertising): 5 articles; 5 depts/columns. Sample copy, $2.50 with 9x12 SASE ($1 postage). Guidelines and theme list available.
- "Preventing Perfectionism in Children." Article explores the dangers of perfectionism in children.
- "Strengthening Father-Daughter Relationships." Article offers steps to help fathers and daughters create more meaningful, positive relationships.
- Sample dept/column: "Leading the Way" tells how PTA members are trained at a conference to step outside their comfort zone.

Rights and Payment
First rights. No payment. Provides 3 author's copies.

Editor's Comments
We are interested in articles on a parent's role in implementing the No Child Left Behind Act, as well as articles on working with principals and administrators.

Pack-O-Fun

Suite 375
2400 Devon
Des Plaines, IL 60018-4618

Managing Editor: Irene Mueller

Description and Readership
The pages of this fun magazine are filled with quick and simple craft projects and activities for elementary-age children. It is read by teachers and group leaders working with children.
- **Audience:** 6–12 years; teachers; parents
- **Frequency:** 6 times each year
- **Distribution:** 67% subscription; 33% newsstand
- **Circulation:** 130,000
- **Website:** www.craftideas.com

Freelance Potential
100% written by nonstaff writers. Publishes 8 free-lance submissions yearly; 20% by unpublished writers, 40% by authors who are new to the magazine. Receives 42 queries and unsolicited mss monthly.

Submissions
Query or send complete ms with instructions and sketches if appropriate. Accepts photocopies. SASE. Responds in 4–6 weeks.
Articles: To 200 words. How-to and craft projects and party ideas.
Depts/columns: Word length varies. Art ideas; projects for children and adults to do together; ideas for vacation Bible school programs; and pictures of projects from readers.
Artwork: B/W line art.
Other: Puzzles, activities, games, skits, and poetry.

Sample Issue
66 pages (10% advertising): 14 crafts and activities; 4 depts/columns. Sample copy, $4.99 with 9x12 SASE (2 first-class stamps). Guidelines available.
- "Pet Lovers Project." Article offers instructions for making a plastic canvas dog and cat note holder.
- "Garden Buddies." Article provides directions for making fun garden pet decorations for clay pots.
- Sample dept/column: "Art Attack" offers project for making an African Safari Sunset Silhouette.

Rights and Payment
All rights. Written material, $10–$15. Artwork, payment rate varies. Pays 30 days after signed contract. Provides 3 contributor's copies.

Editor's Comments
Parents love our inexpensive activities and projects that use common household items. We are looking for easy crafts that children will enjoy and feel good about, and that little hands can make.

Parent and Preschooler Newsletter

North Shore Child & Family Guidance Center
480 Old Westbury Road
Roslyn Heights, NY 11577-2215

Editor: Neala S. Schwartzberg, Ph.D.

Description and Readership
Parents and professionals who care for young children read this newsletter for trusted information on a range of early childhood topics. Everything it publishes is written by professionals who are considered experts in their particular fields.
- **Audience:** Parents, caregivers, and early childhood professionals
- **Frequency:** 10 times each year
- **Distribution:** 100% subscription
- **Circulation:** Unavailable
- **Website:** www.northshorechildguidance.org

Freelance Potential
90% written by nonstaff writers. Publishes 10 free-lance submissions yearly; 50% by authors who are new to the magazine. Receives 5–6 queries monthly.

Submissions
Query with outline. Accepts disk submissions and email queries to nealas@panix.com. SASE. Responds in 1 week.
Articles: 2,000 words. Practical information and how-to articles. Topics include education, self-esteem, discipline, children's health, parenting skills, fostering cooperation through play, and coping with death.
Depts/columns: Staff written.

Sample Issue
8 pages (no advertising): 3 articles; 3 depts/columns. Sample copy, $3 with #10 SASE (1 first-class stamp). Guidelines available.
- "The Power of Poetry." Article explains why poetry not only delights young children, but also nurtures literacy development.
- "Celebrating Children's Strengths Through Poetry." Article describes a Poetry Club that was introduced to teachers working with children with special needs.

Rights and Payment
First world rights. Articles, $200. Pays on publication. Provides 10 contributor's copies.

Editor's Comments
Our newsletter, distributed to an international audience, discusses universal child development themes and features a positive approach to parenting issues. In addition to indicating your subject matter in your query, tell us what qualifies you to write about your topic. Describe your background and enclose some of your published clips.

Parentguide News

13th Floor
419 Park Avenue South
New York, NY 10016

Editor: Anne Marie Evola

Description and Readership
Special directories, articles, and columns filled with information pertinent to the needs and interests of parents fill each issue of this tabloid, which is available free of charge in the New York metropolitan area.
- **Audience:** Parents
- **Frequency:** Monthly
- **Distribution:** Subscription; controlled
- **Circulation:** 210,000
- **Website:** www.parentguidenews.com

Freelance Potential
85% written by nonstaff writers. Publishes 45 freelance submissions yearly; 20% by unpublished writers, 80% by authors who are new to the magazine. Receives 8 queries and unsolicited mss monthly.

Submissions
Query or send complete ms with résumé. Accepts photocopies and computer printouts. SASE. Responds in 3–4 weeks.
Articles: 750–1,500 words. Informational and self-help articles; profiles; humor; and personal experience pieces. Topics include parenting, family issues, social issues, current events, regional issues, popular culture, health, careers, computers, and science.
Depts/columns: 500 words. News of local schools and businesses, travel, reviews, and women's health.

Sample Issue
76 pages (39% advertising): 13 articles; 8 depts/columns; 2 directories; 1 calendar of events. Sample copy, free with 10x13 SASE. Guidelines available.
- "Great Escapes." Article suggests ways to make road trips with children more enjoyable for all involved.
- "Academic Excellence." Article offers a list of practical things parents can do to promote their children's success in school.
- Sample dept/column: "Sun & Fun" includes guidelines for choosing a summer camp and explains how to prepare children for the separation from their parents.

Rights and Payment
Rights negotiable. No payment. Provides 1+ contributor's copies.

Editor's Comments
Although ours is a local publication, the articles we publish address national as well as local issues as they relate to parents of children under the age of 12.

Parenting for High Potential

4921 Ringwood Meadow
Sarasota, FL 34235

Editor

Description and Readership
Parenting for High Potential is published by the National Association for Gifted Children and targets parents who strive to help their children develop their gifts and talents. Each issue also features a special pull-out section for children. Its purpose is to develop a child's potential to the fullest.
- **Audience:** Parents
- **Frequency:** Quarterly
- **Distribution:** Subscription; newsstand
- **Circulation:** Unavailable
- **Website:** www.nagc.org/publications/parenting

Freelance Potential
100% written by nonstaff writers. Publishes 10 freelance submissions yearly.

Submissions
Query or send complete ms. Accepts photocopies, computer printouts, and email submissions to don@creativelearning.com. SASE. Responds in 6–8 weeks.
Articles: Word length varies. Informational articles; profiles; and personal experience pieces. Topics include education and parenting.
Depts/columns: Word length varies. Software and book reviews.

Sample Issue
30 pages: 3 articles; 5 depts/columns. Sample copy, free with 9x12 SASE ($.77 postage). Writers' guidelines available.
- "Natalie: A Story . . . And a Unique Opportunity." Article profiles the challenges in raising a gifted child.
- "Parents as Models: Respecting and Embracing Differences." Article warns parents and educators not to stereotype gifted learners.
- Sample dept/column: "Kids' Kaleidoscope" offers activities for the whole family.

Rights and Payment
First rights. No payment. Provides contributor's copies.

Editor's Comments
We are looking for innovative ideas from parents and advice from experts on topics relating to raising extraordinary children. We suggest writers review several past issues prior to submitting material.

Parenting New Hampshire

P.O. Box 1291
Nashua, NH 03061-1291

Editor: Beth Quarm Todgham

Description and Readership
Information, ideas, and resources that support New Hampshire families can be found in this tabloid. Its articles discuss both regional topics and general parenting issues and concerns.
- **Audience:** Parents
- **Frequency:** Monthly
- **Distribution:** 100% controlled
- **Circulation:** 27,500
- **Website:** www.parentingnh.com

Freelance Potential
70% written by nonstaff writers. Publishes 20–25 freelance submissions yearly; 20% by unpublished writers, 90% by authors who are new to the magazine. Receives 40 queries and unsolicited mss monthly.

Submissions
Query or send complete ms. Accepts photocopies, computer printouts, disk submissions, and email submissions to news@parentingnh.com. Availability of artwork improves chance of acceptance. SASE. Response time varies.
Articles: Word length varies. Informational and how-to articles; and profiles. Topics include parenting, education, maternity and childbirth, special needs, fathering, child development, and health.
Depts/columns: Word length varies. Child development, parenting issues, and medicine.
Other: Submit seasonal material 2 months in advance.

Sample Issue
48 pages (42% advertising): 3 articles; 1 summer camp directory; 14 depts/columns. Sample copy, free. Guidelines available.
- "How to Have a Happy Marriage." Article discusses how the pressures of parenting affect marriage.
- "Family Finances: How Much Should Your Kids Know?" Article looks at how much personal finance information should be shared with children.
- Sample dept/column: "Ten Tips" suggests ten things parents can do to prevent eating disorders.

Rights and Payment
All rights. Articles, $25; other material, payment rate varies. Pays on acceptance. Provides 3 copies.

Editor's Comments
Our editors would like to see personal essays on how families can have fun together, and factual articles on early childhood development and education.

ParentingUniverse.com

Best Parenting Resources, LLC
546 Charing Cross Drive
Marietta, GA 30066

Editor: Alicia Hagan

Description and Readership
Formerly listed as *America's Moms*, this online publication offers articles on topics such as parenting, pregnancy, child development, special needs children, and children's health.
- **Audience:** Women 23–56
- **Frequency:** Daily
- **Distribution:** 100% Internet
- **Hits Per Month:** 1 million+
- **Website:** www.parentinguniverse.com

Freelance Potential
90% written by nonstaff writers. Publishes 500+ freelance submissions yearly. Receives 417 queries, 12–13 unsolicited mss monthly.

Submissions
Query or send complete ms. Accepts photocopies, computer printouts, and email submissions to alicia@parentinguniverse.com. Prefers online submissions through website. SASE. Response time varies.
Articles: Word lengths vary. Informational and how-to articles; profiles; interviews; reviews; and personal experience pieces. Topics include gifted education, pregnancy, parenting, health, fitness, recreation, self-help, and special education.
Depts/columns: Word lengths vary. Parenting tips, guides.

Sample Issue
Sample issues and guidelines available at website.
- "The Truth Behind Having Children." Article lists 9 lessons you'll learn as your baby grows through each stage of childhood, and how hard it is to keep up with them.
- "Life After Television: Teaching Our Children to Play Again." Article discusses how to limit television time and do hands-on activities.

Rights and Payment
Electronic rights. Written material, payment rate varies. Pays on publication. Provides 2 author's copies.

Editor's Comments
We continue to look for articles on topics such as parenting and single parenting, ages and stages of child development, pregnancy, children's health and nutrition, family finances, education, and homeschooling. Also, practical parenting tips, fun activities for little ones, and easy crafts are of interest to us.

ParentLife

1 LifeWay Plaza
Nashville, TN 37234-0172

Editor-in-Chief: William Summey

Description and Readership

This magazine helps parents resolve family concerns by offering articles that present the latest medical and developmental information from a Christian perspective.
- **Audience:** Parents
- **Frequency:** Monthly
- **Distribution:** 90% churches; 10% subscription
- **Circulation:** 100,000
- **Website:** www.lifeway.com

Freelance Potential

90% written by nonstaff writers. Publishes 12 freelance submissions yearly; 5% by unpublished writers, 5% by authors who are new to the magazine. Receives 20 queries and unsolicited mss monthly.

Submissions

Query or send complete ms. Accepts computer printouts and email submissions to parentlife@lifeway.com. SASE. Response time varies.
Articles: 500–1,500 words. Informational and how-to articles; and personal experience pieces. Topics include family issues, religion, education, health, fitness, and hobbies.
Depts/columns: 500 words. Family stories, medical advice, and crafts.
Artwork: Color prints or transparencies.
Other: Accepts seasonal material for Christmas and Thanksgiving.

Sample Issue

50 pages (no advertising): 7 articles; 12 depts/columns. Sample copy, $2.95 with 10x13 SASE. Guidelines available.
- "Real Sex Talk." Informative article tells how to establish an ongoing conversation with your child.
- "Why Do We Have to Move?" Helpful article describes the transition steps involved in a successful family move.
- Sample dept/column: "ParentPower" offers a view on the loyalty issues involved in stepparenting.

Rights and Payment

Non-exclusive rights. Pays on publication. All material, payment rate varies. Provides 1 contributor's copy.

Editor's Comments

We want material that encourages and equips parents with biblical solutions for family issues. We are interested in finding Christian writers who are able to deliver professional-quality articles.

Parents and Children Together Online

Suite 140
2805 East 10th Street
Bloomington, IN 47403

Editor: Mei-Yu Lu

Description and Readership

Stories, poetry, and informational articles for children from preschool through eighth grade are found on this website. It also includes resources for parents and reviews of children's literature. The goal is to promote family literacy and bring parents and children together through reading.
- **Audience:** Parents and children
- **Frequency:** Irregular
- **Distribution:** Internet
- **Circulation:** 10,000
- **Website:** reading.indiana.edu/www/ indexfr.html

Freelance Potential

75% written by nonstaff writers. Publishes 50–80 freelance submissions yearly; 40% by unpublished writers, 60% by authors who are new to the magazine. Receives 12–13 unsolicited mss monthly.

Submissions

Send complete ms. Accepts email submissions to reading@indiana.edu. Availability of artwork improves chance of acceptance. Response time varies.
Articles: 500–1,800 words. Informational articles that expand children's understanding of different lifestyles, cultures, and places. Also publishes articles for parents and children's writers and illustrators.
Fiction: Word lengths vary. Features gender inclusive stories that may be enjoyed by parents and children.
Depts/columns: Word lengths vary. Book reviews.
Artwork: 8x10 B/W and color prints. Line art.
Other: Literary activities for families; poetry.

Sample Issue

Guidelines available at website.
- "Little Hippo." Rhyming story for young children depicts a hippo playing with animal friends.
- "The Flamenco Dancer." Story features a young girl who moves to Spain with her parents.

Rights and Payment

Electronic rights. No payment.

Editor's Comments

Stories should be enjoyable to both children and parents. Various genres are welcome, including retold folktales from different cultures and life stories from one's childhood experience. Practical tips and resources for parents are also always needed.

Parents & Kids

Suite 294
2727 Old Canton Road
Jackson, MS 39216

Editor: Gretchen Cook

Description and Readership
This publication for Mississippi parents appears in two editions—one for the Jackson area and one for the Gulf Coast region. Along with parenting articles, each issue features calendars of local events, directories of regional services, and lists of educational resources.
- **Audience:** Parents
- **Frequency:** 9 times each year
- **Distribution:** 66% schools; 34% controlled
- **Circulation:** 46,000
- **Website:** www.PandKmagazine.com

Freelance Potential
80% written by nonstaff writers. Publishes 80 freelance submissions yearly; 50% by unpublished writers. Receives 33 unsolicited mss monthly.

Submissions
Send complete ms. Accepts email submissions to pkmag@mindspring.com (in text of message and as Microsoft Word attachment). Responds in 6 weeks.
Articles: 700 words. Informational, self-help, and how-to articles. Topics include the arts, computers, crafts and hobbies, health, fitness, multicultural and ethnic issues, recreation, regional news, social issues, special education, sports, and travel.
Depts/columns: 500 words. Travel, cooking, and computers.
Artwork: B/W prints or transparencies. Line art. Prefers electronic files; contact publisher for specifics.
Other: Submit seasonal material 3–6 months in advance.

Sample Issue
32 pages (54% advertising): 4 articles; 1 events guide; 1 directory; 8 depts/columns. Sample copy, free with 9x12 SASE ($1.06 postage). Writers' guidelines available at website.
- "The Power of Loving Touch." Article explains the basics of baby massage.
- Sample dept/column: "Learning Together" relates a family's experience planting a butterfly garden.

Rights and Payment
One-time rights. Articles and depts/columns, $25. Pays on publication. Provides tearsheet.

Editor's Comments
Local writers who can provide articles with a regional angle are invited to submit their work to us.

Parents Express

Pennsylvania Edition

290 Commerce Drive
Fort Washington, PA 19034

Submissions Editor: Daniel Sean Kaye

Description and Readership
Parents Express serves families living in the Philadelphia and southern New Jersey area. Regional resources and events are covered, as well as parenting issues of interest to families with infants through teenagers.
- **Audience:** Parents
- **Frequency:** Monthly
- **Distribution:** 50% schools; 50% other
- **Circulation:** 80,000
- **Website:** www.parents-express.net

Freelance Potential
30% written by nonstaff writers. Publishes 25–35 freelance submissions yearly; 25% by unpublished writers, 75% by authors who are new to the magazine. Receives many queries monthly.

Submissions
Query with clips or writing samples. Accepts photocopies, computer printouts, and email queries to dkaye@montgomerynews.com. Availability of artwork improves chance of acceptance. SASE. Responds in 1 month.
Articles: 300–1,000 words. Informational articles; profiles; and personal experience pieces. Topics include parenting and family life, health, politics, business, entertainment, music, education, and computers.
Depts/columns: 600–800 words. Book and product reviews, local school news, and regional events.
Artwork: B/W or color prints or transparencies.
Other: Submit seasonal material 2 months in advance.

Sample Issue
56 pages (62% advertising): 17 depts/columns; 3 events calendars. Sample copy, free with 10x13 SASE ($2.14 postage). Theme list available.
- Sample dept/column: "Our World" explains how to keep lines of communication open with teens.
- Sample dept/column: "Home Sweet Home" features decorating ideas for kids' rooms.

Rights and Payment
One-time rights. Articles, $35–$200. Depts/columns, payment rate varies. Pays on publication. Provides contributor's copies upon request.

Editor's Comments
We like to see submissions from writers living in this area. We want less "fluff," more in-depth reporting.

Parents' Press

1454 Sixth Street
Berkeley, CA 94710

Editor: Dixie Jordon

Description and Readership
This newspaper for parents who live in the San Francisco Bay area covers the local family scene through events listings and features that spotlight family-centered attractions in the region. Its articles cover a variety of topics that pertain to parenting.
- **Audience:** Parents
- **Frequency:** Monthly
- **Distribution:** 100% controlled
- **Circulation:** 75,000
- **Website:** www.parentspress.com

Freelance Potential
60% written by nonstaff writers. Publishes 12 freelance submissions yearly; 25% by authors who are new to the magazine. Receives 60 unsolicited mss each month.

Submissions
Send complete ms. SASE. Responds in 2 months.
Articles: To 1,500 words. Informational and how-to articles. Topics include child development, education, health, safety, party planning, and regional family events and activities.
Depts/columns: Staff written.
Artwork: B/W prints and transparencies. Line art.
Other: Submit seasonal material 2 months in advance.

Sample Issue
36 pages (63% advertising): 9 articles; 5 depts/columns. Sample copy, $3 with 9x12 SASE ($1.93 postage). Writers' guidelines and theme list/editorial calendar available.
- "Moms in the Marketplace." Article offers advice for moms seeking to reenter the workforce.
- "Adventure Playground." Article reports on a park where kids and parents create things with hammers, nails, paint, and saws.

Rights and Payment
All or second rights. Articles, $50–$500. Pays 45 days after publication.

Editor's Comments
We will consider submissions only from writers who live in the Bay area. This is not a beginner's market, however. We don't publish personal essays, but look instead for articles based on solid research from writers who have professional or personal relationships with the local people, businesses, or institutions featured in their story.

Partners

Christian Light Publications
P.O. Box 1212
Harrisburg, VA 22803-1212

Editor: Etta Martin

Description and Readership
This publication, from Christian Light Publications, promotes the principles of the Mennonite faith to children. Its stories seek to motivate followers to adhere to Christian beliefs and lifestyles.
- **Audience:** 9–14 years
- **Frequency:** Monthly
- **Distribution:** Sunday schools; subscription
- **Circulation:** 6,674
- **Website:** www.clp.org

Freelance Potential
98% written by nonstaff writers. Publishes 200–500 freelance submissions yearly; 5% by unpublished writers, 5% by authors who are new to the magazine. Receives 60–80 unsolicited mss monthly.

Submissions
Send complete ms. Prefers email submissions to partners@clp.org. Accepts photocopies, computer printouts, disk submissions, and simultaneous submissions if identified. SASE. Responds in 6 weeks.
Articles: 200–800 words. Informational articles. Topics include nature, customs, and biblical history.
Fiction: 400–1,600 words. Stories that emphasize Mennonite beliefs and biblical interpretations.
Other: Puzzles and activities with Christian themes; poetry. Submit seasonal material 6 months in advance.

Sample Issue
20 pages (no advertising): 2 articles; 5 stories; 1 poem. Sample copy, free with 9x12 SASE ($.78 postage). Guidelines and theme list available.
- "Ten Ways to Be Great." Article offers ten ways to be a kinder person.
- "Jack and the Earthquake." Story features a young boy who temporarily loses his dog during an earthquake.
- Sample poem: "Let It Be" offers ideas on how to savor the moment.

Rights and Payment
First, reprint, or multiple use rights. Articles and stories, $.03–$.05 per word. Poetry, $.35–$.75 per line. Other material, payment rates vary. Pays on acceptance. Provides 1 contributor's copy.

Editor's Comments
We provide prospective writers with a theme list and ask that submitted material be interesting and inspirational to our young audience.

Pediatrics for Parents

P.O. Box 63716
Philadelphia, PA 19147

Editor: Richard J. Sagall, M.D.

Description and Readership
Self-described as "the newsletter for people who care for children," this publication emphasizes a common-sense approach to pediatric care.
- **Audience:** Parents
- **Frequency:** Monthly
- **Distribution:** 100% subscription
- **Circulation:** 2,000
- **Website:** www.pedsforparents.com

Freelance Potential
70% written by nonstaff writers. Publishes 30 freelance submissions yearly; 50% by unpublished writers, 50% by authors who are new to the magazine. Receives 3 unsolicited mss monthly.

Submissions
Query or send complete ms. Prefers email submissions to articles@pedsforparents.com. Accepts photocopies and computer printouts. SASE. Response time varies.
Articles: 250–1,500 words. Informational articles. Topics include pregnancy, medical advancements, new treatments, wellness, prevention, and fitness.
Depts/columns: Word length varies. New product information and article reprints.
Other: Filler, 150–200 words.

Sample Issue
12 pages (no advertising): 14 articles. Sample copy, $3. Guidelines available.
- "Sleep and Crying Infants." Article discusses the difference in sleep structure between fussy and non-fussy infants.
- "Fluid in Your Child's Ears: When Are Tubes Indicated?" Article examines the reasons a doctor may be concerned about noninfective ear fluid.

Rights and Payment
First rights. Pays on publication. Written material, to $25. Provides 3 contributor's copies and a 1-year subscription.

Editor's Comments
Our articles stress action and accident prevention, and suggest when to call the doctor and when to handle a situation at home. We are looking for material that describes general medical and pediatric problems. All material must be medically accurate and useful to parents with children of all ages. We are not interested in general parenting articles.

Piedmont Parent

P.O. Box 11740
Winston-Salem, NC 27116

Editor: Leigh Ann McDonald Woodruff

Description and Readership
Regional resources and event reports appear in this publication for parents living in North Carolina's Forsyth and Guilford counties. It covers topics relevant to parenting children from birth through the teen years.
- **Audience:** Parents
- **Frequency:** Monthly
- **Distribution:** 100% newsstand
- **Circulation:** 33,000
- **Website:** www.piedmontparent.com

Freelance Potential
50% written by nonstaff writers. Publishes 24–48 freelance submissions yearly; 25% by unpublished writers, 50% by authors who are new to the magazine. Receives 25 unsolicited mss monthly.

Submissions
Send complete ms. Accepts email submissions to editor@piedmontparent.com and simultaneous submissions if identified. SASE. Responds in 2 months.
Articles: 600–900 words. Informational and how-to articles; and interviews. Topics include child development, day care, summer camps, gifted and special education, local and regional news, science, social issues, sports, popular culture, health, and travel.
Depts/columns: 600–900 words. Parenting news and health updates.
Other: Family games and activities.

Sample Issue
36 pages (47% advertising): 6 articles; 4 depts/columns; 1 directory. Sample copy, free with 9x12 SASE ($1.50 postage). Guidelines and theme list available.
- "Help, My Son Doesn't Fit In!" Article offers advice for parents whose teens may be having trouble with peers or with schools.
- "Go, Team!" Article explains how to prepare your child, and yourself, for a successful team sport experience.
- "Island Hopping." Visits three family resorts in Georgia, South Carolina, and North Carolina.

Rights and Payment
One-time rights. Written material, $30. Pays on publication. Provides 1 tearsheet.

Editor's Comments
We want unique, fresh article ideas that are based on research and reliable sources.

Pikes Peak Parent

30 South Prospect Street
Colorado Springs, CO 80903

Editor: Lisa Carpenter

Description and Readership
Entertaining and informative articles that focus on raising children can be found in this tabloid that is distributed free to parents in the Colorado Springs area. It also includes profiles of local people, resources that are available in the region, as well as up-to-date information on local events.
- **Audience:** Parents
- **Frequency:** Monthly
- **Distribution:** Unavailable
- **Circulation:** 35,000
- **Website:** www.pikespeakparent.net

Freelance Potential
5% written by nonstaff writers. Publishes 4 freelance submissions yearly; 2% by authors who are new to the magazine. Receives 5 queries monthly.

Submissions
Query with writing samples. No unsolicited mss. Accepts photocopies, computer printouts, and email queries to parent@gazette.com. SASE. Response time varies.
Articles: 800–1,500 words. Informational and how-to articles. Topics include regional news, local resources, parenting, family life, travel, sports, social issues, and recreation.
Depts/columns: Word length varies. News, health, family issues, profiles, and calendar of events.

Sample Issue
62 pages (50% advertising): 6 articles; 12 depts/columns. Sample copy, free with 9x12 SASE.
- "Beyond Tuition." Article discusses the additional expenses of college life.
- "Hush Little Baby." Article offers strategies to teach children to sleep through the night.
- Sample dept/column: "Father Time" takes a humorous look at April Fools' jokes.

Rights and Payment
Buys all rights on original content, when assigned, and second rights. Written material, payment rates vary. Pays on publication. Provides 1 author's copy.

Editor's Comments
We are currently looking for more child-care stories. Please note that we do not need any more personal essays on parenting as we have enough of these. Keep in mind that we look for material that is well researched and well written.

Pittsburgh Parent

P.O. Box 374
Bakerstown, PA 15007

Editor: Pat Poshard

Description and Readership
General parenting advice and information can be found in this regional magazine. *Pittsburgh Parent* offers informative and upbeat articles on a variety of topics.
- **Audience:** Parents
- **Frequency:** Monthly
- **Distribution:** Subscription; newsstand; schools
- **Circulation:** 65,000
- **Website:** www.pittsburghparent.com

Freelance Potential
90% written by nonstaff writers. Publishes 50 freelance submissions yearly; 80% by unpublished writers, 20% by authors who are new to the magazine. Receives 125 queries and unsolicited mss monthly.

Submissions
Query or send complete ms. Accepts photocopies and simultaneous submissions. SASE. Response time varies.
Articles: Cover story, 2,500–2,750 words. Other material, 400–900 words. Informational articles; profiles; and interviews. Topics include family issues, parenting, education, science, fitness, health, nature, the environment, college, computers, and multicultural subjects.
Depts/columns: Word lengths vary. Book reviews, teen topics, and news for families.
Other: Submit seasonal material 3 months in advance.

Sample Issue
52 pages (65% advertising): 10 articles; 7 depts/columns; 1 special section. Sample copy, free. Guidelines and editorial calendar available.
- "Thinking of Selling Your House?" Article suggests how to spruce up your house before selling it.
- "Making Playtime Safe." Article reminds parents of important playtime safety measures.
- Sample dept/column: "Health" addresses common health concerns.

Rights and Payment
First rights. All material, payment rates vary. Pays 30 days after publication. Provides 1 contributor's copy.

Editor's Comments
This year we are seeking personal experience pieces dealing with parenting issues. All material should relate to the Pittsburgh area.

Plays

P.O. Box 600160
Newton, MA 02460

Editor: Elizabeth Preston

Description and Readership
This drama magazine for young people includes easy skits and plays for elementary thespians, as well as more challenging full-length dramas and monologues for high school theater groups.
- **Audience:** 6–17 years
- **Frequency:** 7 times each school year
- **Distribution:** 100% subscription
- **Circulation:** 5,300
- **Website:** www.playsmag.com

Freelance Potential
100% written by nonstaff writers. Publishes 40–45 freelance submissions yearly; 25% by unpublished writers, 50% by authors who are new to the magazine. Receives 20–22 queries and unsolicited mss each month.

Submissions
Query for adaptations of classics and folktales. Send complete ms for other material. Accepts photocopies and computer printouts, SASE. Responds to queries in 2 weeks, to mss in 4 weeks.
Fiction: One-act plays for high school, to 5,000 words; for middle school, to 3,750 words; for elementary school, to 2,500 words. Also publishes skits, monologues, and dramatized classics. Genres include patriotic, historical and biographical drama; mystery; melodrama; comedy; and farce.
Other: Submit material for seasonal school holidays 4 months in advance.

Sample Issue
64 pages (5% advertising): 8 plays; 1 skit; 1 dramatized classic. Sample copy, free. Guidelines available.
- "The Shop Girl's Revenge." A turn-of-the-century melodrama complete with a maiden in distress, a mustashioed villain, and a hero.
- "Thundermuffs." A humorous skit about a family who enjoys noisy thunderstorms.
- "Hansel and Gretel." Dramatization of a favorite childhood fairy tale.

Rights and Payment
All rights. Written material, payment rates vary. Pays on acceptance. Provides 1 contributor's copy.

Editor's Comments
We like material that can involve a variety of children, from shy performers who can help with props and costumes to the accomplished lead performer.

Pockets

The Upper Room
1908 Grand Avenue
P.O. Box 340004
Nashville, TN 37203-0004

Editor: Lynn W. Gilliam

Description and Readership
The underlying message of the stories, poems, prayers, and activities that appear in this Christian magazine is that God loves and cares for each one of us.
- **Audience:** 6–11 years
- **Frequency:** 11 times each year
- **Distribution:** 100% subscription
- **Circulation:** 98,000
- **Website:** www.pockets.org

Freelance Potential
98% written by nonstaff writers. Publishes 150 freelance submissions yearly; 40% by unpublished writers, 20% by authors who are new to the magazine. Receives 200 unsolicited mss monthly.

Submissions
Send complete ms. Accepts photocopies and computer printouts. Availability of artwork improves chance of acceptance. SASE. Responds in 6 weeks.
Articles: 400–1,000 words. Informational articles; profiles; and personal experience pieces related to the issue's theme. Topics include multicultural and social issues; children involved in environmental, community, and peacemaking issues; persons whose lives reflect their Christian commitment.
Fiction: 600–1,400 words. Stories that demonstrate Christian values.
Depts/columns: Word length varies. Recipes and scripture readings.
Artwork: Color prints; 2–4 photos per submission.
Other: Puzzles, activities, and games. Poetry.

Sample Issue
48 pages (no advertising): 2 articles; 6 stories; 6 depts/columns; 11 activities; 6 poems. Sample copy, free with 9x12 SASE (4 first-class stamps). Guidelines and theme list available at website.
- "Treasure Hunt." Article suggests a way for kids to take notice of the good works God does every day.
- "Always There." Story tells of a boy who is inspired by his little sister to rekindle his relationship with God.

Rights and Payment
First and second rights. Written material, $.14 per word. Poetry, $2 per line. Games, $25–$50. Pays on acceptance. Provides 3–5 contributor's copies.

Editor's Comments
We'd like to see interviews with well-known people about how their faith in God affects their daily lives.

Pointe

23rd Floor
110 William Street
New York, NY 10038

Managing Editor: Jocelyn Anderson

Description and Readership
Read primarily by students of ballet who desire to dance professionally, this magazine covers all aspects of the world of ballet and seeks to create an awareness of ballet.
- **Audience:** 10–18 years
- **Frequency:** 6 times each year
- **Distribution:** Unavailable
- **Circulation:** 40,000
- **Website:** www.pointemagazine.com

Freelance Potential
70% written by nonstaff writers. Publishes 2 freelance submissions yearly; 25% by authors who are new to the magazine. Receives 2 queries monthly.

Submissions
Query. Accepts computer printouts. Responds in 2 weeks.
Articles: 1,200 words. Informational articles; personal experience pieces; photo-essays; profiles; and interviews. Topics include ballet news, events, places, people, and trends.
Depts/columns: 800–1,000 words. Happenings, premieres, opinions, performance information, equipment, and costumes.
Artwork: B/W and color prints or transparencies. Line art.

Sample Issue
96 pages (50% advertising): 4 articles; 7 depts/columns. Sample copy available.
- "Rehearsing for Broadway." Informative article discusses the difference between performing in a professional ballet company versus dancing with a theater group.
- "A Day in the Life of Edward Villella." Article profiles the work Edward Villella, the artistic director for the Miami City Ballet.
- Sample dept/column: "Premiéres" takes a look at some of the new ballets currently in performance.

Rights and Payment
All rights. Written material, payment rates vary. Pays on acceptance. Provides 2 contributor's copies.

Editor's Comments
Easy-to-understand, journalistic articles that focus on ballet dancers, choreographers, companies, and programs are needed. We would like to see short profiles of ballet companies around the world.

Positive Teens

SATCH Publishing
P.O. Box 1136
Boston, MA 02130-0010

Publisher/Editor-in-Chief: Susan Manning

Description and Readership
Featuring articles that accentuate the positive in today's teens, this magazine publishes submissions by writers from twelve to twenty-one years of age.
- **Audience:** 12–21 years
- **Frequency:** 6 times each year
- **Distribution:** Subscription; newsstand; other
- **Circulation:** 30,000
- **Website:** www.positiveteensmag.com

Freelance Potential
85% written by nonstaff writers. Publishes 150–200 freelance submissions yearly; 70% by unpublished writers, 80% by authors who are new to the magazine. Receives 50–60 unsolicited mss monthly.

Submissions
Query or send complete ms. Submissions by teens under 18 must include letter of parental content. Accepts photocopies, computer printouts, disk submissions, fax submissions to 617-522-2961, and email submissions to info@positiveteensmag.com. SASE. Responds in 2–3 months.
Articles: To 1,000 words. Informational articles; personal experience pieces; and opinion pieces. Topics include education, friendship, social issues, youth activism, health, fitness, current events, relationships, and humor.
Fiction: 800–1,000 words.
Depts/columns: Word length varies. Sports, commentaries, arts and entertainment, and book reviews.
Artwork: 8 1/2x11 B/W or color prints. Line art.
Other: Poetry.

Sample Issue
28 pages (no advertising): 5 articles; 11 depts/columns. Sample copy, $3.95 with 9x12 SASE. Guidelines available.
- "Let's Talk About the F Word." Article discusses making decisions about the future.
- Sample dept/column: "Having Our Say" looks at commitment and personal achievement.

Rights and Payment
Permissions for exclusive use for 18 months only. Written material, $5–$30. Artwork, payment rate varies. Payment policy varies.

Editor's Comments
We look forward to submissions by writers from all ethnic, racial, and religious groups.

Potluck Children's Literary Magazine

P.O. Box 546
Deerfield, IL 60015-0546

Editor-in-Chief: Susan Napoli Picchietti

Description and Readership
Short stories, poetry, and book reviews from young serious writers appear in this magazine. It also includes information and tips on improving writing skills, and the business side of writing.
- **Audience:** 8–16 years
- **Frequency:** Quarterly
- **Distribution:** Unavailable
- **Circulation:** Unavailable
- **Website:** www.potluckmagazine.org

Freelance Potential
100% written by nonstaff writers. Publishes 150 free-lance submissions yearly; 95% by unpublished writers, 95% by authors who are new to the magazine. Receives 200 unsolicited mss monthly.

Submissions
Send complete ms. Accepts photocopies, computer printouts, and email submissions to submissions@potluckmagazine.org. No simultaneous submissions. SASE. Response time varies.
Articles: Word length varies. Topics include writing, grammar, and character and story development.
Fiction: To 1,500 words. Genres include contemporary fiction, mystery, folktales, fantasy, and science fiction.
Artwork: 8½x11 color photocopies.
Other: Book reviews, to 250 words. Poetry, to 30 lines.

Sample Issue
48 pages (no advertising): 10 stories; 16 poems; 2 book reviews. Sample copy, $5.80. Guidelines available with SASE, at website, and in each issue.
- "Speakeasy." Story tells of a teen girl's reluctance to welcome her father back in her life.
- "Just Like That." Story follows a young girl and her mother and their daily routine playing 500 Rummy.
- "I Can Do Anything." Story tells how a determined gymnast accomplished what she set out to do.

Rights and Payment
First rights. Provides 1 contributor's copy in lieu of payment.

Editor's Comments
We are preparing young writers for the adult markets of their future by providing them with a means to express themselves freely and creatively and by offering information on ways to expand their abilities.

Prehistoric Times

145 Bayline Circle
Folsom, CA 95630-8077

Editor: Mike Fredericks

Description and Readership
Each issue of this magazine includes a mix of articles, interviews, and reviews on topics related to dinosaurs and other prehistoric mammals. It also showcases artwork from paleoartists, and is read by both collectors and enthusiasts.
- **Audience:** YA–Adult
- **Frequency:** 6 times each year
- **Distribution:** Subscription; other
- **Circulation:** Unavailable
- **Website:** www.prehistorictimes.com

Freelance Potential
40% written by nonstaff writers. Publishes 25 free-lance submissions yearly; 60% by unpublished writers, 40% by authors who are new to the magazine. Receives 4 unsolicited mss monthly.

Submissions
Send complete ms. Accepts email submissions to pretimes@comcast.net (attach file). SASE. Response time varies.
Articles: 1,500–2,000 words. Informational articles. Topics include dinosaurs, paleontology, prehistoric life, drawing dinosaurs, and dinosaur-related collectibles.
Depts/columns: Word lengths vary. Interviews, field news, dinosaur models, media reviews, and in-depth descriptions of dinosaurs and other prehistoric species.

Sample Issue
58 pages (30% advertising): 9 articles; 4 depts/columns. Sample copy, $7. Guidelines available via email to pretimes@comcast.net.
- "Raul Martin." Article features an interview with an up and coming paleoartist of Spain.
- "Super Seventies Saturday-Saurs!" Article takes a look back at the television show *Land of the Lost.*
- Sample dept/column: "Collector's Corner" showcases rare Triceratops souvenirs, a bank, dinosaur set, and a projector.

Rights and Payment
All rights. Written material, payment rates vary. Payment policies vary. Provides contributor's copies.

Editor's Comments
This year we'd like to see more material covering the latest information on dinosaur-related collectibles. Also, we continue to seek interviews with scientists.

Preschool Playhouse

Urban Ministries
P.O. Box 436987
Chicago, IL 60409

Editor: Judith Hull

Description and Readership
Targeting young children living in urban areas, this Christian publication is designed to help present Bible stories and principles to preschoolers that will help them to love the Lord Jesus and follow him. Each issue includes a Bible story and a life-action story that link to a Bible lesson, as well as activities. The publisher also produces a guide for teachers.
• **Audience:** Preschool children
• **Frequency:** Quarterly
• **Distribution:** 100% religious instruction
• **Circulation:** 50,000
• **Website:** www.urbanministries.com

Freelance Potential
80% written by nonstaff writers. Publishes 48 freelance submissions yearly.

Submissions
Send résumé with clips or writing samples. All material written on assignment. SASE. Response time varies.
Articles: Word length varies. How-to articles; personal experience pieces; photo-essays; and Bible stories. Topics include animals, crafts, hobbies, African-American history, multicultural, nature, the environment, religion, and social issues.
Depts/columns: Word length varies. Games, puzzles, fillers.
Artwork: B/W and color prints or transparencies.

Sample Issue
4 pages: 1 Bible story; 1 contemporary story; 2 activities. Sample copy, $2.99. Guidelines available.
• "Jesus Is the Best!" Bible story focuses on teaching children that Jesus is superior to anything.
• "Rhonda." Story tells of how a girl and her family have a special breakfast on weekends, pray each day, and know that Jesus is the best.
• Sample dept/columns: "Knowing" offers an activity on finding the biggest and smallest animals.

Rights and Payment
All rights. Written material, payment rates vary. Pays on publication. Provides 1 contributor's copy.

Editor's Comments
We look for stories and lessons that will encourage students to focus on the reason to be faithful and help teachers be effective. We want preschoolers to come to know Jesus and to go to Him for help as they begin their faith journey.

Primary Street

Urban Ministries
1551 Regency Court
Calumet City, IL 60409

Senior Editor: Judith Hull

Description and Readership
This publication strives to introduce African American students in primary religious education classes to Jesus Christ and His Word. Each issue focuses on a Christian theme and includes a Bible story and activity designed to teach children to follow Jesus.
• **Audience:** 6–8 years
• **Frequency:** Quarterly
• **Distribution:** Subscription; other
• **Circulation:** 30,000
• **Website:** www.urbanministries.com

Freelance Potential
10% written by nonstaff writers. Publishes 48 freelance submissions yearly; 5% by unpublished writers, 4% by authors who are new to the magazine.

Submissions
All material is written by assignment. Query with résumé or writing samples. SASE. Response time varies.
Articles: Word lengths vary. How-to articles; photo-essays; personal experience pieces; Bible stories. Topics include nature, environment, animals, pets, crafts, hobbies, African history, multicultural, ethnic subjects, regional news, and social issues.
Depts/columns: Word lengths vary.
Artwork: B/W and color prints or transparencies.
Other: Puzzles, activities, fillers, games, and jokes.

Sample Issue
4 pages (no advertising): 1 story; 1 Bible story; 2 activities. Sample copy, $2.99 ordered from website. Guidelines available.
• "Isaiah." Story tells how a boy helped his teacher prepare for class after seeing her with a broken arm.
• "God's Fellow Workers." Bible story demonstrates how God wants our work in church to be excellent.
• Sample dept/column: "Craft Kingdom" offers directions for making a memory game that shows how we can serve the church.

Rights and Payment
All rights. Written material, payment rates vary. Pays on publication. Provides 1 contributor's copy.

Editor's Comments
We look for material that supports our mission to help children follow Jesus in their everyday life. Our audience includes both beginning and advanced readers.

Primary Treasure

Pacific Press Publishing
P.O. Box 5353
Nampa, ID 83653-5353

Editor: Aileen Andres Sox

Description and Readership
Stories for children that foster a relationship with God can be found in this publication. It appears as a take-home paper for students attending Sabbath School at Seventh-day Adventist Churches.
- **Audience:** 6–9 years
- **Frequency:** Weekly
- **Distribution:** 100% religious instruction
- **Circulation:** 30,000
- **Website:** www.primarytreasure.com

Freelance Potential
85% written by nonstaff writers. Publishes 40–50 freelance submissions yearly; 10% by unpublished writers, 30% by authors who are new to the magazine. Receives 60 unsolicited mss monthly.

Submissions
Query for serials. Send complete ms for other submissions. Accepts photocopies, computer printouts, email submissions to ailsox@pacificpress.com, and simultaneous submissions if identified. SASE. Responds in 4 months.
Articles: 600–1,000 words. Features true stories about children in Christian settings and true, problem-solving pieces that help children learn about themselves in relation to God and others. All material must be consistent with Seventh-day Adventist beliefs and practices.
Other: Must submit seasonal material 7 months in advance.

Sample Issue
16 pages (no advertising): 1 article; 4 stories; 1 rebus story; 1 Bible lesson; 1 page of daily prayers; 1 puzzle. Sample copy, free with 9x12 SASE (2 first-class stamps). Writers' guidelines available.
- "Monarchs on the Move." Article takes a look at what happens after a caterpillar becomes a butterfly.
- "Seth's Race." Story features a boy with a heart defect who participates in a race and helps a friend.
- "The Take-it-Back Prayer." Story tells of a boy who asks God to make his sister disappear.

Rights and Payment
One-time rights. Written material, $25–$50. Pays on acceptance. Provides 3 contributor's copies.

Editor's Comments
We look for material that is true and positive, has a Christian message, and is a fit for the age we target.

Principal

1615 Duke Street
Alexandria, VA 22314

Director of Publications: Lee Greene

Description and Readership
Elementary and middle school principals find ideas, discussions on current educational issues, and tips on effective administration policies in this publication.
- **Audience:** K–8 school administrators
- **Frequency:** 5 times each year
- **Distribution:** 100% controlled
- **Circulation:** 36,000
- **Website:** www.naesp.org

Freelance Potential
90% written by nonstaff writers. Publishes 20 freelance submissions yearly; 80% by authors who are new to the magazine. Receives 7 queries and unsolicited mss monthly.

Submissions
Query or send complete ms. Accepts computer printouts and email submissions to comdiv@naesp.org. SASE. Responds in 1 month.
Articles: 1,000–1,800 words. Informational and instructional articles; profiles; and opinion and personal experience pieces. Topics include elementary education, gifted and special education, parenting, mentoring, science, and computers.
Depts/columns: 750–1,500 words. Classroom management issues, legal issues, and technology.

Sample Issue
72 pages (30% advertising): 8 articles; 12 depts/columns. Sample copy, $8. Writers' guidelines and theme list available.
- "Leadership for School Improvement." Article describes the increasing pressures on principals to initiate rapid and significant change, and examines leadership skills.
- "Training Teachers to Succeed in a Multicultural Climate." Article looks at teacher factors that contribute to achievement gaps of minority students.
- Sample dept/column: "Tech Support" provides suggestions on how schools can find funding for much needed and required technology.

Rights and Payment
All North American serial rights. No payment. Provides 3 contributor's copies.

Editor's Comments
Remember that we are a magazine, not a scholarly journal, our articles are written in plain English. Each issue contains several pieces on a main theme.

Puget Sound Parent

Suite 215
123 NW 36th Street
Seattle, WA 98119

Editor: Wenda Reed

Description and Readership
This local source for parents offers the latest information on matters of concern to parents and the latest news in the Puget Sound area.
- **Audience:** Parents
- **Frequency:** Monthly
- **Distribution:** 100% newsstand
- **Circulation:** 20,000
- **Website:** www.pugetsoundparent.com

Freelance Potential
40% written by nonstaff writers. Publishes 18 freelance submissions yearly; 15% by unpublished writers, 25% by authors who are new to the magazine. Receives 20 queries monthly.

Submissions
Query with outline. Send queries for local stories to above address. Send queries on national stories to Editor, United Parenting Publications, 15400 Knoll Trail, Suite 400, Dallas, TX 75248. Accepts photcopies, computer printouts, and simultaneous submissions if identified. SASE. Responds in 2 weeks.
Articles: Word length varies. Informational and how-to articles; and personal experience pieces. Topics include family and parenting issues, health, fitness, gifted and special education, regional news, travel, and social issues.
Depts/columns: Word lengths vary. Profiles, essays, and media reviews.

Sample Issue
38 pages (30% advertising): 3 articles; 6 depts/columns. Sample copy, $3. Guidelines and theme list available.
- "Universal Preschool." Article examines the debate around whether to make preschool the official starting point of formal education.
- Sample dept/column: "Family F.Y.I." reviews new products that help teach children about money.

Rights and Payment
Rights vary. Written material, $100–$450. Pays on acceptance. Provides 2 contributor's copies.

Editor's Comments
We're looking for informative articles on parenting issues, and up-to-date information on the area. Articles about interesting people who impact children's lives are on our wish list.

Queens Parent

4th Floor
9 East 38th Street
New York, NY 10016

Executive Editor: Helen Freedman

Description and Readership
This publication contains information about issues, events, and resources relating to New York City. Readers also find useful articles on general parenting.
- **Audience:** Parents
- **Frequency:** Monthly
- **Distribution:** 100% controlled
- **Circulation:** 68,000
- **Website:** www.parentsknow.com

Freelance Potential
95% written by nonstaff writers. Publishes 450 freelance submissions yearly; 25% by authors who are new to the magazine. Receives 75 queries, 75 unsolicited mss monthly.

Submissions
Query or send complete ms. Accepts photocopies, computer printouts, and email submissions to hellonwheels@parentsknow.com is preferred. SASE. Responds to queries in 1 week.
Articles: 800–1,000 words. Informational and how-to articles; profiles; interviews; humor; and personal experience pieces. Topics include family issues, health, fitness, humor, nature, current events, gifted and special education, nutrition, crafts, and regional news.
Depts/columns: 750 words. News and reviews.
Other: Submit all seasonal material 4 months in advance.

Sample Issue
70 pages (60% advertising): 5 articles; 1 activity page; 4 depts/columns; 1 calendar of events. Sample copy, free. Guidelines available.
- "Can Your Child Say 'I'm Sorry'?" Article examines the current world of non-apologies and fear of consequences that provides bad examples to children.
- Sample dept/column: "Reflections" gives an account of one woman's third pregnancy and her experiences during the birth of her son.

Rights and Payment
First New York Area rights. Articles, $50. Pays 2 months after publication. Provides 1 contributor's copy.

Editor's Comments
We are looking for material related to raising children in New York City. Currently we are not accepting parenting humor, travel, or general parenting articles.

Read

Weekly Reader
200 First Stamford Place
Stamford, CT 06912

Managing Editor: Debra Dolan Nevins

Description and Readership
This Weekly Reader publication provides a variety of reading material—including narratives, plays, short stories, and nonfiction—designed to promote classroom discussion. Targeting middle school and high school students, it is distributed in classrooms throughout the country.
- **Audience:** 11–15 years
- **Frequency:** 18 times each year
- **Distribution:** 100% schools
- **Circulation:** 180,000
- **Website:** www.weeklyreader.com

Freelance Potential
60% written by nonstaff writers. Publishes 8–10 freelance submissions yearly; 10% by authors who are new to the magazine. Receives 75 unsolicited mss monthly.

Submissions
Send complete ms with résumé. Accepts photocopies, email submissions to read@weeklyreader.com, and simultaneous submissions if identified. SASE. Responds in 1–2 months.
Articles: 1,000–2,000 words. Informational and factual articles. Topics include popular culture, history, nature, the environment, science, technology, and social issues. Also publishes humor and biographies.
Fiction: Word length varies. Genres include science fiction, historical and contemporary fiction, adventure, fantasy, folklore, mystery, romance, and animal stories.
Other: Language games. Submit seasonal material 9 months in advance.

Sample Issue
32 pages (no advertising): 1 article; 2 stories; 1 puzzle; 1 play. Sample copy, free with 5x7 SASE (3 first-class stamps). Guidelines available.
- "Celebrating the Red, White, and Blue." Article discusses the historical basis of the Fourth of July.
- "'Dino'-Mite Discoveries!" Features facts about a newly discovered dinosaur.

Rights and Payment
First North American and electronic one-time user rights. Written material, payment rate varies. Pays on acceptance. Provides 5 contributor's copies.

Editor's Comments
Material you submit should provide the basis for good teaching possibilities and enjoyable reading.

The Reading Teacher

International Reading Association
800 Barksdale Road
P.O. Box 8139
Newark, DE 19714-8139

Senior Editorial Assistant: Christina Lambert

Description and Readership
Articles, essays, and reports on reading and children's literacy learning make up the contents of this magazine. It is the publication of the International Reading Association, a nonprofit organization dedicated to improving reading instruction and promoting a life-long habit of reading.
- **Audience:** Educators
- **Frequency:** 8 times each year
- **Distribution:** 100% subscription
- **Circulation:** 61,000
- **Website:** www.reading.org

Freelance Potential
99% written by nonstaff writers. Publishes 50 freelance submissions yearly; 20% by unpublished writers, 30% by authors who are new to the magazine. Receives 29 unsolicited mss monthly.

Submissions
Send 2 copies of complete ms in email attachment to rt@reading.org, or submit on disk with 2 hard copies; 1 copy of each must have author information removed. SASE. Responds in 2–3 months.
Articles: 1,000–1,500 words. Informational and how-to articles and personal experience pieces. Topics include literacy, reading education, instruction techniques, classroom strategies, and educational technology.
Depts/columns: Word lengths vary. Teaching tips, book reviews, and short pieces on cultural diversity.

Sample Issue
104 pages (17% advertising): 5 articles; 5 depts/columns. Sample copy, $10. Guidelines available.
- "Storybook Reading." Article describes how teachers can use daily read-alouds to build the vocabulary and comprehension skills of primary-grade students who are learning to speak English.
- Sample dept/column: "Teaching Tips" discusses using a mystery box filled with literary clues about a story to be read; this piques a child's interest, which in turn increases comprehension.

Rights and Payment
All rights. No payment. Provides 5 contributor's copies for articles, 2 copies for depts/columns.

Editor's Comments
We seek submissions of articles, teaching tips, and filler. Please follow our specific guidelines for each.

Reading Today

International Reading Association
800 Barksdale Road
P.O. Box 8139
Newark, DE 19714-8139

Editor-in-Chief: John Micklos, Jr.

Description and Readership
Educators around the world who are members of the International Reading Association turn to this magazine to help their students improve reading skills. It publishes articles pertinent to preschool through adult reading education.
- **Audience:** IRA members
- **Frequency:** 6 times each year
- **Distribution:** 100% subscription
- **Circulation:** 80,000
- **Website:** www.reading.org

Freelance Potential
30% written by nonstaff writers. Publishes 25 freelance submissions yearly; 10% by unpublished writers, 25% by authors who are new to the magazine. Receives 15 unsolicited mss monthly.

Submissions
Prefers query. Accepts complete ms. Accepts photocopies, computer printouts, and simultaneous submissions if identified. SASE. Responds in 1 month.
Articles: 500–1,000 words. Informational and factual articles and interviews. Topics include reading and education, grades K–12 and up.
Depts/columns: To 750 words. Classroom ideas and anecdotes, ideas for administrators, and tips for parents and children reading together.
Artwork: B/W and color prints. Line art and cartoons.
Other: Puzzles, activities, and poetry.

Sample Issue
40 pages (30% advertising): 4 articles; 9 depts/columns. Sample copy, $6. Guidelines available.
- "The Other Five Pillars of 'Effective' Reading Instruction." Article stresses the importance of classroom organization, matching pupils and text, and expert tutoring.
- Sample dept/column: "Looking Back, Moving Forward" reflects on the 50th anniversary of the International Reading Association.

Rights and Payment
One-time rights. Written material, $.20–$.30 per word. Pays on publication. Provides 3 contributor's copies.

Editor's Comments
Articles about successful programs, including community outreach programs, membership recruitment, or partnership efforts, are welcome. We also need practical ideas for principals and reading supervisors.

Real Sports

P.O. Box 8203
San Jose, CA 95155

Submissions Editor: Brian Styers

Description and Readership
Entertaining and informative articles covering female sports are featured in this online publication. It strives to challenge conventional thinking in order to bring coverage of girls' and women's sports to an unprecedented level.
- **Audience:** 9–18 years
- **Frequency:** 6 times each year
- **Distribution:** 100% Internet
- **Circulation:** Unavailable
- **Website:** www.real-sports.com

Freelance Potential
75% written by nonstaff writers. Publishes 40 freelance submissions yearly; 5% by unpublished writers, 50% by authors who are new to the magazine. Receives 2 queries monthly.

Submissions
Query with brief summary. No unsolicited mss. Accepts email queries to content@real-sports.com. SASE. Responds in 2–3 weeks.
Articles: 1,500–2,000 words. Informational and how-to articles; profiles; and interviews. Topics include training, tennis, track and field, basketball, baseball, skating, golf, skiing, soccer, and sports personalities.
Depts/columns: 750–1,000 words. Opinion pieces, book reviews, news, and profiles.

Sample Issue
Guidelines and theme list available.
- "Future for the Fab Three." Article takes a look at what the terrific three of the fab five soccer players are doing now that they retired from the game.
- "Creating a Revival." Article takes a look at how some players are pushing for the return of women's pro soccer.
- "Eight is Enough." Article reports on the decision of the WNBA president Val Ackerman to leave her post at the helm of the women's pro basketball league.

Rights and Payment
First rights. Written material, payment rate varies. Pays on publication. Provides 2–5 contributor's copies.

Editor's Comments
We look for the finest editorial and action-based photojournalism possible to meet the needs of our readers. If you have an idea for a great story that will excite readers, and make them feel like they are a part of the game, send us a query.

Resource

6401 The Paseo
Kansas City, MO 64131

Managing Editor: Shirley Smith

Description and Readership
This quarterly magazine is geared toward the interests of Sunday school teachers who follow the WordAction curriculum. Its articles, stories, and tips help educators extend their knowledge and skills in children's and youth ministries.
- **Audience:** Sunday school teachers
- **Frequency:** Quarterly
- **Distribution:** 100% subscription
- **Circulation:** 30,000
- **Website:** www.nazarene.org

Freelance Potential
85% written by nonstaff writers. Publishes 100 freelance submissions yearly; 5–10% by unpublished writers, 5–10% by authors who are new to the magazine. Receives 12+ unsolicited mss monthly.

Submissions
Send complete ms. Accepts computer printouts and email submissions to ssmith@nazarene.org. SASE. Responds in 5 days.
Articles: 800 words. Informational, how-to, and self-help articles; and personal experience pieces. Topics include religion, education, and Sunday school programs and curriculum.

Sample Issue
24 pages (no advertising): 20 articles. Sample copy, free with 9x12 SASE. Guidelines available.
- "Leading Children to Christ." Article discusses how to introduce Christ when children are ready to accept salvation.
- "You Can Make a Difference." Article suggests that you don't have to be an evangelist to influence the lives of others.
- "VBS and Unchurched Children." Article tells how to use Vacation Bible School as an outreach tool for children in the community.

Rights and Payment
All and reprint rights. Written material, $.05 per word. Pays on publication. Provides 1 contributor's copy.

Editor's Comments
Our publication is a vital source of information that enriches and strengthens teacher's skills. We are looking for fresh material on skill development, inspiration and motivation, spiritual formation, the role of a teacher, building community fellowship, evangelism, outreach, and program development.

Reunions Magazine

P.O. Box 11727
Milwaukee, WI 53211-0727

Editor: Edith Wagner

Description and Readership
This magazine serves as a guide for searching, researching, planning, organizing, and attending family and school reunions.
- **Audience:** Adults
- **Frequency:** 6 times each year
- **Distribution:** Subscription
- **Circulation:** 20,000
- **Website:** www.reunionsmag.com

Freelance Potential
75% written by nonstaff writers. Publishes 100 freelance submissions yearly; 60% by unpublished writers, 80% by authors who are new to the magazine. Receives 20–30 queries and unsolicited mss monthly.

Submissions
Query with outline; or send complete ms. Accepts photocopies, computer printouts, and email submissions to reunions@execpc.com. SASE. Responds in 12–18 months.
Articles: Word length varies. Informational, how-to, and factual articles; personal experience pieces; and profiles. Topics include organizing reunions, choosing locations, entertainment, activities, and genealogy.
Depts/columns: 250–100 words. Resources, opinions, and book reviews.
Artwork: Color prints. JPEG, TIF, or PDF files.
Other: Recipes, cartoons, and filler.

Sample Issue
68 pages (45% advertising): 5 articles; 4 depts/columns; 1 resource directory. Sample copy, $3 with 9x12 SASE. Guidelines and editorial calendar available.
- "Create a Family Folklorama." Article tells how to incorporate family origins and traditions to create a colorful and unforgettable event.
- "VarnHargen Family Goes Where It Started." Article follows a family reunion to Brilon, Germany.
- Sample dept/column: "Alum & I" highlights aspects of the reunion experience.

Rights and Payment
One-time rights. Payment rate and policy vary. Provides contributor's copies.

Editor's Comments
We want to teach readers the nitty gritty about organizing successful reunions. Our audience needs new activities, games, and entertainment ideas, as well as information on interesting locales.

Richmond Parents Monthly

Suite 103
5511 Staples Mill Road
Richmond, VA 23228

Editor: Angela Lehman-Rios

Description and Readership
This regional tabloid is distributed free of charge throughout the Richmond/Tri-Cities area. It includes information on local recreation and entertainment events, as well as parenting and family issues.
- **Audience:** Parents
- **Frequency:** Monthly
- **Distribution:** 100% controlled
- **Circulation:** 30,000
- **Website:** www.richmondparents.com

Freelance Potential
80% written by nonstaff writers. Publishes 70–90 freelance submissions yearly; 5% by authors who are new to the magazine. Receives 50 queries monthly.

Submissions
Query. Accepts email queries to mail@richmond publishing.com. Availability of artwork improves chance of acceptance. Responds in 1–3 weeks.
Articles: 600–1,000 words. Informational and self-help articles. Topics include the arts, camps for children, pets, home and garden, birthday parties, school, education, women's health, and holidays.
Depts/columns: Word length varies. Restaurant reviews, family-related news, and media reviews.
Artwork: Color prints and transparencies.

Sample Issue
30 pages (15% advertising): 5 articles; 9 depts/columns; 1 calendar of events. Sample copy, free. Editorial calendar available.
- "Drama Mama." Interview with a local minister who is also an accomplished actress.
- "Raising a Confident Decision Maker." Article examines how to help children make sound decisions.
- Sample dept/column: "Family Connection" profiles a young boy who is waiting for an adoptive family.

Rights and Payment
One-time rights. Written material, $.12 per word. Pays on publication.

Editor's Comments
We want our newspaper to foster a sense of community among our readers. We look for freelance writers who live in Virginia and know about the resources available to families here. If you fit the bill, send us your ideas for an article about unusual happenings, fun family activities, or a national news event that can be tied to something local.

The Rock

Cook Communications
4050 Lee Vance View
Colorado Springs, CO 80918

Editor: Gail Rohlfing

Description and Readership
This Christian publication is used as a tool in Sunday school classes for middle grade students. It includes a mix of Bible-based fiction, personal experience pieces, and activities that teach the glory of God.
- **Audience:** 10–14 years
- **Frequency:** Weekly during the school year
- **Distribution:** 100% religious instruction
- **Circulation:** 65,000
- **Website:** www.cookministries.com

Freelance Potential
10% written by nonstaff writers. Publishes 2–3 freelance submissions yearly; 20% by unpublished writers, 100% by authors who are new to the magazine.

Submissions
Query with résumé and writing samples. SASE. Response time varies.
Articles: Word lengths vary. Informational articles; personal experience pieces; profiles; and interviews. Also publishes Bible lessons, allegories, and meditations.
Fiction: Word lengths vary. Genres include inspirational, contemporary, and historical fiction; adventure; real-life; and problem-solving stories.
Other: Puzzles, quizzes, activities, and poetry.

Sample Issue
8 pages (no advertising): 2 articles; 1 Bible study; 2 depts/columns. Guidelines available at website.
- "Prayer 911." Article discusses the importance of daily prayer and explores what the Bible tells Christians about praying continually.
- "The Upstairs Prayer." Bible study focuses on how Jesus prayed for the disciples and how to express your concerns and feelings to God.
- Sample dept/column: "Play it Safe" offers summer safety tips on ticks, poison plants, and insect and snake bites.

Rights and Payment
Rights negotiable. All material, payment rates vary. Pays on acceptance. Provides 1 contributor's copy.

Editor's Comments
If you have an idea for something that teaches and reinforces the truth of the Bible, send us a query only as we are currently not accepting any unsolicited manuscripts. Also, check our website periodically for information on any upcoming freelance projects.

RTJ: The Magazine for Catechist Formation

P.O. Box 180
185 Willow Street
Mystic, CT 06355

Editor: Alison Berger

Description and Readership
The goal of this magazine is to encourage and aid catechists to engage all age groups in lifelong catechesis, within and supported by the whole faith community.
• **Audience:** Religion teachers
• **Frequency:** Monthly
• **Distribution:** 100% subscription
• **Circulation:** 32,000
• **Website:** www.religionteachersjournal.com

Freelance Potential
90% written by nonstaff writers. Publishes 35–40 freelance submissions yearly; 10% by unpublished writers, 20% by authors who are new to the magazine. Receives 6–10 unsolicited mss monthly.

Submissions
Query or send complete ms. Accepts disk submissions with hard copy, and email submissions (Microsoft Word for Mac attachments) to aberger@ twentythirdpublications.com. SASE. Responds to queries in 2–3 weeks, to mss in 3–4 weeks.
Articles: 1,300 words. Informational and how-to articles; and personal experience. Topics include theology, the sacraments, liturgical seasons, prayer, scripture, and faith.
Depts/columns: 600 words. Prayers, youth ministry, and Catholic rites and rituals.
Other: 200–300 words. Activities, fillers, and games.

Sample Issue
38 pages (12% advertising): 6 articles; 16 depts/ columns. Sample copy, $3.50 with 9x12 SASE (3 first-class stamps). Guidelines and theme list available.
• "Plan a Lenten Mini-Retreat." Article tells how to organize a family retreat centering on the Triduum.
• "Exploring the Gospels." Informative article suggests ways to encourage children to explore Scripture.
• Sample dept/column: "Survival Guide for New Catechists" offers a humorous, insightful story about a substitute catechist.

Rights and Payment
First North American one-time rights. Articles, $50–$125. Depts/columns, $125. Filler, $20. Pays on acceptance. Provides 3 contributor's copies.

Editor's Comments
Draw from your own experience in teaching or directing a religious education class or program. Be specific in your explanation so others can use your ideas.

Sacramento/Sierra Parent

Suite 5
457 Grass Valley Highway
Auburn, CA 95603

Editor-in-Chief: Shelly Bokman

Description and Readership
The goal of this regional magazine is to share information among families with differing lifestyles and personal beliefs.
• **Audience:** Parents and grandparents
• **Frequency:** Monthly
• **Distribution:** 70% newsstand; 27% schools; 3% subscription
• **Circulation:** 50,000
• **Website:** www.ssparent.com

Freelance Potential
75% written by nonstaff writers. Publishes 75 freelance submissions yearly; 5–10% by unpublished writers, 70% by authors who are new to the magazine. Receives 65 queries monthly.

Submissions
Query with list of topics and writing samples. Accepts email queries to ssparent@pacbell.net. Response time varies.
Articles: 700–1,000 words. Informational and how-to articles; personal experience pieces; and humor. Topics include fitness, family finance, alternative education, family travel, learning disabilities, grandparenting, sports, adoption, and regional news.
Depts/columns: 400–500 words. Child development, opinions, and hometown highlights.
Other: Activities and filler. Submit seasonal material 2–3 months in advance.

Sample Issue
48 pages (50% advertising): 5 articles; 12 depts/ columns. Sample copy, free with 9x12 SASE ($1.29 postage). Guidelines and editorial calendar/theme list available.
• "Strangers in Our Homes." Article discusses the effect of television and other media on children's growth and learning potential.
• Sample dept/column: "Creating Families" examines the issues involved when a stepparent wants to adopt his or her stepchildren.

Rights and Payment
Reprint rights. Articles, $50+. Depts/columns, $25–$40. Pays on publication. Provides copies.

Editor's Comments
We are especially interested in articles that promote a developmentally appropriate, healthy, and peaceful environment for children.

St. Louis Parent

P.O. Box 190287
St. Louis, MO 63119

Editor: Barb MacRobie

Description and Readership
This resource for parents in the St. Louis area offers articles on education, technology, family health, finances, and other parenting issues. It also provides information on regional events and resources.
- **Audience:** Parents
- **Frequency:** 10 times each year
- **Distribution:** Newsstands; hospitals; schools
- **Circulation:** 45,000

Freelance Potential
90% written by nonstaff writers. Publishes 30–50 freelance submissions yearly; 5% by unpublished writers. Receives 5 queries monthly.

Submissions
Query with résumé, outline synopsis, and clips or writing samples. Accepts photocopies, computer printouts, and simultaneous submissions if identified. SASE. Response time varies.
Articles: 700 words. Informational and how-to articles. Topics include education; family health; safety; nutrition; child care; personal finances; and regional resources, services, and events.
Other: Submit seasonal material 6 months in advance.

Sample Issue
18 pages (40% advertising): 6 articles; 1 summer camp directory. Sample copy, free with 9x12 SASE ($1 postage). Writers' guidelines and editorial calendar available.
- "Summer Enrichment Programs Gain Popularity." Article discusses the importance of high school summer programs.
- "Sharing the Gross Fun of Science and Mucus with Your Kids." Article offers a fun interactive science experiment to help kids learn about mucus and the important role it plays in the body.
- "Parents as Teachers (PAT) Benefits Everyone." Article explores the overall benefits of a PAT program for a child's pre-school development.

Rights and Payment
All rights. Articles, $50. Other material, payment rate varies. Pays on acceptance. Provides 2 author's copies.

Editor's Comments
We look for writers who can provide in-depth coverage of hot topics, such as education and technology. All material must have a local slant.

San Diego Family Magazine

P.O. Box 23960
San Diego, CA 92193

Publisher & Editor: Sharon Bay

Description and Readership
Parents and families of the San Diego community find up-to-date information on general parenting issues, as well as topics specific to the region.
- **Audience:** Parents
- **Frequency:** Monthly
- **Distribution:** 99% controlled; 1% other
- **Circulation:** 120,000
- **Website:** www.sandiegofamily.com

Freelance Potential
90% written by nonstaff writers. Publishes 50 freelance submissions yearly; 50% by unpublished writers. Receives 30–50 queries and unsolicited mss monthly.

Submissions
Query or send complete ms with sample clip. Accepts photocopies, computer printouts, Macintosh disk submissions (Microsoft Word), and email submissions to family@sandiegofamily.com. SASE. Responds to queries in 6–8 weeks, to mss in 2–3 months.
Articles: 750–1,000 words. Informational, how-to, and self-help articles. Topics include parenting, gifted and special education, family issues, travel, health, fitness, sports, and multicultural issues. Also publishes humorous articles.
Depts/columns: Word length varies. Book reviews, restaurant reviews, advice, health, and the home.
Artwork: 3x5 or 5x7 B/W glossy prints.

Sample Issue
170 pages (60% advertising): 12 articles; 14 depts/columns; 2 special sections. Sample copy, $4 with 9x12 SASE ($1 postage). Guidelines available.
- "Kids Making a Difference." Article offers ways to promote community service in youngsters.
- "The Mad Scramble." Article suggests how to make an Easter egg hunt unforgettable.
- Sample dept/column: "Gardening Tips" offers ways to enrich your soil for a healthy summer garden.

Rights and Payment
First or second rights and all regional rights. Written material, $1.25 per published column inch. Pays on publication. Provides 1 contributor's copy.

Editor's Comments
While our editorial goal has a distinct regional focus, we also include material on parenting, education, and holidays that will appeal to a wider audience. Please note: we do not accept email or fax queries.

Scholastic Parent & Child

Scholastic Inc.
557 Broadway
New York, NY 10012-3999

Editor-in-Chief: Pam Abrams

Description and Readership
Published by the well-known Scholastic company, this magazine provides a link between school and home learning, with informative articles and activities to develop a love of learning in young children.
• **Audience:** Parents
• **Frequency:** 7 times each year
• **Distribution:** Subscription
• **Circulation:** 1.2 million
• **Website:** www.parentandchildonline.com

Freelance Potential
25% written by nonstaff writers. Publishes 10–15 freelance submissions yearly; 10% by unpublished writers. Receives 5 queries, 5 unsolicited mss monthly.

Submissions
Query or send complete ms. Accepts photocopies and computer printouts. SASE. Responds to queries in 3 months, to mss in 2 months.
Articles: 500–1,000 words. Informational articles. Topics include child development and education.
Fiction: 500–1,000 words. Genres include contemporary, mainstream, and literary fiction.
Depts/columns: Word length varies. Literacy, health, parent/teacher relationships, arts and crafts, child development, and family issues.

Sample Issue
100 pages: 7 articles; 13 depts/columns. Sample copy, $2.95. Guidelines available.
• "Great Investigations." Article provides easy ways to encourage science learning at home and suggests how to promote teachable-moment investigations while away from home.
• "It's a Block Party." Informative article highlights some constructive ideas to enrich childrens' block and building playtime.
• Sample dept/column: "Learning Together" gives instructions for making animal-like foot puppets from socks.

Rights and Payment
All rights. Written material, payment rates vary. Pays on publication. Provides contributor's copies.

Editor's Comments
We continue to need material that can be used by parents and care providers of pre-school programs. Articles on child development and education, as well as ideas for activities, are welcome.

Scholastic Scope

Scholastic Inc.
557 Broadway
New York, NY 10012-3999

Associate Editor: Lisa Feder-Fertel

Description and Readership
Striving to foster an appreciation of literature and improve language arts skills in young adult readers, each issue of this magazine offers a mix of articles, stories, plays, and activities.
• **Audience:** 12–18 years
• **Frequency:** 17 times each year
• **Distribution:** 99% schools; 1% other
• **Circulation:** 550,000
• **Website:** www.scholastic.com/scope

Freelance Potential
45% written by nonstaff writers. Publishes few freelance submissions yearly; 2% by unpublished writers, 10% by authors who are new to the magazine. Receives 17–25 unsolicited mss monthly.

Submissions
Query with clips, outline/synopsis, and résumé for nonfiction. Accepts photocopies and computer printouts. SASE. Response time varies.
Articles: 1,000 words. News and features that appeal to teens. Profiles of young adults who have overcome obstacles, performed heroic acts, or had interesting experiences.
Fiction: 1,500 words. Realistic stories about relationships and family problems, school issues, and other teen concerns. Also accepts science fiction.
Depts/columns: Staff written.
Other: Crossword puzzles and word activities. Submit seasonal material 4 months in advance.

Sample Issue
26 pages (8% advertising): 5 articles; 3 depts/columns; 2 activities; 1 play. Sample copy, $1.75 with 9x12 SASE (2 first-class stamps).
• "Escape from Saigon." Article describes the escape of a young orphan from South Vietnam.
• "I Had to Help." Article tells of a teen's commitment to raising money for Vietnam's needy children.
• "Abuse of Inhalants and Prescription Drugs." Article reports on the rise of inhalant abuse among teens.

Rights and Payment
Rights negotiable. Written material, $100+. Pays on acceptance. Provides contributor's copies on request.

Editor's Comments
This year we are looking for true teen stories written in the first person narrative by teens who have overcome obstacles. We have enough poetry and fiction.

SchoolArts

Davis Publications
2223 Parkside Drive
Denton, TX 76201

Editor: Nancy Walkup

Description and Readership
Teachers and others who are active or interested in art education find information, ideas, and inspiration in each issue of *SchoolArts*. Most of its content is supplied by art teachers with a desire to share their successes and help others create more enriching lessons.
• **Audience:** Teachers, grades K–12
• **Frequency:** 9 times each year
• **Distribution:** 100% subscription
• **Circulation:** 20,000
• **Website:** www.davis-art.com

Freelance Potential
90% written by nonstaff writers. Publishes 120 freelance submissions yearly; 60% by unpublished writers, 60% by authors who are new to the magazine. Receives 33 unsolicited mss monthly.

Submissions
Send complete ms with artwork. Accepts photocopies and computer printouts. SASE. Responds in 6 weeks.
Articles: 300–1,000 words. Informational, how-to, and self-help articles. Topics include teaching art, techniques, art history, projects and activities, curriculum development, and art programs for the gifted, handicapped, and learning disabled.
Depts/columns: Word lengths vary. Media reviews, news, and technology updates.
Artwork: B/W prints or 35mm color slides. B/W line art.

Sample Issue
64 pages (40% advertising): 11 articles; 8 depts/columns; 4 ready-to-use resources. Sample copy, $3. Guidelines and editorial calendar available.
• "The Three Perfections." Article offers a lesson in handscrolls, which combine calligraphy, poetry, and painting.
• Sample dept/column: "Bright Ideas" features short essays contributed by readers.

Rights and Payment
First serial rights. Written material, $25–$150. Other material, payment rates vary. Pays on acceptance. Provides 3 contributor's copies.

Editor's Comments
We're currently looking for articles on interdisciplinary approaches to teaching art, using new technologies, working within budget constraints, staff development programs, and community partnerships.

The School Librarian's Workshop

1 Deerfield Court
Basking Ridge, NJ 07920

Editor: Ruth Toor

Description and Readership
Read by school librarians and media specialists, this publication features practical articles dealing with all aspects of library media, current events, and new technological ideas.
• **Audience:** School librarians
• **Frequency:** 6 times each year
• **Distribution:** 99% subscription; 1% other
• **Circulation:** 7,500+
• **Website:** www.school-librarians-workshop.com

Freelance Potential
35% written by nonstaff writers. Publishes 18 freelance submissions yearly; 15% by unpublished writers, 15% by authors who are new to the magazine. Receives 2 unsolicited mss monthly.

Submissions
Send 2 copies of complete ms. Prefers disk submissions (Microsoft Word); accepts photocopies and computer printouts. No simultaneous submissions. SASE. Responds in 3 weeks.
Articles: To 1,000 words. Informational, how-to, and practical application articles; profiles; and interviews. Topics include librarianship, special education, ethnic studies, computers, technology, social and multicultural issues, and the environment.
Artwork: Line art.
Other: Submit seasonal material 8 months in advance.

Sample Issue
24 pages (no advertising): 17 articles; 3 book reviews. Sample copy, free with 9x12 SASE. Guidelines and theme list available.
• "Research to Go." Article examines ways to introduce students to online resources for exploring career options.
• "Teaching Together." Article presents an activity that combines learning the Dewey Decimal System with the solar system.
• "Bibliographies." Informative article lists books for all age levels that feature a character who learns about responsibility.

Rights and Payment
First rights. No payment. Provides 3 copies.

Editor's Comments
We continue to need timely material on working with other teachers, standards and assessment, current media technology, and department budgeting.

School Library Journal

360 Park Avenue
New York, NY 10010

News & Features Editor: Rick Margolis

Description and Readership
Professionals working in school, public, and private libraries find articles and media reviews in this magazine. Topics include the latest trends in children's literature and media, and issues pertinent to librarians.
- **Audience:** Librarians
- **Frequency:** Monthly
- **Distribution:** 100% subscription
- **Circulation:** 34,500
- **Website:** www.slj.com

Freelance Potential
80% written by nonstaff writers. Publishes 25 freelance submissions yearly; 60% by unpublished writers, 60% by authors who are new to the magazine. Receives 4–6 unsolicited mss monthly.

Submissions
Query or send complete ms. Accepts disk submissions (ASCII or Microsoft Word) and email submissions to rmargolis@reedbusiness.com. SASE. Responds to queries in 1 month, to mss in 3 months.
Articles: 1,500–2,500 words. Informational articles and interviews. Topics include children's and young adult literature, school library management, and library careers.
Depts/columns: 1,500–2,500 words. Book and media reviews; descriptions of successful library programs; and opinion pieces.
Artwork: Color prints, tables, charts, and cartoons.

Sample Issue
140 pages (25% advertising): 5 articles; 4 depts/columns; 17 book and media reviews. Sample copy, $6.75. Guidelines available at website.
- "Charming the Next Generation." Article suggests ways to get toddlers excited about reading.
- "The Good, the Bad, and the Edgy." Article tells how to create a successful magazine collection for teens.
- Sample dept/column: "Up for Discussion" argues that all informational books may not be created equal.

Rights and Payment
First rights. Articles, $400. Dept/columns, $100–$200. Pays on publication. Provides 4 contributor's copies.

Editor's Comments
Please review our guidelines at our website before submitting. If you are interested in reviewing children's literature and are a librarian, contact us.

School Library Media Activities Monthly

17 East Henrietta Street
Baltimore, MD 21230-3910

Publisher: Paula Montgomery

Description and Readership
This magazine helps school library media specialists prepare cooperative lessons with teachers working at the kindergarten through eighth-grade level. Ideas for library and classroom activities appear along with reports on successful strategies.
- **Audience:** School library and media specialists, grades K–8
- **Frequency:** 10 times each year
- **Distribution:** 100% subscription
- **Circulation:** 12,000
- **Website:** www.schoollibrarymedia.com

Freelance Potential
80% written by nonstaff writers. Publishes 30 freelance submissions yearly; 15% by unpublished writers, 25% by authors who are new to the magazine. Receives 4 queries and unsolicited mss monthly.

Submissions
Query or send complete ms. Accepts photocopies, disk submissions, and email submissions to paulam@crinkles.com. SASE. Responds in 2 months.
Articles: 1,000–1,500 words. Informational and factual articles. Topics include media education, information technology, integrating curriculum materials, and library management.
Depts/columns: "Activities Almanac" features short descriptions of media activities. "Into the Curriculum" uses lesson plans. Also publishes media reviews and short articles on media production.
Artwork: B/W transparencies and prints. Line art.

Sample Issue
52 pages (no advertising): 3 articles; 13 depts/columns. Guidelines available.
- "A Multiplicity of Research Models: Alternative Strategies for Diverse Learners." Article discusses ways to customize information skills instruction to meet the needs of diverse learners.
- "If Only You'd Read to Me!" Editorial focuses on a report that stresses the importance of reading to preschool children.

Rights and Payment
All rights. All material, payment rate varies. Pays on publication. Provides 3+ contributor's copies.

Editor's Comments
Brief, daily suggestions for student library activities are needed.

The School Magazine

P.O. Box 1928
Macquarie Centre, NSW 2113
Australia

Editor: Jonathan Shaw

Description and Readership
Striving to produce quality literature for elementary school children, this Australian magazine includes articles and stories. Each issue includes four publications for students at different reading levels.
• **Audience:** 8–12 years
• **Frequency:** 10 times each year
• **Distribution:** 100% subscription
• **Circulation:** 220,000

Freelance Potential
85% written by nonstaff writers. Publishes 100 freelance submissions yearly; 20% by unpublished writers, 30% by authors who are new to the magazine. Receives 50 unsolicited mss monthly.

Submissions
Send complete ms. Accepts computer printouts. IRC. Responds in 6–8 weeks.
Articles: 800–2,000 words. Informational and factual articles. Topics include nature, pets, the environment, history, biography, science, technology, and multicultural and ethnic issues.
Fiction: 800–2,000 words. Adventure; humor; fantasy; horror; mystery; folktales; stories about science and animals; problem-solving and real-life stories; and contemporary, multicultural, and historical fiction.
Depts/columns: Staff written.

Sample Issue
32 pages (no advertising): 1 article; 3 stories; 4 poems; 6 depts/columns. Sample copy, free with IRC ($2 Australian postage). Writers' guidelines available.
• "When Granny Was a Girl." Story tells of a grandmother who shares stories about her youth with her granddaughter.
• "Why Can't We Go Now?" Article describes what goes on at an airport before planes can take off.
• "The Club." Story describes the ill feelings a boy experiences after joining a club at school.

Rights and Payment
One-time serial rights. Written material, $209 (Australian) per 1,000 words. Poetry, payment rate varies. Pays on acceptance. Provides 2 copies.

Editor's Comments
Send us something that is interesting and educational that children will enjoy reading. Please do not send overtly moralistic, "messagey" stories or specifically U.S. cultural events (i.e. Groundhog day).

Science Activities

Heldref Publications
1319 18th Street NW
Washington, DC 20036-1802

Managing Editor: Cheri Williams

Description and Readership
Published for science teachers in kindergarten through grade twelve classrooms, this journal features classroom science projects, experiments, and curriculum ideas, as well as research articles.
• **Audience:** Science teachers
• **Frequency:** Quarterly
• **Distribution:** Subscription; schools; libraries
• **Circulation:** 1,200
• **Website:** www.heldref.org

Freelance Potential
75–80% written by nonstaff writers. Publishes 20–25 freelance submissions yearly; 80% by unpublished writers, 20% by authors who are new to the magazine. Receives 4 queries and unsolicited mss monthly.

Submissions
Query or send 2 copies of complete ms. Accepts photocopies and computer printouts. SASE. Responds in 3 months.
Articles: Word length varies. Informational and how-to articles. Topics include science, nature, technology, and computers.
Depts/columns: Word length varies. Book reviews, computer news, and classroom aids.
Artwork: B/W photos, prints, and slides. Line art and diagrams.

Sample Issue
56 pages (1% advertising): 9 articles. Sample copy, $6 with 9x12 SASE. Guidelines available.
• "Crayfish Investigations." Article offers instructions for using crayfish to introduce the inquiry approach to students in grades 4 to 8.
• "How to Generate Student Excitement in Science." How-to article describes how to flex classroom activities to allow for student interest and participation.
• "Plant Gall Activity." Research article suggests studying galls to arouse students' curiosity in plant-insect interactions.

Rights and Payment
All rights. No payment. Provides 2 copies.

Editor's Comments
We are always looking for articles that show the many facets of inquiry learning. We need innovative manuscripts that provide teachers and educators with classroom-tested projects, experiments, and curriculum ideas that promote science study.

Science and Children

National Science Teachers Association
1840 Wilson Boulevard
Arlington, VA 22201-3000

Managing Editor: Monica Zerry

Description and Readership
Published for science educators, this magazine presents peer-reviewed articles that describe activities and instructional approaches to teaching science.
- **Audience:** Science teachers, pre-K–grade 8
- **Frequency:** 8 times each year
- **Distribution:** 100% subscription
- **Circulation:** 23,000
- **Website:** www.nsta.org/pubs/

Freelance Potential
99% written by nonstaff writers. Publishes 25 freelance submissions yearly; 95% by unpublished writers, 95% by authors who are new to the magazine. Receives 30 unsolicited mss monthly.

Submissions
Accepts submissions from practicing educators only. Send 5 copies of complete ms. Accepts photocopies and IBM or Macintosh disk submissions. SASE. Responds in 6 months.
Articles: To 1,500 words. Informational and how-to articles; personal experience pieces; profiles; interviews; and reviews. Topics include science education, teacher training and techniques, staff development, classroom activities, astronomy, biology, chemistry, physics, and earth science.
Depts/columns: To 1,500 words. "Helpful Hints" and "In the Schools," to 500 words.
Other: Submit seasonal material 1 year in advance.

Sample Issue
68 pages (2 advertising): 5 articles; 14 depts/columns. Sample copy, free. Guidelines available.
- "S'Cool Science." Article reports on a NASA program that depends on students to confirm weather satellite images and information.
- "Hoeked' on Science." Article describes a history lesson and microscope exercises that help students focus on science.
- Sample dept/column: "Science 101" answers teachers' questions about everyday science.

Rights and Payment
All rights. No payment. Provides 3 contributor's copies.

Editor's Comments
We need practicing educators to write about their successful classroom activities and experiences, as well as discuss current issues and concerns in elementary science education.

The Science Teacher

National Science Teachers Association
1840 Wilson Boulevard
Arlington, VA 22201-3000

Managing Editor: Jennifer Henderson

Description and Readership
In each issue of this magazine, members of the National Science Teachers Association share their ideas for creating successful science programs with thousands of their peers who also teach science at the high school level.
- **Audience:** Science educators, grades 7–12
- **Frequency:** 9 times each year
- **Distribution:** 100% controlled
- **Circulation:** 29,000
- **Website:** www.nsta.org/highschool

Freelance Potential
100% written by nonstaff writers. Publishes 50 freelance submissions yearly; 70% by unpublished writers, 30% by authors who are new to the magazine. Receives 30 unsolicited mss monthly.

Submissions
Send 3 copies of complete ms with copy on disk to Nadine Bowser, Manuscript Review Coordinator, at the address above; and 1 copy to Janet Gerking, Field Editor, 443 Valley Stream Drive, Geneva, FL 32732. SASE. Responds in 1 month.
Articles: 2,000 words. Informational articles; classroom projects; and experiments. Topics include science education, biology, earth science, space, computers, social issues, technology, and sports medicine.
Depts/columns: 500 words. Science updates, association news, and science careers.
Artwork: 5x7 or larger B/W glossy prints. Tables, diagrams, and line drawings.

Sample Issue
76 pages (40% advertising): 7 articles; 13 depts/columns. Sample copy, $4.25. Guidelines available.
- "The Sidewalk Project." Article reports on a collaborative effort by high school physics students and their mentors to invent a heated sidewalk.
- "Shell Creek Summers." Article details the efforts of a group of students who spend their summers monitoring water quality at a local watershed.
- Sample dept/column: "Career of the Month" profiles a woman who works as an environmental consultant.

Rights and Payment
First rights. No payment. Provides contributor's copies.

Editor's Comments
We invite submissions from science teachers. Your work can be a significant contribution to science programs.

Science Weekly, Inc.

Suite 202
2141 Industrial Parkway
Silver Springs, MD 20904

Publisher: Dr. Claude Mayberry

Description and Readership
Science Weekly is a classroom periodical for students in kindergarten through grade six. Its format is designed to stimulate students' interest in science and the scientific process. As an instructional tool, it helps students develop cross-curriculum thinking skills.
- **Audience:** Students, grades K–6
- **Frequency:** 14 times each year
- **Distribution:** Subscription; schools
- **Circulation:** 200,000
- **Website:** www.scienceweekly.com

Freelance Potential
100% written by nonstaff writers. 80% by unpublished writers, 20% by new authors.

Submissions
Query with résumé only. No unsolicited mss. All work is assigned to writers in the District of Columbia, Maryland, or Virginia. SASE. Response time varies.
Articles: Word length varies. Informational and factual articles. Topics include space exploration, ecology, the environment, nature, biology, the human body, meteorology, ocean science, navigation, nutrition, photography, physical science, roller coasters, and secret codes.
Other: Theme-related puzzles, games, and activities.

Sample Issue
4 pages (no advertising): 1 article; 6 activities. Sample copy and theme list available.
- "Clouds." Short article explains the different types of clouds, how they are formed, and what they represent in meteorological terms.
- Sample activity: "Raining Cotton Balls" involves estimating how much water a cotton ball "cloud" will hold before it "rains."

Rights and Payment
All rights. All material, payment rate varies. Pays on publication.

Editor's Comments
Each issue of our publication is written for different reading levels to compensate for differences in readiness and language skills among students; each level incudes a set of Teaching Notes. Prospective freelance writers must live in the Washington, D.C. metropolitan area and have a strong background in science and education. We will let you know if your résumé indicates you are suitable for our editorial needs.

Scouting

Boy Scouts of America
1325 West Walnut Hill Lane
P.O. Box 152079
Irving, TX 75015-2079

Editor: Jon C. Halter

Description and Readership
Scout leaders and parents will find articles about successful program activities by and for Cub Scouts, Boy Scouts, and Venturing crews in this publication.
- **Audience:** Scout leaders and parents
- **Frequency:** 6 times each year
- **Distribution:** 100% subscription
- **Circulation:** 1 million
- **Website:** www.scoutingmagazine.org

Freelance Potential
80% written by nonstaff writers. Publishes 2–3 freelance submissions yearly; 2% by unpublished writers, 10% by authors who are new to the magazine. Receives 15+ queries monthly.

Submissions
Query with synopsis or outline and clips; or send complete ms. Responds in 3 weeks.
Articles: 500–1,200 words. Informational and how-to articles; personal experience pieces; profiles; interviews; and humor. Topics include scout programs, leadership, volunteering, nature, social issues and trends, and history.
Depts/columns: 500–700 words. Scouting and family events, anecdotes, and scouting history.
Other: Puzzles.

Sample Issue
48 pages (33% advertising): 6 articles; 7 depts/columns. Sample copy, $2.50 with 9x12 SASE. Guidelines available.
- "This Is What We Do!" Article shows how scouts helped out following five hurricanes in Florida.
- "Havasu Heaven." Article follows a troop of Boy Scouts as they bravely hike to the bottom of the Grand Canyon.
- Sample dept/column: "Family Talk" discusses proper dental care for children.

Rights and Payment
First North American serial rights. Pays on acceptance. Written material, $300–$800. Provides 2 author's copies.

Editor's Comments
We will consider material that will help parents and leaders strengthen their ties with young people. Many of our best article ideas come from volunteer and professional scouters, but most are written by staff members or professional writers assigned by us.

Seattle's Child

Suite 215
123 NW 36th Street
Seattle, WA 98107

Editor: Wenda Reed

Description and Readership
General parenting topics and subjects relevant to Seattle residents are found in this publication. It also contains information on local resources and activities.
- **Audience:** Parents
- **Frequency:** Monthly
- **Distribution:** 100% newsstand
- **Circulation:** 70,000
- **Website:** www.seattleschild.com

Freelance Potential
80% written by nonstaff writers. Publishes 10 freelance submissions yearly; 10% by unpublished writers, 25% by authors who are new to the magazine. Receives 6–7 queries monthly.

Submissions
Query with outline. Send queries for local stories to above address; send queries for national interest stories to Bill Lindsay, United Parenting Publications, 670 Centre Street, Jamaica Plains, MA 02130. Accepts photocopies, computer printouts, and simultaneous submissions if identified. SASE. Responds in 2 weeks.
Articles: Word length varies. Informational and how-to articles; and personal experience pieces. Topics include family and parenting issues, health, fitness, regional news, travel, and social issues.
Depts/columns: Word length varies. Profiles, cooking, and media reviews.

Sample Issue
62 pages (30% advertising): 3 articles; 1 calendar; 6 depts/columns. Sample copy, $3. Guidelines and theme list available.
- "Power Struggles." Article strips away the outer coverings of children's negative actions to reveal what really causes power struggles between parents and their children.
- "An Allergy to Parents." Article discusses why teenagers seem to suddenly disown their parents.
- Sample dept/column: "Viewpoint" examines how the rhetoric of a political campaign affected one child.

Rights and Payment
Rights vary. Written material, $100–$450. Pays on acceptance. Provides 2 contributor's copies.

Editor's Comments
We would like to receive knowledgeable articles on local educational issues that use more than one source of information.

Seek

Standard Publishing Company
8121 Hamilton Avenue
Cincinnati, OH 45231

Editor: Margaret K. Williams

Description and Readership
Older teens and adults are the target audience of this weekly Sunday school publication. Addressing religious and contemporary issues, it offers inspirational stories, articles, and Bible lessons.
- **Audience:** YA–Adult
- **Frequency:** Weekly
- **Distribution:** 100% religious education
- **Circulation:** 27,000
- **Website:** www.standardpub.com

Freelance Potential
85% written by nonstaff writers. Publishes 150–200 freelance submissions yearly; 80% by authors who are new to the magazine. Receives 250 mss monthly.

Submissions
Send complete ms that relates to an upcoming theme (available at website). Prefers email to seek@standardpub.com. SASE. Responds in 3–6 months.
Articles: 400–1,200 words. Inspirational, devotional, and personal experience pieces. Topics include religious and contemporary issues, Christian living, moral and ethical dilemmas, and controversial subjects.
Fiction: 400–1,200 words. Stories about coping with contemporary issues, Christian living, moral and ethical dilemmas, and controversial subjects.
Artwork: 8x10 B/W glossy prints.
Other: Filler, 250 words. Submit seasonal material 1 year in advance.

Sample Issue
8 pages (no advertising): 3 articles; 1 Bible lesson. Sample copy, free with 6x9 SASE. Guidelines and theme list available at website.
- "Don't Get Too Comfortable." Article discusses how church members need to get involved with mission work and outreach in addition to attending service.
- "Keep Reminding Me, Lord." Personal experience piece reflects on how the author was reminded of the importance of telling others about Jesus.

Rights and Payment
First and second rights. Written material, $.05 per word. Artwork, $50. Pays on acceptance. Provides 5 contributor's copies.

Editor's Comments
We look for inspirational pieces that explore living a Christian lifestyle and the importance of faith. Keep in mind that we only accept material for our theme list.

Seventeen

13th Floor
1440 Broadway
New York, NY 10018

Features Editor: Leslie Heilbrunn

Description and Readership
This popular teen magazine offers readers information on current trends in fashion, pop culture, and relationships with family and friends.
- **Audience:** 13–21 years
- **Frequency:** Monthly
- **Distribution:** 70% subscription; 30% newsstand
- **Circulation:** 2 million
- **Website:** www.seventeen.com

Freelance Potential
20% written by nonstaff writers. Publishes 20 freelance submissions yearly; 5% by unpublished writers, 40% by authors who are new to the magazine. Receives 46 queries, 200 unsolicited mss monthly.

Submissions
Send complete ms for fiction. Query with outline and clips or writing samples for other material. Accepts photocopies, computer printouts, and simultaneous submissions if identified. SASE. Response time varies.
Articles: 650–3,000 words. Informational and self-help articles; personal experience pieces; and profiles. Topics include relationships, dating, family issues, current events, social concerns, friendship, and popular culture.
Fiction: 1,000–3,000 words. Stories that feature female teenage experiences.
Depts/columns: 500–1,000 words. Fashion, beauty, health, and fitness.
Other: Submit seasonal material 6 months in advance.

Sample Issue
214 pages (50% advertising): 6 articles; 42 depts/columns. Sample copy, $3.00 at newsstands. Guidelines available.
- "Hilary Duff." Profile of established film and TV star discusses her views on her life and work.
- "Do You Believe in God?" Article reports on what some readers have to say about their beliefs.
- Sample dept/column: "Dear Mom" offers a letter from a young woman to her mother.

Rights and Payment
First rights. Written material, $1–$1.50 per word. Pays on acceptance.

Editor's Comments
We are looking for original first-person essays focusing on personal decisions and relationships, as well as light and funny pieces about unusual situations.

SG: Surf Snow Skate Girl

Suite C
950 Calle Amanecer
San Clemente, CA 92673

Editor: Melissa Larsen

Description and Readership
This sports magazine for girls profiles female athletes who excel at surfing, snowboarding, and skateboarding. Illustrated with action-packed photos, it also offers in-depth articles on technique and detailed pieces that spotlight popular surfing and snowboarding destinations all over the world.
- **Audience:** 13–21 years
- **Frequency:** Monthly
- **Distribution:** Subscription; newsstand .
- **Circulation:** 100,000
- **Website:** www.sgmag.com

Freelance Potential
30% written by nonstaff writers. Publishes 100 freelance submissions yearly.

Submissions
Query. Accepts computer printouts and email submissions to sgmag@primedia.com. SASE. Responds in 2 months.
Articles: 1,500–2,000 words. Informational and how-to articles; profiles; interviews; and personal experience pieces. Topics include surfing, skateboarding, snowboarding, skiing, the beach lifestyle, health, fitness, sports, travel, leisure, nutrition, recreation, and relationships.
Fiction: 300–800 words. Stories with snowboarding, skateboarding, and surfboarding themes.
Depts/columns: 300–800 words. Short profiles, skateboarding tips, fashion, beauty, travel, the environment, industry news, and reader-written poetry.

Sample Issue
112 pages (50% advertising): 4 articles; 18 depts/columns. Sample copy, $2.99. Guidelines available.
- "Oz Surf." Article presents the lowdown on 10 of Australia's famous surfing spots.
- "NZ Snow." Article covers snowboarding conditions in New Zealand.
- Sample dept/column: "D.I.Y." offers instructions for making your own stickers.

Rights and Payment
First rights. All material, payment rate varies. Pays on publication.

Editor's Comments
Query us if you have the expertise to write about the sports we cover or if you have access to talented female athletes who participate in board sports.

Sharing the Victory

Fellowship of Christian Athletes
8701 Leeds Road
Kansas City, MO 64129

Editor: Jill Ewert

Description and Readership
The focus of this magazine is on athletes of the Christian faith whose religious beliefs direct their lives both on and off the playing field. Unknowns as well as recognized athletes are featured.
- **Audience:** Athletes and coaches, grades 7 and up
- **Frequency:** 9 times each year
- **Distribution:** 100% subscription
- **Circulation:** 80,000
- **Website:** www.fca.org

Freelance Potential
75% written by nonstaff writers. Publishes 30 freelance submissions yearly; 25% by unpublished writers, 10% by authors who are new to the magazine. Receives 4 queries and unsolicited mss monthly.

Submissions
Query with outline/synopsis and clips or writing samples; or send complete ms. Accepts photocopies, computer printouts, and IBM disk submissions. Availability of artwork improves chance of acceptance. SASE. Response time varies.
Articles: To 1,200 words. Informational articles; profiles; interviews; and personal experience pieces. Topics include sports, competition, training, and Christian education.
Depts/columns: Staff written.
Artwork: Color prints.
Other: Submit seasonal material 3–4 months in advance.

Sample Issue
38 pages (35% advertising): 7 articles; 11 depts/columns. Sample copy, $1 with 9x12 SASE (3 first-class stamps). Guidelines available.
- "Nate and Kevin Burleson Speak Out from Opposite Sides of the Globe." Article profiles two brothers, both professional athletes, who discuss the role of faith in their upbringing and in their careers.
- "Power to Win." Article comments on the actions some ministries are taking to turn the Super Bowl halftime show into an outreach event.

Rights and Payment
First serial rights. Articles, $150–$400. Pays on publication.

Editor's Comments
Articles focusing on female athletes who are involved with the FCA are particularly needed at this time.

SheKnows.com

Suite 230
7944 East Beck Lane
Scottsdale, AZ 85260

Editor: Nancy Price

Description and Readership
SheKnows is an online network of sites for women, covering topics from parenting to personal finance. It seeks to improve the lives of readers by providing them with information, enlightenment, community interaction, and entertainment.
- **Audience:** Mothers
- **Frequency:** Weekly
- **Distribution:** 100% online
- **Hits per month:** Unavailable
- **Website:** www.sheknows.com

Freelance Potential
50% written by nonstaff writers. Publishes 80–100 freelance submissions yearly. Receives 20 queries, 4 unsolicited mss monthly.

Submissions
Query or send complete ms. Accepts submissions through website only. Responds in 2 months.
Articles: 500–1,200 words. Informational, how-to, and factual articles; personal experience pieces; profiles; and interviews. Topics include parenting, fertility, pregnancy, maternity fashion trends, birth stories, pain management, depression, infants, toddlers, family issues, relationships, romance, entertainment, celebrities, work, health, hobbies, home decor, and money management.

Sample Issue
Sample copy and guidelines available at website.
- "The 21st Century Parent." Article explains why parenting is so difficult in this era, and suggests how parents can arm themselves with the tools they need to become effective parents.
- "The Stranger in Your Child's Life." Article reveals how the media is affecting family solidarity, and how to set limits and enforce guidelines for a greater family connection.

Rights and Payment
First electronic rights. Features, $25–$50. First-person pieces, $10. Pays on publication.

Editor's Comments
We are looking for information from experts in a variety of fields, as well as feature articles written by journalists and others with the appropriate skills. Our sites are primarily written by freelancers. We like articles based on research and interviews that are presented in an accessible format.

Shine Brightly

P.O. Box 7259
Grand Rapids, MI 49510

Managing Editor: Christina Malone

Description and Readership
Published by GEMS Girls' Clubs, this magazine is read by Christian girls. It features inspirational and educational articles and stories.
- **Audience:** 9–14 years
- **Frequency:** 9 times each year
- **Distribution:** 100% subscription
- **Circulation:** 15,500
- **Website:** www.gemsgc.org

Freelance Potential
70% written by nonstaff writers. Publishes 30 freelance submissions yearly; 20% by unpublished writers, 20% by authors who are new to the magazine. Receives 50 unsolicited mss monthly.

Submissions
Send complete ms. Accepts photocopies, computer printouts, and simultaneous submissions if identified. No email submissions. SASE. Responds in 1 month.
Articles: 50–500 words. Informational and how-to articles; personal experience pieces; profiles; and humor. Topics include work ethics, spiritual gifts, community service, stewardship, and contemporary social issues.
Fiction: 400–900 words. Contemporary fiction, romance, mystery, science fiction, and adventure. Also publishes stories about nature, sports, and animals.
Depts/columns: Staff written.
Artwork: 5x7 or larger B/W and color prints.
Other: Puzzles, activities, and cartoons.

Sample Issue
20 pages (no advertising): 1 article; 3 stories; 4 depts/columns; 1 recipe. Sample copy, $1 with 9x12 SASE ($.75 postage). Guidelines available.
- "Too Late for Take Backs." Short story about friends, hurt feelings, and saying I'm sorry.
- "What a Nut!" Article highlights fun historical facts about peanuts.

Rights and Payment
First, second, and simultaneous rights. Articles and fiction, $.02–$.05 per word. Other material, payment rates vary. Pays on publication. Provides 2 copies.

Editor's Comments
We like to see material that relates to girls and their experiences. Articles should build girls up in Christian character, but they should not be preachy. Stretch our readers to see and experience new things.

Single Mother

A Support Group in Your Hands

National Organization of Single Mothers
P.O. Box 68
Midland, NC 28107-0068

Editor: Andrea Engber

Description and Readership
The nonprofit National Organization of Single Mothers publishes this newsletter to provide support, information, and advice. Its articles and columns are written to help single mothers face the daily challenges of parenting.
- **Audience:** Single mothers
- **Frequency:** Quarterly
- **Distribution:** Subscription; membership
- **Circulation:** 3,000
- **Website:** www.singlemothers.org

Freelance Potential
10% written by nonstaff writers. Publishes 6 freelance submissions yearly. Receives 1–2 queries and unsolicited mss monthly.

Submissions
Query or send complete ms. Prefers email submissions to singlemother@singlemothers.org. Accepts photocopies and computer printouts. Availability of artwork improves chance of acceptance. SASE. Responds to queries in 2 weeks, to mss in 3 months.
Articles: Word lengths vary. Informational articles. Topics include parenting, money and time management, absent dads, dating, death, handling ex-families, pregnancy and childbirth, adoption, donor insemination, child support, paternity, custody, and visitation rights.
Depts/columns: Word length varies. Opinion pieces and book reviews.

Sample Issue
16 pages (no advertising): 16 articles; 2 depts/columns. Sample copy, $2.95 with 9x12 SASE.
- "Slacker Moms Unite!" Article defends the position that it's okay to do less, have less, and spend less.
- "Widowed Moms and Kids Can Relate." Article discusses a book called "Our Dad Died."
- Sample dept/column: "Bookshelf" reviews a children's book about an unwanted stepdad.

Rights and Payment
Rights vary. Payment policy and rates vary.

Editor's Comments
Positive, research-based writing that affirms single motherhood is needed. Pieces that depict mothers of diverse social, emotional, cultural, and religious backgrounds are especially welcome.

Skating

United States Figure Skating Association
20 First Street
Colorado Springs, CO 80906

Director of Publications

Description and Readership
In print since 1923, this magazine for members of the U.S. Figure Skating Association includes articles and tips relating to the world of figure skating, as well as coverage of events and news.
- **Audience:** 5 years–Adult
- **Frequency:** 10 times each year
- **Distribution:** Subscription; other
- **Circulation:** 45,000
- **Website:** www.usfigureskating.org

Freelance Potential
70% written by nonstaff writers. Publishes 15 freelance submissions yearly; 10% by unpublished writers, 20% by authors who are new to the magazine. Receives 6 queries and unsolicited mss monthly.

Submissions
Query with résumé, clips or writing samples, and photo ideas; or send complete ms with photos or art ideas. Accepts photocopies, Macintosh zip disk submissions, and email to skatingmagazine@ usfigureskating.org. SASE. Responds in 1 month.
Articles: 750–2,000 words. Informational articles; profiles; and interviews. Topics include association news, competitions, techniques, personalities, and training.
Depts/columns: 600–800 words. Competition results, profiles of skaters and coaches, sports medicine, fitness, and technique tips.
Artwork: B/W or color prints, slides, or transparencies. Electronic images scanned at 300 dpi.

Sample Issue
70 pages: 6 articles; 10 depts/columns. Sample copy, $3 with 9x12 SASE. Guidelines available.
- "Taking the Next Step." Article tells of a coach who learned to skate as an adult after facing challenges resulting from an injury as a young gymnast.
- Sample dept/column: "Health & Fitness" describes methods used in a sports psychology program.

Rights and Payment
First serial rights. Articles, $75–$150. Depts/columns, $75. Artwork, payment rate varies. Pays on publication. Provides 5–10 contributor's copies.

Editor's Comments
Interesting and entertaining articles and profiles of elite skaters are of interest to us, as well as coverage of competitions, and up-and-coming skaters.

Skipping Stones

A Multicultural Magazine

P.O. Box 3939
Eugene, OR 97403-0939

Editor: Arun N. Toké

Description and Readership
A magazine of ecological awareness and cultural diversity, *Skipping Stones* serves as a forum for communication among children around the globe.
- **Audience:** 7–17 years; teachers; parents
- **Frequency:** 5 times each year
- **Distribution:** Subscription; newsstand; schools; libraries
- **Circulation:** 2,500
- **Website:** www.skippingstones.org

Freelance Potential
90% written by nonstaff writers. Publishes 175–200 freelance submissions yearly; 60% by unpublished writers, 75% by authors who are new to the magazine. Receives 167–250 unsolicited mss monthly.

Submissions
Send complete ms with cover letter. Accepts photocopies, computer printouts, Macintosh disk submissions, simultaneous submissions, and email submissions to editor@skippingstones.org. Artwork improves chance of acceptance. SASE. Responds in 3–4 months.
Articles: To 750 words. Essays and contemporary nonfiction. Topics include community service, family relationships, technology, problem-solving, sustainable living, disabilities, role models, and living abroad.
Fiction: To 750 words. Genres include multicultural, inspirational, and historical fiction; and folktales.
Depts/columns: 100–200 words. News, book reviews, opinion pieces, community action, and proverbs.
Artwork: B/W and color prints. Line art.
Other: Puzzles, activities, games, and jokes. Poetry. Submit seasonal material 3 months in advance.

Sample Issue
36 pages (no advertising): 12 articles; 6 stories; 11 depts/columns; 20 poems. Sample copy, $5 with 9x12 SASE ($1 postage). Guidelines available.
- "Semana Santa in Spain." Article tells of a French girl's experience of Holy Week in the Spanish culture.
- "The Basket Weaver." Story of a Navajo woman who helps a mother and her child accept death.

Rights and Payment
First and reprint rights. No payment. Provides up to 4 copies and 25% discount on additional copies.

Editor's Comments
We're in need of authentic African American, Asian American, Latin American, and Native American pieces.

Slap

High Speed Productions
1303 Underwood Avenue
San Francisco, CA 94124

Editor: Mark Whiteley

Description and Readership
Teen fans of skateboarding and the hip-hop music scene enjoy this magazine for its articles and photos covering competitions and profiles of musicians.
- **Audience:** YA
- **Frequency:** Monthly
- **Distribution:** 50% newsstand; 10% subscription; 40% other
- **Circulation:** 130,000
- **Website:** www.slapmagazine.com

Freelance Potential
20% written by nonstaff writers. Publishes 25+ freelance submissions yearly.

Submissions
Send complete ms. Accepts photocopies, computer printouts, IBM or Macintosh disk submissions, and simultaneous submissions if identified. Availability of artwork improves chance of acceptance. SASE. Responds in 2 months.
Articles: Word length varies. Informational and how-to articles; interviews; and personal experience pieces. Topics include skateboarding, contest reports and statistics, skateboard equipment, music, and recreation.
Depts/columns: Word length varies. Short news items, skateboarding tricks, and music news.
Artwork: 35mm B/W negatives; color prints and transparencies. B/W and color line art.
Other: Cartoons and comics about skateboarding and popular music.

Sample Issue
162 pages (40% advertising): 12 articles; 9 depts/columns. Sample copy, free with 9x12 SASE ($1.95 postage). Guidelines and editorial calendar available.
- "Pro on the Rise: Bryan Herman." Article profiles a young skateboard pro on one of the most respected teams.
- Sample dept/column: "Gear" takes a look at backpacks, shoes, a line of clothing, and skateboards.

Rights and Payment
First rights. All material, payment rate varies. Pays on publication. Provides 1 contributor's copy.

Editor's Comments
In order to write for us, you must be familiar with street and skateboard lingo, and know who is hot in the hip-hop scene. Check us out before submitting.

Social Studies and the Young Learner

National Council for the Social Studies
Suite 500, 8555 16th Street
Silver Springs, MD 20910

Editor

Description and Readership
This magazine offers kindergarten through sixth grade social studies educators lesson ideas, read-aloud stories, articles, news, and activities.
- **Audience:** Teachers
- **Frequency:** Quarterly
- **Distribution:** Subscription; newsstand
- **Circulation:** 15,000
- **Website:** www.socialstudies.org

Freelance Potential
95% written by nonstaff writers. Publishes 32 freelance submissions yearly; 30% by unpublished writers, 50% by authors who are new to the magazine. Receives 5 mss monthly.

Submissions
Send complete ms. Accepts photocopies and computer printouts. SASE. Responds in 1 year.
Articles: To 2,000 words. Informational articles; profiles; and personal experience pieces. Topics include current events, gifted education, multicultural and ethnic subjects, social issues, history, and special education.
Fiction: Word lengths vary. Folktales; folklore; multicultural, ethnic, and historical fiction.
Depts/columns: To 500 words. Classroom resources and perspectives on topics related to social studies.
Artwork: B/W and color prints and transparencies. Line art.
Other: Filler, puzzles, and activities.

Sample Issue
32 pages: 3 articles; 3 depts/columns. Sample copy, $7.50. Guidelines, theme list, and editorial calendar available.
- "Social Studies in Motion: Learning with the Whole Person." Article takes a look at using kinesthetic activities in classrooms to integrate action into the learning process.
- Sample dept/column: "Classroom Resources" takes a look at a program that explores the concepts of hero and celebrity and what a real hero is.

Rights and Payment
All rights. No payment.

Editor's Comments
We look for articles, projects, and activities that allow students to explore the world and help them gain a deeper understanding of important social issues.

South Florida Parenting

6501 Nob Hill Road
Tamarac, FL 33321

Managing Editor: Vicki McCash Brennan

Description and Readership
Serving parents in the Miami-Dade, Broward and Palm Beach area, this publication covers topics related to parenting such as education, finances, health, travel, child development, and family issues. In addition, it also includes crafts and information on regional events and resources.
- **Audience:** Parents
- **Frequency:** Monthly
- **Distribution:** Controlled; schools; other
- **Circulation:** 110,000
- **Website:** www.sfparenting.com

Freelance Potential
85% written by nonstaff writers. Publishes 90 freelance submissions yearly; 10% by authors who are new to the magazine. Receives 83 unsolicited mss each month.

Submissions
Send complete ms. Accepts photocopies, computer printouts, and email submissions to vmccash@ sfparenting.com. SASE. Responds in 2–3 months.
Articles: 800–2,000 words. Informational and how-to articles; profiles; interviews; and personal experience pieces. Topics include family life, travel, parenting, education, leisure, music, health, and regional events.
Depts/columns: To 750 words. Family finance, health, nutrition, and advice on infants and preteens.

Sample Issue
178 pages (60% advertising): 2 articles; 11 depts/columns; 1 calendar. Guidelines available.
- "Moms Who Blog." Article discusses weblogs, (online journals), for moms.
- "Dad Duty." Article offers suggestions for fathers-to-be on how they can support their pregnant wives.
- Sample dept/column: "With the Kids" offers craft ideas for father's day gifts.

Rights and Payment
One-time regional rights. Written material, $75–$300. Pays on publication. Provides copies upon request.

Editor's Comments
We are currently looking for thorough, well-sourced, well-researched features on current issues in parenting, and are not interested in personal essays, or one-source reprint offers, as we have enough of these. Material should have a regional or local slant. Most of the writers we use are from the areas we feature.

Sparkle

P.O. Box 7259
Grand Rapids, MI 49510

Managing Editor: Christine Malone

Description and Readership
The material presented in *Sparkle* magazine entertains young girls while imparting valuable lessons about the Christian faith. It is published by a non-profit organization that is associated with Dynamic Youth Ministries.
- **Audience:** Girls, 6–9 years
- **Frequency:** 3 times each year
- **Distribution:** Unavailable
- **Circulation:** 2,700
- **Website:** www.gemsgc.org

Freelance Potential
85% written by nonstaff writers. Publishes 9 freelance submissions yearly; 50% by unpublished writers, 50% by authors who are new to the magazine. Receives 20 unsolicited mss monthly.

Submissions
Send complete ms. SASE. Responds in 4–6 weeks.
Articles: 100–400 words. Informational articles. Topics include animals, sports, music, musicians, famous people, interaction with family and friends, service projects, and dealing with school work.
Fiction: 100–400 words. Genres include adventure, mystery, and contemporary fiction. Also publishes stories about animals.
Other: Puzzles, games, recipes, party ideas, short humorous pieces, cartoons, and inexpensive craft ideas.

Sample Issue
15 pages (no advertising): 2 articles; 2 stories; 6 activities; 1 Bible lesson. Sample copy, free. Writers' guidelines available.
- "God's Care for Animal Babies." Article looks at child-care customs of wolves, elephants, and monkeys.
- "Loose Tooth?" Article explains tooth loss in humans and in other mammals.
- "Princess Slug." Story tells of a slug who creates beautiful pictures with her slimy trails.

Rights and Payment
Rights policy varies. Articles, $20. Other material, payment rates vary. Pays on publication. Provides 2 contributor's copies.

Editor's Comments
We look for material that presents the Christian life realistically. Show our young readers how God is at work in their lives and in the world around them.

Spider
The Magazine for Children

Cricket Magazine Group
P.O. Box 300, 315 Fifth Street
Peru, IL 61354

Submissions Editor

Description and Readership
Top-quality stories, poems, and nonfiction for beginning and early readers appear in *Spider,* which seeks work created by the world's best children's authors and illustrators.
- **Audience:** 6–9 years
- **Frequency:** Monthly
- **Distribution:** Subscription; newsstand
- **Circulation:** 70,000
- **Website:** www.cricketmag.com

Freelance Potential
97% written by nonstaff writers. Publishes 50 freelance submissions yearly; 30% by unpublished writers, 50% by authors who are new to the magazine. Receives 300 unsolicited mss monthly.

Submissions
Send complete ms; include bibliography for nonfiction. Accepts photocopies, computer printouts, and simultaneous submissions if identified. SASE. Responds in 2–3 months.
Articles: 300–800 words. Informational and how-to articles; profiles; and interviews. Topics include nature, animals, science, technology, history, multicultural issues, foreign cultures, and the environment.
Fiction: 300–1,000 words. Easy-to-read stories. Genres include humor, fantasy, fairy tales, folktales, realistic and historical fiction, and science fiction.
Other: Recipes, crafts, puzzles, games, brainteasers, and math and word activities. Poetry, to 20 lines.

Sample Issue
32 pages (no advertising): 5 stories; 6 activities; 1 poem. Sample copy, $5 with 9x12 SASE. Writers' guidelines available.
- "Fabulous Frederic." Story features a boy who learns to perfect his magic-act skills.
- "Stone Soda Bread." Story tells of a hungry stranger who tricks the villagers into preparing a feast when he shares his recipe for bread made from a stone.

Rights and Payment
All rights. Articles and fiction, $.25 per word. Poetry, to $3 per line. Other material, payment rate varies. Pays on publication. Provides 2 contributor's copies.

Editor's Comments
We'd like to reach as many children's authors as possible for original work, but our standards are very high and we will only consider top-quality material.

Spirit

Sisters of St. Joseph of Carondelet
1884 Randolph Avenue
St. Paul, MN 55105-1700

Editor: Joan Mitchell

Description and Readership
Catholic teens receive this take-home paper in weekly religious education classes. Each issue includes an article that reflects on the Gospel reading for that week, an invitation to readers to share their experiences of God, and suggestions for ways to build Christian community.
- **Audience:** YA
- **Frequency:** 28 times each year
- **Distribution:** 100% subscription
- **Circulation:** 25,000
- **Website:** www.goodgroundpress.com

Freelance Potential
50% written by nonstaff writers. Publishes 6–10 freelance submissions yearly; 50% by unpublished writers. Receives 16 queries and unsolicited mss monthly.

Submissions
Query or send complete ms. Accepts photocopies, computer printouts, and simultaneous submissions if identified. SASE. Responds to queries in 1 month, to mss in 6 months.
Articles: To 1,200 words. Informational and factual articles. Topics include peer pressure, moral dilemmas, social problems, risk taking, dating, eating disorders, drug and alcohol abuse, physical handicaps, family issues, community service, missionary work, and youth ministry. Also publishes profiles of adults who exemplify Christian values.
Fiction: To 1,200 words. Genres include contemporary fiction, about issues that affect teens.

Sample Issue
4 pages (no advertising): 3 articles; 4 activities. Sample copy, free. Guidelines available.
- "Asking for Faith." Article relates how a teen who didn't believe in God prayed for faith and received an understanding of God that makes sense to him.
- "Keeping Faith." Article explains that faith doesn't give us the power to change circumstances; faith is about God being there for us.

Rights and Payment
All rights. Written material, $200. Pays on publication. Provides 5–10 contributor's copies.

Editor's Comments
We'd like to see articles about youth service projects in parishes, schools, or neighborhoods. Be sure to include photos and quotes from the teens involved.

233

SportingKid

Suite 300
3650 Brookside Parkway
Alpharetta, GA 30022

Editor: Michael J. Pallerino

Description and Readership
As the official publication of the National Alliance for Youth Sports, this magazine includes articles that cover many aspects of sports. It strives to provide readers with information that details the important role of sports in the lives of children.
- **Audience:** Parents
- **Frequency:** 6 times each year
- **Distribution:** Subscription; newsstand
- **Circulation:** 400,000
- **Website:** www.sportingkid.com

Freelance Potential
20–30% written by nonstaff writers. Publishes 10 freelance submissions yearly; 10% by authors who are new to the magazine. Receives 50 queries monthly.

Submissions
Query or send complete ms. Accepts email submissions to editor@sportingkid.com. Queries must be pasted into the email message; manuscripts must be attached in a Microsoft Word document. Responds in 1 month.
Articles: Word length varies. Informational and how-to articles and personal experience pieces. Topics include all sports played by children, coaching, and training.
Depts/columns: Word length varies. The culture of youth sports, new product information, profiles of prominent sports figures, and essays from a parent's perspective.

Sample Issue
40 pages: 7 articles; 9 depts/columns. Sample copy and guidelines available at website.
- "Sports as Life." Article discusses the values and lessons that sports can provide and instill in the lives of children.
- "Hang in There." Article discusses finding the underlying reason why a child may want to quit a sport.
- Sample dept/column: "Health & Wellness" takes a look at strength training for children.

Rights and Payment
First and electronic rights. All material, payment rate varies. Pays on publication.

Editor's Comments
We look for material that shows how sports can positively affect the lives of young people. Profiles of athletes and interviews of players also interest us.

Sports Illustrated for Kids

Time & Life Building
1271 Avenue of the Americas
New York, NY 10020

Managing Editor: Neil Cohen

Description and Readership
This magazine covers the world of sports for middle-grade kids. A good part of each issue spotlights star athletes—collegiate, pro, or high school—as well as up-and-coming younger athletes. Other articles cover timely, sports-related news and issues.
- **Audience:** 8–14 years
- **Frequency:** Monthly
- **Distribution:** 71% subscription; 27% controlled; 2% newsstand
- **Circulation:** 1.1 million
- **Website:** www.sikids.com

Freelance Potential
30% written by nonstaff writers. Publishes 20 freelance submissions yearly. Receives 17 queries monthly.

Submissions
Query or send complete ms. Send for writers' guidelines to determine which department your material should be sent to. SASE. Responds in 2 months.
Articles: Lead articles and profiles, 500–700 words. Short features, 500–600 words. Topics include professional and aspiring athletes, fitness, health, safety, sports tips, hobbies, science, technology, and multicultural issues.
Depts/columns: Word length varies. Events coverage, humor, team profiles.
Other: Poetry and drawings created by kids. Trivia, puzzles, and games.

Sample Issue
70 pages (24% advertising): 11 articles; 9 depts/columns; 1 calendar of events; 1 poster. Sample copy, $3.50 with 9x12 SASE to *Sports Illustrated for Kids*, P.O. Box 830609, Birmingham, AL 35283. Guidelines available.
- "Mercury Rising." Article profiles Diana Taurasi, the WNBA's hottest new star, of the Phoenix Mercury.
- Sample dept/column: "Warmup" examines how Baylor's win of the 2005 NCAA title signals a change in women's college basketball.

Rights and Payment
All rights. Articles, $100–$1,500. Depts/columns, payment rate varies. Pays on acceptance. Provides contributor's copies.

Editor's Comments
Freelancers may query with specific story ideas, but please note that most of our content is staff written.

Stone Soup

The Magazine by Young Writers and Artists

P.O. Box 83
Santa Cruz, CA 95063

Editor: Gerry Mandel

Description and Readership

Stone Soup publishes stories, poems, book reviews, and art by young people through age thirteen. Its goal is to stir the imaginations of readers, and inspire writers to create.
- **Audience:** 8–14 years
- **Frequency:** 6 times each year
- **Distribution:** 50% subscription; 25% newsstand; 25% schools
- **Circulation:** 20,000
- **Website:** www.stonesoup.com

Freelance Potential

100% written by nonstaff writers. Publishes 65 freelance submissions yearly; 90% by unpublished writers, 90% by authors who are new to the magazine. Receives 1,200 unsolicited mss monthly.

Submissions

Send complete ms. Accepts submissions by writers under 14 years of age. No simultaneous submissions. SASE. Responds in 6 weeks only if interested.
Fiction: To 2,500 words. Multicultural, ethnic, and historical fiction, adventure, mystery, suspense, and science fiction.
Depts/columns: Word length varies. Book reviews.
Artwork: Color art.
Other: Poetry, line length varies.

Sample Issue

48 pages (no advertising): 8 stories; 2 poems, 2 book reviews. Sample copy, $5.75. Guidelines available.
- "The View from Santa Chiara." Story about a young artist who discovers her talent at the hands of an elderly painter.
- "Muslim Girl." Short story reminds us of what freedom really means.
- Sample dept/column: "Book Review" highlights new titles of interest to readers.

Rights and Payment

All rights. Written material, $40. Artwork, $25. Pays on publication. Provides 2 contributor's copies.

Editor's Comments

Whether your work is about imaginary situations or real ones, use your own experiences and observations to give your work depth and a sense of reality. If we are considering your submission, you will hear from us. If you don't, it means we were not able to use your work at this time.

Story Friends

Mennonite Publishing Network
616 Walnut Avenue
Scottdale, PA 15683-1999

Editor: Susan Reith Swan

Description and Readership

This general-interest magazine for children includes articles, poems, stories, and activities that reinforce Christian values.
- **Audience:** 4–9 years
- **Frequency:** Monthly
- **Distribution:** 100% subscription
- **Circulation:** 5,000
- **Website:** www.mph.org

Freelance Potential

90% written by nonstaff writers. Publishes 70 freelance submissions yearly; 10% by unpublished writers, 50% by authors who are new to the magazine. Receives 83 unsolicited mss monthly.

Submissions

Send complete ms. Accepts photocopies, computer printouts, and simultaneous submissions if identified. SASE. Responds in 2–3 months.
Articles: 125–300 words. Informational articles. Topics include nature, history, and religion.
Fiction: 300–800 words. Genres include contemporary and multicultural fiction that portray Christian family values, and stories about religious holidays.
Depts/columns: Book reviews, activities, puzzles, and recipes.
Artwork: Color slides and illustrations.
Other: Poetry, 6–12 lines.

Sample Issue

16 pages (no advertising): 3 stories; 1 rebus; 3 poems; 5 depts/columns; 1 activity. Sample copy, free with 9x12 SASE (2 first-class stamps). Guidelines available.
- "One is Enough?" Story shares how a boy learns that a small amount goes a long way when you share.
- "The Turtle Adventure." Story tells of a boy who guides baby sea turtles to the ocean.
- Sample dept/column: "Let's Cook" offers a recipe for making easy fruit kabobs.

Rights and Payment

One-time rights. Fiction, $.03–$.05 per word. Other material, payment rate varies. Pays on acceptance. Provides 2 contributor's copies.

Editor's Comments

We look for stories that focus on the positive power of love and caring. Submissions should show children resolving their own conflicts.

Story Mates

Christian Light Publications
P.O. Box 1212
Harrisonburg, VA 22803-1212

Editor: Crystal Shank

Description and Readership
This Christian publication is produced by Christian Light Publications and serves as a take-home paper for children of the Mennonite faith. Its stories, activities, and poems all relate to the Mennonite doctrine and seek to supplement Sunday school lessons.
- **Audience:** 4–8 years
- **Frequency:** Monthly
- **Distribution:** Subscription; religious instruction
- **Circulation:** 6,278
- **Website:** www.clp.org

Freelance Potential
90% written by nonstaff writers. Publishes 200 freelance submissions yearly. Receives 50 unsolicited mss monthly.

Submissions
Send complete ms. Accepts photocopies, computer printouts, and email submissions to storymates@clp.org. SASE. Responds in 6 weeks.
Fiction: 800 words. Stories related to Sunday school lessons and true-to-life stories. 120–150 words. Picture stories.
Other: Biblical puzzles, activities, and crafts. Poetry, word length varies. Submit seasonal material 6 months in advance.

Sample Issue
6 pages (no advertising): 3 stories; 1 poem; 1 puzzle; 1 activity. Sample copy, free with 9x12 SASE ($.80 postage). Guidelines and theme list available.
- "Questions and Choices." Story about a young boy and his grandfather.
- "He's Going to Bite!" Story about a young girl who is afraid of dogs, but learns to overcome her fear.

Rights and Payment
First, reprint, or multiple-use rights. Fiction, $.03–$.05 per word. Poetry, $.35–$.75 per line. Other material, payment rates vary. Pays on acceptance. Provides 1 contributor's copy.

Editor's Comments
We target young Mennonite children between the ages of 4–8. All material must be suitable for that age range, as well as follow the tenants of the Mennonite faith. We seek inspirational and interesting stories, poems, and activities that reflect the moral lessons of the Bible and encourage Christian living. Writers must complete a questionnaire, which accompanies our guidelines.

Storytelling Magazine

National Storytelling Network
Suite 5
132 Boone Street
Jonesborough, TN 37659

Managing Editor: Grace Hawthorn

Description and Readership
The craft of storytelling comes alive in this publication. Targeting professional story tellers, teachers, and librarians, it offers news and applications on oral story-telling tradition as well as read-aloud stories.
- **Audience:** Adults
- **Frequency:** 6 times each year
- **Distribution:** 90% controlled; 10% newsstand
- **Circulation:** 6,000
- **Website:** www.storynet.org

Freelance Potential
50% written by nonstaff writers. Publishes 100 freelance submissions yearly. Receives 4 unsolicited mss each month.

Submissions
Send complete ms. Accepts photocopies, disk submissions (Microsoft Word), and simultaneous submissions if identified. Responds in 4 months.
Articles: 1,000–2,000 words. Informational and how-to articles; and personal experience pieces. Topics include storytelling research and analysis, story origins, and ethnic multicultural issues.
Depts/columns: 500 words. Noteworthy storytelling projects, resources, and reports on activities and events.

Sample Issue
48 pages (25% advertising): 12 articles; 2 stories; 16 depts/columns. Sample copy, $6 (includes postage).
- "I Lost Myself in Space." Essay recounts the author's memories of trying the high dive and her father's kind words of encouragement.
- "The Apple Tree's Discovery." Story tells of how an apple tree longs for stars on its branches, and later discovers it has them.
- Sample dept/column: "The Center Connection" reports on a pilot program to inspire and empower people to collect, craft, and share their stories.

Rights and Payment
First North American serial rights. No payment. Provides 2 contributor's copies.

Editor's Comments
The majority of our material comes from our readers, who are members of the National Storytelling Network. However, we will consider manuscripts from others who are experienced with oral storytelling applications and can provide us with something new.

Student Assistance Journal

Suite F
1270 Rankin Drive
Troy, MI 48083

Editor: Susan Hipsley

Description and Readership

As the official journal of the National Student Assistance Association, this publication offers insightful and practical information for professionals and other youth workers to use to enhance their program's effectiveness and techniques.
- **Audience:** Student assistance personnel, K–12
- **Frequency:** 4 times each year
- **Distribution:** Unavailable
- **Circulation:** 10,000
- **Website:** www.prponline.net

Freelance Potential

90% written by nonstaff writers. Publishes 12 freelance submissions yearly; 50% by unpublished writers. Receives 3 queries monthly.

Submissions

Query if outside the field. Professionals should send complete ms. Accepts photocopies, computer printouts, IBM DOS-compatible disk submissions (WordPerfect), and simultaneous submissions if identified. SASE. Responds only if interested.

Articles: 1,500 words. Informational and how-to articles; and personal experience pieces. Topics include high-risk students, special education programs, drug testing, substance abuse prevention, school violence, legal issues, federal funding, and staff development.

Depts/columns: 750–800 words. Book reviews, events, commentaries, short news items, legal issues, media resources, and related research.

Sample Issue

34 pages (20% advertising): 3 articles; 9 depts/columns. Sample copy, free. Guidelines available.
- "To Test or Not to Drug Test." Article takes a look at the lessons learned from three schools that implemented random student drug testing.
- Sample dept/column: "Groupwork" discusses how engaging students in a timeline activity can help them focus on setting and achieving goals.

Rights and Payment

First rights. No payment. Provides 5 author's copies.

Editor's Comments

We are looking for information on evaluating programs, and fresh articles on prevention at the elementary level. Our readers look to us for the latest information on how to implement proven techniques that can be easily applied to their practice.

Student Leader

Oxendine Publishing
P.O. Box 14081
Gainesville, FL 32604-2097

Editor: Anna Campettelli

Description and Readership

Subtitled "The Forum for America's Emerging Leaders," this magazine helps high school and college students improve leadership skills and effectively run student organizations.
- **Audience:** High school and college students
- **Frequency:** 3 times each year
- **Distribution:** Schools; subscription
- **Circulation:** 130,000
- **Website:** www.studentleader.com

Freelance Potential

10% written by nonstaff writers. Publishes 10 freelance submissions yearly; 50% by unpublished writers, 80% by authors who are new to the magazine. Receives 5 queries monthly.

Submissions

Query only. Accepts photocopies, computer printouts, email submissions to info@studentleader.com, and simultaneous submissions. Availability of artwork improves chance of acceptance. SASE. Responds in 6 weeks.

Articles: 1,000 words. Informational articles. Topics include organizational management, service projects, fund-raising, student motivation, interpersonal skills, promoting special events, editorial standards, communication, and volunteerism.

Depts/columns: 250 words. Short updates and reports on college activities.

Artwork: Color prints and 35mm slides.

Sample Issue

32 pages (50% advertising): 8 articles; 1 dept/column. Sample copy, $3.50 with 9x12 SASE ($1.07 postage). Guidelines and editorial calendar available.
- "Young at Heart." Article profiles a 57-year-old college student who assumed leadership of the Associated Students Union at Contra Costa College.
- "Mental Fitness." Article offers advice for dealing with the stress faced by student leaders.

Rights and Payment

All rights. All material, payment rate varies. Pays on publication. Provides 1 contributor's copy.

Editor's Comments

We want positive, practical articles that student leaders can use in their work. Relevant topics include fund-raising, organizing students, and building relationships with school administrators and the media.

Student Leadership

P.O. Box 7895
6400 Schroeder Road
Madison, WI 53707-7895

Editorial Assistant: Shelley Soceka

Description and Readership
Christian college students who participate in and lead intervarsity student fellowship groups find articles, stories, and poems that address Christian lifetstyle issues in this magazine.
- **Audience:** 18+ years
- **Frequency:** 3 times each year
- **Distribution:** 95% controlled; 5% subscription
- **Circulation:** 10,000
- **Website:** www.ivcf.org/slj.

Freelance Potential
98% written by nonstaff writers. Publishes 3 freelance submissions yearly; 85% by unpublished writers, 5% by authors who are new to the magazine. Receives 8 unsolicited mss monthly.

Submissions
Send complete ms. Accepts photocopies, computer printouts, and simultaneous submissions if identified. Availability of artwork improves chance of acceptance. SASE. Responds in 6 months.
Articles: Word length varies. Informational, self-help, and how-to articles; and personal experience pieces. Topics include campus life, ministry, religion, leadership, student outreach programs, dating, relationships, popular culture, college, racial reconciliation, careers, and social issues.
Depts/columns: Word length varies. Trends and cultural observations, ideas and notes from chapters, and fellowship strategies.
Other: Poetry, no line limits.

Sample Issue
32 pages (no advertising): 3 articles; 1 story; 4 depts/columns. Sample copy, $4 with 9x12 SASE ($1.25 postage). Guidelines and theme list available.
- "Busy Sickness." Article describes a college student's struggle to resist piling on too many responsibilities.
- "The Medical Missionary." Story features a young man who struggles with how to best help his friend.
- Sample dept/column: "Spotlight" offers an eclectic mix of campus thoughts and trends.

Rights and Payment
First rights. Written material, $50–$100. Pays on acceptance. Provides 2 contributor's copies.

Editor's Comments
We are looking for quality poetry that reflects honest spiritual growth and tension, yet steers clear of preachiness.

Suburban Parent

Middlesex Publications
850 Route 1
North Brunswick, NJ 08902

Editor: Melodie Dhondt

Description and Readership
Timely articles on all aspects of parenting, reports on upcoming regional events and activities, and reviews of local resources for central New Jersey are included in this tabloid newspaper.
- **Audience:** Parents
- **Frequency:** Monthly
- **Distribution:** 96% controlled; 4% other
- **Circulation:** 78,000
- **Website:** www.njparentweb.com

Freelance Potential
80% written by nonstaff writers. Publishes 12 freelance submissions yearly; 20% by unpublished writers, 40% by authors who are new to the magazine. Receives 60 queries monthly.

Submissions
Query with writing samples. Accepts photocopies, computer printouts, and simultaneous submissions if identified. SASE. Responds in 2–8 weeks.
Articles: 700–1,000 words. Informational and how-to articles. Topics include parenting, family issues, cultural events, pregnancy, childbirth, sports, careers, financial concerns, and dining and media reviews.
Artwork: B/W or color prints.
Other: Submit seasonal material 4 months in advance.

Sample Issue
30 pages (60% advertising): 9 articles; 5 depts/columns; 1 calendar of events. Sample copy, free with 9x12 SASE. Writers' guidelines and editorial calendar available.
- "Opening Day Blues." Article offers suggestions for an easy transition into life at summer camp.
- "Avoiding Seasonal Allergies." Article reports on ways to reduce the potential for allergies.
- Sample dept/column: "Just for Fun" includes reviews of cool new clothes and accessories.

Rights and Payment
Rights policy varies. Articles, $30. Artwork, payment rate varies. Pays on acceptance. Provides 1+ contributor's copies.

Editor's Comments
Writers who are familiar with the offerings of New Jersey are needed for articles on topics of interest to parents and their families. Material that is specific to our region, yet tied to national concerns, will be considered by our editorial staff.

SuperScience

Scholastic Inc.
555 Broadway
New York, NY 10012-3999

Editor: Nancy Honovich

Description and Readership
Published by Scholastic, this classroom resource magazine helps teach science concepts through clearly presented articles and hands-on activities and experiments. Each issue includes a teachers' guide with cross-curriculum tie-ins.
- **Audience:** Classrooms, grades 3–6
- **Frequency:** 8 times each year
- **Distribution:** 100% schools
- **Circulation:** 250,000
- **Website:** www.scholastic.com/superscience

Freelance Potential
75% written by nonstaff writers. Of the freelance submissions published yearly, 50% are by authors who are new to the magazine. Receives 1 query monthly.

Submissions
Query with résumé and clips. No unsolicited mss. Accepts photocopies. SASE. Response time varies.
Articles: 300–1,000 words. Informational and how-to articles; personal experience pieces; profiles; and interviews. Topics include earth, physical, and life science; health; technology; chemistry; nature; and the environment.
Depts/columns: Word length varies. Science news.
Artwork: 8x10 B/W or color prints. Line art.
Other: Puzzles and activities.

Sample Issue
16 pages (no advertising): 2 articles; 1 story; 3 activities; 1 puzzle. Sample copy, free with 9x12 SASE. Guidelines and editorial calendar available.
- "Dinner Time!" Informative article discusses how various animals digest their food.
- "Mmmm . . . Chocolate!" Article reports on what it takes to transform a cacao bean into a sweet treat.
- Sample dept/column: "Hands On" provides an easy-to-do test for determining how cocoa butter affects chocolate.

Rights and Payment
First rights. Articles, $75–$600. Other material, payment rate varies. Pays on publication. Provides 2 contributor's copies.

Editor's Comments
We do not accept unsolicited manuscripts. If you have an idea you think we can use, query us. We like to see material for topics that excite young students, such as special effects, tornadoes, the solar system, glaciers, and natural hazards.

Surfing

Suite C
950 Calle Amanecer
San Clemente, CA 92673

Editor: Evan Slater

Description and Readership
Experienced young adult and adult surfers are the primary audience for this magazine. It offers articles that help readers improve their surfing skills, as well as features that portray the surfing lifestyle. Most of its readers are male.
- **Audience:** YA–Adult
- **Frequency:** Monthly
- **Distribution:** Newsstand; subscription
- **Circulation:** 105,000
- **Website:** www.surfingthemag.com

Freelance Potential
35% written by nonstaff writers. Publishes 15 freelance submissions yearly; 50% by unpublished writers. Receives 6 unsolicited mss monthly.

Submissions
Query or send complete ms. Accepts computer printouts, Macintosh disk submissions (Quark XPress or Microsoft Word), and simultaneous submissions if identified. SASE. Responds in 1 month.
Articles: 2,000–3,000 words. Informational and how-to articles; profiles; and interviews. Topics include surfing destinations, techniques, equipment, surfing personalities, fashion, nature, the environment, and music.
Depts/columns: 35–500 words. New product information and opinion pieces.
Artwork: Color prints.

Sample Issue
160 pages: 3 articles; 10 depts/columns. Sample copy, $3.99 at newsstands. Guidelines available.
- "Shark Myths." Article dispels myths and presents facts about shark behavior in the wake of recent shark attacks off the coast of Florida.
- "Ponto Beach Development Update." Reports on surfers' concerns regarding the development of a section of the California coastline.

Rights and Payment
One-time rights. Written material, $.10–$.25 per word. Pays on publication. Provides 2 contributor's copies.

Editor's Comments
We look for articles that focus on surfing from the viewpoint of the surfer and present unusual experiences to our readers. News from the world of surfing and reports on surfing locations are needed, as well as lifestyle pieces.

SW Florida Parent & Child

2442 Dr. Martin Luther King, Jr. Boulevard
Fort Myers, FL 33901

Editor: Connie Ramos-Williams

Description and Readership
This magazine offers parents in southwest Florida local information as well as general interest articles and personal experience essays. It also includes reviews and activities in its editorial mix.
- **Audience:** Parents
- **Frequency:** Monthly
- **Distribution:** 100% controlled
- **Circulation:** 25,000
- **Website:** www.swflparentchild.com

Freelance Potential
50% written by nonstaff writers. Publishes 40–50 free-lance submissions yearly; 5% by unpublished writers, 10% by authors who are new to the magazine. Receives 25 queries and unsolicited mss monthly.

Submissions
Query or send complete ms. Prefers email submissions to parentchild@earthlink.net. Accepts photo-copies and computer printouts. SASE. Response time varies.
Articles: Word length varies. Informational articles; profiles; and personal experience pieces. Topics include family issues, parenting, education, travel, sports, health, fitness, computers, and social and regional issues.
Depts/columns: Word length varies. Dining, travel, parenting, education, and nutrition.

Sample Issue
56 pages (50% advertising): 3 articles; 14 depts/columns. Guidelines available.
- "Egg Hunters." Humorous personal experience essay about a family's first Easter egg hunt.
- "Families on the Move" is a special section that offers tips about moving.
- Sample dept/column: "A Dad's View" tells of one dad's view of coaching and kids' sports.

Rights and Payment
All rights. Written material, $25–$40. Pays on publication.

Editor's Comments
We seek to provide a community resource for local parents that is informative and entertaining. Send us tips on local family-friendly establishments or an informative article on child-rearing, family issues, or education. Please note that we prefer email submissions over fax or hard copy.

Swimming World and Junior Swimmer

Suite 200
90 Bell Rock Plaza
Sedona, AZ 86351

Editor-in-Chief: Dr. Phillip Whitten

Description and Readership
Focusing on competitive swimming, this magazine includes inspirational stories, training and technique tips, interviews, profiles, swim drills, medical advice, and articles on nutrition and fitness. Each issue also includes a section by and for kids.
- **Audience:** All ages
- **Frequency:** Monthly
- **Distribution:** 90% subscription; 10% newsstand
- **Circulation:** 59,000
- **Website:** www.swiminfo.com

Freelance Potential
75% written by nonstaff writers. Publishes 5–10 free-lance submissions yearly; 5% by unpublished writers, 25% by new authors. Receives 16+ queries monthly.

Submissions
Query. Accepts photocopies, disk submissions (WordPerfect 3.1), and email submissions to philw@swimmingworld.com. SASE. Responds in 2 months.
Articles: 500–3,500 words. Informational and how-to articles; profiles; and personal experience pieces. Topics include swimming, training, competition, medical advice, swim drills, nutrition, dryland exercise, exercise physiology, and fitness.
Depts/columns: 500–750 words. Swimming news, new product reviews, and nutrition advice.
Artwork: Color prints and transparencies. Line art.
Other: Activities, games, and jokes. Submit seasonal material 1–2 months in advance.

Sample Issue
62 pages (30% advertising): 3 articles; 10 depts/columns. Sample copy, $4.50 with 9x12 SASE ($1.80 postage). Writers' guidelines available.
- "Color NCAAs Orange and Blue." Article takes a look at the teams competing in the NCAA championship and who is favored to win.
- Sample dept/column: "Swim Parent" discusses what parents need to know about the recruiting process and shares the experiences of three families.

Rights and Payment
All rights. Written material, $.12 per word. Artwork, payment rate varies. Pays on publication. Provides 2–5 contributor's copies.

Editor's Comments
We look for articles that will inform, instruct, and inspire our readers who love the sport of swimming.

Synapse

25 Beacon Street
Boston, MA 02108

Editor

Description and Readership
Appearing both online and in print, this thematic magazine features articles, essays, poetry, and artwork by teens who are part of the youth organization of the Unitarian Universalist Association.
- **Audience:** 14–21 years
- **Frequency:** 3 times each year online/1 time print
- **Distribution:** 100% subscription
- **Circulation:** 2,500
- **Website:** www.uua.org/yruu/synapse

Freelance Potential
85% written by nonstaff writers. Of the freelance submissions published yearly, 90% are by unpublished writers.

Submissions
Send complete ms with résumé. Accepts disk submissions (Quark) and email submissions to YRUU@uua.org. Responds in 1 month.
Articles: Word length varies. Informational articles and personal experience and opinion pieces. Topics include current events, social issues, popular culture, regional events, youth programs, history, and ethnic and multicultural issues.
Depts/columns: Word length varies. Readings by Unitarian Universalist youth, sermons, homilies, religious and spiritual reflections, and social action news.
Other: Puzzles, activities, games, and jokes related to Unitarian Universalism.

Sample Issue
40 pages (7% advertising): 7 articles; 10 depts/columns; 1 event calendar. Sample copy and guidelines available at website.
- "What the SWAT." Article discusses the lack of sexual orientation in non-discrimination policies and how to get involved in making a change.
- "Flashback: A Call to Action." Article takes a look at how sexual education was presented in schools in the past and a new curriculum being developed.
- Sample dept/column: "Learn About" discusses the history of the Unitarian Universalist Association.

Rights and Payment
All rights. No payment.

Editor's Comments
We are looking for writers to share their creativity with the world of Young Religious Unitarian Universalists. Check our website for our next upcoming theme.

Syracuse Parent

5910 Firestone Drive
Syracuse, NY 13206

Editor: Brittany Jared

Description and Readership
Highlighting local events and resources, and including general interest articles on parenting issues, this tabloid is distributed to New York families.
- **Audience:** Parents
- **Frequency:** Monthly
- **Distribution:** 70% controlled; 20% schools; 10% subscription
- **Circulation:** 22,500
- **Website:** www.syracuseparent.com

Freelance Potential
40% written by nonstaff writers. Publishes 15 freelance submissions yearly; 25% by unpublished writers, 10% by authors who are new to the magazine. Receives 8 queries monthly.

Submissions
Query. Accepts photocopies and computer printouts. SASE. Responds in 4–6 weeks.
Articles: 800–1,000 words. Informational and how-to articles; personal experience and practical applications pieces; profiles; interviews; and humor. Topics include parenting, family issues, animals, pets, education, health, current events, regional news, social issues, nature, the environment, computers, music, travel, and sports.
Depts/columns: Staff written.
Other: Submit seasonal and holiday material 3–4 months in advance.

Sample Issue
22 pages (50% advertising): 9 articles; 8 depts/columns. Sample copy, guidelines, and editorial calendar, $1 with 9x12 SASE. Guidelines available.
- "2nd Annual Duck Race." Report on local event to raise funds for a program to improve interracial relationships among diverse individuals.
- "Rest Stop, Road Trip Theme for Taste of Cazenovia." Article highlights an upcoming community event and fundraiser.
- Sample dept/column: "@ Your Library" discusses New York State's Summer Reading Program for students in elementary grades through high school.

Rights and Payment
First rights. Articles, $25–$30. Pays on publication.

Editor's Comments
Parenting is all about retaining your sense of humor; share your humor with us.

Take Five Plus

The General Council of the Assemblies of God
1445 North Boonville Avenue
Springfield, MO 65802-1894

Editor: Carey Huffman

Description and Readership
This religious magazine for teens seeks to strengthen a connection to God by providing daily devotionals based on scripture readings. Each devotional contains an anecdote that helps teens relate to the subject matter.
- **Audience:** 12–19 years
- **Frequency:** Quarterly
- **Distribution:** 90% religious instruction;
  10% subscription
- **Circulation:** 25,000
- **Website:** www.radiantlife.org

Freelance Potential
80% written by nonstaff writers. Of the freelance submissions published yearly; 5% are by unpublished writers, 10% are by authors who are new to the magazine.

Submissions
All material is assigned. Send letter of introduction and résumé, church background, and clips or writing samples. Accepts photocopies and computer printouts. SASE. Responds in 3 months.
Articles: 200–235 words. Daily devotionals based on scripture readings.
Artwork: Accepts material from teenagers only. 8x10 B/W prints and 35 mm color slides. 8x10 or smaller color line art.
Other: Poetry by teens, to 20 lines.

Sample Issue
128 pages (no advertising): 90 devotionals; 3 poems.
Guidelines and sample devotional available on request for sample assignment.
- "Where the Green Is." Devotional based on Jeremiah that likens nature to our relationship with God.
- "What Is Worship?" Devotional identifies the meaning of Christian worship.

Rights and Payment
First rights. Written material, $.05 per word. Artwork, payment rate varies. Pays on publication. Provides 2 contributor's copies.

Editor's Comments
If you are interested in writing for us, send us a letter of introduction and request writers' guidelines and a sample assignment. We are looking for devotionals with connections to contemporary issues that teens face.

Tar Heel Junior Historian

North Carolina Museum of History
4650 Mail Service Center
Raleigh, NC 27699-4650

Editor: Doris McLean Bates

Description and Readership
North Carolina children in grades four, eight, and eleven learn about the state's geography, history, and government in *Tar Heel Junior Historian*. Photographs and illustrations that accompany each article, as well as related activities, enhance the learning experience.
- **Audience:** 9–18 years
- **Frequency:** Twice each year
- **Distribution:** 100% North Carolina schools
- **Circulation:** 9,000
- **Website:** http://ncmuseumofhistory.org

Freelance Potential
50% written by nonstaff writers. Publishes 15 freelance submissions yearly; 40% by unpublished writers, 20% by authors who are new to the magazine.

Submissions
Query. No unsolicited mss. SASE. Response times vary.
Articles: 700–1,000 words. Informational articles; profiles; interviews; and personal experience pieces. Topics include regional history and social, multicultural, and ethnic issues.
Fiction: Word lengths vary. Genres include historical, ethnic, and multicultural fiction; folktales; and folklore.
Artwork: B/W and color prints or transparencies. Line art.
Other: Puzzles, activities, and word games.

Sample Issue
38 pages (no advertising): 10 articles; 3 activities.
Sample copy, $4 with 9x12 SASE ($2 postage).
Guidelines and theme list available.
- "Assigned Places." Article explains segregation as it existed in North Carolina during the 1920s.
- "Radio Begins." Article discusses the invention of the radio and explores how radio broadcasting developed during the 1920s.
- "A New Woman Emerges." Article takes a look at the significant changes that occurred for women in politics, the home, the workplace, and in education during the 1920s.

Rights and Payment
All rights. No payment. Provides 10 author's copies.

Editor's Comments
Themes for our issues are determined two to three years in advance. You may query us if you are a scholar of North Carolina history, geography, or government.

Teacher Librarian

15200 NBN Way
Blue Ridge Summit, PA 17214

Managing Editor: Kim Tabor

Description and Readership
Founded in 1973, this magazine keeps school library professionals up-to-date with the latest information on library services available to children and young adults.
- **Audience:** Professional librarians and educators
- **Frequency:** 5 times each year
- **Distribution:** 100% subscription
- **Circulation:** 10,000
- **Website:** www.teacherlibrarian.com

Freelance Potential
60% written by nonstaff writers. Publishes 10 freelance submissions yearly; 25% by unpublished writers, 50% by authors who are new to the magazine. Receives 6 queries and unsolicited mss monthly.

Submissions
Query or send complete ms with résumé, abstract, and bibliography. Accepts photocopies, computer printouts, disk submissions, and email to editor@ teacherlibrarian.com. SASE. Responds in 2 months.
Articles: 2,000+ words. Informational and analytical articles and profiles. Topics include library programming issues, library management, audio/visual materials, cooperative teaching, and young adult services.
Depts/columns: Staff written.

Sample Issue
64 pages (20% advertising): 12 articles; 13 depts/columns; 14 book reviews. Writers' guidelines and editorial calendar available.
- "State Funded Informational Databases: You May Lose Them Even if You Visit Them." Article discusses ways to help prevent state funding from being withdrawn.
- "Money, Money, Money: Taking the Pain out of Grant Writing." Article offers tips and tricks for finding, writing, and obtaining grants for K–12 educators.
- "Using Technology to Facilitate Assessment of Library Education." Article discusses using technology to improve data collection and analysis in the assessment process.

Rights and Payment
All rights. Written material, $100. Pays on publication. Provides 2 contributor's copies.

Editor's Comments
We look for original articles on topics related to library services for children. In addition to charts, figures and tables, we welcome cartoons and photos.

Teacher Magazine

Editorial Projects in Education
Suite 100
6935 Arlington Road
Bethesda, MD 20814

Senior Editor: Mark Toner

Description and Readership
This publication showcases successful educational programs around the country while also offering commentary, news, and book reviews. *Teacher Magazine* targets educators working in kindergarten through high school classrooms.
- **Audience:** Teachers
- **Frequency:** 6 times each year
- **Distribution:** Subscription; controlled
- **Circulation:** 120,000
- **Website:** www.teachermagazine.org

Freelance Potential
40% written by nonstaff writers. Publishes 35–40 freelance submissions yearly; 80% by unpublished writers, 20% by authors who are new to the magazine. Receives 40 unsolicited mss monthly.

Submissions
Send complete ms. Accepts computer printouts. SASE. Responds in 3 months.
Articles: To 3,000 words. Educational articles; commentary; opinion pieces; and personal experience pieces. Topics include K–12 education, professional development, classroom teaching, literacy, technology, and bilingual education.
Depts/columns: 1,000–1,250 words. "Viewpoints" features opinion pieces on precollegiate education. "First Person" offers school-related personal experiences.

Sample Issue
72 pages: 6 articles; 12 depts/columns. Sample copy, $4. Guidelines available.
- "What They Did on Their Summer Vacation." Article tells how some teachers take advantage of their summer breaks to take on new challenges and slip into new identities.
- Sample dept/column: "Kids Books" reviews books on travel, adolescent strength, and whales.

Rights and Payment
First rights. Written material, payment rate varies. Pays on publication. Provides 3 contributor's copies.

Editor's Comments
While most of our magazine is written by our staff writers, we will consider exceptionally well-written articles that describe innovative educational ideas. Our opinion pieces and columns are also open to freelance writers.

Teachers & Writers

7th Floor
5 Union Square West
New York, NY 10003-3306

Publication Director: Christopher Edgar

Description and Readership
This magazine offers practical articles on ideas and strategies for teaching the art of writing in grades kindergarten through twelve.
- **Audience:** Teachers
- **Frequency:** 5 times each year
- **Distribution:** 100% subscription
- **Circulation:** 3,000
- **Website:** www.twc.org

Freelance Potential
70% written by nonstaff writers. Publishes 25 freelance submissions yearly; 5% by unpublished writers, 50% by authors who are new to the magazine. Receives 10 unsolicited mss monthly.

Submissions
Send complete ms. Accepts photocopies, computer printouts, and simultaneous submissions if identified. No email submissions. SASE. Response time varies.
Articles: 750–5,000 words. Practical and theoretical articles featuring innovative teaching ideas; and fresh approaches to familiar teaching methods. Topics include teaching writing in conjunction with the visual arts; teaching oral history; and teaching writing to senior citizens. Also publishes translations.
Depts/columns: Word length varies. Information on events and book reviews.
Other: Submit seasonal material 6 months in advance.

Sample Issue
28 pages (no advertising): 3 articles; 2 depts/columns. Sample copy, $4. Guidelines available.
- "Fur on the Whale." Article discusses the purpose of writing workshops.
- "The Literary Anatomy." Article takes a look at the history of the essay genre and the evolution of the research essay.
- Sample dept/column: "Passwords" explores the teachings of Wallace Stevens.

Rights and Payment
First serial rights. Written material, $20 per printed column. Pays on publication. Provides 10 copies.

Editor's Comments
Our readers turn to us for the latest information on new teaching methods. Send us something practical and theoretical. Keep in mind that our readers tend to be bright, motivated, creative teachers.

Teaching PreK–8

40 Richards Avenue
Norwalk, CT 06854

Editorial Director: Patricia Broderick

Description and Readership
Published for elementary and middle-grade teachers, this magazine offers teaching strategies, activities, and classroom projects.
- **Audience:** Teachers, pre-K–grade 8
- **Frequency:** 8 times each year
- **Distribution:** 100% subscription
- **Circulation:** 125,000
- **Website:** www.teachingk-8.com

Freelance Potential
80% written by nonstaff writers. Publishes 30–32 freelance submissions yearly; 95–98% by unpublished writers, 95% by authors who are new to the magazine. Receives 2,000 unsolicited mss monthly.

Submissions
Send complete ms. Accepts photocopies and computer printouts. No simultaneous submissions. SASE. Responds in 1 month.
Articles: To 1,000 words. Informational and how-to articles; and personal experience pieces. Topics include gifted and special education, curriculum development, classroom management, character education, and teaching methods, math, social studies, science, and language arts.
Depts/columns: Staff written.
Artwork: Color prints. No digital images.

Sample Issue
82 pages (50% advertising): 11 articles; 20 depts/columns. Sample copy, $4.50 with 9x12 SASE (10 first-class stamps). Guidelines and theme list available.
- "Mysteries of the Misunderstood." Profile of children's book author and illustrator Janell Cannon.
- "A Writer's Bag of Tricks." Article provides several simple strategies for great writing ideas.

Rights and Payment
All North American serial rights. Written material, $20–$50. Artwork, payment rate varies. Pays on publication. Provides 2 contributor's copies.

Editor's Comments
We like to see material detailing specific teaching strategies for elementary and middle-grade subjects. Send us solid, fact-based articles with fresh ideas that can be applied in today's diverse and varied classrooms. Please make sure that your ideas have been tested and successfully used in the classroom.

Teachers Interaction

Concordia Publishing House
3558 South Jefferson Avenue
St. Louis, MO 63118-3698

Editor: Thomas A. Nummela

Description and Readership
This resourceful tool for Sunday school teachers and administrators offers teaching strategies and ideas for spreading the glory of God's Word with children in preschool through sixth grade.
- **Audience:** Sunday school teachers
- **Frequency:** Quarterly
- **Distribution:** 70% subscription; 30% churches
- **Circulation:** 12,000
- **Website:** www.cph.org

Freelance Potential
95% written by nonstaff writers. Publishes 20 freelance submissions yearly; 10% by unpublished writers, 20% by authors who are new to the magazine. Receives 4 unsolicited mss monthly.

Submissions
Query or send complete ms; include Social Security number. Prefers email submissions to tom.nummela@cph.org. Accepts photocopies and computer printouts. SASE. Responds in 3 months.
Articles: To 1,100 words. How-to articles and personal experience pieces. Topics include education, theology, teaching methods, and child development.
Depts/columns: 400 words. Mission stories, grade-specific teaching tips, and classroom ideas.
Other: Practical ideas for teachers, 100–200 words. Submit seasonal material 10 months in advance.

Sample Issue
30 pages (no advertising): 5 articles; 10 depts/columns. Sample copy, $4.99. Guidelines available.
- "Scheduling Considerations." Article discusses the consequences of having a worship service the same time as Sunday school.
- "Sunday Morning Struggles." Article reports on congregations who have tried adding another service to accommodate the growing worship attendance.
- Sample dept/column: "Parents as Teachers" discusses the importance of forgiveness for sins.

Rights and Payment
All rights. Articles, $55–$110. "The Teacher's Toolbox," $20–$40. Pays on publication. Provides 1 contributor's copy.

Editor's Comments
We have a constant need for practical, original, and creative ideas that our readers can use in class, such as crafts, object lessons, games, and puppet scripts.

Teachers of Vision

Christian Educators Association International
P.O. Box 41300
Pasadena, CA 91114

Contributing Editor: Judy Turpen

Description and Readership
Educational articles that inspire and provide practical ideas that Christian educators can use in the classroom can be found in this publication.
- **Audience:** Christian teachers
- **Frequency:** 6 times each year
- **Distribution:** 90% controlled; 10% newsstand
- **Circulation:** 10,000
- **Website:** www.ceai.org

Freelance Potential
70% written by nonstaff writers. Publishes 25 freelance submissions yearly; 5% by unpublished writers, 80% by new authors. Receives 4–5 mss monthly.

Submissions
Send complete ms with brief biography. Prefers email submissions to judy@ceai.org (RFT files). Accepts letter-quality computer printouts and disk submissions (RTF files or Microsoft Word) with hard copy. SASE. Responds in 2–3 months.
Articles: 400–1,000 words. How-to articles, personal experience pieces, and documented reports, 800–1,000 words. Topics include issues related to education, educational philosophy, and methodology. Interviews with noted Christian educators, 500–800. Teaching techniques, news, and special events, 400–500 words.
Depts/columns: 100–200 words. Reviews of books, videos, curricula, games, and other curricula resources for K–12 teachers.
Other: Submit seasonal material 4 months in advance.

Sample Issue
16 pages (1% advertising): 7 articles; 6 depts/columns. Sample copy, free with 9x12 SASE (5 first-class stamps). Guidelines available.
- "I Search, I Understand." Article discusses a project where students search to learn about a subject.
- "Getting Creative About Creativity." Article takes a look at how to be a more creative teacher.
- Sample dept/column: "In the School of Prayer" discusses turning to God for creative ideas.

Rights and Payment
First and electronic rights. Articles, $20–$40. Reviews, $5. Pays on publication. Provides 3 copies.

Editor's Comments
We are looking for more information on secondary education. Material must be up-to-date.

Teaching Elementary Physical Education

Human Kinetics Publishers
P.O. Box 5076
Champaign, IL 61825-5076

Senior Editor: Steve Stork

Description and Readership
Tips, reviews, and the latest resources for physical education teachers can be found in this magazine. It strives to present material that will allow educators to create fun programs that will get kids moving.
- **Audience:** Physical education teachers
- **Frequency:** 6 times each year
- **Distribution:** 95% subscription; 5% other
- **Circulation:** 4,000+
- **Website:** www.humankinetics.com

Freelance Potential
100% written by nonstaff writers. Publishes 78 freelance submissions yearly; 20% by unpublished writers, 30% by authors who are new to the magazine. Receives 8 unsolicited mss monthly.

Submissions
Query with clips; or send complete ms. Accepts photocopies, and computer printouts. SASE. Responds in 1–4 weeks.
Articles: 2–12 double-spaced pages. Informational, how-to, personal experience, and self-help articles. Topics include health, fitness, physical education, liability, accountability, motivation, and public relations.
Depts/columns: 200–500 words. Early childhood issues, book reviews, and technology tips.

Sample Issue
32 pages (25% advertising): 2 articles; 12 depts/columns. Sample copy, $4 with 9x12 SASE. Guidelines available.
- "Where Are Our Elementary School Health and Physical Education Programs?" Article discusses the national guidelines and future directions for elementary school physical education.
- "Sport for All." Article describes a new program of physical activity and sports readiness activities for preschool, elementary, and middle school students.
- Sample dept/column: "Technology Tips" discusses the benefits of using a handheld computer.

Rights and Payment
First or one-time rights. No payment. Provides 1 contributor's copy.

Editor's Comments
We are looking for specific ideas for activities in physical education lessons. Material should be fresh and practical. Please note that we do not need theoretical articles by university professionals.

Teaching Theatre

2343 Auburn Avenue
Cincinnati, OH 45219

Editor: James Palmarini

Description and Readership
Articles covering topics related to teaching theatre arts to middle and high school students can be found in this magazine. Each issue features a mix of articles on curriculum ideas, play suggestions, advanced work on acting, directing, and professional development.
- **Audience:** Theatre teachers
- **Frequency:** Quarterly
- **Distribution:** 80% controlled; 20% other
- **Circulation:** 4,500
- **Website:** www.edta.org

Freelance Potential
60% written by nonstaff writers. Publishes 10–14 freelance submissions yearly; 20% by unpublished writers, 50% by authors who are new to the magazine. Receives 5 queries monthly.

Submissions
Query with outline. Accepts photocopies and computer printouts. SASE. Responds in 1 month.
Articles: 1,000–3,000 words. Informational articles and personal experience pieces. Topics include theatre education, the arts, and curriculum materials.
Depts/columns: Word lengths vary. "Promptbook" features classroom exercises, ideas, technical advice, and textbook or play suggestions.

Sample Issue
32 pages (no advertising): 3 articles; 2 depts/columns. Sample copy, $2 with 9x12 SASE ($2 postage). Guidelines available.
- "Plays on Video for You and Your Class." Article offers a list of plays on video that will help students get a better understanding of what theatre is and how it works.
- "Stories of Life and Death." Article takes a look at how a playwright and some students embarked on a project to make theatre from biology.
- Sample dept/column: "News & Notes" takes a look at what is happening in the world of theatre, including an Anniversary Homecoming Convention, and the President's push for an increase to the NEA.

Rights and Payment
One time rights. Written material, payment rate varies. Pays on publication. Provides 5 contributor's copies.

Editor's Comments
We look for informative and creative material for our readers, who are experienced and skilled educators.

Teach Kids!

P.O. Box 348
Warrenton, MO 63383-0348

Editor: Elsie Lippy

Description and Readership

Formerly listed as *Evangelizing Today's Child*, this publication offers articles and ideas for Christian educators to aid them in teaching children ages 4–11.
- **Audience:** Christian educators
- **Frequency:** 6 times each year
- **Distribution:** 75% subscription; 25% other
- **Circulation:** 12,000
- **Website:** www.teachkidsmag.com

Freelance Potential

75% written by nonstaff writers. Publishes 50 freelance submissions yearly; 5% by unpublished writers, 20% by authors who are new to the magazine. Receives 8–9 queries and unsolicited mss monthly.

Submissions

Query with outline; or send complete ms. Accepts photocopies, computer printouts, or email submissions to editor@teachkidsmag.com. SASE. Responds to queries in 1 month, to mss in 2 months.
Articles: 800–900 words. How-to, factual, and idea pieces. Topics include Christian education, religion, teaching techniques, and understanding children.
Fiction: 800–900 words for stories written at the third- and fourth-grade level. Features contemporary stories with scriptural solutions to problems faced by children.
Depts/columns: "Easy Ideas" offers creative teaching ideas teachers can use with children ages 4–11, 200–300 words.

Sample Issue

56 pages (25% advertising): 4 articles; 10 depts/columns; 6 teaching tools; 6 reproducibles. Sample copy, $3. Guidelines available with SASE.
- "Can You Hear Me Now?" Article offers ways to help children hear the meaning of God's Word and respond appropriately.
- Sample dept/column: "Add Some Seasoning" offers instructions for making a Mother's Day craft.

Rights and Payment

All, first, one-time, or electronic rights. Written material, payment rates vary. Pays within 60 days of acceptance. Provides 1 contributor's copy.

Editor's Comments

We need hands-on creative preschool teaching ideas for children ages 4–5 that are theme related, as well as creative pieces for our "Easy Ideas" department.

Tech Directions

Prakken Publications
832 Phoenix Drive
P.O. Box 8623
Ann Arbor, MI 48107

Managing Editor: Susanne Peckham

Description and Readership

Established in 1941, this magazine features articles that focus on technology that can be applied to classroom teaching. It is read by professionals that work in vocational, industrial, and technological schools.
- **Audience:** Teachers and administrators
- **Frequency:** 10 times each year
- **Distribution:** 98% controlled; 2% subscription
- **Circulation:** 43,000
- **Website:** www.techdirections.com

Freelance Potential

80% written by nonstaff writers. Publishes 40 freelance submissions yearly; 50% by unpublished writers, 50% by authors who are new to the magazine. Receives 16 unsolicited mss monthly.

Submissions

Query or send complete ms. Accepts photocopies, computer printouts, and Macintosh compatible email to susanne@techdirections.com. SASE. Responds to queries in 1 week, to mss in 1 month.
Articles: To 3,000 words. Informational and how-to articles; and new product information. Topics include vocational and technical career education, technology, electronics, graphics, industrial arts, manufacturing, and computers.
Depts/columns: Word lengths vary. Legislative news, tool reviews, and new product information.

Sample Issue

52 pages (40% advertising): 6 articles; 8 depts/columns. Sample copy, $5 with 9x12 SASE (2 first-class stamps). Writers' guidelines and editorial calendar available.
- "Sparking Student Interest–Fire as Technology." Article describes a classroom activity that deals with fire production as an aspect of technology.
- "Heavy Truck Driver." Article offers information about careers for truck drivers.
- Sample dept/column: "Technology Today" takes a look at different types of artificial hearts.

Rights and Payment

All rights. Articles, $50 for first page, $25 for each additional page. Pays on publication. Depts/columns, to $25. Provides 3 contributor's copies.

Editor's Comments

We need more hands-on project articles for technology and applied science education.

Techniques

Connecting Education and Careers

1410 King Street
Alexandria, VA 22314

Editor: Susan Reese

Description and Readership
People involved in the field of technical education read this magazine for articles that portray well-run career and technical programs around the country. It also offers teaching tips and resources, updates on legislation that affects this field, and news from the Association for Career and Technical Education.
- **Audience:** Educators
- **Frequency:** 8 times each year
- **Distribution:** 80% membership; 15% schools; 5% subscription
- **Circulation:** 35,000
- **Website:** www.acteonline.org

Freelance Potential
50% written by nonstaff writers. Publishes 10–20 freelance submissions yearly; 15% by unpublished writers, 30% by authors who are new to the magazine. Receives 8 unsolicited mss monthly.

Submissions
Query or send complete ms. Prefers email submissions to susan@printmanagementinc.com. Accepts photocopies, computer printouts, and disk submissions (Microsoft Word). SASE. Responds in 4 months.
Articles: To 2,000 words. Informational and how-to articles; profiles; and reviews. Topics include technology, careers, education, computers, college, current events, science, math, and social studies.
Depts/columns: 500–850 words. Organizational news, opinion pieces, and legislative updates.
Artwork: Color prints and transparencies. Line art.
Other: Submit material about the end of the school year in March.

Sample Issue
62 pages (30% advertising): 6 articles; 8 depts/columns. Writer's guidelines and theme list available at website.
- "Building a Culinary Arts Academy." Profiles the work of a family and consumer sciences teacher.
- Sample dept/column: "Information Technology Update" offers news of interest to career educators.

Rights and Payment
All and Internet rights. Articles, payment rate varies. Depts/columns, $500. Pays on publication.

Editor's Comments
Our departments and columns offer the best opportunities to writers who are new to us.

Technology & Learning

CMP Media, Inc.
600 Harrison Street
San Francisco, CA 94107

Managing Editor: Mark Smith

Description and Readership
The publication explores innovative ways to use technology to teach and inspire students. Its subscribers are education professionals working with students in kindergarten through grade 12.
- **Audience:** Education and technology coordinators
- **Frequency:** 11 times each year
- **Distribution:** 70% subscription; 30% newsstand
- **Circulation:** 85,000
- **Website:** www.techlearning.com

Freelance Potential
50–60% written by nonstaff writers. Publishes 44 freelance submissions yearly; 5% by authors who are new to the magazine. Receives 5–8 queries monthly.

Submissions
Query with outline and clips or writing samples. Accepts photocopies and computer printouts. SASE. Responds in 3 months.
Articles: 1,200–2,500 words. Informational and how-to articles. Topics include technology, education, research, teaching, and controversial issues in education and technology. Also publishes reviews of software used in education.
Depts/columns: To 600 words. Teaching ideas, technology primers, and news.
Other: Comics.

Sample Issue
68 pages (40% advertising): 12 articles; 2 depts/columns; 1 pull-out calendar. Sample copy, $3 with 9x12 SASE ($3 postage). Guidelines and editorial calendar available.
- "Shaping E-Learning Policy." Article examines how public schools are developing formal policies regarding online learning options.
- "Miracle Workers." Article tells how new technologies are helping students who have severe communication disorders.

Rights and Payment
First rights. Articles, $400–$600. Software reviews, $150. Depts/columns, payment rate varies. Pays on publication. Provides 1 contributor's copy.

Editor's Comments
We prefer material that will appeal to educators nationwide; don't send articles that have a specific local focus. You should have extensive classroom experience if you wish to write for us.

Teen

3000 Ocean Park Boulevard
Santa Monica, CA 90405

Editor: Jane Fort

Description and Readership
Stories of teens facing dramatic situations, updates on Hollywood's teen celebrities, and articles about boys, dating, health, and well-being are among the features that appear regularly in *Teen* magazine.
- **Audience:** 12–16 years
- **Frequency:** Quarterly
- **Distribution:** 100% newsstand
- **Circulation:** 650,000
- **Website:** www.teenmag.com

Freelance Potential
60% written by nonstaff writers. Of the freelance submissions published yearly, 5% are by authors who are new to the magazine. Receives 10 queries monthly.

Submissions
Query for nonfiction. Send complete ms for fiction. Accepts photocopies, computer printouts, and simultaneous submissions if identified. SASE. Responds in 2 months.
Articles: 800 words. Informational and how-to articles and personal experience pieces. Topics include relationships, beauty, fashion, music, popular culture, recreation, the arts, crafts, current events, and social issues.
Fiction: 1,000 words. Genres include romance and inspirational fiction.
Depts/columns: Word lengths vary. Advice.

Sample Issue
112 pages (10% advertising): 4 articles; 1 story; 32 depts/columns; 1 book excerpt; 2 quizzes. Sample copy, $3.99 at newsstands.
- "I Had Breast Cancer." Personal experience piece tells of a 17-year-old girl who discovered she had breast cancer.
- "Your Summer Sanity Survival Guide." Article offers suggestions for beating summer boredom.
- Sample dept/column: "Your Horror Stories" features readers' contributions that describe their most mortifying moments.

Rights and Payment
All rights. Written material, payment rates vary. Pays on publication. Provides 2 contributor's copies.

Editor's Comments
Rare is the article for teenage girls that tackles an original subject. We look instead for articles that approach a familiar topic in a fresh, innovative way.

Teenage Christian E-Magazine

P.O. Box 2227
Brentwood, TN 37024-2227

Editor: Ben Forrest

Description and Readership
This online Christian magazine for youth provides readers with entertaining articles and stories that are relevant to their devotion to Jesus and the teachings of the Bible.
- **Audience:** YA–Adult
- **Frequency:** Unavailable
- **Distribution:** 100% Internet
- **Hits per month:** Unavailable
- **Website:** www.teenagechristian.net

Freelance Potential
50% written by nonstaff writers. Publishes 30 freelance submissions yearly. Receives 4–6 queries and unsolicited mss monthly.

Submissions
Query or send complete ms. Accepts email submissions to teenagechristian@bellsouth.net. Response time varies.
Articles: 450–700 words. Informational articles, profiles, interviews, photo essays, and personal experience pieces. Topics include health, fitness, multicultural and ethnic issues, relationships, music, popular culture, religion, and social issues.
Depts/columns: Word lengths vary. Advice, entertainment, sports, and music.

Sample Issue
Guidelines available at website.
- "She's at the Top." Article profiles Tori Allen, the world's fastest woman speed climber.
- "A Storm, a Whisper." Story features a young girl who struggles with whether or not to tell an adult about her friend's alcohol abuse.
- Sample dept/column: "Missions" offers advice on how to share the Christian faith with friends.

Rights and Payment
All rights. Payment policy and rates vary. Contributor's copies available at website.

Editor's Comments
As of July 2005, we have ceased printing and become a web-only publication. We are looking for articles and stories that speak to our Christian youth audience. We publish material that helps guide and support them in their Bible study, mission, and spiritual growth. Topics of interest to our audience are famous people, real-life scenarios, entertainment, and sports.

Teen Graffiti

P.O. Box 452721
Garland, TX 75045-2721

Publisher: Sharon Jones-Scaife

Description and Readership

Produced by volunteers and interns of the nonprofit organization Teens Reaching Teens, this magazine seeks to offer tweens and teens useful and entertaining information about health, school, current events, and social issues.
- **Audience:** 12–19 years
- **Frequency:** 6 times each year
- **Distribution:** 100% subscription
- **Circulation:** Unavailable
- **Website:** www.teengraffiti.com

Freelance Potential

70% written by nonstaff writers. Publishes 30–40 freelance submissions yearly.

Submissions

Query or send complete ms. Prefers email submissions to publish@teengraffiti.com. Accepts photocopies and computer printouts. SASE. Response time varies.
Articles: 250 words. Informational articles; personal experience and opinion pieces; and essays. Topics include college, careers, current events, popular culture, health, and social issues.
Depts/columns: 100–200 words. Educational tips, advice, and resource information from teachers about English, reading, science, math, writing, and computers. Teen-to-teen advice and book, music, and movie reviews.
Artwork: B/W and color prints accepted from teens only.
Other: Poetry written by teens.

Sample Issue

22 pages (3% advertising): 1 article; 12 depts/columns; 4 poems. Sample copy, $2.75. Guidelines included with each issue.
- "A Successful School Year Starts Now." Article helps teens transition from summer vacation to school.
- Sample dept/column: "Keepin' It Real" warns teens about the dangers of meningococcal meningitis.
- Sample dept/column: "Advice" suggests that being confident can help students reach their potential.

Rights and Payment

One-time rights. No payment.

Editor's Comments

We accept submissions from teachers who are members of our council, and teenagers.

Teen Light

6118 Bend of River Road
Dunn, NC 28334

Publisher: Annette Dammer

Description and Readership

Teen Light is a Christian arts magazine written entirely by teens. Each issue showcases a variety of creative efforts, including short fiction, true-to-life stories, journal entries, poetry, photography, and opinion pieces. Available online and in print, it also serves as a resource guide to publishing opportunities, artist contests, writers' workshops, and college scholarships.
- **Audience:** 10–21 years
- **Frequency:** Internet, weekly; print, quarterly
- **Distribution:** Internet; religious instruction; schools; subscription; churches
- **Circulation:** 4,000
- **Website:** www.teenlight.org

Freelance Potential

50% written by nonstaff writers. Publishes 24 freelance submissions yearly; 75% by unpublished writers, 50% by authors who are new to the magazine. Receives 20 queries monthly.

Submissions

Query with brief introduction. Accepts email submissions to publisher@teenlight.org (no attachments). Responds in 2 weeks.
Articles: To 500 words. Informational and self-help articles; profiles; devotionals; testimonials; photo-essays; and personal experience pieces. Topics include the arts, college, popular culture, and social issues.
Fiction: 500 words. Publishes contemporary fiction.
Artwork: B/W and color JPG files.
Other: Poetry. Submit seasonal material 6 months in advance.

Sample Issue

32 pages (15% advertising): 10 articles; 1 book review; 9 poems. Sample copy, $1.75 with 9x12 SASE. Guidelines available.
- "God Is Big!" Article reveals how a teen learned to magnify her concept of God.
- "They're Alive!" Article compiles comments from four teen writers on how to make characters come alive.

Rights and Payment

Non-exclusive rights. No payment. Provides 3 copies.

Editor's Comments

If you're a teenager thinking about submitting, we encourage you to send us your work. If you'd like to be considered for a staff writer position, mention that too, and fill us in on your previous writing experience.

Teen Times

1910 Association Drive
Reston, VA 20191

Communications Manager: Beth Carpenter

Description and Readership
Articles and photos capturing the activities and events of the Family, Career and Community Leaders of America can be found in this magazine for students. In addition, it includes articles on topics such as careers, education, health, and leadership skills.
- **Audience:** 10–18 years
- **Frequency:** Quarterly
- **Distribution:** 98% schools; 2% other
- **Circulation:** 220,000
- **Website:** www.fcclainc.org

Freelance Potential
50% written by nonstaff writers. Publishes 20 freelance submissions yearly; 100% by unpublished writers.

Submissions
Query or send complete ms. Accepts photocopies, and computer printouts. Availability of artwork improves chance of acceptance. SASE. Response time varies.
Articles: Word lengths vary. Informational and how-to articles; profiles; and photo-essays. Topics include careers, health, fitness, recreation, regional news, and member information.
Depts/columns: Word lengths vary. Leader profiles, event coverage, issues for action, news and updates.
Artwork: Color prints and transparencies.
Other: Puzzles, activities, and games.

Sample Issue
20 pages (12% advertising): 7 articles; 10 depts/columns. Sample copy available with 9x12 SASE. Editorial calendar available.
- "Picture This." Article offers tips on how to take effective pictures.
- "Road Trip." Article provides tips to help travelers stay safe and healthy.
- Sample dept/column: "Ideas, Etc." highlights a safe driving educational campaign, a service award winner, and a fundraising idea.

Rights and Payment
All rights. No payment. Provides contributor's copies upon request.

Editor's Comments
We continue to seek coverage of family, career and leadership activities and success stories. Writing must be geared towards middle, junior, and high school students who are members of FCCLA.

Teen Tribute

1 Barber Greene Road
Dons Mills, Ontario M3C 2AZ
Canada

Submissions: Robin Stevenson

Description and Readership
Canadian teens read *Teen Tribute* for updates on their favorite celebrities. The magazine also includes movie and film industry news, articles about popular culture, and fashion and beauty tips.
- **Audience:** 14–18 years
- **Frequency:** Quarterly
- **Distribution:** 90% newsstand; 10% subscription
- **Circulation:** 310,000
- **Website:** www.tribute.ca

Freelance Potential
10% written by nonstaff writers. Publishes 5–10 freelance submissions yearly; 1% by authors who are new to the magazine. Receives 2 queries monthly.

Submissions
Query with clips or writing samples. No unsolicited mss. Availability of artwork improves chance of acceptance. SAE/IRC. Responds in 1–2 months.
Articles: 400–500 words. Informational articles; profiles; and personal experience pieces. Also publishes photo-essays. Topics include movies, the film industry, entertainment, the arts, music, popular culture, and social issues.
Depts/columns: Word length varies. Media reviews; fashion and beauty tips.
Artwork: Color prints or transparencies.

Sample Issue
38 pages (50% advertising): 3 articles; 2 depts/columns. Sample copy, $1.95 Canadian with 9x12 SASE ($.86 Canadian postage).
- "Simply Simpson." Article profiles Jessica Simpson and talks about her first big-screen appearance in *The Dukes of Hazzard*.
- "Secrets of the Sisterhood." Interviews the four stars of the movie *The Sisterhood of the Traveling Pants*.
- "About a Boy." Article features an interview with the lead singer of a popular Toronto band.

Rights and Payment
First North American serial rights. Written material, $75–$100 Canadian. Artwork, payment rate varies. Pays on acceptance. Provides 1 contributor's copy.

Editor's Comments
We're primarily interested in profiles of celebrities and news about the film industry. You must have access to inside information about popular culture and stars to write for us.

Teen Voices

P.O. Box 120-027
Boston, MA 02112-0027

Editor-in-Chief: Ellyn Ruthstrom

Description and Readership
The power of young women's voices are displayed through writing and artwork on the pages of this magazine. It strives to empower and connect young women to make positive changes that matter.
- **Audience:** Young adult women
- **Frequency:** Twice each year
- **Distribution:** Newsstand; other
- **Circulation:** 55,000
- **Website:** www.teenvoices.com

Freelance Potential
95% written by nonstaff writers. Publishes 100 freelance submissions yearly; 95% by unpublished writers, 95% by new authors. Receives 167 mss monthly.

Submissions
Accepts articles written by teenage girls only. Send complete ms. Response time varies.
Articles: Word length varies. Informational and self-help articles. Topics include family relationships, teen motherhood, the arts, popular culture, the media, surviving sexual assault, coping with disabilities and chronic illness, and experiences from teens around the world.
Fiction: Word length varies. Short stories.
Depts/columns: 500 words. News important to teens.
Artwork: B/W and color prints. Line art. Various art for features, as assigned.
Other: Poetry.

Sample Issue
58 pages (8% advertising): 8 articles; 4 poems; 6 depts/columns. Sample copy, $5. Writers' guidelines and editorial calendar available.
- "Teens Tackle Teasing." Article discusses what teens across they country are saying about teasing, bullying and harassment.
- "Crimes Of Fashion or Freedom." Article takes a look at school dress codes and uniform rules across the country and the reasons behind them.
- Sample dept/column: "Top 10" offers ways to be all-around healthy.

Rights and Payment
First or one-time rights. No payment. Provides 5 contributor's copies.

Editor's Comments
We are looking for quality short stories with teen girl protagonists, written by teen women.

Teenwire.com

434 West 33rd Street
New York, NY 10001

Editor: Susan Yudt

Description and Readership
Maintained by Planned Parenthood Federation of America, this website for teens provides open, honest information on sexual health. Its goal is to provide the facts about issues of concern, so teens can make responsible choices.
- **Audience:** 13–21 years
- **Frequency:** Unavailable
- **Distribution:** 100% online
- **Hits per month:** 800,000
- **Website:** www.teenwire.com

Freelance Potential
90% written by nonstaff writers. Publishes 100–156 freelance submissions yearly; 10% by unpublished writers, 25% by new authors.

Submissions
Query with brief biography and clips or writing samples. Accepts email queries to twstaff@ppfa.org (include "Write for Teenwire" in subject line). Responds in 1 week.
Articles: 500 words. Informational and factual articles; profiles; interviews; and Spanish pieces. Topics include teen relationships, sexual health, birth control, pregnancy, sexually transmitted diseases, teen activism, international youth issues, the arts, colleges, careers, current events, music, popular culture, recreation, substance abuse, social concerns, and multicultural and ethnic issues.
Other: Puzzles, games, and quizzes.

Sample Issue
Sample copy and guidelines available at website.
- "Saving Sex Ed: Shelby Knox." Article profiles a teen crusader for sex education as a way to reduce teen pregnancy and sexually transmitted infections.
- "The Truth About Virginity Pledges." Article by a high school student who reveals the pros and cons pledging to remain a virgin until marriage.
- "Surviving Valentine's Day." Article tells how to make it through a lovey-dovey holiday, whether you feel that way or not.

Rights and Payment
All rights. Articles, $.50 per word to $250. Pays on acceptance.

Editor's Comments
We continue to need information on hot teen issues, including drugs and alcohol use, and gay relationships.

Texas Child Care

P.O. Box 162881
Austin, TX 78716-2881

Editor: Louise Parks

Description and Readership
A professional publication for adults who work with or care for children, *Texas Child Care* offers articles on child development theory and professional development. Its intention is to support adults caring for children in foster homes, group homes, child-care centers, and early childhood classrooms everywhere.
- **Audience:** Child-care workers and parents
- **Frequency:** Quarterly
- **Distribution:** 80% controlled; 20% subscription
- **Circulation:** 32,000
- **Website:** www.childcarequarterly.com

Freelance Potential
50% written by nonstaff writers. Publishes 12–15 freelance submissions yearly; 10% by unpublished writers, 50% by authors who are new to the magazine. Receives 2–3 unsolicited mss monthly.

Submissions
Send complete ms. Accepts email submissions to editor@childcarequarterly.com. Responds in 3 weeks.
Articles: 2,500 words. Informational articles. Topics include child care, education, program administration, infant care, professional development, and issues and activities relating to school-age children.
Depts/columns: Word lengths vary. News and updates about child care, parenting, and licensing information.
Other: Submit seasonal material 6 months in advance.

Sample Issue
44 pages (no advertising): 6 articles; 8 depts/columns. Sample copy, $6.50. Guidelines available at website.
- "Find the Beat." Article provides instructions for making simple rhythm instruments.
- "Is It Just Me or Is It Noisy in Here?" Article discusses sound management in child-care centers and early childhood classrooms.
- Sample dept/column: "Back to Basics" offers suggestions for setting up an art center that supports investigation and experimentation.

Rights and Payment
All rights. No payment. Provides 2 contributor's copies.

Editor's Comments
We continue to seek hands-on activities in the areas of math and science, as well as articles about the emotional development of young children.

Theory Into Practice

169 Ramseyer Hall
29 West Woodruff Avenue
Ohio State University
Columbus, OH 43210

Editor: Anita Woolfolk Hoy

Description and Readership
Engaging articles on educational topics are featured in this thematic journal for professionals. If offers a scholarly forum based on concepts and ideas that can be applied in the classroom.
- **Audience:** Educators
- **Frequency:** Quarterly
- **Distribution:** 65% schools/libraries; 35% other
- **Circulation:** 2,000
- **Website:** www.coe.ohio-state.edu/tip

Freelance Potential
100% written by nonstaff writers. Publishes 38 freelance submissions yearly; 10% by unpublished writers, 90% by authors who are new to the magazine. Receives 2 queries and unsolicited mss monthly.

Submissions
Query or send 2 copies of complete ms. Accepts photocopies. SASE. Responds in 1–2 months.
Articles: 3,000–4,000 words. Factual and informational articles. Topics include educational technology, cultural diversity, literary theory, teacher quality, cooperative learning, children's literature, mentoring, classroom communication, foreign languages, community service, and curriculum theory.

Sample Issue
142 pages (3% advertising): 11 articles. Sample copy, $12. Guidelines and theme list available.
- "Becoming a Self-Regulated Learner: An Overview." Article discusses students' self-regulation, including individual differences in learning, structure and functions, and methods to guide students to learn.
- "Individualizing Instruction in Self-Regulated Learning." Article describes how teachers can provide instruction that promotes students' successful navigation through academic work.

Rights and Payment
All rights. No payment. Provides 2 author's copies.

Editor's Comments
We look for material that is logically developed, with examples used freely to support difficult material. Avoid technical jargon. We encourage authors to include research and case studies to support ideas. Illustrations, tables, and diagrams should be used only when essential to the article. We utilize a thematic format, but will consider top-notch material on any educational topic. Most of our work is solicited.

Thrasher

1303 Underwood Avenue
San Francisco, CA 94124

Editor: Jake Phelps

Description and Readership

This magazine is dedicated to the sports of skate-boarding and snowboarding. Each issue includes articles, profiles, and information for young adult males.
- **Audience:** 12–20 years
- **Frequency:** Monthly
- **Distribution:** 30% subscription; 30% newsstand; 40% other
- **Circulation:** 200,000
- **Website:** www.thrashermagazine.com

Freelance Potential

20% written by nonstaff writers. Publishes 20 free-lance submissions yearly; 100% by unpublished writers. Receives 6–10 unsolicited mss monthly.

Submissions

Send complete ms. Accepts photocopies, computer printouts, IBM and Macintosh disk submissions, and simultaneous submissions if identified. Availability of artwork improves chance of acceptance. SASE. Responds in 1 month.
Articles: To 1,500 words. Informational articles; profiles; and interviews. Topics include skateboarding, snowboarding, sports, and music.
Fiction: To 2,500 words. Stories with skateboarding and snowboarding themes.
Depts/columns: 750–1,000 words. Skateboarding and snowboarding news, tips, and techniques.
Artwork: Color prints or transparencies; 35mm B/W negatives. B/W or color line art.

Sample Issue

248 pages (45% advertising): 11 articles; 9 depts/columns. Sample copy, $3.99. Guidelines available.
- "Shreddings for Heddings." Article looks at a skate session to raise money for the legal counsel of skateboarder Neil Heddings.
- "Goin' AM." Article highlights new boarders on the scene across the U.S.
- Sample dept/column: "On Board" offers news, jokes, poems, and stats about skateboarders.

Rights and Payment

First North American serial rights. Written material, $.10 per word. Artwork, payment rate varies. Pays on publication. Provides 2 contributor's copies.

Editor's Comments

Writers that understand the board sports scene are appreciated. Style must reflect the interest of our readers.

Three Leaping Frogs

P.O. Box 2205
Carson City, NV 89702

Publisher: Ellen Hopkins

Description and Readership

Written for elementary school children, *Three Leaping Frogs* is a newspaper offering stories, poems, articles, and news for northern Nevada readers. It publishes material on science, animals, math, nature, holidays, and history.
- **Audience:** 7–12 years
- **Frequency:** Monthly
- **Distribution:** 100% schools
- **Circulation:** 35,000
- **Website:** www.goshawkroad.org

Freelance Potential

70% written by nonstaff writers. Publishes 50 free-lance submissions yearly; 50% by unpublished writers, 60% by authors who are new to the magazine. Receives 16–40 unsolicited mss monthly.

Submissions

Send complete ms. Prefers email submissions to goshawkroad@goshawkroad.org. Accepts computer printouts. SASE. Responds in 3 months.
Articles: 500 words. Informational articles, profiles, and interviews. Topics include animals, nature, math, fitness, hobbies, and history. Also publishes biographies and regional news.
Fiction: 1,000 words. Genres include mystery, adventure, historical and multicultural fiction, and science fiction.
Depts/columns: 300 words. Science experiments and advice.
Other: Puzzles, activities, games, and jokes. Poetry. Submit seasonal material 6 months in advance.

Sample Issue

8 pages (no advertising): 10 articles; 2 depts/columns; 3 poems; 1 activity. Sample copy, $1 with 9x12 SASE ($.57 postage). Writers' guidelines and theme list available.
- "The Mother of Civil Rights." Article details the life of Rosa Parks.
- "Dressed for Winter." Article describes the adaptations of animals that live in the Arctic.

Rights and Payment

First rights. No payment. Provides 5 contributor's copies.

Editor's Comments

Keep it short—under 600 words. And remember that most of our fiction is written by our young readers.

Tidewater Parent

258 Granby Street
Norfolk, VA 23510

Editor: Jennifer O'Donnell

Description and Readership
Families living in Virginia's Tidewater Peninsula area find information about regional resources, child development, and family-oriented events in this publication. It is distributed free through schools, libraries, and doctors' offices.
- **Audience:** Parents
- **Frequency:** Monthly
- **Distribution:** 50% schools; 50% other
- **Circulation:** 48,000
- **Website:** www.tidewaterparent.com

Freelance Potential
90% written by nonstaff writers. Publishes 40 freelance submissions yearly; 10% by unpublished writers, 50% by authors who are new to the magazine. Receives 6 unsolicited mss monthly.

Submissions
Send complete ms. Will accept previously published mss that can be reprinted. Accepts photocopies and computer printouts. SASE. Response time varies.
Articles: 800–1,200 words. Informational and how-to articles. Topics include parenting, education, child health and development, family travel, and safety.
Depts/columns: Staff written.
Other: Send seasonal material 2–3 months in advance.

Sample Issue
36 pages (50% advertising): 2 articles; 8 depts/columns; 1 events calendar. Sample copy, $2. Guidelines and theme list available.
- "Breastfeeding 911." Article discusses the services offered by the seven La Leche League groups in the Hampton Roads area.
- "Nanny to the Rescue." Reports on local reaction to the television hit, *Supernanny*.
- "Mind Games." Reviews books that explore the wonders of the teenage mind.

Rights and Payment
Rights vary. Written material, $25 per word. Kill fee, 50%. Pays on publication. Provides 1 contributor's copy.

Editor's Comments
Articles that are written in an approachable, informal style are preferred. Avoid long paragraphs and difficult vocabulary. It's always a good idea to use real-life situations and experiences that readers can relate to.

Tiger Beat

Suite 700
6430 Sunset Boulevard
Hollywood, CA 90028

Editor: Leesa Coble

Description and Readership
This teen magazine provides information on today's hottest young celebrities. Each issue includes articles and photos, news, the latest in fashion and beauty, quizzes, gossip, and posters.
- **Audience:** 10–16 years
- **Frequency:** Monthly
- **Distribution:** 90% newsstand; 10% subscription
- **Circulation:** 200,000
- **Website:** www.tigerbeatmag.com

Freelance Potential
5% written by nonstaff writers. Publishes 2 freelance submissions yearly; 50% by authors who are new to the magazine. Receives 8 queries monthly.

Submissions
Query with résumé and clips for celebrity angles only. Accepts photocopies, computer printouts, and simultaneous submissions if identified. SASE. Responds in 3 months.
Articles: To 700 words. Interviews; and profiles. Topics include celebrities in the film, television, and recording industries.
Depts/columns: Staff written.
Artwork: Color digital.
Other: Short updates on young celebrities. Submit seasonal material 3 months in advance.

Sample Issue
82 pages (12% advertising): 17 articles; 16 depts/columns; 9 posters. Sample copy, $3.99 at newsstands.
- "Under Jessie's Skin." Article takes a look at what makes singer Jessie McCartney lose his cool.
- "Sister Knows Best." Article reports on the relationship between sisters Hilary and Haylie Duff.
- "What's Luck Got to Do With It?" Article spotlights some of the luckiest young celebrities in Hollywood including Hilary Duff, Ashlee Simpson, and Raven.

Rights and Payment
All rights. Written material, payment rates vary. Pays on publication. Provides 2 contributor's copies.

Editor's Comments
We keep our readers happy by providing them with exclusive information and the latest news on their favorite celebrities. We are looking for celebrity angles and interviews that appeal to our tween audience. We do not publish non-celebrity related topics.

Time For Kids

Time-Life Building
22nd Floor
1271 Avenue of the Americas
New York, NY 10020

Editor: Martha Pickerill

Description and Readership
Time Magazine publishes this children's version of the newsmagazine for kindergarten through high school students. Each issue covers news and current events in a lively and engaging format.
• **Audience:** 5–18 years
• **Frequency:** Weekly
• **Distribution:** 100% schools
• **Circulation:** 4.1 million
• **Website:** www.timeforkids.com

Freelance Potential
4% written by nonstaff writers. Publishes 4 freelance submissions yearly. Receives many queries and unsolicited mss monthly.

Submissions
Query with résumé. No unsolicited mss. SASE. Response time varies.
Articles: Word length varies. Informational and biographical articles. Topics include world news, current events, animals, education, health, fitness, science and technology, math, social studies, geography, multicultural and ethnic issues, music, popular culture, recreation, regional news, sports, travel, and social issues.
Depts/columns: Word lengths vary. Short news items and profiles.
Artwork: Color prints and transparencies.
Other: Theme-related activities.

Sample Issue
8 pages (no advertising): 3 articles; 4 depts/columns. Subscription, $3.95.
• "Too Young to Work." Article looks at the issue of child labor in the United States.
• "Baseball Takes a Hit." Article examines the problem of illegal steroid use among professional baseball players.
• Sample dept/column: "Spotlight" profiles well-known poet Ted Kooser.

Rights and Payment
All rights. Written material, payment rates vary. Pays on publication.

Editor's Comments
We are interested in engaging and informative material that is written in a clear and concise manner. Recently, articles about kids' health and fitness, and bullying, have been submitted in overwhelming numbers.

Today's Catholic Teacher

Suite 300
2621 Dryden Road
Dayton, OH 45439

Editor-in-Chief: Mary Noschang

Description and Readership
This magazine is a source of information on issues of concern and interest to educators in Catholic schools, from community needs to national trends.
• **Audience:** Educators, grades K–8
• **Frequency:** 6 times each year
• **Distribution:** 90% schools; 10% religious instruction
• **Circulation:** 50,000
• **Website:** www.peterli.com

Freelance Potential
95% written by nonstaff writers. Publishes 20 freelance submissions yearly; 50% by authors who are new to the magazine. Receives 16+ queries and unsolicited mss monthly.

Submissions
Query or send complete ms. Accepts photocopies, computer printouts, disk submissions with hard copy, email submissions to mnoschang@peterli.com, and simultaneous submissions if identified. SASE. Responds to queries in 1 month, to mss in 3 months.
Articles: 600–1,500 words. Informational, how-to, and self-help articles. Topics include technology, fundraising, character education, classroom management, curriculum development, administration, and educational issues and trends.
Depts/columns: Word length varies. Opinions, news items, software, and teaching tools.
Artwork: 8x10 B/W or color slides, prints, or transparencies accepted.
Other: Classroom-ready reproducible activity pages.

Sample Issue
46 pages (45% advertising): 4 articles; 15 depts/columns; 1 activity page. Sample copy, $3. Guidelines and editorial calendar available.
• "Integration Issues for 21st-Century Teachers." Article discusses how to prepare students to use technology efficiently and effectively.
• Sample dept/column: "Great Ideas" offers workable classroom ideas from teachers and principals.

Rights and Payment
All rights. Written material, $100–$250. Pays on publication. Provides contributor's copies.

Editor's Comments
Our readers are interested in private education in general, and Catholic education in particular. Our articles offer practical solutions to common problems.

Today's Christian Woman

465 Gundersen Drive
Carol Stream, IL 60188

Associate Editor: Lisa Ann Cockrel

Description and Readership
This magazine seeks to help women deal with the contemporary issues and hot topics that impact their lives, and provide a biblical perspective to all types of personal and professional relationships.
- **Audience:** Women
- **Frequency:** 6 times each year
- **Distribution:** Subscription; newsstand
- **Circulation:** 250,000
- **Website:** www.todayschristianwoman.com

Freelance Potential
75% written by nonstaff writers. Publishes 30–50 freelance submissions yearly; 25% by authors who are new to the magazine. Receives 10 queries each month.

Submissions
Query with résumé and summary. Accepts photocopies and computer printouts. No simultaneous submissions. SASE. Responds in 2 months.
Articles: 1,000–2,00 words. Informational and self-help articles; personal experience pieces; and humor; Topics include parenting, family issues, spiritual living, contemporary women's concerns, and turning points in life.
Depts/columns: 100–300 words. Reviews, faith, parenting, and first-person narratives.

Sample Issue
72 pages (25% advertising): 8 articles; 12 depts/columns. Sample copy, $5 with 9x12 SASE ($3.19 postage). Guidelines available.
- "Balancing Act." Profile of Christian recording artist/author Rebecca St. James.
- "Confessions of a Perfect Christian Woman." True story explains how genuine confession leads to radical forgiveness through Christ.
- Sample dept/column: "Mom Time" answers questions on parenting topics.

Rights and Payment
First rights. Written material, $.20 per word. Pays on acceptance. Provides 2 contributor's copies.

Editor's Comments
We have readers who are actively involved in a church and knowledgeable about the Bible, as well as those who are exploring Christianity or are new believers. Articles should be practical and contain a distinct evangelical Christian message.

Today's Parent

8th Floor
1 Mount Pleasant Road
Toronto, Ontario M4Y 2YS
Canada

Managing Editor: Sarah Moore

Description and Readership
Canadian parents of children from birth to teenagers look to *Today's Parent* for informative and up-to-date articles on all aspects of parenting and childrearing. Book reviews and recipes are also included in its mix.
- **Audience:** Parents
- **Frequency:** 11 times each year
- **Distribution:** Subscription; newsstand; other
- **Circulation:** 215,000
- **Website:** www.todaysparent.com

Freelance Potential
Of the freelance submissions published yearly, many are by unpublished writers and authors who are new to the magazine. Receives several queries monthly.

Submissions
Query with clips or writing samples; include information on article length. No unsolicited mss. Accepts photocopies and computer printouts. SAE/IRC. Response time varies.
Articles: 1,800–2,500 words. Informational how-to, and self-help articles. Topics include parenting, family life, child development, health, nutrition, pregnancy, and childbirth.
Depts/columns: Word length varies. First-person parenting accounts and essays, cooking with kids, child behavior, teen issues, updates of interest to families.

Sample Issue
154 pages (15% advertising): 5 articles; 15 depts/columns; 1 special section on children's fiction. Sample copy, $4.50 (Canadian) at newsstands.
- "10 Parenting Habits." Article identifies ten habits that parents may not know they have.
- "Will Power." Article examines why planning ahead for your death will benefit your children.
- Sample dept/column: "Cooking with Kids" offers ideas for tasty, kid-friendly finger foods.

Rights and Payment
All North American serial rights. Articles, $700–$1,500. Depts/columns, payment rate varies. Pays on publication. Provides 2 contributor's copies.

Editor's Comments
We look for material that does not underestimate readers' intelligence and that helps them feel that they are not alone in the joys and frustrations of parenting. We seek to provide readers with options; not solutions or perfect answers.

Toledo Area Parent News

1120 Adams Street
Toledo, OH 43624

Editor: Misty Walker

Description and Readership
Distributed free at locations throughout the Toledo, Ohio region, this tabloid offers informative, thought-provoking articles on parenting issues, health, education, and social issues. In addition, it keeps readers up-to-date on local events, offers resources in the region, and reviews family-oriented restaurants.
- **Audience:** Parents
- **Frequency:** Monthly
- **Distribution:** 100% controlled
- **Circulation:** 81,000
- **Website:** www.toledoparent.com

Freelance Potential
75% written by nonstaff writers. Publishes 8–10 freelance submissions yearly; 10% by unpublished writers, 20% by authors who are new to the magazine. Receives 4 queries and unsolicited mss monthly.

Submissions
Query with clips; or send complete ms. Accepts photocopies and computer printouts. SASE. Responds in 1 month.
Articles: 700–2,000 words. Informational articles; profiles; and interviews. Topics include family issues, parenting, teen issues, education, social issues, health, and fitness.
Depts/columns: Word length varies. Brief news items related to family, and opinion essays.

Sample Issue
38 pages (60% advertising): 2 articles; 8 depts/columns; 1 calendar. Sample copy, free with 9x12 SASE. Guidelines available.
- "Bag the Bad Lunch." Article reports on the problem of childhood obesity and the focus on improving school lunch programs.
- "Summer Camp Guide." Article offers descriptive reviews of summer camps for kids.
- Sample dept/column: "Food Fight" focuses on local family restaurants: food, entertainment, and kid-friendly additions.

Rights and Payment
All North American serial rights. Written material, $30–$200. Pays on publication.

Editor's Comments
We are looking for more hard-hitting news stories relative to the local area about kids and teens. We have enough material on obesity and dental care.

Transitions Abroad

P.O. Box 745
Bennington, VT 05201

Editor/Publisher: Sherry Schwarz

Description and Readership
Serving as a planning guide for cultural immersion travel, *Transitions Abroad* provides practical, first-hand information to readers who are preparing to spend an extended time abroad working or furthering their education. It has been in publication since 1977.
- **Audience:** YA–Adult
- **Frequency:** 6 times each year
- **Distribution:** 75% subscription; 25% newsstand
- **Circulation:** 12,000
- **Website:** www.transitionsabroad.com

Freelance Potential
95% written by nonstaff writers. Publishes 150–180 freelance submissions yearly; 30% by unpublished writers, 30% by authors who are new to the magazine. Receives 100 queries, 50 mss monthly.

Submissions
Prefers query with outline; accepts complete ms with bibliography. Prefers email submissions to editor@ transitionsabroad.com. Accepts photocopies. SASE. Responds in 1–2 months.
Articles: To 1,500 words. Informational and how-to articles. Topics include overseas travel for teens, families, and seniors, as well as overseas study and employment programs.
Depts/columns: Word length varies. Responsible travel, budget travel, and volunteer travel.

Sample Issue
80 pages (50% advertising): 37 articles; 3 depts/columns. Sample copy, $4.95. Guidelines and editorial calendar available at website.
- "A Land of Myths and Faith." Article reports on a Guatemalan family that has been creating magnificent carpets for the Good Friday processions for 48 consecutive years.
- "Keep Copies of Key Documents in Your Backpack." Article outlines a three-tiered security system overseas travelers can use to protect their possessions.

Rights and Payment
First rights. Written material, $.05 per word. Artwork, payment rate varies. Pays on publication. Provides 2 contributor's copies.

Editor's Comments
We welcome full articles as well as brief summaries on any topic related to work, study, travel, or living abroad. Be concise, and feel free to include critical evaluations.

Treasure Valley Family Magazine

13191 West Scotfield Street
Boise, ID 83713-0899

Publisher: Liz Buckingham

Description and Readership
This magazine, distributed free to Idaho families, focuses on issues related to parenting children under the age of 12. Its articles and departments cover educational issues, parental involvement, health, family fun, travel, and crafts.
- **Audience:** Parents
- **Frequency:** 10 times each year
- **Distribution:** 100% controlled
- **Circulation:** 19,500
- **Website:** www.treasurevalleyfamily.com

Freelance Potential
100% written by nonstaff writers. Publishes 10 freelance submissions yearly; 5% by authors who are new to the magazine. Receives 17 mss monthly.

Submissions
Send complete ms. Accepts email submissions to magazine@treasurevalleyfamily.com. Responds in 3–4 months.
Articles: To 1,500 words. How-to articles and personal experience pieces. Topics include regional news, gifted and special education, health, travel, fitness, crafts, hobbies, the arts, and recreation.
Fiction: Word lengths vary. Inspirational and historical fiction.
Depts/columns: 700–800 words. Regional news, book reviews, family advocacy, and crafts.
Artwork: Color prints and transparencies. Line art.
Other: Filler on health and safety, activities, and games. Submit seasonal material 6 months in advance.

Sample Issue
58 pages (45% advertising): 9 articles; 8 depts/columns. Sample copy, $1.50 with 9x12 SASE. Guidelines available.
- "Tween Time." Article addresses issues of interest to parents of girls between the ages of 9 and 12.
- "Misbehavior Isn't a Problem—It's a Symptom." Article argues that bad behavior is a sign that a child's emotional needs aren't being met.

Rights and Payment
First rights. All material, payment rate varies. Pays on publication. Provides 2 contributor's copies.

Editor's Comments
We want articles that will be of interest to parents living in Boise, Meridian, Eagle, and Nampa, Idaho.

Tulsa Kids Magazine

Suite 100
1820 South Boulder Avenue
Tulsa, OK 74119-4409

Editor: Betty Casey

Description and Readership
This family-friendly magazine offers parents accurate information on topics such as physical and mental health, education, and entertainment. It also includes information on local resources and events.
- **Audience:** Families
- **Frequency:** Monthly
- **Distribution:** 80% newsstand; 15% schools; 3% religious instruction; 2% subscription
- **Circulation:** 20,000
- **Website:** www.tulsakids.com

Freelance Potential
99% written by nonstaff writers. Publishes 100+ freelance submissions yearly; 5% by unpublished writers, 1% by authors who are new to the magazine. Receives 100 unsolicited mss monthly.

Submissions
Send complete ms. Accepts photocopies, computer printouts, disk submissions, and simultaneous submissions if identified. SASE. Responds in 2–3 months.
Articles: 500–800 words. Informational articles; profiles; interviews; humor; and personal experience pieces. Topics include family life, education, parenting, recreation, entertainment, college, health, fitness, careers, crafts, and social issues.
Depts/columns: 100–300 words. News, book reviews, safety, and family cooking.

Sample Issue
36 pages (50% advertising): 2 articles; 8 depts/columns; 1 calendar. Sample copy, free with 10x13 SASE ($.75 postage). Guidelines available.
- "Route 66 Diner Delicacies." Article reviews *The Route 66 Cookbook* and offers some recipes.
- "Moms on the Mother Road." Article describes some fun spots to visit while vacationing with the family on Route 66.
- Sample dept/column: "Zero to Three" discusses brain development in babies.

Rights and Payment
One-time rights. Written material, $25–$100. Payment policy varies. Provides 1 contributor's copy.

Editor's Comments
We look for up-to-date articles that address the concerns and needs of parents of children from prenatal through adolescence, as well as information on family-oriented recreational activities within the region.

Turtle
Magazine for Preschool Kids

Children's Better Health Institute
1100 Waterway Boulevard
P.O. Box 567
Indianapolis, IN 46206-0567

Editor: Terry Harshman

Description and Readership
Articles, activities, and puzzles that educate and entertain preschool children are found in *Turtle*. Published by the Children's Better Health Institute, it encourages children to live a healthy lifestyle.
- **Audience:** 2–5 years
- **Frequency:** 6 times each year
- **Distribution:** 100% subscription
- **Circulation:** 382,000
- **Website:** www.turtlemag.org

Freelance Potential
20% written by nonstaff writers. Publishes 20 freelance submissions yearly.

Submissions
Send complete ms. Accepts photocopies and computer printouts. SASE. Responds in 2–3 months.
Articles: To 500 words. Informational articles. Topics include science, health, fitness, and medicine.
Fiction: To 100 words for rebus stories. Genres include mystery; adventure; fantasy; humor; problem-solving stories; and contemporary, ethnic, and multicultural fiction.
Other: Puzzles, activities, and games. Poetry.

Sample Issue
36 pages (6% advertising): 1 article; 3 stories; 10 activities; 1 rebus; 1 book review; 1 poem. Sample copy, $1.75 with 9x12 SASE. Guidelines available.
- "Against the Odds." Rebus story about a boy's safe landing on homeplate at his baseball game.
- "Veggie Election 2004." Article features interesting facts about corn.
- Sample dept/column: "Action Time" asks kids to act out the movements of different aquatic life.

Rights and Payment
All rights. Articles and fiction, $.22 per word. Other material, payment rate varies. Pays on publication. Provides up to 10 contributor's copies.

Editor's Comments
We are dedicated to informing and educating preschool children through fun and lively articles, stories, puzzles, games, and recipes. Send us something that is easy-to-follow and promotes healthy living in children and adults. Although our activities may require parental assistance, please make sure that your material is age appropriate.

Tuscaloosa Christian Family

P.O. Box 66
Northport, AL 35476

Editor: Craig Threlkeld

Description and Readership
A community publication, *Tuscaloosa Christian Family* is available free of charge at various locations throughout the Tuscaloosa area. Its positive perspective appeals to parents seeking to enhance their family life as well as to those seeking ways to contribute to the local Christian community.
- **Audience:** Parents
- **Frequency:** Monthly
- **Distribution:** 95% newsstand; 5% other
- **Circulation:** 10,000

Freelance Potential
30% written by nonstaff writers. Publishes 60 freelance submissions yearly; 5% by unpublished writers. Receives 8 queries monthly.

Submissions
Query with photos if applicable. Accepts photocopies, computer printouts, and email queries to editorial@ tuscaloosachristianfamily.com. SASE. Responds in 2 months.
Articles: 500 words. Informational and how-to articles; profiles; interviews; humor; and personal experience pieces. Topics include current events, health, fitness, recreation, regional news, religion, social issues, and travel.
Fiction: 500 words. Genres include inspirational and humorous fiction.
Depts/columns: 500 words. Book and music reviews, family finances, mission news, and working with youth.
Artwork: Color prints or transparencies.
Other: Activities. Submit seasonal material 2 months in advance.

Sample Issue
30 pages: 3 articles; 14 depts/columns; 1 calendar; 2 activities. Sample copy, free with 9x12 SASE ($3 postage). Editorial calendar available.
- "Alabama's Mark Gottfried." Article explores the faith life of the University of Alabama's basketball coach.
- Sample dept/column: "Are We There Yet?" offers getaway ideas for Mom and Dad.

Rights and Payment
Rights vary. No payment. Provides 1 contributor's copy.

Editor's Comments
We can always use inspirational profiles of local people who understand the importance of family life.

Twins

Suite 101
11211 East Arapahoe Road
Centennial, CO 80112

Managing Editor: Sharon Withers

Description and Readership
This magazine has been an important resource to parents since 1984. Each issue brings helpful tips and real-life advice on parenting twins and multiple births.
- **Audience:** Parents
- **Frequency:** 6 times each year
- **Distribution:** 60% subscription; 37% controlled; 3% newsstand
- **Circulation:** 56,000
- **Website:** www.twinsmagazine.com

Freelance Potential
80% written by nonstaff writers. Publishes 80 freelance submissions yearly; 25% by new authors. Receives 21 queries and unsolicited mss monthly.

Submissions
Query or send complete ms. Accepts photocopies, computer printouts, and simultaneous submissions if identified. SASE. Responds in 3 months.
Articles: 800–1,300 words. Informational and how-to articles; profiles; and personal experience pieces. Topics include parenting, family life, health, fitness, education, music, the arts, house and home, nutrition, diet, sports, social issues, crafts, and hobbies.
Depts/columns: To 800 words. News, new product information, opinion pieces, and short items on child development.

Sample Issue
54 pages (30% advertising): 8 articles; 13 depts/columns. Sample copy, $5.50. Guidelines available.
- "Pumping Primer." Article discusses different types of breast pumps and tips for expressing milk.
- "Separate or Together in School?" Article discusses school placement for twins and the importance of meeting the needs of the children.
- Sample dept/column: "The First Year" takes a look at some of the milestones babies reach in their first year of life.

Rights and Payment
All rights. All material, payment rate varies. Kill fee, 10% or $100. Pays on publication. Provides 1 contributor's copy.

Editor's Comments
We are looking for positive, helpful articles on raising twins from birth to age six from writers who are parents of multiples. Please double-check statistical information and facts, and list all references.

Twist

270 Sylvan Avenue
Englewood Cliffs, NJ 07632

Entertainment Editor: Jamie Harkin

Description and Readership
Twist offers the latest news and gossip from the young celebrity world. Young readers find news and tips on a variety of pop culture topics, as well as advice on beauty, fashion, and relationships.
- **Audience:** 14–19 years
- **Frequency:** 10 times each year
- **Distribution:** Subscription; newsstand
- **Circulation:** 1 million
- **Website:** www.twistmagazine.com

Freelance Potential
5% written by nonstaff writers. Publishes 30 freelance submissions yearly; 5% by unpublished writers, 5% by authors who are new to the magazine. Receives 20 unsolicited submissions monthly.

Submissions
Query. Accepts computer printouts. Responds in 2–3 weeks.
Articles: Word length varies. Informational articles; and humor. Topics include popular culture, music, celebrities, fashion favorites, beauty tips, health, fitness, nutrition, sex, and relationships.
Depts/columns: Word lengths vary. Embarrassing moments, new fashion and beauty products, advice, and horoscopes.

Sample Issue
98 pages (25% advertising): 15 articles; 16 depts/columns. Sample copy, $2.99 with 9x12 SASE. Writers' guidelines available.
- "Your Freaky Dreams Explained!" Article reveals the possible meaning behind various dreams.
- "I'm Scared to Turn 18!" Article about why Hilary Duff is apprehensive to become an adult, and what she loves about her mom, Susan.
- Sample dept/column: "Guys Decoded" takes a look at what four American Idol contestants' hairdos say about their personalities.

Rights and Payment
First North American serial rights. Written material, payment rates vary. Pays on acceptance. Provides 2 contributor's copies.

Editor's Comments
We are no longer running real-life stories, and are currently seeking original quizzes and celebrity interviews. All material must speak to our readers in a hip and upbeat manner.

U Magazine

United States Automobile Association
9800 Fredericksburg Road
San Antonio, TX 78288-0264

Editor: Shari Biediger

Description and Readership
A free publication sent to dependents of USAA members, *U Magazine* provides its readers with articles and activities that encourage responsible citizenship and healthy lifestyle habits.
- **Audience:** 9–12 years
- **Frequency:** Quarterly
- **Distribution:** 99% controlled; 1% other
- **Circulation:** 440,000
- **Website:** www.usaa.com

Freelance Potential
90% written by nonstaff writers. Publishes 5 freelance submissions yearly. Receives 1 query monthly.

Submissions
Query with résumé and clips or writing samples. Accepts photocopies. SASE. Responds in 6 weeks.
Articles: Word lengths vary. Informational, how-to, and self-help articles; profiles; interviews; and personal experience pieces. Topics include hobbies, history, mathematics, music, popular culture, current events, science, technology, social issues, the arts, travel, money management, and safety issues.
Other: Puzzles, activities, games, and jokes.

Sample Issue
16 pages (no advertising): 5 articles; 5 activities. Sample copy, free with 9x12 SASE ($2 postage). Guidelines and theme list available.
- "Coach Mom." Article looks at the advantages and some of the drawbacks of having parents coach their children's sports teams.
- "My Favorite Sport." Article profiles a 10-year-old girl who has been playing baseball for five years.
- "Who Wins?" Article presents five sticky situations involving sports players or teams and asks the reader to think about the best ways to settle them.

Rights and Payment
All rights. Written material, payment rates vary. Pays on acceptance. Provides 25 contributor's copies.

Editor's Comments
We rarely publish fiction, and yet we're getting too many fiction submissions at this time. Instead, we'd like to see quizzes, games, interactive lists, or activities centered around an issue's theme. Most of what we publish is written in-house, but we'll consider assigning stories to writers who submit published clips and appropriate article queries.

The Universe in the Classroom

Astronomical Society of the Pacific
390 Ashton Avenue
San Francisco, CA 94112

Editor: Suzanne Chippindale

Description and Readership
Written specifically for teachers, librarians, and others involved in the education of children, this online newsletter calls attention to current astronomical events and makes the subject of astronomy interesting and understandable.
- **Audience:** Teachers
- **Frequency:** Quarterly
- **Distribution:** 100% Internet
- **Hits per month:** 10,000
- **Website:** www.astrosociety.org

Freelance Potential
90% written by nonstaff writers. Publishes 4 freelance submissions yearly; 50% by unpublished writers, 75% by authors who are new to the magazine. Receives 1 query monthly.

Submissions
Query with outline. Accepts photocopies and computer printouts. Availability of artwork improves chance of acceptance. SASE. Responds in 1 month.
Articles: 3,000 words. Informational articles. Topics include astronomy, teaching methods, and astrobiology.
Artwork: Color prints and transparencies.
Other: Classroom activities.

Sample Issue
Sample copy available at website.
- "A Flag for Mars." Article explains the importance of dedication to the study of flag history, which includes colors used to design a new flag and symbolism.
- "Sharing the Night Sky with Your Students." Article written by a teacher provides suggestions for conducting successful nighttime observations with your students.

Rights and Payment
One-time rights. No payment.

Editor's Comments
We exist to help teachers explain astronomy to their students in easily understood terms. If you have the scientific background and know-how to achieve this, send us a query. We look for articles written in layperson's terms, and we ask that you include at least one hands-on activity designed to enhance understanding of your subject. We're interested in any topic that imparts knowledge of our vast universe.

U*S* Kids

Children's Better Health Institute
1100 Waterway Boulevard
P.O. Box 567
Indianapolis, IN 46206-0567

Editor: Daniel Lee

Description and Readership
By providing creative and imaginative articles and stories, this magazine helps young readers learn good lifestyle habits.
- **Audience:** 6–8 years
- **Frequency:** 8 times each year
- **Distribution:** 100% subscription
- **Circulation:** 230,000
- **Website:** www.uskidsmag.com

Freelance Potential
50% written by nonstaff writers. Publishes 12 freelance submissions yearly; 70% by unpublished writers, 70% by authors who are new to the magazine. Receives 58 unsolicited mss monthly.

Submissions
Send complete ms. Accepts photocopies and computer printouts. SASE. Responds in 6 weeks.
Articles: 400 words. Factual and informational articles. Topics include health, exercise, nutrition, safety, hygiene, and drug education.
Fiction: 300–400 words. Genres include historical and contemporary fiction; mystery; fantasy; adventure; and folktales.
Depts/columns: Staff written.
Other: Activities and puzzles. Poetry, to 24 lines. Submit seasonal material 6 months in advance.

Sample Issue
36 pages (3% advertising): 3 articles; 2 stories; 3 puzzles; 1 dept/column. Sample copy, $2.95 with 9x12 SASE (2 first-class stamps). Guidelines available.
- "The Coolest Kid in Class." Story features a hip boy who thinks that his new glasses make him uncool.
- "The Eyes Have It." Factual article describes how the human eyeball works.
- "Warm Your Toes with a Hat." Article explains how the body stays warm.

Rights and Payment
All rights. Articles and fiction, to $.20 per word. Other material, payment rates vary. Pays on publication. Provides 5 contributor's copies.

Editor's Comments
We like to see material that helps readers learn good personal habits. We need stories about real kids who are doing something a bit out of the ordinary, as well as informative articles that explore the natural wonders of the world.

U.25 Magazine

9800 Fredericksburg Road
San Antonio, TX 78288

Editor: Carol Barnes

Description and Readership
Published for young members of the United Services Automobile Association (USAA), *U.25 Magazine* promotes responsible driving and lifestyle habits through informative articles on a wide array of topics.
- **Audience:** 18–24 years
- **Frequency:** Quarterly
- **Distribution:** 100% controlled
- **Circulation:** 440,000
- **Website:** www.usaa.com

Freelance Potential
90% written by nonstaff writers. Publishes 5–10 freelance submissions yearly. Receives 5 queries monthly.

Submissions
Query with résumé and clips for feature articles. Send complete ms for shorter pieces. Accepts photocopies and computer printouts. SASE. Responds in 6–8 weeks.
Articles: 1,000 words. Shorter pieces 300 words. Informational and how-to articles; profiles; interviews; and personal experience pieces. Topics include college, careers, saving and investing money, driving, and lifestyle issues.
Depts/columns: Word length varies. Short news items, USAA programs, and driving information.
Other: Activities, games.

Sample Issue
32 pages: 4 articles; 3 depts/columns. Sample copy, free with 9x12 SASE ($1.80 postage). Writers' guidelines available.
- "What's Messing with You?" Article offers tips on how to be more organized.
- "Star Treps." Article profiles several successful, young entrepreneurs.
- Sample dept/column: "Bits.Bytes" explores the comeback of knitting as a relaxation method.

Rights and Payment
All rights. Feature articles, $500. Other material, payment rates vary. Pays on acceptance.

Editor's Comments
We are interested in material on the latest trends in college, careers, money, and driving. Send us something that will give our readers ideas on how to become successful, contributing members of society who maximize their potential.

Vegetarian Baby & Child

47565 323rd Avenue
Cass Lake, MN 56633

Editor: Melanie Wilson

Description and Readership
Articles, product reviews, interviews, and recipes
make up the contents of this online magazine for
parents who have chosen the vegetarian or vegan
lifestyle for themselves and their children.
- **Audience:** Parents
- **Frequency:** Quarterly
- **Distribution:** 100% Internet
- **Hits per month:** Unavailable
- **Website:** www.vegetarianbaby.com

Freelance Potential
95% written by nonstaff writers. Publishes 50 freelance submissions yearly. Receives 2 queries, 1–2
unsolicited mss monthly.

Submissions
Query or send complete ms. Accepts photocopies,
computer printouts, and email submissions to
melanie@vegetarianbaby.com (Microsoft Word attachments). SASE. Response time varies.
Articles: 350–1,500 words. Informational and how-to
articles; profiles; interviews; and personal experience
pieces. Topics include general nutrition, vegetarian
pregnancy, dealing with friends and family, living with
non-vegetarians, health, child care, activism, and
support networks.
Depts/columns: Word lengths vary. Q&As, recipes,
and book and new product reviews.
Other: Activities, games, and crafts for children.

Sample Issue
Sample copy and guidelines available at website.
- "Why We Scream for Ice Cream." Article traces the
  history of ice cream from its earliest form as an iced
  drink in biblical times to its evolution into the
  creamy treat we enjoy today.
- "Green Smoothies: An Easy Way to Love Greens."
  Article cites the health benefits of green vegetables
  and explains that mixing them in a blender with fruit
  makes them much more pleasant to consume.

Rights and Payment
First rights. Articles, $10. Pays on publication.

Editor's Comments
We're interested in receiving "healthy kid" stories from
our readers. These should be 400–800 words in
length and include your child's age, advice for other
parents, quotes from your child or other adults, challenges you've overcome, and your original recipes.

Vegetarianteen.com

47565 323rd Avenue
Cass Lake, MN 56633

Editor: Melanie Wilson

Description and Readership
Teens who follow a vegan or vegetarian diet, physi-
cians, nutritionists, and counselors who work with
youth provide the articles that appear in this online
publication. *Vegetarianteen.com* advocates a
vegan/vegetarian lifestyle and offers advice and
encouragement to its teen readers.
- **Audience:** YA–Adult
- **Frequency:** Quarterly
- **Distribution:** 100% Internet
- **Hits per month:** Unavailable
- **Website:** www.vegetarianteen.com

Freelance Potential
95% written by nonstaff writers. Publishes 50 freelance submissions yearly; 50% by authors who are
new to the magazine. Receives 20–25 queries,
10–15 unsolicited mss monthly.

Submissions
Query or send complete ms. Accepts photocopies,
computer printouts, and email submissions to
melanie@vegetarianbaby.com (Microsoft Word attachments). Availability of artwork improves chance of
acceptance. SASE. Response time varies.
Articles: 350–1,200 words. Informational and how-to
articles; profiles; interviews; and personal experience
pieces. Topics include health, food, fitness, family
issues, animal activism, and nutrition.
Depts/columns: Word lengths vary. Recipes and book
and product reviews.

Sample Issue
Sample copy and guidelines available at website.
- "I Changed for a Man . . . But I Still Have a Mind of
  My Own." Personal essay tells how a teen's relationship with her vegetarian boyfriend led her to investi-
  gate vegetarianism and eventually give up meat.
- "My Transformation." Essay reveals how a teen gave
  up his junk-food diet and, along with his mom,
  embarked on an all-raw vegan lifestyle.

Rights and Payment
Rights vary. Written material, $15. Payment policy
varies.

Editor's Comments
We always need "how I went veg" stories as well as
material for our food diaries section, which details
what you eat each day and includes recipes. Tell us
how you're different now that you've given up meat.

VegFamily

9436 Deer Lodge Lane
Las Vegas, NV 89129

Editor: Erin Pavlina

Description and Readership
This e-zine is available to readers around the world who are seeking information about offering nutritionally-sound vegan meals to their children.
- **Audience:** YA-Adult
- **Frequency:** Monthly
- **Distribution:** 100% Internet
- **Hits per month:** 90,000
- **Website:** www.vegfamily.com

Freelance Potential
50% written by nonstaff writers. Publishes 40 free-lance submissions yearly; 90% by unpublished writers, 50% by authors who are new to the magazine. Receives 5 queries monthly.

Submissions
Query. Accepts email submissions to contact@ vegfamily.com. Responds in 2 weeks.
Articles: 500–1,500 words. Informational, self-help, and how-to articles; profiles; interviews; and personal experience pieces. Topics include health, fitness, nature, the environment, social issues, and vegan parenting.
Fiction: 500–2,000 words. Genres include inspirational fiction, animal stories, and stories with nature and environmental themes.
Depts/columns: Word lengths vary. Recipes and book and product reviews.
Artwork: JPEG and GIF files.
Other: Activities. Submit seasonal material 2 months in advance.

Sample Issue
Sample copy and guidelines available at website.
- "Ten Tips for Perfect Vegan Baking." Article explains ten important steps for producing delicious cookies, cakes, and muffins.
- Sample dept/column: "Recipes" offers recipes for fettuccine skillet, Mexicali corn, blueberry pie, and vegan ice cream.

Rights and Payment
All electronic rights. Articles, $20. Pays on publication.

Editor's Comments
You don't have to be a professional author to write for us; you must simply be willing to share information. In addition to articles about vegan foods, we also cover topics such as dealing with pediatricians and the risks and benefits of prenatal testing.

Ventura County Parent Magazine

Suite O
3477-D Old Conejo Road
Newbury Park, CA 91320

Editor & Publisher: Hillary Lynn

Description and Readership
This magazine provides support and resources to parents around Ventura County. It includes up-to-date information on parenting, child development, social issues, local community events, and health matters.
- **Audience:** Parents
- **Frequency:** Monthly
- **Distribution:** 89% controlled; 11% subscription
- **Circulation:** 42,000
- **Website:** www.vcparent.com

Freelance Potential
60% written by nonstaff writers. Publishes 40 free-lance submissions yearly; 10% by unpublished writers; 10% by authors who are new to the magazine. Receives 250 queries, 8 unsolicited mss monthly.

Submissions
Query with sample paragraph; or send complete ms. Accepts disk submissions (Macintosh compatible) and email submissions to info@vcparent.com. SASE. Responds to queries in 2 months, to mss in 6 weeks.
Articles: 1,000–1,500 words. Informational articles and personal experience pieces. Topics include animals, crafts, hobbies, pets, the arts, computers, current events, education, health, fitness, social issues, popular culture, and news.
Fiction: 1,000–1,500 words. Publishes real-life and problem-solving fiction.
Depts/columns: 600 words. Health and safety news, media reviews, and Internet tips.
Artwork: B/W or color prints. Line art.
Other: Activities and filler on local topics.

Sample Issue
30 pages (44% advertising): 3 articles; 7 depts/columns; 1 camp directory. Sample copy, free with 12x14 SASE. Guidelines and theme list available.
- "In beTween." Article shares ideas for kids to make money over the summer.
- Sample dept/column: "Healthwise" offers information on pool safety, bees, sunscreen, and traveling.

Rights and Payment
Exclusive regional rights. Written material, $35–$100. Artwork, payment rate varies. Pays on publication. Provides 1 contributor's copy.

Editor's Comments
We are looking for more articles and tips on tween issues and the Internet, as well as education.

The Village Family

501 40th Street S
Fargo, ND 58103

Editor: Laurie Neill

Description and Readership
This publication from the Village Family Service Center is dedicated to improving the quality of life of residents of the Fargo, ND, and Moorhead, MN, areas. Its articles educate families and encourage them to develop and maintain positive, constructive relationships.
• **Audience:** Parents, 25–50 years
• **Frequency:** 6 times each year
• **Distribution:** Subscription; other
• **Circulation:** 25,000
• **Website:** www.thevillagefamily.org

Freelance Potential
70% written by nonstaff writers. Publishes 30 freelance submissions yearly.

Submissions
Query or send complete ms with brief author bio. Accepts photocopies, computer printouts, and email to magazine@thevillagefamily.com. SASE. Response times vary.
Articles: To 1,500 words. Informational, self-help, and how-to articles; profiles; interviews; and personal experience pieces. Topics include current events, health, fitness, recreation, regional news, social issues, sports, and travel.
Depts/columns: Word lengths vary. Medical updates, media reviews, humorous essays, crafts, recipes, money matters, and family issues.

Sample Issue
46 pages: 3 articles; 8 depts/columns; 1 calendar of events. Guidelines available.
• "Domestic Violence: It Hurts More Than You Can Imagine." Article explores why domestic violence occurs and what can be done to stop it.
• "Homelessness Right Here at Home." Article reports that homelessness is on the rise in the Fargo-Moorhead area and across the country.
• Sample dept/column: "Money Matters" discusses debt settlement scams.

Rights and Payment
First and electronic rights. Written material, $.07–$.10 per word. Reprints, $30–$50. Pays on publication.

Editor's Comments
Please remember that we receive a large volume of material and a response is not always possible. If we decide to use your submission, we will contact you.

Voice of Youth Advocates

Suite 200
4501 Forbes Road
Lanham, MD 20706

Editor-in-Chief: Cathi Dunn MacRae

Description and Readership
Self-proclaimed as "the library magazine serving those who serve young adults," this professional journal offers informational articles and book reviews on a wide range of genres for young readers.
• **Audience:** Professionals who work with youth
• **Frequency:** 6 times each year
• **Distribution:** 90% subscription; 10% other
• **Circulation:** 6,400
• **Website:** www.voya.com

Freelance Potential
85% written by nonstaff writers. Publishes 50 freelance submissions yearly; 70% by unpublished writers, 60% by authors who are new to the magazine. Receives 5 queries monthly.

Submissions
Query with résumé, synopsis, and market analysis. Accepts photocopies, computer printouts, and email queries to cmacrae@voya.com. Availability of artwork improves chance of acceptance. SASE. Responds in 2–4 months.
Articles: 800–3,000 words. Informational and how-to articles; book reviews; and book lists. Prints one book list annually. Topics include young adult literature, contemporary authors, and library programs.
Other: Submit seasonal material 1 year in advance.

Sample Issue
80 pages (20% advertising): 4 articles; 160 book reviews. Sample copy, free with 9x12 SASE. Writers' guidelines available with SASE and at website.
• "Let's (Not) Get It On." Article critically examines the role of girls and sexuality in YA fiction.
• "Teen Realm." Article profiles one school that has an entire section of the library set aside for teens.
• Sample dept/column: "Top Shelf Fiction for Middle School Readers" reviews the year's best YA fiction.

Rights and Payment
All rights. Articles, $50–$100. Pays on publication. Provides 3 contributor's copies.

Editor's Comments
We are seeing too much in the way of YA literary criticism and misdirected submissions from writers who are not familiar with the magazine. Please take the time to review a few issues and then submit a detailed query, résumé, synopsis, and market analysis.

Voices from the Middle

National Council of Teachers of English
1111 West Kenyon Road
Urbana, IL 61801-1096

Production Editor: Carol Schanche

Description and Readership
This professional journal from the National Council of Teachers of English provides the research base for, and practical examples of, best-practice classroom strategies and theory for language arts teachers working with students in the middle grades.
- **Audience:** Teachers
- **Frequency:** Quarterly
- **Distribution:** 90% subscription; 10% other
- **Circulation:** 11,000
- **Website:** www.ncte.org/pubs/journals/vm

Freelance Potential
60% written by nonstaff writers. Publishes 30 freelance submissions yearly; 60% by unpublished writers, 85% by authors who are new to the magazine. Receives 20 unsolicited mss monthly.

Submissions
Send 3 copies of complete ms. Accepts photocopies, computer printouts, and email submissions to cschanche@ncte.org (indicate issue for which you are submitting in the subject line). SASE. Responds in 3–5 months.
Articles: 2,500–4,000 words. Educational and personal experience articles related to the issue's theme. Topics include middle school language arts and English instruction.
Depts/columns: Staff written.
Artwork: B/W prints or transparencies. Line art.

Sample Issue
80 pages (9% advertising): 8 articles; 12 depts/columns. Sample copy, $6. Guidelines and theme list available.
- "A Hand Up: What I Wouldn't Give to Be That Good." Discusses how standardized testing eliminates the most motivating factor in learning: creativity.
- "The Odd Fish Story." Article explains how visual/verbal tools can help all students, not just "different learners."

Rights and Payment
First and second rights. No payment. Provides 2 contributor's copies.

Editor's Comments
Each issue of our journal is devoted to one topic or concept related to literacy and learning at the middle school level. We prefer articles that include charts, diagrams, or photos of students working.

Washington Families Magazine

Suite 550
485 Spring Park Place
Herndon, VA 20170

Managing Editor: Marae Leggs

Description and Readership
Activity calendars, museum guides, and reports on things to see and do in the Washington, D.C. area are found in this family publication. It also offers articles on health, education, and other parenting topics.
- **Audience:** Parents
- **Frequency:** Monthly
- **Distribution:** 100% controlled
- **Circulation:** 100,000
- **Website:** www.washingtonfamilies.com

Freelance Potential
75% written by nonstaff writers. Publishes 90 freelance submissions yearly; 50% by unpublished writers, 50% by authors who are new to the magazine. Receives 100 queries and unsolicited mss monthly.

Submissions
Query or send complete ms. Accepts Macintosh disk submissions and email submissions to editor@familiesmagazines.com. SASE. Response time varies.
Articles: 500–700 words. How-to and self-help articles and personal experience pieces. Topics include parenting, family life, relationships, fitness, crafts, hobbies, the arts, gifted and special education, music, multicultural and ethnic issues, social issues, music, recreation, and travel.
Depts/columns: Word length varies. Travel, health, and news of interest to families.
Artwork: B/W prints or transparencies. Line art.
Other: Submit seasonal material 6 months in advance.

Sample Issue
114 pages (50% advertising): 14 articles; 2 depts/columns; 4 resource guides; 2 events calendars. Sample copy, $4 with 9x12 SASE. Guidelines and editorial calendar available online.
- "Dads in Delivery." Article explores the roles of fathers in the delivery room and offers resources for expectant and new dads.
- "A Healthy Diet for Your Little Athlete." Features hints for good nutrition.

Rights and Payment
Regional rights. Articles, $35–$50. Depts/columns, rate varies. Pays on publication. Provides 1 copy.

Editor's Comments
We enjoy humor in our articles, but we don't publish "fluff." Material should always be informative.

Washington Parent

Suite N720
4701 Sangamore Road
Bethesda, MD 20186

Editor: Margaret Hut

Description and Readership
This resource for local parents seeks to educate and support families living in the Washington, D.C. metropolitan area.
- **Audience:** Families
- **Frequency:** Monthly
- **Distribution:** 93% controlled; 7% subscription
- **Circulation:** 75,000
- **Website:** www.washingtonparent.com

Freelance Potential
98% written by nonstaff writers. Publishes 20 freelance submissions yearly. Receives 100 queries and unsolicited mss monthly.

Submissions
Query. Accepts disk submissions (Microsoft Word or WordPerfect) and email submissions to washpar@washingtonparent.com (Microsoft Word or WordPerfect attachments). SASE. Response time varies.
Articles: 1,000–2,000 words. Informational and how-to articles. Topics include regional news and events, parenting, family issues, local entertainment, gifted and special education, child development, health, fitness, the environment, and multicultural and ethnic issues.
Depts/columns: Word lengths vary. Family travel, book and media reviews, education, topics relating to children with special needs, and short news reviews.

Sample Issue
130 pages (63% advertising): 9 articles; 10 depts/columns. Sample copy, guidelines and editorial calendar available.
- "The Littlest Campers." Article offers advice on how to know when your child is ready for camp.
- "Ready, Set, Go Potty!" Article discusses ways to successfully potty train a toddler.
- Sample dept/column: "Ages & Stages" offers ways to soothe a child's fear.

Rights and Payment
First rights. Written material, payment rates vary. Pays on publication. Provides 3 contributor's copies.

Editor's Comments
We are looking for informative, useful articles that deal with raising children of all ages. Our readership consists of local parents, so in addition, material must be relative to the area. Please verify that all information, (addresses, phone numbers, etc.) is correct.

Weatherwise

1319 Eighteenth Street NW
Washington, DC 20036

Managing Editor: Lynn Elsey

Description and Readership
The pages of this educational magazine include informational articles and photos on topics related to the weather. It also includes reviews of books and weather instruments. All material has a scientific basis.
- **Audience:** Students–Adults
- **Frequency:** 6 times each year
- **Distribution:** 100% subscription
- **Circulation:** 20,000
- **Website:** www.weatherwise.org

Freelance Potential
20% written by nonstaff writers. Publishes 10 freelance submissions yearly; 5% by unpublished writers, 10% by authors who are new to the magazine. Receives xxqueries monthly.

Submissions
Query with résumé, cover letter, and clips. Accepts email queries to lelsey@heldref.com. Availability of artwork improves chances of acceptance. Responds in 2 months.
Articles: Word length varies. Informational articles; photo essays, and reviews. Topics include storms, storm tracking, safety issues, and other topics related to the weather. All material has a scientific basis.
Depts/columns: Word length varies. Book reviews and resources, weather highlights, forecasts, history, and questions/answers about types of weather.
Artwork: Color prints or transparencies.

Sample Issue
82 pages: 6 articles; 8 depts/columns. Writers' guidelines available.
- "Name That Storm." Article discusses the history of the process of assigning names to storms.
- "Safeguarding the Spectator." Article takes a look at the dangers of lightning to large outdoor audiences and recommendations for safety guidelines.
- Sample dept/column: "Reviews & Resources" offers a review of the book *The Children's Blizzard*, a weekly calendar, and a handheld windmeter.

Rights and Payment
All rights. Pays on publication. Written material, payment rate varies. Artwork, payment rate varies.

Editor's Comments
We seek photo-essays on memorable weather events, as well as articles that define the power, excitement, and beauty of the ever-changing weather.

Wee Ones

Editor: Jennifer Reed

Description and Readership
This children's website features stories, articles, artwork and illustrations, puzzles, games, and activities designed to help children read and learn. All links are carefully selected for age appropriateness.
- **Audience:** 5–10 years
- **Frequency:** 6 times each year
- **Distribution:** Internet
- **Hits per month:** 40,000+
- **Website:** www.weeonesmag.com

Freelance Potential
100% written by nonstaff writers. Publishes 200 freelance submissions yearly; 50% by unpublished writers, 50% by authors who are new to the magazine. Receives 80 unsolicited mss monthly.

Submissions
Send complete ms. Accepts only email submissions to submissions@weeonesmag.com (attachments for artwork only). Responds in 1–4 weeks.
Articles: 500 words. Informational and how-to articles. Topics include animals, pets, the arts, crafts, hobbies, current events, health, fitness, history, music, multicultural issues, nature, the environment, sports, travel, and recreation. Also publishes biographical articles.
Fiction: 500 words. Genres include contemporary, historical, and multicultural fiction; adventure; mystery; and suspense. Also publishes humor, and sports and read-along stories.
Artwork: Line art.
Other: Submit seasonal material 6 months in advance.

Sample Issue
Guidelines available at website.
- "Snow-it-All." Article describes the different kinds of snowflakes and also provides a snowy craft.
- "Loops, Whirls, and Arches." Article explains about the uniqueness of fingerprints.
- "Life on Ferry Farm." Article tells about George Washington's childhood farm.

Rights and Payment
Nonexclusive worldwide, electronic, and reprint rights. Written material, $.05 per word. Pays on publication.

Editor's Comments
For 2006, we need more mysteries and stories about sports that kids and parents can read together.

Westchester Family

Suite 102
141 Halstead Avenue
Mamaroneck, NY 10543

Editor: Jean Sheff

Description and Readership
This local resource for parents of children in Westchester County contains articles on a variety of parenting topics, from education to traveling. It also features interviews and profiles of interesting people, along with local tips on dining and entertainment.
- **Audience:** Parents
- **Frequency:** Monthly
- **Distribution:** 96% controlled; 4% subscription
- **Circulation:** 59,000
- **Website:** www.westchesterfamily.com

Freelance Potential
80% written by nonstaff writers. Publishes 40 freelance submissions yearly; 40% by authors who are new to the magazine. Receives 50 queries monthly.

Submissions
Query with clips. Accepts photocopies and computer printouts. SASE. Response time varies.
Articles: 800–1,200 words. Informational articles; humor; profiles; interviews; photo-essays; and personal experience pieces. Topics include gifted education, music, recreation, regional news, social issues, special education, travel, and women's issues.
Depts/columns: 400–800 words. News and reviews.

Sample Issue
82 pages (52% advertising): 2 articles; 6 depts/columns. Sample copy, free with 9x12 SASE. Guidelines available.
- "The Youngest Athletes." Article advises parents on how to encourage a love of sports in children.
- "Going Organic." Article offers tips on how and why to buy organic products.
- Sample dept/column: "Education" examines the latest news about the No Child Left Behind Act.

Rights and Payment
First rights. Written material, $25–$200. Pays on publication. Provides 1 contributor's copy.

Editor's Comments
Parents of this suburb of New York City read our magazine for in-depth, well-researched articles as well as accurate local information. We would like to hear from you if you are familiar with the area and have an interesting topic to explore or new information to share. We are also open to queries for articles and tips for our website. Check our guidelines for details.

Westchester Parent

Suite 21
901 North Broadway
North White Plains, NY 10603

Editor: Reneé Cho

Description and Readership
This publication serves as a resource guide for parents who live in Westchester and Rockland counties in New York and in the Connecticut towns of Greenwich and Stamford. In addition to events calendars and reviews of local entertainment, each issue also provides articles on child care and family matters.
- **Audience:** Parents
- **Frequency:** Monthly
- **Distribution:** 100% controlled
- **Circulation:** 66,000
- **Website:** www.parentsknow.com

Freelance Potential
90% written by nonstaff writers. Publishes 15 freelance submissions yearly; 5% by unpublished writers, 20% by authors who are new to the magazine. Receives 95 queries, 8 unsolicited mss monthly.

Submissions
Query or send complete ms. Accepts photocopies, computer printouts, and email submissions to renee@parentsknow.com. SASE. Response times vary.
Articles: 800–1,000 words. Informational, self-help, and how-to articles; profiles; interviews; and personal experience pieces. Topics include parenting, family life, child development, animals, pets, the arts, computers, crafts, hobbies, current events, gifted and special education, health, fitness, recreation, regional news, and travel.
Depts/columns: 750 words. Short news items, family travel pieces, and media reviews.
Other: Submit seasonal material 4 months in advance.

Sample Issue
60 pages: 5 articles; 10 depts/columns; 1 calendar of events. Sample copy, free with 10x13 SASE. Guidelines available via email.
- "Should Kids Have Cell Phones?" Article questions whether cell phones increase safety or vulnerability.
- Sample dept/column: "Family Travel" spotlights the family attractions in Baltimore.

Rights and Payment
First New York area rights. Articles, $75. Depts/columns, payment rates vary. Pays 2 months after publication. Provides 1 contributor's copy.

Editor's Comments
We welcome unsolicited submissions, especially from freelancers experienced in writing about family issues.

West Coast Families

224-280 Nelson Street
Vancouver, British Columbia V6B 2E2
Canada

Editor: Michelle Froese

Description and Readership
In print for 13 years, this tabloid offers families living in the Vancouver area informative tips and advice on parenting issues, as well as fun family activities, and regional events and resources.
- **Audience:** Families
- **Frequency:** 8 times each year
- **Distribution:** 93% controlled; 5% schools; 2% subscription
- **Circulation:** 50,000
- **Website:** www.westcoastfamilies.com

Freelance Potential
70% written by nonstaff writers. Publishes 50 freelance submissions yearly; 25% by authors who are new to the magazine. Receives 25 queries monthly.

Submissions
Query. Accepts photocopies, computer printouts, Macintosh disk submissions, and email submissions to info@westcoastfamilies.com. SAE/IRC. Response time varies.
Articles: 600–800 words. Informational, self-help, and how-to articles; and personal experience pieces. Topics include family life, parenting, recreation, travel, religion, current events, health, fitness, education, sports, hobbies, science, technology, nature, animals, and pets.
Depts/columns: Staff written.
Other: Puzzles, activities, jokes, and games. Submit seasonal material 3 months in advance.

Sample Issue
30 pages (8% advertising): 12 articles; 7 depts/columns; 3 contests. Sample copy, free with 9x12 SASE ($1.45 Canadian postage). Guidelines and editorial calendar available.
- "It Takes a Village." Article discusses factors to consider when deciding whether the timing is right to become a foster parent.
- "Reflections of a Single Dad." Essay shares the author's thoughts on being a single dad.

Rights and Payment
Rights policy varies. Articles, $40–$60. Other material, payment rate varies. Pays on acceptance or publication. Provides contributor's copies upon request.

Editor's Comments
We are looking for articles on family finances and technology, as well as family-friendly travel pieces.

What If?

19 Lynwood Place
Guelph, Ontario N1G 2V9
Canada

Managing Editor: Mike Leslie

Description and Readership
Written by and for young Canadians, *What If?* encourages and supports young authors by providing a place for them to share their writing and read the work of others.
- **Audience:** 12–21 years
- **Frequency:** 5 times each year
- **Distribution:** 60% schools; 20% subscription; 20% newsstands
- **Circulation:** 25,000
- **Website:** www.whatifmagazine.com

Freelance Potential
90% written by nonstaff writers. Publishes 100 freelance submissions yearly; 90% by unpublished writers, 90% by authors who are new to the magazine. Receives 200 unsolicited mss monthly.

Submissions
Send complete ms with résumé. Accepts photocopies, computer printouts, email to editor@whatifmagazine.com (Microsoft Word), and simultaneous submissions if identified. Availability of artwork improves chance of acceptance. SAE/IRC. Responds in 3 months.
Articles: To 1,000 words. Opinion pieces and editorials.
Fiction: To 3,000 words. Topics include mystery; suspense; fantasy; humor; and contemporary, inspirational, real-life, and science fiction.
Depts/columns: 500 words. Crafts and cooking.
Artwork: Full color prints. Line art.
Other: Poetry, to 20 lines.

Sample Issue
48 pages (3% advertising): 4 articles; 6 stories; 3 editorials; 8 poems; 5 depts/columns. Sample copy, $7.50 with 9x12 SAE. Guidelines available.
- "The Art of Getting Published." Article offers pointers on how to get your work published.
- "Selling Cookies." Story features Girl Scouts who meet a lonely elderly couple while selling cookies.
- Sample dept/column: "Viewpoint" offers one reader's opinion about the paradoxical nature of individuality.

Rights and Payment
First rights. No payment. Pays on publication. Provides 2 contributor's copies.

Editor's Comments
We are looking for mystery, suspense, and adventure stories written by Canadians, 19 years old and younger.

What's Hers

108-93 Lombard Avenue
Winnipeg, Manitoba R3B 3B1
Canada

Editor: Barbara Chabai

Description and Readership
Formerly known as *What*, this redesigned magazine now focuses on what's hot, hip, and cool for teenage girls and young adults. Each issue includes serious articles on world events, light pieces on popular culture, and profiles of well-known personalities.
- **Audience:** 14–18 years
- **Frequency:** 5 times each year
- **Distribution:** 100% schools
- **Circulation:** 180,000
- **Website:** www.whatshers.com

Freelance Potential
40–45% written by nonstaff writers. Publishes 25–30 freelance submissions yearly; 5% by unpublished writers, 20% by authors who are new to the magazine. Receives 20 queries monthly.

Submissions
Query with clips. No unsolicited submissions. SAE/IRC. Response time varies.
Articles: 300–1,700 words. Informational and factual articles; profiles; interviews; and humor. Topics include current events, popular culture, entertainment, health, social issues, and relationships.
Depts/columns: 300–1,700 words. Trends, sports, and ordinary in extraordinary situations.
Artwork: Color prints or transparencies.

Sample Issue
38 pages (60% advertising): 2 articles; 10 depts/columns. Sample copy, $1.42 Canadian with 9x12 SAE/IRC. Guidelines available.
- "Guys We Love." Article profiles popular young men from stage, screen, and sound.
- "Identity Crisis." Article discusses the disturbing increase in stolen identities.
- Sample dept/column: "HERstory" tells about a teen who underwent breast reduction surgery.

Rights and Payment
First rights. Written material, to $500. Pays 30 days after publication. Provides 2 contributor's copies.

Editor's Comments
Focus your article on what teens want to know about the world. Material should be written in a light, conversational format that is easy to read and understand. If the topic is complicated, use descriptions that readers can relate to; don't assume that the audience knows everything.

What's His

108-93 Lombard Avenue
Winnipeg, Manitoba R3B 3B1
Canada

Editor: Dan Kenning

Description and Readership
Formerly known as *What*, this redesigned magazine for teenage boys and young adults includes serious articles on world events, light pieces on popular culture, and profiles of well-known personalities.
- **Audience:** 14–18 years
- **Frequency:** 5 times each year
- **Distribution:** 100% schools
- **Circulation:** 100,000
- **Website:** www.whatshis.com

Freelance Potential
40–45% written by nonstaff writers. Publishes 25–30 freelance submissions yearly; 5% by unpublished writers, 20% by authors who are new to the magazine. Receives 20 queries monthly.

Submissions
Query with clips. No unsolicited submissions. SAE/IRC. Response time varies.
Articles: 300–1,700 words. Informational and factual articles; profiles; interviews; and humor. Topics include current events, popular culture, entertainment, health, social issues, and relationships.
Depts/columns: 300–1,700 words. Trends, sports, and ordinary in extraordinary situations.
Artwork: Color prints or transparencies.

Sample Issue
22 pages (60% advertising): 2 articles; 10 depts/columns. Sample copy, $1.42 Canadian with 9x12 SAE/IRC. Guidelines available.
- "We're Drawn to Amanda Walsh." Profile of a young TV actress.
- "Cabinet Makers." Tongue-in-cheek article about how to become a politician, win friends, and influence people.
- Sample dept/column: "Level 4" reviews and rates new video games on the market.

Rights and Payment
First rights. Written material, to $500. Pays 30 days after publication. Provides 2 contributor's copies.

Editor's Comments
Our readers know what's going on in the world. Find a way to give them more information without lecturing. Material should be written in a light, conversational tone that is easy to read and understand. We will consider all topics of interest to young adult males, such as home, school, and relationships.

What's Up Kids?

496 Melter Road
Ridgeville, Ontario L0S 1M0
Canada

Managing Editor: Susan Pennell-Sebekos

Description and Readership
Educational and fun activities for children ages birth through thirteen, along with articles on family issues, parenting, travel, and education can be found in this Canadian magazine for families.
- **Audience:** Parents and children
- **Frequency:** 6 times each year
- **Distribution:** Subscription; newsstand
- **Circulation:** 200,000
- **Website:** www.whatsupkids.com

Freelance Potential
80% written by nonstaff writers. Publishes 30 freelance submissions yearly; 5% by unpublished writers, 60% by authors who are new to the magazine. Receives 29 queries monthly.

Submissions
Query. Accepts email queries to editor@whatsupkids.com. Response time varies.
Articles: Word lengths vary. Informational articles. Topics include education, family issues, travel, fitness, nutrition, and health.
Depts/columns: Word lengths vary. Brief informational items on fathers, health, finance, and news.

Sample Issue
62 pages (15% advertising): 12 articles; 10 depts/columns; 1 kids' section.
- "Booster Seat Safety." Article reports on the proper use of safety restraint systems for children.
- "Homework Tips." Article offers key ways parents can help children develop good study habits.
- Sample dept/column: "Planet Earth" offers a story about a big spruce tree and its impact on the environment when it was unnecessarily cut down.

Rights and Payment
All rights. Payment policy varies. Provides contributor's copies.

Editor's Comments
We continue to seek family-friendly travel pieces, articles on family issues, and activities. We strive to provide something for all members of the family and look for exceptional articles for parents and fun and challenging activities and games for our kids' section. If you are a Canadian writer, and have an idea for something new that will bring our readers up-to-date on a hot parenting topic, send us a well-written query that will highlight your experience.

Winner

55 West Oak Ridge Drive
Hagerstown, MD 21740

Editor: Jan Schleifer

Description and Readership
Preventive drug education and lifestyle-skills training for middle school students are the focus of this magazine. Each issue includes articles on drug facts, life skills, and real-world advice.
- **Audience:** 8–12 years
- **Frequency:** 9 times each year
- **Distribution:** 80% subscription; 20% other
- **Circulation:** 10,000
- **Website:** www.listenmagazine.org

Freelance Potential
15% written by nonstaff writers. Publishes 50 freelance submissions yearly; 5% by unpublished writers, 20% by authors who are new to the magazine. Receives 8 queries monthly.

Submissions
Send complete ms. Accepts email submissions to jschleifer@rhpa.org. Responds in 1 month.
Articles: 500–600 words. Informational, how-to, and self-help articles; and profiles. Topics include family issues; sports; peer pressure; tobacco, drug and alcohol abuse; life skills; social issues; and personal relationships.
Fiction: 600 words. True-life stories and positive lifestyles and problem solving.
Artwork: Color prints and transparencies. Line art.
Other: Puzzles, games, and filler.

Sample Issue
16 pages (no advertising): 2 articles; 2 stories; 5 activities; 1 comic. Sample copy, $2 with 9x12 SASE (2 first-class stamps). Guidelines available at website.
- "Dangerous Dieting." Story features a girl who may be suffering from an eating disorder.
- "John's Big Choice." Story tells of a boy who makes the right choice about smoking.
- "He Needed a Clear Mind." Essay describes a trip to Hawaii to film an underwater lava flow.

Rights and Payment
First rights. Articles, $80. Pays on acceptance. Provides 3 contributor's copies.

Editor's Comments
We are looking for articles that present facts about a specific drug or drug-related behavior, and that give advice on how to steer clear of drugs and fit into society. We ask that with each article you include two or three thought questions and a pencil activity.

Wire Tap Magazine

c/o Independent Media Institute
77 Federal Street
San Francisco, CA 94107

Associate Editor: Kristina Rizga

Description and Readership
News articles, essays, opinion pieces, and poems which address social and political issues from a youth perspective are presented in this online magazine.
- **Audience:** 6–12 years
- **Frequency:** 6 times each year
- **Distribution:** Online
- **Hits permonth:** Unavailable
- **Website:** http://www.alternet.org/wiretap

Freelance Potential
95% written by nonstaff writers. Publishes 50 freelance submissions yearly. Receives 10 queries each month.

Submissions
Query. Accepts photocopies, computer printouts, and email submissions to editor@wiretapmag.com (no attachments). SASE. Responds time varies.
Articles: Word lengths vary. Informational articles; profiles; interviews; and personal experience pieces. Topics include social issues and politics.
Depts/columns: Word length varies. Reviews, politics, news.
Other: Poetry.

Sample Issue
Guidelines available at website.
- "Empty Words." Article offers an undercover look at the conservatives of the future, from a progressive point of view.
- "The Political Power of the Midwest." Article reports on a young native of Ohio who offers a long-term plan for transforming politics in the Midwest.
- Sample dept/column: "No Road For You" discusses why an elected official wants to bar cities from giving their residents quick and easy Internet access.

Rights and Payment
Electronic rights. Written material, $50–$100 for assigned pieces. No payment for unsolicited submissions.

Editor's Comments
New, young writers are welcome. We prefer writing that is written in a personal voice, is well researched and carefully written, and has an activist spin to it. We look for editorial that addresses the issues that are of interest to our audience of progressive and socially conscious youth. To get an idea of what we are looking for, check out our website for article samples.

Writers' Journal

P.O. Box 394
Perham, MN 56573

Editor: Leon Ogroske

Description and Readership
In print for 25 years, this resourceful magazine for writers includes informational articles on writing skills, the business side of writing, marketing, and publishing. It also offers contest information, as well as reviews of books, computer software, and poetry.
- **Audience:** YA–Adult
- **Frequency:** 6 times each year
- **Distribution:** 90% newsstand; 10% subscription
- **Circulation:** 23,000
- **Website:** www.writersjournal.com

Freelance Potential
90% written by nonstaff writers. Publishes 60 freelance submissions yearly; 50% by unpublished writers, 70% by authors who are new to the magazine. Receives 16 queries and unsolicited mss monthly.

Submissions
Query or send ms. Accepts photocopies, and computer printouts. SASE. Responds in 2–6 months.
Articles: 1,000–2,000 words. Informational and how-to articles; profiles; and interviews. Topics include fiction writing, travel writing, technical writing, business writing, writing skills, interviewing, research, record keeping, and finances.
Depts/columns: Photography tips and marketing ideas, 1,200–2,000 words. Software reviews, 500–750.
Other: Poetry. Fiction contest, various genres.

Sample Issue
66 pages (10% advertising): 11 articles; 1 story; 13 depts/columns; 2 poems. Sample copy, $5 with 9x12 SASE. Guidelines available.
- "The Query Letter." Article offers information on how to write a query letter that will sell an article.
- "Rejection or Refusal?" Article takes a look at the difference between rejection and refusal letters, and the reasons for getting them.
- Sample dept/column: "Computer Business" explores feasible wireless options available to writers.

Rights and Payment
One-time rights. Written material, $20; plus 1-year subscription. Pays on publication. Provides contributor's copies upon request.

Editor's Comments
We are looking for more articles that will provide readers with good descriptions of different genre writing.

Yes Mag

3968 Long Gun Place
Victoria, British Columbia V8N 3A9
Canada

Managing Editor: Jude Isabella

Description and Readership
Focusing on Canadian science and scientists, this magazine features theme-related articles, projects, and experiments, as well as software and book reviews.
- **Audience:** 8–14 years
- **Frequency:** 6 times each year
- **Distribution:** 85% subscription; 15% newsstand
- **Circulation:** 22,000
- **Website:** www.yesmag.ca

Freelance Potential
70% written by nonstaff writers. Publishes 30 freelance submissions yearly; 15% by unpublished writers, 25% by authors who are new to the magazine. Receives 15 queries monthly.

Submissions
Query. Accepts email submissions to editor@yesmag.ca. Response time varies.
Articles: Features, 800–1,200 words. Short, theme-related articles, 400–800 words. Informational articles, 250 words. Topics include astronomy, engineering, math, science, technology, plants and animals, and the environment.
Depts/columns: 250 words. Short items on current science, technology, and environmental events.

Sample Issue
28 pages (9% advertising): 5 articles; 5 depts/columns. Sample copy, $4 with SAE/IRC. Guidelines and theme list available.
- "Artificial Power." Article about how science and technology have improved prosthetics.
- "The Thinking Human's Guide to Other Animals." Article discusses how animals think.
- Sample dept/column: "Bug Beat" looks at the world of termites.

Rights and Payment
First rights. Written material, $.20 per word. Other material, payment rate varies. Pays on publication. Provides 1 contributor's copy.

Editor's Comments
We are looking for imaginative, fun, well-researched pieces that help readers discover the adventure of science and technology. Prospective writers have the best chance of acceptance with a submission to "Science and Technology Watch," a regular column of short pieces on recent science, technology, and environmental news.

Young Adult Today

P.O. Box 436987
Chicago, IL 60643-6987

Submissions Editor: Aja Carr

Description and Readership
Targeting young African American adults, this religious publication contains weekly Bible study guides that help students of Urban Ministries' Christian education programs master scriptural passages and apply them to everyday life.
- **Audience:** 18–24 years
- **Frequency:** Quarterly
- **Distribution:** 100% subscription
- **Circulation:** 19,000
- **Website:** www.youngadulttoday.com

Freelance Potential
95% written by nonstaff writers. Publishes 52 freelance submissions yearly; 50% by unpublished writers, 50% by authors who are new to the magazine. Receives 20 queries monthly.

Submissions
Query with résumé. No unsolicited mss. All articles and Bible lessons are assigned. SASE. Responds in 2 months.
Articles: To 400 words. Lessons consist of discussion pieces, questions, devotional readings, and Bible study guides that explain how to apply the lessons learned from scripture to modern life.

Sample Issue
80 pages (4% advertising): 1 article; 13 life application stories; 13 Bible study guides. Sample copy, $2.25 with 9x12 SASE ($.87 postage). Guidelines provided on assignment.
- "Learning to Live." Article profiles several people who have made contributions to society.
- "Jesus: The Reason To Be Faithful." Bible study guide explains how and why to be faithful to God.
- "Select Good Leaders." Bible study guide teaches why we should appreciate church leaders.

Rights and Payment
Rights negotiable. Written material, $150 per lesson. Pays on publication.

Editor's Comments
Our mission is to provide quality Christian educational services which will empower God's people, especially within the African American community, and to evangelize and equip people for serving Christ. If you would like to write for us, send us a detailed query on the scripture that you would like to write about, along with a résumé.

Young Adult Today Leader

P.O. Box 436987
Chicago, IL 60643-6987

Submissions Editor: Aja Carr

Description and Readership
This journal is read by teachers of the Urban Ministries' religious education program. Each issue contains Bible lessons that correspond to scriptural passages and targets the African American community.
- **Audience:** Teachers
- **Frequency:** Quarterly
- **Distribution:** Unavailable
- **Circulation:** 12,000
- **Website:** www.youngadulttoday.com

Freelance Potential
95% written by nonstaff writers. Publishes 52 freelance submissions yearly; 50% by unpublished writers, 50% by authors who are new to the magazine. Receives 20 queries monthly.

Submissions
Query with résumé. All work is done on assignment. No unsolicited mss. SASE. Responds in 2 months.
Articles: Devotionals, 400 words. Topics include current events and social issues as they relate to Christianity and the Bible.

Sample Issue
80 pages (no advertising): 1 article; 26 teaching plans with daily lessons. Sample copy, $2.25 with 9x12 SASE ($.87 postage). Guidelines available.
- "Jesus Fulfills the Plan of Salvation." Bible study guide teaches students to recognize their position in God's creation and understand the meaning of sacrifice.
- "Be Faithful to Teaching." Bible study guide helps students understand how to grow in their commitment to God.
- "Faithfulness and Discipline." Bible study guide motivates students to remain faithful in spite of life's challenges.

Rights and Payment
Rights negotiable. Written material, $150. Pays on publication.

Editor's Comments
Our mission is to motivate teachers to provide quality Christian education to African American young people, which will help empower and motivate them to be better Christians and to spread the word of God. Send your detailed query and résumé only. We assign all material and do not accept unsolicited manuscripts. Please read a few issues of our journal to get a feel for the style of our publication.

Young Rider

P.O. Box 8237
Lexington, KY 40533

Editor: Lesley Ward

Description and Readership
Good horse grooming, riding techniques, profiles of celebrity riders, and overall information on equestrian matters appear in this magazine for enthusiasts.
- **Audience:** 6–14 years
- **Frequency:** 6 times each year
- **Distribution:** 70% subscription; 30% newsstand
- **Circulation:** 92,000
- **Website:** www.youngrider.com

Freelance Potential
20% written by nonstaff writers. Publishes 20 freelance submissions yearly; 30% by unpublished writers, 80% by authors who are new to the magazine. Receives 15 queries monthly.

Submissions
Query. Prefers word documents attached to emails. SASE. Responds in 2 weeks.
Articles: Word length varies. Factual, informational, and how-to articles; and profiles. Topics include riding, horses, careers, training, technique, and general horse care.
Fiction: 1,200 words. Stories that feature horses and youth themes.
Artwork: Color prints, transparencies, and high-resolution digital images.

Sample Issue
64 pages (28% advertising): 10 articles; 1 story; 5 depts/columns. Sample copy, $3.99 with 9x12 SASE ($1 postage). Writers' guidelines and editorial calendar available.
- "Island Pony." Article brings to life the experience one young rider had of going to Chincoteague Island and buying a wild pony during the annual roundup.
- "Amy Tryon." Article chronicles the life of this Olympic equestrian superstar in her riding pursuits, along with her full-time job as a firefighter.
- "Haley and the Law." Short story portrays a young rider who reluctantly rides again after being thrown off her horse.

Rights and Payment
First rights. Pays on publication. Written material, $.10 per word. Artwork, payment rate varies. Provides 2 contributor's copies.

Editor's Comments
We need short stories that are funny, with a bit of conflict and resolution, that appeal to young teens.

Young Salvationist

The Salvation Army
P.O. Box 269
Alexandria, VA 22313-0269

Editor-in-Chief: Marlene Chase

Description and Readership
Articles and stories with a Christian worldwide view that address contemporary teen issues can be found between the covers of this magazine.
- **Audience:** 13–21 years
- **Frequency:** 10 times each year
- **Distribution:** 80% controlled; 20% subscription
- **Circulation:** 43,000
- **Website:** www.salpubs.com

Freelance Potential
80% written by nonstaff writers. Publishes 50 freelance submissions yearly; 5% by unpublished writers, 10% by authors who are new to the magazine. Receives 40 unsolicited mss monthly.

Submissions
Send complete ms. Accepts photocopies, computer printouts, simultaneous submissions, and email submissions to ys@usn.salvationarmy.org. SASE. Responds in 2 months.
Articles: 1,000–1,500 words. How-to, inspirational, and personal experience pieces; profiles; interviews; and humor. Topics include religion and issues of relevance to teens.
Fiction: 500–1,200 words. Genres include adventure; fantasy; romance; humor; and religious and science fiction—all written from a Christian perspective.
Other: Submit seasonal material 6 months in advance.

Sample Issue
22 pages (no advertising): 6 articles; 2 stories. Sample copy, free with 9x12 SASE (3 first-class stamps). Guidelines and theme list available with #10 SASE or at website.
- "The Blues Sisters." Story features three best friends who support each other during the emotional periods in their lives.
- "Coping with Your Parents' Divorce." Article discusses problems children of divorced parents face.

Rights and Payment
First and second rights. Written material, $.15 per word for reprint rights. Pays on acceptance. Provides 4 contributor's copies.

Editor's Comments
We are looking for more articles on a variety of serious, real-life teen issues with concrete examples in narratives. We are seeing too many submissions on superficial issues such as lying and cheating.

Youth & Christian Education Leadership

1080 Montgomery Avenue
Cleveland, TN 37311

Editor: Wanda Griffith

Description and Readership
Informative and inspiring articles for Christian education workers are featured in this magazine. It is read by Sunday school teachers and leaders, youth pastors, children's church leaders, and others involved in the Christian ministry profession.
- **Audience:** Adults
- **Frequency:** Quarterly
- **Distribution:** 100% subscription
- **Circulation:** 13,000
- **Website:** www.pathwaypress.org

Freelance Potential
85% written by nonstaff writers. Publishes 10 freelance submissions yearly; 90% by unpublished writers, 10% by authors who are new to the magazine. Receives 8 queries and unsolicited mss monthly.

Submissions
Prefers complete ms with author biography. Accepts queries. Accepts disk submissions (Microsoft Word or WordPerfect), and email to Wanda_Griffith@ pathwaypress.org. SASE. Responds in 3 weeks.
Articles: 500–1,000 words. Informational and how-to articles; profiles; interviews; and personal experience pieces. Topics include current events, humor, music, religion, social issues, psychology, family parenting, and multicultural and ethnic subjects.
Depts/columns: Staff written.

Sample Issue
30 pages (2% advertising): 14 articles; 6 depts/columns. Sample copy, $1 with 9x12 SASE (2 first-class stamps). Guidelines available.
- "Pathways to Preteens." Article takes a look at different learning styles of preteens.
- "Current Events in Sunday School: Discussing Natural Disasters, Terrorism and War." Article offers guidelines for discussing disturbing world events with children in the classroom.

Rights and Payment
First rights. Written material, $25–$50. Kill fee, 50%. Pays on publication. Provides 1–10 author's copies.

Editor's Comments
We are interested in receiving more teaching articles and prefer articles that quote experts and include real-life examples. We are also interested in practical how-to's giving nuts and bolts guidelines for effective ministry. We currently have enough devotionals.

Youth Today

4th Floor
1200 17th Street NW
Washington, DC 20036

Editor: Patrick Boyle

Description and Readership
Topics of interest to youth service workers can be found in this independent newspaper. It includes articles, news, research analysis, book and video reviews, and resources for running successful youth programs and agencies.
- **Audience:** Youth workers
- **Frequency:** 10 times each year
- **Distribution:** 75% subscription; 25% controlled
- **Circulation:** 26,000
- **Website:** www.youthtoday.org

Freelance Potential
50% written by nonstaff writers. Publishes 25 freelance submissions yearly; 10% by authors who are new to the magazine. Receives 3 queries monthly.

Submissions
Query with résumé and clips. Responds in 3 months.
Articles: 1,000–2,500 words. Informational articles; news and research reports; profiles of youth workers and youth programs; and business features. Topics include foster care, child abuse, youth program management, violence, adolescent health, juvenile justice, job training and school-to-work programs, after-school programs and mentoring, and other social issues related to youth development.
Depts/columns: Book and video reviews; news briefs; opinion pieces; and people in the news.

Sample Issue
40 pages (50% advertising): 10 articles; 14 depts/columns. Sample copy, $5. Guidelines available.
- "Mentoring." Article reports on a paid mentoring program by the Friends of the Children.
- "Service-Learning." Article discusses the history and direction of the Giraffe Project, which inspires kids with stories about heroes who stick their neck out.
- Sample dept/column: "Web Watch" offers valuable websites for youths and youth workers.

Rights and Payment
First and Internet rights. Written material, $.50–$.75 per word. Pays on acceptance. Provides 2 contributor's copies.

Editor's Comments
Our readers turn to us to provide them with youth programs that have proven to be effective, as well as information and resources they can use to help them successfully manage a youth agency.

Youthworker

Suite 300
104 Woodmont Boulevard
Nashville, TN 37205

Editor: Will Penner

Description and Readership
Youthworker is a Christian publication for the professional and personal concerns of serious youth workers in church and parachurch settings.
- **Audience:** Adults working with youth
- **Frequency:** 6 times each year
- **Distribution:** 100% subscription
- **Circulation:** 20,000
- **Website:** www.youthworker.com

Freelance Potential
50% written by nonstaff writers. Publishes 20 freelance submissions yearly; 10% by unpublished writers. Receives 60 queries monthly.

Submissions
Query with short biography. Accepts photocopies, computer printouts, disk submissions (Microsoft Word), fax submissions to 615-385-4412, and email submissions to will@youthspecialties.com (include "Query" in subject field). SASE. Responds in 6–8 weeks.
Articles: Word lengths vary. Informational and practical application articles; personal experience pieces; and reviews. Topics include youth ministry, theology, helping youth, spreading the word, student worship, family ministry, popular culture, education, family issues, the media, and volunteering.
Depts/columns: Word length varies. National and regional trends, quotes from youth workers.

Sample Issue
68 pages (30% advertising): 7 articles; 7 depts/columns. Sample copy, $8. Guidelines available at website.
- "Am I an Adult or Not?" Article stresses that there's more to being a teenager than just growing up.
- "Communication That Builds Trust." First-person piece compares student ministry to learning to swim.

Rights and Payment
All rights. Written material, $15–$200. Pays on publication. Provides 1 contributor's copy.

Editor's Comments
We are looking for articles written by youth workers for youth workers. If you want to write for us, read a few recent issues. All material must be crisp, focused, and provocative, with a definite slant to those youth workers who especially (but not exclusively) work in churches. Make your article authentic. We would rather you explore a problem than solve it.

Yu-Gi-Oh

15850 Dallas Parkway
Dallas, TX 75248

Editorial Director: Doug Kale

Description and Readership
As the official guide to Yu-Gi-Oh cards, games, and memorabilia, this magazine offers articles, reviews, and information on upcoming products and releases. It is read by young adult and adult collectors.
- **Audience:** YA–Adult
- **Frequency:** Monthly
- **Distribution:** 80% newsstand; 20% subscription
- **Circulation:** 250,000
- **Website:** www.beckettyugioh.com

Freelance Potential
50% written by nonstaff writers. Publishes 20 freelance submissions yearly; 10% by unpublished writers, 1% by authors who are new to the magazine.

Submissions
Prefers query with outline and clips. Accepts complete ms. Accepts photocopies and computer printouts. SASE. Responds in 1–2 months.
Articles: 500–1200 words. Informational articles; profiles; and reviews. Includes information on collecting Yu-Gi-Oh cards and memorabilia.
Fiction: Word lengths vary. Stories on Yu-Gi-Oh.
Depts/columns: 500–750 words. News and reviews.

Sample Issue
88 pages: 11 articles; 11 depts/columns. Sample copy, $9.99. Guidelines available.
- "A Dueling Destiny." Article describes a new game that requires players to become familiar with the use of Yu-Gi-Oh cards and common dueling techniques.
- "Tips for Buying Yu-Gi-Oh Cards." Article lists helpful hints for buying cards online and at hobby shops.
- Sample dept/column: "Yu-Gi-Oh! News Flash!" offers information on rare cards, new releases, re-releases, and products.

Rights and Payment
First North American serial rights. Articles and fiction, $150–$350. Depts/columns, $50–$200. Provides 2 contributor's copies.

Editor's Comments
Our readers turn to us to find out the latest information covering the world of Yu-Gi-Oh. We look for material that will keep them up-to-date with reviews of the latest games; tips for collecting, buying, and selling; memorabilia; and what is hot in the market. Articles detailing rare cards are also of interest to us.

Additional Listings

Additional Listings

We have selected the following magazines to offer you additional publishing opportunities. These magazines range from general interest publications to women's magazines to craft and hobby magazines. While children, young adults, parents, or teachers may not be their primary target audience, these publications do publish a limited amount of material that relates to children and families.

These listings also serve to keep you informed of the magazines that would not be considered good markets at this time. Such listings would include magazines that were closed to queries and freelance submissions at the time we went to press, as well as magazines that are in the process of reviewing their focus.

As you review the listings that follow, use the Description and Readership section as your guide to the particular needs of each magazine. This section offers general information about the magazine and its readers' interests, as well as the type of material it usually publishes. The Freelance Potential section will provide information about the publication's receptivity to freelance manuscripts.

After you survey the listings to determine if your work meets the magazine's specifications, be sure to read a recent sample copy and the current writers' guidelines before submitting your material.

Adventures

6401 The Paseo
Kansas City, MO 64131

Submissions: Denise Willemin

Description and Readership
This colorful take-home magazine is used in conjunction with the educational programs of the Church of the Nazarene. Its lively stories and activities supplement the lesson of the day. Circ: Unavailable.
Website: www.wordaction.com

Freelance Potential
50% written by nonstaff writers. Publishes 15 freelance submissions yearly; 10% by unpublished writers, 10% by authors who are new to the magazine. Receives 25 queries.
Submissions and Payment: Writers' guidelines and theme list available. Query. SASE. Accepts photocopies and computer printouts. SASE. Responds in 4–6 weeks. Articles, word lengths and payment rates vary. Pays on acceptance. All North American serial rights. Provides 2 contributor's copies.

AKC Family Dog

American Kennel Club
260 Madison Avenue
New York, NY 10016

Managing Editor: Erika Mansourian

Description and Readership
Owners of purebred dogs who enjoy sharing life with their pet find up-to-date information on all aspects of raising a happy and well-behaved dog in this magazine. It is published six times each year. Circ: 40,000.
Website: www.akc.org

Freelance Potential
90% written by nonstaff writers. Publishes 50 freelance submissions yearly; 2% by unpublished writers, 10% by authors who are new to the magazine. Receives 5–10 queries monthly.
Submissions and Payment: Sample copy and guidelines, $3.95 with 9x12 SASE. Query with outline. Accepts computer printouts and email to familydog@ akc.org (Microsoft Word attachments). SASE. Responds in 1–2 months. Articles, 1,000–2,000 words; $125– $500. Depts/columns, staff written. Pays on publication. First North American serial rights.

The ALAN Review

College of Liberal Arts & Sciences
Department of English
Arizona State University, P.O. Box 870302
Tempe, AZ 85287

Editor: Dr. James Blasingame

Description and Readership
The Assembly on Literature for Adolescents publishes this magazine three times each year for teachers, librarians, and others interested in young adult literature. Circ: 2,500.
Website: www.alan-ya.org

Freelance Potential
90% written by nonstaff writers. Publishes 25 freelance submissions yearly; 50% by unpublished writers. Receives 4 unsolicited mss monthly.
Submissions and Payment: Guidelines available in magazine. Sample copy, free. Send 3 copies of complete ms with disk (ASCII or Microsoft Word 5.1 or higher). Accepts simultaneous submissions if identified. Availability of artwork improves chance of acceptance. SASE. Responds in 2 months. Articles, to 3,000 words. Depts/columns, word lengths vary. No payment. All rights. Provides 2 contributor's copies.

All About Kids Parenting Magazine

Suite 101
1077 Celestial Street
Cincinnati, OH 45202

Editor: Tom Wynne

Description and Readership
Parents in the greater Cincinnati area have been reading this monthly publication since its launch in 1987. Each issue offers helpful tips, national news, and local stories about events, education, health, and all facets of parenting and family life. Freelance submissions are welcome, particularly from local writers. Circ: 120,000.
Website: www.aak.com

Freelance Potential
100% written by nonstaff writers. Publishes 30 freelance submissions yearly.
Submissions and Payment: Guidelines available at website. Send complete ms. Accepts disk submissions and email submissions to editor@aak.com (text files only; hard copy must be submitted by mail). SASE. Response time varies. Articles and depts/columns, word lengths and payment rates vary. Payment policy and rights vary. Provides 1 contributor's copy.

Amazing Kids

PMB 485
1158 26th Street
Santa Monica, CA 90403

Editor: Alyse Rome

Description and Readership
Dedicated to the belief that every child has the potential to achieve "amazing" status, this website presents the writings of kids and teens and spotlights their achievements. It is currently seeking volunteers to research and write stories for its "Amazing Kids of the Month" section. Hits per month: 640,000.
Website: www.amazing-kids.org

Freelance Potential
40% written by nonstaff writers. Publishes 70 freelance submissions yearly; 90% by unpublished writers, 70% by authors who are new to the magazine. Receives 250 queries and unsolicited mss monthly.
Submissions and Payment: Sample copy available at website. Query or send complete ms. Accepts email submissions to info@amazing-kids.org. SASE. Response time varies. Articles, word length varies. All rights. No payment.

American History

Primedia
Suite D2
741 Miller Drive SE
Leesburg, VA 20175

Editorial Director: Roger Vance

Description and Readership
Six times a year, *American History* offers stories and articles that educate as well as entertain history enthusiasts and the general public. It features articles about the people and places that have influenced the nation we are today. Circ: 100,000.
Website: www.thehistorynet.com

Freelance Potential
80% written by nonstaff writers. Publishes 30 freelance submissions yearly; 50% by authors who are new to the magazine. Receives 100 queries monthly.
Submissions and Payment: Sample copy and guidelines, $6 with return label. Query with 1–2 page proposal. Accepts photocopies and computer printouts. SASE. Responds in 10 weeks. Articles and stories, 3,000 words; $.20 per word. Reviews, 250 words; $75. Pays on acceptance. All rights. Provides 5 contributor's copies.

The Apprentice Writer

Box GG
Susquehanna University
Selinsgrove, PA 17870-1001

Writers' Institute Director: Gary Fincke

Description and Readership
This literary publication appears annually, and presents the best writing, photography, and graphics produced by high school students across the U.S. Circ: 10,500.
Website: www.susque.edu/writers (click on writers' institute)

Freelance Potential
100% written by nonstaff writers. Publishes 80 freelance submissions yearly; 95% by unpublished writers, 95% by authors who are new to the magazine. Receives 5,000 unsolicited mss monthly.
Submissions and Payment: Sample copy, $3 with 9x12 SASE ($1.17 postage). Send complete ms. Accepts photocopies, computer printouts, and simultaneous submissions if identified. SASE. Responds during the month of May. Articles and fiction, 7,000 words. Poetry, no line limits. No payment. First rights. Provides 2 contributor's copies.

Art Jewelry

21027 Crossroads Circle
Waukesha, WI 53187

Editorial Assistant: Amy Robleski

Description and Readership
Launched in 2004, this magazine publishes articles to inspire jewelry makers at all levels of ability. It needs how-to articles on working with metal, wire, clay, glass, and other media. Circ: Unavailable.
Website: www.artjewelrymag.com

Freelance Potential
60% written by nonstaff writers. Of the freelance submissions published yearly, 50% are by unpublished writers, 90% are by authors who are new to the magazine. Receives 30 queries monthly.
Submissions and Payment: Guidelines available. Sample copy, $5.95. Query with jewelry samples or photos. Accepts computer printouts and email queries with JPEG images to editor@artjewelrymag.com. SASE. Responds in 1–2 months. Written material, word lengths and payment rates vary. Pays on acceptance. All rights. Provides 2 contributor's copies.

Athens Parent

P.O. Box 1251
Athens, GA 30603

Editor: Cynthia Hamilton

Description and Readership
A variety of topics of interest to parents and grandparents are addressed in this publication for Athens, Georgia, families. Departments and columns tackle teen issues, fathering, and pregnancy/infancy issues while features cover such things as health, education, and family finances. Published eight times each year, it welcomes submissions from freelance writers. Circ: Unavailable.
Website: www.athensparent.com

Freelance Potential
100% written by nonstaff writers. Publishes several freelance submissions yearly.
Submissions and Payment: Query. Accepts photocopies, computer printouts, and email submissions to mail@athensparent.com. SASE. Response time varies. Articles and depts/columns, word lengths vary; payment rate varies. Publication policy varies. First rights.

BC Parent Magazine

P.O. Box 72086
4479 West 10th Avenue
Vancouver, British Columbia V6R 4P2
Canada

Editor: Elizabeth Shaffer

Description and Readership
Parents and caregivers living in British Columbia read this newsmagazine eight times each year for up-to-date, trustworthy information on topics related to raising children from birth to the teen years. Its editors are currently seeking submissions on the following topics: adoption, baby care, maternity issues, sports, teens, education, computers, money matters, family issues, health, and women's issues. Circ: Unavailable.
Website: www.bcparent.com

Freelance Potential
80% written by nonstaff writers. Publishes 25 freelance submissions yearly.
Submissions and Payment: Guidelines available. Send complete ms. Accepts email submissions to editor@bcparent.com (RTF format). Response time varies. Articles, 500–1,000 words; $85. Pays on acceptance. First rights.

Beta Journal

National Beta Club
151 Beta Club Way
Spartenburg, SC 29306-3012

Editor: Lori Guthrie

Description and Readership
Five times each year, students in elementary school through high school who are members of the National Beta Club receive this magazine, which covers academics, leadership, and service to others. Circ: 300,000.
Website: www.betaclub.org

Freelance Potential
50% written by nonstaff writers. Publishes 2–4 freelance submissions yearly; 80% by unpublished writers. Receives 1 unsolicited ms monthly.
Submissions and Payment: Send complete ms. Accepts computer printouts and email submissions to lguthrie@betaclub.org. Availability of artwork improves chance of acceptance. SASE. Responds in 2 months. Articles and fiction, 700–1,000 words; $25–$50. B/W prints, transparencies, and line art; payment rate varies. Pays on publication. Rights policy varies. Provides 10 contributor's copies.

Beyond Centauri

P.O. Box 782
Cedar Rapids, IA 52406

Editor: Tyree Campbell

Description and Readership
A science fiction and fantasy magazine for readers ages 10 and up, this quarterly seeks to nurture imagination and creativity in the next generation by publishing stories, poems, and illustrations created by younger readers. Adult submissions are also reviewed. Circ: Unavailable.
Website: www.samsdotpublishing.com

Freelance Potential
100% written by nonstaff writers. Publishes 35–50 freelance submissions yearly.
Submissions and Payment: Sample copy and guidelines, $6. Query or send complete ms. Accepts photocopies, computer printouts, and email submissions to beyondcentauri@samsdotpublishing.com (RTF attachments). SASE. Responds to queries in 2 weeks, to mss in 2–3 months. Articles, 500 words. Fiction, 2,000 words. Poetry, to 100 lines. Written material, $3–$5. Pays on publication. First North American serial rights.

The Big Country Peacock Chronicle

RR 1 Box 89K-112
Aspermont, TX 79502

Editor-in-Chief: Audrey Yoeckel

Description and Readership
This interactive e-zine is dedicated to the preservation of community values and folk cultures. Its focus is on traditional arts and crafts, artists, writers, information, resource links, and mutual support. Most of the material it publishes is contributed by new writers. At this time, its editors are looking for children's book reviews, historic pieces, and poetry. Hits per month: Unavailable.
Website: www.peacockchronicle.com

Freelance Potential
25% written by nonstaff writers. Publishes 10–12 freelance submissions yearly; 80% by authors who are new to the magazine.
Submissions and Payment: Sample copy available at website. Query or send complete ms. Accepts email submissions to audrey@peacockchronicle.com. Response time varies. Articles, word lengths vary. No payment. Electronic rights.

Bird Times

7-L Dundas Circle
Greensboro, NC 27407

Executive Editor: Rita Davis

Description and Readership
This magazine appears six times a year, offering articles that educate as well as entertain bird owners. Topics covered include basic care and training. It also features human interest stories. Circ: 20,000.
Website: www.birdtimes.com

Freelance Potential
90% written by nonstaff writers. Publishes 30–40 freelance submissions yearly; 10% by unpublished writers, 50% by authors who are new to the magazine. Receives 10 queries, 15–20 unsolicited mss monthly.
Submissions and Payment: Sample copy, $5 with 9x12 SASE (4 first-class stamps). Query with clips; or send complete ms. Accepts photocopies and computer printouts. SASE. Responds in 1 month. Articles, 1,200–2,000 words. Depts/columns, 600–800 words. Written material, $.10 per word. Pays on publication. All rights. Provides 1 contributor's copy.

Biography Today

615 Griswold Street
Detroit, MI 48226

Managing Editor: Cherie D. Abbey

Description and Readership
Targeting readers ages 9 to 14, *Biography Today* is a compilation of the life stories of world personalities who are capturing the interest of young people. It appears six times each year with biographical sketches of political figures, stars of the entertainment industry, athletes, scientists, authors, and business leaders. Its accessible, tell-all writing style helps to interest even the most reluctant readers. Circ: 9,000.
Website: www.biographytoday.com

Freelance Potential
50% written by nonstaff writers. Publishes several freelance submissions yearly. Receives 1 query monthly.
Submissions and Payment: Sample copy and guidelines, $19 with 9x12 SASE. Query with résumé. SASE. Responds in 2 months. Articles, 2,000–5,000 words. Payment rates and policies vary according to author's experience. All rights. Provides 2 copies.

Black Woman and Child

P.O. Box 47045
300 Borough Drive
Toronto, Ontario M1P 4P0
Canada

Editor

Description and Readership
This magazine was launched in 2005 for women of African descent seeking pregnancy and parenting information rooted in African culture. Appearing six times each year, it welcomes unsolicited submissions that meet the needs of its target audience. Circ: Unavailable.
Website: www.blackwomanandchild.com

Freelance Potential
25% written by nonstaff writers. Publishes 15 freelance submissions yearly.
Submissions and Payment: Guidelines available. Query or send complete ms. Accepts photocopies, computer printouts, and email submissions to bwac@nubeing.com (text files). No simultaneous submissions. SAE/IRC. Response time varies. Articles, 750–1,500 words. Depts/columns, word lengths vary. Written material, payment rates vary. Pays on publication. Rights policy varies.

B'nai B'rith Magazine

7th Floor
2020 K Street NW
Washington, DC 20006

Managing Editor: Elana Harris

Description and Readership
Articles on issues relating to Jewish life and communities in North America and Israel can be found in this quarterly magazine. It seeks stories that demonstrate creation and innovation in Jewish life. Circ: 100,000.
Website: www.bnaibrith.org

Freelance Potential
50% written by nonstaff writers. Publishes 12–15 freelance submissions yearly; 10% by unpublished writers, 50% by authors who are new to the magazine. Receives 10 queries monthly.
Submissions and Payment: Sample copy and guidelines, $3 with 9x12 SASE (3 first-class stamps). Query with clips. Accepts computer printouts and email to bbm@bnaibrith.org. SASE. Responds in 2–4 weeks. Articles, 1,000–3,000 words. Depts/ columns, word lengths vary. Written material, payment rates vary. Pays on publication. First North American serial rights.

Brain, Child

P.O. Box 5566
Charlottesville, VA 22905

Editors: Jennifer Niesslein & Stephanie Wilkinson

Description and Readership
Subtitled "The Magazine for Thinking Mothers," *Brain, Child* is a quarterly publication that portrays modern motherhood as it really is. Unlike typical parenting publications, it steers clear of parenting advice in favor of reflections on what motherhood does to one's mind and soul. Readers' stories are welcome. Circ: 30,000+.
Website: www.brainchildmag.com

Freelance Potential
Publishes many freelance submissions yearly.
Submissions and Payment: Sample copy and guidelines, $5. Query or send ms. Accepts photocopies, computer printouts, simultaneous submissions, and email to editor@brainchildmag.com. SASE. Responds in 2 months. Features, 3,000 words. Personal essays, 800–4,500 words. Fiction, 1,500–4,500 words. Book reviews, 200 words. Written material, payment rates vary. Pays on publication. Electronic rights.

Caledonia Times

Box 278
Prince Rupert, British Columbia V8J 3P6
Canada

Editor: Debby Shaw

Description and Readership
With a focus on Christian writing, this small paper offers short stories, articles, and poetry for an audience of young adult and adult readers. Nonfiction topics covered include regional news and social issues. Fiction may be inspirational in nature or problem-solving. *Caledonia Times* is published 10 times each year. Circ: 1,259.

Freelance Potential
90% written by nonstaff writers. Publishes 10 freelance submissions yearly. Receives many unsolicited mss each month.
Submissions and Payment: Send complete ms. Accepts computer printouts and email submissions to synodofc@citytell.net. SAE/IRC. Responds in 2–4 weeks. Articles and fiction, 500–750 words. Depts/columns, word lengths vary. No payment. All rights. Provides 5 contributor's copies.

Canoe & Kayak Magazine

Suite 3
10526 NE 68th Street
Kirkland, WA 98033

Editor

Description and Readership
This magazine for paddlesports enthusiasts appears six times each year. Freelancers are invited to submit essays for its "Take Out" department. Circ: 67,000.
Website: www.canoekayak.com

Freelance Potential
90% written by nonstaff writers. Publishes 25 freelance submissions yearly; 5% by unpublished writers, 25% by authors who are new to the magazine. Receives 20 queries and unsolicited mss monthly.
Submissions and Payment: Sample copy and guidelines, free with 9x12 SASE (7 first-class stamps). Query or send complete ms. Accepts computer printouts, IBM or Macintosh disk submissions, and email submissions to editor@canoekayak.com. SASE. Responds in 6–8 weeks. Articles, 700–2,500 words. Depts/columns, 500–1,200 words. Written material, $.13–$.50 per word. Pays on publication. All rights. Provides 1 author's copy.

Catalyst Chicago

Independent Reporting on Urban Schools

Suite 500
332 South Michigan Avenue
Chicago, IL 60604

Editorial Contact: Veronica Anderson

Description and Readership

Read by education professionals and targeting the Chicago and urban school reform community, this nonprofit newsmagazine tracks the progress, problems, and politics of school reform in Chicago. It is published nine times each year and all articles are assigned. Circ: 7,000.
Website: www.catalyst-chicago.org

Freelance Potential

20% written by nonstaff writers. Publishes 45 freelance submissions yearly; 20% by authors who are new to the magazine. Receives 4 unsolicited submissions monthly.
Submissions and Payment: Sample copy and guidelines, $2. Query or send letter of introduction, résumé, and clips. Accepts photocopies and computer printouts. SASE. Response time varies. Articles, to 2,300 words; $1700. Pays on acceptance. All rights. Provides 1 contributor's copy.

Cat Fancy

Bow Tie Magazines
3 Burroughs
Irving, CA 92618

Managing Editor: Sandy Meyer

Description and Readership

Published monthly, this magazine seeks articles on cat culture, the human-animal bond, and feline personalities, as well as cat events. Circ: 270,000
Website: www.catfancy.com

Freelance Potential

95% written by nonstaff writers. Publishes 60 freelance submissions yearly; 10% by unpublished writers, 30–40% by authors who are new to the magazine. Receives 65+ queries monthly.
Submissions and Payment: Guidelines available. Query with clips. No unsolicited mss. Availability of artwork improves chance of acceptance. Accepts email queries to queries@bowtieinc.com. Responds in 1–3 months. Articles, 600–1,000 words. Depts/columns, 600 words. Artwork, 35mm slides or high resolution digital photos with contact sheets. Payment rates vary. Pays on publication. First rights. Provides 2 copies.

Challenge ☆

Pearson Education Australia
P.O. Box 1024
South Melbourne, VIC 3205
Australia

Editor: Petra Poupa

Description and Readership

A magazine for readers between the ages of 11 and 14, *Challenge* appears quarterly with fiction, nonfiction, plays, and poetry. Its editors seek fiction that features characters the same age as its readers, who particularly enjoy adventure stories, fiction with relationship themes, and humorous fiction. Circ: 20,000.
Website: www.pearsoned.com.au/schools

Freelance Potential

50% written by nonstaff writers. Publishes 15 freelance submissions yearly.
Submissions and Payment: Guidelines available. Send complete ms. Accepts photocopies, computer printouts, disk submissions, simultaneous submissions, and email to magazines@pearsoned.com.au. SAE/IRC. Responds in 3 months. Articles, 200–600 words. Fiction, 400–1,000 words. Written material, $80–$200. Pays on publication. First Australian serial rights.

Chickadee

Bayard Press Canada
2nd Floor, 49 Front Street East
Toronto, Ontario M5E 1B3
Canada

Submissions Editor

Description and Readership

Beginning readers will find exciting articles about animals, science, sports, and social studies in this magazine, published ten times each year. Each issue is based on a theme and includes articles, stories, word and math puzzles, science experiments, activities and crafts. Circ: 85,000.
Website: www.owlkids.com

Freelance Potential

5% written by nonstaff writers. Publishes 1 freelance submission yearly; 5% by unpublished writers, 20% by authors who are new to the magazine. Receives 83 unsolicited mss each month.
Submissions and Payment: Sample copy, $4. Guidelines and theme list available. All material is assigned. SAE/IRC. Responds in 6 weeks. Fiction, 650–700 words; $250. Pays on acceptance. All rights. Provides 2 contributor's copies.

Child Life

Children's Better Health Institute
P.O. Box 567
Indianapolis, IN 46206-0567

Editor: Jack Gramling

Description and Readership
The goal of *Child Life* is to promote good health and physical fitness in its readers. Its contents include fiction, health-related articles, poetry, recipes, quizzes, and nonfiction designed to entertain and educate its young readers, ages nine to eleven. At this time, most of its published material is from reprints but its editors are interested in seeing poetry submissions from children. Circ: 35,000.
Website: www.childlifemag.org

Freelance Potential
25% written by nonstaff writers. Publishes several freelance submissions yearly.
Submissions and Payment: Sample copy, $2.95 with 9x12 SASE (4 first-class stamps). Not currently accepting submissions for articles and stories.

Chirp

Bayard Press Canada
2nd Floor, 49 Front Street East
Toronto, Ontario M5E 1B3
Canada

Submissions Editor

Description and Readership
Subtitled "The See and Do, Laugh and Learn Magazine," *Chirp* is published nine times each year. Children ages two to six will find stories, activities, recipes, puzzles, and games that enhance their understanding of the world around them. It does not accept unsolicited submissions. Circ: 60,000.
Website: www.owlkids.com

Freelance Potential
10% written by nonstaff writers. Publishes 1–3 freelance submissions yearly; 1% by unpublished writers, 10% by authors who are new to the magazine. Receives many unsolicited submissions each month.
Submissions and Payment: Sample copy, $3.50. Guidelines available. All material is assigned. SAE with $2 IRC. Response time varies. Written material, 300–400 words; payment rates vary. Pays on publication. First and second rights.

Cincinnati Family

Suite 900
895 Central Avenue
Cincinnati, OH 45202

Editor-in-Chief: Susan Brooke Day

Description and Readership
This regional publication serves as a guide for families in the Cincinnati area. In addition to articles that cover parenting topics, each issue calls attention to local resources that can help make the job of raising a family easier. Programs and events for children and parents are also publicized. *Cincinnati Family* is published monthly. Circ: 75,000.
Website: www.cincinnatifamilymagazine.com

Freelance Potential
75% written by nonstaff writers. Publishes 36 freelance submissions yearly.
Submissions and Payment: Query or send complete ms. Accepts photocopies, computer printouts, and email submissions to shang@cincyradio.com. SASE. Response time varies. Articles and depts/columns, word lengths and payment rates vary. Pays on publication. First rights.

Classic Toy Trains

21027 Crossroads Circle
Waukesha, WI 53187

Editor: Neil Besougloff

Description and Readership
Articles that cover all aspects of collecting and operating toy trains appear in this magazine, which is published nine times each year. Circ: 68,000.
Website: www.classictoytrains.com

Freelance Potential
60% written by nonstaff writers. Publishes 40–50 freelance submissions yearly; 20% by unpublished writers, 20% by authors who are new to the magazine. Receives 8 queries, 5 unsolicited mss monthly.
Submissions and Payment: Sample copy, $4.95 ($3 postage). Prefers query. Accepts complete ms. Accepts photocopies, computer printouts, disk submissions (Microsoft Word), and email submissions to editor@classictoytrains.com. SASE. Responds in 3 months. Articles, 500–5,000 words; $75 per page. Depts/columns, word lengths and payment rates vary. Pays on acceptance. All rights. Provides 1 contributor's copy.

Clubhouse

P.O. Box 15
Berrien Springs, MI 49103

President/Editor: Elaine Trumbo

Description and Readership

A religious magazine, *Clubhouse* is published monthly for readers ages 9 to 12. Each issue offers articles and short stories with biblical themes. Poetry and activities are also included. At this time, the magazine is undergoing editorial changes and is not accepting new material. Check its website for updates to this policy. Circ: 500.
Website: www.yourstoryhour.org/clubhouse

Freelance Potential

85% written by nonstaff writers. Publishes several freelance submissions yearly; 75% by unpublished writers, 95% by authors who are new to the magazine.
Submissions and Payment: Sample copy, free with 6x9 SASE (2 first-class stamps). Send complete ms. Accepts photocopies and computer printouts. SASE. Response time varies. Articles and fiction, 1,500 words. B/W line art. All material, payment rates vary. Pays after publication. All rights.

Coins

700 East State Street
Iola, WI 54990

Editor: Robert Van Ryzin

Description and Readership

This is the magazine coin collectors turn to for authoritative information about their hobby. Each monthly issue provides articles about coin history, personal experience essays from coin collectors, coin value guides, and coin show reports. Queries from numismatists and knowledgeable collectors are welcome. Circ: 60,000.
Website: www.collect.com

Freelance Potential

40% written by nonstaff writers. Publishes 70 freelance submissions yearly; 5% by authors who are new to the magazine. Receives 3–5 queries monthly.
Submissions and Payment: Sample copy and guidelines, free. Query. Accepts photocopies and computer printouts. SASE. Responds in 1–2 months. Articles, 1,500–2,500 words, $.04 per word. Work for hire. Pays on publication. All rights. Provides contributor's copies upon request.

Coastal Family Magazine ☆

5 Oglethorpe Professional Boulevard, Suite 100
Savannah, GA 31406

Editor: Laura Gray

Description and Readership

Published monthly by Coastal Empire Media, Inc., this parenting publication covers child development issues, education, family finances, travel, books, and the media for families living in the Savannah, Georgia, region. In addition to factual articles, *Coastal Family Magazine* offers profiles and interviews, party planning guides, humor, how-to's, and personal experience pieces. Circ: Unavailable.
Website: www.coastalfamily.com

Freelance Potential

Publishes several freelance submissions yearly.
Submissions and Payment: Guidelines available. Query. Accepts photocopies, computer printouts, and email submissions to editor@coastalfamily.com. SASE. Response time varies. Articles and depts/columns, word lengths vary; payment rate varies. Payment policy varies. All rights.

College and Junior Tennis

Port Washington Tennis Academy
100 Harbor Road
Port Washington, NY 10050

Webmaster: Marcia Frost

Description and Readership

This e-zine provides, coaches, players, and fans with the latest scores, rankings, and results of the national and international junior tennis circuit. It also publishes a comprehensive directory of every college in the U.S. with a tennis program, as well as in-depth interviews of today's junior tennis stars. Hits per month: 500,000.
Website: www.collegeandjuniortennis.com

Freelance Potential

10% written by nonstaff writers. Publishes 5 freelance submissions yearly; 1% by authors who are new to the magazine. Receives 2 unsolicited mss monthly.
Submissions and Payment: Sample copy, free at website. Send complete ms. Accepts email submissions to marcia@collegeandjuniortennis.com. Responds in 2–14 days. Articles, to 700 words. Games and 1-page puzzles. Written material, $25–$50. One-time rights.

Comet

Pearson Education Australia–Schools Division
P.O. Box 1024
South Melbourne, VIC 3205
Australia

Editor: Petra Poupa

Description and Readership
This quarterly magazine offers emergent and early readers stories, pictures, and activities that make learning to read fun. Its editors seek contemporary fiction, mystery, suspense, and humor, and nonfiction on topics such as animals, health, and nature. Circ: 20,000.
Website: www.pearsoned.com.au/schools

Freelance Potential
50% written by nonstaff writers. Publishes 15 freelance submissions yearly.
Submissions and Payment: Guidelines available. Send complete ms. Accepts photocopies, computer printouts, disk submissions, simultaneous submissions if identified, and email submissions to magazines@pearsoned.com.au. SAE/IRC. Responds in 3 months. Articles, 200–600 words. Fiction, 400–1,000 words. Written material, $80–$220. Pays on publication. First Australian rights.

Community Education Journal

Suite 91-A
3929 Old Lee Highway
Fairfax, VA 22030

Editor: Valerie A. Romney

Description and Readership
The National Center for Community Education publishes this journal each quarter to address the issues involved with adult education, after-school programs, and summer educational programs. Submissions that describe successful programs are encouraged. Circ: 2,500.
Website: www.ncea.com

Freelance Potential
98% written by nonstaff writers. Publishes 24 freelance submissions yearly; 30% by unpublished writers, 60% by authors who are new to the magazine. Receives 1–2 unsolicited mss monthly.
Submissions and Payment: Sample copy, guidelines, and theme list, $5. Send 5 copies of complete ms. Accepts computer printouts and email submissions to varomney@hotmail.com. SASE. Responds in 1–2 months. Articles, 1,500–2,000 words. No payment. All rights. Provides 5 contributor's copies.

Cookie

7 West 34th Street
New York, NY 10001

Acquisitions: Dani Fisher

Description and Readership
Described as an "anti-parenting magazine," *Cookie* is written for sophisticated parents who are welcoming a baby into their established lifestyles. Launched in November of 2005, it covers health, development, beauty, and fitness for parents with children up to the age of six. Its editors currently seek fitness stories for women who are trying to squeeze exercise time into their busy days. Writers are encouraged to submit queries that explain how they plan to organize their material. Circ: Unavailable.
Website: www.fairchildpub.com

Freelance Potential
50% written by nonstaff writers.
Submissions and Payment: Query. Accepts photocopies and computer printouts. SASE. Response time varies. Articles, word lengths and payment rates vary. Pays on publication. Rights policy varies.

Cool! Magazine

P.O. Box 80886
Lansing, MI 48820

Editor: Kathy Andres

Description and Readership
Published monthly and available free of charge, *Cool! Magazine* serves the residents of Eaton, Ingham, and Clinton counties in Michigan with articles that highlight positive aspects of the area. Its editors currently seek stories on social responsibility, the transition from high school to college, and career planning. Circ: Unavailable.
Website: www.cool-community.com

Freelance Potential
80% written by nonstaff writers. Of the freelance submissions published yearly, 80% are by authors who are new to the magazine. Receives 2 queries and unsolicited mss monthly.
Submissions and Payment: Sample copy, free. Query or send complete ms. Accepts computer printouts and email to info@cool-community.com. SASE. Response time varies. Articles, word lengths, payment rates, and payment policies vary. First and electronic rights.

Creative Child Magazine ☆

#C111
4522 Woodman Avenue
Sherman Oaks, CA 91423

Editor

Description and Readership
Published every other month, *Creative Child Magazine* provides parents with the latest information on ways to nurture a child's creativity and helpful tips for raising well-balanced children. It features articles on health, safety, gifted and special education, and family activities that stimulate a child's learning. Circ: Unavilable.
Website: www.creativechildonline.com

Freelance Potential
25% written by nonstaff writers. Publishes 20 freelance submissions yearly.
Submissions and Payment: Sample copy, available with 9x12 SASE (4 first-class stamps). Query. Accepts photocopies, computer printouts, and email queries to info@creativechildonline.com. SASE. Responds in 1–3 months. Articles and depts/columns, word lengths vary. Written material, payment rates vary. First and electronic rights. Provides contributor's copies.

Cyberteens Zeen

Able Minds, Inc.
1750-1 30th Street #170
Boulder, CO 80301

Editor

Description and Readership
Poetry, articles, and stories appropriate for teens and created by writers under the age of 19 appear in this e-zine. Humor and upbeat articles are especially welcome, as are submissions accompanied by photos or illustrations. Hits per month: Unavailable.
Website: www.cyberteens.com

Freelance Potential
100% written by nonstaff writers. Publishes 300 freelance submissions yearly. Receives many unsolicited mss monthly.
Submissions and Payment: Sample copy available at website. Query or send complete ms. Accepts photocopies, computer printouts, and email submissions to editor@cyberteens.com (no attachments). Availability of artwork improves chance of acceptance. SASE. Response time varies. Written material, to 10 pages. Artwork, TIFF or JPEG format. No payment. All rights.

Discoveries

WordAction Publishing Company
6401 The Paseo
Kansas City, MO 64131

Editorial Assistant: Sarah Weatherwax

Description and Readership
Published by WordAction Publishing Company, this weekly full-color story paper correlates directly with the WordAction Sunday School curriculum for children ages 8 to 10. In January 2007, it will resume submission reviews and will consider stories that demonstrate Scriptural application and character building. All themes and outcomes should conform to the theology of the Evangelical churches. Circ: 35,000.

Freelance Potential
70% written by nonstaff writers.
Submissions and Payment: Not currently accepting submissions. Will resume submission reviews in January 2007. Query or send complete ms. Accepts photocopies and computer printouts. SASE. Responds in 6–8 weeks. Articles, 150 words; $15. Stories, to 500 words; $.05 per word. Multiple-use rights. Pays on publication. Provides 4 contributor's copies.

Dog Fancy

Bowtie, Inc.
P.O. Box 6050
Mission Viego, CA 92690-6050

Managing Editor: Hazel Barrowman

Description and Readership
This monthly magazine offers practical and informative articles on canine breeding, health, training, behavior, and care for owners, breeders, and fanciers of all breeds of dogs. Circ: 270,000.
Website: www.dogfancy.com

Freelance Potential
80% written by nonstaff writers. Publishes 20–25 freelance submissions yearly; 25% by authors who are new to the magazine. Receives 100 queries monthly.
Submissions and Payment: Guidelines available. Sample copy, $4.50 at newsstands. Query with résumé, outline, and writing samples. No unsolicited mss. Responds in 6–8 weeks. Articles, 1,200–1,800 words. Depts/columns, 650 words. All material, payment rates vary. Pays on publication. First North American serial rights. Provides 2 contributor's copies.

Dollhouse Miniatures

5th Floor
420 Boylston Street
Boston, MA 02116

Editor: Lauren Walker

Description and Readership
Hobbyists who make or collect small-scale reproductions find ideas and information, as well as reviews of new products, in each monthly issue of *Dollhouse Miniatures*. Circ: 25,000.
Website: www.dhminiatures.com

Freelance Potential
75% written by nonstaff writers. Publishes 120 freelance submissions yearly; 30% by unpublished writers, 30% by authors who are new to the magazine. Receives 20 queries monthly.
Submissions and Payment: Guidelines available at website. Sample copy, $4.95 with 9x12 SASE ($1.95 postage). Query with outline. Accepts computer printouts and email queries to editor@dhminiatures.com. SASE. Responds in 1 month. Articles and depts/columns, word lengths and payment rates vary. Pays on acceptance. All rights. Provides 1 contributor's copy.

Early Years

Suite 103
3035 Valley Avenue
Winchester, VA 22601

Submissions: Jennifer Hutchinson

Description and Readership
Nine issues of this newsletter are distributed each year through preschool and kindergarten classrooms. *Early Years* offers busy parents quick and easy access to important information about parenting young children and helping them adjust to school. Circ: 60,000.
Website: www.rfeonline.com

Freelance Potential
100% written by nonstaff writers. Publishes 80 freelance submissions yearly; 28% by unpublished writers. Receives 3 queries monthly.
Submissions and Payment: Sample copy, free with 9x12 SASE ($.77 postage). Query with résumé and clips. Accepts photocopies and computer printouts. SASE. Responds in 1 month. Articles, 225–300 words. Depts/columns, 175–200 words. Written material, $.60 per word. Pays on acceptance. All rights. Provides 5 contributor's copies.

Earthwatch Institute Journal

3 Clock Tower Place
Maynard, MA 01754-0075

Editor: Philip Johansson

Description and Readership
This quarterly journal educates, inspires, and empowers readers through diverse examples of Earthwatch in action around the world. Its goal is to make field science relevant to its constituents, to show them why it matters and what they can do. Through features, interviews, and human-interest articles, it gives readers a broader perspective on the world. Circ: 25,000.
Website: www.earthwatch.org

Freelance Potential
30% written by nonstaff writers. Publishes 2–3 freelance submissions yearly. Receives 4–5 queries, 2–3 unsolicited mss monthly.
Submissions and Payment: Sample copy and writers' guidelines available. Query or send complete ms. Prefers email submissions to pjohansson@earthwatch.org. SASE. Response time varies. Articles, $500–$1,000. First rights. Pays on publication.

Education in Focus

P.O. Box 202
Warrenton, VA 20188

Editor: Joe David

Description and Readership
Today's education is the subject of this magazine. Its articles and essays cover a variety of educational practices, including homeschooling, community education, traditional classrooms, and the Montessori method. The editors encourage writers with classroom experience to submit insightful, factual material that will enlighten readers to specific concerns in education and direct them toward solutions. Circ: 1,000.
Website: www.bfat.com

Freelance Potential
80% written by nonstaff writers. Publishes 4 freelance submissions yearly.
Submissions and Payment: Query. Accepts photocopies, computer printouts, simultaneous submissions if identified, and email submissions to staff@bfat.com. SASE. Response time varies. Articles, word lengths and payment rates vary. Pays on acceptance. First rights.

The Education Revolution

417 Roslyn Road
Roslyn Heights, NY 11577

Executive Director: Jerry Mintz

Description and Readership
The focus of this quarterly publication is on learner-centered educational options that follow the interest of the child rather than an arbitrary curriculum. Articles appearing in *The Education Revolution* cover a broad spectrum of educational alternatives, including the Montessori method and homeschooling. They provide information and guidance to students, parents, schools, and organizations regarding their educational choices. Circ: 700.
Website: www.educationrevolution.org

Freelance Potential
20% written by nonstaff writers. Publishes 10 freelance submissions yearly; 40% by authors who are new to the magazine. Receives 15 queries monthly.
Submissions and Payment: Query. SASE. Responds in 1 month. Written material, word lengths vary. No payment. No rights.

The Elementary School Journal ☆

University of Missouri
College of Education
211-F Townsend Hall
Columbia, MO 65211-1150
Managing Editor

Description and Readership
Published five times per year, this academic journal features original studies containing data about school and classroom processes in elementary or middle schools. With an audience of teacher educators, researchers, and practitioners, *The Elementary School Journal* contains articles dealing with both educational theory and research and their implications for teaching practice. Circ: 2,200.
Website: www.journals.uchicago.edu/ESJ

Freelance Potential
Publishes several freelance submissions yearly.
Submissions and Payment: Sample copy, $13.50. Writers' guidelines available at website. Send four copies of complete ms with an abstract of 100-150 words. Accepts computer printouts. SASE. Articles, word length and response time varies. Rights and payment policy varies.

EFCA Today

901 East 78th Street
Minneapolis, MN 55420

Editor: Diane McDougall

Description and Readership
This Christian magazine is the official publication of the Evangelical Free Church of America and is read by pastors, clergy, elders, deacons, and volunteers. It appears quarterly, and each issue follows an editorial theme that is aimed at promoting spiritual growth and religious commitment. Circ: 30,000.
Website: www.efca.org/magazine

Freelance Potential
90% written by nonstaff writers. Publishes several freelance submissions yearly.
Submissions and Payment: Sample copy and guidelines, $1 with 9x12 SASE (5 first-class stamps). Query. Accepts photocopies, computer printouts, and email queries to dianemc@journeygroup.com. SASE. Response time varies. Articles, 200–700 words. Cover theme articles, 300–1,000 words. Written material, $.23 per word. Pays on acceptance. First rights.

Encyclopedia of Youth Studies ☆

130 Essex Street
South Hamilton, MA 01982

Editor: Dean Borgman

Description and Readership
Youth ministers, social workers, teachers, and others who work with young people find information on all topics pertaining to youth culture in this online encyclopedia of research articles, profiles, interviews, and personal experience essays. Contributions from experienced youth workers are needed. Hits per month: Unavailable.
Website: www.centerforyouth.org

Freelance Potential
50% written by nonstaff writers. Publishes 25 freelance submissions yearly; 85% by unpublished writers, 85% by authors who are new to the magazine. Receives 4 queries, 2–3 unsolicited mss monthly.
Submissions and Payment: Sample copy and guidelines available at website. Query or send complete ms. Accepts email submissions to cys@centerforyouth.org. Responds to queries in 1 week, to mss in 1 month. Articles, 600 words. No payment. All rights.

Entertainment Magazine ☆

P.O. Box 3355
Tucson, AZ 85722

Publisher: Robert Zucker

Description and Readership
Entertainment Magazine highlights local and national entertainment, Tucson and Phoenix tourism, and regional community information and resources. Its editors are interested in current entertainment and travel news and feature articles specific to the Arizona area; personality profiles; and music, film, and book reviews. Hits per month: 30,000
Website: www.emol.org

Freelance Potential
67% written by nonstaff writers. Publishes many freelance submissions yearly.
Submissions and Payment: Sample copy, available online. Query. Accepts photocopies, computer printouts, and email queries to publisher@emol.org. Digital JPG or GIF images, 72–300 dpi. SASE. Responds in 5–7 days. Articles, word lengths vary. No payment.

Explore

Pearson Education Australia–Schools Division
P.O. Box 1024
South Melbourne, VIC 3205
Australia

Articles Editor: Petra Poupa

Description and Readership
Offering fiction, nonfiction, plays, poetry, and activities, *Explore* is a quarterly publication tailored to readers between the ages of 8 and 10. It covers a variety of topics of interest to this age group. Circ: 20,000.
Website: www.pearsoned.com/au/schools

Freelance Potential
50% written by nonstaff writers. Publishes 15 freelance submissions yearly.
Submissions and Payment: Guidelines available at website. Query or send complete ms. Accepts photocopies, computer printouts, disk submissions, simultaneous submissions if identified, and email submissions to magazines@pearsoned.com.au. SAE/IRC. Responds to queries in 1 month, to mss in 3 months. Articles, to 500 words; $100–$220. Fiction, to 800 words; $80–$200. 35mm color transparencies. Pays on publication. First Australian rights.

Family Energy ☆

P.O. Box 1780
Evanston, IL 60204

Submissions Editor

Description and Readership
The focus of this magazine is on family health, fitness, and fun. Experienced parents as well as experts provide informational and how-to articles, essays, news articles, and interviews with famous or fascinating people. New writers are welcome to query as long as they are passionate about the magazine's subject matter. *Family Energy* is published six times each year. Circ: Unavailable.
Website: www.familyenergy.com

Freelance Potential
Publishes several freelance submissions yearly.
Submissions and Payment: Sample copy available at newsstands. Guidelines available at website. Query with list of sources to be interviewed. Accepts email queries to editors@iparenting.com (no attachments). Response time varies. Articles, 600–1,200 words; payment rate varies. Pays 30 days after acceptance. All rights.

Family-Life Magazine

P.O. Box 351
Philo, CA 95466

Editor

Description and Readership
Formerly known as *Sonoma Parents Journal*, this monthly magazine is distributed throughout Sonoma, Mendocino, and Lake counties in California. In addition to serving as a directory of community resources of interest to families, it also includes articles and columns intended to enhance parenting skills. Circ: 28,000.
Website: www.theparentsjournal.com

Freelance Potential
40% written by nonstaff writers. Publishes 20 freelance submissions yearly; 10% by unpublished writers. Receives 10+ unsolicited mss monthly.
Submissions and Payment: Guidelines and editorial calendar available. Send complete ms. Accepts email submissions to patty@family-life.us (text only attachments). Response time varies. Articles and depts/columns, word lengths and payment rates vary. Pays on publication. One-time rights.

FamilyRapp.com

P.O. Box 117
Oxted RH8 0FN
United Kingdom

Submissions: Cathy Baillie & Jane Rouse

Description and Readership

A weekly online magazine for parents, *FamilyRapp.com* specializes in articles on all aspects of parenting children between the ages of 3 and 13. In addition to parenting topics, other subjects covered include education, health, the holidays, family day trips, and social issues. Its editors look for seven new articles in these categories to publish each week. Book reviews also appear regularly. Hits per month: Unavailable.
Website: www.familyrapp.com

Freelance Potential

90% written by nonstaff writers. Publishes 320 freelance submissions yearly. Receives 5 queries monthly.
Submissions and Payment: Sample copy and guidelines available at website. Send complete ms. Accepts email submissions to info@familyrapp.com. Response time varies. Articles, 500–1,000 words. No payment. One-time and electronic rights.

Fantastic Stories of the Imagination

P.O. Box 329
Brightwaters, NY 11718

Editor-in-Chief: Edward J. McFadden

Description and Readership

The stories and poetry that appear in this quarterly belong to the science fiction or fantasy genres. Mixed-genre stories with science fiction or fantasy elements also appear. The magazine is currently overstocked and closed to submissions until 2008. Circ: 7,000.
Website: www.dnapublications.com

Freelance Potential

100% written by nonstaff writers. Publishes 50 freelance submissions yearly; 10% by unpublished writers. Receives 450 unsolicited mss monthly.
Submissions and Payment: Sample copy, $5 with 9x12 SASE. Send complete ms. Accepts photocopies and computer printouts. SASE. Responds in 1–8 weeks. Fiction, 2,000–15,000 words. Depts/columns, word lengths vary. Poetry, no line limits. Written material, $.01–$.05 per word. Payment policy varies. First North American serial rights. Provides 1 contributor's copy.

Farm & Ranch Living

5925 County Lane
Greendale, WI 53129

Editor: Nick Pabst

Description and Readership

Photo-illustrated articles about today's farmers fill the pages of this bimonthly publication. It focuses on the people who operate farms, rather than the technical side of farming. Circ: 350,000.
Website: www.farmandranchliving.com

Freelance Potential

90% written by nonstaff writers. Publishes 36 freelance submissions yearly; 50% by unpublished writers, 50% by authors who are new to the magazine. Receives 10 queries and unsolicited mss monthly.
Submissions and Payment: Sample copy, $2. Query or send complete ms. Accepts photocopies, computer printouts, and email to editors@farmandranchliving.com. Photos improve chance of acceptance. SASE. Responds in 6 weeks. Articles, 1,200 words. Depts/columns, 350 words. Written material, $10–$150. Pays on publication. One-time rights. Provides 1 copy.

Fido Friendly

P.O. Box 10219
Costa Mesa, CA 92627

Editor: Nick Svelosky

Description and Readership

A travel magazine, *Fido Friendly* is written for people who take their dogs along on trips. Each quarterly issue spotlights U.S. and Canadian destinations that welcome dogs and includes state- and city-specific information. Hotel, restaurant, and campsite reviews are regular features. Circ: 30,000.
Website: www.fidofriendly.com

Freelance Potential

100% written by nonstaff writers. Publishes 4 freelance submissions yearly; 10% by unpublished writers, 60% by authors who are new to the magazine. Receives 10 queries monthly.
Submissions and Payment: Sample copy and guidelines, $4.95. Query with sample paragraph. Accepts email queries to nick@fidofriendly.com. SASE. Responds in 1 month. Articles, 800–1,200 words; $.10 per word. Pays on publication. First rights. Provides 1 copy.

57 Story Lane

P.O. Box 11487
Southport, NC 28461

Editor: Monica F. Celinski

Description and Readership
This website created by writers for writers allows them to receive feedback and advice from other writers and readers. By submitting fiction, nonfiction, editorials, and poetry, writers have the opportunity of having their work read and reviewed online by fellow writers to help them improve their craft. Hits per month: Unavailable.
Website: www.57StoryLane.com

Freelance Potential
100% written by nonstaff writers. Publishes many freelance submissions yearly. Receives many unsolicited mss monthly.
Submissions and Payment: Writers' guidelines and submission form available at the website. Send complete ms. Accepts submissions through the website only. Responds in 10 days. Articles, fiction, and poetry, word lengths vary. No payment. Perpetual but nonexclusive rights.

Gay Parent Magazine

P.O. Box 750852
Forest Hills, NY 11375-0852

Editor: Angeline Acain

Description and Readership
Published six times per year, this magazine's readership consists of gay and lesbian parents. It features articles on parenting, travel activities, and family-oriented features written by gay parents. Circ: 10,000.
Website: www.gayparentmag.com

Freelance Potential
2% written by nonstaff writers. Publishes 5 freelance submissions yearly. Receives 1 unsolicited ms each month.
Submissions and Payment: Sample copy and guidelines, $3.50. Send complete ms. Prefers email submissions to acain@gis.net. Availability of artwork improves chance of acceptance. SASE. Response time varies. Articles, 500–1,000 words. Color prints or transparencies. Written material, $50. One-time rights. Pays on publication. Contributor's copies available on request.

FineScale Modeler

21027 Crossroads Circle
P.O. Box 1612
Waukesha, WI 53187

Editor: Mark Thompson

Description and Readership
How-to articles written to help modelers advance their skills appear in this hobbyist magazine. Published ten times each year, it seeks submissions from knowledgeable modelers on all aspects of the craft. Circ: 60,000.
Website: www.finescale.com

Freelance Potential
85% written by nonstaff writers. Publishes 40 freelance submissions yearly; 20% by authors who are new to the magazine. Receives 30 queries, 10–20 mss monthly.
Submissions and Payment: Sample copy, $4.95 with 9x12 SASE. Query or send complete ms. No simultaneous submissions. Accepts photocopies, computer printouts, disk submissions with hard copy, and email submissions to editor@finescale.com. SASE. Responds in 1–4 months. Articles, 750–3,000 words. Depts/columns, word lengths vary. Written material, $40–$60 per page. Pays on acceptance. All rights. Provides 1 author's copy.

Girlfriend Magazine

35-51 Mitchell Street
McMahons Point, New South Wales 2060
Australia

Editorial Assistant: Belinda Frizza

Description and Readership
This monthly magazine offers celebrity news, fashion reports, and articles on relationships, current events, and social issues for its readership of 14- to 17-year-old girls. Circ: 112,000.
Website: www.girlfriend.com.au

Freelance Potential
30% written by nonstaff writers. Publishes 36 freelance submissions yearly; 25% by unpublished writers, 15% by authors who are new to the magazine.
Submissions and Payment: Sample copy, $4.50. Send complete ms. Accepts photocopies, computer printouts, and email submissions to girlfriendonline@pacpubs.com.au. SAE/IRC. Responds in 3 weeks. Articles, 1,500–2,000 words. Fiction, 2,000 words. Depts/columns, 500 words. Color prints or transparencies. All material, payment rates vary. Pays on publication. Exclusive rights. Provides 3 contributor's copies.

Good Housekeeping

Hearst Corporation
250 West 55th Street
New York, NY 10019

Executive Editor: Judith Coyne

Description and Readership
This monthly magazine reviews timely queries for health narratives and for features about people involved in inspiring or heroic pursuits. Queries should demonstrate careful research and a fresh angle. Circ: 6 million.
Website: www.goodhousekeeping.com

Freelance Potential
80% written by nonstaff writers. Publishes 50+ freelance submissions yearly. Receives 1,500–2,000 queries monthly.
Submissions and Payment: Guidelines available. Sample copy, $5.50 at newsstands. Query with résumé and clips for nonfiction; SASE. Send complete ms for fiction; mss not returned. Accepts computer printouts. Responds in 4–6 weeks. Articles, 750–2,500 words; to $2,000. Essays, to 1,000 words; to $750. Pays on acceptance. All rights for nonfiction; first North American serial rights for fiction. Provides 1 contributor's copy.

Grandparents Magazine

281 Rosedale Avenue
Wayne, PA 19087

Editor: Katrina Hayday Wester

Description and Readership
Grandparents Magazine is an e-zine that was created for grandparents and anyone who loves them. Each issue is updated monthly and includes articles, song lyrics, and links to children's activities, along with personal experience pieces, profiles, and interviews. Topics include recreation, travel, life lessons, social issues, religion, relationships, and health and fitness. Circ: Unavailable.
Website: www.grandparentsmagazine.net

Freelance Potential
Publishes several freelance submissions yearly.
Submissions and Payment: Sample copy and guidelines available at website. Query. SASE. Accepts email queries to content@grandparentsmagazine.net. Response time varies. Articles, word length varies. No payment. Electronic rights.

Grand Rapids Family

Suite 201
549 Ottawa Avenue NW
Grand Rapids, MI 49503

Editor: Carole Valade

Description and Readership
Informational articles about family matters, personal experience essays, profiles of outstanding local kids and teens, and interviews with local family professionals fill each issue of this parenting monthly published for the residents of West Michigan. A guide to local kid-friendly events appears in each issue. Circ: 30,000.
Website: www.grfamily.com

Freelance Potential
20% written by nonstaff writers. Publishes 15 freelance submissions yearly.
Submissions and Payment: Guidelines available with #10 SASE. Query or send complete ms. Accepts photocopies and computer printouts. SASE. Responds to queries in 2 months, to mss in 6 months. Articles and depts/columns, word lengths and payment rates vary. B/W or color prints; $25. Pays on publication. Kill fee, $25. All rights.

Grrr!

c/o PETA
501 Front Street
Norfolk, VA 23510

Editorial Coordinator: Robyn Wesley

Description and Readership
Grrr! is published quarterly by the organization People for the Ethical Treatment of Animals (PETA) and is devoted to promoting an appreciation and respect for animals. Written material includes articles, personal opinion pieces, interviews, and profiles. Its target audience is children between the ages of four and fourteen. All material is by assignment only and *Grrr!* is currently not accepting article submissions. Circ: 55,000.
Website: www.petakids.com

Freelance Potential
5% written by nonstaff writers. Publishes few freelance submissions yearly. Receives 1 query monthly.
Submissions and Payment: Sample copy, free. No unsolicited mss. Responds in 1 month. Articles; word lengths, payment rates, and payment policies vary. All North American serial rights.

Harford County Kids

Suite 100
124 North Main Street
Bel Air, MD 21014

Editor

Description and Readership
Educational and health issues, family finances, family dining, and local events and resources are covered in this publication for parents living in Bel Air and other Harford County, Maryland, communities. Profiles of area families can also be found regularly in this monthly. Circ: Unavailable.
Website: www.harfordcountykids.com

Freelance Potential
100% written by nonstaff writers. Publishes 20 freelance submissions yearly.
Submissions and Payment: Guidelines available. Query. Accepts photocopies, computer printouts, and email submissions to joanf@aboutdelta.com. SASE. Response time varies. Articles and depts/columns, word lengths and payment rates vary. Pays on publication. First electronic rights. Provides 1 contributor's copy.

Home & School Connection

Suite 103
3035 Valley Avenue
Winchester, VA 22601

Submissions: Jennifer Hutchinson

Description and Readership
A newsletter that is published monthly and distributed through schools, *Home & School Connection* offers short, easy-to-read articles that convey valuable tips for parents who want to help their children succeed in school. Circ: 3 million.
Website: www.rfeonline.com

Freelance Potential
100% written by nonstaff writers. Publishes 80 freelance submissions yearly; 28% by unpublished writers, 14% by authors who are new to the magazine. Receives 3 unsolicited mss monthly.
Submissions and Payment: Sample copy, free with 9x12 SASE ($.77 postage). Query with résumé and 3 clips. SASE. Responds in 1 month. Articles, 225–300 words. Depts/columns, 175–200 words. Written material, $.60 per word. Pays on acceptance. All rights. Provides 5 contributor's copies.

High School Years

Suite 103
3035 Valley Avenue
Winchester, VA 22601

Submissions Editor

Description and Readership
Distributed through high schools, this monthly newsletter offers short, practical articles that can be quickly read by busy parents. With a goal to promote success during the high school years, it covers topics such as after-school jobs, post-high school plans, and other issues of concern to parents of teenagers. Circ: 300,000.
Website: www.rfeonline.com

Freelance Potential
100% written by nonstaff writers. Publishes 80 freelance submissions yearly; 28% by unpublished writers. Receives 3 unsolicited mss monthly.
Submissions and Payment: Sample copy, guidelines, and editorial calendar, free with 9x12 SASE. Query with résumé and 3 clips. SASE. Responds in 1 month. Articles, 225–300 words. Depts/columns, 175–200 words. Written material, $.60 per word. Pays on acceptance. All rights. Provides 5 contributor's copies.

Hot Rod

6420 Wilshire Boulevard
Los Angeles, CA 90048

Editor: David Frieburger

Description and Readership
Covering high-performance cars for an audience of hands-on hot rod enthusiasts, this magazine includes informational articles on racing events and how-to pieces on topics such as building custom cars, car maintenance, and vehicle repairs. *Hot Rod* is published monthly. Circ: 680,000.
Website: www.hotrod.com

Freelance Potential
15% written by nonstaff writers. Publishes 24 freelance submissions yearly. Receives 24 queries monthly.
Submissions and Payment: Sample copy, $3.50 at newsstands. Guidelines available. Query. SASE. Response time varies. Articles, 3,000 characters per page; $250–$300 per page. Depts/columns, word length varies; $100 per page. B/W and color prints and 35mm color transparencies; payment rate varies. Pays on publication. All rights.

I.D.

Cook Communications Ministries
4050 Lee Vance View
Colorado Springs, CO 80918

Editor: Gail Rohlfing

Description and Readership
A weekly paper used in young adult Sunday school classes, *I.D.* presents its readers with stories that illuminate biblical concepts. While it does not review unsolicited manuscripts, freelancers who would like to try writing for this market may submit a letter of inquiry to the editor, along with a résumé and list of publishing credits. Circ: 61,000.
Website: www.cookministries.org

Freelance Potential
30% written by nonstaff writers.
Submissions and Payment: Guidelines available. Query with résumé. All articles are assigned. Accepts photocopies and computer printouts. SASE. Responds in 6 months. Articles, 600–1,200 words; $50–$300 depending on experience. Color and B/W prints; payment rate varies. Pays on acceptance. Rights policy varies. Provides 1 contributor's copy.

Indian Life Newspaper

P.O. Box 3765
RPO Redwood Centre
Winnipeg, Manitoba R2L 1L6
Canada

Editor: Viola Jones

Description and Readership
This Christian newspaper, published six times per year, is an evangelical tool to help the North American Indian church with the social, cultural, and spiritual needs of its people. Circ: 20,000.
Website: www.indianlife.org

Freelance Potential
80% written by nonstaff writers. Publishes 10 freelance submissions yearly; 2% by unpublished writers, 25% by authors who are new to the magazine. Receives 23 unsolicited mss monthly.
Submissions and Payment: Sample copy, $2.50 with #9 SAE (4 first-class stamps). Prefers query. Accepts complete ms. Accepts photocopies, disk submissions, and email submissions to jim.editor@indianlife.org. SAE/IRC. Responds in 1 month. Articles, 250–2,000 words. Written material, $25–$100. First rights. Pays on publication. Provides 15 contributor's copies.

I Love Cats

16 Meadow Hill Lane
Armonk, NY 10504

Editor: Lisa Allmendinger

Description and Readership
Feature stories about cats, tips for cat owners, unusual cat happenings, and feline health and behavior are in in each bimonthly issue of this magazine. It is interested in profiles of cat owners and humorous stories.
Circ: 25,000
Website: www.iluvcats.com

Freelance Potential
95% written by nonstaff writers. Publishes 120 freelance submissions yearly; 50% by unpublished writers, 75% by authors who are new to the magazine. Receives 208 unsolicited queries and mss monthly.
Submissions and Payment: Sample copy and guidelines, $5 with 9x12 SASE. Query or send complete ms. Accepts computer printouts and email to ilovecatseditor@sbcglobal.net. SASE. Responds in 1–2 months. Articles and fiction, 500–1,000 words; $25–$150. Pays on publication. All rights. Provides 1 contributor's copy.

Inside Kung-Fu

CFW Enterprises
4201 Vanowen Place
Burbank, CA 91505

Editor: Dave Cater

Description and Readership
Covering the martial arts for readers of all ages, *Inside Kung-Fu* appeals to practitioners under the age of 20 in particular. Each monthly issue delves into technique and the traditional forms of fighting. Circ: 110,000.
Website: www.cfwenterprises.com

Freelance Potential
80% written by nonstaff writers. Publishes 100 freelance submissions yearly; 25% by unpublished writers, 75% by authors who are new to the magazine. Receives 42 queries monthly.
Submissions and Payment: Sample copy and guidelines, $2.95 with 9x12 SASE. Query. Accepts computer printouts, IBM or Macintosh disk submissions, and email queries to davecater@cfwenterprises.com. SASE. Responds in 4–6 weeks. Articles, 1,500 words. Depts/columns, 750 words. Written material, payment rate varies. Pays on publication. First rights.

Inspirationstation Magazine

1119 South Despelder #6
Grand Haven, MI 49417

Publisher: Kevin Collier

Description and Readership
Published online six times each year, this Christian e-zine offers faith-based stories for readers ages 7 to 14. Its entertaining, uplifting fiction includes fantasy stories that feature talking creatures as well as inspirational stories with compelling human characters. Although most of the content is written by staff, new writers find exposure for their work if they are chosen to fill a guest author spot. Hits per month: 2,400.
Website: www.inspirationstation.faithweb.com

Freelance Potential
10% written by nonstaff writers. Publishes 12 freelance submissions yearly.
Submissions and Payment: Sample copy available at website. Query or send complete ms. Accepts email submissions to kevinscottcollier@hotmail.com. Response time varies. Articles, word lengths vary. No payment. Rights policy varies.

Jam Rag

Suite 240
22757 Woodward
Ferndale, MI 48220

Co-Editor & Publisher: Tom Ness

Description and Readership
A free newspaper available monthly in the Detroit area, *Jam Rag* seeks articles from writers passionate about music and the local music community. Circ: 12,000.
Website: www.jamrag.com

Freelance Potential
70% written by nonstaff writers. Publishes 250 freelance submissions yearly; 50% by unpublished writers, 50% by authors who are new to the magazine. Receives 20 unsolicited mss monthly.
Submissions and Payment: Sample copy and guidelines, free with 9x12 SASE ($.75 postage). Query or send complete ms. Accepts photocopies, computer printouts, disk submissions, and simultaneous submissions if identified. Availability of artwork improves chance of acceptance. SASE. Response time varies. Articles, word lengths vary; $10–$50. Pays on publication. One-time rights. Provides 1 contributor's copy.

Junior Storyteller

P.O. Box 205
Masonville, CO 80541

Editor: Vivian Dubrovin

Description and Readership
Boys and girls in elementary through junior high school who want to be storytellers find plays, crafts, and finformation on the craft of storytelling in this magazine. The goal of *Junior Storyteller* is to promote the art through complete storytelling projects. Circ: 500.
Website: www.storycraft.com

Freelance Potential
30% written by nonstaff writers. Receives several queries and unsolicited mss monthly.
Submissions and Payment: Sample copy, $3.50 with 6x9 SASE. Query. Accepts photocopies, computer printouts, and email to jrstoryteller@directway.com. Availability of artwork may improve chance of acceptance. SASE. Response time varies. Articles and fiction, 500–1,000 words; $50–$125. Artwork, line art. Pays on acceptance. First rights. Provides 10 contributor's copies.

Kahani

P.O. Box 590155
Newton Centre, MA 02459

Editor: Monika Jain

Description and Readership
Subtitled "A South Asian Literary Magazine for Children," *Kahani* looks at the experiences of South Asian children in America through its stories and articles. The stories it seeks may involve cultural conflicts or simply portray South Asian kids as cool protagonists instead of secondary characters. Mystery, adventure, and humorous stories are welcome as long as they feature well-developed characters, not stereotypes. *Kahani* is published six times each year. Circ: Unavailable.
Website: www.kahani.com

Freelance Potential
Publishes several freelance submissions yearly.
Submissions and Payment: Guidelines available at website. Send complete ms. Accepts email submissions to writers@kahani.com. Response time varies. Articles and fiction, word lengths vary. No payment. Rights vary.

Kansas 4-H Journal

116 Umberger Hall
KSU
Manhattan, KS 66506-3417

Editor: Rhonda Atkinson

Description and Readership
Published ten times each year, this journal is read by 4-H members, leaders, and parents of members. Up-to-date reports on 4-H events are covered, as well as how-to articles, activities, photo essays, and personal experience pieces. Writers must be involved in 4-H events. Circ: 14,000.

Freelance Potential
60% written by youth 4-H writers. Publishes 100 freelance submissions yearly; 10% by unpublished writers, 20% by authors who are new to the magazine. Receives 58 queries and unsolicited mss monthly.
Submissions and Payment: Sample copy and editorial calendar, $5. Query or send complete ms. Accepts photocopies and computer printouts. SASE. Response time varies. Articles, 500 words. Written material, payment rates vary. Payment policy varies. Rights negotiable.

Kentuckiana Parent

525 West Broadway
P.O. Box 740031
Louisville, KY 40201

Editor

Description and Readership
This regional parenting publication for families who have children between the ages of four and eleven was launched in March 2005. Family recreation, education, health and fitness, and regional news are among the topics it addresses regulary. The editors are primarily interested in ideas for family-oriented activities, articles and columns about health issues, and movie reviews. Circ: 25,000.
Website: www.kentuckianaparent.com

Freelance Potential
10–15% written by nonstaff writers. Publishes 10–15 freelance submissions yearly.
Submissions and Payment: Guidelines available. Query or send complete ms. Accepts photocopies and computer printouts. SASE. Response time varies. Articles and depts/columns, word lengths and payment rates vary. Payment policy and rights vary.

Keyboard

2800 Campus Drive
San Mateo, CA 94403

Editor-in-Chief: Ernie Rideout

Description and Readership
Published monthly, *Keyboard* presents articles written to help amateur and professional keyboardists improve their musical abilities. Circ: 61,000.
Website: www.keyboardmag.com

Freelance Potential
10–20% written by nonstaff writers. Publishes 120 freelance submissions yearly; 35% by unpublished writers, 50% by authors who are new to the magazine. Receives 60 unsolicited mss monthly.
Submissions and Payment: Sample copy and guidelines, free with 9x12 SASE. Send complete ms with résumé. Accepts photocopies, computer printouts, and email submissions to keyboard@musicplayer.com. SASE. Responds in 3 months. Articles, 500–3,000 words. Depts/columns, 400–800 words. All material, payment rate varies. Pays on acceptance. All rights. Provides 5 contributor's copies.

Kids

341 East Lancaster Avenue
Downingtown, PA 19335

Editor: Bob Ludwick

Description and Readership
This monthly newspaper for Chester County is sponsored by the county's public schools. Its purpose is to keep the educational community of parents, teachers, and students aware of the events taking place in local schools. Reports on successful programs, profiles of outstanding teachers, and announcements of notable student accomplishments are some of its regular features. Circ: 43,000.

Freelance Potential
90% written by nonstaff writers. Publishes 120 freelance submissions yearly; 20% by unpublished writers. Receives several queries monthly.
Submissions and Payment: Sample copy and editorial calendar, free with 9x12 SASE. Query with résumé. Accepts photocopies and computer printouts. SASE. Responds in 1 week. Articles and depts/columns, to 500 words. No payment. All rights. Provides 2 copies.

Kidsandkaboodle.com

1169 Mount Rushmore Way
Lexington, KY 40515

Editor: Jennifer Anderson

Description and Readership
This regional, online magazine offers parents and families living in central Kentucky valuable information on parenting, safety, and child development. It is currently seeking informational articles on health, fitness, and pregnancy. It does not need vacation tips or personal opinion essays. Circ: 50,000.
Website: www.kidsandkaboodle.com

Freelance Potential
20% written by nonstaff writers. Publishes 20 freelance submissions yearly; 50% by unpublished writers, 50% by authors who are new to the magazine. Receives 3–4 queries and unsolicited mss monthly.
Submissions and Payment: Sample copy available at website. Send complete ms. Accepts email submissions to editor@kidsandkaboodle.com. SASE. Response time varies. Written material, word lengths vary. Payment rates and policies vary. All rights.

Kid's Directory

P.O. Box 21226
Little Rock, AR 72221-1226

Publisher: Jennifer Robins

Description and Readership
Primarily a directory of family services, this monthly publication has been available to central Arkansas parents since 1991. Its purpose is to provide information about local events and services of interest to families with children under the age of 13. A segment of the directory is devoted to family-related book, music, software, and video reviews, for which the publisher will consider submissions from freelance writers. Circ: 19,000.
Website: www.littlerockkidsdirectory.com

Freelance Potential
100% written by nonstaff writers. Publishes 6 freelance submissions yearly. Receives 2 queries, 2 unsolicited mss monthly.
Submissions and Payment: Sample copy, free with 6x9 SASE ($1.06 postage). Query or send complete ms. SASE. Response time varies. Articles, word length, payment rate, and payment policy vary. All rights.

The Kids' Storytelling Club ☆

Editor: Vivian Dubrovin

Description and Readership
This online magazine for young storytellers, teachers, librarians, parents, and youth group leaders features informational, how-to, and bilingual articles as they relate to storytelling. Reports of young storytellers, clubs, or classes that promote youth storytelling are on its wish list. Circ: 4,000
Website: www.storycraft.com

Freelance Potential
70% written by nonstaff writers. Publishes many freelance submissions yearly; many by unpublished writers, most by authors who are new to the magazine.
Submissions and Payment: Sample copy, free at website. Query. Accepts photocopies, computer printouts, and email submissions to jrstoryteller@directway.com. SASE. Response time varies. Articles, 500 words. Fiction, 250–500 words. Written material, $25. Pays on acceptance. First rights.

Kiwibox.com

Suite 1602
330 West 38th Street
New York, NY 10018

Submissions Editor: Jasmine Kurjakovie

Description and Readership
Designed and managed by teens, this website features contributions from writers between the ages of 14 and 21. Any topic of interest to young adults is considered, including technology, dating, sports, the music scene, fashion, films, and social issues. Offering fiction as well, the site publishes contemporary, multicultural, and inspirational fiction; fantasy; horror; romance; and science fiction. Hundreds of freelance submissions are published at this website, which is updated every two weeks. Hits per month: 1 million.
Website: www.kiwibox.com

Freelance Potential
90% written by nonstaff writers.
Submissions and Payment: Sample copy available at website. Send complete ms. Accepts email submissions to editor@kiwibox.net. Responds in 2 weeks. Articles, 350 words. Fiction, length varies. No payment. All rights.

Knucklebones

N7450 Aanstad Road
P.O. Box 5000
Iola, WI 54945-5000

Editor: Sarah Gloystein Peterson

Description and Readership

Launched in September 2005, *Knucklebones* appears six times each year for people who enjoy board games, card games, brainteasers, and other intellectual diversions. Each issue offers reviews, interviews, games, and puzzles for its readers' entertainment. Circ: Unavailable.
Website: www.kbones.com

Freelance Potential

90% written by nonstaff writers. Publishes 150–175 freelance submissions yearly, 25% by unpublished writers, 100% by authors who are new to the magazine.
Submissions and Payment: Guidelines available with SASE or by email. Prefers query; accepts complete ms. Accepts photocopies, computer printouts, and email submissions to editor@kbones.com. SASE. Response time varies. Articles and depts/columns, word lengths and payment rates vary. Pays on publication. First and electronic rights.

The Lamp–Post

1106 West 16th Street
Santa Ana, CA 92706-3715

Senior Editor: David G. Clark

Description and Readership

This quarterly is a literary review of C. S. Lewis, his contemporaries and circle of influence, his theology, and scholarship. Published by the Southern California C.S. Lewis Society, *The Lamp-Post* features nonfiction, interviews, essays, scholarly articles, fiction, book reviews about Lewis and his circle of friends, and poetry related to this famous author. Circ: 100.

Freelance Potential

90% written by nonstaff writers. Publishes 10–12 freelance submissions yearly; 20% by unpublished writers, 60% by authors who are new to the magazine. Receives 1–2 unsolicited mss monthly.
Submissions and Payment: Sample copy, $3. Send complete ms. Accepts email to dgclark@adelphia.net (Microsoft Word or rich text format). Responds in 3 days. Articles, fiction, and poetry, length varies. No rights. No payment. Provides 2 contributor's copies.

Little Rock Family

122 East Second Street
Little Rock, AK 72201

Submissions Editor

Description and Readership

Timely, local information of interest to parents living in central Arkansas is presented in this monthly publication. It mixes articles on health care, education, and family relationships with special sections, such as a Public School Guide, a Private School Guide, and a Summer Camp Guide. Activity and event calendars are also included in each issue. *Little Rock Family* has won more than 30 Awards of Excellence from Parenting Publications of America. Circ: 20,000.
Website: www.littlerockfamily.com

Freelance Potential

100% written by nonstaff writers. Publishes several freelance submissions yearly.
Submissions and Payment: Query. Accepts photocopies and computer printouts. SASE. Response time varies. Articles and depts/columns, word lengths and payment rates vary. Payment policy varies. First rights.

Metro Augusta Parent

825 Russell Street
Augusta, GA 30904

Editor: Rebecca Murphy

Description and Readership

A free monthly, *Metro Augusta Parent* publishes a calendar that includes activities, events, sport sign-ups, after-school programs, support groups, and classes. Book and movie reviews, party guides, family dining guides, and local resources are also part of the editorial mix. Published monthly, it has a strong regional slant. Circ: Unavailable.
Website: www.augustaparent.com

Freelance Potential

100% written by nonstaff writers. Publishes 10 freelance submissions yearly.
Submissions and Payment: Query. Accepts photocopies, computer printouts, and email submissions to editor@augustaparent.com. SASE. Response time varies. Articles and depts/columns, word lengths and payment rates vary. Payment policy varies. First rights. Provides 1 contributor's copy.

MetroFamily Magazine

Suite C-152
306 South Bryant
Edmond, OK 73034

Editor: Denise Springer

Description and Readership
Launched in 1998 and circulated monthly throughout
central Oklahoma, this magazine provides local parenting information in the form of factual articles, lists of
family-centered events and activities, and community
resources. Circ: 20,000.
Website: www.metrofamilymagazine.com

Freelance Potential
60% written by nonstaff writers.
Submissions and Payment: Sample copy and guidelines, free with 10x13 SASE. Query or send complete
ms. Accepts photocopies, computer printouts, and
email queries to editor@metrofamilymagazine.com.
SASE. Responds to queries in 3 weeks, to mss in
1 month. Articles, 300–600 words; $25–$50. Depts/
columns, 600 words; $25–$35. Pays on publication. Kill
fee, 100%. First North American serial rights. Provides 1
contributor's copy.

Metro Parent

P.O. Box 13660
Portland, OR 97213

Editor: Marie Sherlock

Description and Readership
Available in the Portland area, this monthly magazine
provides articles on baby and child care along with a
calendar of local events and activities that parents and
children can enjoy together. Freelance writers who live
in the region are invited to query. Circ: 36,000.
Website: www.metro-parent.com

Freelance Potential
75% written by nonstaff writers. Publishes 50 freelance
submissions yearly; 5% by unpublished writers. Receives
20 queries monthly.
Submissions and Payment: Sample copy and theme
list, $2. Query with outline. Accepts photocopies, com-
puter printouts, simultaneous submissions if identified,
and email submissions to editor@metro-parent.com.
SASE. Responds in 1 month. Articles and depts/
columns, word lengths and payment rates vary. Pays on
publication. Rights policy varies.

Middle Years

Suite 103
3035 Valley Avenue
Winchester, VA 22601

Submissions Editor: Jennifer Hutchinson

Description and Readership
Easy-to-follow tips and short articles on parenting
middle-grade students, particularly in regard to handling
school-related issues, make up the content of this
monthly newsletter. New writers stand a good chance of
publication with a submission to its "Parent to Parent"
or "Activity" departments. Circ: 1 million.
Website: www.rfeonline.com

Freelance Potential
100% written by nonstaff writers. Publishes 80 freelance submissions yearly. Receives 3 queries monthly.
Submissions and Payment: Sample copy and guidelines, free with 9x12 SASE ($.77 postage). Query with
résumé and 3 clips. Accepts photocopies and computer
printouts. SASE. Responds in 1 month. Articles, 225–
300 words. Depts/columns, 175–200 words. Written
material, $.60 per word. Pays on acceptance. All rights.
Provides 5 contributor's copies.

Model Airplane News

Air Age Publishing
100 East Ridge Road
Ridgefield, CT 06877-4606

Editor-in-Chief: Debra Cleghorn

Description and Readership
Model Airplane News appears monthly and provides
informational and how-to articles on all aspects of
model airplanes, from building and design to flying
techniques. Circ: 95,000.
Website: www.modelairplanenews.com

Freelance Potential
90% written by nonstaff writers. Publishes 100 freelance submissions yearly; 33% by authors who are new
to the magazine. Receives 12–24 queries monthly.
Submissions and Payment: Sample copy and guidelines, $3.50 with 9x12 SASE. Query with outline and
biography describing model experience. Accepts photocopies and computer printouts. Availability of artwork
improves chance of acceptance. SASE. Responds in
6 weeks. Articles, 1,700–2,000 words; $175–$600.
Pays on publication. All North American serial rights.
Provides up to 6 contributor's copies.

Mommy Too! Magazine

2525 Booker Creek Road #13B
Chapel Hill, NC 27514

Editor: Jennifer James

Description and Readership
An online publication that is updated monthly, this magazine celebrates mothers of color. Its publishing standards are high, but the editors encourage submissions from long-time as well as first-time writers. Any topic related to parenting or the varied aspects of being a mom is considered. Subscribers: 12,000.
Website: www.mommytoo.com

Freelance Potential
35% written by nonstaff writers. Publishes 50–60 freelance submissions yearly.
Submissions and Payment: Sample copy and guidelines available at website. Query or send complete ms. Accepts submissions through the website and email submissions to mommytoo@email.com. Response time varies. Articles, 600 words minimum. Essays, fiction, and poetry, word length varies. No payment. Electronic rights.

Natural Family Online ☆

Suite 119
2413 West Algonquin Road
Algonquin, IL 60102-9402

Editor: Lisa Poisso

Description and Readership
This informational magazine serves as a nuts-and-bolts, how-to guide to attachment parenting and natural family living. Published online and updated monthly, it seeks articles that offer tips, tools, and strategies for implementing natural parenting on a daily basis. It does not publish birth stories. On rare occasions it may publish an educational essay. Hits per month: 20,000.
Website: www.naturalfamilyonline.com

Freelance Potential
60% written by nonstaff writers. Publishes 60 freelance submissions yearly; 10% by unpublished writers, 50% by authors who are new to the magazine.
Submissions and Payment: Sample copy and guidelines available at website. Query. Accepts email queries to editor@naturalfamilyonline.com. Response time varies. Articles, 500–750 words; $10–$25. Pays on publication. 60-day electronic and archival rights.

National PAL CopsNkids Chronicles

National Association of Police Athletic Leagues
Suite 301, 618 U.S. Highway 1
North Palm Beach, FL 33408

Creative Services Editor

Description and Readership
This quarterly magazine targets professionals working for Police Athletic Leagues across the United States. Striving to prevent criminal and violent behavior in youths, it reports on successful programs and events that have taught young people alternatives to violence. Regularly covered topics include violence prevention, social and ethnic topics, sports, and crime prevention. Ideas for games and competitions are also covered. Circ: 21,000.
Website: www.nationalpal.org

Freelance Potential
75% written by nonstaff writers.
Submissions and Payment: Sample copy, free. Query or send complete ms. Accepts computer printouts and email submissions to copnkid@nationalpal.org. SASE. Response time varies. Articles, word lengths vary. No payment. All North American serial rights.

Natural Jewish Parenting

P.O. Box 466
Sharon, MA 02067

Editor: Yael Resnick

Description and Readership
Dedicated to Jewish families and their physical, emotional, and spiritual health, *Natural Jewish Parenting* is enjoyed quarterly by socially conscious parents. Circ: 5,000.
Website: www.naturaljewishparenting.com

Freelance Potential
90% written by nonstaff writers. Publishes 40 freelance submissions yearly; 50% by unpublished writers, 80% by authors who are new to the magazine. Receives 8 unsolicited mss monthly.
Submissions and Payment: Guidelines available. Sample copy, $5 with 9x12 SASE ($1.65 postage). Send complete ms. Accepts computer printouts and email submissions to njpmail@mindspring.com. SASE. Responds in 1–2 months. Articles, 1,000–3,500 words. Depts/columns, 500–1,500 words. Written material, $.04—$.05 per word. Pays on publication. First and second rights. Provides 1 contributor's copy.

Neapolitan Family Magazine

P.O. Box 110656
Naples, FL 34108

Editor

Description and Readership
Families in Naples and Collier counties in Florida find this free monthly publication at various distribution points throughout the area. It covers family issues and local events of interest to parents and kids. Circ: 10,000.
Website: www.neafamily.com

Freelance Potential
95% written by nonstaff writers. Publishes 10–12 freelance submissions yearly. Receives 10–15 queries, 25–30 unsolicited mss monthly.
Submissions and Payment: Guidelines and editorial calendar available at website. Sample copy, free with 9x12 SASE. Query or send complete ms. Prefers email submissions to NeapolitanFamily@aol.com. Accepts photocopies and computer printouts. SASE. Responds in 1 month. Articles and depts/columns, word lengths and payment rates vary. Pays on publication. Rights policy varies.

The Numismatist

American Numismatic Association
818 North Cascade Avenue
Colorado Springs, CO 80903-3279

Editor & Publisher: Barbara J. Gregory

Description and Readership
This monthly magazine provides collectors and hobbyists of all levels with informational articles on medals, paper money and coins. Circ: 29,500.
Website: www.money.org

Freelance Potential
60% written by nonstaff writers. Publishes 36 freelance submissions yearly; 20% by unpublished writers, 10% by authors who are new to the magazine. Receives 4 unsolicited mss monthly.
Submissions and Payment: Sample copy and guidelines, free with 9x12 SASE ($2.50 postage). Send complete ms with biography. Accepts photocopies, computer printouts, disk submissions, and email submissions to magazine@money.org. SASE. Responds in 8–10 weeks. Articles, to 3,500 words; $3.60 per published column inch. Pays on publication. Perpetual non-exclusive rights. Provides 5 author's copies.

Our Little Friend

Pacific Press Publishing
P.O. Box 5353
Nampa, ID 83653-5353

Editor: Aileen Andres Sox

Description and Readership
This weekly Sabbath school paper for children ages one through six offers stories consistent with Seventh-day Adventist practices and beliefs. Circ: 40,000.
Website: www.ourlittlefriend.com

Freelance Potential
100% written by nonstaff writers. Publishes 50 freelance submissions yearly; 10% by unpublished writers, 10% by authors who are new to the magazine. Receives 40+ unsolicited mss monthly.
Submissions and Payment: Sample copy and guidelines, free with 9x12 SASE (2 first-class stamps). Send complete ms. Accepts photocopies, computer printouts, simultaneous submissions if identified, and email submissions to ailsox@pacificpress.com. SASE. Responds in 4 months. Articles and fiction, 500–650 words; $25–$50. Pays on acceptance. One-time rights. Provides 3 contributor's copies.

Owl

Bayard Press Canada
2nd Floor, 49 Front Street East
Toronto, Ontario M5E 1B3
Canada

Submissions Editor

Description and Readership
Owl is published nine times each year and features articles about animals, science, people, and technology for children ages eight and up. Circ: 104,000.
Website: www.owlkids.com

Freelance Potential
60% written by nonstaff writers. Publishes 1–3 freelance submissions yearly; 5% by unpublished writers, 10% by authors who are new to the magazine. Receives 50 queries each month.
Submissions and Payment: Sample copy, $4.28. Accepts query with résumé, outline, clips, or writing samples. Accepts photocopies and computer printouts. All material is assigned. Include $1.50 IRC for reply. Responds in 2–3 months. Articles, 500–1,000 words; $200–$500 Canadian. Depts/columns, word lengths and payment rates vary. Payment policy and rights policies vary. Provides 1 contributor's copy.

Palm Beach Conservative ☆

Suite 16
3676 Collin Drive
West Palm Beach, FL 33406

Editor: Dennis Lombard

Description and Readership
This monthly tabloid takes a biblical worldview on national and international news, entertainment, home, family, and people. It offers positive and practical articles on parenting and education, as well as contemporary and humorous fiction. Circ: 6,000.
Website: www.myconservative.com

Freelance Potential
80% written by nonstaff writers. Publishes 25 freelance submissions yearly; 75% by authors who are new to the magazine. Receives 60 unsolicited mss monthly.
Submissions and Payment: Sample copy, $3. Send complete ms. Accepts photocopies, computer printouts, and simultaneous submissions. SASE. Responds in 1 month. Articles and fiction, 500–750 words. Depts/columns, word lengths vary. Written material, payment rates vary. Pays on publication. One-time and electronic rights. Provides contributor's copies on request.

Parents

Gruner & Jahr
375 Lexington Avenue
New York, NY 10017

Editor

Description and Readership
This widely circulated parenting magazine strives to bring its readers practical parenting information that appeals to a broad spectrum of families. It includes personal parenting experiences as well as advice from experts on topics such as health, child care, education, behavior, and pregnancy. Circ: Unavailable.
Website: www.parents.com

Freelance Potential
20% written by nonstaff writers. Publishes 50 freelance submissions yearly. Receives 100 queries monthly.
Submissions and Payment: Sample copy, $3.50 with 9x12 SASE (4 first-class stamps). Query with clips. Accepts photocopies and computer printouts. SASE. Responds in 6 weeks. Articles and depts/columns, word lengths and payment rates vary. Pays on publication. Rights policy varies. Provides 2 contributor's copies.

ParentingHumor.com

P.O. Box 2128
Weaverville, NC 28787

Editor

Description and Readership
Available online and updated weekly, this e-zine avoids typical child-rearing fare in favor of articles that focus on the upbeat side of parenting—the humorous side in particular. Contributors don't need writing credentials to have their work accepted here. As long as the content is family-rated, new writers with a funny story to tell stand a good chance of publication. Hits per month: Unavailable.
Website: www.parentinghumor.com

Freelance Potential
98% written by nonstaff writers. Publishes 250 freelance submissions yearly. Receives 25 queries monthly.
Submissions and Payment: Sample copy, guidelines, and submission form available at website. Query. Accepts email to staff@parentinghumor.com. Response time varies. Articles, to 700 words. No payment. One-time electronic rights. Offers an author's biography and a link to the author's website.

Parents' Choice

Parents' Choice Foundation
Suite 303
201 West Padonia Road
Timonium, MD 21093

Editor: Claire Green

Description and Readership
Parents interested in making informed decisions about which new products are right for their children consult this electronic magazine, which is updated monthly. In each issue, parents find products that are fun, safe, and socially sound—products that help kids grow mentally, morally, and physically. Hits per month: 750,000.
Website: www.parentschoice.org

Freelance Potential
80% written by nonstaff writers. Publishes 4 freelance submissions yearly; 90% by unpublished writers, 15% by authors who are new to the magazine.
Submissions and Payment: Sample copy available at website. Query or send complete ms. Accepts photocopies, computer printouts, and simultaneous submissions if identified. SASE. Response time varies. Articles, 800–1,000 words; $200–$400. Pays on acceptance. All rights.

Passport

WordAction Publishing
6401 The Paseo
Kansas City, MO 64131

Editorial Assistant: Sarah Weatherwax

Description and Readership
This paper is published weekly and is used to supplement Christian education programs for pre-teens. It relates to the lesson of the day and follows the Church of the Nazarene's doctrine. Circ: 55,000.
Website: www.nazarene.org

Freelance Potential
90% written by nonstaff writers. Publishes 30 freelance submissions yearly; 20% by unpublished writers, 20% by authors who are new to the magazine. Receives 20 queries and unsolicited mss monthly.
Submissions and Payment: Sample copy, free with 5x7 SASE. Query with author information; or send complete ms. Accepts photocopies and computer printouts. SASE. Responds in 4–6 weeks. Articles, 400–500 words. Fiction, 600–800 words. Written material, $15–$25. Pays on publication. Rights policy varies. Provides 2 contributor's copies.

Pogo Stick

1300 Kicker Road
Tuscaloosa, AL 35404

Editor: Lillian Kopaska-Merkel

Description and Readership
Pogo Stick is a quarterly magazine for readers up to the age of seventeen. It is exclusively written by children for children and includes contemporary, multicultural, and ethnic fiction; and fantasy; as well as adventure stories, mystery, and poetry. Submissions from adults will not be considered. Circ: Unavailable.

Freelance Potential
99% written by nonstaff writers. 49% by unpublished writers, 99% by authors who are new to the magazine. Receives unsolicited mss each month.
Submissions and Payment: Guidelines available. Sample copy, $3. Send complete ms. Three manuscripts per child per submission. Accepts photocopies and computer printouts. SASE. Responds in approximately 1 month. Written material to 2,000 words. No payment. All rights. Provides 1 contributor's copy.

Plum Magazine

Suite 1600
100 Park Avenue
New York, NY 10017

Submissions: Mary Jane Horton

Description and Readership
The American College of Obstetricians and Gynecologists publishes this magazine annually for pregnant women over the age of 35. Serving as a patient education tool, it covers topics as they relate to older mothers, such as fertility and conception, prenatal testing, smoking cessation, and postpartum health. Circ: Unavailable.
Website: www.plummagazine.com

Freelance Potential
95% written by nonstaff writers. Of the freelance submissions published yearly, 100% are by authors who are new to the magazine.
Submissions and Payment: Guidelines available at website. Query or send complete ms. Accepts email submissions to editor@plummagazine.com. Response time varies. Articles and depts/columns, word lengths and payment rates vary. Pays on publication. All rights. Provides 1 contributor's copy.

Prairie Messenger

Box 190
100 College Drive
Muenster, Saskatchewan S0K 2Y0
Canada

Associate Editor: Maureen Weber

Description and Readership
This weekly Catholic journal has a strong ecumenical focus that encompasses a wide range of spiritualities. Its articles discuss political, social, and economic processes in light of the Gospel. Circ: 7,100.
Website: www.stpeters.sk.ca/prairie_messenger

Freelance Potential
40% written by nonstaff writers. Publishes 3 freelance submissions yearly. Receives 2 queries and unsolicited mss monthly.
Submissions and Payment: Sample copy and guidelines, $1 with 9x12 SAE/IRC. Query or send complete ms. Accepts email submissions to pm.canadian@ stpeters.sk.ca. Responds in 1 month. Articles, 700 words; payment rate varies. Depts/columns, 700 words; $50 (Canadian). Color prints or transparencies and line art; rates vary. Pays at the end of each month. First rights.

PTO Today

Racquetball

Suite 6A
200 Stonewall Boulevard
Wrentham, MA 02093

Editor-in-Chief: Craig Bystrynski

Description and Readership
Founded in 1999, *PTO Today* targets parents and advisors working with parent/teacher organizations at the kindergarten through eighth-grade level. It focuses on providing expert advice and information about resources to parent group leaders. Published six times each year, it seeks ideas for starting up and improving parent/teacher oganizations (regardless of their acronym) and increasing volunteerism among parents. Circ: 80,000.
Website: www.ptotoday.com

Freelance Potential
Publishes several freelance submissions yearly.
Submissions and Payment: Guidelines available. Email queries to craigb@ptotoday.com. Responds in 2 months. Articles, word lengths vary; payment rate varies. Pays on publication. First and electronic rights. Provides 1 contributor's copy.

1685 West Uintah
Colorado Springs, CO 80904

Executive Assistant: Heather Fender

Description and Readership
Coaches, players, tournament directors, and fans find the latest tournament coverage, profiles of outstanding players, and informative articles on technique and strategy in this magazine. It appears six times per year and is published by the United States Racquetball Association. Circ: 40,000.
Website: www.usa.racquetball.org

Freelance Potential
25% written by nonstaff writers. Publishes 10 freelance submissions yearly.
Submissions and Payment: Sample copy and guidelines, $4. Prefers query; accepts mss. Accepts photocopies and computer printouts. SASE. Responds in 9 weeks. Articles, 1,500–2,000 words. Depts/columns, 500–1,000 words. Written material, $.03–$.07 per word. Pays on publication. One-time rights.

Radio Control Boat Modeler

Air Age Publishing
100 East Ridge Road
Ridgefield, CT 06877-4606

Executive Editor: Matt Higgins

Description and Readership
Every other month, fans of radio control boats find detailed information on all aspects of their hobby in this magazine. Among its features are how-to articles, product reviews, and event coverage. Circ: 55,000.
Website: www.rcboatmodeler.com

Freelance Potential
70% written by nonstaff writers. Publishes 20–25 freelance submissions yearly; 75% by unpublished writers. Receives 15 queries monthly.
Submissions and Payment: Sample copy and guidelines, free with 9x12 SASE. Query with outline and brief biography. Accepts photocopies, computer printouts, and email queries to rcboatmodeler@airage.com. Availability of artwork improves chance of acceptance. B/W prints and 35mm slides. SASE. Responds in 1–3 months. Articles, 1,000–2,000 words; $50–$500. Pays on publication. All rights. Provides 2 author's copies.

Radio Control Car Action

Air Age Publishing
100 East Ridge Road
Ridgefield, CT 06877-4606

Technical Editor: Peter Vieira

Description and Readership
Radio-controlled car hobbyists with a serious interest in improving their skills find cutting-edge advice from RC experts, comparison test results, and in-depth product reviews in each monthly issue of this magazine. Race reports are also included. Circ: 140,000.
Website: www.rccaraction.com

Freelance Potential
50% written by nonstaff writers. Publishes 50 freelance submissions yearly. Receives 35 mss monthly.
Submissions and Payment: Sample copy and guidelines, $4.50. Send complete ms with available artwork. Accepts photocopies, computer printouts, and disk submissions (ASCII). Accepts 35mm color slides for complete projects; B/W prints for step-by-step articles. SASE. Responds in 2 months. Articles, 700–1,500 words; $75–$500. Pays on publication. All rights. Provides 2 contributor's copies.

Rainbow Kids

Suite S
1821 Commercial Drive
Harvey, LA 70058

Editor: Martha Osborne

Description and Readership

Published online each month and updated weekly, *Rainbow Kids* provides information for families before, during, and after adoption. Articles and personal essays are submitted by people who read the e-zine closely and regularly. Topics covered include preparing for adoption, adopting special-needs and older children, and sibling adoption. Hits per month: Unavailable.
Website: www.rainbowkids.com

Freelance Potential

80% written by nonstaff writers. Publishes 40 freelance submissions yearly; 50% by authors who are new to the magazine.
Submissions and Payment: Sample copy and guidelines available at website. Query or send complete ms. Accepts email to martha@rainbowkids.com. Responds in 2–3 days. Articles, word lengths vary. No payment. Electronic rights.

Read, America!

3900 Glenwood Avenue
Golden Valley, MN 55422

Editor & Publisher: Roger Hammer

Description and Readership

Reading program coordinators working with new readers, developing readers, and remedial readers, both in clinical and classroom settings, receive this quarterly newsletter. Its intent is to change educational content, theory, and practice to make these areas more compatible with the ways children learn. Circ: 10,000.
Website: www.readamerica.net

Freelance Potential

50% written by nonstaff writers. Publishes 100 freelance submissions yearly; 80% by unpublished writers, 100% by authors who are new to the magazine. Receives 125 unsolicited mss monthly.
Submissions and Payment: Sample copy and guidelines, $7.50. Send complete ms. No simultaneous submissions. SASE. Responds in 2 months. Articles and fiction, to 1,000 words. Written material, $50. Pays on acceptance. All rights.

Realiteen Magazine

1022 Stirling Road
Silver Springs, MD 20901

Editor: Christine Virgin

Description and Readership

Music, spirituality, health, fitness, popular culture, entertainment, recreation, and social issues are some of the topics covered by this magazine that is written from a biblical perspective. Targeting young adults between the ages of 14 and 18, it seeks real life stories from its teen readers. *Realiteen* publishes six issues per year. Circ: 125,000.
Website: www.realiteenmagazine.com

Freelance Potential

20% written by nonstaff writers. Publishes 20 freelance submissions yearly.
Submissions and Payment: Guidelines available. Query. Accepts photocopies, computer printouts, and email submissions to christine@realiteenmagazine.com. SASE. Response time varies. Articles and depts/columns, word lengths and payment rates vary. Pays on publication. First rights.

Recreational Ice Skating

Ice Skating Institute
Suite 140, 17120 North Dallas Parkway
Dallas, TX 75248-1187

Editor: Lori Fairchild

Description and Readership

Skaters between the ages of 6 and 15 read this quarterly membership publication, which offers profiles of other skaters and skating teams and interviews with professional and competitive skaters. Circ: 50,000.
Website: www.skateisi.org

Freelance Potential

20% written by nonstaff writers. Publishes 10 freelance submissions yearly; 80% by unpublished writers, 90% by authors who are new to the magazine. Receives 1 query and unsolicited ms monthly.
Submissions and Payment: Sample copy and guidelines, $4. Query or send complete ms. Accepts photocopies, computer printouts, simultaneous submissions if identified, and email submissions to lfairchild@skateisi.org. SASE. Responds in 2–4 weeks. Articles, 500–1,000 words. Depts/columns, to 400 words. No payment. One-time rights. Provides author's copies.

Redbook

Hearst Corporation
224 West 57th Street
New York, NY 10019

Articles Department

Description and Readership
Young married women who define themselves as smart, capable, and happy with their lives read this popular monthly magazine. Detailed queries that include a list of sources or experts to be consulted are accepted from freelance writers, as are first-person essays that describe pivotal moments in a woman's life. Circ: 2.3 million.
Website: www.redbookmag.com

Freelance Potential
5% written by nonstaff writers. Publishes 10 freelance submissions yearly; 2% by unpublished writers. Receives 830+ queries monthly.
Submissions and Payment: Sample copy, $2.99 at newsstands. Query with clips. Accepts photocopies and computer printouts. SASE. Responds in 3–4 months. Articles, 1,000–3,000 words; $.75–$1 per word. Depts/columns, 1,000–1,500 words; payment rate varies. Pays on acceptance. All rights.

Research in Middle Level Education

College of Education
Southwest Missouri State University
Springfield, MO 65804

Editor: David Hough

Description and Readership
Twice each year, the National Middle School Association updates this online publication for university professors, public school teachers, and school administrators. The purpose of the journal is to publish current research on educational issues related to the middle grades. Hits per month: 30,000.
Website: www.nmsa.org

Freelance Potential
95% written by nonstaff writers. Publishes 10 freelance submissions yearly; 90% by unpublished writers, 50% by authors who are new to the magazine. Receives 6 unsolicited mss monthly.
Submissions and Payment: Sample copy, $20. Send 5 full-binded copies of complete ms including title and 150–200 word abstract. Accepts computer printouts. SASE. Responds in 1 week. Articles, 1,500–2,500 words. No payment. All rights. Provides 1 contributor's copy.

Reptiles

P.O. Box 6050
Mission Viejo, CA 92690

Editor: Russ Case

Description and Readership
This guide for owners of reptiles and amphibians is published monthly. Articles submitted by experts provide detailed instructions for beginning or intermediate enthusiasts who care for these pets in captivity. Circ: 50,000.
Website: www.reptilesmagazine.com

Freelance Potential
60% written by nonstaff writers. Publishes 55 freelance submissions yearly; 50% by unpublished writers, 40% by authors who are new to the magazine. Receives 10 queries monthly.
Submissions and Payment: Sample copy, $3.99 at newsstands. Query or send complete ms. Accepts photocopies and computer printouts. No simultaneous submissions. SASE. Responds in 2–3 months. Articles and depts/columns, word lengths and payment rates vary. Payment policy varies. First North American serial rights. Provides contributor's copies.

Riot ☆

Suite 505
252 West 38th Street
New York, NY 10018

Submissions Editor

Description and Readership
Boys between the ages of 8 and 14 who enjoy humorous, edgy, irreverent articles read *Riot*. Launched as a quarterly in 2005 and published monthly in 2006, the magazine focuses on topics such as sports, games, and entertainment. Fiction is also included, particularly science fiction, fantasy, and stories about superheros and sports. Its editors are open to queries from new writers who understand what appeals to tween boys. Circ: Unavailable.
Website: www.riot101.com

Freelance Potential
Publishes several freelance submissions yearly.
Submissions and Payment: Sample copy and guidelines available. Query. Accepts email queries to publishinginfo@riot101.com. Response time varies. Articles, fiction, and depts/columns, word lengths and payment rates vary. Pays on publication. Rights vary.

Rugby Magazine

Suite 1200
459 Columbus Avenue
New York, NY 10024

Editor: Ed Hagerty

Description and Readership
This monthly magazine is read by male and female rugby players, coaches, and enthusiasts. It is currently looking for "profiles of interesting people who happen to play rugby." Circ: 10,500.
Website: www.rugbymag.com

Freelance Potential
50% written by nonstaff writers. Publishes 50 freelance submissions yearly; 75% by unpublished writers; 75% by authors who are new to the magazine. Receives 200 unsolicited submissions monthly.
Submissions and Payment: Sample copy and guidelines, $4 with 9x12 SASE ($1.70 postage). Query or send complete ms. Accepts photocopies, computer printouts, disk submissions, or email to rugbymagazine@aol.com. SASE. Responds in 2 weeks. Written material, word lengths and payment rates vary. Pays on publication. All rights. Provides 3 contributor's copies.

Saturday Evening Post

1100 Waterway Boulevard
Indianapolis, IN 46202

Executive Editor: Ted Kreiter

Description and Readership
This health magazine features articles on medical issues, prevention, and solutions, as well as general-interest articles on family oriented material. It is published six times each year. Circ: 450,000.
Website: www.satevepost.org

Freelance Potential
10% written by nonstaff writers. Publishes 10 freelance submissions yearly; 10% by unpublished writers. Receives 30–40 queries, 200 unsolicited mss monthly.
Submissions and Payment: Sample copy, $4 with 9x12 SASE. Query with clips or writing samples for articles; send complete ms for fiction. Accepts photocopies, computer printouts, and simultaneous submissions. SASE. Responds in 3–8 weeks. Articles, to 3,000 words. Fiction, 2,500–3,000 words. Depts/columns, 10–200 words. Written material, payment rates vary. Pays on publication. All rights. Provides 1 copy.

Scholastic Choices

Scholastic Inc.
557 Broadway
New York, NY 10012-3999

Editor: Bob Hugel

Description and Readership
Students in grades seven through twelve receive this publication six times each year from their classroom teachers. Each issue provides guidance on subjects of concern to these emerging young adults and helps them make positive, healthful life choices. Circ: 200,000.
Website: www.scholastic.com

Freelance Potential
90% written by nonstaff writers. Publishes 30–40 freelance submissions yearly; 10% by unpublished writers. Receives 5 queries, 5 unsolicited mss monthly.
Submissions and Payment: Guidelines available. Query or send complete ms. Accepts photocopies, computer printouts, and email to choicesmag@scholastic.com. SASE. Responds to queries in 3 months, to mss in 2 months. Articles, 500–1,000 words; payment rate varies. Pays on publication. All rights. Provides 10 contributor's copies.

Scholastic DynaMath

Scholastic Inc.
557 Broadway, Room 4052
New York, NY 10012-3999

Editor: Matt Friedman

Description and Readership
Students in grades three through six find fun-to-do math activities, puzzles, and games in each issue of this take-home paper that is distributed eight times each year. Circ: 200,000.
Website: www.scholastic.com

Freelance Potential
10% written by nonstaff writers. Publishes 5 freelance submissions yearly; 25% by unpublished writers, 25% by authors who are new to the magazine. Receives 4 queries and unsolicited mss monthly.
Submissions and Payment: Sample copy and guidelines, $4 with SASE. Query with outline and synopsis; or send complete ms. Accepts photocopies, computer printouts, and simultaneous submissions if identified. SASE. Responds in 1–2 months. Articles, to 600 words; $250–$400. Puzzles, $25–$50. Pays on acceptance. All rights. Provides 3 contributor's copies.

Scholastic Math Magazine

Scholastic Inc.
557 Broadway
New York, NY 10012-3999

Editor: Jack Silbert

Description and Readership
Written for middle school students, this monthly magazine uses examples from popular culture to explain mathematical concepts and spark an interest in solving mathematical problems. Topics covered include using math in careers, calculating batting averages, and understanding profit. Circ: 200,000.
Website: www.scholastic.com/classmags

Freelance Potential
40% written by nonstaff writers. Publishes 3 freelance submissions yearly; 5% by unpublished writers. Receives 2 queries monthly.
Submissions and Payment: Sample copy and guidelines, free with 9x12 SASE (3 first-class stamps). Query. Accepts photocopies and computer printouts. SASE. Responds in 2–3 months. Articles, 600 words; $300+. Depts/columns, 140 words; $35. Pays on publication. All rights.

SchoolNet Magazine

Room 441
155 Queen Street
Ottawa, Ontario K1A 0H5
Canada

Submissions Editor

Description and Readership
Published by Canada's SchoolNet, this magazine serves as a resource for professionals involved in preparing students for a knowledge-based society. Its purpose is to help teachers and media specialists convey information and communication technology to their students. Promoting the goals of Canada's SchoolNet, the magazine strives to help students experience classrooms without walls, communication without borders, and information without limits. Circ: Unavailable.
Website: www.schoolnet.ca/magazine

Freelance Potential
80% written by nonstaff writers. Publishes 10 freelance submissions yearly.
Submissions and Payment: Query. Accepts photocopies and computer printouts. SAE/IRC. Response time varies. Articles and depts/columns, word lengths and payment rates vary. Payment policy varies.

Scholastic News

Scholastic Inc.
555 Broadway
New York, NY 10012

Submissions Editor, editions 1–3: Rebecca Bonder
Submissions Editor, editions 4–6: Suzanne Freemon

Description and Readership
Distributed by classroom teachers, *Scholastic News* keeps elementary school students informed of world events through age-appropriate articles written in six editions—one for each grade from one through six. New issues are published weekly and cover topics related to the curriculum, current events, and people in the news. Circ: Unavailable.
Website: www.scholastic.com

Freelance Potential
5% written by nonstaff writers.
Submissions and Payment: Query or send complete ms with résumé. Accepts photocopies, computer printouts, and simultaneous submissions if identified. SASE. Availability of artwork improves chance of acceptance. Responds in 1–3 months. Articles, to 500 words; $75–$500. Pays on publication. All rights. Provides 3+ contributor's copies.

Science World

Scholastic Inc.
557 Broadway
New York, NY 10012-3999

Editor: Patricia Janes

Description and Readership
Science World appears 14 times each year and offers articles on life science, earth science, and physical science for junior high and high school students. Circ: 400,000.
Website: www.scholastic.com

Freelance Potential
50% written by nonstaff writers. Publishes 2 freelance submissions yearly; 10% by authors who are new to the magazine. Receives 10 queries, 50 unsolicited queries and mss monthly.
Submissions and Payment: Sample copy and guidelines free with 9x12 SASE. All articles are assigned. Query with list of publishing credits and clips or writing samples. SASE. Accepts photocopies and computer printouts. SASE. Responds in 2 months. Articles, to 750 words; $200–$650. Depts/columns, 200 words; $100–$125. Pays on publication. All rights. Provides 2 contributor's copies.

Scott Stamp Monthly

Scott Publishing Company
P.O. Box 828
Sidney, OH 45365

Editor: Michael Baadke

Description and Readership
Scott Stamp Monthly serves every stamp collector, from beginner to advanced, with informative articles covering all aspects of the hobby. Each monthly issue also includes listings for new stamp issues. Circ: 24,000.
Website: www.scottonline.com

Freelance Potential
75% written by nonstaff writers. Publishes 120 freelance submissions yearly; 10% by unpublished writers, 15% by authors who are new to the magazine. Receives 15 queries and unsolicited mss monthly.
Submissions and Payment: Sample copy and guidelines, $3.50 with 9x12 SASE ($1.95 postage). Prefers query. Accepts mss. Accepts computer printouts and disk submissions (Microsoft Word). SASE. Responds in 1 month. Articles, 1,200–2,000 words; $75–$150. Depts/columns, word lengths and payment rates vary. Pays on publication. First rights. Provides 1 copy.

Sesame Street Magazine

One Lincoln Plaza
New York, NY 10023

Editor: Rebecca Herman

Description and Readership
Published 11 times each year for children ages two through five, this magazine offers humorous fiction, and nonfiction on the topics of animals, music, the arts, health, and exercise. In general, *Sesame Street Magazine* does not accept freelance material. Prospective writers wishing to write for this publication should send a résumé or query letter that details their qualifications. Circ: 800,000.
Website: www.sesamestreet.com

Freelance Potential
99% written by nonstaff writers. Receives 4 queries monthly.
Submissions and Payment: Query or send résumé only. No unsolicited mss. Accepts photocopies and computer printouts. SASE. Response time varies. Written material, word lengths and payment rates vary. Pays on publication. All rights. Provides copies.

Shameless Magazine

P.O. Box 68548
360A Bloor Street W
Toronto, Ontario M5S 1X1
Canada

Editor: Nicole Cohen

Description and Readership
Teenage girls looking to get involved in the world around them find practical ways to make a difference in the pages of this publication. Offering three issues each year, *Shameless Magazine* is rooted in feminism and guided by a teen advisory board. It covers contemporary music, films, sports, and technology, and reports on successful, strong women role models. Circ: Unavailable.
Website: www.shamelessmag.com

Freelance Potential
30% written by nonstaff writers. Publishes 25 freelance submissions yearly.
Submissions and Payment: Guidelines available at website. Query with clips. Prefers email to submit@ shamelessmag.com. Accepts photocopies and computer printouts. SAE/IRC. Response time varies. Articles, 650–2,000 words. Profiles, 300–500 words. No payment. First and electronic rights.

Shasta Parent

P.O. Box 1602
Mount Shasta, CA 96067

Editor: Pam Newman

Description and Readership
This monthly, regional parenting publication provides positive editorial content of interest to families with a variety of beliefs and lifestyles. *Shasta Parent* strives to keep its editorial content respectful of familial and cultural diversity. It is filled with event guides and informative articles. Circ: Unavailable.
Website: www.shastaparent.com

Freelance Potential
100% written by nonstaff writers. Publishes 20 freelance submissions yearly.
Submissions and Payment: Guidelines available at website. Send complete ms. Accepts photocopies, computer printouts, and email submissions to pn@shastaparent.com. SASE. Response time varies. Articles, 700–1,000 words. Depts/columns, 300–500 words. Written material, $40–$70. Pays on publication. First rights.

Simply You Magazine

P.O. Box 284
Phillips, WI 54555-0284

Editor

Description and Readership
This teen and young adult e-zine designed to enhance body, mind, and spirit is published six times each year. It offers helpful articles, stories, poetry, quizzes, product reviews, celebrity gossip, personal advice, and message boards. Hits per month: 10,000.
Website: www.simplyyoumagazine.com

Freelance Potential
25% written by nonstaff writers. Publishes 9–15 freelance submissions yearly; 50% by unpublished writers, 65% by authors who are new to the magazine. Receives 3–4 unsolicited mss monthly.
Submissions and Payment: Sample copy and guidelines, free with business-size SASE. Send complete ms. Accepts email to yourfriends@simplyyoumagazine.com. Responds in 1–2 months. Articles, word length varies. All rights. No payment. Provides 1 contributor's copy.

Skiing

Suite 200
929 Pearl Street
Boulder, CO 80302

Executive Editor: Evelyn Spence

Description and Readership
This magazine is published seven times each year. It features informational articles, reviews, and information on other winter sporting activities. Circ: 400,000.
Website: www.skiingmag.com

Freelance Potential
60% written by nonstaff writers. Publishes 50 freelance submissions yearly; 2% by unpublished writers, 5% by authors who are new to the magazine. Receives 12 queries monthly.
Submissions and Payment: Sample copy and guidelines, $2.50 with 9x12 SASE ($1 postage). Query with clips or writing samples. No simultaneous submissions. Accepts photocopies and computer printouts. SASE. Responds in 2–4 months. Articles and depts/columns, word lengths vary. Written material, $.75 per word. Pays on acceptance. First universal and all media rights. Provides contributor's copies.

Small Town Life Magazine ☆

1046 Barnett Hill Road
Punxsutawney, PA 15767

Editor: Jennifer Forrest

Description and Readership
A magazine the whole family can enjoy, *Small Town Life* is filled with features, recipes, puzzles, and other upbeat material that focuses on the positive. One of the magazine's specific goals is to provide opportunities for new writers to break into print. *Small Town Life* appears on newsstands six times per year. Circ: Unavailable.
Website: www.smalltownlifemagazine.com

Freelance Potential
90% written by nonstaff writers. Publishes 60 freelance submissions yearly; 25% by authors who are new to the magazine.
Submissions and Payment: Sample copy, $5 with 9x12 SAE. Guidelines available at website. Query or send complete ms. Accepts disk submissions and email submissions to editor@smalltownlifemagazine.com. SASE. Response time varies. Articles, 3–4 pages. Depts/columns, 500–750 words. No payment. First rights.

Supertwins

P.O. Box 306
East Islip, NY 11730

Editor: Maureen A. Doolan Boyle

Description and Readership
Members of MOST (Mothers of Supertwins) receive this publication every quarter. Written for higher order multiple birth families (families with triplets, quadruplets, etc.), it strives to inform and support parents through practical articles and inspiring profiles of other families with multiples. Circ: Unavailable.
Website: www.MOSTonline.org

Freelance Potential
50% written by nonstaff writers. Publishes 16 freelance submissions yearly.
Submissions and Payment: Sample copy, $5 with 9x12 SASE. Query or send complete ms. Accepts photocopies, computer printouts, and email to info@mostonline.org. No simultaneous submissions. SASE. Response time varies. Articles and depts/columns, word lengths and payment rates vary. Pays on publication. Rights vary. Provides 2 contributor's copies.

TAP: The Autism Perspective ☆

Suite 243
10153½ Riverside Drive
Toluca, CA 91602

Publisher: Nicki Fisher

Description and Readership
This quarterly was founded in response to the growing prevalence of autism spectrum disorder and the ever-increasing need for up-to-date information on new therapies, treatments, and services. It is especially interested in inspirational stories, new perspectives on autism, and articles on legislation and advocacy. Its readers include both parents and professionals. Circ: Unavailable.
Website: www.theautismperspective.com

Freelance Potential
Publishes several freelance submissions yearly.
Submissions and Payment: Query. Accepts photocopies, computer printouts, and email submissions to info@theautismperspective.com. SASE. Response time varies. Articles and depts/columns, word lengths and payment rate varies. Payment policy varies. All rights. Provides 1 contributor's copy.

Teen People

Time Life Building
35th Floor
Rockefeller Center
New York, NY 10020-1393

Editor: Amy Barnett

Description and Readership
This counterpart to *People* magazine was launched in 1998 to focus on popular personalities of the pre-teen and young adult age groups. Published ten times each year, it heavily emphasizes fashion and beauty as well. Quizzes and book excerpts, articles on relationships and other issues important to teens, and stories that spotlight interesting, unknown young adults make up the balance of its editorial content. Freelance submissions are rarely accepted, but if you're a magazine journalist, they may consider your query. Circ: 1.6 million.
Website: www.teenpeople.com

Freelance Potential
Publishes few freelance submissions.
Submissions and Payment: Sample copy, $3.99 at newsstands. Query. SASE. Response time varies. Articles and depts/columns, word lengths and payment rates vary. Pays on acceptance. All rights.

Think & Discover ☆

P.O. Box 408
Fort Madison, IA 52627

Editor: Donna Borst

Description and Readership
Students in grades one through four benefit from the creative ideas presented in every issue of this magazine, which is published five times each year. Seeking to challenge its young readers, *Think & Discover* seeks story starters, logic puzzles, creative writing exercises, problem-solving scenarios, and enrichment activities for the core curriculum. All submissions must feature hands-on activities for the reader. Circ: 1,200.
Website: www.menageriepublishing.com

Freelance Potential
99% written by nonstaff writers. Publishes 60–100 freelance submissions yearly.
Submissions and Payment: Guidelines available. Query. Accepts email queries to donna@menageriepublishing.com. Response time varies. Articles and activities, word lengths and payment rates vary. Pays on publication. First rights. Provides 1 copy.

Tiny Tummies

P.O. Box 5756
Napa, CA 94581

Editor: Sanna Delmonico

Description and Readership
Tiny Tummies keeps readers abreast of the latest trends in nutrition and includes informative articles on raising healthy children, children's food issues, recipes, and healthy diet tips. It is published six times each year. Circ: 10,000.
Website: www.tinytummies.com

Freelance Potential
30% written by nonstaff writers. Publishes 10 freelance submissions yearly; 15% by authors who are new to the magazine. Receives 3 queries and unsolicited mss monthly.
Submissions and Payment: Sample copy, $1; also available at website. Query or send complete ms. SASE. Response time varies. Articles and depts/columns, word lengths vary. Payment rates and policies vary. Rights policy varies.

Today's Christian

465 Gundersen Drive
Carol Stream, IL 60188

Editorial Coordinator: Cynthia Thomas

Description and Readership
Articles with a Christian angle and spiritual reflection pieces appear in this general interest magazine that is published six times each year. Circ: 145,000.
Website: www.todays-christian.com

Freelance Potential
40% written by nonstaff writers. Publishes 25–30 freelance submissions yearly; 10% by unpublished writers, 10% by authors who are new to the magazine. Receives 150 unsolicited mss monthly.
Submissions and Payment: Sample copy, free with 6x9 SASE (4 first-class stamps). Send complete ms. Accepts photocopies, computer printouts, and email submissions to tceditor@todays-christian.com. SASE. Responds in 2 months. Articles, 700–2,800 words. Depts/columns, word length varies. Written material, $.15–$.25 per word. Pays on acceptance. First serial rights. Provides 2 contributor's copies.

Total Reader

Suite 200
3214 50th Street Court NW
Gig Harbor, WA 98335

Editor: Karie Youngdahl

Description and Readership
Total Reader serves as an online tool for measuring and improving the reading levels of students in grades three through twelve. The site helps teachers assess a student's reading ability and points them toward appropriate texts for improving the current level of skill. Hi/lo material is needed from freelance writers, especially articles on science, technology, and history. Science fiction, fantasy, adventure stories, and contemporary fiction are also welcome. Hits per month: Unavailable.
Website: www.totalreader.com

Freelance Potential
25% written by nonstaff writers. Publishes 20 freelance submissions yearly.
Submissions and Payment: Send complete ms. Accepts email to trsubmissions@edgate.com. Response time varies. Articles and fiction, 200–1,200 words; $25–$75. Payment policy varies. Rights vary.

Toy Farmer

7496 106th Avenue SE
LaMoure, ND 58458-9404

Editorial Assistant: Cheryl Hegvik

Description and Readership
Collectors with a serious interest in farm toys read this monthly magazine for information about the history of farm toys, toy company stories, reports on new farm toys, and profiles of other collectors. Circ: 27,000.
Website: www.toyfarmer.com

Freelance Potential
80% written by nonstaff writers. Publishes 50 freelance submissions yearly; 20% by unpublished writers, 20% by authors who are new to the magazine. Receives several queries monthly.
Submissions and Payment: Sample copy, guidelines, and editorial calendar, $5 with 9x12 SASE. Query with writing samples. Accepts computer printouts and disk submissions. SASE. Responds in 1 month. Articles, 1,500 words. Depts/columns, 800 words. Written material, $.10 per word. Pays on publication. First rights. Provides 2 contributor's copies.

Toy Tips Magazine

9663 Santa Monica Boulevard
Beverly Hills, CA 90210

Publisher: Marianne M. Szymanski

Description and Readership
The goal of this quarterly publication is to present parents with unbiased information about new toys. Product reviews focus on toy safety, durability, learning value, age appropriateness, and enjoyment. Circ: 6.6 million.
Website: www.toytips.com

Freelance Potential
15% written by nonstaff writers. Publishes 4 freelance submissions yearly; 5% by authors who are new to the magazine. Receives 2–4 queries, 2 unsolicited mss each month.
Submissions and Payment: Sample copy and guidelines, $3 with 9x12 SASE. Query or send complete ms. Accepts email submissions to comments@toytips.com. Availability of artwork improves chance of acceptance. SASE. Responds in 1 month. Articles and depts/columns, 200 words. Color prints or transparencies. No payment. All rights. Provides 10 contributor's copies.

True Love

Sterling/McFadden Publishing
11th Floor
333 Seventh Avenue
New York, NY 10001

Editor-in-Chief: Alison Way

Description and Readership
The first-person stories in *True Love* feature some aspect of love or romance. Most of the stories are contributed by long-time readers of the magazine who have a firm grasp of its particular editorial tone and style. New issues appear 10 times each year. Circ: 200,000.
Website: www.truestorymail.com

Freelance Potential
100% written by nonstaff writers. Publishes 120 freelance submissions yearly; 40% by unpublished writers. Receives 35 unsolicited mss monthly.
Submissions and Payment: Sample copy, $2.99 at newsstands. Guidelines available. Send complete ms. No simultaneous submissions. Accepts photocopies and computer printouts. SASE. Responds in 6–9 months. Articles, 2,000–10,000 words; $.03 per word; no byline. Poetry, to 24 lines; $2 per line. Pays on publication. All rights. Provides 1 contributor's copy.

Verve Girl ☆

Suite 245
401 Richmond Street West
Toronto, Ontario M5V 1X3
Canada

Editor-in-Chief: Jaishree Drepaul

Description and Readership
Published seven times each year by Youth Culture Group, *Verve Girl* includes informational, self-help, and how-to articles; personal experience pieces; profiles; and interviews on topics of interest to young women ages 14 to 18. Available in French and English editions, it currently seeks articles on college, careers, health, fitness, fashion, beauty, music, recreation, education, the environment, and social issues. Profiles of real-life teen heroes are also of interest to the editors. Circ: 150,000 English; 30,000 French.

Freelance Potential
15% written by nonstaff writers. Publishes 10–20 freelance submissions yearly.
Submissions and Payment: Query. Accepts photocopies and computer printouts. SASE. Response time varies. Articles and depts/columns, word lengths and payment rates vary. Pays on publication. Rights vary.

Vegetarian Journal

P.O. Box 1463
Baltimore, MD 21203

Managing Editor: Debra Wasserman

Description and Readership
Vegetarian Journal, published quarterly, offers articles on healthy living, nutrition, fitness, and natural foods. It is read by those interested in vegetarian living or healthy recipes without the use of meat products. Circ: 20,000.
Website: www.vrg.org

Freelance Potential
50% written by nonstaff writers. Publishes 12 freelance submissions yearly; 5% by unpublished writers, 15% by authors who are new to the magazine. Receives 8–10 queries and unsolicited mss monthly.
Submissions and Payment: Guidelines available. Query or send complete ms. Accepts photocopies and computer printouts. SASE. Response time varies. Articles, 1,200–2,000 words. Depts/columns, 600–800 words. Written material, word lengths and payment rates vary. Pays on acceptance. First rights. Provides 2 contributor's copies.

Vibrant Life

55 West Oak Ridge Drive
Hagerstown, MD 21740

Editor: Charles Mills

Description and Readership
Vibrant Life combines the physical, mental, and spiritual aspects of a healthy lifestyle in a practical, Christian approach. It is published 6 times each year. Circ: 28,500.
Website: www.vibrantlife.com

Freelance Potential
60% written by nonstaff writers. Publishes 18 freelance submissions yearly; 50% by unpublished writers, 50% by authors who are new to the magazine. Receives 30 queries, 40 unsolicited mss monthly.
Submissions and Payment: Sample copy and guidelines, $1 with 9x12 SASE (3 first-class stamps). Prefers complete ms; accepts queries. Accepts photocopies and computer printouts. SASE. Responds in 1 month. Articles, 1,000 words. Depts/columns, word length varies. Written material, $50–$400. Pays on acceptance. First world and reprint rights. Provides 3 contributor's copies.

Volta Voices

Alexander Graham Bell Association
for the Deaf and Hard of Hearing
3417 Volta Place NW
Washington, DC 20007-2778

Editor

Description and Readership
Individuals who are hearing impaired, their families, and professionals who work in related fields are among the readers of this magazine. Appearing six times each year, it reports on issues such as school programs, legislation, discrimination, and new technology—all as they relate to the hearing impaired. Circ: 5,500.
Website: www.agbell.org

Freelance Potential
90% written by nonstaff writers. Publishes 6 freelance submissions yearly; 50% by unpublished writers. Receives 2 unsolicited mss monthly.
Submissions and Payment: Sample copy, free with 9x12 SASE ($.58 postage). Send complete ms. Accepts computer printouts and Macintosh disk submissions (Microsoft Word or WordPerfect 5.1) with hard copy. SASE. Responds in 1–3 months. Articles, 500–2,000 words. No payment. All rights. Provides 2 copies.

Wanna Bet?

North American Training Institute
Suite 702
314 West Superior Street
Duluth, MN 55802

Submissions

Description and Readership
Published online and updated monthly, *Wanna Bet?* addresses middle school kids who are worried about gambling. Articles offer age-appropriate messages about betting, gambling, and the problems that gambling can lead to. Other articles discuss healthy alternatives to gambling. Topics of current interest include the rising popularity of poker playing among kids and how a parent's gambling addiction can affect a family. Hits per month: 60,000.
Website: www.wannabet.org

Freelance Potential
25% written by nonstaff writers. Publishes 12–15 freelance submissions yearly.
Submissions and Payment: Sample copy available at website. Query or send ms. Accepts email submissions to info@wannabet.org. Response time varies. Articles, word length varies. No payment. Electronic rights.

WaterSki

Suite 200
460 North Orlando Avenue
Winter Park, FL 32789

Editor: Todd Ristorcelli

Description and Readership
Waterskiers looking for in-depth information on technique and destinations read this magazine, which is published 10 times each year. Circ: 320,000.
Website: www.waterskimag.com

Freelance Potential
10% written by nonstaff writers. Publishes 6–10 freelance submissions yearly; 10% by unpublished writers. Receives 1 query, 1 unsolicited ms monthly.
Submissions and Payment: Sample copy and guidelines, $3 with 9x12 SASE. Query with résumé, outline, and clips; or send complete ms. Accepts photocopies, computer printouts, and IBM disk submissions. SASE. Responds in 2 months. Articles, 1,000–2,500 words; $300–$500. Depts/columns, 650–850 words; payment rate varies. Artwork, $75–$500. Pays on publication. Kill fee, 50%. First or one-time rights. Provides 10 contributor's copies.

The Water Skier

USA Water Ski
1251 Holy Cow Road
Polk City, FL 33686-8200

Editor: Scott Atkinson

Description and Readership
Water skiing enthusiasts look forward to this magazine's illustrated articles on technique, training, and tournaments, and profiles of USA Water Ski teams and athletes. In its nine issues per year, it also covers the activities of USA Water Ski's eight divisions: 3-event, Barefoot, Collegiate, Disabled, Kneeboard, Show Skiing, Ski Racing, and Wakeboard. Circ: 35,000.
Website: www.usawaterski.org

Freelance Potential
25% written by nonstaff writers. Publishes 3–5 freelance submissions yearly; 60% by authors who are new to the magazine. Receives 1 query monthly.
Submissions and Payment: Sample copy, $1.25 with 9x12 SASE. Query. SASE. Responds in 1 month. Articles, 1,000 words. Fiction, 500–1,000 words. Written material, payment rate varies. Pays on publication. All rights. Provides 1 contributor's copy.

West Tennessee Parent and Family ☆

245 West Lafayette Street
Jackson, TN 38301

Editor: Jacque Hillman

Description and Readership
First published in April 2005, *West Tennessee Parent and Family* is a monthly publication. Distributed free throughout western Tennessee, it features practical and fun ideas for families. Its articles and departments focus on day trips, craft and snack ideas, book reviews, and pet tips. Event, activity, and storytime calendars can also be found in each issue. In addition to factual articles, it includes self-help and how-to pieces, interviews, and photo essays. Circ: Unavailable.
Website: www.wtnparent.com

Freelance Potential
100% written by nonstaff writers. Publishes 25 freelance submissions yearly.
Submissions and Payment: Query or send complete ms. SASE. Response time varies. Articles and depts/columns, word lengths and payment rate varies. Payment policy varies. All rights.

With

The Magazine for Radical Christian Youth

P.O. Box 347
722 Main Street
Newton, KS 67114

Editor: Carol Duerksen

Description and Readership
This inspirational Mennonite publication for young adults features first-person stories, humor, and realistic and speculative fiction. Circ: 4,000.
Website: www.withonline.org

Freelance Potential
100% written by nonstaff writers. Publishes 60 submissions yearly; 5% by unpublished writers, 5% by new authors. Receives 80 queries and mss monthly.
Submissions and Payment: Sample copylines, $, free with 9x12 SASE (4 first-class stamps). Query with clips or writing samples for how-to and first-person stories. Send complete ms for other material. Accepts photocopies, computer printouts, and simultaneous submissions if identified. SASE. Responds to queries in 1 month. All material, payment rates vary. Pays of acceptance. Simultaneous and reprint rights.

Wild West

Primedia History Group
Suite D-2
741 Miller Drive SE
Leesburg, VA 20175

Editor: Greg Lalire

Description and Readership
Lively articles about the settlement of the American West fill each issue of this magazine, which is published six times each year. It appeals to history enthusiasts as well as to high school teachers, who often use the magazine as a teaching tool. Circ: 80,000.
Website: www.thehistorynet.com

Freelance Potential
90% written by nonstaff writers. Publishes 60 freelance submissions yearly; 10% by unpublished writers, 30% by new authors. Receives 25 queries monthly.
Submissions and Payment: Sample copy and guidelines, $6. Query with résumé, outline, illustration ideas, source lists, and clips or writing samples. Accepts photocopies and computer printouts. SASE. Responds in 4–6 months. Articles, to 3,500 words; $300. Depts/columns, to 2,000 words; $150. Pays on publication. All rights.

World Around You

#6 Kendall School
Gallaudet University
800 Florida Avenue NE
Washington, DC 20002

Editor: Cathryn Caroll

Description and Readership
Appearing five times each year, this magazine targets students who are deaf or hard of hearing. It is published by the world's only university for undergraduate students who are deaf or hard of hearing. It provides informational articles on careers, reports on the achievements of hearing-impaired adults and young adults, and personal experience pieces. Circ: 3,000.
Website: www.gallaudet.edu

Freelance Potential
10% written by nonstaff writers. Publishes 3–5 freelance submissions yearly. Receives 4 queries monthly.
Submissions and Payment: Sample copy, $2 with 9x12 SASE. Query. Accepts photocopies, computer printouts, and simultaneous submissions if identified. SASE. Responds in 1 month. Written material, word lengths and payment rates vary. Pays on publication. Rights negotiable. Provides 5 contributor's copies.

Young & Alive

P.O. Box 6097
Lincoln, NE 68506

Editor: Gaylena Gibson

Description and Readership
This magazine for sight-impaired young adults offers Christian stories and articles in large print. *Young & Alive* is published quarterly. Circ: 25,000.
Website: www.christianrecord.org

Freelance Potential
90% written by nonstaff writers. Publishes 50 freelance submissions yearly; 5–10% by unpublished writers, 50% by authors who are new to the magazine. Receives 40–50 queries and unsolicited mss monthly.
Submissions and Payment: Sample copy, free with 8x10 SASE (5 first-class stamps). Guidelines available. Query. Accepts photocopies, computer printouts, and simultaneous submissions. SASE. Responds in 11–12 months. Articles, 800–1,400 words. Depts/columns, word length varies. Written material, $.03–$.05 per word. Pays on acceptance. One-time rights. Provides 2 contributor's copies.

Your Child

155 5th Avenue
New York, NY 10010-6802

Editor: Kay E. Pomerantz

Description and Readership
Parents of young Jewish children find articles on parenting, religion, family issues, social issues, popular culture, music, and recreation in this conservative newsletter published by the United Synagogue of Conservative Judaism. It appears three times each year and welcomes freelance submissions of media reviews and personal experience pieces. Circ: 3,000.
Website: www.uscj.org

Freelance Potential
Of the freelance submissions published yearly, 50% are by unpublished writers.
Submissions and Payment: Sample copy, free with 9x12 SASE ($.55 postage). Send complete ms. Accepts photocopies. Availability of artwork improves chance of acceptance. SASE. Response time varies. Articles, word lengths vary. 8x10 B/W transparencies; line art. No payment. All rights. Provides 1 contributor's copy.

Young-Expressions Magazine

Suite B-2
810 East Jackson Boulevard
Jackson, MO 63755

Editor: Lisa Cooley

Description and Readership
This e-zine targets young adult readers with its articles on beauty, health, fashion, and lifestyles. Other regular features include reviews of games, music, and television programs. Much of its content is contributed by teens, who are invited to submit stories, articles, essays, drawings, paintings, or photos. Young people age 17 and under must include parental permission to publish with their submissions. Hits per month: Unavailable.
Website: www.young-expressions.com

Freelance Potential
50% written by nonstaff writers. Publishes 20–25 freelance submissions yearly.
Submissions and Payment: Guidelines available at website. Send complete ms. Accepts email submissions to submit@young-expressions.com. Response time varies. Articles, 500–2,000 words. No payment. Rights vary.

ZooGoer

Friends of the National Zoo Communications Office
National Zoological Park
3001 Connecticut Avenue NW
Washington, DC 20008

Associate Editor: Shannon Lyons

Description and Readership
Enlightening and entertaining readers is the goal of this publication. Published six times each year, it features articles on natural history, wildlife, biology, and conservation. Circ: 30,000
Website: www.fonz.org/zoogoer.htm

Freelance Potential
70% written by nonstaff writers. Publishes 14 freelance submissions yearly; 10% by authors who are new to the magazine. Receives 1 unsolicited ms monthly.
Submissions and Payment: Guidelines available. Query with synopsis and clips or writing sample; or send complete ms. Accepts computer printouts, disk submissions (Microsoft Word), and email submissions to shannon@fonz.org. SASE. Responds in 1–2 months. Articles, 2,500–3,000 words. Depts/columns, 800–1,500 words. Written material, $.50 per word. Pays on publication. First rights. Provides 5–8 copies.

Contests and Awards

Selected Contests and Awards

Entering a writing contest will provide you with a chance to have your work read by established writers and qualified editors. Winning or placing in a contest or an award program can open the door to publication and recognition of your writing. If you don't win, try to read the winning entry if it is published; doing so will give you some insight into how your work compares with its competition.

For both editors and writers, contests generate excitement. For editors, contests are a source to discover new writers. Entries are more focused because of the contest guidelines, and therefore more closely target an editor's current needs.

For writers, every contest entry is read, often by more than one editor, as opposed to unsolicited submissions that are often relegated to a slush pile.

And you don't have to be the grand-prize winner to benefit—non-winning manuscripts are often purchased by the publication for future issues.

To be considered for the contests and awards that follow, your entry must fulfill all of the requirements mentioned. Most are looking for unpublished article or story manuscripts, while a few require published works. Note special entry requirements, such as whether or not you can submit the material yourself, need to be a member of an organization, or are limited in the number of entries you can send. Also, be sure to submit your article or story in the standard manuscript submission format.

For each listing, we've included the address, the contact, a description, the entry requirements, the deadline, and the prize. In some cases, the 2006 deadlines were not available at press time. We recommend that you write to the addresses provided or visit the websites to request an entry form and the contest guidelines, which usually specify the current deadline.

Abilene Writers Guild Annual Contest

Abilene Writers Guild
P.O. Box 2562
Abilene, TX 79604

Description
Open to all writers, this annual contest accepts entries in the categories of children's stories, memoirs, adult fiction, nonfiction articles, inspirational pieces, poetry, novel, and genre fiction.
Website: www.abilenewritersguild.org
Length: Varies for each category.
Requirements: Entry fees, $10 for novel categories; $5 for all other categories. Accepts photocopies and computer printouts. All entries must include a cover sheet with author's name, address, and telephone number. Author's name should not appear on manuscript itself. Send an SASE or visit the website for further guidelines and category information.
Prizes: Winners receive cash prizes ranging from $35 to $100.
Deadline: Submissions are accepted during July only.

Amy Writing Awards

The Amy Foundation
P.O. Box 16091
Lansing, MI 48901

Description
These annual awards recognize creative writing that presents the biblical position on issues affecting the world today in a sensitive, thought-provoking manner. The competition is open to all writers and eligible entries will have been published in a secular, non-religious publication, but must contain Scripture.
Website: www.amyfound.org
Length: No length requirements.
Requirements: No entry fee. All entries must contain quotes from the Bible. Send an SASE or visit the website for complete guidelines.
Prizes: First-place winner receives a cash award of $10,000.
Deadline: December 31.

Amazing Kids! Annual Essay Contest

Amazing Kids!
PMB 485
1158 26th Street
Santa Monica, CA 90403

Description
Sponsored by the Internet publication *Amazing Kids!*, this essay contest is open to children and young adults ages 5 to 17 and features a different theme each year.
Website: www.amazing-kids.org
Length: No length requirements.
Requirements: No entry fees. Prefers email submissions to essays@amazing-kids.org. Will accept photocopies and computer printouts. All entries must include author's name, address, and a parent or guardian's permission to enter the contest. Visit the website or send an SASE for complete guidelines and current theme.
Prizes: Winners receive publication of their essay in the September issue of *Amazing Kids!*
Deadline: August 15.

Isaac Asimov Award

University of South Florida
School of Mass Communications
4202 East Fowler
Tampa, FL 33620

Description
Open to undergraduate students, this annual award looks to promote and encourage the writing of high-quality science fiction and fantasy. It accepts previously unpublished entries only.
Website: www.asimovs.com
Length: 1,000–10,000 words.
Requirements: Open to full-time college students only. Entry fee, $10. Limit three entries per competition. Entries should include a cover sheet with author's name, address, and university. Author's name should not appear on the entry itself.
Prizes: Winner receives a cash prize of $500 and will be considered for publication in *Asimov's Science Fiction Magazine*.
Deadline: December 15.

AuthorMania.com Writing Contests

Cindy Thomas
AuthorMania.com
Rt. 4 Box 201-A
Buna, TX 77612

Description

AuthorMania.com sponsors a fiction contest and poetry contest each year. The contests are open to writers living in the U.S. and look for original, unpublished material. Entries must be written in English and may be on any subject, but must not include violence or hate.
Website: www.authormania.com
Length: Fiction, to 5,000 words. Poetry, no length limits.
Requirements: Entry fee, $20. Multiple entries will be accepted provided each is accompanied by a separate entry fee. Accepts photocopies and computer printouts. Manuscripts will not be returned. Send an SASE or visit the website for complete guidelines.
Prizes: Fiction contest winner receives a cash award of $1,000. Poetry contest winner receives a cash award of $400.

Baker's Plays High School Playwriting Contest

Baker's Plays
P.O. Box 699222
Quincy, MA 02269-9222

Description

This annual contest accepts submissions from high school students only. It looks to acknowledge playwrights at the high school level and to insure the future of American theater. Each entry should receive a public reading or production prior to submission.
Website: www.bakersplays.com
Length: No length requirements.
Requirements: No entry fee. Plays must be accompanied by the signature of a sponsoring high school English teacher. Accepts photocopies and computer printouts. Include an SASE for return of manuscript. Visit the website or send an SASE for complete guidelines and entry form.
Prizes: Cash prizes ranging between $100 and $500 are awarded. The first-place winner will also have their play produced.
Deadline: January 30.

AWA Contests

Cumberland College
6000 College Station Drive
Williamsburg, KY 40769

Description

The Appalachian Writers Association presents these contests that offer several different awards in categories that include short story, essay, and playwriting. The competition is open to members of AWA and accepts previously unpublished material only.
Length: Lengths vary for each award category.
Requirements: No entry fee. Entrants may submit up to 3 entries per category. Accepts photocopies and computer printouts. Submit two copies of each entry. Manuscripts will not be returned. Visit the website or send an SASE for specific category guidelines and further information.
Prizes: First-place winners in each award category receive a cash award of $100. Second- and third-place winners receive cash awards of $50 and $25, respectively.
Deadline: June 1.

Waldo M. and Grace C. Bonderman Youth Theatre Playwriting Competition

Indiana University–Purdue University at Indianapolis
CA305, 425 University Blvd., Suite 309
Indianapolis, IN 46202-5140

Description

This annual competition accepts plays that are intended for a young audience (third grade through high school). Scripts previously produced are not eligible for this competition.
Website: www.liberalarts.iupui.edu/bonderman
Length: 45-minute running time.
Requirements: No entry fee. Limit one entry per competition. Accepts photocopies and computer printouts. For dramatizations or adaptations, written proof is required that the original work is in the public domain or that permission has been granted by the copyright holder. Send an SASE or visit the website for more details.
Prizes: Awards will be presented to 10 finalists. Four cash awards of $1,000 are also awarded to the playwrights whose plays are selected for development.
Deadline: September 1.

ByLine Magazine Contests

Contests, *ByLine* Magazine
P.O. Box 5240
Edmond, OK 73083-5240

Description

ByLine sponsors several writing contests each month in various categories including children's story, personal essay, genre fiction, and character sketch.
Website: www.bylinemag.com/contests.asp
Length: Lengths vary according to category.
Requirements: Fees vary according to category but range from $3 to $5. Multiple entries are accepted. Accepts photocopies and computer printouts. Send an SASE or visit the website for complete category information and further guidelines.
Prizes: Cash prizes ranging from $10 to $70 are presented to the winners. Runners-up also receive cash awards in each category. Winning entries for the Annual Literary Awards are published in *ByLine,* and receive a cash award of $250.
Deadline: Deadlines vary according to category.

Canadian Writer's Journal ☆ Short Fiction Contest

Box 1178
New Liskeard, Ontario P0J 1P0
Canada

Description

Sponsored by *Canadian Writer's Journal,* this short story contest accepts original, unpublished stories in any genre.
Website: www.cwj.ca
Length: To 1,200 words.
Requirements: Entry fee, $5. Multiple entries are accepted. Accepts photocopies and computer printouts. Author's name should not appear on manuscript. Include a cover sheet with author's name, address, and title of entry. Manuscript will not be returned. Send an SASE or visit the website for further guidelines.
Prizes: First-place winners receive a cash prize of $100. Second- and third-place winners receive cash prizes of $50 and $25, respectively.
Deadline: September 30.

Calliope Fiction Contest

Calliope
P.O. Box 466
Moraga, CA 94556-0466

Description

This contest accepts entries of short fiction that display creativity, good storytelling, and appropriate use of language for the target audience.
Length: To 2,500 words.
Requirements: Entry fee, $2 per story for non-subscribers; first entry is free for subscribers. Limit 5 entries per competition. Accepts photocopies and computer printouts. Manuscript will not be returned. Enclose an SASE for winners' list. Send an SASE for current contest theme and complete guidelines.
Prizes: First-place winner receives a cash award of $75. Second- and third-place winners receive $25 and $10, respectively. All winners are published in *Calliope* (requires one-time rights). Winners also receive certificates and a 1-year subscription to *Calliope*.
Deadline: Entries are accepted between April 15 and September 30.

CAPA Competition

c/o Daniel Uitti
Connecticut Authors and Publishers
223 Buckingham Street
Oakville, CT 06779

Description

This competition is open to residents of Connecticut. It accepts previously unpublished entries in the categories of children's story, short story, personal essay, and poetry.
Website: http://aboutcapa.com
Length: Children's stories and short stories, to 2,000 words. Personal essays, to 1,500 words. Poetry, to 30 lines.
Requirements: Entry fee, $10 for 1 story or essay or up to 3 poems. Multiple entries are accepted. Submit four copies of manuscript. Manuscripts will not be returned. Visit the website or send an SASE for complete guidelines.
Prizes: First-place winner in each category receives a cash prize of $100. Second-place winners receive a cash award of $50.
Deadline: May 31.

Children's Writer Contests

Children's Writer
95 Long Ridge Road
West Redding, CT 06896-1124

Description
Children's Writer sponsors two contests each year with different themes for original, unpublished fiction and nonfiction. Entries are selected and judged on originality, writing quality, characterization, plot, and age-appropriateness.
Website: www.childrenswriter.com
Length: Requirements vary for each contest; usually 500–1,000 words.
Requirements: Entry fee, $10 for non-subscribers (entry fee includes an 8-month subscription); no entry fee for subscribers. Multiple entries are accepted. Manuscripts are not returned. Visit the website or send an SASE for current themes and further requirements.
Prizes: Cash prizes vary per contest. Winning entries are published in *Children's Writer.*
Deadline: February and October of each year.

Shubert Fendrich Memorial Playwriting Contest

Pioneer Drama Service, Inc.
P.O. Box 4267
Englewood, CO 80155-4267

Description
Held in honor of the founder of Pioneer Drama Service, this contest honors its winners with publication and a royalty advance. Plays may be on any subject that is appropriate for family viewing.
Website: www.pioneerdrama.com
Length: Running time, 20 to 90 minutes.
Requirements: No entry fee. Cover letter must accompany all submissions. Include title, synopsis, cast list breakdown, proof of production, number of sets and scenes, and, if applicable, musical score and tape. Any writers currently published by Pioneer Drama Service are not eligible. Send SASE for contest guidelines and information.
Prizes: Winner receives a $1,000 royalty advance in addition to publication.
Deadline: March 1. Winners will be announced in June.

CNW/FFWA Florida State Writing Competition

CNW/FFWA
P.O. Box A
North Stratford, NH 03590

Description
This annual competition is open to all writers and presents awards in several categories including children's literature short story, children's nonfiction, novel chapter, nonfiction book chapter, and poetry.
Website: www.writers-editors.com
Length: Vary according to category.
Requirements: Entry fees vary for each category. Multiple entries are accepted, as long as each entry is accompanied by an entry fee. Use paper clips only. Author's name must not appear on manuscript. Send an SASE or visit the website for complete contest guidelines, specific category information, and official entry form.
Prizes: First- through third-place winners will be awarded in each category. Winners receive cash awards ranging from $50 to $100.
Deadline: March 15.

Focus on Writers Contest

3rd Floor
828 I Street
Sacramento, CA 95814

Description
Open to residents of California, this competition offers writers the opportunity to test their writing talents against other writers. It looks for high-quality, unpublished submissions of short stories, nonfiction articles, books/articles for children, and first chapter of a young adult novel.
Website: www.saclib.org
Length: Length limits vary for each category.
Requirements: Entry fee, $5. Multiple entries are accepted. Accepts photocopies and computer printouts. Author's name should not be included on manuscript. Include a 3x5 index card with author's name, address, and title of entry. Send an SASE or visit the website for guidelines.
Prizes: First-place winners in each category receive $200. Second- and third-place winners receive $100 and $50, respectively.

Foster City International ☆ Writing Contest

Foster City Recreation Dept.
650 Shell Boulevard
Foster City, CA 94404

Description
This annual contest accepts original, unpublished entries in the categories of children's story, fiction, humor, poetry, and personal essay.
Website: www.geocities.com/fostercity_writers/
Length: Children's stories and fiction, to 3,000 words. Humor and personal experience piece, to 2,000 words. Poetry, to 500 words.
Requirements: Entry fee, $12. Multiple entries are accepted under separate cover. Accepts photocopies, computer printouts and email submissions to fostercity_writers@yahoo.com (RTF or Microsoft Word attachments). Check website for further category information.
Prizes: First-place winners in each category receive a cash award of $100.
Deadline: December 17.

Friends of the Library Writing Contest

130 North Franklin
Decatur, IL 62523

Description
The Friends of the Library Writing Contest accepts material in the categories of fiction, juvenile fiction, essay, and poetry (both rhymed and unrhymed). It is co-sponsored by Hutton Publications and the Decatur Public Library.
Website: www.decatur.lib.il.us
Length: Fiction and juvenile fiction, to 3,000 words. Essay, to 2,000 words. Poetry, to 40 lines.
Requirements: Entry fee, $3 per piece. Limit 5 entries per competition. Accepts photocopies and computer printouts. Include an SASE for winners' list. Send an SASE or visit the website for complete guidelines and category information.
Prizes: Winners in each category receive cash prizes ranging from $20 to $50.
Deadline: September 25.

Frontiers in Writing Contest

Panhandle Professional Writers
P.O. Box 8066
Amarillo, TX 79114

Description
The Frontiers in Writing Contest presents awards annually in several categories including juvenile/young adult short story; juvenile/young adult novel; historical novel; and screenplay. The competition is open to all writers and accepts original, unpublished work only.
Length: Varies for each category.
Requirements: No entry fee. Accepts photocopies and computer printouts. Author's name must not be on manuscript. Include an entry form (available at website or with an SASE) with each submission.
Prizes: First-place winners in the short story categories receive $75; novel category winners receive $100. Second- and third-place winners receive cash awards ranging from $25 to $75.
Deadline: April 1.

John Gardner Memorial Prize for Fiction

Harpur Palate
English Department, Binghamton University
Box 6000
Binghamton, NY 13902-6000

Description
This competition was created to honor John Gardner for his dedication to the creative writing program at Binghamton University. Presented annually, it welcomes the submission of previously unpublished short stories in any genre.
Website: http://harpurpalate.binghamton.edu
Length: To 8,000 words.
Requirements: Entry fee, $10 (checks should be made out to *Harpur Palate*). Multiple entries are accepted under separate cover only. Include a cover letter with name, address, phone number, email address, and title. Manuscripts will not be returned. Send an SASE or visit the website for further information.
Prizes: Winner receives a cash award of $500 and publication in *Harpur Palate*.
Deadline: March 1.

Lorian Hemingway
Short Story Competition

P.O. Box 993
Key West, FL 33041

Description

Writers of short fiction are encouraged to enter the Lorian Hemingway Short Story Competition. The goal of this competition is to help writers who have not yet achieved major success in the world of publishing.
Website: www.shortstorycompetition.com
Length: To 3,000 words.
Requirements: Entry fee, $10 postmarked by May 1; $15 per submission postmarked between May 1 and May 15. Multiple entries are accepted. Accepts photocopies and computer printouts. Send an SASE for complete guidelines and further information.
Prizes: First-place winner receives a cash award of $1,000. Second- and third-place winners each receive a cash award of $500.
Deadline: May 15.

Highlights for Children
Fiction Contest

Fiction Contest
803 Church Street
Honesdale, PA 18431

Description

This annual contest has a commitment to raise the quality of writing for children. It looks for well-written short stories for children ages two through twelve. Stories should not contain violence, crime, or derogatory humor.
Website: www.highlights.com
Length: To 500 words.
Requirements: No entry fee. Multiple entries accepted. Accepts photocopies and computer printouts. Include SASE for manuscript return. Send SASE for further guidelines.
Prizes: Winners receive a cash award of $1,000 and publication in *Highlights for Children* (requires all rights).
Deadline: Entries must be postmarked between January 1 and February 28.

Insight Writing Contest

Insight Magazine
55 West Oak Ridge Drive
Hagerstown, MD 21740-7390

Description

This annual contest values and recognizes the mechanics of good writing, particularly that with a spiritual message. It accepts entries of short nonfiction and poetry that are of interest to young people ages 14 to 22.
Website: www.insightmagazine.com
Length: From 1,500 to 2,000 words (no longer than seven pages).
Requirements: No entry fee. Accepts photocopies and computer printouts. Author's name must not be included on the manuscript. Include cover letter with title, category, name, address, phone number, and Social Security number. Multiple submissions accepted. Include SASE for return of entry.
Prizes: Winners receive cash awards ranging from $150 to $250 and publication in *Insight*. All other entries will be considered for purchase.
Deadline: June 1.

Magazine Merit Awards

The Society of Children's Book Writers & Illustrators
8271 Beverly Boulevard
Los Angeles, CA 90048

Description

The Magazine Merit Awards look to honor previously published fiction and nonfiction. The purpose of these awards is to recognize outstanding original magazine work for young people published during that calendar year.
Website: www.scbwi.org
Length: No length requirements.
Requirements: No entry fee. SCBWI members only. Submit 4 copies of the published work showing proof of publication date. Include 4 cover sheets with member's name as listed by SCBWI, mailing address, phone number, entry title, category, name of publication, and date of issue.
Prizes: Winners in each category receive a plaque. Honor certificates are also awarded.
Deadline: Entries are accepted between January 31 and December 15 of each year.

Milkweed Fiction Prize

Milkweed Editions
Suite 400
430 First Avenue North
Minneapolis, MN 55401-1473

Description
Sponsored by Milkweed Editions, this prize is awarded to the best fiction manuscripts received during each calendar year. Manuscripts can be a collection of short stories or individual stories previously published in magazines or anthologies.
Website: www.milkweed.org
Length: No length requirement.
Requirements: No entry fee. Manuscripts previously submitted to Milkweed Editions should not be resubmitted. Individual stories previously published in magazines or anthologies are eligible.
Prizes: Winner receives a $10,000 cash advance.
Deadline: Ongoing.

National Children's Theatre Festival

Actors' Playhouse at Miracle Theatre
280 Miracle Mile
Coral Gables, FL 33134

Description
The Actors' Playhouse at Miracle Theatre invites the submission of original musical scripts targeting children ages 3 to 12. Entries are judged on content, music, and originality.
Website: www.actorsplayhouse.org
Length: 45–60 minute running time.
Requirements: Entry fee, $10. Multiple submissions are accepted under separate cover. Accepts photocopies and computer printouts. Include an SASE for return of manuscript. Visit the website or send an SASE for guidelines.
Prizes: Winner receives a cash award of $500 and a full production of their play (requires performance rights for a limited time).
Deadline: August 1.

NWA Nonfiction Contest

National Writers Association
3140 S. Peoria #295
Aurora, CO 80014

Description
The purpose of this contest is to encourage the writing of nonfiction and recognize those who excel in this field. The competition opens each October.
Website: www.nationalwriters.com
Length: To 5,000 words.
Requirements: Entry fee, $18. Multiple entries are accepted under separate cover. Accepts photocopies and computer printouts. All entries must be accompanied by an entry form (available with an SASE or at the website).
Prizes: First-place winner receives $200. Second- and third-place winners receive $100 and $50, respectively.
Deadline: December 31.

NWA Short Story Contest

National Writers Association
3140 S. Peoria #295
Aurora, CO 80014

Description
This short story contest is sponsored by the National Writers Association. It accepts previously unpublished manuscripts and looks to encourage the development of creative skills, and recognize and reward outstanding ability in this field.
Website: www.nationalwriters.com
Length: To 5,000 words.
Requirements: Entry fee, $15. Multiple entries are accepted under separate cover. Accepts photocopies and computer printouts. All entries must be accompanied by an entry form (available with an SASE or at the website).
Prizes: First-place winner receives $250. Second- and third-place winners receive $100 and $50, respectively.
Deadline: July 1.

Pacific Northwest Writers Association Literary Contest

P.O. Box 2016
Edmonds, WA 98020-9516

Description
These contests are sponsored by the Pacific Northwest Writers Association and accept entries in several categories including juvenile/young adult novel, juvenile short story, adult genre novel, and nonfiction/memoir.
Website: www.pnwa.org
Length: Length limits vary for each category.
Requirements: Entry fee, $35 for members; $45 for non-members. Limit one entry per category. Accepts photocopies and computer printouts. Send two copies of manuscript. Author's name should not appear on manuscript. Include a 3x5 index card with author's name, address, and title of entry. Send an SASE or visit the website for guidelines and specific category information.
Prizes: Winners in each category receive a cash prize of $1,000 and publication of their entry.
Deadline: February 22.

Pockets Annual Fiction Contest

Attn. Lynn Gilliam
Box 340004
1908 Grand Avenue
Nashville, TN 37203-0004

Description
Open to all writers, this competition accepts previously unpublished entries only. Historical and biblical fiction are not accepted.
Website: www.pockets.org
Length: From 1,000 to 1,600 words.
Requirements: No entry fee. Multiple entries are accepted. Accepts clear photocopies and computer printouts. Manuscripts must list accurate word count on cover sheet. Entries not adhering to the contest word lengths will be disqualified. Send an SASE for return of manuscript. Visit the website or send an SASE for complete competition guidelines.
Prizes: Winner receives a cash award of $1,000 and publication in *Pockets Magazine*.
Deadline: Submissions must be postmarked between March 1 and August 15.

Science Fiction/Fantasy Short Story Contest

Science Fiction Writers of Earth
P.O. Box 121293
Fort Worth, TX 76121

Description
Looking to promote the art of short story writing, this contest is sponsored by Science Fiction Writers of Earth. It is open to previously unpublished members of SFWoE.
Website: http://home.flash.net/~sfwoe/
Length: From 2,000 to 7,500 words.
Requirements: Entry fee, $5 for first entry; $2 for each subsequent entry. Entry fee includes 1 year membership to SFWoE. Accepts photocopies and computer printouts. Send an SASE or visit the website for complete guidelines.
Prizes: First-place winner receives publication on the SFWoE website. First- through third-place winners receive cash awards ranging from $50 to $200. Special awards are also presented for outstanding work from younger authors.
Deadline: October 30.

Seven Hills Writing Contests

Tallahassee Writers' Association
P.O. Box 32328
Tallahassee, FL 32315

Description
This writing competition accepts entries in the categories of children's literature, essay, memoir, and short story. It is open to all writers and accepts previously unpublished material only.
Website: www.twaonline.org
Length: Children's literature, memoir, and short stories, to 2,500 words. Essays, to 1,000 words.
Requirements: Entry fee, $15 for members; $20 for non-members ($5 each additional entry). Submit 3 copies of each entry. Accepts photocopies and computer printouts. Author's name should not appear on manuscript. Send an SASE or visit the website for further guidelines.
Prizes: Winning entries will be published in *Seven Hills* and receive honor certificates.
Deadline: Submissions are accepted between January 1 and September 30.

Seventeen Magazine Fiction Contest

Seventeen Magazine
13th Floor
1440 Broadway
New York, NY 10018

Description
Open to writers between the ages of 13 and 21, this contest is sponsored by *Seventeen Magazine*. It accepts original short story entries that exemplify creativity, originality, and writing ability.
Website: www.seventeen.com
Length: To 2,000 words.
Requirements: No entry fee. Multiple entries are accepted. Accepts photocopies and computer print-outs. Send an SASE or visit the website for complete guidelines.
Prizes: Grand-prize winner receives a cash prize of $1,000 and publication in *Seventeen Magazine*. Cash prizes and possible publication are awarded to second- and third-place winners.
Deadline: December 31.

Mary Shelley Prize for Imaginative Fiction

Mary Shelley Award
N3310 Asje Road
Cambridge, WI 53523

Description
In its first year, this biennial contest looks for original fantasy, horror, mystery, and science fiction entries. Entries should strive to take creative risks to gain the attention of the judges.
Website: www.rsbd.net
Length: To 3,500 words.
Requirements: Entry fee, $10 ($15 if you wish to receive the issue of *Rosebud* where the winning entry will appear). Accpets photocopies and computer print-outs. Visit the website or send an SASE for complete details.
Prizes: Winner receives a cash prize of $1,000 and publication in *Rosebud*. Runner-ups may also receive publication.
Deadline: October 1.

Skipping Stones Awards

Skipping Stones
P.O. Box 3939
Eugene, OR 97403

Description
The Skipping Stones Awards look to cultivate awareness of our multicultural world without perpetuating stereotypes or biases. Entries should promote cooperation, non-violence, and an appreciation of nature. Entries may be published magazine articles, books, or educational videos.
Website: www.efn.org/~skipping
Length: No length requirements.
Requirements: Entry fee, $50. Send 4 copies of each entry. Only entries produced in the preceding year are eligible. Send an SASE, visit the website, or send email to Editor@SkippingStones.org for complete guidelines.
Prizes: Cash prizes are awarded to first- through fourth place winners. Winners are announced in April and reviewed in the summer issue of *Skipping Stones*.
Deadline: January 15.

Southwest Writers Contests

Southwest Writers Workshop
3721 Morris NE
Albuquerque, NM 87110

Description
The Southwest Writers Workshop sponsors these annual contests in several categories including middle-grade short story, children's picture book, screenplay, genre story, and young adult short story. The competition accepts unpublished material only.
Website: www.southwestwriters.org
Length: vary for each category.
Requirements: Entry fee, $25 for members; $45 for non-members. Accepts photocopies and computer printouts. Multiple entries are accepted under separate cover. Author's name should only appear on entry form (available at website or with an SASE). Send an SASE or visit the website for complete category information and further guidelines.
Prizes: Winners receive cash awards ranging from $75 to $150.
Deadline: May 1.

Stepping Stones Writing Contest

P.O. Box 8863
Springfield, MO 65801-8863

Description

This annual contest promotes writing for children by giving writers an opportunity to submit their work for competition. Entries are judged on clarity, punctuation, grammar, and imagery that are suitable for children. All entries must be unpublished and may be either fiction or poetry.

Length: Fiction, to 1,500 words. Poetry, to 30 lines.
Requirements: Entry fee, $8 for first entry; $3 for each additional entry. Multiple entries are accepted under separate cover only. Accepts photocopies and computer printouts. For additional information and official entry forms, send an SASE.
Prizes: First-place winner receives a cash award of $140 and publication in *Hodge Podge*. Second-through fourth-place winners receive cash awards ranging from $15 to $50.
Deadline: July 31.

Sydney Taylor Manuscript Competition

Association of Jewish Libraries
c/o Rachel Glasser
315 Maitland Avenue
Teaneck, NJ 07666

Description

Established to encourage aspiring writers of Jewish children's books, this competition looks for fiction manuscripts of interest to children ages 8 to 11. Entries must have a universal appeal and should reveal positive aspects of Jewish life.
Website: www.jewishlibraries.org
Length: From 64 to 200 pages.
Requirements: No entry fee. Limit one entry per competition. Accepts photocopies and computer printouts. Send an SASE or vsit the website for complete guidelines and submission information.
Prizes: Winner receives cash award of $1,000 and possible publication.
Deadline: December 31.

Utah Original Writing Competition

617 E. South Temple
Salt Lake City, UT 84102

Description

Each year this competition looks to promote and reward excellence from Utah's finest writers. The competition presents awards in several categories including juvenile book, juvenile essay, short story, biography, and general nonfiction. It accepts previously unpublished work from Utah writers only.
Website: http://arts.utah.gov/literature-program/
Length: Varies for each category.
Requirements: No entry fee. Limit one entry per category. Accepts photocopies and computer printouts. Manuscripts will not be returned. Send an SASE or visit the website for complete category guidelines.
Prizes: Winners receive cash prizes ranging from $300 to $5,000.
Deadline: June 24. Winners are notified in September.

Vegetarian Essay Contest

The Vegetarian Resource Group
P.O. Box 1463
Baltimore, MD 21203

Description

Sponsored by The Vegetarian Resource Group, this competition awards prizes in three age categories: 14–18; 9–13; and 8 and under. Entrants should base their submissions on interviews, research, or personal opinion. Entrants need not be vegetarian to enter.
Website: www.vrg.org
Length: 2–3 pages.
Requirements: No entry fee. Limit one entry per competition. Accepts photocopies, computer printouts, and handwritten entries. Send an SASE or visit the website for complete guidelines.
Prizes: Winners in each category receive a $50 savings bond and publication in *The Vegetarian Journal* (requires all rights).
Deadline: May 1. Winners are announced at the end of the year.

Jackie White Memorial National Playwriting Competition

309 Parkade Avenue
Columbia, MO 65202

Description
Held annually, this competition looks to encourage the writing of family-friendly plays. It accepts quality, unpublished scripts that are suitable for both children and adults and that challenge the talents of the participating actors.
Website: www.cectheatre.org
Length: Full-length plays only; running time, 1 to 1½ hours.
Requirements: Entry fee, $10. Multiple entries are accepted. Accepts photocopies and computer printouts. Include a brief synopsis of the play. Send an SASE for return of manuscript. Visit the website or send an SASE for guidelines.
Prizes: Winner receives a cash award of $500 and the possible production of the winning entry.
Deadline: June 1.

Tennessee Williams One-Act Play Competition

Tennessee Williams New Orleans Literary Festival
Suite 328
938 Lafayette Street
New Orleans, LA 70113

Description
This competition looks to celebrate and honor previously unpublished playwrights. Entries should be one-act plays that demonstrate the strength of the work.
Website: www.tennesseewilliams.org
Length: One act; 1-hour in length.
Requirements: Entry fee, $25 per piece. Accepts photocopies, computer printouts, and multiple submissions. All entries must be typed and must include an entry form, available with an SASE or at the website. Send an SASE or visit the website for guidelines.
Prizes: Winner receives a cash prize of $1,000 and a reading and staging of their winning entry.
Deadline: Entries are accepted between September 1 and December 15.

Paul A. Witty Short Story Award

International Reading Association
P.O. Box 8139
Newark, DE 19714-8139

Description
Each year the Paul A. Witty Short Story Award is given to an author of an original short story published for the first time during the calendar year. Entries should serve as a literary standard that encourages young readers to read periodicals.
Website: www.reading.org
Length: No length requirements.
Requirements: No entry fees. Accepts photocopies accompanied by a copy of the periodical. No more than three entries per magazine. Publishers or authors may nominate a short story and send it to the designated Paul A. Witty Award Subcommittee Chair. For additional information and award guidelines, send an SASE, or email exec@reading.org.
Prizes: $1,000 given to winner at the annual IRA Convention.
Deadline: December 1.

John Wood Community College Creative Writing Contest

1301 S. 48th Street
Quincy, IL 62305

Description
This contest accepts entries in several categories including nonfiction, fiction, traditional rhyming poetry, and non-rhyming poetry. This competition focuses on promoting the work of beginning writers.
Website: www.jwcc.edu
Length: Nonfiction and fiction, to 2,000 words. Poetry, limit 2 pages.
Requirements: Entry fees range from $5 to $7 depending on category. Accepts photocopies and computer printouts. Author's name should not be included on manuscript itself. Include a 3x5 index card with author's name, address, and telephone number.
Prizes: Cash prizes are awarded to the first- through third-place winners. All winners may also receive publication of their winning entries.
Deadline: April 1.

Writers at Work Fellowship Competition

P.O. Box 540370
North Salt Lake, UT 84054-0370

Description
This fellowship competition is open to emerging writers in the genres of fiction, nonfiction, and poetry. It is open to previously unpublished entries only.
Website: www.writersatwork.org
Length: Fiction and nonfiction, to 5,000 words. Poetry, to 10 pages (up to 6 poems).
Requirements: Entry fee, $15. Accepts photocopies and computer printouts. Multiple entries are accepted under separate cover only. Indicate contest category on outside envelope. Manuscripts will not be returned. Visit the website or send an SASE for complete guidelines.
Prizes: Winners in each category receive a cash prize of $1,500 and publication in *Quarterly West*. Honorable mentions are also awarded.
Deadline: March 1.

Writer's Digest Annual Writing Competition

4700 East Galbraith Road
Cincinnati, OH 45236

Description
In its 74th year, this annual competition accepts works in several categories including children's fiction, feature article, genre short story, memoir/personal essay, and stage play script.
Website: www.writersdigest.com
Length: Children's fiction, to 2,000 words. Other categories, word lengths vary.
Requirements: Entry fee, $10. Multiple submissions are accepted under separate cover. Accepts photocopies and computer printouts. Author's name, address, phone numbers, and category should appear in the upper left corner of the first page. Manuscripts are not returned. Visit the website or send an SASE for complete category list and guidelines.
Prizes: Winners will be published in a short story collection by Outskirts Press.
Deadline: June 1.

The Writing Conference, Inc. Writing Contests

P.O. Box 664
Ottawa, KS 66067-0664

Description
Open to children and young adults, these contests accept entries of short stories, short nonfiction, and poetry. The goal of these contests is to encourage a love of writing among young people.
Website: www.writingconference.com
Length: No length requirements.
Requirements: No entry fee. Limit one entry per competition. Accepts photocopies and computer printouts. Visit the website or send an SASE for further information.
Prizes: Winners in each category receive publication in *The Writer's Slate*.
Deadline: January.

Writing for Children Competition

Writers' Union of Canada
Suite 200, 90 Richmond Street
Toronto, Ontario M5E 1C7
Canada

Description
This competition looks to discover, encourage, and promote new and emerging writers. It is open to Canadian residents and entries must target children, and may be either fiction or nonfiction.
Website: www.writersunion.ca
Length: To 1,500 words.
Requirements: Entry fee, $15 per piece. Multiple entries are accepted. Accepts photocopies and computer printouts. Send an SASE or visit the website for complete competition guidelines.
Prizes: Winner receives a cash prize of $1,500 and the Writers' Union of Canada will submit the winning entry to several children's publishers.
Deadline: April.

Indexes

2006 Market News

New Listings ☆

Abilene Writers Guild
  Annual Contest
Above & Beyond
All About Kids Parenting
  Magazine
Amazing Journeys
  Magazine
Anime
Art Jewelry
Athens Parent
Atlanta Sporting Family
Bay State Parent
BC Parent Magazine
Becoming Family
Beyond Centauri
Big Country Peacock
  Chronicle
Bird Times
Black Woman and Child
B'nai B'rith Magazine
Brain, Child
Byronchild
Canadian Writers Journal
  Short Fiction Contest
Cappers
Challenge
Christian Work at Home
  Moms Ezine
Coastal Family Magazine
Comet
Cookie
Cool! Magazine
Cousteau Kids
Creative Child Magazine
The Dabbling Mum
Education in Focus
Eduguide
Edutopia

Elementary School
  Journal
Encyclopedia of Youth
  Studies
Entertainment Magazine
Explore Magazine
The Family Digest (IN)
Family Energy
Fido Friendly
57 Story Lane
Fort Myers Magazine
Foster City International
  Writing Contest
Grand Rapids Family
  Magazine
Gwinnett Parents
  Magazine
Harford County Kids
Healthy Beginnings
Healthy Choices
Healthy Growing
Higher Things
The Illuminata
InQuest Gamer
Inspirationstation
  Magazine
Junior Storyteller
Kahani
Kentuckiana Parent
The Kids Storytelling
  Club
Knucklebones
Little Rock Family
Long Island Mothers
  Journal
Magic the Gathering
Mentoring Bigtime
Metro Augusta Parent

MetroFamily
Mission
MomsVoice.com
Moo-Cow Fan Club
MotherVerse Magazine
Natural Family Online
Neopets
New & Fox Valley Kids
The Northland
Palm Beach Conservative
Parenting for High
  Potential
ParentingUniverse.com
Plum Magazine
PTO Today
Rainbow Kids
Realiteen Magazine
Riot
Shasta Parent
Mary Shelley Prize for
  Imaginative Fiction
Small Town Life
  Magazine
Tap: The Autism
  Perspective
Think & Discover
Total Reader
Verve Girl
Wanna Bet?
Weatherwise
West Tennessee Parent
  & Family
What's Hers
What's His
Young-Expressions
  Magazine
Yu Gi Oh

2006 Market News (cont.)

Deletions and Name Changes

Able Ezine: Unable to contact

American Adrenaline: Unable to contact

American Journal of Health Education: Unable to contact

American Kids Parenting Magazine: Ceased publication

America's Moms: See **ParentingUniverse.com**

And Baby: Ceased publication

Baseball Parent: Unable to contact

Bay Area Parent: Unable to contact

Blackgirl Magazine: Unable to contact

Career World: Unable to contact

Children's Magic Window: Ceased publication

Children's Mission: Not accepting freelance submissions

Church Worship: Ceased publication

Circles of Peace, Circles of Justice: Unable to contact

City Parent: Unable to contact

Class Act: Ceased publication

CosmoGirl!: Unable to contact

Discovery: Unable to contact

Discovery Trails: Ceased publication

Dolphin Log: See **Cousteau Kids**

Eclectic Homeschool Online: Unable to contact

Edge for Kids: Unable to contact

Encounter: Unable to contact

English Journal: Unable to contact

Family Digest (CA): Unable to contact

Family Digest Baby: Unable to contact

Fox Valley Kids: See **New & Fox Valley Kids**

Gball: Ceased publication

Georgia Family: Unable to contact

Going Forth: Unable to contact

Haunted Attraction Magazine: Unable to contact

Home Times: See **Palm Beach Conservative**

In The Family: Ceased publication

Jackson Christian Family: Unable to contact

Kid's Domain: Unable to contact

Kids Tribute: Unable to contact

Kid Zone: Unable to contact

LA Family Magazine: Unable to contact

LAPregnancy.com: Unable to contact

Leaders in Action: Suspended publication

Moms Help Moms: Unable to contact

Monterey County Family: No response

Northwest Family News: Ceased publication

ParenTeacher Magazine: Unable to contact

Parenting: Unable to contact

Parents' Monthly: Ceased publication

Pray Kids!: Ceased publication

Quilt It for Kids: Not accepting new material

Ranger Rick: Unable to contact

Ruminator Review: Unable to contact

Sharing Space: Unable to contact

Sister 2 Sister: Unable to contact

SloppyNoodle.com: Unable to contact

Storyworks: Unable to contact

Sugar: Unable to contact

Surfer: Unable to contact

Susquehanna Valley Parent: Unable to contact

Teens in Motion News: Unable to contact

Teens on Target: Unable to contact

Today's Parent (CA): See **Bay State Parent**

Varsity Communications: Unable to contact

Welcome Home: Suspended publication

Western New York Family Magazine: Unable to contact

Woman's Day: Unable to contact

Women Today Magazine: Unable to contact

Wonder Years: Unable to contact

Word Dance Magazine: Unable to contact

Working Mother: Unable to contact

World Kid Magazine: Ceased publication

Yin Magazine: Unable to contact

YM: Ceased publication

YoungBucksOutdoors.com: Unable to contact

Young Dancer: Unable to contact

Young Money: Unable to contact

Young Voices: Unable to contact

Your Stepfamily: Unable to contact

Fifty+ Freelance

Y ou can improve your chances of selling by submitting to magazines that fill their pages with freelance material. Of the 618 freelance markets listed in this directory, we have listed 175 markets that buy at least 50% of their freelance material from writers who are new to the magazine. Of course, there are no guarantees; but if you approach these magazines with well-written manuscripts targeted to their subject, age range, and word-limit requirements, you can increase your publication odds.

Abilities
Adoptalk
Amazing Kids!
American Careers
American History
American Libraries
American String Teacher
AppleSeeds
The Apprentice Writer
Art Jewelry
Arts & Activities
Austin Family
Babybug
Bay Area Baby
Boys' Quest
Brio and Beyond
Busy Family Network
Calliope
Camping Magazine
Cappers
Celebrate
Characters
Chicago Parent
Child Care Information
    Exchange
Childhood Education
Children and Families
Children's Digest
Children's Playmate
Child Welfare Report
Christian Work at Home
    Moms Ezine
The Claremont Review
The Clearing House
Cleveland/Akron Family
Club Connection
Clubhouse
College Bound Teen
    Magazine
Columbus Parent
Community Education
    Journal
Connect
Cousteau Kids
Creative Kids
Cricket
The Dabbling Mum
Dance Magazine
Dane County Kids
Davey and Goliath

Devo'Zine
Dig
Dimensions
Dimensions of Early
    Childhood
Dovetail
Dramatic Publishing
The Edge
Educational Horizons
Education Forum
The Education Revolution
Education Week
Eduguide
Elementary School Writer
Exceptional Parent
Faces
Face Up
The Family Digest (IN)
Farm & Ranch Living
Faze Teen
Footsteps
Fort Myers Magazine
Gifted Education Press
    Quarterly
Go-Girl
Green Teacher
Group
Guideposts Sweet 16
Gumbo Magazine
Highlights for Children
The High School Journal
High School Writer (Junior
    High Edition)
High School Writer (Senior)
Hopscotch
Hudson Valley Parent
I Love Cats
Inside Kung-Fu
Insight
InTeen
InTeen Teacher
International Gymnast
Jack And Jill
Journal of School Health
Juco Review
Kansas School Naturalist
Keynoter
KidsandKaboodle.com
Kids Life
Ladybug

The Lamp-Post
Leadership for Student
    Activities
Live
Long Island Mothers Journal
Lowcountry Parent
Mentoring Bigtime
Mission
Momentum
MOMSense
Moo-Cow Fan Club
Mothering
Mother Verse Magazine
Mr. Marquis' Museletter
My Friend
Nashville Parent Magazine
New & Fox Valley Kids
New Expression
New Moon
Nick Jr. Family Magazine
No Crime
Northern Michigan Family
    Magazine
The Old Schoolhouse
    Magazine
On Course
Our Children
Pack-O-Fun
Palm Beach Conservative
Parent and Preschooler
    Newsletter
Parentguide News
Parenting New Hampshire
Parents and Children
    Together Online
Parents Express-Pennsylvania
Plays
Positive Teens
Potluck Children's Literary
    Magazine
Prehistoric Times
Principal
Recreational Ice Skating
Reptiles
Reunions Magazine
The Rock
Sacramento/Sierra Parent
SchoolArts
School Library Journal
Science Activities

Science and Children
Seek
Seventeen
Simply You Magazine
Sparkle
Stone Soup
Story Friends
Student Leader
Suburban Parent
SuperScience
Teacher Librarian
Teachers & Writers
Teachers of Vision
Teaching PreK–8
Tech Directions
Teen Light
Texas Child Care
Theory into Practice
Three Leaping Frogs
Tidewater Parent
Today's Catholic Teacher
The Universe in the
    Classroom
U*S*Kids
VegFamily
Vibrant Life
The Village Family
Voice of Youth Advocates
Voices from the Middle
Washington Families
    Magazine
The Water Skier
Wee Ones E-Magazine
Westchester Family
What If?
What's Up Kids?
Writers' Journal
Young Adult Today
Young Rider

Category Index

To help you find the appropriate market for your manuscript or query letter, we have compiled a category and subject index listing magazines according to their primary editorial interests. Pay close attention to the markets that overlap. For example, when searching for a market for your rock-climbing adventure story for 8- to 12-year-old readers, you might look under the categories "Adventure Stories" and "Middle-grade (Fiction)." If you have an idea for an article about blue herons for early readers, look under the categories "Animals/Pets" and "Early Reader (Nonfiction)" to find possible markets. Always check the magazine's listing for explanations of specific needs.

For your convenience, we have listed below all of the categories that are included in this index. If you don't find a category that exactly fits your material, try to find a broader term that covers your topic.

Adventure Stories
Animals (Fiction)
Animals/Pets (Nonfiction)
Audio/Video
Bilingual (Nonfiction)
Biography
Boys' Magazines
Canadian Magazines
Career/College
Child Care
Computers
Contemporary Fiction
Crafts/Hobbies
Current Events
Drama
Early Reader (Fiction)
Early Reader (Nonfiction)
Education/Classroom
Factual/Informational
Fairy Tales
Family/Parenting
Fantasy
Folktales/Folklore
Games/Puzzles/Activities
Geography
Gifted Education
Girls' Magazines
Health/Fitness

Historical Fiction
History
Horror
How-to
Humor (Fiction)
Humor (Nonfiction)
Inspirational Fiction
Language Arts
Mathematics
Middle-grade (Fiction)
Middle-grade (Nonfiction)
Multicultural/Ethnic
  (Fiction)
Multicultural/Ethnic
  (Nonfiction)
Music
Mystery/Suspense
Nature/Environment
  (Fiction)
Nature/Environment
  (Nonfiction)
Personal Experience
Photo Essays
Popular Culture
Preschool (Fiction)
Preschool (Nonfiction)
Profile/Interview
Read-aloud Stories

Real-life/Problem-solving
Rebus
Recreation/Entertainment
Regional
Religious (Fiction)
Religious (Nonfiction)
Reviews
Romance
Science Fiction
Science/Technology
Self-help
Services/Clubs
Social Issues
Special Education
Sports (Fiction)
Sports (Nonfiction)
Travel
Western
Writing
Young Adult (Fiction)
Young Adult (Nonfiction)
Young Author (Fiction)
Young Author
  (Nonfiction)

Factual/Informational

Humor (Fiction)

Multicultural/ Ethnic (Fiction)

Multicultural/ Ethnic (Nonfiction)

Music

Magazine and Contest Index

The following codes have been used to indicate each publication's readership: **YA**=Young adults, **A**=Adults, **E**=Educators (including librarians, teachers, administrators, student group leaders, and child-care professionals), **F**=Family (general interest), **P**=Parents. We have listed age ranges when specified by the editor.

If you do not find a particular magazine, turn to Market News on page 336.

★ indicates a newly listed magazine